5.03.199_

Liewe Hein

Dankie vir al jou geduld
met ons!

Liefde

Jou Skoonma

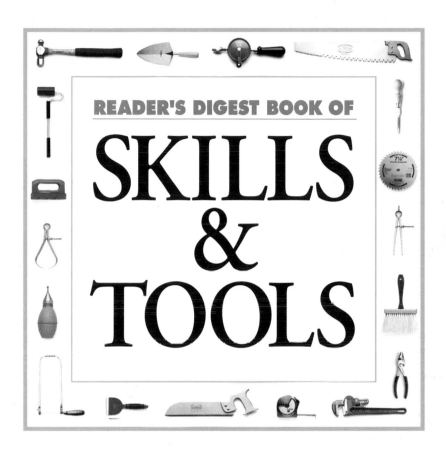

READER'S DIGEST BOOK OF
SKILLS
&
TOOLS

READER'S DIGEST BOOK OF

SKILLS
&
TOOLS

The Reader's Digest Association
South Africa (Pty) Limited, Cape Town

READER'S DIGEST BOOK OF SKILLS & TOOLS

**Reader's Digest
Book of Skills & Tools**
was edited and produced by
The Reader's Digest Association
South Africa (Pty) Ltd
130 Strand Street
Cape Town
8001

South African Edition

Editor
Brian Johnson Barker

Art Editor
Stuart Nix

Project Co-ordinator
Carol Adams

Proofreader
Ethné Clarke

Contributors and Consultants

William Barker
Daniel Basovitch
Judy Beyer
Terence Beyer
Ralph Brophy
Bob Buteyn
Victor DeMasi
John de Villiers
Phil Englander
Charles N Farley
Allan E Fitchett
George Frechter
Eugene Goeb
Wayne Hawk
Colleen Jacobs
Walter Kurzmann
Peter Legnos
Frances le Roux
Jim McCann
Tim McCreight
Charles McRaven
Susan Moore
Rose-Ann Myers
Americo Napolitano
Gerald Persico
Lawrence D Press
Meryl Prichard
Henry H Printz
Michael Raffio
Vernon Robins
Michael Sapienza
Seth Stem
Max Widan
Bob Wilcoxson

Acknowledgments

The publishers wish to thank the following South African companies and organizations for the assistance they provided:

A A Ball (Pty) Ltd
Baltic Timber Co (Pty) Ltd
The Building Centre
Colorwall (Pty) Ltd
Columbia D C M (Pty) Ltd
Concrete Masonry Association
Corobrik
F B R Plastics (Pty) Ltd
Handles & Hinges (Pty) Ltd
Hawkes & Findlay (Pty) Ltd
Gordons Power Tool Hardware
Non-Ferrous Metal Works
Permoseal (Pty) Ltd
P G Bison Ltd
Plascon Paints (Cape) (Pty) Ltd
Portland Cement Institute
Ramset Fasteners (Africa) (Pty) Ltd
Rare Woods (S A)
The Robins Forge
South African Bureau of Standards
S A Ladder (Pty) Ltd
Tal (Pty) Ltd
Wardkiss Homecare

The acknowledgments and credits that appear on the facing page are hereby made a part of this copyright page.

Reader's Digest and the Pegasus logo
are registered trademarks of
The Reader's Digest Association, Inc.

Additional photographs
James de Villiers, pp 16, 18, 19, 20, 70, 72, 81, 94, 95, 99, 104, 105, 108, 118, 126, 127, 128, 129, 218, 268
Janek Szymanowski, p 287

Additional artwork
Dave Snook, pp 104, 105, 110, 178, 257, 305, 348, 349

ISBN 1-874912-36-X

The publishers cannot accept any responsibility for any act or omission arising from consulting this book.

The following organizations and individuals provided assistance in the preparation of the original edition:

Aberdeen's Magazine of Masonry Construction
Adjustable Clamp Company
Advanced Technology Inc
AIN Plastics, Inc
Allcraft Tool & Supply Company, Inc
American Clamping Corp
American Machine & Tool Co, Inc
American Saw & Mfg Company
American Stone and Supply, Inc
American Tool Companies, Inc
Ames Lawn and Garden Tools
Andrite Wondrastone Distributing Co, Inc
Armstrong World Industries, Inc
Arrow Fastener Company, Inc
Ball & Ball
Barrasso & Sons, Inc
Richard J. Bell Company, Inc
S A Bendheim Company, Inc
Black & Decker
Boise Cascade Corp
Botolpher & Lee, Inc
BP Chemicals, Inc–Filon Products
Brass Accent by Urfic, Inc
Brick Institute of America
Bridge City Tool Works, Inc
C & A Wallcoverings
Central Hardware & Electric Corp
Central Supply Inc
Colonial Bronze Co
Concrete Paver Institute
Congoleum Corp
Albert Constantine & Son, Inc
CooperTools
Delta International Machinery Corp
Ray Donarski
Tom Doyle
Dremel Power Tools

Eldorado Stone Corporation
Empak Company
Fibre Glass Evercoat Co Inc
Flexi-Wall Systems
Florian Glass
Formica Corporation
Freud, Inc
Garden State Flooring
Garrett Wade Company
GB Electrical, Inc
GE Plastics
Glen-Gery Corporation
The Glidden Co
Grinnell Concrete Pavingstones
Grizzly Imports, Inc
Hafele America Co
Hager Hinge Co
Harris-Tarkett, Inc
Hebron Brick Supply Co
HEWI, Inc
Hitachi Power Tools U S A Limited
Hi Way Concrete Products
Hyde Tools
Ilco Unican Corp
Inter Design Inc
International Wallcoverings Ltd
The Irwin Company
Ives: a Harrow Company
Johnson Level and Tool Manufacturing Company, Inc
Jolie Papier Ltd
Kentile Floors Inc
Kentucky Mill Work
Kentucky Wood Floors, Inc
Keystone Retaining Walls Systems Inc
Kwikset, a Black & Decker Company
Lasco Panel Products, Div of Tomkins Industries, Inc
Laticrete International
C R Laurence Company Inc
Lazon Paints & Wallcoverings

L B I, Inc
McFeely's
Makita U S A Inc
Mannington Floors
Marion Tool Corp
Marshalltown Trowel Company
Middletown Plate Glass Co Inc
Milwaukee Electric Tool Corp
Monterey Shelf, Inc
Benjamin Moore & Co
Mosaic Supplies
Musolf Distributing, Inc
National Concrete Masonry Association
National Manufacturing Company
National Oak Flooring Manufacturers' Association
National Particleboard Association
National Wood Flooring Association
New Hippodrome Hardware Corp
NicSand, Inc
Owens-Corning Fiberglas Corp
Padco, Inc
Paxton Hardware
Pfister Industries
Pittsburgh Corning Corporation
Plexi-Craft Quality Products Corp
Porter-Cable Professional Power Tool Corporation
Potlatch Corporation
Power-Flo Products
PPG Industries
Red Devil, Inc
Cynthia Rees Ceramic Tile Showroom
Rickel Do-It-Yourself Home Centers
Ridge Tool Company
Rio Grande Albuquerque

Robbins, Inc
Roofing Industry Educational Institute
Roysons Corporation
Ryobi America Corp
Sandvik Saws and Tools
S-B Power Tool Company
Schlage Lock Company
Shur-line, Inc
R&G Sloane Manufacturing Co
Solo Metal Works Ltd
South Street Ready-Mix Concrete
Stanley Tools
The L S Starrett Company
John Sterling Corp
Stone Products Corporation
StoneWall™ Landscape Systems, Inc
Structural Stone Company, Inc
Tahran Painting & Decorating Center
Target Products Inc
TECO/Lumberlok
3M Do-It-Yourself Division
Tremont Nail Company
Triangle Tool Group Inc
Unicorn Universal Woods Ltd
Unilock N Y Inc
Vaughan & Bushnell Mfg Co
Vermont American Tool Co
V T Industries, Inc
Wallcoverings Association
Wedge Innovations
R D Werner Company, Inc
Wilde Tool Co, Inc
Willson Safety Products
Ralph Wilson Plastics Co
Wood Moulding and Millwork Producer's Association
F W Wostbrock Hardwood Floor Company, Inc
Wright Products Corp

Photo credits

Andrite Wondrastone Co, Inc, p 203 (all)
W Cody/West Light, p 202 (bottom, left)
The Family Handyman, p 287 (top 3)
R D Werner Company Inc, p 87 (extension ladder)

Warning

All do-it-yourself activities involve a degree of risk. Skills, tools, materials, and site conditions vary widely. Although the editors have made every effort to ensure accuracy, the reader remains responsible for the selection and use of tools, materials, and methods. Always obey laws and local regulations, follow manufacturers' operating instructions and observe safety precautions.

ABOUT THIS BOOK

The READER'S DIGEST BOOK OF SKILLS & TOOLS is tailor-made for you if you enjoy working with tools or if you want to brighten up your home. Whether you're thinking about paving your patio, covering a counter with laminate, painting or papering a wall, or simply having the fun and satisfaction of building something useful and beautiful, this book will fulfil a dual purpose. It will tell you how to do the job and show you what tools and materials you'll need.

The book is divided into eight major sections. The first two, *Tools* and *Hardware,* consist of galleries of colour photographs of well over a thousand tools and articles of hardware, with explanations of their use. Included are all the standard hammers and saws, pliers and screwdrivers and nails and hinges, but there are also specialized and unusual tools, such as a textured paint roller, an around-the-corner bit for drilling curved holes in tight corners, a screw pitch gauge, and a variety of router templates. On any given spread (two facing pages in the opened book) the tools and hardware are photographed at the same focus so that their sizes relative to one another are completely accurate – except that tools enclosed in a ruled box are either much larger or much smaller than the other items on the page.

Each of the six sections that follow is devoted to the skills needed to use these tools and articles of hardware to work with a particular type of material or group of materials. Colour photographs show you either the raw materials or the effects that can be created by using them, including woods, metals, mouldings, wood finishes, concrete and concrete blocks, stones, pavers, ceramic and vinyl tiles, plastic laminates, fibreglass, glass and glass blocks, paints and wallcoverings, and flooring of every type. Each picture gallery is followed by full step-by-step instructions on working with the materials, giving all the information a beginner needs, and including advanced techniques as well. In the tradition of other Reader's Digest do-it-yourself books, these instructions are brought to life with vivid illustrations – in this case, hundreds of full-colour drawings that include all the details you'll need to see.

The READER'S DIGEST BOOK OF SKILLS & TOOLS is not a project book that provides blueprints for specific jobs, but it can teach you how to work with a wide variety of tools and materials, giving you the skills and confidence to create your own projects. And when you do, you'll have fun indulging your creative impulses and derive a great deal of satisfaction from the completed work. Although this book is not intended as a manual for large construction jobs (it has no information on electrical work, plumbing, or house-building), the skills it teaches can be put to good use, helping you to save money by doing much of the work in even the largest of projects, leaving only the heavy-duty and highly technical work to the professionals.

Rounding out the book are sections on organizing a safe workshop, working safely with tools, planning a project (including standard measurements for furniture and open spaces in your home), understanding basic electrics and how to convert figures from one system of dimensions into another.

And, in case you do want to tackle a large project, there's also help on selecting and working with a contractor.

CONTENTS

Metalworking

Masonry

A shop with a sturdy workbench, basic tools, adequate safety equipment and plenty of well-organized, easily accessible storage space will make it easier and safer for you to complete most jobs. Plan the space with extra room so that you can add tools and accessories as you gain experience and move into more advanced types of work.

Choosing the space. The ideal shop is a closed but well-ventilated room specifically created for that purpose. With such an area, you can lock the door to keep tools and materials from unauthorized use, and save time by letting tools and unfinished projects sit until you are ready to work again.

A workshop should measure at least 2,5 × 3 m. Build a new structure or convert a storage shed, spare room, or disused servant's quarters. Garage and basement workshops work well if you add a wall or a large sliding door to separate the shop from cars, water heaters or laundry facilities. An attic shop may be good for small work, but it is difficult to move in large tools and materials, and the roof beams may not take the heavy loads. Before moving any heavy equipment into your attic, reinforce the joists.

Electrical work. Once you have selected your space, have a professional electrician put in the proper wiring. Install bright overhead fluorescent fixtures, and use droplights or clamp-on lamps to focus light on your workbench and large power tools. If possible, install an exhaust fan above the workbench area.

Be sure you have strategically placed electric outlets for all your power tools, including dedicated circuits for heavy machinery that will not be moved. By installing extra outlets, you can avoid the dangerous practice of running cords on the floor or draping them across benches and tools. If you must run a cord across the floor, cover it with a brightly coloured wooden bridge to protect the cord and keep it from tripping anyone. Never allow a power cord to rest on a damp surface. At the outset, make sure that the circuits are connected to an earth leakage relay (ELR) on the main switchboard. In case of a fault in the electrical earthing (such as a loose live wire touching the metal housing of an earthed tool), the ELR will 'trip' to cut the power off and protect you from shock.

Avoid using extension cords, if at all possible. If using one is unavoidable, be sure that it has a three-prong plug and exceeds the capacity of the tool's cord. To keep the extension and tool cords from unplugging, tie the ends together in a loose knot before plugging them into each other.

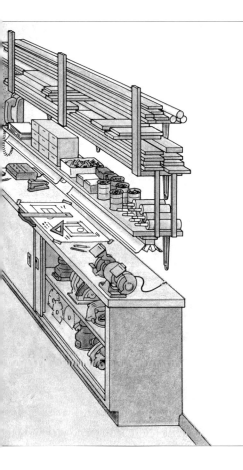

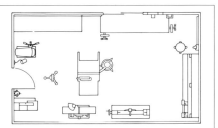

Set up your workshop so that the workbench is convenient to your large power tools and major storage areas. In a larger space, position the workbench in the centre of the shop; if you have a table saw, leave enough space around it to handle large sheets of plywood, and include a roller stand or some other type of table extension. If you mount your large power tools on tables with locking castors, you'll be able to store them out of the way when not in use.

For holding workpieces stationary, install a bench vice and hold-downs for the types of jobs you plan to do. If your shop has a concrete floor, place thick rubber mats or carpet scraps in front of your bench and large power tools to prevent tired legs and cold feet when standing for long periods.

For support when measuring and cutting long framing materials and sheet materials such as plywood, panelling and wallboard, you might want to include a good set of sawhorses in your shop. You can also place a sheet of plywood across sawhorses and instantly create an additional work surface for painting, staining and finishing work in the shop or on a job site.

Storage. Tools, hardware and materials should never be left lying about when not in use. A cluttered space is an invitation to fire or accidents.

Store everything in a safe but convenient place. On the wall above or near your bench, install a pegboard panel with hooks for hanging hand tools, arranging them so that those most used are the closest. Be sure to position the hooks in such a way that tools can be removed easily without interfering with one another.

Install metal or wooden shelves for small power tools, use labelled coffee tins or jars for nails and screws, and reserve a long shelf or a dry area on the floor for planks and other materials. Add cartons for waste materials you want to recycle. More sophisticated storage could include large toolboxes, multiple-unit containers or bins for fasteners and other hardware, wood racks and bins, and built-in shelves, cupboards, and drawers. Arrange the tools and materials you use most often so that they are the most accessible.

Store flammable and toxic materials (such as paints, thinners, glues and oils) in a locked fireproof metal cabinet firmly attached to a wall. To protect the environment, check with your local government on how to dispose of these materials properly.

Other safety precautions. Install a fire extinguisher and smoke alarms in the shop. Choose an extinguisher rated A-B-C-D, which is designed to fight wood, oil, petrol, chemical and electrical fires. Check periodically that the extinguisher's expiry date has not passed and that the batteries in the smoke detectors are good.

Keep a first-aid kit handy and a list of emergency numbers by the telephone. Install childproof switches on your large power tools so that they cannot be inadvertently turned on. You can buy a device that encases and locks the tool's plug or a locking switch that lets you send power to the tool only by turning a key, which you can keep out of the reach of children.

Setting up a workbench. The focus of any shop is the workbench. It must be sturdy and large enough to handle the type of work you plan to

do. You can purchase a bench or, better still, build one to fit your space and to suit your particular needs.

You can make a simple workbench for occasional small projects by attaching a set of metal bench legs (sold at home improvement centres) to an expanse of particleboard or chipboard. For the serious do-it-yourselfer or craftsman, however, a sturdier bench is called for. Workbenches or kits to make them are available from woodwork suppliers. Or you can make one with 50 × 100 mm planks, and use a sheet of particleboard with a layer of hardwood for the top to provide a solid surface. Add storage areas underneath the bench by installing shelves, doors, wooden or plastic drawers, and slide-out bins. Workbench plans ranging from simple to elaborate can be found in various books and magazines and at home improvement centres.

Choose tools that suit your budget, space, experience and the type of work you plan to do. Quality tools are expensive, but you needn't buy a lot of them at first. Start with a few basic hand and power tools, learn to use them and, as you gain experience, add others. Hire tools that you will use only once.

Tool maintenance. Take care of your tools to keep them safe and effective. Sharpen, clean, or replace blades, bits and other cutters before they become damaged or dull. A sharp tool cuts smoothly, accurately and safely.

Follow the manufacturer's procedures to keep power tools in good working order. Most power tools are permanently lubricated and sealed and require no oiling. On a few tools, however, you may have to oil certain parts, and you may be able to replace worn brushes or power cords or defective switches. Check your owner's manual.

To clean a power tool, unplug it and wipe it with a damp cloth or sponge. Never submerge the tool in water or clean it with solvents. If a tool's air vents become clogged, remove the debris with compressed air or a vacuum cleaner.

If you have cordless tools, use only the battery and charger that came with the tool. Never charge or store a tool where the temperature is close to freezing point or above 40°C. Batteries rely on chemical reactions that slow down in the cold and stop altogether at freezing point. High temperatures release vapours from the battery and diminish its capacity.

Tool storage. Store cutting tools where their sharp edges won't be damaged, cause injury, or damage other tools. To prevent rust from accumulating on tools, store them in a dry place. Spray a rust-inhibiting coating on steel tools or put camphor tablets (mothballs) or rust-preventive paper in toolboxes and cabinets. Camphor vapour coats the tools with a rust-preventive film, and the paper gives off a protective vapour or absorbs moisture.

Toolboxes come in a variety of sizes. A small or medium-size box with a handle and removable tray is used to store small tools and to transport them to a job site. Larger boxes with drawers, trays and compartments store a variety of tools and hardware. Some have castors for easy mobility in the shop.

When working outside the shop, use a carpenter's pouch, or tool belt, to store and carry basic tools and hardware. A canvas nail apron holds nails, screws, other fasteners and small tools.

Clothing. Dress appropriately in your workshop and have any helpers do the same. Wear proper footwear, preferably sturdy leather shoes or boots with non-slip soles. Sandals and open-toed or canvas shoes are inappropriate. Roll long sleeves up above the elbows, tie long hair back, and never wear dangling jewellery or loose-fitting clothing, especially when operating power tools; they can become entangled in the tool and cause serious injury. Wear gloves when working with rough materials, sharp edges, hot metal or broken glass and when unloading supplies or cleaning up.

Do not wear gloves when handling most tools. A hand tool may slip from your grasp or twist around and injure you; a power tool's cutter may catch a glove and drag your hand in with it.

Wear kneepads when installing tiles, doing masonry work, or working on other projects that require kneeling for long periods. If you don't have kneepads, kneel on a folded blanket or thick newspaper while working.

Eye and ear protection. Wear adequate eye protection whenever you do sawing, grinding, filing, chiselling or any other work that involves dust, flying chips or harmful liquids that might splash into your eyes. Safety glasses give general protection, but goggles are more efficient and can be worn over prescription spectacles. For full protection, use a face shield.

Whenever you operate power tools or perform noisy tasks such as hammering, wear hearing protectors or earplugs. They filter out damaging noise but allow you to hear voices.

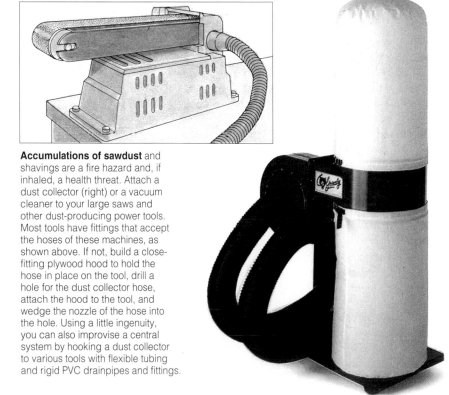

Accumulations of sawdust and shavings are a fire hazard and, if inhaled, a health threat. Attach a dust collector (right) or a vacuum cleaner to your large saws and other dust-producing power tools. Most tools have fittings that accept the hoses of these machines, as shown above. If not, build a close-fitting plywood hood to hold the hose in place on the tool, drill a hole for the dust collector hose, attach the hood to the tool, and wedge the nozzle of the hose into the hole. Using a little ingenuity, you can also improvise a central system by hooking a dust collector to various tools with flexible tubing and rigid PVC drainpipes and fittings.

Safe work habits. Whether you're working with hand or power tools, think about safety before and with every move you make. Keep your mind on your work, avoid distractions, work at a comfortable pace and stop before you get tired. Avoid potentially dangerous operations that you don't feel totally comfortable performing. Don't smoke in the shop.

Keep children, visitors and pets out of your workshop, especially when you are operating power tools. They could cause an accident by distracting you or getting in your way.

Tools are dangerous if used improperly. To ensure safety, always read and follow the owner's manual or instructions that came with the tool. Be careful to use the right tool for the job; never force a tool to work beyond its capacity or your ability. When working with power tools, observe the safety rules listed at right.

Clearing the air. Wood, metal, concrete and other workshop dust is hazardous when inhaled. Dust created from sanding some woods, including pressure-treated woods, and some stains and finishes can cause harm when it comes in contact with the skin and eyes.

Ventilate your shop by opening windows and doors or by turning on an exhaust fan. Use a dust mask for jobs that generate dust and a respirator for work involving toxic fumes (such as using glues and strippers) or when working with insulation.

The most effective dust masks are those marked with the SABS stamp – the South African Bureau of Standards. They are generally thicker than the cheaper masks and have two straps for a tighter seal. Respirators are available with interchangeable colour-coded cartridges to filter out the harmful effects of toxic dust and the fumes from specific materials, such as paints, lacquers and adhesives.

Use a dust collector or vacuum cleaner often to keep dust and debris from accumulating, and attach one to all the machines you can.

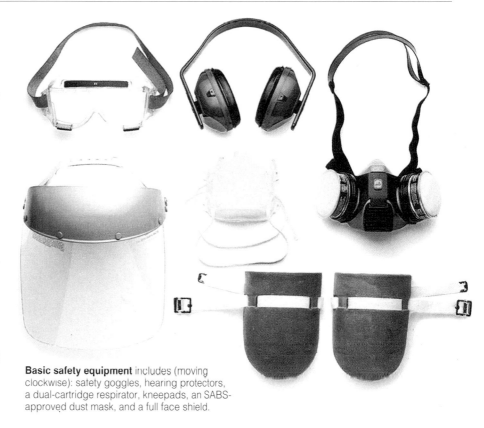

Basic safety equipment includes (moving clockwise): safety goggles, hearing protectors, a dual-cartridge respirator, kneepads, an SABS-approved dust mask, and a full face shield.

SAFETY WITH POWER TOOLS

To promote safety when working with power tools, always take the following precautions:
▷Make sure that the tool you are using is double insulated and properly earthed.
▷Don't operate a tool if you are tired or under the influence of medication, drugs or alcohol.
▷Mentally run through the procedures for using a tool before switching it on.
▷Never ignore, override or remove safety devices, such as blade guards, splitters and anti-kickback mechanisms on saws.
▷Don't saw wet wood, and be especially careful when sawing warped or knotty wood.
▷Check wood for nails, screws and loose knots before cutting or drilling.
▷Support large workpieces during operations. When cutting long planks or large plywood panels, get an assistant or use a roller stand to support the piece at the outfeed side of a saw.
▷Clamp all work securely in place.
▷Use feather boards, push sticks or jigs to move stock past a whirling cutter.
▷Leave no foreign items on the tool's table.
▷Remove adjusting keys and wrenches from a tool before turning on the power.
▷Before plugging in a tool, make sure the power switch is off, tighten all of its clamps, knobs, nuts and levers, and make sure its cutters are securely attached.
▷Never operate a power tool while standing on a wet surface.

▷Keep children and pets out of the workshop when operating power tools.
▷Keep your fingers, hands and other parts of your body well out of the path of cutters.
▷Keep power cords away from cutters.
▷Maintain a firm footing; never reach so far with a portable tool that you become unbalanced. Don't reach over the cutter of any tool.
▷Stand to one side of a saw in case the blade binds and causes the tool to kick back.
▷When you finish making a cut, turn off the tool and let the cutters come to a stop naturally if the machine has no brake. Never slow down or stop a cutter with a piece of wood.
▷Never touch a moving cutter.
▷If a cutter stalls, switch off the power and unplug the tool before trying to free the cutter.
▷If you are interrupted while using a power tool, finish the operation you are working on and switch the tool off before responding.
▷Never clear scraps from a saw table with your fingers; use a long stick.
▷Turn off and unplug tools when not in use or when making adjustments, performing maintenance, or changing cutters or accessories.
▷Sharpen or replace any dull or damaged cutters as soon as possible.
▷Never use the power cord to carry a tool or to pull out its plug.
▷Don't be overconfident, or you will become careless and have an accident.

TOOLS

MEASURING TOOLS

For any job that requires accuracy – from making a simple wooden box to installing a built-in entertainment centre – a good set of measuring tools is important for taking lengths, widths and angles. Even a small miscalculation can make a difference in the appearance or operation of the finished work; improperly measured pieces will not fit together smoothly when assembled. And if the first step is off, the error can compound itself as you continue, resulting in a significant blunder. A basic assortment of rules, gauges and callipers is a must for any workshop.

Folding carpenter's rule is useful for measurements where a rigid rule is necessary. Hinged sections fold for easy storage. Some are made of plastic, others of hardwood with brass fittings, and some have a sliding extension for inside and depth measurements. Common lengths for this rule are 1 m and 2 m.

Steel rule has metric graduations. An accurate straightedge makes the rule suitable for use as a guide for scribing and cutting when straight lines are important. It comes in lengths from 150 mm to 1 m.

Retractable tape houses a spring-loaded metal rule in a small case. The rule is usually replaceable. A lip at the end of the rule catches on the workpiece, making long measurements a one-person job. When measuring walls, it is useful to have a broad-bladed tape that will stand up against a vertical surface (right). Standard lengths are available from 2 to 5 m.

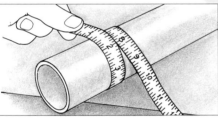

Wrap tape around odd-shaped object; align edges. Start measuring at 2 units; subtract 2 from total.

Micrometer, a high-precision metalworking tool, measures inside or outside diameters in graduations down to 0,005 mm. This example measures outside diameters.

Some models have a brass extension for making inside measurements. Add reading on the rule and on the extension for total distance.

Screw pitch gauge offers an easy way to identify the number of threads on a screw, bolt, nut or in a threaded hole. A series of notched metal blades held in a case correspond to the shape and spacing of the threads. Hold the various blades against the threads until a perfect snug fit is achieved. The number on the blade indicates the correct size.

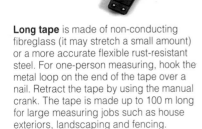

Long tape is made of non-conducting fibreglass (it may stretch a small amount) or a more accurate flexible rust-resistant steel. For one-person measuring, hook the metal loop on the end of the tape over a nail. Retract the tape by using the manual crank. The tape is made up to 100 m long for large measuring jobs such as house exteriors, landscaping and fencing.

Electronic distance measurer sends an ultrasonic pulse up to 80 m. When it hits a flat surface, the pulse returns to the tool, which displays the distance. The more expensive and accurate models are a useful tool for interior designers and painters who have to make cost estimates based on area.

Gauge plate comes in different gauge systems to check the thickness of sheet metal or of wire. To use one, push the wire or sheet-metal edge into the slots until you find the right size. The number by the slot shows the gauge.

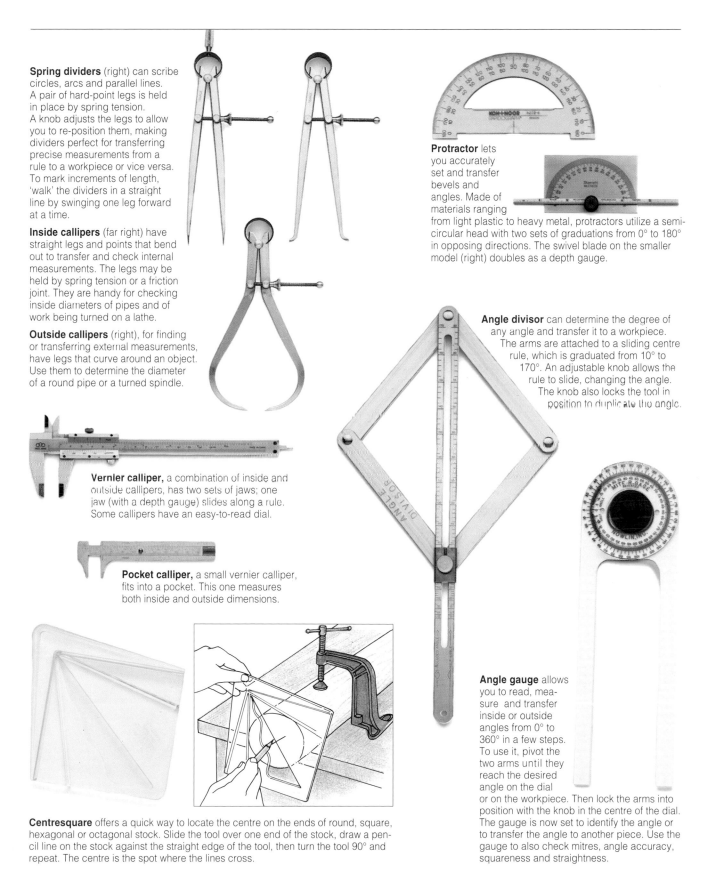

Spring dividers (right) can scribe circles, arcs and parallel lines. A pair of hard-point legs is held in place by spring tension. A knob adjusts the legs to allow you to re-position them, making dividers perfect for transferring precise measurements from a rule to a workpiece or vice versa. To mark increments of length, 'walk' the dividers in a straight line by swinging one leg forward at a time.

Inside callipers (far right) have straight legs and points that bend out to transfer and check internal measurements. The legs may be held by spring tension or a friction joint. They are handy for checking inside diameters of pipes and of work being turned on a lathe.

Outside callipers (right), for finding or transferring external measurements, have legs that curve around an object. Use them to determine the diameter of a round pipe or a turned spindle.

Vernier calliper, a combination of inside and outside callipers, has two sets of jaws; one jaw (with a depth gauge) slides along a rule. Some callipers have an easy-to-read dial.

Pocket calliper, a small vernier calliper, fits into a pocket. This one measures both inside and outside dimensions.

Centresquare offers a quick way to locate the centre on the ends of round, square, hexagonal or octagonal stock. Slide the tool over one end of the stock, draw a pencil line on the stock against the straight edge of the tool, then turn the tool 90° and repeat. The centre is the spot where the lines cross.

Protractor lets you accurately set and transfer bevels and angles. Made of materials ranging from light plastic to heavy metal, protractors utilize a semi-circular head with two sets of graduations from 0° to 180° in opposing directions. The swivel blade on the smaller model (right) doubles as a depth gauge.

Angle divisor can determine the degree of any angle and transfer it to a workpiece. The arms are attached to a sliding centre rule, which is graduated from 10° to 170°. An adjustable knob allows the rule to slide, changing the angle. The knob also locks the tool in position to duplicate the angle.

Angle gauge allows you to read, measure and transfer inside or outside angles from 0° to 360° in a few steps. To use it, pivot the two arms until they reach the desired angle on the dial or on the workpiece. Then lock the arms into position with the knob in the centre of the dial. The gauge is now set to identify the angle or to transfer the angle to another piece. Use the gauge to also check mitres, angle accuracy, squareness and straightness.

Many jobs involve laying out angles and curves as well as straight lines. To lay out a design properly, you will need specialized tools and gauges. Protractors and compasses are most commonly used for drawing curves, but other tools are available. A number of combination tools are handy for multiple uses. To transfer points and cutting lines on your work, you will need various scribers, awls, punches, chalk lines and gauges.

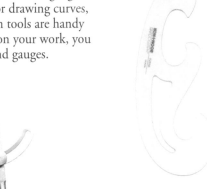

French curves, made of clear acrylic, are used to draw irregular shapes and perspective details. Simply trace along the desired edge to make matching curves in as many locations as you wish.

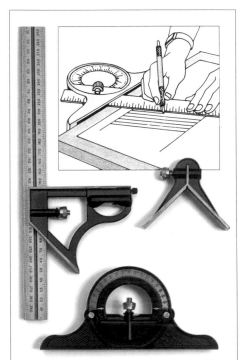

Compass draws arcs and circles. Insert a pencil into the tool's short leg, set the distance between the two legs to the desired radius, position the metal pivot point at the centre of the projected circle and swing the pencil over the surface.

Sliding T-bevel is an adjustable gauge for setting, testing and transferring angles. The handle is made of wood or plastic. The metal blade pivots and can be locked at any angle by loosening and tightening the wing nut. Set the angle from an existing one, or set it using a protractor. The end of the blade is angled at 45° for use on mitred corners.

Combination tool or engineer and carpenter's square consists of a rule, protractor head and centre finder. To use protractor, lock it onto rule at correct angle, set flat face of head along edge of work, and scribe line as shown. To use centre finder, lock it onto rule, position its ends on circle, and draw line using rule; reposition and repeat.

Trammel points draw large circles and arcs. Attach them to a steel rule, board or bar so that the distance between them is equal to the radius of the circle or arc you wish to draw, and use the assembly like a compass.

Another combination tool does the job of several individual tools: rule, square, protractor, bevel, pitch-to-distance indicator, plumb and level – in fact, four separate levels allow readings from various positions. The revolving turret, in which the steel rule is mounted, shows degrees on one side and pitch on the other. The tool illustrated is well made, but multiple combination tools sometimes don't match up to their manufacturer's claims.

Direct-read compass has a graduated scale for more accuracy in setting. The drawing lead can be replaced with a steel point for scribing metal.

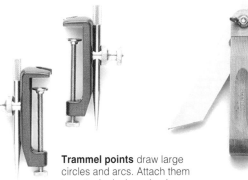

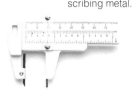

Flexible curve is a bendable vinyl-wrapped bundle of lead strips for forming, transferring and duplicating unusual shapes. Bend the tool into any shape, hold it in position, and trace the design in as many places as you wish.

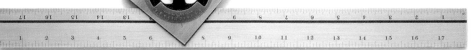

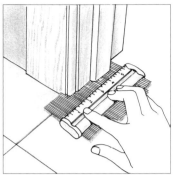

Profile gauge or contour gauge duplicates and transfers an irregular design to a template or piece of stock. The tool is made of a series of movable metal or plastic pins that take on the contour of whatever object they are pressed against.

Metal scriber makes light marks on soft metal. Use it to mark layout and cutting lines or even to write an instruction or direction that will be hidden later.

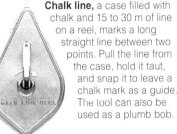

Awl makes small holes for starting nails, drill bits, and screws, and can be used in place of a pencil for marking very fine layout and cutting lines. The steel shank is sharpened to a point; the tool's handle is plastic or wood. The awl also pierces holes in leather or vinyl.

Automatic centre-punch operates on a spring so that you need not hit it with a hammer. Grasp the tool in one hand and push down firmly where you want a mark.

Chalk line, a case filled with chalk and 15 to 30 m of line on a reel, marks a long straight line between two points. Pull the line from the case, hold it taut, and snap it to leave a chalk mark as a guide. The tool can also be used as a plumb bob.

Punches are steel marking instruments that are used by striking them with a hammer. The centre punch (top) and the sharper prick punch (centre) have bevelled points for starting holes in metal and wood. The pin punch (bottom) has a straight flank and flat tip for knocking out the small pins sometimes used to assemble parts.

Pounce wheels make light perforation marks in wood when rolled across its surface. They can be used with carbon paper for drawing dotted lines.

Electronic stud finder locates studs behind wall-coverings by measuring changes in the wall's density. Also available are inexpensive magnetic finders that react to the screws or nails that secure wallcoverings to the studs. Either type can be thrown off by steel pipes or wires in the wall.

Marking gauge scribes a line on wood parallel to the edge. Set the distance you wish to mark from the edge of the stock by sliding the gauge's fence to the correct point on the beam, which often has a graduated scale. Place the face of the fence against the edge of the wood and draw the pin along the stock. Both a wooden and a metal gauge are shown here. You can set the two slides on the metal gauge for different measurements and use them alternately.

Mortise gauge scribes double lines on the ends of wood for laying out mortises. Lock the gauge's fence at the exact measurement, hold the face of the fence against the side of the stock, and draw the pin across it.

Pantograph copies a design and enlarges it or reduces it in the process. Clamp the tool to a drawing table or flat board, set it up as shown, and adjust it to get the desired scale. Use one hand to trace over the original design with the stylus and the other hand to guide the pencil as it draws the copy.

SQUARES

A type of layout and measuring tool, the square is essential for accurately marking and assembling a project. If it's made in two pieces, the metal or wooden handle is called the stock; on a one-piece model, the metal handle is called the tongue. To lay out and mark cuts, place the handle parallel to the object and draw a line against the blade. Models with the blade set at a 90° angle to the handle can also check squareness after cutting and assembling the workpiece. Some models have blades set at different angles.

Carpenter's square is practical for laying out many types of projects. It's made from one piece of steel and incremented in millimetres. Other markings indicate commonly used angles. Sizes go up to a 600 mm blade and a 400 mm tongue.

Dovetail square comes in two ratios: 8:1 for hardwood, 6:1 for softwood. Use it to set angled lines for both the pins and the tails of a dovetail, and to lay out vertical lines.

Mitre square has a blade set at a 45° angle for laying out and marking lines. It is especially handy for mitre cuts. The opposite angle is set at 135°.

Engineer's square, a metalworking version of the try square (below), has a notch cut into the handle near the blade to make room for burrs when scoring metal.

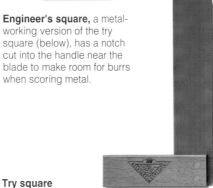

Try square for woodworking lets you lay out cutting lines at 90° angles and check the squareness of adjoining surfaces and of planed timber. The most useful model has a blade 200 mm long.

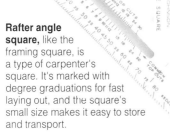

Rafter angle square, like the framing square, is a type of carpenter's square. It's marked with degree graduations for fast laying out, and the square's small size makes it easy to store and transport.

Framing square, a specialized version of the carpenter's square, has tables and formulas imprinted on it for making quick calculations, including those for area and volume.

Combination square combines several features of measuring and marking tools. Its blade and sliding adjustable head incorporate a try square, a 45° mitre square, and a level in one compact unit.

Adjustable T-square is suitable for laying out square and angled lines on large surfaces such as plywood and other sheet materials. Some have a 1,2 m-long handle; a 550 mm pivoting blade locks in position at any angle. Smaller models are used by boat navigators.

LEVELS AND PLUMBS

Whether you're hanging a sink, setting a fence post or putting up a wall, keeping surfaces level and plumb is vital. A spirit level has one or more clear vials filled with a liquid. When you rest the level on a surface, a bubble in the liquid shows that the surface is 'true' when it floats in an area marked on the vial. Longer levels are usually more accurate than shorter ones.

Digital level (right) does everything other levels do but does it electronically. Lights on older models flash red for not level or green for level. Newer models feature a simulated bubble display plus a digital readout of degrees of slope, as well as the gradient of stairs and roofs, and a percentage of slope for drainage problems on decks and masonry.

Torpedo level (below), a shorter 200 to 250 mm version of a carpenter's level, is preferred by plumbers because it can fit into most restricted places. It usually has three bubble vials – which can be read through both top and side windows – to show levelness, plumb and 45° angle. Some models are grooved on the bottom for rest-ing on pipes and shafts.

Carpenter's level (left, centre) comes with a varying number of vials to check horizontal level and vertical plumb. The vials may be adjustable or replaceable. Frames are usually made of aluminium, brass, magnesium, plastic or wood. Some frames are magnetized to keep hands free for moving the workpiece. Before buying a level, test it on a known level surface. The standard lengths are 450, 600 and 800 mm and 1 m. To check the drop of a sloped surface, place a 1 m level on the surface; use wood blocks to level the tool. Every cm of wood block equals a fall about 21 mm per m.

Mason's level (left), similar to a carpenter's level, includes special features such as heavy-duty bubble vials, a hardwood and brass body, and protective rubber end plates. Standard lengths are 450, 600 and 900 mm, and 1 and 2 m for checking across concrete and brick.

Water level, when attached to a garden hose and filled with water, establishes level heights at a distance that is limited only by the length of the hose. To use it, screw a tube onto each end of the hose; then fill the hose with water. Hold up one tube until the liquid reaches a desired height; the water in the other tube will adjust itself to the same height.

Line level is a handy miniature level with hooks that attach to a taut line stretched between two points. It has a standard vial, and is very useful in masonry, fencing and landscaping projects.

Angle level uses a dial and needle indicator (like a compass) to determine levelness and various degrees of angle. Some models attach magnetically to a metal straightedge, square or other metal surface.

Circular level, a 360° disc-shaped level, is also called a bull's-eye level. It's useful for shimming furniture and appliances, and for levelling caravans and boats. The bubble is centred in a circle when level.

Plumb bob has a weight attached to a line. To establish plumb (a straight vertical line), suspend the line from a height and drop the weight to the ground. Let the weight steady before checking plumb – for example, when aligning wallcoverings or panelling.

HAMMERS AND MALLETS

Most hammers come in a variety of head weights and handle lengths. Choose a quality tool that is precision balanced, fits your hand, matches your strength and is designed for the work you are doing. A quality hammer will have a forged steel head and a hardwood, fibreglass, graphite or steel handle. Avoid dangerous cast heads and softwood handles. Faces may be milled (corrugated) to prevent glancing blows and flying nails, but a milled face cannot be used on finished work or it will mar the surface. Most handles are contoured for comfort and some have slip-resistant grips.

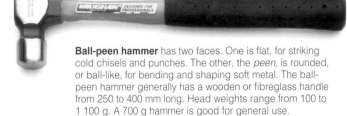

Ball-peen hammer has two faces. One is flat, for striking cold chisels and punches. The other, the *peen,* is rounded, or ball-like, for bending and shaping soft metal. The ball-peen hammer generally has a wooden or fibreglass handle from 250 to 400 mm long. Head weights range from 100 to 1 100 g. A 700 g hammer is good for general use.

Ripping hammer or 'wood-chipper' is similar to a curved-claw hammer except that its claw is almost straight. Although not as effective a nail puller as the curved-claw hammer, it is excellent for prying apart or tearing out boards, lath or sheet materials. The handle is usually from 250 to 425 mm long and the head weighs up to 750 g. Some hammers have magnetized heads to hold nails.

Curved-claw hammer, most familiar of all hammers, can be used for driving common or finishing nails, but concrete nails or case-hardened cut nails can damage it. Heads may be 300, 500, 600, 700 or 800 g. Handle length and thickness vary with head weight.

Soft-faced hammer or blow mallet will not mar surfaces because its 25 to 60 mm head has replaceable soft and hard plastic faces. It is used for joining, seaming, panelbeating and for assembling and dismantling wood or soft metal projects.

Upholsterer's hammer, or tack hammer, is a small lightweight tool that holds and sets tacks, small nails and brads. It usually has a wooden handle up to 300 mm long. The head, weighing up to 250 g, has a magnetic face on one end and a striking face, or a small claw, on the other. This hammer is used on cabinetwork, moulding, trim and upholstery.

Bricklayer's hammer usually has a square flat face for setting bricks in mortar and a chisel-shaped face for scoring and cutting bricks and chipping away excess mortar. The head commonly weighs 500 g and the wood or tubular steel handle may be up to 360 mm long.

Cross-peen, or Warrington, hammer has a head with a flat face and a tapered peen. This balanced hammer is a traditional cabinet-maker's tool. You can hold a nail in place with two fingers and start tapping it in with the peen face without smashing your fingers. The head weighs 200 or 225 g and handle lengths vary from 250 to about 375 mm.

Nail set, a punch-shaped tool, countersinks nails in wooden cabinets, mouldings and trim. Position its point over the head of the nail and strike the top with a hammer. Points range in diameter from 1 to 6 mm to accommodate the various nailhead sizes.

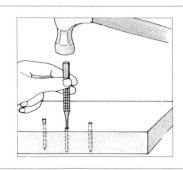

Jeweller's hammer is a lightweight tool that is ideal for working on models, miniatures and jewellery. Head is 50 to 75 mm long, and handle length up to 250 mm.

Sledgehammer breaks up concrete or drives heavy spikes, stakes or chisels into stone, brick or the ground by the sheer weight of its solid steel head, which ranges from 3,6 to 6,3 kg. The wood or fibreglass handle may be between 250 mm and 1 m in length. Heavy sledges are used primarily for demolition tasks.

Heavy-duty framing hammer, a construction tool for assembling and dismantling framing members, has an even narrower and straighter claw than the standard framing hammer. The hammer has a 425 mm-long hatchet handle, which gives more leverage and is less likely to twist in your hand. The head weighs about 800 g. The model shown here has a milled face.

Club hammer, a broad double-faced construction hammer, is often used by brick and blocklayers. Useful for striking cold and brick chisels, the metal head typically weighs 1,8 kg, and the handle (usually wood) is 250 mm long.

Carpenter's wooden-head mallet, used mainly for assembling woodworking components and striking chisels, is also good for installing metal parts on equipment without marring them. Its head varies from 60 to 150 mm in length and is usually made of beech or other hard wood.

Rubber mallet is used primarily in assembling components and beating out dents in metal. The barrel-shaped head is usually made of solid black rubber or non-marking white rubber, weighing 200 to 600 g. The handle is wood, or metal with a rubber grip and is up to 325 mm long.

Carver's mallet drives chisels and other carving tools into wood or stone. Its heavy head (500 g to over 1 kg) is made from a single piece of hard, dense wood, usually from 100 to 150 mm long. Store in a plastic bag to keep it from drying out.

Dead-blow hammer head is filled with steel shot and oil that absorb energy when the hammer impacts, eliminating any rebound in demolition and assembly work. The head weighs 225 g to 2 kg and the handle is 250 to 350 mm long.

Two-faced mallet has one round face and a tapering wedge face. The round face can be used to shape sheet metal into bowls or other concave shapes when hammering inside a wooden form. The wedge face shapes, or 'raises', metal over a solid stake.

Rawhide mallet consists of a round head of compressed rawhide, weighing 100 to 900 g, and its wooden handle is usually about 300 mm long. It has the same uses as a carpenter's wooden-head mallet.

METALWORKING HAMMERS AND HAMMERING SURFACES

Because so much metalworking involves hammering, a large number of specialized metalworking hammers are available. Before using a hammer to shape metal, be sure that the face is clean and free of pits or scale; the tiniest defect in the hammer head can be imprinted on the work many times over. It's a good idea to keep a piece of polishing cloth handy to wipe off the face of the hammer as you work. Before storing a metalworking hammer for a long time, coat the face with petroleum jelly, wax or oil.

Chasing hammer drives chisel-like tools into the top surface of sheet metal to indent decorative designs into it. The work is done in a pitch-filled bowl. The head of the hammer generally weighs up to 250 g.

Embossing hammer or light raising hammer is used to get into awkward areas and to imprint decorative bulges in the metal. Its head is 100 to 150 mm long and weighs 85 g to about 500 g.

Raising hammer shapes deep metal objects, such as bowls or vases, by striking their outer surfaces over solid metal stakes. Standard and extra-narrow heads are available, running from 100 to 150 mm long and generally weighing 250 to 500 g.

Planishing hammer flattens and toughens sheet metal as it adds texture to it. The head is 50 to 200 mm long and weighs from 50 to about 550 g. Some have one square and one round face.

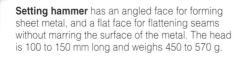

Setting hammer has an angled face for forming sheet metal, and a flat face for flattening seams without marring the surface of the metal. The head is 100 to 150 mm long and weighs 450 to 570 g.

Forging hammer is used to shape metal rods or bars. The head is 100 to 150 mm long and weighs 85 to 500 g. It generally has one slightly domed or flat face and one wedge-shaped face.

Blacksmith's hammer, the traditional tool for shaping heated metal on an anvil, is also used for driving spikes, stakes, rivets and hardened nails, for striking cold chisels, and for any job that requires a heavy striking face. The head weighs 750 g to 2 kg, and one of its faces is flat and the other is wedge-shaped.

Anvil (far right), one of the oldest and most used metal-shaping surfaces, is available in a wide variety of sizes.The familiar shape is flat on top and coned on one end. Metal is also shaped on solid steel stakes, which weigh from 2 to 25 kg. The crossbar of a T-stake may be curved, tapered or shaped like the horns of a bull. Mushroom stakes and flat circular stakes are also widely used. To hold a stake while hammering against it, slide it into a bolted-down holder, like the one shown, or into a special opening in your workbench or anvil. Rectangular blocks and cone-shaped mandrels are also used as hammering surfaces.

There are a number of other hammerlike tools and driving tools that are related to the hammer. The hatchet, of course, is used for chopping rather than driving or shaping, but many hatchets have a hammer face opposite the cutting face. Other hand and power tools are used for driving brads and staples, and large pry bars and nail pullers do the work that is too difficult for the claws on standard hammers.

Power stapler provides the fastest and easiest way to staple large or thick materials. Simply place the unit against a surface and pull the trigger to drive in a staple. There are cordless and standard models.

Drywall hatchet, a combination hammer and hatchet, is used to trim, position and attach wallboard to wall plugs or studs. Use the flat head of the tool to drive and set nails on flat surfaces and close to corners. Use the bevelled slot to pull nails, and the sharp hatchet face to make cutouts and score breaks in wallboard. The handle is 300 to 450 mm long, and the head generally weighs 300 to 400 g.

Half hatchet, a combination hammer and hatchet, includes a bevelled slot for pulling nails and normally comes with a wood handle that is 300 to 450 mm long. The head weighs 550 g to 1 kg. Like the drywall and shingling hatchet, it is uncommon in South Africa.

Brad nailer holds small nails in its magnetized spring loaded barrel while you drive them in by pushing the handle.

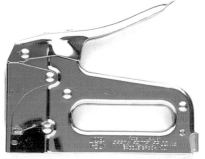

Hand stapler drives staples with a squeeze of the handle. Use it to attach paper-covered insulation, hang plastic sheets, upholster furniture, install screening or for any major stapling job in your home or workshop.

Shingling hatchet is a special tool for installing wooden shingles. The sharp face cuts the shingles, and a gauge on the side of the face spaces the shingles evenly; move the screw to the desired depth. The handle is 350 mm long and the head weighs 400 g.

Power brad nailer drives and countersinks brads up to 30 mm long with the pull of a trigger – and without marring the surface.

Pry bar utilizes two angled blades. One blade is used as a nail puller, and the other as a prying tool for removing moulding and trim and for separating materials that are nailed together. It is 300 to 750 mm long.

Nail puller removes deeply embedded nails, exerting more leverage with its 400 mm length than a claw hammer can. Some models are articulated to give more leverage and some have a cushioned grip.

Hammer tacker drives a staple in one motion. Simply strike the tool against the surface to be stapled. Various sizes of staples can be used in a hammer tacker.

Although a number of hand-powered drilling tools are available, every workshop should have at least one electric drill. Equipped with the right bit or attachment, an electric drill can bore holes in almost any material and do the work of other tools as well. The size of a drill is determined by the largest bit shank its chuck accepts. A drill may run at a single speed, two or three set speeds, or at variable speeds, which you set to suit the job. Generally, the larger the drill, the slower it runs but the greater its turning power, or torque. Before drilling, make sure the work is firmly supported and clamped down. Make a starter hole with a centre punch, awl or nail to keep the bit from wandering.

Brace works by manually cranking the centre handle as you apply pressure towards the bit. The brace is suitable for boring large holes in wood and for driving and removing screws. The bits must have a special end that is designed to fit into the brace's chuck jaw.

Hand drill bores holes in wood, soft metal and plastics, using twist or countersink bits with 6,4 mm shanks. A hand crank turns an interlocking gear to rotate the bit; reverse it to withdraw the bit.

Push drill operates with a repetitive pushing motion that turns a bit and bores a pilot hole up to 1,1 mm in diameter. You can use the tool with one hand, leaving the other free to hold the work or guide the tool. The drill accepts drill points. In this model, the points are stored in the handle; a knurled knob opens the handle.

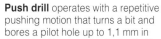

Miniature hand drill holds high-speed steel bits as small as 0,5 mm. This model has a collet on both ends to accept the bits. A miniature drill is especially handy for working on models, miniatures and jewellery. You can use it to make pilot holes for screws.

Standard electric hand drill comes with 6,4, 10 and 13 mm chucks to hold bits. Select a reversible drill so that you can back out bits or loosen screws, and get one with variable speeds if you want to use it with the various available accessories. Because of its high speed, the 6,4 mm model is good for boring small holes, but the 10 mm drill (top, left) can handle most household jobs, making it a better choice for the homeowner. The 13 mm drill (left) can bore larger holes, but because it runs at a lower speed, it's unsuitable for sanding and grinding.

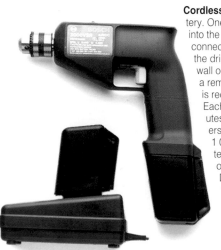

Cordless drill is powered by a battery. One type has a battery built into the handle. Recharge it by connecting the transformer to the drill and plugging it into a wall outlet. The other type has a removable battery pack that is recharged in a separate unit. Each pack takes about 45 minutes to charge and, manufacturers claim, can be charged up to 1 000 times. Buy an extra battery so that you can recharge one while using the other. Don't charge (or store) a tool where the temperature is below freezing or above 40°C. For longer battery life, turn the drill off when you're not using it.

Close-quarters drill has the same capabilities as a standard 10 mm electric drill, but its 55° angled chuck and unique, well-balanced body shape also allow access to hard-to-reach areas. A paddle switch allows you to control speed up to 1 300 rpm. Another switch on the bottom of the drill controls forward and reverse directions.

Drill-screwdriver, as the name implies, both drills and drives screws. Its motor has greater torque for driving screws without burning out; it also powers the drill through tough materials quickly. The cordless type shown here is easier to manipulate and can be used without awkward cords far from an electric outlet.

Drywall driver is designed specifically for driving drywall screws through wallboard and into wooden studs or plugs. The driver tip has a depth stop. Set the torque so that it doesn't overtighten the screw and tear the material or damage the screwhead. Cordless models are available.

Drill press incorporates an electric drill and worktable in one unit. Both freestanding and bench-top models are available, but either type must be bolted down. The machine's throat capacity (the distance between its rear post and the centre of the bit) determines the maximum size of the workpiece it can accept. Secure the work on the machine's table; lower the bit into the work by pulling down on the handle. The permanently positioned drill and adjustable worktable make the drill press the most accurate method of drilling square and angled holes. It's also ideal for sanding and shaping attachments.

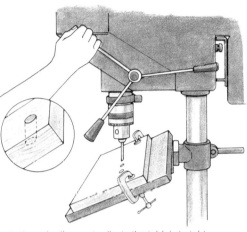

A clamp by the post adjusts the table's height; a clamp under the table adjusts its angle. Clamp smaller work and sheet metal to the table; to guide larger pieces, secure a jig to the table.

Hammer drill can bore into concrete and brick. This tool simultaneously spins a bit and creates a hammering action, which is rated in bpm (blows per minute). The variable speed feature can turn out up to 40 000 bpm. Most models are reversible and can be quickly switched to a standard rotary-action drill. Some are cordless. A depth stop and a detachable side handle may be included.

D-handle drill is suitable for driving auger bits and for other jobs where high torque is desirable. It comes with a 13 mm chuck and with single, double or variable-speed control. The D-shaped spade handle and side handle provide a secure grip for precise control on large jobs.

Right-angle drill has a right-angled head for operating in tight spaces where a standard drill body will not fit. The side handle helps support the tool. The angled head on this 13 mm model can be removed to use the drill straight on; some models do not have this feature. Use high speed for drilling small holes and low speed for large ones.

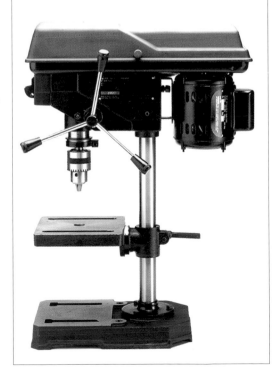

DRILL BITS

In order for them to be versatile – so they can make holes of different sizes and in a variety of materials – drills are designed to accept specialized bits. There are bits for wood, ferrous and non-ferrous metals, plastic, wallboard, concrete, masonry, glass and tile. Some bits make extra-smooth and accurate entrances and exits, which is desirable in fine woodworking; other less expensive bits make accurate holes when used properly, but can create rough exits if too much pressure is applied. Most types of bits are available in a wide range of sizes and quality. For the best results, always use the bit that is recommended for a specific job.

Screw pilot bit comes in several sizes to drill shank and pilot holes for a specific-size wood screw. In the same step you can also create a countersink to recess the screwhead or a counterbore to hide the screwhead. The tapered bit (right) creates a snug fit for wood screws.

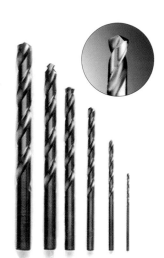

Adjustable screw pilot bit has a depth stop or a collar with a setscrew on its side. To set the bit for a flush, countersink or counterbore hole, release the setscrew to move the depth stop. On the model with a collar, body and thread cutters are also adjustable. Before tightening the setscrew, make sure the flat sides of all the cutting elements face the screw. The bits come in various sizes to match the diameters of different screws.

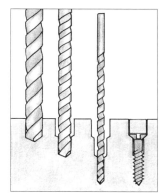

To counterbore a screw without a screw pilot bit, use twist bits slightly narrower than the screw threads and the same width as the head and body. Use a mallet to tap a glued plug into the hole.

Twist bit made of carbon steel is designed for wood. For metal, use hardened bits or bits coated with titanium. Lubricate the bit with machine oil when drilling steel or iron, with paraffin when drilling aluminium.

Brad-point bit, the best choice for wood, has a centre point to position it for the exact, clean holes that are required for fine woodworking applications, especially dowelling. Wide flutes eject wood chips to prevent clogging.

Countersink bit has an angled tip to form a recess for screwheads in wood, plastic, steel, iron and soft metals. Also use it to deburr and chamfer materials. Lubricate tip before applying the bit to metal.

Glass/tile bit has carbide tip for drilling holes in glass and tile. Drill slowly through pool of turpentine held in by putty dam.

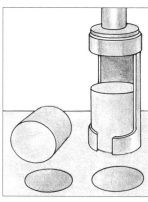

Spade bit has a centre locating point and two sharp flat cutting edges, which work with a scraping action, to bore holes in wood. Start the drill at a low speed; as the bit enters the wood, slowly increase the speed. It can leave a rough, splintered exit hole.

Masonry bit is designed for drilling holes at speeds below 400 rpm in masonry, concrete, brick, tile, slate and plaster. The carbide-tipped bit has spiral-shaped flutes to channel dust quickly and efficiently.

Plug cutter cuts out cylindrical shapes from hardwood to cover screw- and nailheads in counterbored holes. The plug should be at least 4 mm deep, but not more than 13 mm deep. Use the bit with a drill press only.

Forstner bit drills shallow hole with a sharp outside rim, leaving smooth-sided holes in wood. It has a small centre spur that enables the bit to create a nearly flat-bottomed hole. To form a mortise, cut overlapping holes. Use the bit in a drill press only.

Reamer bit is tapered to allow the tip to fit into an already existing hole, whether the material is wood or metal. As the bit moves into the hole, it enlarges the hole. The bit is also useful for removing burrs from metal tubing.

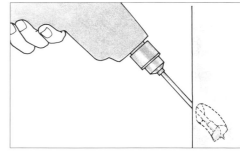

Around-the-corner bit has an angled cutting surface that lets you drill curved holes in tight corners. Gradually feed bit straight into the wood for 13 mm before turning drill to angle the hole. Set the drill at 850 to 1 000 rpm for softwood; for hardwood, set it at 600 to 850 rpm.

Pilot hole and screw-driver bits come as a set to use with electric hand drills and screw-drivers. First make the pilot hole. After the drill comes to a full stop, expose the screwdriver bit by sliding the ring toward the tip of the bit and then pulling off the pilot hole bit.

Self-feeding multispur bit drills holes large enough to run conduit or pipes through wood. To provide a fast feeding action, a replaceable threaded screw point pulls the bit to the work. The bit fits 13 mm drills only and requires very high torque.

Drill saw bit drills and cuts holes in both wood and metal. After the tip of the bit drills the hole, the teeth on the side of the bit cut the opening. It can also enlarge already existing holes. For metal, lubricate the tip before drilling.

Auger bit fits into the chuck of a hand brace. The tip of the bit has a point to start holes. The flutes prevent clogging by quickly ejecting wood chips as you drill, an ideal feature for making mortises.

Adjustable bit, or expansion bit, uses adjustable cutters to drill varying diameter holes. It's used to drill holes in wood for installing pipes and wiring, and in areas where a rough cut will suffice. To adjust the cutter, release the setscrew; then use the scale on the cutter to determine the hole size, and secure the setscrew.

Fly cutter, or circle cutter, is used on a drill press for cutting circles. A shank holds an arm with a cutter; the cutter can be set to different diameters.

Step bit incorporates up to 13 diameters in one bit. As the bit penetrates the stock, it drills a larger hole, deburring the hole at the same time. Use it in wood, soft metal and plastic (up to 4 mm thick).

Acrylic plastic bit has a tip that can prevent splintering when drilling in plastic. Use scrap ply-wood or plastic under the work as a backing board. With the work securely clamped to a bench or table, drill slowly with steady pressure. As you near the other side of the work, reduce drill pressure.

Hole saw with tempered hardened-steel teeth cuts large holes in wood, metal, plastic and wallboard. The saw is mounted on a hole saw arbor (right). The arbor is inserted into a drill. The bit extends slightly beyond the saw teeth to locate the centre; then the saw is pushed into the stock.

Although it isn't necessary to acquire accessories for your drill, they can make the tool more accurate and easier to use, and they can turn the drill into a driver, shaper, sander, grinder or polisher. Some accessories attach to or hold the drill housing, while others fit into the chuck. If you already have a tool such as a sander or grinder, it's best to use that tool for the appropriate job. But if you don't have the additional tools, these attachments are a suitable substitute.

Chuck key comes with an electric drill to lock bits. Hand-tighten bit in chuck; insert key into holes in chuck and turn clockwise. Always remove key before using drill.

Keyless drill chuck operates without a chuck key by hand-tightening only. You can attach it to a drill that has a standard chuck or purchase one as a replacement part. Some drills are sold with this type of chuck already attached.

Flexible shaft extends the shaft of an electric drill by about 1 m, making the drill more manageable for intricate work and for operations in tight places. One end fits into the drill chuck; the other has its own chuck, usually 6 or 8 mm, for small bits, rotary rasps and files, and sanding and buffing attachments.

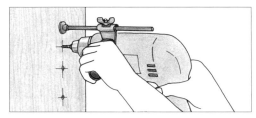

Depth stop and drill stop are guides for drilling holes to a specific depth. A steel or plastic drill stop (left) slides onto a bit; a depth stop (right) attaches to the body of an electric hand drill or to a secondary handle and is set to the right position. When either stop contacts the work surface, it stops the penetration of the bit.

Drill gauge, a template for measuring the size of a drill bit, has holes from 1 to 13 mm. Insert a bit into each hole until you find the one that fits best. The dimension is marked near the hole.

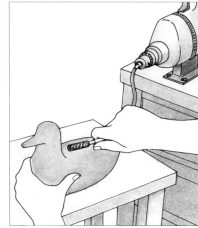

When using a flexible shaft with an electric hand drill, make sure the drill is in a stand secured to a bench. The shaft can also be used with a drill press.

Right-angle drive aids buffing and sanding, and allows drilling in tight areas where the entire length of a drill cannot fit. Some can also either double or halve drill speed. The drive fits between the drill and the chuck.

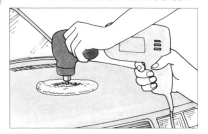

Bit extension adds to the length of a flat or hexagonal bit shaft, allowing you to drill deep holes and to make holes in recessed and hard-to-reach places with a spade or auger-type bit. Insert the bit shank into one end of the extension, and secure it with one or two setscrews. Make sure the bit is seated in a pilot hole before you start drilling. The extension comes in several lengths up to 450 mm.

Drill case, available in many styles, organizes bits for quick access. Look for a case that indicates bit size near the bit slot. This model clips onto the drill cord. To remove a bit, rotate the lid until the hole in the lid aligns with the desired bit. Tip the case to slide out the bit.

Screwdriver bits let you drive screws with an electric drill; these tempered bits have grooved tips to hold screws more securely.

Screwdriver attachment has a clutch mechanism that stops the drill when the screw is driven or pressure is slackened. Fit the attachment to the drill chuck of a variable-speed drill and a screwdriver bit into the attachment.

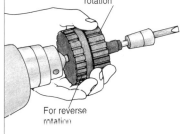

Speed reducer fits on a single-speed electric drill to allow variable-speed operation for screw and nut driving. Hold the reducer's housing when operating. One collar allows forward rotation of the bit; the other collar reverses the direction of rotation.

Rotary files and rasps fit drill presses and flexible shafts. They come in a wide range of shapes; use ones with large teeth for wood, with small teeth for metal.

Wire wheel, with wires extending from its circumference, can rotate at speeds of up to 3 000 rpm. You can use it on any size electric drill to remove paint, rust or stains from wood or metal.

Nail spinner attaches to a drill to start finishing nails. The pilot hole formed by the spinning nail prevents the wood from splitting and tearing as it is driven in. A similar job can be performed by pre-drilling small holes. Use a hammer to finish the job.

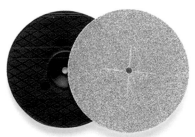

Drum sander sands curves and irregular shapes in wood, metal, fibreglass and plastic. Lock its shank into the chuck of an electric drill or a drill press. The drum varies in diameter from 13 mm to over 75 mm and in length up to 75 mm.

Wire cup brush incorporates wire strands into a circular brush. When mounted in an electric hand drill, it becomes a power scraper for removing paint, rust, or stains from wood or metal. Do not exceed maximum speed of 2 500 rpm.

Flap wheel sander has a number of sandpaper strips attached to a wheel. The spinning strips conform to the flat or contoured surface of the wood, metal, fibreglass or plastic workpiece for sanding and buffing. It's available in various sandpaper grits.

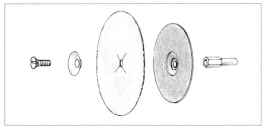

Sandpaper discs convert an electric hand drill to a sander. Some discs are used in combination with a backer pad and wheel arbor. Some systems work with self-adhesive sandpaper or have a Velcro backing. The sandpaper is available with garnet and aluminium oxide, and with coarse to fine grits.

Buffing pad is a soft pad for polishing metals. It is usually made of wool or polyester; most pads are washable and re-usable.

Fibre disc sands, grinds and cuts paint, rust, metal, tile, brick, concrete, and plastic. The disc is made of silicon carbide and attaches to any electric hand drill with a standard backer pad and wheel arbor (right, bottom). Although in some situations it can be used freehand, mounting the drill on a drill stand will allow greater control and safety.

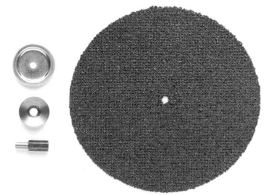

Drilling often requires precision boring that is difficult to achieve when holding an electric hand drill, even with steady hands. A variety of drill stands provides the necessary firm support for drilling holes at any angle. A drill stand also frees both hands to guide the workpiece. With certain drill accessories, such as a rotary rasp attached to a flexible shaft, a stand is essential.

Drill guides ensure accurate hole placement for a variety of drilling applications. The guides on the facing page, except for the spring-action hinge bit and the mortising attachment, can be used either with an electric hand drill or with a drill press.

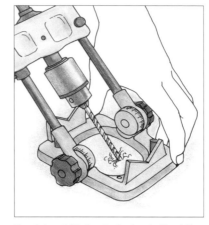

Vertical drill stand is a framework that supports an electric hand drill and turns it into a small bench-top drill press. It has all the basic drill press features: a scaled depth stop, a pull-down handle operation, and a worktable. On some models a mounting bracket swivels the drill to a horizontal position for grinding. On other models the worktable can be tilted to make angled cuts. Before using the stand, bolt it securely to a workbench.

Precision drill stand attaches to the drill in place of the chuck. Its chuck is mounted on a crosspiece that slides up and down two rods, which are attached to a flat base. The rods can be adjusted and locked into place at 5° intervals in order to drill holes at various angles. A collar on one rod acts as a depth stop.

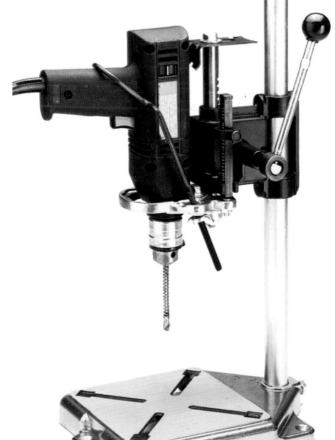

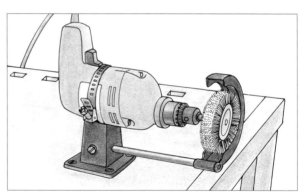

Horizontal drill stand is a base and shield unit that, when bolted to a workbench, holds electric hand drills in a horizontal position. The user's hands are free to hold and manipulate the material being worked. With various attachments, the drill can then be used for sanding, grinding, wire-brushing or polishing. The stand also allows the drill to be operated with a flexible shaft (p 30).

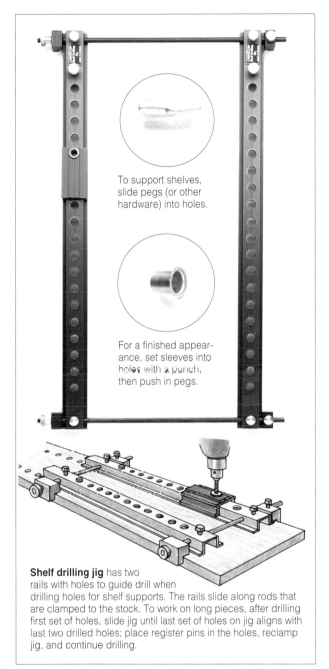

To support shelves, slide pegs (or other hardware) into holes.

For a finished appearance, set sleeves into holes with a punch, then push in pegs.

Shelf drilling jig has two rails with holes to guide drill when drilling holes for shelf supports. The rails slide along rods that are clamped to the stock. To work on long pieces, after drilling first set of holes, slide jig until last set of holes on jig aligns with last two drilled holes; place register pins in the holes, reclamp jig, and continue drilling.

Spring-action hinge (Vix) bit has a bit centred in a guide. The bit fits in an electric hand-drill chuck and is used for drilling pilot holes for hinge screws. First tape the hinges in position. Then place the bit in a hole in the hinge; the guide centres the bit. Push on the drill to extend the bit from the guide. A setscrew lets you adjust the depth of the pilot hole or replace the high-speed drill bit. The bit can drill into wood, metal and plastic.

Doweling jig centres any number of holes in ends or edges of wooden workpieces of almost any thickness. The jig clamps to the workpiece; a centred hole guide shows where to drill the hole. The holes accommodate standard-diameter dowels.

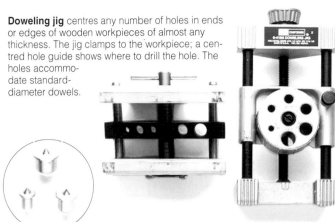

Dowel centres align corresponding dowel holes in wood workpieces that are to be joined. Drill holes in one workpiece; push dowel centres into the holes, align with the second workpiece, and push. The points on the dowel centres leave marks to show where to drill holes in the second workpiece.

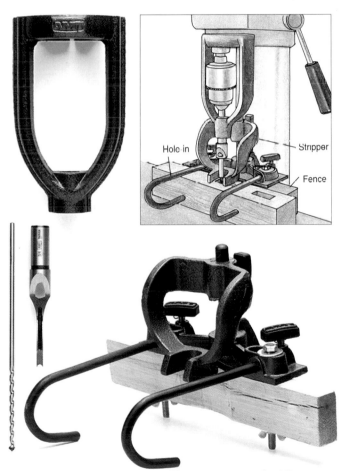

Mortising attachment is bolted on a quill above the chuck of a drill press. A bit removes waste; a chisel shapes the mortise. The attachment includes a fence for guiding the work, and a stripper and hold-ins to support it. When using the attachment, run the drill press at normal speed and work down to final depth in 4 mm increments. As the chisel finishes each cut, move workpiece to continue the mortise.

SCREWDRIVERS

Used to insert, remove, loosen and tighten screws, screwdrivers come in many widths and lengths, with different-shaped shanks and with a variety of tips. Screws are driven by torque, or turning power, not by downward pressure. The larger the handle diameter, the more torque per turn. Always match the screwdriver tip to the size and type of screw. To drive a screw, hold it and the screwdriver in a straight line. A screwdriver performs under normal use without marring the tip or the screwhead. Never use a screwdriver as a crowbar, punch or chisel; doing so can damage the tool and the workpiece.

Round-shank screwdriver has a cylindrical *shank,* the steel rod between the tip and handle. The round shape lets you quickly turn the screwdriver by supporting the shank with one hand while rotating the handle with the other.

Stubby screwdriver, designed to be used in restricted areas, has a very short shank. Its large handle permits a firm grip to improve torque.

Square-shank screwdriver is used to drive screws that require a great deal of torque. With an adjustable wrench, grip the square shank and turn the screwdriver; but be careful not to apply too much torque, or the screwhead may be stripped or broken. A rubber sleeve over a plastic fluted handle on some screwdrivers also increases torque by enlarging the grip.

Cabinetmaker's screwdriver has a fat oval handle that is preferred for woodworking. It fits neatly into the palm of the hand. The parallel-sided tip fits into recessed holes to turn slotted flat-head screws without marring the work.

Electrician's screwdriver, designed for working on electrical appliances and equipment, is made with a long shank to reach into deep electrical boxes. It has a plastic tube around the shank to protect the user from electrical shock. Before starting work, unplug appliance or turn off power.

Standard (slotted) screwdriver, the most common type, fits slotted screws. The flared, or winged, tip (left) is best for round- or oval-head screws. Parallel-sided tip (see cabinetmaker's) is best for flat-head screws.

Phillips screwdriver, the most common type of cross-head screwdriver, is made to fit snugly into a Phillips-head screw. The cross design of the tip provides a better grip than the straight-tip style.

Torx screwdriver, widely used in automobile repair work, has a star-shaped tip that can be useful for replacing such parts as taillight lenses. Torx screws are also found in household appliances and garden equipment.

Hex-drive screwdriver conforms to screws that can also be operated with hex (Allen) keys. Suitable for socket-head screws that are recessed, the screwdriver is available in inch and metric sizes.

Ball-end hex-drive screwdriver, for socket-head screws, has a round tip that can be angled up to 25° from the surface. This makes it useful for reaching screws in tight spots. The screwdriver can drive the screw without stripping it.

Pozidriv screwdriver, one of the specialized cross-head screwdrivers, has a square end instead of a pointed tip. Popular in the automotive industry, it's also used for screws in appliances.

Clutch-drive screwdriver has an hourglass-shaped tip that is especially suitable for applications that require extra holding power, as in cars and appliances. It is also used for security to discourage disassembly by unauthorized persons.

Nutdriver operates in the same way as a screwdriver to turn hexagonal nuts and bolts. It comes with a screwdriver-style handle. Some models come in colour-coded or marked sets to make it easy to identify the size.

Robertson screwdriver, usually colour-coded according to size, can reach screws that are sunk below the surface in furniture and in mobile homes, caravans and boats. The square drive in this screwdriver transmits high torque power.

Expansion-tip screwdriver holds a slotted screw as you start to drive it. To use this tool, insert the tip into the screw slot and slide the collar over the split blade, forcing the halves to wedge against each other and to lock into and hold the screw.

Offset screwdriver, handy for driving screws in hard-to-reach spots, is operated with a cranking action. The tips are set at 45° or 90° from the shank; they may be slotted or Phillips – or the screwdriver may have one of each. A ratchet model (far left) lets you drive the screw with a back-and-forth motion without removing the screwdriver.

Cordless power screwdriver, with interchangeable tips, lets you drive a large number of screws without the fatigue of hand-driving. To drive or remove screws, a switch allows you to change the direction of rotation. This model has a locking shaft to permit hand operation as a standard screwdriver for extra torque. To recharge the screwdriver, plug it into a charging unit or place a battery in the unit. Mains current models are also available.

Adjustable power screwdriver has a hinge in the middle of its body, which can be snapped into two positions: the conventional straight line of a screwdriver or an angled pistol-grip hold. The torque can also be adjusted on this cordless tool.

Jeweller's screwdriver is ideal for small screws in items like spectacles. To use it, apply pressure to the screwdriver's head with your index fingertip; turn the tool's body with your other fingers.

Magnetic screwdriver accepts interchangeable tips, which come in common types and sizes. A magnetic end holds the tips in place. Some models have a ratchet operation for fast work at high torque, as well as a switch for reversing the direction of the drive. The handle may be hollow to store the tips.

Spiral ratchet screwdriver lets you turn a screw by repeatedly pushing the handle. A ratchet switch changes the direction of rotation of the shank to allow for both driving and removing screws. The knurled collar just below the switch locks the shank in the retracted position for use as a conventional screwdriver. In some models the handle provides storage for extra tips.

Screw holder, an attachment that snaps onto most round-shank screwdrivers, allows the placement of screws where fingers cannot reach. To start a screw, slip it between the holder jaws. Before driving the screw in all the way, slide the holder up the shank, out of the way. It's available in several sizes.

Bradawl (top) and **gimlet** (bottom) are tools for boring pilot holes in wood, thereby making it easier to drive a screw. To use either tool, turn it clockwise. The pilot hole should be narrower and shorter than the screw, leaving enough material for the screw threads to bite into. Gimlets are available in various screw sizes.

Whether they grip a hard-to-hold workpiece or cut wire or other objects, all pliers have the same design: handles on one side of a pivot joint, which allows a scissor-type action, and jaws on the other side. Always use a pair of pliers for the job it was intended to do. The smaller long-nose pliers are delicate; forcing them to do work beyond their capacity can render them useless. Use pliers to turn nuts only in an emergency; pliers can strip the nut, making it difficult to remove with the proper tool. Unless explicitly stated, do not assume that pliers designed for electrical work are insulated, even if the handles have a plastic, rubber or similar coating.

Slip-joint pliers have both serrated teeth and coarse contoured teeth to grip objects of different shapes. They can be set in two positions to vary the jaw size.

Curved thin-nose slip-joint pliers are made with a specially shaped nose to let you see the work. As with many slip-joint pliers, they have wire cutters in the jaws.

Angle-nose pliers, slip-joint pliers with three adjustable settings, have an offset head for hard-to-reach areas where added leverage is needed.

Tongue-and-groove pliers grip flat, square, round or hexagonal objects with serrated teeth. The jaws are set by slipping the curved ridge into the desired groove.

Straight-jaw locking pliers clamp firmly onto objects. A knob in one handle controls the jaws' width and tension. Close handles to lock the pliers; release a lever to open them.

Large tongue-and-groove pliers, also known as 'pump pliers', are often used for holding pipes and give more leverage because of long handles. The jaws stay parallel at all settings.

Long-nose pliers, or snipe-nose pliers, are used to hold small objects, especially in electrical work. Narrow flat jaws may have serrated teeth. They can fit into confined areas and can grip parts. Some models have a wire cutter.

Needle-nose pliers, a smaller version of long-nose pliers, may have smooth, thin tapered jaws that won't mar or scratch. They are ideal for working with soft metals, especially in jewellery. Some have serrated teeth, and some have spring-tensioned handles.

Curved needle-nose pliers are also ideal for working on jewellery or small electrical items. The bent nose holds the workpiece away from the pliers and in the user's line of vision.

Round-nose pliers, favoured by both electricians and jewellers, have smooth, tapered round jaws designed for bending thin wire and sheet metal into different-size loops.

Needle-nose end-cutting pliers work best for cutting thin wire. The cutting area is at the tip of the jaws for cutting items flush or in tight areas.

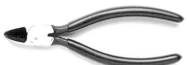

Side cutters, also known as diagonal-cutting nippers, are designed for cutting wire and thin metal. The cutting area is positioned on the side edge of the jaws to cut precise wire lengths and for cutting flush against a surface or in cramped spaces where larger tools can't fit.

End nippers, or end-cutting pliers, a larger oval-head version of the needle-nose end-cutting pliers, cut heavier wire. Their design keeps knuckles out of the way and cuts work flush. They also come with angled jaws.

Fence pliers combine several features in one tool to help install wire fencing. The head has wire-cutting slots on each side; the jaws are for pulling and stretching wire mesh; the tool's hammer is suitable for driving staples; and the claw pulls out staples.

Tile nippers chip, shape and trim irregular contours in ceramic tile up to 10 mm thick. They are ideal for shaping tiles to fit around plumbing fixtures.

Bolt cutters are heavy-duty metal-cutting pliers that chop soft to medium-hard materials such as rods, bolts and wire. The handles may be from 200 mm to almost 1 m long. Handle length and pivot mechanism provide the leverage needed to cut through metals. Use both hands to operate the tool.

Wire stripper removes insulation from wire. To stop the blades from cutting into the wire, adjust a screw in a handle; it blocks the handles and the jaws. A band holds the handles closed when not in use.

Wire stripper and cutter removes insulation from a wire and cuts it. To strip a section of wire, place it in a hole, squeeze the handles, and pull off the insulation. To cut the wire, set it between the jaws' sharp flat edges.

Tweezers and tongs

While not technically pliers, these holding tools are necessary for delicate work as well as for protecting hands from heat and chemicals.

Tweezers are used for holding small objects. They are ideal for miniature work and making jewellery, and they can help remove wood or metal splinters. Tweezers come with straight or curved blades and with sharp, rounded or flat points that are either smooth or serrated.

Automatic wire stripper cuts and strips wire with one squeeze of the handles – unlike other strippers that require you to pull off the insulation after cutting it. This stripper has two sets of jaws: one pair holds the wire; the other pair cuts and pulls off the insulation, exposing enough bare wire for a connection.

Lineman's pliers are a combination of flat-jaw pliers and wire cutters. The outermost portion of the jaws is flat and serrated for a solid grip when pulling and twisting wire. The inner portion of the jaws is a basic cable and wire cutter.

Soldering tweezers are fireproof fine-point tools for holding small pieces of metal during soldering. These cross-locking models can double as clamps. To push the ends apart, apply pressure to the centre part of the tool, the point where the arms overlap.

Multipurpose electrician's pliers measure, strip and cut wire, crimp wire connectors and cut machine screws. Models vary in functions; buy one that will suit your needs best. As with other wire strippers, the handles do not insulate against electricity.

Copper tongs hold soldered metal while positioning it in a bath of pickling solution for cleaning. Because iron contaminates the solution, iron tongs are not suitable for this job.

Turning tools that fit around nuts, bolts or pipe fittings, spanners and wrenches provide the needed leverage to loosen and tighten the fasteners. A spanner may be fixed (fit only one size of nut or bolt) or adjustable (expandable to fit different sizes). A fixed spanner comes in English or metric sizes and is used on the exactly corresponding size nut or bolt. No matter how close the size might seem, using a spanner that is 'almost right' can damage the hardware. To make hard-to-reach nuts and bolts accessible, one side of the heads on some fixed spanners is open to let the spanner slide into place. Ring spanners and closed tubular box spanners are stronger and less likely to slip. They come with 8 points to fit square nuts or with 6 or 12 points to fit hex nuts.

Obstruction spanner is a double open-end spanner that has a standard open head on one end of the shaft and a head of the same size on the other end with the opening angled up to 90°. The angled head allows the user to reach fasteners that are otherwise hard to reach.

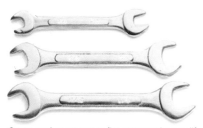

Open-end spanner or flat spanner has a different opening at each end. The openings are close in size, and may match one on the previous- or following-size spanner, providing two same-size heads – one to turn the nut, the other to hold the bolt. Extra-thin spanners are available to fit into tight spots.

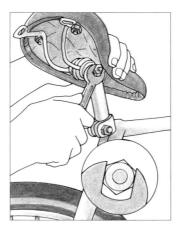

Combination spanner gives you a choice of two different ends of the same size to loosen or tighten a nut or bolt. Use the ring end when the job calls for strength and the speedier open end when less torque is needed.

Crow's-foot wrench, an open-end spanner head without a handle, has a square hole that accepts either a socket spanner handle or an extension. Depending on the type of handle used, the head can be used parallel to the handle or set at an angle, making it exceptionally useful for tightening or loosening nuts in odd positions.

Flare-nut spanner for copper and brass fittings slides over tubing, then down to the fitting. It has a better grip than an open-end spanner.

Torque wrench turns nuts and bolts to an exact tightness. It is ideal for tightening a number of fasteners to the same degree to avoid warping. A scale is attached to the handle of one standard model. The torque (turning force) is indicated by a pointer that remains stationary as the handle bends under stress. All models accept standard square-drive sockets and adapters. Measuring units and the amount of torque vary.

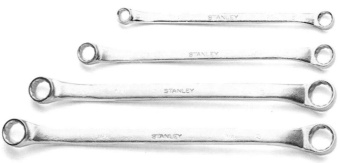

Offset double ring spanner is designed for hex or square nuts and bolts. Its handle curves away from the work surface, leaving room for gripping. The box ends fit more securely around the fastener than the open-end type. After each turn, lift and re-position the wrench before continuing.

Combination box wrench, resembling a dog bone, has five different openings on each head. The handle provides little leverage, making it suitable only for light work. Its compact size is ideal for carrying on bicycle trips.

Cranked spanner handle uses a cranking motion to remove or install nuts or bolts. Its 13 mm shaft accepts socket heads, adapters and extensions. The grip remains stationary while the shaft is turned clockwise for tightening fasteners, counterclockwise for loosening.

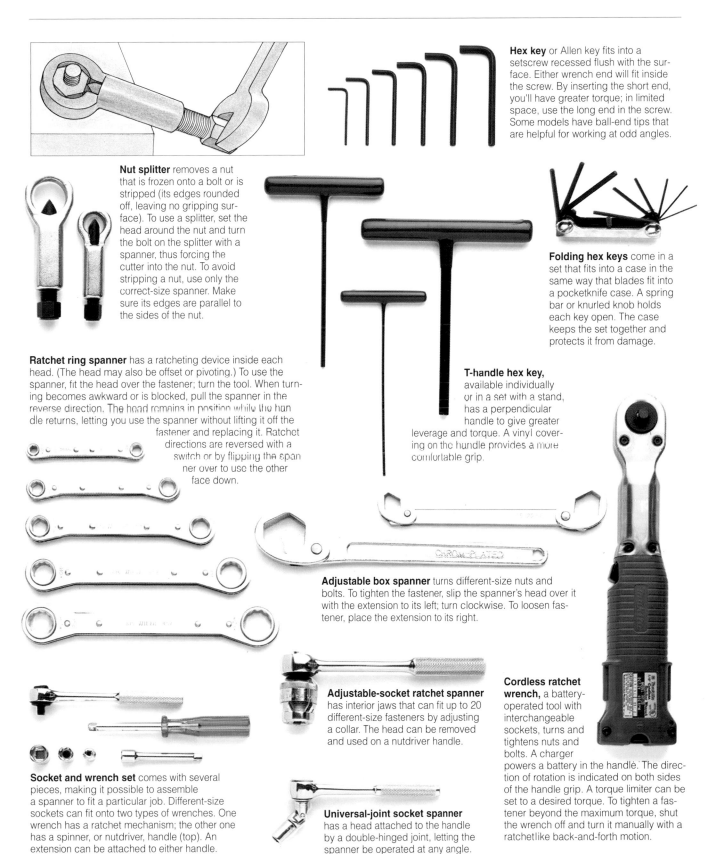

Hex key or Allen key fits into a setscrew recessed flush with the surface. Either wrench end will fit inside the screw. By inserting the short end, you'll have greater torque; in limited space, use the long end in the screw. Some models have ball-end tips that are helpful for working at odd angles.

Nut splitter removes a nut that is frozen onto a bolt or is stripped (its edges rounded off, leaving no gripping surface). To use a splitter, set the head around the nut and turn the bolt on the splitter with a spanner, thus forcing the cutter into the nut. To avoid stripping a nut, use only the correct-size spanner. Make sure its edges are parallel to the sides of the nut.

Folding hex keys come in a set that fits into a case in the same way that blades fit into a pocketknife case. A spring bar or knurled knob holds each key open. The case keeps the set together and protects it from damage.

Ratchet ring spanner has a ratcheting device inside each head. (The head may also be offset or pivoting.) To use the spanner, fit the head over the fastener; turn the tool. When turning becomes awkward or is blocked, pull the spanner in the reverse direction. The head remains in position while the handle returns, letting you use the spanner without lifting it off the fastener and replacing it. Ratchet directions are reversed with a switch or by flipping the spanner over to use the other face down.

T-handle hex key, available individually or in a set with a stand, has a perpendicular handle to give greater leverage and torque. A vinyl covering on the handle provides a more comfortable grip.

Adjustable box spanner turns different-size nuts and bolts. To tighten the fastener, slip the spanner's head over it with the extension to its left; turn clockwise. To loosen fastener, place the extension to its right.

Adjustable-socket ratchet spanner has interior jaws that can fit up to 20 different-size fasteners by adjusting a collar. The head can be removed and used on a nutdriver handle.

Cordless ratchet wrench, a battery-operated tool with interchangeable sockets, turns and tightens nuts and bolts. A charger powers a battery in the handle. The direction of rotation is indicated on both sides of the handle grip. A torque limiter can be set to a desired torque. To tighten a fastener beyond the maximum torque, shut the wrench off and turn it manually with a ratchetlike back-and-forth motion.

Socket and wrench set comes with several pieces, making it possible to assemble a spanner to fit a particular job. Different-size sockets can fit onto two types of wrenches. One wrench has a ratchet mechanism; the other one has a spinner, or nutdriver, handle (top). An extension can be attached to either handle.

Universal-joint socket spanner has a head attached to the handle by a double-hinged joint, letting the spanner be operated at any angle.

ADJUSTABLE WRENCHES

Designed to accept pipes, pipe fittings, bolts and nuts, the adjustable wrench may have two jaws – one fixed, the other movable – or a strap or chain that grips the object to loosen or tighten it. Use one of these wrenches when the right-size fixed spanner is not available or for special tasks such as reaching under a basin. An adjustable wrench usually works best with pressure put on the stationary jaw, not the movable one.

Shifting spanner, also known as an adjustable spanner, is a versatile smooth-jaw wrench for turning nuts, bolts, small pipe fittings and chrome-faced pipe fittings. Some models have calibrated faces so that the spanner can be set to turn a fastener of a known size.

Pipe wrench turns threaded pipes. The upper jaw is adjusted by turning the knurled knob. Both jaws have serrated teeth for gripping power. When using the wrench, turn it so that you apply pressure on the movable jaw. That jaw is spring-loaded and slightly angled; it allows you to release the grip and re-position the wrench, without re-adjusting the jaw, when you remove the pressure.

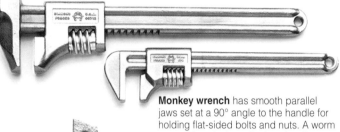

Monkey wrench has smooth parallel jaws set at a 90° angle to the handle for holding flat-sided bolts and nuts. A worm gear with a single rack of teeth adjusts the movable jaw to the desired opening.

Spud wrench loosens and tightens fittings on drain traps, sink strainers, toilet connections and large odd-shaped nuts. After adjusting the jaws, lock them in place with the wing nut.

Chain-locking clamp and wrench can turn irregularly shaped items and can also clamp objects together up to 150 mm in diameter. Wrap the chain around the object and slide it under the tool's hook. Adjust the thumbscrew to tighten or loosen the chain. Lock the chain in position by squeezing the handles; un-lock it by squeezing the lever inside one of the handles.

Chain wrench fits around any large pipe or oddly shaped item. Wrap the chain around the object, secure it on the hook in the handle, and pull the wrench downward (with the hook on top).

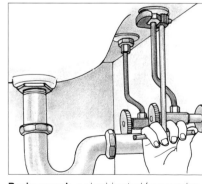

Basin wrench, a plumbing tool for removing and installing basin taps, has a long handle that reaches up from under a sink to turn nuts on fittings and taps. The hinged jaw re-positions itself after each turn. Buy one with a reversible jaw.

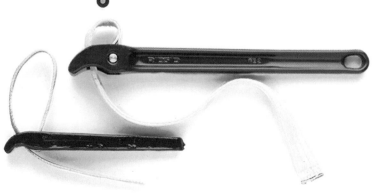

Strap wrench has canvas webbing that wraps around pipes without marring their finish. Hold the wrench with the claw pointing down; loop the strap around the pipe, then into the opening. Pull the wrench toward the free end of the strap.

A clamping tool that holds work steady, the vice is attached, permanently or temporarily, to a work surface. Specialized woodworking vices have smooth wood or metal jaws; metalworking vices have serrated teeth on steel jaws. Be sure to match the vice to the job; improper use can damage the vice or the workpiece. To protect the workpiece, fasten a jaw face between it and the jaws of the vice. For woodworking, use wood or hardboard jaw faces. If the work is metal, bend smooth sheet metal (at least as wide as the jaws) to a right angle over the jaws, or use a fibre liner.

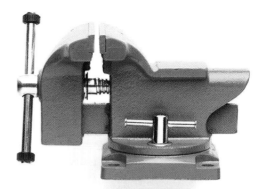

Machinist's vice is permanently bolted to a benchtop for metalworking. Many models incorporate a small anvil and have a swivel base that locks in place. Some vices can hold round pipe with round serrated pipe jaws located under the flat jaws.

Woodworker's bench vice has a screw-and-slide adjustment mechanism that mounts on the underside of a workbench, preferably near a leg for stability. The jaws and handle are exposed at the bench edge. The flat smooth jaws have holes for attaching wood faces to protect the workpiece. The wood or metal handle slides from side to side for easy turning and often has a quick release mechanism.

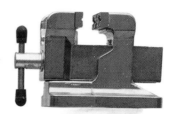

Drill press vice, when bolted on a drill press work-table, holds small and round metal pieces securely for drilling. Some mod els tilt for drilling angled holes.

Hold-down applies downward pressure on woodwork. It can be mounted on a workbench, along the edge or middle of the top surface or on the bench's side, or on a machine table for a drill press or table saw. The tool usually hooks onto mounting bolts permanently set in the bench. It can be used in unlimited locations by installing additional bolts. Simply remove the tool from one bolt and hook it onto another.

Bench holdfast has a long shaft that slides through a metal collar, which is counterbored in the bench for re-inforcement. An arm is attached to the shaft with a pivot; a screw tightens the holdfast. Set a few collars along the edges of the bench for flexibility when positioning the tool.

Clamp-on vice, a small portable machinist's vice that is suitable for light-duty use, attaches to the edge of a workbench with a screw-clamp mechanism. The vice can be stored when not in use and set up quickly whenever it's needed.

Bench dogs, whether metal or wood, clamp work in a bench vice. One dog fits into a hole in the bench (you may have to make it); the other dog fits in the movable vice jaw, or it may be part of the vice.

Whenever you need extra hands to hold pieces together temporarily, clamps are the tools of choice. Use them to grip corresponding parts while driving nails or drilling holes for screws, to test-fit pieces before gluing them, or to brace a freshly glued assembly until the glue dries.

Clamps come in many sizes and styles. Some have specific applications, while others are used in a wide array of situations. Every workshop should have a variety of top-quality clamps; buy them in pairs as you need them. The more clamps you have, the better. According to one rule of thumb, too many clamps are just enough. When using clamps, be sure to apply pressure evenly from two sides to avoid twisting the work.

G-clamp, one of the most common types of clamps, is named for its G-shaped appearance. A *shoe* at one end of the screw holds the work against the frame; at the other end is a T-handle. To tighten the screw against the work or change the size of the opening, adjust the screw by turning the T-handle.

Deep-throat G-clamp is shaped for clamping toward the centre of the workpiece, distributing pressure evenly. The deep throat is particularly useful for holding wide pieces where the shallow-throat frame of a standard G-clamp won't fit. As with most clamps, attach a piece of scrap wood to each jaw with double-stick tape to keep the jaws from marring the work.

Square-frame G-clamp is a variation of the standard G-clamp. The square inside perimeter of the frame allows the clamp to fit around the corners of a square workpiece, but it still applies full pressure to the work.

Edge clamp has two or three screws extending from the frame to exert right-angle pressure on the edge or side of a workpiece. A three-way edge clamp (shown) is more versatile for positioning the workpiece. The right-angle, or centre screw can be positioned on or off centre on varying thicknesses of workpieces.

Spring clamp operates with hand pressure to open the jaws. Spring pressure forces the jaws closed when the handles are released, allowing the jaws to grip the work. Some models have plastic-coated handles for easier opening and coated tips to protect the workpiece.

Small parallel clamp operates in a similar way to the hand-screw clamp (right), but its jaws are set in a parallel position. It's ideal for working with small or thin pieces without interfering with the workspace.

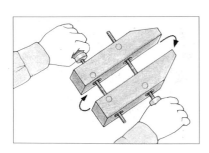

Hand-screw clamp can spread pressure over a broad surface area. Each jaw works independently, allowing them to angle towards or away from each other or to remain parallel. Set the jaws slightly wider than desired by holding the spindles and rotating the clamp. Slip the jaws over the work and tighten the rear spindle.

Speed clamp consists of a bar with a fixed jaw and a sliding jaw. A spring-locking device secures the sliding jaw in place. Set the workpiece against the fixed jaw and slide the other jaw to the work (with the screw set away from the work). Once the clamp is positioned, tighten the screw to hold the work securely.

Cam-action clamp has a sliding jaw that adjusts quickly to the size of the work. A handle in the movable jaw is set in a perpendicular position to lock the jaw and work in place. The jaws are padded with cork to prevent damaging the work surface. Its light weight makes this clamp suitable for most delicate work.

Universal clamp holds two pieces of 15- or 22 mm stock together for gluing. One jaw has a friction grip for holding the stock in place; the other jaw has a screw for increasing the clamp pressure. The clamp is best suited for long work where bar clamps are not practicable.

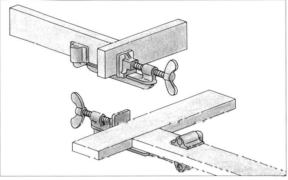

The Universal clamp at top is handy for clamping shelves and drawer supports to the furniture carcass; the one at bottom is useful for holding butt joints and T-joints.

Pipe clamp comes in a kit to fit onto 15 or 22 mm iron pipe. The length of the clamp is determined by the length of the pipe. A sliding jaw operates with a spring locking device; a middle jaw is controlled by a screw set in a third, fixed jaw.

Scrap wood

Pipe saddles hold 22 mm pipes. Mounted on sawhorses and gripping pipe clamps, they support a work surface. On a workbench, they create a clamping station. A thumbscrew retains the pipe.

Reversible pipe clamp has a sliding jaw that can also be used in the reverse direction, applying pressure away from the clamp instead of between the clamp jaws. As with the standard pipe clamp, set the work against the middle jaw first, with the screw drawn back; set the sliding jaw; then tighten the screw.

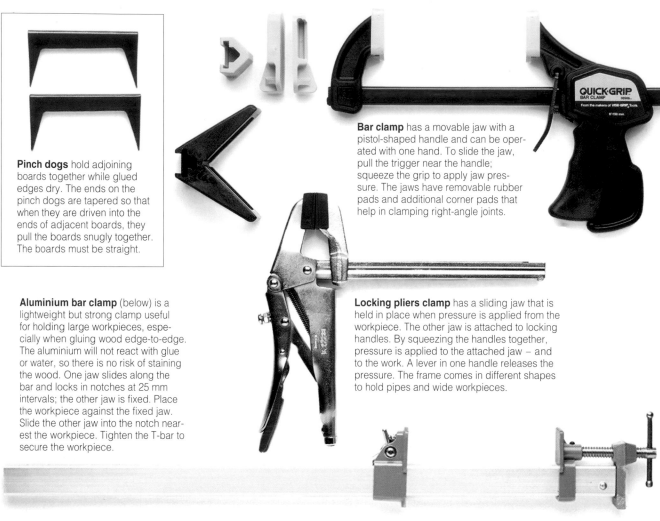

Pinch dogs hold adjoining boards together while glued edges dry. The ends on the pinch dogs are tapered so that when they are driven into the ends of adjacent boards, they pull the boards snugly together. The boards must be straight.

Bar clamp has a movable jaw with a pistol-shaped handle and can be operated with one hand. To slide the jaw, pull the trigger near the handle; squeeze the grip to apply jaw pressure. The jaws have removable rubber pads and additional corner pads that help in clamping right-angle joints.

Aluminium bar clamp (below) is a lightweight but strong clamp useful for holding large workpieces, especially when gluing wood edge-to-edge. The aluminium will not react with glue or water, so there is no risk of staining the wood. One jaw slides along the bar and locks in notches at 25 mm intervals; the other jaw is fixed. Place the workpiece against the fixed jaw. Slide the other jaw into the notch nearest the workpiece. Tighten the T-bar to secure the workpiece.

Locking pliers clamp has a sliding jaw that is held in place when pressure is applied from the workpiece. The other jaw is attached to locking handles. By squeezing the handles together, pressure is applied to the attached jaw – and to the work. A lever in one handle releases the pressure. The frame comes in different shapes to hold pipes and wide workpieces.

Double-action edge-gluing clamp applies even pressure across the faces and to the edges of tabletops and other flat workpieces. Use several clamps to ensure a flat surface when gluing boards edge-to-edge. To assemble the work, a linking device attached to the bottom bar swings out of the way, allowing you to remove the top bar. Once the work is in place, set the top bar on the work; fit the linking device in the notch in the top bar. (Some models have several notches for adustments; you can add your own.) A screw forces the two bars and the linking device to apply equal pressure.

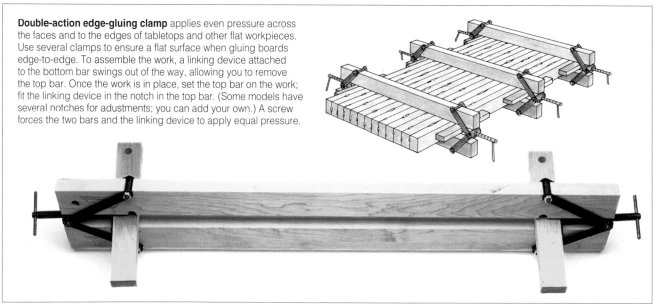

Band clamp applies even pressure around regular and irregular shapes. Loop the 25 mm-wide nylon band around the workpiece and pull it snug by hand. To apply pressure, tighten the bolt in the clamp head with a wrench or screwdriver. A quick-release device loosens the band. Steel cornerpieces allow the band to tighten evenly around the workpiece without catching on sharp corners.

Framing clamp holds all four 90° corners of a frame while glue dries. L-shaped corner blocks have grooves to allow excess glue to escape. To use the clamp, screw the threaded rods into the blocks and adjust them to the frame size; then thread knurled nuts onto the rods near the blocks. Place the clamp around the object; adjust the pressure with the knurled nuts. The clamp fits frames up to 1,2 m square, and can also be used for clamping boxes, small shelf units, and other rectangular workpieces.

Web clamp has a broad canvas band that can be set around irregular shapes. Wrap the band around the workpiece; weave the loose band ends into the head, passing the rollers and looping around the cams. Then pull the band snug at both ends; the cams will lock the band in place. To exert pressure against the work, rotate the screw. While the band clamp (above) is suitable for lightweight jobs such as clamping chairs and picture frames, the web clamp is better for heavy-duty applications such as clamping sofa frames.

Mitre clamp is designed to hold joints. One type (above) has a removable jaw that rotates, allowing the clamp to be set at different angles. A handle adjusts its placement. By turning a second handle, swivel jaws apply pressure to the work. Another type has screws that press the jaws toward the work.

KNIVES, SNIPS AND SCRAPERS

Cutting and scraping tools are necessities for everything from opening taped boxes to removing chipped paint from walls. There are two basic types of knives. One has a sharp blade for cutting materials; the other type has a larger, duller blade for applying compounds to walls and ceilings. Scrapers also have sharp blades; they help remove material from a surface. When using a cutting tool, always make sure that the blade is sharp. A dull blade can damage the material it's used on and cause injury to the user.

Utility knife has a variety of blades to cut wood, vinyl and other materials. A good straight-handle model has a button that adjusts the length of the blade and retracts the blade into the handle for safety. Replacement blades are often stored in the handle. To expose a stored blade in the offset-handle model, unscrew the cap and pivot the sides.

Snap-blade knife has blades that can be snapped off when dull. The end cap pulls off to allow insertion of the blade cartridge. To snap off a blade, use a slot in the end cap. A locking button adjusts blade position and retracts it into handle.

Razor knife holds a replaceable standard single-edge razor blade. It's ideal for trimming and cutting wallcoverings, paper and similar materials. The model at left has an attachment to cut overlapping pieces for a perfect butt.

Carpet knife has a blade shape that's best for trimming carpeting in tight areas, such as in corners and around doorjambs, vents and pipes. Use the back edge of the blade to tuck carpet under moulding.

Vinyl knife has a blade ideal for scoring hard and soft vinyl and other similar floorcoverings.

Flooring knife is also handy for shaping flooring materials, and it can score wallboard. Use the blade edge for scraping.

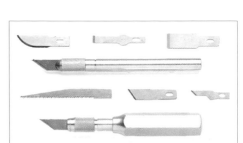

Hobby knife has numerous blades for various tasks, and the handle comes in different sizes. A large handle helps cut hard materials; a small handle is better for precision cuts. Loosen the knurled collar to change blades. Depending on the blade and handle, the knife can cut paper, plastic, wood, cloth and metal.

Plastic cutter has angled blade edges for scoring acrylic and other brittle materials. Turn the tool over to use it in an offset position.

Shavehook scrapes paint from mouldings. Blades may also be teardrop-shaped or triangular to fit different mouldings. Some models have interchangeable blades; others come in sets.

Roofing knife, for scoring and cutting asphalt shingles, tar paper and other roofing materials, can also be used for wallboard and insulation. The model with the straight blade can pry apart asphalt shingles.

Window scraper removes paint from windowpane without damaging the putty. Hold the scraper so that the wheels glide against the window trim; blade scrapes off paint.

Razor-blade scraper uses a single-edge razor blade to scrape paint and stickers off windowpanes. One model (left) has a retractable blade. The blade on the other model (far left) can be locked in several different positions.

Four-edge blade scraper (above) is for quick paint and varnish removal. Use the knob to apply extra pressure. Two blade edges scrape at a time. Turn blade over or replace it when dull.

Utility-blade scraper (left) has a guide to help remove paint from window frames and flat surfaces.

Glazier's putty knife combines two functions in one tool. Use the heavy-duty flat chisel blade to remove old putty from a window. Apply and smooth down new putty with the slotted V-blade. To create a bevelled edge, hold the tool with the blade at a slight angle.

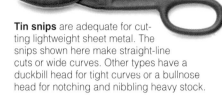

Tin snips are adequate for cutting lightweight sheet metal. The snips shown here make straight-line cuts or wide curves. Other types have a duckbill head for tight curves or a bullnose head for notching and nibbling heavy stock.

Putty knife has a flexible blade to spread and smooth wood putty and filler, glazing or spackling compound, patching plaster, and other similar materials. A knife with a stiff blade scrapes away paint, glue, vinyl and paper wallcoverings and other materials.

Aviation snips cut sheet metal with less effort than tin snips. A compound lever mechanism provides greater control with less hand pressure. The serrated jaws prevent slippage and withstand heavy use. All aviation snips cut straight lines. Specific heads also cut left curves, right curves and a combination of all three cuts. The grips are colour-coded: yellow for combination cuts, red for left-hand curves and green for right-hand curves. A latch holds the jaws closed.

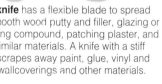

Painter's five-in-one tool has a blade that functions as a paint scraper, putty remover and spreader, gouger and paint-roller cleaner. Use it when making repairs, installing window glass, painting and hanging wallcoverings.

Hacking knife has a blade that is thicker on one side for use with a hammer. It's most often used for cutting sheets of corrugated-iron roofing Hold the slightly angled blade tip with the point against the roofing sheet. Drive a hammer against the thicker edge of the blade to make the cut.

Electric nibblers use a replaceable die and punch combination to cut aluminium, stainless steel and corrugated steel. The nibblers can make straight, right-curve and left-curve cuts. To make an internal cut, first drill a starter hole.

Joint knife, with a large blade for spreading and smoothing wide areas of joint compound over wallboard tape, can also be used to patch wallboard and to smooth wallcoverings.

Right-angle joint knife lets you apply joint compound smoothly to inside corners where walls meet. The handle is offset to allow clearance for fingers.

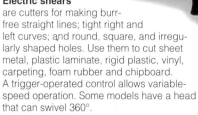

Electric shears are cutters for making burr-free straight lines; tight right and left curves; and round, square, and irregularly shaped holes. Use them to cut sheet metal, plastic laminate, rigid plastic, vinyl, carpeting, foam rubber and chipboard. A trigger-operated control allows variable-speed operation. Some models have a head that can swivel 360°.

The best handsaws are made of fine-tempered steel and have well-shaped wooden handles. The main difference among handsaws is the shape, number and pitch of their teeth, which make them suitable for cutting wood across the grain or with it, along curved lines, or through metal, plastic or wallboard. To prevent binding, saw teeth are usually set, or angled, away from the blade so that the path, or kerf, it cuts is slightly wider than the blade's thickness. Most saws are graduated according to the old imperial measure of teeth per inch (tpi). Generally the more points or teeth per inch a saw has, the smoother and slower it cuts. The number of teeth per inch is always one less than the number of points. Most American and European saws cut on the push stroke.

Wallboard saw makes cutouts in plasterboard for electrical outlets or appliances. The average blade is 150 to 240 mm long with about 10 tpi. The sharp point allows you to make plunge cuts without first drilling a hole to accept the blade.

Crosscut saw has knifelike teeth that slice through wood fibres, cutting stock across the grain. The standard blade is 660 mm long with 7 to 12 tpi. For a smooth cut, use a saw with the highest tpi measure.

Saw set can be used to bend the teeth of a handsaw to the angle needed to effect the desired cut. Sharpen the saw first. Then turn the wheellike anvil of the saw set to the proper angle, position the jaws of the saw set over a saw tooth, and squeeze the tool's handles together; a plunger will push the saw tooth against the anvil.

Backsaw or tenon saw is a crosscut saw for making joints, especially mitres and tenons. The squared end and thick rib along its back keep the blade rigid while cutting. Standard blades are 200 to 350 mm long with 11 to 14 tpi.

Plywood saw has a fine-tooth blade that reduces tearing of the outer plies of a sheet of plywood. An extra set of teeth on the curved upper edge of the blade lets you start a cut on the inside of a panel (away from the edge) without having to drill a starting hole. The standard plywood saw blade is 280 mm long and has 14 tpi.

Ripsaw cuts parallel to wood grain by gouging a groove in the wood with coarse teeth shaped like miniature chisels. The standard blade is 660 mm long and has 4 to 7 tpi. A ripsaw with 5,5 tpi gives a smooth, fast cut.

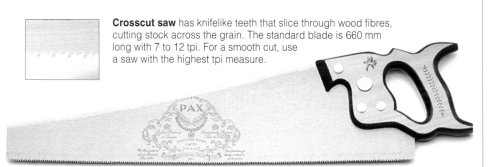

General-purpose saw makes both crosscuts and rip cuts in wood and is ideal if you can have only one saw. Its teeth have three bevelled sides, providing razor-sharp cutting, and deep gullets (spaces between the teeth), which make it easier to clear chips away fast. The blade is 660 mm long with 9 tpi, and cuts fast and smooth.

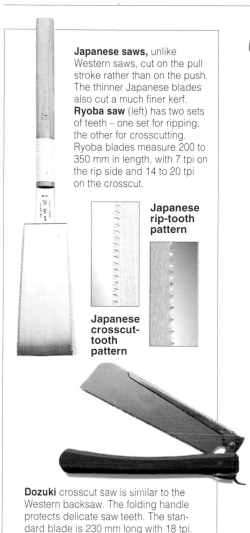

Japanese saws, unlike Western saws, cut on the pull stroke rather than on the push. The thinner Japanese blades also cut a much finer kerf.

Ryoba saw (left) has two sets of teeth – one set for ripping, the other for crosscutting. Ryoba blades measure 200 to 350 mm in length, with 7 tpi on the rip side and 14 to 20 tpi on the crosscut.

Japanese rip-tooth pattern

Japanese crosscut-tooth pattern

Dozuki crosscut saw is similar to the Western backsaw. The folding handle protects delicate saw teeth. The standard blade is 230 mm long with 18 tpi.

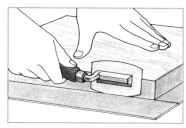

Veneer saw is a small double-edged tool for cutting thin hardwood veneers. Its narrow curved blade facilitates precision work, and its elevated offset handle makes it possible to cut flush with a surface. The blade is 75 mm long and has 13 tpi.

French flush-cut saw is designed for trimming the ends of dowels, tenons and other protrusions flush with a surface. Its 150 mm blade is double-edged, with 11 tpi on one side and 20 tpi on the other. To avoid marring the surface adjacent to the cut, the teeth have no downward set, but are angled upward slightly to help the blade clear the cut.

Frame saw or wooden bowsaw is used for cutting curved edges. The twisted cord at the top of the frame supplies tension to keep the blade from wobbling during cutting. By rotating the handles, you can turn the blade to cut at any angle. Blades range from 200 to 300mcm long with 8 to 16 tpi.

Dovetail saw is a small backsaw with a straight handle and fine teeth set to cut a narrow kerf, making it ideal for fine joints. The blade is 250 to 300 mm long with 16 to 20 tpi.

Folding pocket saw is a handle that accepts a variety of saw blades that cut wood, metal, plastic and other materials. It folds to protect the blade's edge and has storage space for extra blades.

Bowsaw is a heavy-duty tool for cutting logs or for coarse sawing of green wood, dry or seasoned wood, or other building materials. The tubular steel frame holds the blade under tension, which can be controlled with the quick-release lever. The replaceable blades are made up of pegged teeth and gullets to allow cutting in both directions.

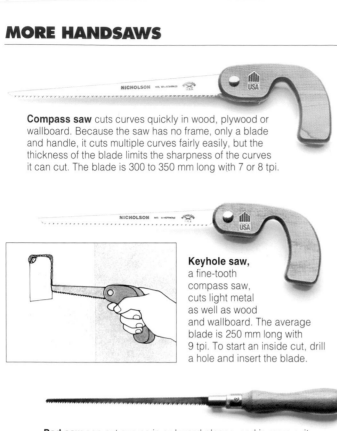

Compass saw cuts curves quickly in wood, plywood or wallboard. Because the saw has no frame, only a blade and handle, it cuts multiple curves fairly easily, but the thickness of the blade limits the sharpness of the curves it can cut. The blade is 300 to 350 mm long with 7 or 8 tpi.

Keyhole saw, a fine-tooth compass saw, cuts light metal as well as wood and wallboard. The average blade is 250 mm long with 9 tpi. To start an inside cut, drill a hole and insert the blade.

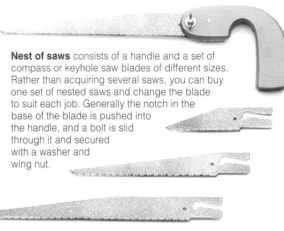

Nest of saws consists of a handle and a set of compass or keyhole saw blades of different sizes. Rather than acquiring several saws, you can buy one set of nested saws and change the blade to suit each job. Generally the notch in the base of the blade is pushed into the handle, and a bolt is slid through it and secured with a washer and wing nut.

Slotting saw has 150 mm-long blade with fine teeth (25 tpi) for cutting very narrow grooves. It is especially handy for creating delicate dovetails and for model work.

Pad saw can cut curves in awkward places, and is more suitable than a compass or keyhole saw for cutting tight curves. The blade of the pad saw is generally 100 to 250 mm long with 8 tpi. It can be inserted into the handle so that it cuts on the pull stroke (like a Japanese saw) for greater control.

Curved pruning saw, a knifelike pruning tool, can be folded to protect the blade when not in use. The tempered steel blade is 250 mm long, with long slender reverse teeth (5 tpi) set for cutting on the pull stroke.

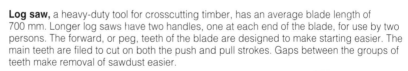

Pruning saw has a blade of specially hardened and tempered steel for cutting branches. The straight 450 mm-long blade of the saw shown here has two cutting edges. One edge has coarse teeth for sawing green wood more easily. The opposite edge has crosscut teeth (7 tpi) for finish strokes and cutting deadwood.

Plastic pipe handsaw doubles as a tool for cutting PVC and fibre-cement pipe and a general-purpose saw for cutting plywood, panelling and wallboard. The blade is 300 mm long with 10 tpi set for cutting on either the push or pull stroke. Replace the blade by removing the screw in the handle, slide out the old blade, slide in the new, and replace the screw.

Log saw, a heavy-duty tool for crosscutting timber, has an average blade length of 700 mm. Longer log saws have two handles, one at each end of the blade, for use by two persons. The forward, or peg, teeth of the blade are designed to make starting easier. The main teeth are filed to cut on both the push and pull strokes. Gaps between the groups of teeth make removal of sawdust easier.

Hacksaw, the traditional handsaw for cutting metal, has extra-hard teeth, a sturdy frame with a pistol-grip handle, and a narrow blade from 200 to 400 mm long with 14 to 32 tpi. When installing a new blade, apply tension to it by turning the wing nut in the handle. In this model you can store extra blades in the hollow top of the frame.

Adjustable hacksaw accepts blades of various sizes – pull the front part of the frame out as on a trombone. When using a hacksaw, steady the front of the frame with your free hand.

Coping saw has a steel frame and a narrow, flexible 150 mm-long blade that can be rotated at any angle to cut small curves in wood. The blade, which has 12 to 18 tpi, is pulled taut by turning the handle of the frame. To make an inside cut, drill a starting hole and slip the blade through it before attaching it to the saw frame.

Mini-hacksaw consists only of a handle that holds whole or broken hacksaw blades. Use it to cut metal in awkward places where a full-size saw will not fit. The blade is held steady by a screw on the handle.

Rod saw is a wire with carbide chips permanently affixed. It can be attached to a hacksaw frame for cutting glass, ceramic, plastic, masonry, marble, fibreglass and metal. Because it can cut in any direction, it is ideal for curves and for shaping tiles to fit around door frames or plumbing fixtures.

Fretsaw is a deep-throated coping saw for cutting further in from the edge of the stock than a normal coping saw can do. Because the blade is extra fine (up to 32 tpi), it can cut intricate curves. When installing a blade, fasten one end in the frame, press the frame against the edge of a workbench or table to bend the frame in slightly, attach the other end of the blade to the frame, and then release the frame to put tension on the blade and keep it taut.

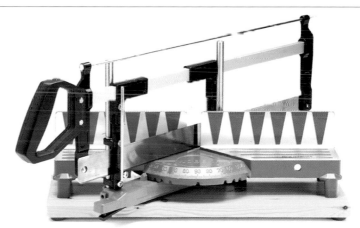

Mitre box holds a backsaw blade in the proper position to make cuts at precise angles. It is often used to cut mitres in moulding. The simplest mitre box is merely a U-shaped wooden structure with a slot through its sides at a 90° angle. The more precise unit shown here comes with its own saw and with clamps to hold work of various sizes and shapes. A dial lets you set the angle of the saw.

Jeweller's saw cuts lightweight sheet metal, such as silver. Its thin, flexible blade is usually 125 to 150 mm long with up to 80 tpi. Install a new blade as shown at left for a fretsaw.

Flexible pocket saw resembles a burred wire with a handle on each end. It comes in a plastic carrying case. This versatile saw cuts in any direction and can be used on wood, plastic, rubber, bone and even ice. To use it, loop the blade over the object to be cut, and alternately pull on one handle and then the other, while applying pressure.

In general, a power saw gives a quicker and more precise cut than a handsaw. A jigsaw cuts with a blade that moves up and down; a reciprocating saw cuts with an additional front-to-back motion. A variety of blades allows either saw to cut different materials. After making a cut with a portable power saw, wait for the blade to stop moving before setting the saw down.

To cut very tight convex or concave curves, first saw straight lines in the waste material, then cut along the curved line. The pieces of waste material will drop off as the blade makes the cut, giving extra clearance for the saw blade to continue.

Jigsaw can cut straight lines with a guide, but it excels in making curved cuts. With the proper blade, it can cut wood and most other materials. Desirable features are adjustable orbital action (to clear away chips and allow higher cutting speed), variable-speed control from 500 to 3 200 strokes per minute (spm) for cutting different materials, a baseplate that can be tilted for bevel cuts, and an anti-chip device.

Reciprocating saw, also known as a sabre saw or all-purpose saw, is a heavy-duty power saw used mainly for rough cutting. The rapid pistonlike motion cuts wood, plaster, PVC pipe, metal and other materials. Some models may operate at only one speed, in most cases 2 000 strokes per minute (spm). Others have two speeds, (usually 1 900 and 2 500 spm), while electronic models cut at variable speeds, with a typical range being from around 500 to 2 500 spm.

Scrolling jigsaw, a version of the jigsaw, has a blade holder that pivots for cutting intricate curves and contours without the operator turning the body of the saw. The saw has an automatic scrolling mode, in which the blade turns in the direction the saw is guided, a manual scrolling setting that lets you control the blade with the top-mounted knob, and settings for normal blade positions.

Jigsaw blades are gauged by the number of teeth per inch (tpi). The more tpi, the smoother the cut. Blades with fewer tpi make a rougher but quicker cut. The narrower the blade, the tighter the turning radius. Select the blade to fit the job. At top (from left to right) are blades for wood: crosscut, rough-cut, extra-fine, scrolling (also for plastic) and rough-cut for thick planks and logs. At bottom (from left to right) are a flush-cut blade for wood, and medium, fine and extra-fine blades for cutting metal. Other blades are available for cutting ceramic tile, fibreglass, leather and plaster.

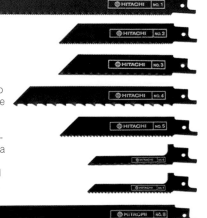

Reciprocating saw blades range in length from 50 to about 300 mm. Some can cut wood as thick as 300 mm, others metal up to 20 mm thick. Use the shortest blade that will do the job. From top to bottom, the first three blades are for cutting steel pipe of different thicknesses and diameters. They are followed by two blades for cutting wood of various thicknesses, a blade for cutting curves in iron, a blade for cutting curves in wood and a blade for cutting vinyl pipe.

The tool of choice for making intricate and accurate curved and piercing cuts, the scroll saw is indispensable for creating inlay and marquetry pieces and for making miniatures and fretwork. The saw cuts with a blade suspended between two chucks mounted in arms that move up and down. To reduce teeth marks and blade breakage, look for a saw that holds the blade with a constant-tension arm. Single-speed models are available, but multiple-speed and variable-speed scroll saws are more versatile. Mount the saw on a benchtop if it doesn't have its own stand.

Scroll saw blades have ends designed to fit into chucks. Pin-end blades are easier to mount than the smooth ones, but not all saw chucks accept them. All blades can cut very tight curves. Basic blades cut solid wood, plywood, veneer, plastic and some fibrous materials. Very fine blades cut thin non-ferrous metals. A unique spiral-shaped blade allows you to saw in any direction without turning the work.

Sawdust blower keeps workpiece clear of debris, allowing a clear view of the cut. The lock knob holds the drop foot in place. The foot can be raised, but it must rest on the work when the saw is running.

Tension control sets tautness of the blade; turn it to increase or reduce the blade tension. To convert a smooth-end blade to fit a pin-end chuck, use the blade gauge (right of knob) to attach adapters.

Table adjustment control lets you tilt the saw's table to make bevel cuts up to a 45° angle. Some models can be adjusted up to 45° in the opposite direction.

To change a blade, first loosen the blade by releasing the tension control. The top end of the blade fits into the upper chuck (top). On some models, you can cut pieces longer than the saw's throat depth by rotating the pin-end blade 90° and feeding the wood away from the throat. (Chuck systems differ.) The bottom end of the blade fits into the lower chuck (right). To reach the lower chuck, remove the table insert (replace it before using saw).

Ideal for curve cutting and for re-sawing (making a board thinner), the band saw can also be used to make straight or regular cuts in wood, plastic and metal. Its blade is looped around a set of wheels; the bottom wheel drives the blade into the work. Before buying a band saw, think about how you'll use it. It should have adequate throat capacity (the distance from the blade to the left vertical support); this determines the widest board it can cut. The saw should also have suitable cutting depth (the distance from the worktable to the upper blade guard set at its highest position). Cutting depth in smaller band saws runs up to 1,27 m; in larger models, it can be greater than 2,3 m. A variable-speed saw allows better cutting control.

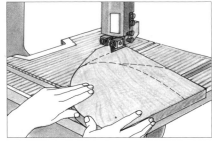

If the blade is too wide to make a curved cut, first cut several passes to remove waste material. If the cut doesn't finish at another edge of the work, turn the saw off at the end of the cut and back the blade out; otherwise, the blade may be pulled off the wheels.

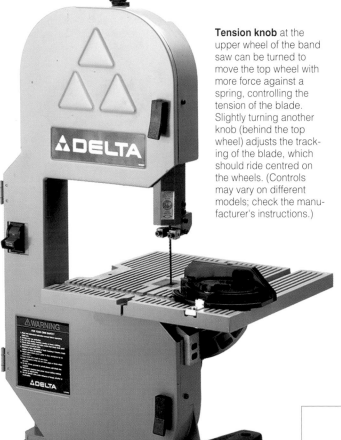

Tension knob at the upper wheel of the band saw can be turned to move the top wheel with more force against a spring, controlling the tension of the blade. Slightly turning another knob (behind the top wheel) adjusts the tracking of the blade, which should ride centred on the wheels. (Controls may vary on different models; check the manufacturer's instructions.)

Upper blade guide and guard move up and down to accommodate work of various thicknesses. The guide should be positioned about 4 mm above the work. The upper blade guide and another one under the table help to keep the blade aligned.

Table-tilting lock holds the table at various angles up to 45°. A scale below the table shows the angle. When re-adjusting the table for a 90° cut, use a square to make sure the table is set at 90° to the blade.

Blade is reached by opening a door or removing a panel on the side of the saw. Blades come in various widths with different numbers of teeth. The more teeth on the blade, the smoother the cut; fewer teeth allow a faster but coarser cut. Generally, use the widest blade possible.

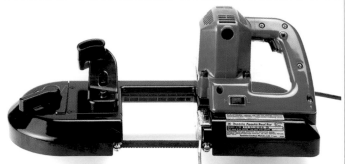

Portable band saw can be used on a workpiece that's too large to fit on a standard band saw's worktable; it's also easier to move to a work site. This saw has a 100 mm cutting-depth and variable-speed control. When using it, hold the saw with two hands; clamp the work securely, leaving clearance for the saw. You can buy a stand to hold it, freeing your hands.

CIRCULAR SAWS

The circular saw is used for fast straight cuts in wood or other materials, depending on the blade chosen (pp 58–59). The saw has one of two types of gears: the standard helical gear or the powerful worm-drive gear (not shown); the latter is used mostly in construction. The size of the saw is identified by the diameter of the largest blade it accepts: from 152 to 235 mm (about 180 mm is average). Select a saw that you can handle comfortably and still accomplish your work; a heavy saw can be tiring and hard to control.

Cordless circular saw This battery-powered model has a water reservoir and diamond blade, making it ideal for cutting tiles. When cutting, make sure that you use enough water to keep the blade and the work cool. Other small saws are made specifically for cutting (chasing) grooves in masonry or concrete walls.

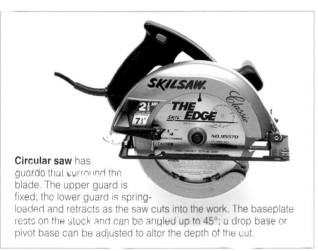

Circular saw has guards that surround the blade. The upper guard is fixed; the lower guard is spring-loaded and retracts as the saw cuts into the work. The baseplate rests on the stock and can be angled up to 45°; a drop base or pivot base can be adjusted to alter the depth of the cut.

Sliding compound mitre saw has a blade assembly that slides along a rod, allowing you to cut wide stock by pulling the assembly toward you. The saw can make mitre cuts up to 45°, and it tilts to one side to make compound cuts, also up to 45° angles. Some models handle stock up to 300 mm wide.

Mitre saw combines a portable mitre table and a circular saw to make straight and angled cuts. The saw pivots and locks in position to cut angles from 0° to 45° right and left. Stops are set for common angles. Some models handle stock up to 75 mm thick and 100 mm wide. Maximum stock width decreases as saw angle increases. Some models can also make compound cuts.

Ideal for making precise straight and angled cuts, the table saw can rip and crosscut long boards and wide panels. A circular blade (pp 58–59) protrudes through a slot in the table; the work is pushed into the blade. (In one model, you can also pull the blade into the work.) The diameter of the largest blade the saw can use establishes its size. The 250 mm table saw is the most common. While a benchtop model (shown) is portable and requires less space, a floor model makes smoother, more accurate cuts.

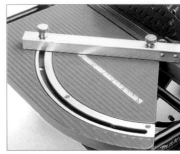

Blade guard shields the user's hands from the blade and prevents flying chips. The spreader, suspended from the blade guard assembly, keeps the kerf (the cut in the work-piece) open behind the blade. If the kerf is allowed to close, the blade will be pinched by the workpiece, jam, and cause the work to kick back and injure the operator.

Mitre gauge can be adjusted to use as a guide for making crosscuts and angled cuts up to 45°. For a long board, support the weight of the work with one hand; while the saw is running, push the mitre gauge with the work into the blade with the other hand. For a mitre gauge that comes with other table saw models, see band saws, p 54.

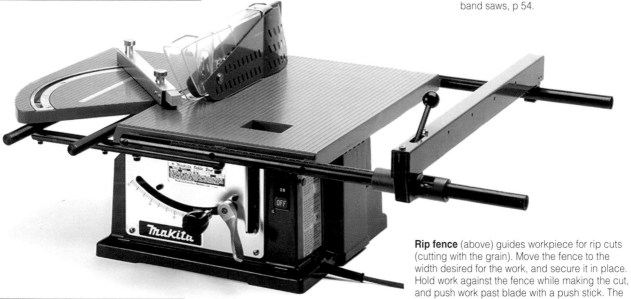

Rip fence (above) guides workpiece for rip cuts (cutting with the grain). Move the fence to the width desired for the work, and secure it in place. Hold work against the fence while making the cut, and push work past blade with a push stick. The mitre gauge must be removed to make a rip cut.

Depth of cut is adjusted by moving the blade up or down. On this model, you turn a knob to move the blade. (Some table saws use cranks.) You can also tilt the blade to make bevelled cuts up to 45°. A scale indicates the degree of the angle.

Safety accessories are essential for preventing accidents while you use a table saw. Use the push stick (top) to keep fingers away from the saw blade. The spring-loaded wheel (centre) is one of a pair that helps hold and guide work on the table and prevent kickback. The wheels are attached to a fence – one wheel on each side of the blade. The feather board (bottom) holds the work against the fence while you make rip cuts. (Use two feather boards on a large table saw.)

RADIAL ARM SAWS

The blade assembly of a radial arm saw is suspended from an arm and can be rotated, angled and tilted to make a variety of cuts. The saw excels in making crosscuts – especially in long boards – and you can turn the blade housing and use it horizontally. With the proper attachments (use only those designed for your model), you can turn a radial arm saw into a sander, router and drill press. The size of the saw is based on the diameter of the largest blade (pp 58–59) it will accept; 250 mm is a versatile size for a home workshop. Before operating the saw, make any adjustments suggested in the manufacturer's manual.

Kerf spreader   Pawl

Saw guard covers blade to prevent injury to user – a safety feature found on all radial arm saws. This guard is made of clear plastic; others are made of steel. Attached to the guard is an anti-kickback pawl for making rip cuts. If the work starts to move backward, the pawl grips it. A kerf spreader behind the blade keeps the cut open during rip cuts, preventing the blade from jamming in the work.

Worktable can be covered with a protective sheet of 6 mm hardboard. To cut completely through the work, the blade must penetrate into the worktable surface or the protective sheet. As you need them, cut kerfs (slots) in the table and fence to allow clearance for the blade. The radial arm saw shown is a portable model. It is easy to store and transport to work sites. A heavy-duty floor model, however, will make more accurate cuts.

Arm lock and gauge allow arm to be set in preset stops for making mitre cuts up to 22,5° left and 45° right (models vary). The arm can also be locked at other angles between stops.

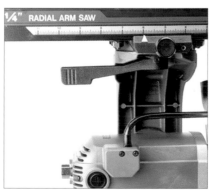

Yoke controls are used to turn blade assembly to position it for rip sawing. The carriage lock knob secures the carriage in place along the arm, thus setting the width of the cut.

Bevel controls can be adjusted to tilt blade assembly up to 90° in either direction for making a bevelled crosscut or rip cut. Adjust arm and bevel controls to make compound cuts.

Having a variety of blades will expand the capabilities of your circular saw, table saw or radial arm saw. Blades fall into two categories: standard steel, which must be sharpened often, and carbide tipped. The latter stay sharp longer, but are more brittle and can be damaged if badly handled. The number of teeth, the grind of each tooth and the gullet depth (the space between teeth) determine the smoothness and speed of a blade's cut. Generally, large teeth make a fast, rough rip cut. Small, pointed teeth cut slowly and smoothly. To avoid kickback, some blades have a hump behind each tooth. Shown here is a range of standard 7,25 inch- (184 mm-) diameter blades. You must match both blade size and arbor holes to your tool.

Rip has large square chisel teeth for making clean cuts parallel to the grain of hardwood and softwood.

Crosscut has small pointed teeth for making smooth cuts perpendicular to the grain in hardwood, softwood and plywood.

Combination, with alternating large pointed teeth, can make rip cuts, crosscuts, and mitre cuts in all wood materials without your having to change blades.

Chisel-tooth combination has large teeth for making fast, rough rip cuts.

Hollow-ground planer provides clearance for cut because blade body is thinner than cutting edge; its combination-ground teeth make smooth crosscuts and mitre cuts.

Hollow-ground plywood has alternating fine bevel-ground teeth for splinter-free cuts in plywood and panelling.

Plywood/panelling Small alternating top-bevel-ground teeth make smooth cuts in plywood and panelling.

Non-ferrous metal/plastic cutter has alternating top-bevel-ground teeth for cutting brass, aluminium, copper and plastics. Lubricate with oil or wax before use.

Thin kerf minimizes waste by making fine cuts in woods under 18 mm thick; it has carbide-tipped teeth. This model, for combination cuts, has vents to prevent overheating.

Combination thin kerf has large carbide-tipped alternating bevel-ground teeth with antikickback humps. Use it for smooth rip cuts and crosscuts in most woods.

Framing thin kerf, with large carbide-tipped square chisel teeth and anti-kickback humps, is for smooth rip cuts in most woods.

Finishing thin kerf has small carbide-tipped alternating bevel-ground teeth with anti-kickback humps for making fine crosscuts in most woods.

Nail cutter, with large carbide-tipped teeth, can make rough cuts through nails that may be embedded in wood. It's ideal for cutting old timber for re-use.

Non-ferrous metal cutter has carbide-tipped teeth for cutting aluminium, copper, lead and brass. Lubricate with oil or wax before use.

Non-stick coating is added to hooked carbide-tipped teeth for fine cuts in solid wood, plywood veneers and plastic.

Dado set includes saw blades and chippers, which are assembled to cut rebates and grooves in solid wood and plastic laminate. An adjustable dado head comes assembled; it can be reset for various groove widths. Use dado blades on table and radial arm saws only.

A woodworking tool that is basically a blade in a holder, the plane can trim and smooth wood, bevel, round off and straighten irregular edges. Special-purpose planes can cut grooves for joints and shave wood into decorative shapes.

Choose a plane that will accomplish the particular job. Make sure the plane has a readily accessible and easy-to-use depth-adjusting knob or wheel; look for a frog – the underlying plate – that fully supports the blade. For surfacing passes, pick a plane with a grooved sole; to plane edges, use one with a flat sole.

Jack plane has a wide blade and 350 to 380 mm-long body for initial smoothing. To use it on freshly cut wood, set the cap holding the blade about 3 mm from the cutting edge. For further smoothing, move cap to 1,5 mm of the cutting edge. Adjust the blade with the lateral lever and adjusting knob. To remove the blade, release the wedge iron; remove the wedge- and cap-irons.

Steel jointer plane is used for edge joining and the initial levelling of wide boards. It has a 560 to 580 mm-long sole to prevent the tool from following bumps and dips. To change the depth of cut, move the blade by adjusting the lateral lever and the knurled adjusting knob.

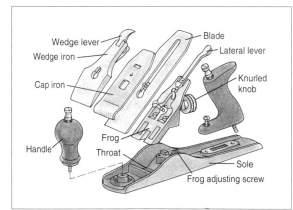

Wood jointer plane has a fence to guide the tool for squaring and truing wood edges for tight fits. It's ideal for preparing wood for edge-to-edge gluing. To turn the tool into a smoothing plane, unscrew the fence and remove it.

Smoothing plane finishes a surface after rough planing. Because the sole is only 180 to 230 mm long, the plane is suitable for working small areas of wood with tricky grain patterns.

Raised panel plane creates a panelled look with an angled sole and blade. It cuts 50 mm-wide strips and comes in right- and left-handed models. A wedge holds the blade in place. To adjust the blade, tap it with a wooden mallet.

Scrub plane removes large amounts of wood quickly. Its convex-shaped blade is held in place with a wooden wedge. Use short repetitive passes, moving diagonally across the grain. Finish the work with a smoothing plane.

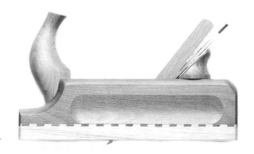

Gent's plane is designed for general finishing work. The handle at the front of the plane is held to give extra pushing power. It's smaller than the standard cabinet-maker's smoothing plane. Although this design makes the plane lighter and less tiring to use, it also makes it unsuitable for heavy-duty work.

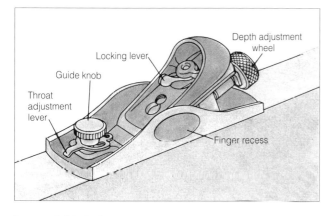

Depth adjustment wheel

Locking lever

Guide knob

Throat adjustment lever

Finger recess

Block plane cuts and trims wood and makes fine finishing cuts. An adjusting wheel under the palm-rest controls positioning of the blade. Because of its smaller size, the block plane can be used with one hand.

Low-angle block plane, one of several varieties of the block plane, is used for shaping fine trim work and end grain. The blade rests at a 12° angle for finer cuts on cross grains and end grains. The plane is adjustable for making rougher cuts.

Bullnose plane, for fine woodworking, makes stopped rebates and grooves. The short nose in front of the blade allows cutting in cramped quarters.

Palm plane fits into places where a standard-size plane will not fit. It's very useful for intricate detail work. Another model has a raised handle.

Violin plane, for fine detail work, may have a straight blade or come in a set with matching convex- and concave-shaped blades.

Edge plane has an L-shaped body that works like a fence to form true square edges in wood. The blade is skewed for a smooth cut, preventing wood tearout.

Rebate plane shapes a rebate in wood. There are two blade positions: centre for general use and forward for bullnose applications. Spurs permit work on cross grain. Some models feature an adjustable, detachable fence.

Side rebate plane forms sides of rebates and grooves. Two blades allow movement in both directions, and a depth gauge adjusts up to 13 mm deep.

Shoulder plane has sole and body sides at perfect right angles. As the name implies, it trims and squares the shoulders of tenon and rebate joints.

Chamfer plane cuts a 45° bevel, or chamfer, on the corner of a square piece. Adjust the width of the bevel cut with the threaded rods and nuts. Scales at the front and back ensure precise blade adjustment. The V-shaped sole is set at a 90° angle.

Butt mortise plane cuts mortises for hinges, strike plates, deadbolt locks and similar hardware. It makes accurate square cuts with ease.

Edge finishing plane comes in two versions: one cuts round edges, the other chamfered edges. The front blade makes a rough cut; the rear one finishes it. To set the blades, insert a hex key in openings on the side and on top.

Three-in-one plane is a combination rebate, bullnose, and stop rebate plane in one tool. The bullnose head (left) makes it easier to control the depth of cut in tight areas. To convert the plane, unscrew one head and attach the other; the screw is located inside the head. To increase the mouth width, add the shims (centre).

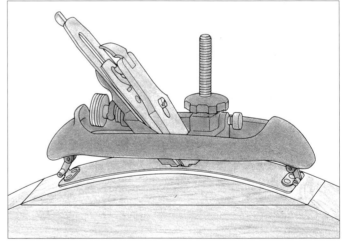

Circular plane, also called a compass plane, has a flexible sole for planing concave and convex surfaces. Place the plane on the work; then, using the adjusting knob to turn the threaded rod, position the sole to fit the contour desired for the work. Once the sole is set, adjust the blade to the correct setting.

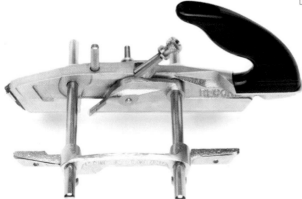

Plough combination plane uses an adjustable fence to guide it across the work edge while cutting grooves or rebates. A conversion kit allows the plane to make bead and tongue cuts. Cutters are available in different widths and styles.

Router plane cuts grooves and other flat-bottomed depressions to a precise depth. It also surfaces the bottom of grooves. Some models have an adjustable, detachable guide fence for general or bullnose (close-quarters) work on straight and curved grooves.

SPOKESHAVES AND DRAWKNIVES

Although all these woodworking tools perform the same basic functions, shaving and shaping wood, each of them is specialized for creating a flat, concave or convex surface. In general, spokeshaves are better suited for finishing workpieces, drawknives for roughing out stock. Most of these tools are held with two hands; the worker pushes or pulls the instrument against the work. To create smooth cuts and prevent injury, keep the cutting edges sharp. When using the tools, make sure you follow the grain of the wood.

Adjustable straight spokeshave should have two adjustment nuts to change the blade depth. A third adjustment nut holds a *lever cap,* which applies pressure to the blade. Loosen the nut before adjusting the blade depth. This spokeshave is for flat or convex surfaces. With practice, you need do little sanding after using a spokeshave.

Convex spokeshave (far left) carves a recessed area into a surface. Use it for work that requires hollowing out wood.

Concave spokeshave (left) has a curved blade for shaving rails, posts and chair legs. The shape it creates fits around the shape carved by the convex spokeshave.

Chamfering spokeshave (far left), guided by two fences, cuts a bevel, or chamfer, on squared work. Thumbscrews adjust the fences.

Combination spokeshave (left) incorporates both a straight and a concave blade. Although this tool performs the same functions as the two individual spokeshaves, its blades are narrower.

Small spokeshave is useful for working in areas where bigger tools won't fit and for creating fine detail. It comes with a flat, round or spoon-shaped sole. The blade may be flat or convex. To adjust the blade or to remove it for sharpening, remove the screw and washer.

Cabinet scraper holds a blade in a body that resembles a spokeshave. (Some scraper blades are used without a holder.) A thumbscrew is used to adjust the blade. The tool smooths knots and removes dried glue and paper-thin layers of wood.

Inshave, a type of drawknife, has a deeply curved blade for hollowing out wood. It's a tool for making recesses but is less controllable than a spokeshave. Use it for initial smoothing of wood.

Drawknife removes large or small quantities of wood, depending on how it's pulled by the user. Handles and blades vary. Smaller drawknives are better carving tools; the larger ones have better handle grips for heavy-duty jobs.

Scorper, originally for smoothing inside barrels and buckets, has a circular blade. Use the scorper with one hand to hollow out recesses in wood seats and bowls.

Push knife is a variation of the drawknife. Grasp the handles to push the straight blade through the wood; or with the blade in the reverse position, pull the knife toward you. The blade's tang passes through the handle for added strength – a feature to look for in any type of drawknife.

The portable power plane is ideal for jobs such as shaving down door edges. But if your projects call for perfect-fitting joinery and workpieces, a power jointer and a thickness planer should also be part of your workshop. (Both tools require accurate adjustments to be effective.) With them you can cut boards to less than standard thicknesses, and you can also buy less expensive rough-sawn timber and smooth its surface yourself. On a jointer, first flatten and straighten a surface, then straighten and square its edges. Finally give the piece an overall equal thickness with the planer. If the work calls for strong joints, it's ready for the biscuit joiner.

Portable power plane is the perfect tool for removing a small amount of stock from a door that no longer swings open because of new carpeting or the wood swelling in humid weather. Balance the door with hand-screw clamps, and use scrap wood to create a wider base.

Portable power plane is often used for smoothing and squaring the edges of wood. A set of two rotating blades removes up to 3 mm of stock per pass – make a series of passes to remove more wood. Planes are sized according to the width of cut they can make. Maximum cutting width ranges from 50 to 150 mm, depending on the model. As you plane a workpiece, apply even pressure throughout the pass; at the end of the pass let up slightly on the plane's front end to avoid digging into the work. Besides straightening edges, the plane can also make chamfers and tapers. A fence can be attached to the plane to cut specific angles.

Jointer flattens, straightens and squares boards from 100 to 200 mm wide. The machine consists of an infeed table, cutter head, outfeed table and fence. The height of the infeed table is adjustable to change the depth of cut up to 3 mm. A guard (open here to show cutter) protects your hands as you feed the work across the cutter; but if the top edge of a board is lower than the fence top, use push blocks. The fence adjusts up to 45° left and right for bevelling and chamfering. The tool is available in small benchtop models and larger floor models.

Push blocks are absolutely essential safety tools when working with the jointer. (They can also be used with a table or radial arm saw.) The ones shown have foam pads to grip the work securely, and their handles are angled to keep hands away from the fence.

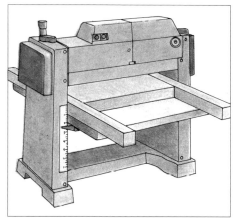

To plane workpieces that are smaller than the manufacturer's recommendations, use a glue gun to fix scrap wood to the sides of the work. (Make sure the assembly isn't too wide to fit through the planer.) After planing, tap on the scrap wood to break it off the workpiece.

Biscuit joiner

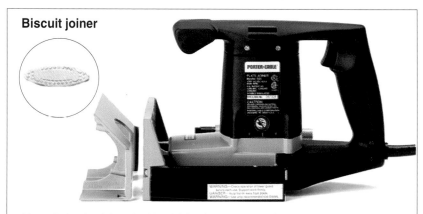

Also called a plate joiner, the biscuit joiner is a unique tool for strengthening butt, mitre and edge joints in wood. A blade cuts corresponding grooves into each of two workpieces; oval-shaped 'biscuits' of wood or plastic fit into the grooves and, with a little glue, create a strong joint. (Glue causes the biscuit to expand for a tight fit.) Biscuit joints can be aligned before the glue dries by shifting the pieces laterally. Biscuits are available in several sizes; use the largest one that fits the joint.

Thickness planer sizes stock to a desired thickness after one surface has been straightened or flattened on the jointer. The stock is placed on the table and fed automatically by rollers past rotating blades. It's best to make several passes, removing a small amount of stock each time. The type of wood, its width and the feed rate determine the amount of stock that can be removed. The slower the feed, the more cuts per centimetre. The more cuts per centimetre, the smoother the surface. The thickness planer is available in benchtop models that accept stock from 100 to 300 mm wide and from thin veneers to about 150 mm thick. Heavier machines can accept stock from 300 to 900 mm wide and 3 mm to 200 mm thick. The planer may operate on single-speed, two-speed or variable-speed feed rates. Some planers have blades with a cutting edge on both sides. When one side becomes dull, remove any debris and re-install the blade with the sharp side in the cutting position. Before changing a blade, make sure that you unplug the machine.

An adaptable woodworking tool, the router can be used to make decorative edges or surfaces, top-quality joinery, and freehand or pattern-assisted carvings. It comes with collet sizes from 6 to 12 mm, and equivalent sizes in imperial measure. Speeds range from 5 000 to 27 000 rpm and power output from 500 to 1 850 W. A larger collet, for accepting matching bit shanks, gives greater versatility. But biggest is not always best – higher-powered machines slow down less under load, but can be tiring to use for long periods. Router bits may be used singly or in combinations to cut hundreds of different profiles and grooves. A solid or bearing-tip on some bits makes it easier to follow the edge of the work. High-speed steel bits cost much less than tungsten carbide bits, but they need to be sharpened much more frequently.

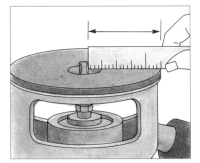

Standard router with 655 W motor and 6 or 8 mm collet. The motor adjusts up and down. To change the depth of the cut, loosen the knob and re-position the motor in the base. When the motor is on, make sure fingers stay clear of the sharp high-speed bits. Never use drill bits in a router.

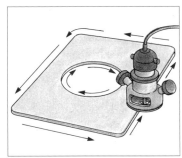

Because bit sizes vary, measure from bit to edge of base before setting a fence or guide. Mark the same distance from the cutting edge.

The router bit spins clockwise and must feed into the work. For cuts on an edge, move the router from left to right; guide it counterclockwise around a continuous piece. For inside cuts, move it clockwise.

Plunge router, ideal for making interior cuts, is supported with two posts extending up from the base. After setting the depth stop, set the router over the work at the starting point and start the motor; release the plunge locking lever and lower the bit into the work. Some models have variable-speed control.

Retrofit plunge base replaces the base on a standard router with a 90 mm-diameter motor. When attached to the motor, the standard router becomes a plunge router. The plunge base also has a locking lever and a multiposition depth stop.

Laminate trimmer finishes plastic laminate edges on countertops, backsplashes, cabinet doors, and shelves. Attachments include an offset base (top, centre) to reach into corners, an adjustable base (top, right) to set trimmer at 0° to 45° angles, and a slitter (bottom, right) to cut laminate sheets.

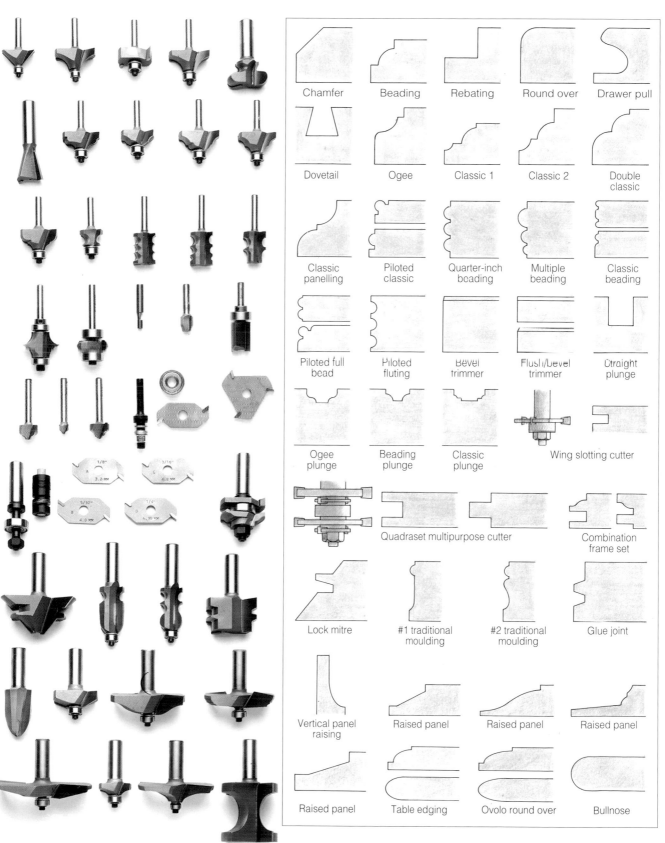

Chamfer

Beading

Rebating

Round over

Drawer pull

Dovetail

Ogee

Classic 1

Classic 2

Double classic

Classic panelling

Piloted classic

Quarter-inch beading

Multiple beading

Classic beading

Piloted full bead

Piloted fluting

Bevel trimmer

Flush/bevel trimmer

Straight plunge

Ogee plunge

Beading plunge

Classic plunge

Wing slotting cutter

Quadraset multipurpose cutter

Combination frame set

Lock mitre

#1 traditional moulding

#2 traditional moulding

Glue joint

Vertical panel raising

Raised panel

Raised panel

Raised panel

Raised panel

Table edging

Ovolo round over

Bullnose

ROUTER GUIDES AND TEMPLATES

To make perfect cuts and shapes, a router is often used with a guide or template. Before routing with one of these accessories on the actual workpiece, practise on scrap wood until you feel comfortable with it. Because bits vary in width, when setting up a guide or template, always calculate the distance with the bit in place in the collet (p 66).

Pantograph guides a router to transfer designs from templates to signs, plaques and other flat surfaces. To use it, attach the router to the pantograph, turn on the router, then trace the design with the stylus; the router will duplicate the design on the workpiece. Some models include letter templates and drawings. You can also make your own templates.

Roller edge guide and guide bushings come in a kit. The roller edge guide, attached to a special baseplate (right), has a bearing that lets you shape decorative profiles when using unpiloted bits. It's also useful for trimming laminate and for edging irregular shapes. Guide bushings (left) and retainer (top) protect precision dovetail, letter and butt-hinge templates. Never use the roller edge guide and a guide bushing together.

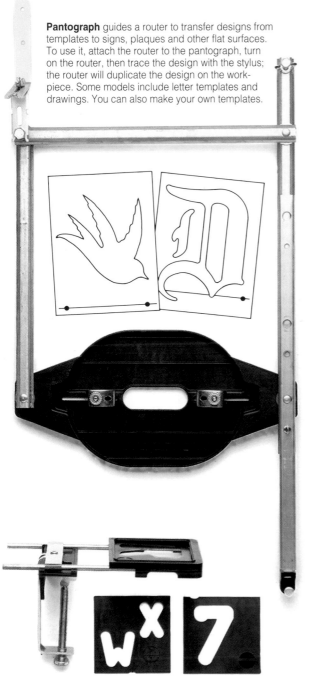

Straight-and-circular guide directs the router for making cuts parallel to the edge of the work. Use it to make straight or circular plunge cuts. The guide has an adjustable fence for straight cuts; an adjustable trammel point holds the guide in place to make circular cuts. Wing nuts are used to make the adjustments. This model also has a micrometer adjustment for accuracy.

Letter templates are used with a guide bushing and a straight, V-groove, or cove router bit to engrave letters and numbers in wooden signs. A bracket clamps the template and work to a workbench. Letter styles and sizes vary.

Router table transforms a router into a stationary shaper for precision work. Invert the router and mount it underneath the table; make sure the cutter protrudes up through the hole in the centre of the table. To rout the work surface or edge, place its good face down on the table and push it into the bit. The table includes a cutter safety guard, a guide fence for edging and slotting, and a mitre gauge for angles and crosscuts.

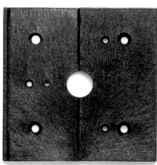

Edge-joining guide is a two-piece base-plate that replaces your router's standard base. To create a perfect edge joint, make a separate pass against each of the two workpieces, using the enclosed bit.

Mortise-and-tenon jig makes perfect-fitting round mortise-and-tenon joints for constructing furniture and door frames. The jig can create up to three consecutive mortises-and-tenons without being moved. The joints can also be angled or mitred. A piloted mortise-and-tenon bit is included.

Dovetail template guides router to make strong dovetail joints for fine furniture, cabinet and drawer construction. It's used in conjunction with a guide bushing and a dovetail router bit. The guide bushing follows the template as the router bit cuts a series of evenly spaced fan-shaped pins and matching recesses simultaneously in the two workpieces. It makes both flush and rebate dovetails.

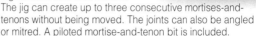

Butt-hinge template fits on doorjambs and edges to rout mortises for butt hinges from about 60 to 140 mm wide. It comes in a kit with three templates, letting you make up to three mortises at a time. Adjustable link rails slide into the templates; markings indicate proper placement on 2 to 2,15 m-tall doors. One template has a gauge for the top mortise. Before using a router with the templates, attach a butt-hinge guide to its base.

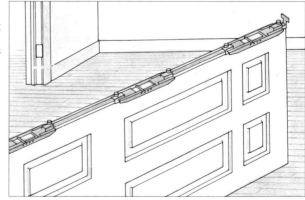

Universal precision positioning jig can become an adjustable fence to make accurate finger and dovetail joints on a router table, and it can act as an adjustable stop for other cuts. The jig (left) can be quickly set at exact stops as small as 1 mm apart, up to 200 mm. It also operates as a fence on a table saw and has other applications for a radial arm saw and drill press. The multifunction precision gauge (left, top) sets the bit-to-fence alignment and establishes the depth of the cut with the same accuracy as the jig.

CHISELS, GOUGES AND LATHES

When kept sharp and free of corrosion, a chisel or gouge will last a lifetime. Chisels come in a variety of sizes for working on wood, metal and stone. They are hand-driven or driven with a mallet. The steel blades may have straight or bevelled sides. Straight sides are stronger than bevelled, but a bevelled blade can reach into tight places. The blade shape may be square, round or skewed for specific tasks. Gouge blades are curved to make concave or convex cuts. Store chisels and gouges where their blades cannot be damaged by hitting each other or other tools. Never place one where it can be knocked to the floor; the sharp blade can cause a cut.

Butt chisel has a short blade that makes it easier to work with than a standard chisel. It is hand- or lightly mallet-driven. The bevelled sides and straight cutting edge make it ideal for undercutting to create dovetail joints.

Mortise chisel has a thick rigid blade, straight cutting edge and square sides to make mortises and similar joints. The sturdy reinforced handle is struck with a mallet to remove waste.

Skew chisel uses a slicing motion to finish cuts in tight spaces and to trim close to adjacent surfaces. The angled cutting edge (about 60°) gives the chisel its name; the skew on the blade may be right- or left-handed or both. The blade sides are straight for strength. This chisel is hand-driven only.

Framing chisel has bevelled sides and a straight cutting edge; it flexes slightly when used in hard-to-reach spaces. You strike the hoop-reinforced handle with a mallet to remove waste when cutting mortises, dovetails and similar joints.

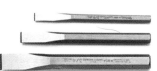

Corner chisel, resembling a punch, is used primarily with a mallet. Another model has a handle for striking and for handwork. The L-shaped cutting edge cleans out square holes and corners with angles of 90° and more; it also trims and fine-tunes mortises.

Swan-neck mortise chisel has a blade shaped to clean out grooves and small mortises. Using a chisel slightly smaller than the mortise, set the blade's cutting edge along the mortise's bottom edge. The tool can be used in mortises to 150 mm deep.

Dogleg chisel with a straight, right skew or left skew cutting edge works like a small paring or carving chisel. Uses include fine-tuning joints and adding detail to fine woodwork.

Cold chisel for metalwork is struck with a hammer to cut sheet metal and to chop off rivets, bolts and nails. You can also use one to reach a plumbing fixture by chipping away ceramic tile.

Flooring chisel cuts and lifts flooring materials for removal or repair; it's ideal for tongue-and-groove flooring. The wide blade distributes pressure evenly to prevent damage to adjacent boards.

Paring chisel is ideal for cleaning grooves and slicing away small amounts of stock. The straight cutting edge has bevelled sides to reach tight spaces. It's made for hand use only; do not strike it with a mallet.

Cabinet scrapers are thin steel plates that remove very fine shavings to give a smooth finish without producing dust that might clog the grain of the wood. They come in various shapes and cut-control is determined by finger pressure. Re-sharpen with a file or burnishing tool.

Crank-neck paring chisel has an offset blade to allow you to hold the tool flat against the work surface, even in the middle of the work, and still have clearance to hold the handle.

Blind-nail chisel lifts up a small sliver of wood. After hammering the nail in place, glue the sliver over the nailhead.

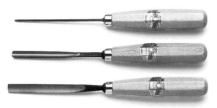

Carving chisel, sold separately or in sets, is used for cutting intricate designs into wood and for sculpting. Some carving chisels are designed to be struck. Their cutting edges include gouge, parting, skew, straight, paring and V-groove.

Chip-carving knives have blades in a variety of designs for creating low-relief carving and for whittling. Often sold in sets, the knives can be conveniently stored in a canvas pouch.

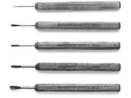

Miniature carving chisel is for extra-fine detail work. It comes with the same variety of blades as standard carving chisels.

Cabinetmaker's carving chisel has a handle that fits into the palm of your hand.

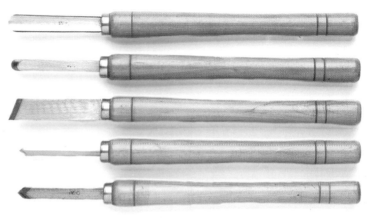

Adze is a sculptor's tool for quickly shaping large pieces of wood. One end of the head has an axelike blade; the other end is shaped like a gouge. The adze is available in several sizes; with only the axe or the gouge blade, or with the two combined.

Lathe chisels are used with a lathe to create turned woodwork such as chair legs and rails. A basic set of chisels includes, from top to bottom: gouge for rounding and cutting coves (concave curves); round-nose chisel to form coves and hollows; skew chisel to cut beads (convex curves) and to smooth straight or tapered cylinders; spear point chisel to cut V-grooves and square shoulders; and parting tool for sizing cuts and to separate the turned work from the waste stock.

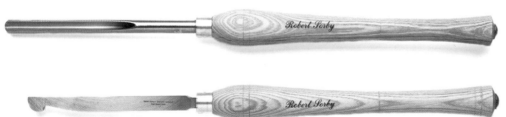

Deep-throat gouge is for bowl work on a lathe. Handled properly, it leaves a smooth finish that needs no sanding.

Finishing scraper is used for inside finishing of work turned on a lathe. It may have a round- or square-shaped blade.

Lathe is ideal for turning wood stock into a cylindrical shape. The headstock holds the wheel; a motor turns the wheel, which turns a spindle. The tailstock also has a spindle. Depending on the model, the headstock or tailstock spindle is adjustable. Centres on the spindles grip the work. As the work turns, a chisel held on the tool rest by the user shaves or scrapes it. For bowls and other flat round pieces, attach the work to a faceplate mounted on the headstock spindle; rotate the tool rest 90°.

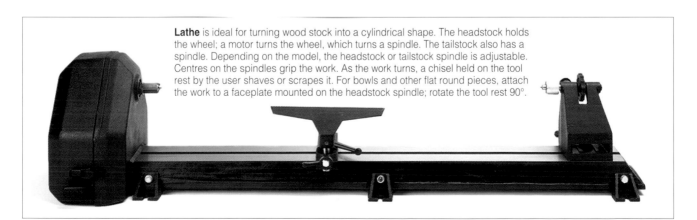

FILES AND RASPS

Depending on the individual tool, a file or rasp can sharpen, shape or smooth while removing metal or wood. Cut, coarseness, length and shape determine the tool's use. The *cut* refers to the pattern of the teeth. A single-cut file has parallel diagonal rows of ridgelike teeth for smoothing and sharpening metal; a double-cut file has a second set of rows that cross the first for rapid removal of metal stock. The rasp has straight or random rows of individual teeth for fast rough removal of wood or soft metal stock. Files are available in several grades – rough, bastard, second cut, smooth and extra smooth. Generally the longer the tool, the coarser its cut. The shape, or profile, of a file or rasp can make it useful for specific jobs.

Flat file (near right), a general-purpose file for fast removal of metal, has a slightly tapered shape and a rectangular profile. It has double-cut faces (above) with a single cut along the edges.

Hand file (near centre) is similar to flat file, but it has parallel edges; one edge is *safe,* or uncut, to keep it from marring the work.

Pillar file (far centre), a thin file, fits into narrow grooves and slots.

Square file (far right) is shaped to fit into recesses, angles, and square mortises and holes for filing. Like the flat file, it tapers toward the end.

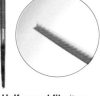

Half-round file (top, far left) has a round and a flat side to file large concave and flat surfaces.

Round file (top, near left) shapes small curves and enlarges and smooths holes. A tapered one is called a rat-tail file.

Triangular file (left) has three sides. Each side is flat and has a single cut.

Saw files sharpen saw-blade teeth. From left to right are a chain-saw file, veneer knife file, crosscut file, cant-saw file (for saw blades with teeth angled less than 60°) and taper file (for blades with 60° angle teeth).

Cabinet file (above) has ridge-like teeth staggered in parallel rows. Wood-carvers and cabinet-makers use it for sculpting.

Wood file (above, right), a half-round file, has teeth that are slightly coarser than those of the cabinet file.

Long-angle lathe file (far left) has a single cut (above) that can leave a smooth finish on lathe metalwork.

Mill file (left, centre) is used for lathe metalwork, for fine finishing of metals, for draw-filing and for sharpening cutters and saw blades.

Auger bit file (near left) is for maintaining the cutting edges on auger drill bits.

Three-square (triangular) file (far left) is tapered and has three flat sides for filing metal at angles under 90°.

Knife file (left, centre) is for working on metal pieces with acute angles.

Warding file (left) has a narrow tip to fit into tight areas.

Rifflers – files and rasps used for woodcarving and metalcrafts – shape and remove stock in irregular and tight spaces. They vary in size and come in the same shapes, coarsenesses and cuts as standard files and rasps. Some rifflers have handles, and some are double-ended, with a file at one end and a rasp at the other.

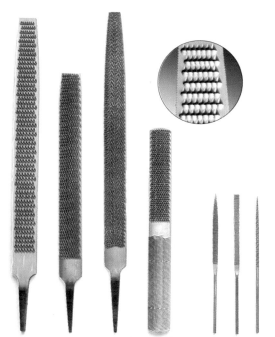

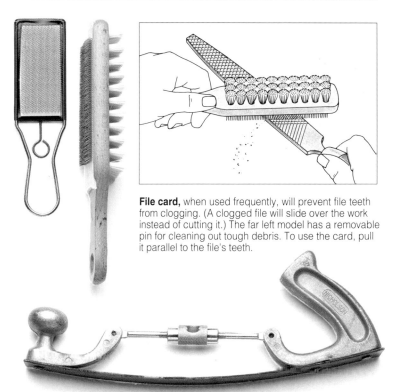

File card, when used frequently, will prevent file teeth from clogging. (A clogged file will slide over the work instead of cutting it.) The far left model has a removable pin for cleaning out tough debris. To use the card, pull it parallel to the file's teeth.

Rasps have individual teeth, instead of ridges, to rough out shapes and remove stock quickly. They work best on wood but can also be used on leather and soft metals. From left to right are a wood rasp with a rectangular profile and coarse teeth, a cabinet rasp with a half-round profile and medium teeth, a patternmaker's cabinet rasp that also has a half-round profile but fine teeth, and a four-in-one rasp, which combines a half-round and a flat profile —each side has a file end and a rasp end. The rat-tail rasp (not shown) has a round profile. Small rasps are ideal for working in restricted spaces.

Flexible file holder provides easy two-handed gripping and filing power. Secure a file in the holder, then adjust the holder to bend outward or inward to suit the stock surface. It can hold files that are from 300 to 360 mm long.

File handle fits on the file's tang, the pointed end of the file, allowing a better hold on the file and protecting the user from the sharp tang. Handles are usually purchased separately from the file. This model has a screw on one end that controls jaws at the other end.

Surform file, like the rasp, has individual teeth punched into metal for cutting wood. The resulting hole near each of the teeth allows shavings to pass through, preventing clogging. The tool can also be used to cut, shave and shape hardboard, some roofing tiles, rigid plastics, fibreglass, aluminium, copper and brass.

Surform plane shapes, planes and removes stock with a two-handed pushing action. The blades cannot be sharpened but are replaceable; remove the screw usually found beside the handle. Blades come in fine, regular, and medium cuts and in grits from coarse to fine. Use the plane on wood, plywood, chipboard, plaster, vinyl and linoleum. The regular-cut blade has a feature on one edge for cutting inside corners; the other edge does not cut.

Surform shaving tool works with a pull stroke. Change the depth of cut by adjusting hand pressure. Unlike the other Surforms, the blade simply clips into place.

Surform pocket plane fits comfortably into the palm of your hand. Use it to trim narrow surfaces and to get into tight corners.

Round Surform file is useful for enlarging holes and shaping curved surfaces.

Surform file-plane has a handle that unscrews and moves, allowing the tool to be held and used like a file or a plane.

SANDING TOOLS

Hand and power sanders fitted with abrasive papers can shape workpieces, remove imperfections in wood, and create smooth surfaces prior to finishing. They can also help remove unwanted paint, rust and finishes from wood, metal and other surfaces. Hand-sanding is made easier with blocks and pads that hold the abrasive. Power-assisted sanding takes less time but sometimes requires extra skill; you can hire large power sanders, especially floor models. Always wear a dust mask and protective glasses when power-sanding, even if the sander has a dust collection system. Start a power sander before the abrasive touches the work surface. Raise it before switching off, and wait until the sander stops moving before setting it down. Empty the dust bag often, and particularly before sanding metal after wood – sparks may ignite wood dust.

Sanding block holds abrasive sheets. It pulls apart to anchor the sheet ends between the two sections.

Flexible block can be adjusted to the contour of the workpiece. To change its shape, pull the two ends of the block apart or push one end under the other.

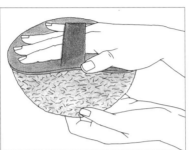

Sanding pad is secured to your hand with a strap, making it convenient for sanding large surfaces, and 150 mm abrasive discs are attached to the pad with Velcro. The pad's flexibility allows you to bend it to the work's shape.

Fibre block is designed to hold self-adhesive abrasive sheets that grip onto a felt backing. Replacing the sheet is as easy as pulling off the old one  and sticking on the new one. The block itself has a large handle with a comfortable grip. Use the straight end of the base to sand into tight corners. The rounded end can fit into a concave surface.

Palm orbital sander, for preparing a wood surface before applying a finish, works with an orbital motion. A soft pad (covered with an abrasive sheet) moves in quick, tight circles while the housing remains stationary. The sander's small size allows for one-handed use; hold the base flush to the work. Some models accept adhesive-backed abrasive sheets; a quarter-sheet square pad for fitting in corners is available. The sander may come with a dust bag.

Pole sander, when attached to an extension pole, is used for reaching ceilings and upper parts of walls. Abrasive sheets are held in place with metal clips.

Eccentric orbital sander, available in single- and variable-speed models, quickly removes stock with coarse abrasive paper; its eccentric action creates a swirl-free finish when using fine abrasive paper.

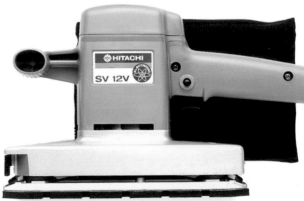

Finishing sander has a second handle for steadier, two-handed operation. It's available in one-, two- and variable-speed models. Apply light pressure when sanding; excessive pressure can overload the motor. Clamp one-third of an abrasive sheet to the pad.

Belt disc sander, which should be bolted to a workbench, lets you sand, buff and sharpen narrow pieces of straight, curved and odd-shaped stock. The belt sander can be raised to fit a job. Attach a buffing belt to polish metals and other materials. The disc sander, with an adjustable worktable, smooths the ends or convex edges of workpieces. Use the mitre gauge for precise sanding. Grinding attachments are available.

Portable belt sander uses a continuous loop of abrasive sheet for fast sanding of large, flat areas of wood, for trimming off excess wood, and for stripping old paint and finish. Two drumlike rollers control the belt. The back roller is powered by the motor; the front roller is spring-loaded to correct the belt tension. The longer and wider the belt, the heavier and more powerful the tool. Look for a model with a dust collection bag. Before buying a belt sander, hold it to check its feel – is it comfortable? Make sure the sander doesn't twist in your hands when you start it. When using the sander, keep the tool level as you move it across the work.

Offset disc sander is also a polisher and grinder. The sander smooths wood and metal surfaces and removes old paint and rust. A wool bonnet fits over the rubber backing pad for polishing painted metal, varnished wood and other surfaces. The sander comes in one-, two- and variable-speed models; lower speeds are recommended for polishing. When grinding, only part of the flexible disc should contact the metal surface, as shown at right.

ABRASIVES

Also known as sandpaper, abrasive paper comes with aluminium oxide, emery, garnet, or silicon carbide particles, or grit, glued to a paper or cloth backing (which is graded by weight). The paper comes in pre-cut sizes or in sheets that can be folded and torn to size; it's graded by numbers that reflect the size of the grit. The higher the number, the finer the grit. Grades include extra-coarse (30–40), coarse (50–60), medium (80–100), fine (120–150), very fine (160–240), extra-fine (280–320), superfine (360–400), and ultrafine (above 400). Other abrasives include metal wools and polishing powders, such as pumice and rottenstone (not shown).

Disc-shaped papers, like other abrasive papers, come in coarse, medium and fine grits. Use coarse-grit papers for fast stock removal; fine-grit papers are best for sanding finishes on wood, metal and plastic surfaces.

Precut abrasive papers come in the same grits and coarsenesses as the standard large sheets, but they are cut to fit specific sanders (pp 74–75). Clockwise, the papers fit a sanding block, finishing sander, orbital palm sander with a square pad, portable belt sander and workbench belt sander. The papers are attached by a form of clamping, an adhesive backing or with Velcro. Most papers have a closed coat – the paper is completely covered with grains. But to prevent the paper from being clogged with fibres when working on softwoods, try to find an open-coat paper with only 70 per cent surface coverage.

Abrasive sheets (from top to bottom) are *aluminium oxide paper,* a tough, durable synthetic abrasive for smoothing wood, metal, plastic and fibreglass, and for removing paint; *emery cloth,* a fine natural abrasive set on cloth, for metalworking; *garnet paper,* with a natural grit that fractures during use to form new cutting edges, for heavy and moderate smoothing on hard- and softwoods, and for preparing wood for sealing and finishing; and *silicon carbide paper,* which uses a synthetic abrasive that cuts fast and smooth, for wet- or dry-sanding between coats of varnish, paint and other finishes on wood and metal. (Water reduces clogging and extends the life of silicon carbide paper.) The last example is *aluminium oxide* bonded to a pad; it can be rinsed and used a number of times, wet or dry.

Steel wool can clean, strip and buff metal, wood and other surfaces. It is graded by number: 4 is extra-coarse, 0 is fine, and 0000 is superfine. Wools made of bronze and copper are corrosion-resistant, making them ideal for work that is exposed to water.

Sanding screen can be used in the hand or on a pole. Use it for the initial sanding when working with plaster patching compounds. The open screen allows dust to pass through to prevent clogging.

WALLCOVERING TOOLS

To hang wallcoverings with professional results, you'll find that the tools shown on this page will be helpful. A clean flat surface is necessary to lay the wallcovering down for pasting. If you don't have a large 1,5 × 1 m table, make a temporary one by setting plywood on sawhorses (cover it with a plastic sheet, such as a drop cloth); or if you plan to do a substantial amount of wallcovering, buy a pasting table that folds up for storage. For pre-pasted wallcoverings, you'll need an inexpensive plastic water tray, or you might be able to use your bath.

Paste brush with 75 mm-long bristles applies paste to wall-coverings that are not pre-pasted. The brush is 150 mm wide. It comes in wallcovering kits, but you can also purchase the brush separately.

Smoothing brush flattens the wallcovering to create a uniform surface without wrinkles and air pockets. The long-bristle brush works best on paper, cloth and such delicate coverings as cork, silk and grass cloth; the gentle bristles won't tear them. The short-bristle model is appropriate for the sturdier vinyl wallcoverings. Both are 300 mm wide.

Seam roller smooths edges of wallcoverings (except embossed). Use rollers with oval barrels for seams, tapered barrels for corners, and flat barrels for door and window frames.

Touching-up kit has a tapered-tip syringe (far left) to repair curled wallcovering corners. To remove an air bubble, slit it with a knife; then inject paste behind the bubble with the needle-tip syringe (left). Smooth down the repair with a seam roller or smoother. Wash area if wallcovering is washable.

Smoother is used on vinyl wallcoverings to produce a uniformly smooth surface and to remove air bubbles. It can also serve as a spreader for spackling compound or as a trim guide. Rounded corners will not mar the work.

Corner trimmer (far left) has an attachment to guide cuts at corners, ceiling lines, and skirting boards.

Casing knife (left) trims wallcoverings around outlets, vents, skirting, and window and door frames.

Wallpaper trimmer (above) comes with a straightedge to remove selvage edges and to cut wallcoverings to size.

Wallcovering shears have sharp blades to cut wallcoverings with great accuracy. The handles are designed to provide a comfortable grip.

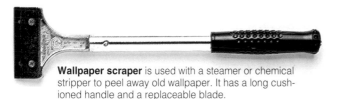

Wallpaper scraper is used with a steamer or chemical stripper to peel away old wallpaper. It has a long cushioned handle and a replaceable blade.

Wallpaper steamer speeds up the task of removing old wallpaper. Hold the unit against the wallpaper, letting the steam saturate the paper just enough to soften the paste. Then use a scraper to remove the paper.

PAINTING TOOLS

By taking the time to select the right tools and use the correct techniques, an amateur painter can turn a so-so project into one with outstanding results. Choose the appropriate paint applicators from among the various bristle and foam brushes, rollers, pads and power sprayers. Each applicator has its own benefits, depending on the type of finish being applied, the size of the area being covered, and the quality and speed of application desired. Special accessories, including tools for preparing the surface and cleaning up afterwards, also help to make painting tasks easier and to produce professional-looking results.

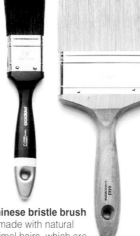

Chisel-edge brush has angled bristles for painting clean edges. Hold the brush so that the ends of the bristles apply the paint. With a steady hand, pull the brush with the shorter bristles leading the way.

Chinese bristle brush is made with natural animal hairs, which are preferred for applying enamel paint, varnish and stain. A good brush will provide long service if treated and cleaned properly.

Wall brush is at least 100 mm wide to cover broad areas. To speed the job, use the widest brush possible without using one wider than the work. This brush, with synthetic polyester bristles (others may be nylon), can apply PVA or enamel paint, varnish and stain.

Trim brush, available with natural or synthetic bristles for enamel or PVA finishes, comes in several widths up to 50 mm. The brush can apply paint to such detail work as skirting boards, door and window trim, and mouldings. It also 'cuts in' paint where rollers cannot reach – such as in corners and where the walls and ceiling meet.

Edger pad has compact fibres to disperse paint quickly and evenly along trim areas. It spreads paint faster than a brush but slower than a roller. One model (right) has guide wheels and a removable pad for cleaning.

Corner pad with two sides angled at 90° is especially designed for painting the inside corners of walls and between walls and ceilings, as well as other right-angle intersections. For other trims, hold the pad with only one side against the work surface.

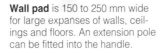

Wand and sponge applicators can fit into restricted areas. To change angle of handle on wand applicator (left), press the button; move pad to the other side. The sponge applicator (right) uses disposable pads.

Wall pad is 150 to 250 mm wide for large expanses of walls, ceilings and floors. An extension pole can be fitted into the handle.

Pad paint tray can be hung over step- or extension ladder rungs. To avoid overloading pad with paint, roll the pad over the revolving wheel in the tray

Trim rollers have specialized applications. The 75 mm-wide roller (below) comes with its own paint tray for quick touch-up jobs and hard-to-reach areas. Another roller (centre) applies paint in corners. The third roller (right) is for narrow surface areas.

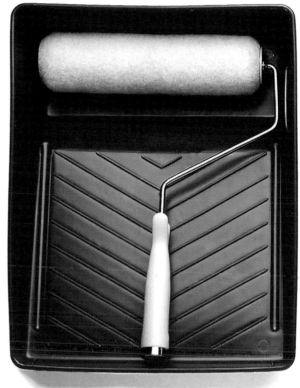

Pipe roller has an indented centre groove in the cover to conform to the contour of water-pipes. Make sure you apply only heat-resistant paint to hot-water pipes.

Roller and paint tray make it possible to apply paint and other finishes to broad surfaces quickly and economically. The roller uses less paint than a brush, requires less effort to spread a smooth, even coat, and leaves no brush marks. With the paint tray set on a flat surface, pour paint into the deeper well section. Slip a roller cover onto the frame. Place the roller in the well; pull it up to the grooved area, applying slight pressure and rolling it to squeeze out excess paint.

Splatter-shield roller reduces splatters. End caps hold the roller cover in a handle and housing unit. To remove the roller cover, you may have to pry out tight-fitting end caps. The handle can be connected to an extension pole.

Texture roller has a cover made from pieces of leather; only the edges of the leather come in contact with the surface, creating a pattern. The cover fits only on a special-size frame. Roller and frame are usually purchased as a unit.

Trim guard keeps paint off adjoining straight surfaces. Hold it perpendicular to the work with the long edge touching it. The roller cover should fit into its curved shape to let you apply paint to the edge of the work.

Roller covers slide onto a frame or the end caps of a splatter-shield roller. If cleaned properly, most roller covers may be used several times. Roller covers come in various naps for use with PVA and enamel paints and for special applications.

Extension pole screws into a threaded roller or pad handle, allowing you to reach ceilings and upper wall areas without using a ladder. It also eliminates bending or kneeling when painting floors and sealing driveways. Extension poles may be 2 m or longer, and some telescope still further.

Self-feeding roller comes with a lid and filling tube that fit on a paint tin. Attach the extension pole (assembled with roller cover and splatter shield) to the lid. Pull pole sections apart to draw paint into handle. Detach pole from lid; push pole section in to send paint to roller. Self-feeding brushes are also obtainable.

Electric paint roller employs an electric pump to apply paint, requiring even less effort than using a self-feeding roller. The pump feeds paint directly from the tin to the roller through a hose. A push button on the roller handle starts and stops the flow of paint. Not widely available, electric rollers may be ordered on special request and are useful for larger jobs.

Pouring spout fits on a standard 5 litre paint tin. It allows you to pour the paint into a tray without spilling or dripping.

Lid openers come in several patterns and quickly open standard paint tins of various sizes without damaging the lipped lid.

Paint mixer locks into the chuck of almost any standard electric drill. With more consistency and less mess than stirring by hand, the blades easily mix and blend paint, driveway and roofing sealers, and joint compound in the tin.

Paint sprayer applies paint, stain, varnish and other liquids with a fine mist for fast, even and run-free covering. It's useful for hard-to-paint objects such as window shutters and wickerwork.

Paint glove, for applying paint to unusually shaped items, is first slipped onto a hand. Dip the glove into paint, then spread the paint over the work.

Graining comb creates a pattern in wet stain or paint to simulate wood grain. The comb comes in different sizes; the steel teeth vary in width.

Rubber grainer has concentric circles imprinted on a rubber base. Experiment with dragging and rolling it in wet stain or glaze to create your own effect.

Three-in-one graining comb has three combs with rubber teeth combined in one tool. This tool is especially suited to round and curved surfaces.

Spiked cleaner helps separate bristles when cleaning a brush. For proper maintenance, always clean a brush before the paint hardens.

Wire brush prepares wood, metal and other surfaces for painting by removing loose paint, rust, corrosion and other hardened materials. This model has a built-in scraper on the back of the handle.

Paint sponges come in various shapes to apply paints and stains. Depending on the sponge surface, it will leave a smooth or textured pattern.

Striping brush utilizes natural camel bristles that are cut and set in the ferrule to come to a point. Drag the brush through wet stain or glaze to create a wood-grain or marbling effect. The brush can also be used with a steady hand to create delicate line work.

Stippling brush is pounced over a stencil to leave a decorative pattern on walls, furniture and other surfaces. Be careful not to overload the bristles with paint.

Varnish brushes have natural bristles for applying varnish, shellac and other finishes. One brush (right) has bristles with an oval profile to hold varnish and to provide best edge control. The badger-hair brush (far right) can hold more varnish with its 'split end' bristles

Masking tool dispenses a 150 mm-wide paper strip (or a 450 mm-wide plastic drop cloth) with masking tape along one edge. Use it to protect surfaces that you don't intend to paint.

Radiator brush is a thin-handled brush with an angled head that makes it easier to reach awkward and out-of-the-way places. Different types are made of natural or synthetic bristle and commonly available widths are 25, 50 and 75 mm.

Heat gun focuses a controlled amount of heat, usually at a working temperature of 500°C, to soften paint so that you can remove it with a scraper. Also use the heat gun to remove glued-down tiles and to bend plastic. On models with variable settings, start with a low temperature and work your way up.

LADDERS AND SAWHORSES

To reach high places or to create extra surfaces for holding your work, a few ladders and sawhorses – and perhaps a portable work-centre – are a great help. Some manufacturers grade their ladders as domestic or industrial, or as light, medium or heavy duty according to the number of steps, but no uniform standards or descriptions are applied. Aluminium ladders require almost no maintenance but are relatively expensive. With wooden ladders, ensure that the wood is kept oiled or sealed and the support wires are tightened regularly.

Caution: Fully open a stepladder and lock its braces before using it. Make sure the ladder is secure and steady. Always face a ladder and hold on when climbing or descending. Never use a broken or damaged ladder. Never work on a ladder outdoors during windy or inclement weather. Keep the ladder far away from electrical or other wires. Never work with two people on a ladder, or underneath someone on a ladder.

Tripod stepladder, available in heights from 1,2 to 3,7 m, is handy for reaching high corners where the two back legs of a standard stepladder would push you too far away. The single back leg of a tripod ladder also fits between studs of unfinished walls, allowing you to get as close to the wall as you like. The front legs are braced to balance the ladder.

Stepladder, which comes in heights ranging from 1,2 to 5 m, supports itself with a hinged framework and has a fold-out shelf for holding paint and tools. The ladder can be made of wood (usually saligna), aluminium or glass-reinforced plastic (GRP). A GRP ladder (shown) is lightweight, as is an aluminium one, but it does not conduct electricity as does a metal or a wet wooden ladder.

Sawhorses come ready-made, or you can make your own with 50 x 100's and the bracket kit shown above. Hook-on hardware bins and tool hangers are also available. Use two sawhorses to support a large workpiece, or lay a sheet of plywood across them to make a temporary workbench.

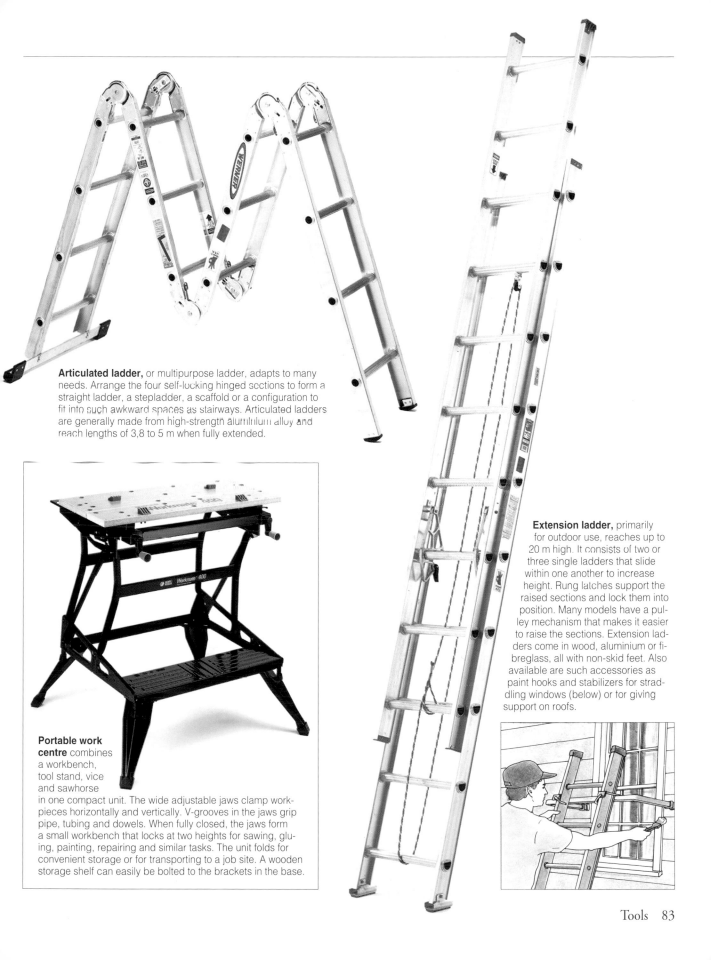

Articulated ladder, or multipurpose ladder, adapts to many needs. Arrange the four self-locking hinged sections to form a straight ladder, a stepladder, a scaffold or a configuration to fit into such awkward spaces as stairways. Articulated ladders are generally made from high-strength aluminium alloy and reach lengths of 3,8 to 5 m when fully extended.

Portable work centre combines a workbench, tool stand, vice and sawhorse in one compact unit. The wide adjustable jaws clamp work-pieces horizontally and vertically. V-grooves in the jaws grip pipe, tubing and dowels. When fully closed, the jaws form a small workbench that locks at two heights for sawing, gluing, painting, repairing and similar tasks. The unit folds for convenient storage or for transporting to a job site. A wooden storage shelf can easily be bolted to the brackets in the base.

Extension ladder, primarily for outdoor use, reaches up to 20 m high. It consists of two or three single ladders that slide within one another to increase height. Rung latches support the raised sections and lock them into position. Many models have a pulley mechanism that makes it easier to raise the sections. Extension ladders come in wood, aluminium or fibreglass, all with non-skid feet. Also available are such accessories as paint hooks and stabilizers for straddling windows (below) or for giving support on roofs.

TOOLS FOR SHARPENING

You can sharpen dulled tools on a variety of sharpening stones and grinding wheels and polish metalwork with buffing wheels and a buffing compound. Grinding and buffing wheels are made to fit the chucks of electric drills (for light jobs) or the arbors of a bench grinder (most grinders have two arbors). Before using a wheel, check it by rapping it with a screwdriver handle and listening for a ringing sound. If it makes a buzzing sound, the wheel is chipped or cracked; replace it. Although the grinder has guards, always wear a face shield for necessary extra protection. When turning on the power, stand to one side of the wheel in case it shatters. To prevent overheating, use light pressure and cool the work often in water. Keep your grinding wheels true and even by dressing them with the appropriate tool. After cleaning a stone, store it in a closed box (re-apply oil to an oilstone before storing it).

Benchstone, made of silicon carbide or aluminium oxide, has coarse grit on one side, medium on the other. Lubricate it with water or oil. If you start with oil, don't switch to water for later uses.

Japanese waterstone sharpens quickly because worn particles on the stone break away, exposing new sharp particles. Before using a medium- or coarse-grit stone, soak in water for about 6 hours; soak a fine-grit stone for 5 minutes. Continue to apply water as you work.

Slipstone, with its wedge-shaped profile, has a flat surface for honing straight edges and a round side for irregular shapes. It's ideal for gouge chisels and carving tools. To use the stone, move it against the stationary tool. Some stones are supplied in a wooden box.

Arkansas stone, one of many natural stones, comes in four grades: Washita, soft, hard and black hard. Lubricate the stone with oil.

Gouge stone is contoured to fit the round edge of a gouge chisel. Depending on your stone selection, apply water or a light mineral oil to the stone. Rub the stone against the gouge.

Lubricating oil is applied to oilstones to increase grinding speed and to prevent the pores in the stones from clogging. When twhe stone becomes sticky, clean off the oil with paraffin or ammonia.

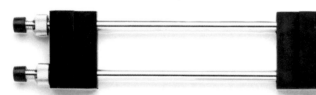

Stone holder keeps stone in place when honing. Grooved rubber soles prevent the holder from skidding. Set the stone in the holder and turn the two knurled wheels to secure it.

Bevel setter and guide sets blades of chisels, planes and spokeshaves to 25 different angles. Place the guide on the setter with the work edge under the angle block. When it's parallel, secure the work.

Burnisher forms burr, or hooked edge, on scraper. Use round (centre) or triangular (bottom) type for general burnishing; only round type with curved scrapers. Dresser (top) is for touch-ups.

Honing guide holds a chisel or plane blade at a set angle for honing. Turn the top knob to hold the blade in place; set the angle of the guide by adjusting the side knob. Wheels let you slide the tool along the stone.

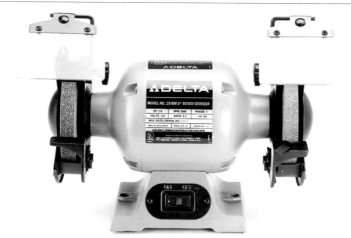

Tapered spindle fits into a bench grinder to hold accessories. The cone-shaped buffer comes in different grades of coarseness and in various shapes. To buff nooks and crannies in metals, use irregularly shaped buffers; to polish rings, use narrow ones.

Bench grinder mounts on a workbench or pedestal stand. It has a tool rest for each of the two wheels, spark deflectors and protective shields. Grinders come in different sizes. Always match the diameter of the wheel to the correct grinder.

Buffing compounds, when applied to their own buffing wheels, create final finishes. From top to bottom are emery cake, to remove rust from metals; tripoli, to buff brass, steel, aluminium and pewter; white rouge, to add lustre to chrome, steel and nickel; and red rouge to polish silver and other precious metals.

Bench grinder wheels vary in materials. The stone wheel (top) is available in different grits for sharpening. The wire wheel (centre) can turn the grinder into a stripper to remove rust and paint from small objects. The buffing wheel (bottom) is suitable for applying a polished finish to metal surfaces.

Strop, a two- or four-sided tool covered with leather and slate, gives the finishing touch to a honed blade or tool. On the four-sided version, three of the sides are covered with different grades of leather.

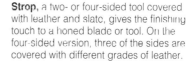

Wheel dressers come in a number of styles to re-surface a grinding wheel. The silicon carbide stick (above) cleans and restores a clogged wheel. When the wheel has worn unevenly, hold a hooded star wheel dresser (far left) against it. To true a grinding wheel, use the diamond wheel dresser (left), holding it against the bench grinder's tool rest or a home-made jig.

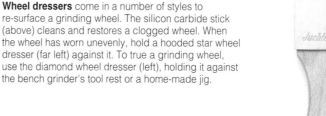

Drill bit sharpener, powered by a standard electric drill (not a cordless drill), sharpens steel twist bits and masonry bits. Set drill in holder, fitting the spindle of sharpener into its chuck; use collet to hold the bit.

SOLDERING TOOLS

Soldering uses heat to melt a bonding material (solder) and join metal pieces to one another. Soldering irons, guns and pencils are electric heat-generating tools. Propane or acetylene and butane gas-powered torches produce a flame with significantly more heat. When working with any of these heat-producing tools, be extremely cautious. Keep a fire extinguisher handy, wear eye protection and other protective clothing, avoid explosive atmospheres and keep the flame away from flammable materials and surfaces.

Soldering gun electrically heats small areas and is ideal for soldering electronic circuits. The interchangeable tip heats quickly when the trigger is depressed, and cools when it is released.

Electric soldering iron has interchangeable tips that come in a variety of shapes to fit the job. The iron shown is for heavy jobs, such as stained-glass work. Smaller soldering pencils are available for electrical work and light metalworking jobs.

Cordless soldering iron holds enough butane gas for up to 4 hr of work. Ignite it by pushing a button, and use it as a soldering iron or as a hot-air tool. Keep cover on tool when not in use.

Soft solder comes as solid wire or wire with flux at its centre. Use acid-core solder (top, left) to join pieces that can be washed to get rid of the corrosive flux; rosin-core solder (bottom, left) for electronic work; and lead-free solid-core solder (right) for water pipes.

Hard solder flows (melts) at higher temperatures than soft solder. Cut strips, wire or sheets into tiny chips before using.

Flux is brushed onto metal before soldering to prevent oxidation and help the solder flow. Use a non-corrosive rosin flux for electronic work, a zinc chloride flux for all other soft soldering, and a fluoride or borax-based flux for hard soldering.

Oxygen/fuel torch uses two tanks that combine propane or acetylene gas and oxygen gas or solid oxygen pellets to fuel an extremely hot flame (up to 2 750°C) for heavy soldering, cutting metal, brazing and welding.

Soldering iron rest can be attached to the edge of the workbench to provide a safe base for the hot iron. Always place the iron on the stand when not using it. Some irons come with small stands of their own.

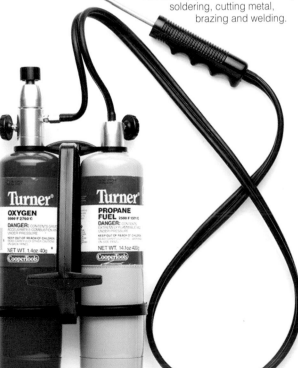

Torch lighter eliminates dangerous match lighting. Squeezing the trigger causes a spark that ignites the propane or butane gas.

Propane torch uses propane gas that mixes with the surrounding air to produce a hot flame (about 1 375°C) Different tips are available for soldering, removing paint from metal and other jobs requiring localized heat.

Binding wire of black iron can be tied around pieces being soldered to hold them in place. Select 26-gauge wire for general use.

SHEET-METAL TOOLS

Because of sheet metal's strength, malleability and versatility, a number of specialized tools are available to cut, bend, shape, join and stretch it. In addition to the ones illustrated below, you'll need a number of the tools shown on the preceding pages, including a punch or metal scriber and a micrometer to mark and measure the metal; snips, electric nibblers, and saws to cut it; drills to make holes in it; various hammers, mallets, stakes and an anvil to beat and shape it; and a machinist's vice to hold it steady while cutting and bending it.

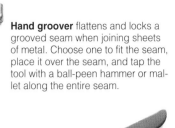

Hand groover flattens and locks a grooved seam when joining sheets of metal. Choose one to fit the seam, place it over the seam, and tap the tool with a ball-peen hammer or mallet along the entire seam.

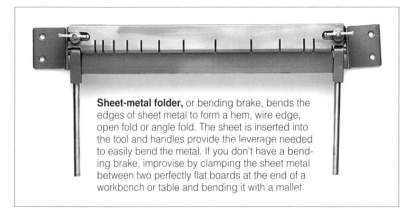

Sheet-metal folder, or bending brake, bends the edges of sheet metal to form a hem, wire edge, open fold or angle fold. The sheet is inserted into the tool and handles provide the leverage needed to easily bend the metal. If you don't have a bending brake, improvise by clamping the sheet metal between two perfectly flat boards at the end of a workbench or table and bending it with a mallet

Hand seamer bends and flattens sheet-metal edges. Use it to bend sheets into boxes or similar shapes, to fold over sharp edges to form a hem or add rigidity, and to fold over interlocking seams to join multiple sheets.

Hand notcher makes a clean V-shaped cut in sheet metal without slippage. The compound-action handles produce the necessary leverage for fast and easy cutting.

Annealing bowl filled with charcoal chips makes a good surface for annealing metal or holding small pieces while soldering. Filled with pitch, it is used as a bed for chasing or repoussé work

Hand punch applies almost 1 000 kg of pressure to cut holes in sheet metal, plastic or leather. The powerful jaws push small metal punches into cylindrical dies, which are interchangeable to create different-size holes.

Chasing and repoussé tools are small blunt punches and chisels that etch decorative designs into metal.

Circle cutter consists of a number of cylindrical pins and a slotted metal base with holes of different sizes. Insert sheet metal into the slot in the base and punch a hole with the pin and a hammer.

Pop riveter fastens metal to metal, plastic to metal, or heavy-gauge fabric to itself or to metal by inserting metal fasteners, called rivets, into pre-drilled holes.

Sandbag can be used as a malleable backing when beating dents out of metal. Simply hold the damaged section against the bag and gently beat out the dent with a mallet.

OTHER METALWORKING TOOLS

If you work with steel or alloy pipes and copper tubing, you'll need specialized tools for bending, cutting and joining the sections. To cut threads into metal rods or plates, you'll also need a set of taps and dies. These tools are made of hardened steel and can cut neatly into any softer metal, and they can also be used to restore damaged threads in appliances and vehicle parts. Special large-size dies and diestocks are available for threading copper tubing or steel pipes. Finally, if you are working on metal jewellery, you'll find specialized tools to help you do the job. In addition to the tools shown here, you may need smooth-jaw pliers for handling delicate pieces.

Pipe bender provides leverage to bend copper tubing and steel pipe to a maximum of 180°. Push a metal bar into top of bender to form handle. Insert tubing or pipe into curved channel, step on tread and pull handle until spirit levels in bender indicate the degree of bend you want.

Pipe- or tubing- cutter produces clean cuts on copper tubing or steel pipe. These cutters come in sizes to fit pipe and tubing of different diameters. Some cutters, such as the one above, have built-in reamers to remove burrs after cutting.

Spring-type pipe bender aids in bending thin-wall pipe or tubing, such as copper and aluminium, without crimping, flattening or creasing it. The bender is a tightly wound wire coil about 300 mm long and is available in standard pipe diameters. With a twisting motion, slide the bender onto the pipe, then bend it slowly with your hands or over your knee.

Pipe reamer shaves away rough edges and burrs left inside ends of pipes or tubing after cutting. Turn the reamer as you push it into the pipe. Reamer bits for electric drills are also available.

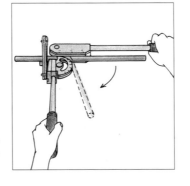

Lever bender is operated with two hands to bend tubing. Grasp the tool by its form handle and swing the shoe handle out. Slide tubing into groove of wheellike bending form, and slowly pull the shoe handle back in until the tubing is bent to the desired angle.

Flaring tool widens ends of copper, brass and aluminium tubing to take flared fittings. A double bar–type clamp (below) holds tubing while a cone-shaped ram (right) is driven into the tubing to flare it to angle of 45°.

Plumber's die and diestock are used to thread brass and steel pipe. Secure the pipe in a vice; fix the die (left) in the diestock (above), and slide it over the pipe. Pressing into the pipe, turn the diestock clockwise until the die begins to cut. Add cutting oil to the end of the pipe, and continue turning the diestock without applying pressure. Add more oil from time to time.

Taps cut or restore internal threads in holes in metal so that threaded fasteners can be used.

Tap wrenches turn the taps in the metal. T-handled wrench (left) gives less leverage than larger model (above).

Diestock is a special wrench for turning die as you thread metal rods or fasteners. This model has an adapter disc that can be inserted to convert the tool to a tap wrench.

Thread-restoring file renews damaged right- or left-handed external threads on any diameter screw, pipe or rod.

Draw plate is clamped in a vice and wire is drawn through the holes with pliers to change its shape or make it thinner. You can pull the wire through successively smaller holes until the desired gauge is reached.

Dies cut external threads on screws, bolts and rods. Sets including a range of dies and taps, a diestock and a tap wrench are available. There are also adjustable dies that can be made larger or smaller with the turn of a screw.

Dapping punch comes in various sizes for use in chasing or repoussé or to shape thin metal on a dapping die (below). Strike the punch with a ball-peen hammer.

Three-in-one tap tree cuts and cleans threads in thin metal or plastic. It is handy for threading electrical boxes. The replaceable taps come in various sizes.

Dapping die has depressions of various sizes along its polished steel faces for forming silver or other metal for jewellery. Tap the metal into the recess with a dapping punch.

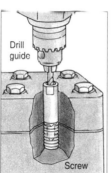

Bolt extractors remove broken screws or bolts. Drill hole in fastener and turn extractor (left, above) with a spanner. Slide collar over type at centre before using spanner. With both types, the drill guides at right aid in drilling into hard-to-reach fasteners.

Swage block lets you shape wire or metal strips into square, rectangular, triangular or curved shapes. Lay the metal in the appropriate groove and gently hammer it into shape.

Bending jig holds bar metal firmly in place while you hammer it into curves. Secure the jig in a vice and arrange the pins for the curve you want.

Bracelet bender, an alternative to the mandrel (below), holds a strip of metal in its upturned end as you bend it around the curve of the tool to shape an open-end bracelet.

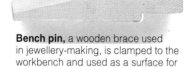

Bench pin, a wooden brace used in jewellery-making, is clamped to the workbench and used as a surface for sawing or filing small metal pieces.

Bracelet mandrel is a form for shaping bracelets. Bend the metal around the mandrel with your hands, and finish by beating it with a mallet. Turn the bracelet upside down for final beating.

Mandrel cradle holds a bracelet or a ring mandrel in a horizontal position. To use the cradle for a ring mandrel, insert the narrow end of the mandrel into the hole in one end of the cradle.

Ring mandrel works in same way as the bracelet mandrel, but it is graduated to help you shape a ring into the proper size. Turn the ring upside down occasionally to compensate for the mandrel's taper.

CONCRETE-WORKING TOOLS

To work with concrete, you'll need a number of general-purpose tools, including measuring and levelling tools, a steel square, a hammer and a saw for building forms, and buckets for measuring cement and adding it to the mixture. In addition, you'll need the specialized tools shown below. If you're sinking a pier footing or a post base, you may need a post-hole digger; and if you're mixing your own concrete, a mortar box. Plastic or metal mortar boxes resembling children's sandboxes are available commercially, or you can make one by nailing together a frame of boards and adding a marine plywood bottom. For larger jobs, rent a rotating-drum mixer or have the mixed concrete delivered.

Screed, or screed board, is the first tool used to level freshly poured concrete. When using one, rest its ends on the tops of the forms. Wooden screeds and lightweight aluminium screeds (like the one shown here) are sold in standard lengths, but a long, straight 50 x 100 will also do the job.

Float smooths concrete after screeding by drawing sand and cement to the surface and pushing aggregate below. Steel and wooden floats (above) are available commercially, or you can make your own, using a piece of flat wood 300 x 150 x 19 mm. Screw a smooth wooden handle to one surface.

Edger finishes and rounds the sharp edges of concrete slabs and paths. The ends of the blade are straight, curved, or a combination of straight and curved for various applications.

Groover cuts grooves in paths, driveways and patio floors to control the cracking caused by expansion and contraction.

Square-edged shovel is preferred to a garden spade for concrete work. To eliminate air pockets when filling forms, pull the shovel blade up and down in the concrete; press the concrete against the forms with the back of the shovel.

Mortar hoe is used to mix concrete and mortar and to spread concrete. The large holes in the blade aerate the mixture for a better consistency.

Post-hole digger digs deep, narrow holes without disturbing the surrounding area.

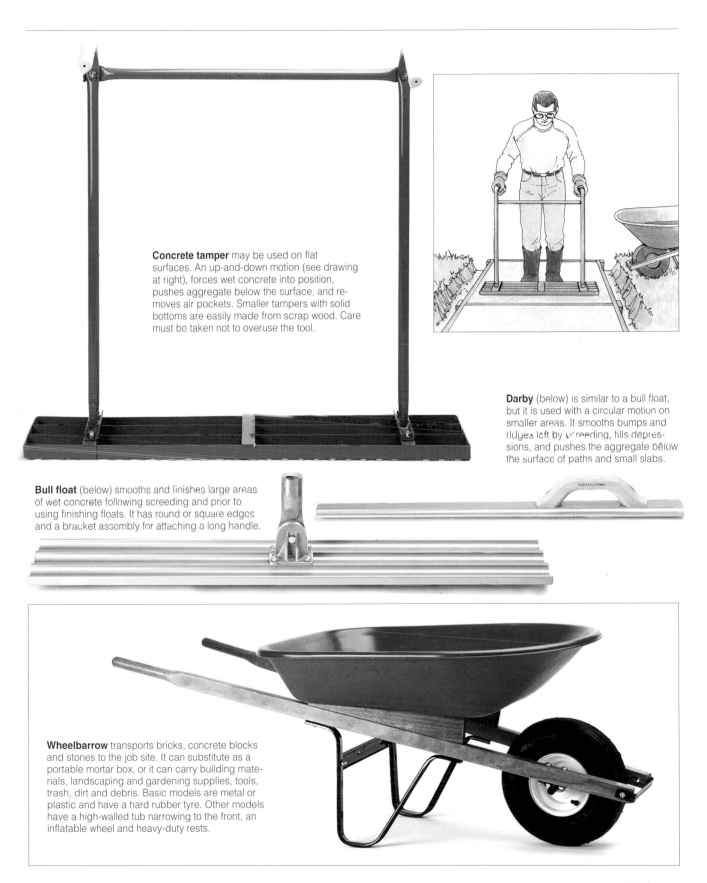

Concrete tamper may be used on flat surfaces. An up-and-down motion (see drawing at right), forces wet concrete into position, pushes aggregate below the surface, and removes air pockets. Smaller tampers with solid bottoms are easily made from scrap wood. Care must be taken not to overuse the tool.

Darby (below) is similar to a bull float, but it is used with a circular motion on smaller areas. It smooths bumps and ridges left by screeding, fills depressions, and pushes the aggregate below the surface of paths and small slabs.

Bull float (below) smooths and finishes large areas of wet concrete following screeding and prior to using finishing floats. It has round or square edges and a bracket assembly for attaching a long handle.

Wheelbarrow transports bricks, concrete blocks and stones to the job site. It can substitute as a portable mortar box, or it can carry building materials, landscaping and gardening supplies, tools, trash, dirt and debris. Basic models are metal or plastic and have a hard rubber tyre. Other models have a high-walled tub narrowing to the front, an inflatable wheel and heavy-duty rests.

The best trowels have blades cast from a single piece of high-grade steel and handles made of wood, plastic or leather. Trowels with welded blades are less expensive, but they warp and break easily. When buying a trowel, check the quality of the blade by striking it against a hard object and listening for a ringing sound. A long ring indicates a good blade. Also consider the tool's weight, size, balance, flexibility and the angle of its handle. After using a trowel, scrape off all mortar with another trowel or a wire brush, and thoroughly rinse and dry the tool. Rub wooden or leather handles with linseed oil.

Concrete finishing trowel is used to smooth a surface after the concrete has begun to set. Hold the trowel nearly level and move it in sweeping arcs across the surface. Make two passes for an extra-smooth surface.

Gauging trowel mixes mortar and applies small amounts in confined areas. It is used principally to replace crumbled mortar and to patch concrete. In addition, its rounded nose makes it useful for tucking and pushing material into tight areas.

Bucket trowel comes in handy for scooping mortar out of a bucket or mortar box. It is also good for buttering bricks and for small smoothing jobs.

Pool trowel, or round trowel, is a special variation of the concrete finishing trowel. The blade is rounded to prevent it from accidentally digging into the wet concrete, making it ideal for smoothing.

Corner trowels are available for shaping concrete around internal and external corners. The handle is located at the centre of the 90° bend in the blade to balance the tool and allow you to apply equal pressure to both sides of the corner.

Step trowel shapes the inside angles on concrete steps. The gentle bend in the blade allows for rounded edges. Trowels for outside angles are also available.

Pointing trowel applies mortar to joints in brick and concrete block work. This smaller version of the brick trowel is also useful for filling small cavities and repairing old crumbling mortar joints.

Brick trowel, or mason's trowel, spreads mortar onto bricks or concrete blocks with a technique call *buttering*. The shape of the blade also makes it ideal for smoothing small patches in concrete.

Tile setter is a brick trowel with an extra-wide blade which holds a greater amount of mortar and smooths more easily than the standard brick trowel. It is the best tool for buttering large bricks and blocks.

Margin trowel works mortar into tight spaces and corners where a larger pointed trowel will not fit.

BRICKLAYING TOOLS

When working with bricks, concrete blocks or even stones, you'll need a number of specialized tools including some of the trowels on the facing page and a number of the hammers, levels, and measuring and squaring tools covered earlier in this section. You'll also need tools for carrying, cutting, aligning and cleaning the bricks, and tools for working with mortar, as shown on this page. Finally, you'll need a hawk or mortar board – a flat board with a handle for holding mortar as you work. You can buy a hawk (not shown) or easily make one by cutting a square of plywood and screwing a section of thick dowel or broomstick under its centre. You'll also need a plastic or wooden box for mixing mortar.

Tuck pointer is used to pack mortar neatly between bricks or concrete blocks when re-pointing – restoring crumbling mortar in masonry walls.

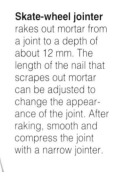

Skate-wheel jointer rakes out mortar from a joint to a depth of about 12 mm. The length of the nail that scrapes out mortar can be adjusted to change the appearance of the joint. After raking, smooth and compress the joint with a narrow jointer.

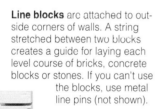

Jointer shapes mortar in a joint just before it dries, removing excess mortar and providing durability. Standard convex jointer (above, top) leaves a rounded groove. Grapevine jointer (above) leaves a pattern. Sled-runner jointer (left, top) is used for long horizontal joints. V jointer (left, bottom) leaves a V-shaped groove; it also comes without a handle.

Line blocks are attached to outside corners of walls. A string stretched between two blocks creates a guide for laying each level course of bricks, concrete blocks or stones. If you can't use the blocks, use metal line pins (not shown).

Brick tongs make transporting bricks from supply pile to work area easy and fast. The handle quickly adjusts to hold 6 to 10 bricks. There are also tongs (not shown) that pick up a single concrete block.

Brick chisel, or brick bolster cuts brick, stone, or concrete block to size and shape when struck with a hammer. A bolster with a 100 mm-wide blade is the most common. The electrician's bolster has a 55 mm-blade and is used for cutting grooves in masonry.

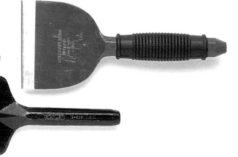

Mason's brush finishes off rough spots in wet joints and cleans brick and concrete block surfaces prior to applying mortar. Joints can be weakened if dust and debris are not removed.

Joint chisel cleans out hardened mortar. Hold chisel in a gloved hand and strike with a hand-drilling hammer. The direction the taper in the blade faces determines if chisel will cut deep or run shallow along joint.

Rub brick is a grooved silicon-carbide stone mounted on a base and handle. Use it to smooth rough areas and to remove form marks from dried concrete.

Although this section has covered hundreds of tools, there are still many more available for working with specific materials. On this and the facing page you'll find just a few of the additional tools that can make a particular job easier. Whether it's gluing, veneering, tiling, or working with glass or plastic, these tools are worth the money if you'll be putting them to a lot of use. Because some tools are such great timesavers, they can be worth buying even if they are used only once or twice, but you may find it more cost-effective to hire them. Buy tools selectively, only as you need them. With time, you'll find that your workshop will be well stocked.

Glue brushes are made with natural hog bristles and long handles that make it easier to reach into restricted areas. Unlike brushes that use metal ferrules, the bristles are attached to the handles with glue and string so that rust stains cannot mar the workpiece; this is especially handy when working on fine woodwork. Brushes come in various sizes.

Tar brush is an inexpensive applicator commonly made with coir 'bristles'. It is used for spreading bitumen and similar sealing compounds. This brush is meant to be used only once and then discarded.

Glue roller applies semi-liquid glues quickly and evenly to flat surfaces and edges. Remove the stopper before applying glue. Holding the bottle in your hand, squeeze it as you roll the tool over the work. The harder you squeeze, the more glue will come out. Re-stopper the reservoir and wash the roller in hot soapy water after use. Dried glue can be removed with a dull-bladed tool.

Hot-melt glue gun heats a glue stick that is inserted into an opening at the rear of the gun. By squeezing the trigger, melted glue can be applied to the work. This model is powered by a charger, which also serves as a resting stand. A variety of sticks is available for gluing different materials, including wood, ceramic and plastic.

Tap reseating tool solves the problem of taps that leak even when a new washer has just been fitted. The tool's tapering thread screws into the tap body and gently rotating the central spindle until it turns smoothly will cut a new smooth surface on the washer seat.

Screwdriver bits for hand brace are useful where extreme torque needs to be applied. First check that the bit blade fits the slot exactly.

Veneer roller applies pressure evenly as it is rolled on veneer that's being glued to a surface. It may be up to 180 mm wide. Use a narrow roller for joining seams.

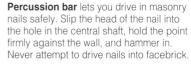

Percussion bar lets you drive in masonry nails safely. Slip the head of the nail into the hole in the central shaft, hold the point firmly against the wall, and hammer in. Never attempt to drive nails into facebrick.

Old toothbrushes are handy for removing dirt from a variety of surfaces. Create your own shapes to reach awkward places by standing the stems in boiling water to soften them, then bend and stretch them to the shapes you require.

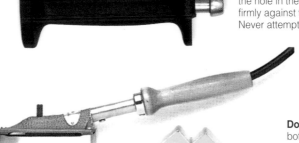

Edge-banding iron uses heat to seal heat-activated veneer strips along plywood edges. As you work, set iron on rest to free your hands. Edge trims come in various wood finishes.

Double-edge trimmer cuts both edges of veneer strips on surface edges that are up to 30 mm wide. Set tool over work; press its sides together; slide it in direction of arrows.

Miniature rotary tool accepts attachments to carve, grind, polish, drill and engrave wood, metal, glass and tile. Use it hand-held, or hang it from the hook and attach a flexible shaft. The tool also comes in a cordless model.

Woodburning tool has a 20 to 100 W element and a range of tips to create designs in wood by darkening the wood colour. For greater control over the markings, buy a separate rheostat. A light soldering iron may suffice for small jobs.

Tile cutter scores and cuts ceramic tile. The long throat accepts tiles up to 300 mm wide. A replaceable wheel under the handle scores the tile as the handle is pulled along a bar. A breaker bar ensures a clean break.

Fibreglass roller has spiral grooves in the roller to work out air bubbles that may form when applying resin to fibreglass cloth. It's available in several sizes, with aluminium or plastic rollers.

Caulking gun holds a tube of caulk or adhesive. To apply the material to the work, squeeze the trigger. The bar will exert pressure on a disc, pushing material out of the tube. Use the spring-loaded clip to release the bar.

Glass cutter wheel scores a line on glass. Separate the glass by holding it on each side of the score with your thumbs and index fingers and bending it until it snaps. The notches can be used to snap thin strips.

Speed wrench, or one-handed spanner comes in several sizes, each of which fits a wide range of nuts – metric or imperial, hex or square. Quick to operate, it doesn't need to be lifted off the nut between strokes, whether tightening or loosening.

Plastic tube cutter is bolted onto a workbench or other flat surface to cut plastic tubing or rubber hoses. Place the work in the V-shaped rest on the bottom arm of the tool. As the top arm is moved down onto the tubing or hose, the blade cuts the work.

Laminate roller has a smooth rubber roller to apply pressure to laminate while gluing it to the work, thus creating a strong bond.

Breast drill is used for drilling into hard material such as rock, concrete or masonry. Pressure is usually applied by the operator pressing with his chest against the concave T-bar and grasping the steadying handle. Most models can be run at one of two speeds through a permanently sealed and lubricated gearbox.

HARDWARE

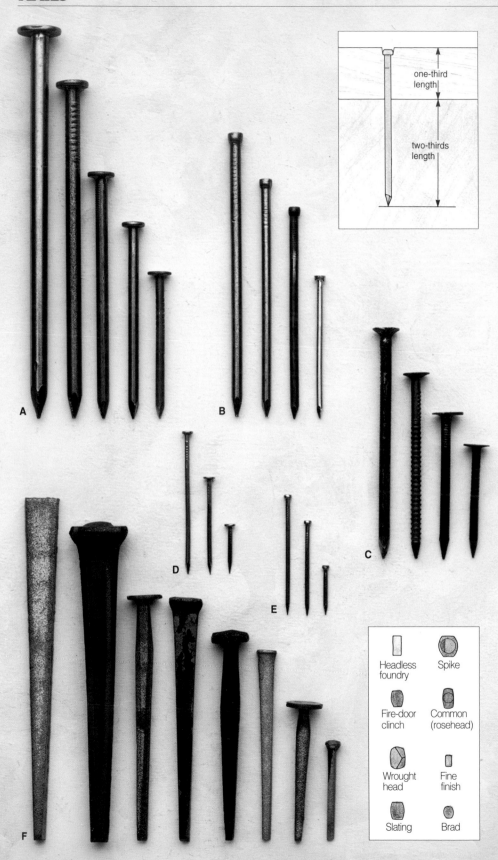

one-third length

two-thirds length

Fasteners are the most common items of hardware, and the nail, used primarily to join items permanently, is the most common fastener. Nails come in a number of metals, styles and sizes for driving into different materials. Nails are sorted according to type, length and thickness, and are usually sold by weight.

When nailing a thinner piece of material to a thicker one (left), use nails whose length is 3 times the thickness of the thinner piece. If the pieces are of the same thickness, use nails the length of the combined thicknesses minus 6 mm.

Common nail (A), a heavy-duty fastener with a flat head that won't pull through the work, is used in carpentry and roof framing. The box nail (not shown), a lighter version of the common nail, is used in thin wood to keep it from splitting.

Finishing nail (B) is a thin small-headed nail for cabinet-making and attaching trim. The nailhead is usually driven below the surface and filled over. The casing nail (not shown) is a heavy finishing nail. It has more holding power than the standard finishing nail, and is used for door and window casings or trim.

Drywall nail (C) has a sharp point and broad head for installing wallboard partitions. In ceilings and other areas under pressure, use the ringed type, which has more holding power. The length of a drywall nail is sometimes given in inches and its diameter in gauge numbers. The higher the gauge, the thinner the nail.

Wire nail (D) is a small, usually soft version of the common nail and is perfect for light jobs.

Wire brad (E) is a small finishing nail that is used for fine work. It is frequently driven below the surface of the work with a punch, and the hole above filled in.

Antique-style nails (F) are available with a variety of different shanks and heads for restoring old furniture and attaching antique hinges. The head styles of the antique nails in the photograph are shown in the drawing at left.

Headless foundry

Spike

Fire-door clinch

Common (rosehead)

Wrought head

Fine finish

Slating

Brad

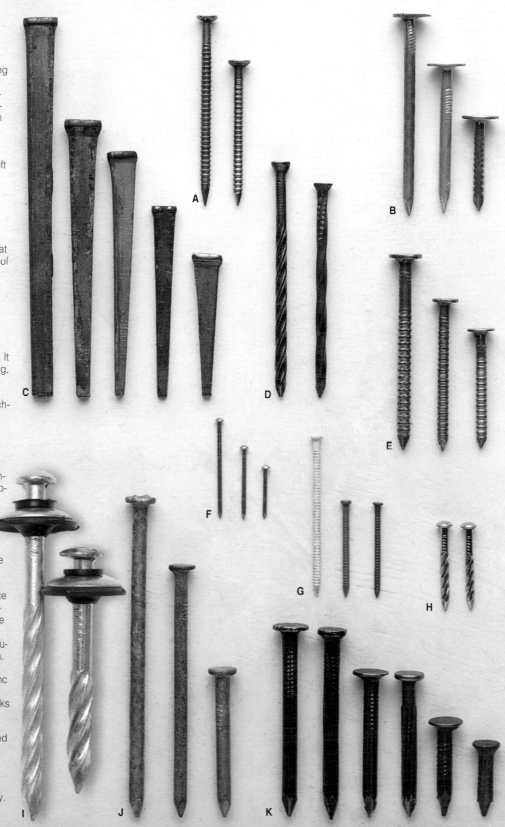

Ring underlay or annular nail (A) has a shank that is ringed with deep, closely spaced grooves. The wood's fibres wedge themselves into these grooves, resulting in maximum holding power in soft or medium woods. It's ideal for use in the installation of subflooring, because the increased holding power keeps the subflooring from squeaking or pulling loose.

Clout nail (B), has a large flat head that keeps it from working through soft roofing materials, such as asphalt shingles. It is generally galvanized to prevent rusting.

Cut flooring nail (C) comes in either steel or iron and is used for installing tongue-and-groove floorboards. Its flat sides and blunt tip minimize splitting of hardwood flooring.

Spiral-fluted flooring nail (D) turns like a screw when driven in, gripping tightly to eliminate squeaking.

Boat nail (E) is a ringed, or annular, fastener made of rust-resistant metal. It is ideal for outdoor use where a strong, rust-free bond is needed.

Escutcheon nail (F) is used for attaching keyhole plates and other backplates, or escutcheons. Sizes usually range from 15 to 20 mm.

Panelling nail (G), a hard, thin nail, often ribbed, is ideal for securing panelling to wall plugs. It is sometimes obtainable in different colours to match the panelling material.

Moulding nail (H), similar to the wire brad, is used to attach moulding. Generally the heads of these nails are countersunk and filled.

Galvanized roofing screw (I), despite its name, is a nail. With a rain-excluding washer under its domed head, the spiral shaft is driven by hammer through roofing material such as corrugated iron and into the rafter beneath.

Galvanized nail (J) is coated with zinc to prevent rusting. Use it when exposure to weather is a factor, as on decks or patios.

Masonry nail (K) is made of hardened steel that resists bending. The nail is used mostly for temporarily holding strips to concrete or masonry walls. The shank may be plain, or it may be fluted to help the nail grip more tightly. For a more permanent construction, screws and wall plugs are preferred.

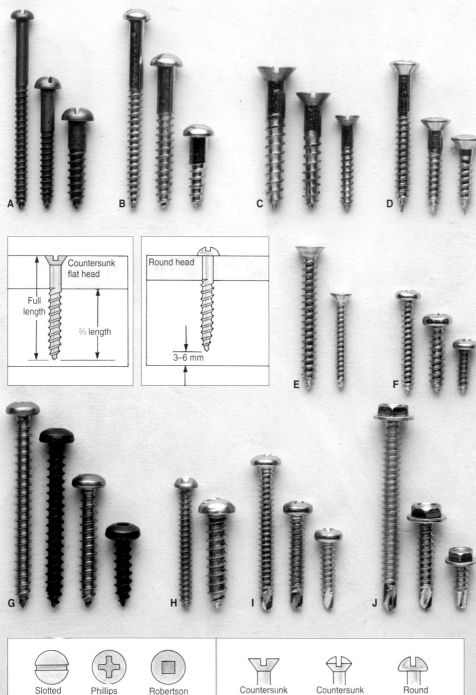

There are five considerations when choosing a screw: the type and thickness of the material to be fastened, the size of the screw, the material it is made of, the shape of its head and the type of drive. Screws are available for fastening wood, wallboard, masonry and sheet metal. Screw size is determined by the diameter of the smooth shank (gauge) and the length of the screw measured from the tip to the part of the head that is flush with the surface when driven in. Gauge does not vary with length – thus a 25 mm 8-gauge screw has the same size head and shank as a 75 mm 8-gauge screw. Screws come in many metals, such as steel or brass, and in a variety of finishes. There are various types of heads and drives (see below) and some combination drives, which can be driven by either of two types of driver, such as slotted and Phillips. The one-way screw cannot easily be unscrewed, and so is used for security. Robertson (square) and star-drive screws are found mainly on cars and appliances.

Wood screw holds two pieces of wood together, providing a strong joint that can be dismantled. Shown are brass and zinc-plated round-head screws with slotted drives (**A, B**), flat-head screws with slotted drives (**C**), and oval-head screws with Phillips drives (**D**). When determining screw size, consider the thickness of the woods being fastened. Two-thirds of the screw should enter the second piece; the screw should be 3 to 6 mm shorter than the combined thicknesses of the materials being fastened.

Sheet-metal screw fastens two pieces of metal together. Shown are flat-head (**E**) and pan-head (**F**) screws with Phillips drives, pan-head screws with Robertson (**G**), and one-way drives (**H**), and self-tapping screws with Phillips drive pan heads (**I**) and hex washer heads (**J**). Self-tapping screws have sharp winged tips that cut threaded holes in the metal as they are driven, pulling the second piece in tight.

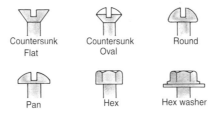

Screw drives of six major types are used on the various screws. Use a screwdriver with the proper tip to drive them. Use a spanner to drive a hex-drive screw.

Slotted · Phillips · Robertson · Star · One-way · Hex

Screwheads come in various shapes. Flat-head is flush with the surface when countersunk; oval head is partly countersunk; the others rest on top. Hex-heads come with or without attached washers.

Countersunk Flat · Countersunk Oval · Round · Pan · Hex · Hex washer

Drywall screw (A), a thin, sharp fastener with a bugle-shaped head, cuts through wallboard and anchors itself in wood or metal plugs, holding the partition tighter than a nail can. Its Phillips or Robertson drive lets you countersink the screw without tearing the wallboard's surface paper.

Lag screw (B), or lag bolt, is a heavy-duty wood screw that comes up to 150 mm long, in diameters of 5, 6, 8, 10 and 12 mm. Use a lag screw if you need a screw with lots of holding power. Lag screws are available with hex heads (shown) or square heads. Drive with a ring spanner or socket.

Concrete screw has sharp, widely spaced threads that are driven directly into concrete without an anchor. The screws shown have hex washer heads **(C)** and flat heads **(D).**

Post and screw (E) is used to join case units, such as kitchen cabinets, or to put together frames or assemblies that may later need to be taken apart and re-assembled. The screw is driven through the two pieces, and the cap is pushed into a recess in the second piece and screwed on. A light plastic version of this hardware is used on acrylic plastic.

Thumbscrew (F) is a machine screw (p 102) with a wide thin head that can be grasped with thumb and forefinger and turned into a threaded plate or bracket. It is used in areas that require frequent adjustment by hand.

Hanger screw (G) is a fastener for installing dropped ceilings with acoustic tiles. Screw the threaded end into a joist and hook the wire that supports the metal grid of the dropped ceiling into the hole in the unthreaded end.

Hanger bolt (H) has machine-screw threads on one end and has regular screw threads on the other. To install one, drill a pilot hole in the wood, and thread two nuts side by side onto the machine-screw end of the hanger bolt, locking them together. Grasp the nuts with a wrench, and drive the screw in.

Dowel screw (I) is used mainly for attaching table legs and other furniture work. Pre-drill holes, grasp the screw with locking pliers with taped jaws, and screw it into the top of a table leg; then screw the leg into the tabletop.

Finishing washer (J) supplies a hard surface against which to tighten flathead screw without damaging wood.

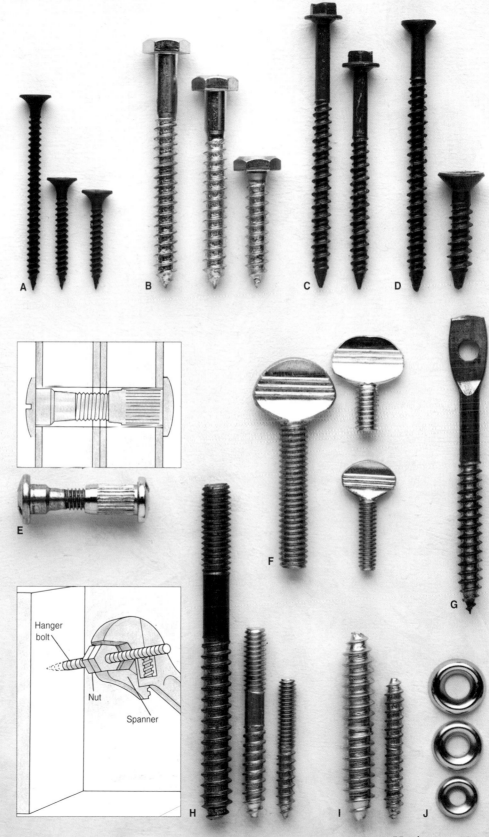

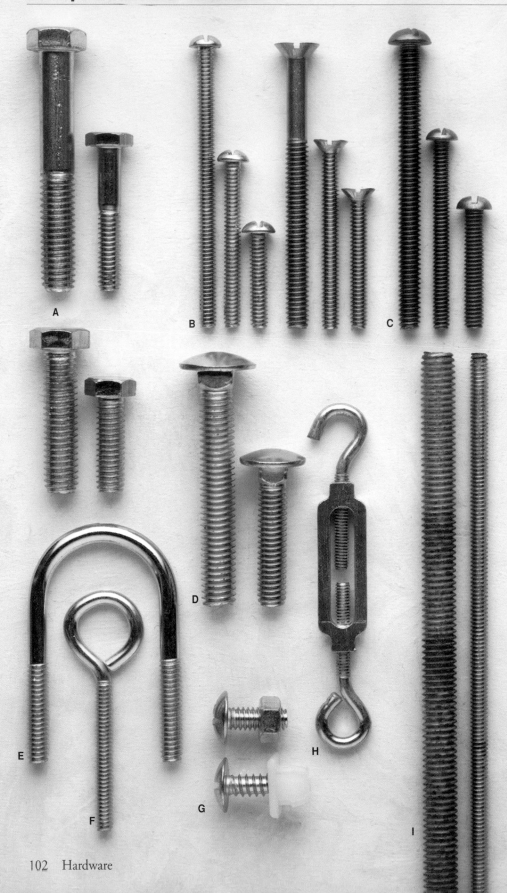

A bolt used with one or two washers and a nut or piece of threaded metal makes a bond that is strong but also easy to take apart. A bolt should protrude through the outside of the nut when assembled, with at least one thread showing. Metric, American and imperial sizes are used, and a bolt's size may be given as the diameter in inches or gauge number, followed by the number of threads per inch and the length of the bolt in inches; for example, $1/4-20 \times 1$. Metric descriptions are similar, except that they commence with the letter M and that the second figure represents the pitch of the thread (p 16). A bolt with a diameter of 8 mm, a thread pitch of 1,25 and a length of 60 mm is represented as $M8 \times 1,25 \times 60$. The larger the bolt, the coarser the thread.

Machine bolt (A) is a strong bolt with a hex or square head.

Stove bolt (B) has a round or flat slotted head that can be countersunk.

Machine screw (C) is similar to a stove bolt, but is often screwed into threaded metal rather than into a nut.

Carriage bolt (D) is used in woodworking and sheet-metal work. It has a smooth round head and square shoulders that sink into the wood or fit in a hole, keeping the bolt from turning.

U-bolt (E) holds pipes and other objects firmly against a wall or ceiling.

Eye-bolt (F) holds wires, ropes and other objects in place.

Licence-plate fastener (G) is a short machine screw with a nut or plastic backplate for attaching licence plates.

Turnbuckle (H) has threaded hooks or eyes that move in or out when the sleeve is turned, exerting pull on a diagonal to keep a gate straight.

Threaded rod (I), or all thread, joins objects over a span of up to 1 m. It is available with fine or coarse threads.

Flat washer (A) is used under a bolt head or nut to spread the load and protect the surface. A large flat washer with a small hole is a fender washer. It can cover a hole that is larger than the bolt being used in it, eliminating the need for filling the hole.

Lock washer (B), also known as a split washer or spring washer, exerts a slight springlike pressure because of its near-spiral shape; this keeps a nut from loosening. When bolting pieces of wood together, it's best to use a flat washer under a lock washer.

Toothed washer (C) has external or internal teeth (or both), which give additional gripping power to a bolt. The washer can also be shaped for use with a flat-head machine screw.

Hex nut (D) screws onto the threaded end of a bolt to tighten the bolt against the pieces being fastened. It may be screwed on over a washer.

Square nut (E) is basically the same as a hex nut, except that it has only four sides instead of six.

Cap nut (F) is a decorative nut that covers the end of the bolt and conceals any exposed threads.

Knurled nut (G) can be turned by hand for fast assembly and disassembly. Its milled circumference makes it easy to grip between thumb and forefinger. Two styles are shown.

Lock nut (H) has a fibrelike lining next to the threads that prevents the nut from coming loose when subjected to vibration or stress.

Push nut (I), or axle nut, is used to cover the end of a rod or to hold a small wheel on an axle. It has no threads, but is simply pushed on. Plastic push nuts with steel spring inserts are also available.

T-nut (J) permits the easy driving of machine screws in wood. Drill a hole and hammer the T-nut into place, with its prongs penetrating the wood.

Wing nut (K) is used to fasten units that will be repeatedly disassembled and re-assembled. Always drive a wing nut with your fingers. Using pliers may damage the nut.

Threaded insert (L) screws into the wood and becomes a receptacle for a bolt to screw into. It is easier to conceal than a T-nut.

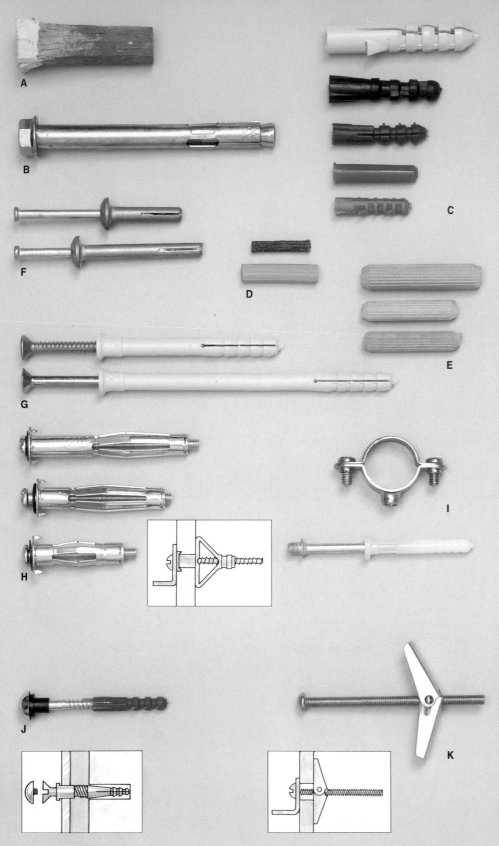

Anchors, shields and toggles are available in various sizes to give a firm grip both in solid walls (masonry or concrete) and in cavity walls. Most fasteners depend for their grip on the expansion or controlled collapse of a metal or nylon shield by driving in a bolt or screw. It's important that the hole drilled for the fastener should be correct – it will not grip well in a hole that is either too large or too small. Before inserting the fastener, clean the hole of all loose debris with a narrow screwdriver blade, a test-tube brush or by inserting a drinking straw and blowing.

Softwood plugs (A) are an emergency solution only. They tend to rotate and may rot, split or shrink.

Metal sleeve anchor (B) will hold firm in brick, blocks and concrete.

Plastic split anchor (C) expands and grips the sides of the hole when a screw is driven into it.

Plastic plug (D) is made of sturdy plastic for heavier jobs than the fibre plug (above).

Joiner's dowels (E) are a useful standby. White glue in the hole will help expand the plug for a tighter grip.

Nail anchor (F) holds best in base material such as brick or stone.

Frame fixing anchor (G) has a pin that can be driven by hammer or Phillips screwdriver.

Hollow-wall anchor (H), or Molly bolt, is a machine screw in a sleeve that collapses against the inside surface of the wall as you drive in the screw.

Pipe clip (I) is retained by threading it onto the head of the steel nail in its plastic expanding sleeve.

Mirror fixing screws (J) include domed covers, plastic split anchors and flanged rubber collars.

Toggle bolt (K) is a machine screw with spring-loaded wings that pass through the hole, then open against the inner surface of wall or ceiling. The wings fall off if the screw is removed.

Cavity fixing (A) is a light plastic variation of the Molly bolt (H opposite).

Plastic toggle (B) comes with flexible guide strip (removed when installed) and combined collar and washer.

Segmented metal shield (C) forms the basis of a range of sturdy fastenings. In most, a bolt passes through the length of the shield to a threaded cone or wedge at the end of the shield. Tightening the bolt draws the cone further into the shield, forcing its segments apart and thus providing a powerful grip. A binding of spring-steel wire holds the assembly together and allows controlled expansion. Several specialized forms of bolt are available.

Hook and eye bolts (D) provide anchors for a variety of hanging features, from light-fittings to ceilings.

Loose-bolt anchor E) consists of a machine screw and segmented metal shield anchor. When installed, the bolt can be removed and replaced without affecting the firmness of the anchor.

Projecting-bolt anchor (F) is a variation of the segmented metal shield in which the cone that expands the shield forms the base of the bolt that remains firmly fixed in the wall.

Connector plates (G) strengthen woodworking joints with widely spaced prongs driven straight into the wood.

Corrugated fastener (H) holds lightweight butt and mitre joints, such as those on screens and picture frames.

Blind rivet (I) joins sheet metal to sheet metal. It is installed through predrilled holes with a riveting tool.

Split pin (J) holds thin rods or shafts. Push it through a hole in the shaft, fold the legs out on the other side of the hole, and wrap them around the shaft.

Tack (K) is used to attach carpet or fabric to wood and for other light jobs.

Upholstery tack (L) comes in a variety of colours and with decorative heads to complement the style of the furniture.

Staple (M) comes in various forms for use on fabrics and other materials.

Insulated saddles (N) are used to position and retain electrical wiring against walls and woodwork.

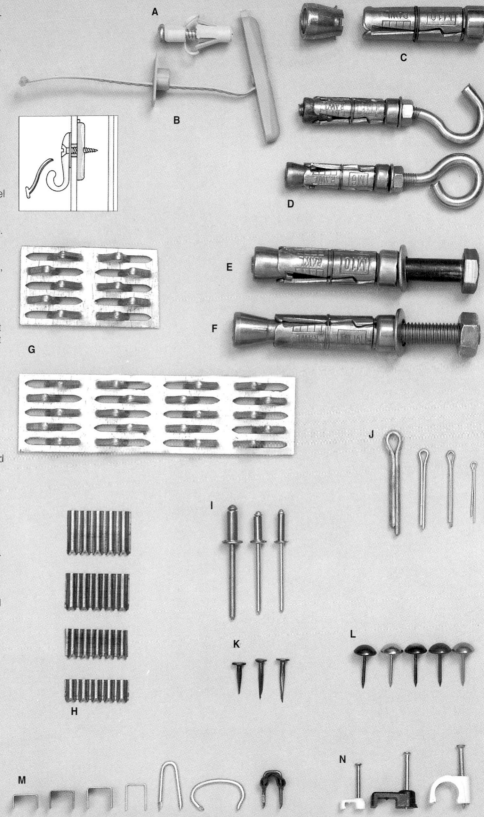

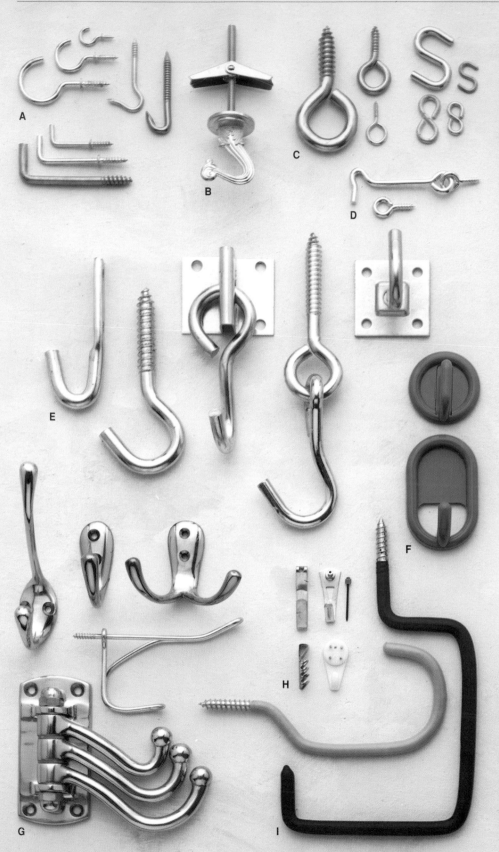

Whether you want to hang a coffee cup or support a clothesline, you'll be able to find a hook of the right shape and size to do the job. Use large hooks for heavy objects; a small hook may pull away from the surface when it's supporting a heavy load. Before installing a hook that screws into place, make a pilot hole with a nail or drill.

Screw hook (A) has a threaded end that screws into wood, walls or ceilings. The open end supports various items. The rounded-tip hook is for household uses; the pointed-tip hook is for suspended ceilings. The L-shaped hook supports wide objects.

Toggle hook (B) combines an ornamental hook with a toggle bolt for hanging a lamp or plant from a ceiling.

Screw eye (C) has a ring-shaped end. Use it alone by fitting objects through the ring or link an S- or 8-hook to it. The linking hook can hold the object.

Hook and eye (D) has a hook attached to a screw eye that screws into a gate or door. The hook fits into another screw eye to keep the gate or door closed; a hook with a clasp (not shown) provides extra security.

Rope hook (E) comes in various designs. From left to right are a general-purpose hook with two holes in the flat stem for screws, a porch-swing hook that is screwed into the porch roof, a hammock hook with a plate to secure it to a flat surface, a hammock hook with a screw eye for a round surface, and a clothesline hook that slips through a plate that is screwed to a flat surface.

Self-adhesive hook (F) made of plastic is for lightweight objects. To install it, wipe the surface clean, remove the lining paper and press hook in place.

Coat hook (G) may have one, two or more hooks in various directions for hanging coats and hats. The three-hook model has pivoting hooks.

Picture hanger (H) is nailed to a wall. Attach a wire to the back of a picture frame to hang it on the hook.

Heavy-duty hook (I) is for hanging objects in a garage or workshop. For items like bicycles, use them in pairs.

BRACKETS

Sets of two or more brackets are indispensable for supporting a variety of items. Before mounting the brackets, accurately position and level their supports.

Curtain and blind brackets come in pairs. To install a café rod, screw the first brackets shown **(A)** above a window for an outside mount, or attach socket brackets **(B)** to window jambs for an inside mount. Screw roller blind brackets **(C)** inside the jambs (or on other models, outside the jambs or on the wall). A U-shaped curtain rod fits onto outside-mount brackets **(D)**; slip the opening in the rod over the bracket's hook and push the rod into place.

Rail brackets, screwed into wall studs or plugs, support handrails, footrails and landing rails. A flat rail rests on a cranked rail bracket **(E)**; a round rail slips through a post rail bracket **(F)** or its end fits into a flanged bracket **(G)**.

Shelf brackets (H) are attached to a wall to support a horizontal piece (usually 20 mm-thick softwood or plywood) for storing or displaying items. The almond-colour bracket has a decorative cover that slips over the metal support. Among many attractive designs are hard plastic brackets (not shown) in Victorian cast-iron patterns.

Spade pins (I) slip into holes drilled in a cabinet's sides, two for each end of a shelf. Make sure that all four holes align horizontally.

Shelf clips (J) are shown inserted in a bookcase strip (near right). They support shelves in cabinets or bookcases – use two clips at each end of a shelf. Screw four strips in place (you can recess them) and use a level to check plumb. Fit clips into slots at identical heights on each strip. Available in various lengths, strips can be cut to size.

Brackets (K) slide into slots in a wall-mounted standard (far right) to support shelves. Screw the standards into wall studs or plugs, using a level to check plumb. Push the bracket's hooks through the slots in the standard and force down. Some brackets have a thumbscrew for extra-firm fitting.

Spring-loaded folding bracket (L) can be raised and locked in place for an extra work surface. Light pressure on the release lever allows you to fold the surface out of the way.

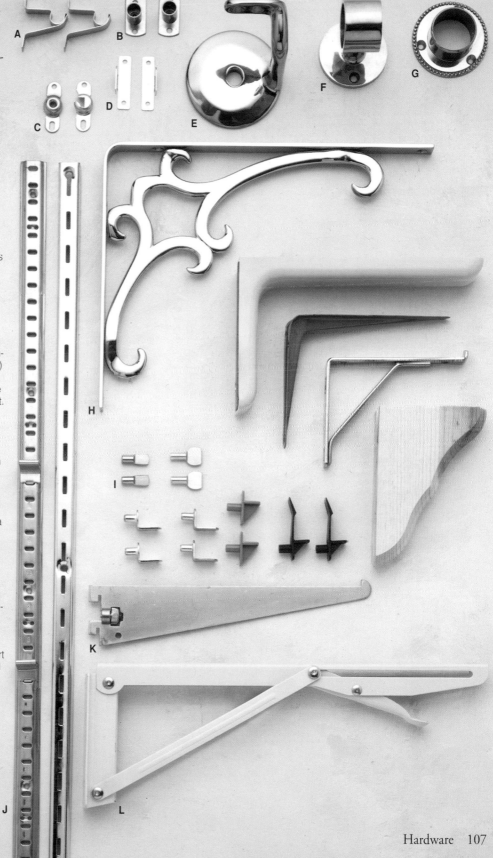

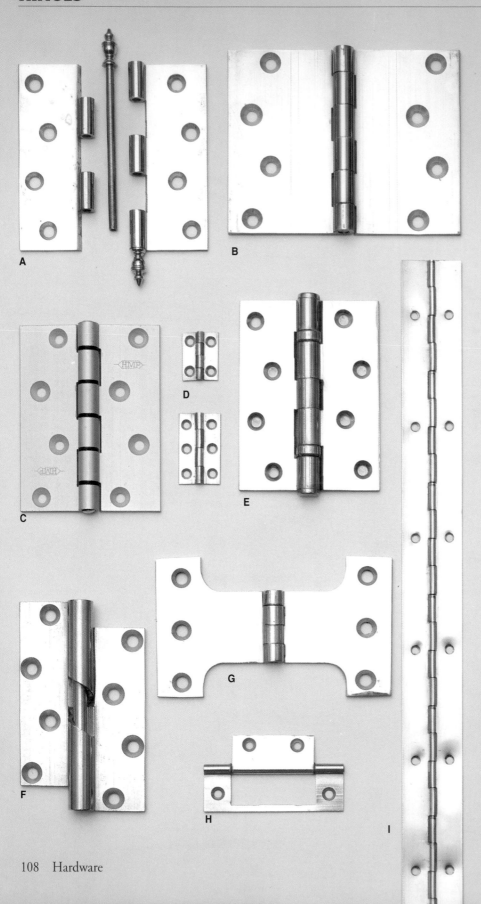

Most hinges have two leaves held together with a pivot pin inside knuckles or a barrel. Surface-mounted hinges create a slight gap between the door and frame when the door is closed. Recessed leaves are mortised flush with the surface. On heavy doors, fit a third hinge midway, to resist warping and to maintain lock alignment. Hinges may be measured by the length of the leaf and the width of both leaves when open, increasing in graduations of 6 and 12 mm.

Loose-pin butt hinge (A) has a detachable pin to allow for door removal without unscrewing the hinge. Some butt hinges have a fixed pin, so the leaves cannot be separated.

Projection hinge (B) is a variation of the parliament hinge (G), but the rectangular profile with long hinge-pin makes it suitable for heavier weights.

Aluminium butt hinge (C) is used for hanging patio doors and has nylon bearings for smooth operation.

Small butt hinge (D) may have a fixed or a loose pin. It's often used on small boxes. Attach it with nails or screws.

Ball-bearing hinge (E), for heavy doors, has a ball-bearing assembly that's permanently lubricated.

Rising butt hinge (F) has a barrel that is split diagonally. As you open the door, one leaf rides up the other, slightly raising the door to swing clear of carpets. The weight of the door also produces a self-closing effect. Rising butts are obtainable for both left- and right-opening doors.

Parliament hinge (G), usually made of brass, comes in a variety of sizes for doors and shutters that fold back flat against a wall.

Flush hinge (H), for a lightweight door, is surface-mounted but doesn't create a gap. To install the type shown, screw the small leaf to the door, the large leaf to the frame.

Piano hinge (I) is used for table flaps and chest tops where extra strength is important. Sold in various lengths, the hinge may be cut to fit. It can be surface-mounted or recessed.

H-hinge (A), generally used on furniture, cabinet doors and small chests, can be mounted vertically or horizontally. The H-hinge below is sometimes referred to as a snake hinge.

Lift-off hinge (B) lets you remove a door without unscrewing the hinge or removing the pin. It comes in a variety of sizes and styles for cabinets and house doors. It is commonly used on dressing-table mirrors or on any hinged object that may need to be removed frequently.

Backflap hinge (C) is a fixed-pin butt hinge with wide leaves that provide better support for flaps and lids. It can be recessed into wood.

Box hinge (D) is small enough to use on delicate jewellery-box lids. The hinge opens only to a 90° angle, preventing the lid from tipping over.

Drop-leaf hinge (E), similar to the backflap hinge, is traditionally used on folding table flaps. The hinge's longer leaf should be screwed to the flap, and the shorter leaf to the fixed board.

Butler's-tray hinge (F) comes with rounded or square corners. It's a small, sturdy hinge for trays and small tables with folding flaps. The hinge is recessed and its surface is flat when open, with no protruding barrel. In the 'up' position, a steel spring holds the leaves at 90°.

Strap hinge (G) is designed for surface mounting. It's available in plain and ornamental styles. Larger sizes are used where strong support is needed – for example, on heavy chest lids, gates and doors.

Desk hinge (H), a straight strap hinge, is most often found recessed into well-made desk lids and flaps.

Card-table hinge (I) looks similar to the desk hinge but has a 180° stop, making it suitable for small table flaps that fold out of the way.

Single strap hinge (J) comes in large heavy-duty sizes for doors, gates, boxes and chests. The steel one shown here is sometimes called a T-hinge. The small decorative hinge is for small boxes.

H-and-L hinge (K) is surface-mounted on a cabinet door. A larger version is available for regular-weight house doors; another variation of the hinge allows you to mortise the jamb leaf.

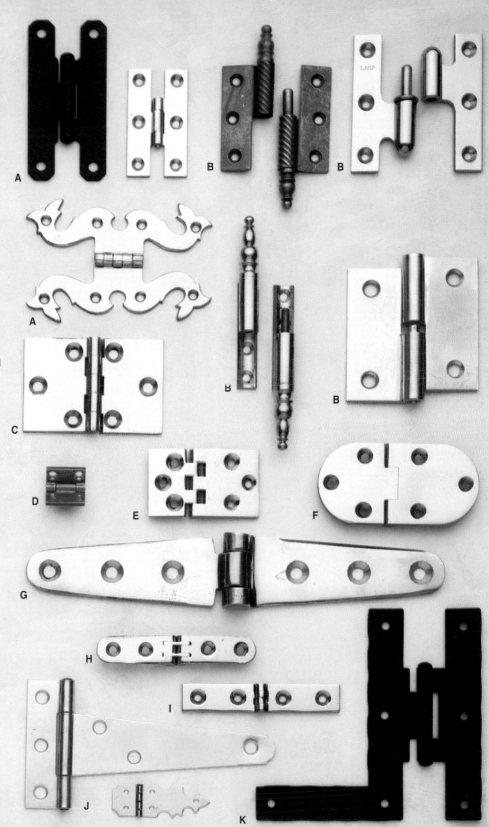

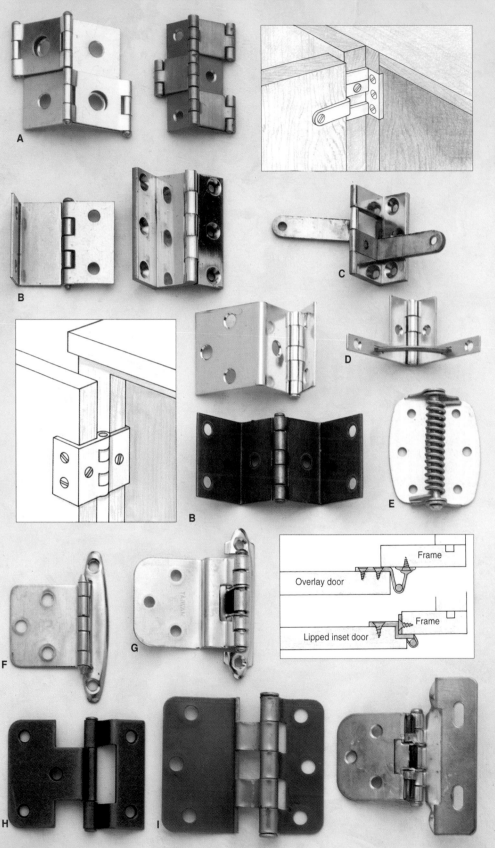

Double-acting hinge (A) is mounted along the side edges of a folding door or screen. The two linked sets of leaves and barrels permit the panels to swing open from both directions. To avoid binding, the leaves of the hinge (less the barrels) must be equal to or less than the thickness of the work.

Wrap-around hinge (B), a version of the fixed-pin butt hinge, is used on flush inset cabinet doors. The size of the hinge must match the door thickness. For extra support, the right-angle leaf attaches to both the edge and the back of the door. Only the barrel shows when the door is closed. The back-to-back wrap-around hinge (bottom) has two right-angle leaves for even greater strength. One leaf is attached to the door, the other leaf to the frame. This hinge is also suitable for a flush inset cabinet door.

Double-flap cranked hinge (C) is mounted on a cabinet's centre stile, or partition, to hold two doors. Each door, which overlays half the stile, can be opened independently 180°.

Quadrant hinge (D) is recessed in mortises made in the edges of a small box. It holds the lid open at 100°.

Spring hinge (E) has a coiled spring that returns a door to the closed position. Surface-mount it on a cabinet door and on other places where self-closing doors are desirable.

Overlay hinge (F), for a cabinet door, has a short leaf that is mounted on the exterior surface of the cabinet frame. The long leaf is attached to the back of the door. The hinge allows the door to overlay the frame.

Inset cabinet hinge (G) is similar to the overlay hinge, but the long leaf is offset so that it can be used on a lipped cabinet door. Concealed under the barrel is a spring that, when activated, snaps the door shut.

Semi-concealed overlay hinge (H), for a cabinet door, is almost hidden when the door is closed. A short leaf is offset so that the leaf can be mounted inside the cabinet frame. When the door is closed, only the barrel shows. Use it on overlay doors.

Semi-concealed inset hinge (I), when mounted on a lipped cabinet door, is hidden except for the barrel. The spring-loaded hinge (near left) snaps the door shut when you release it.

Pivot hinge (A) mounts at top and bottom of overlay cabinet door and against cabinet frame. Elongated screw holes permit easy adjustment. When the door is closed, only the pivot pin is visible. Mount the hinge at top as shown; mount both halves of the hinge at bottom horizontally.

Knife hinge (B) comes in a variety of sizes for use on objects as small as a jewellery box or as large as a 100 kg door. The hinge is recessed into two mortises at the top or bottom of the door, making it almost invisible. With the offset knife hinge (bottom), only the pivot point shows.

Double spring-action hinge (C) is a self-closing hinge that allows the door to swing in both directions. It comes in numerous sizes for a variety of doors. Some types must be mounted to a strip that you hang from the doorjamb.

Glass-door hinge (D), unlike some other hinges for glass cabinet doors, requires no drilling in glass. One leaf is screwed to the cabinet frame. The bottom edge of the glass door slides into the other leaf. Secure it in place with a setscrew. A spring-loaded catch in the hinge holds the door closed.

Flush-fitting flap hinge (E) provides a gap-free joint on cabinets and other furniture with down-swinging flaps. For a flush fit, recess the hinge into the bottom edges of the cabinet frame and the flap.

Concealed hinge (F) comes in a variety of styles for small cabinet doors and other lightweight applications. It is mounted in a recess made with a drill or router. When the hinge is closed, the leaves lie flat together; the knuckles slide out of sight into gaps in the leaves. Select the hinge size that is close to but less than the thickness of the cabinet stock.

Face-frame hinge (G) has a baseplate that is attached to the front of a cabinet's frame. The cup is recessed into the door. To re-position the door vertically or horizontally, adjust the screws in the baseplate. The hinge can swing open to 105°.

European-style concealed hinge (H), a face-frame hinge that swings open to 176°, is for inset and overlay cabinet doors. A cup is recessed into the door, and the baseplate is attached to the cabinet side. Loosen the screws to adjust alignment of the door.

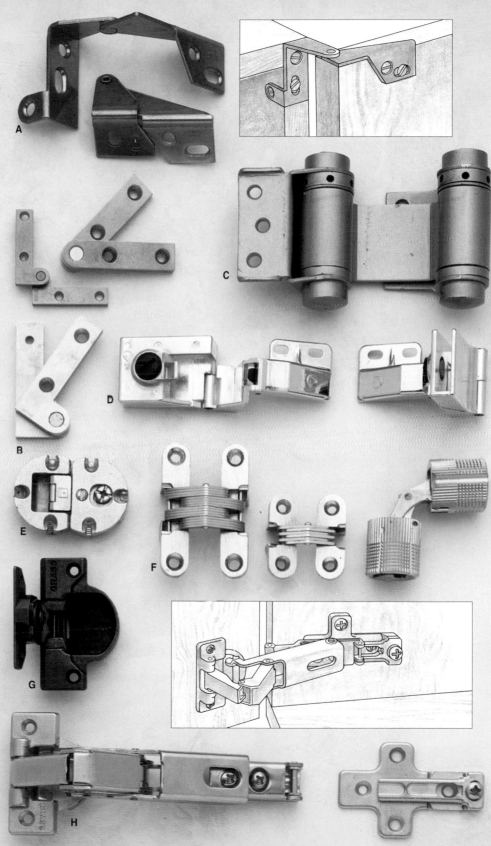

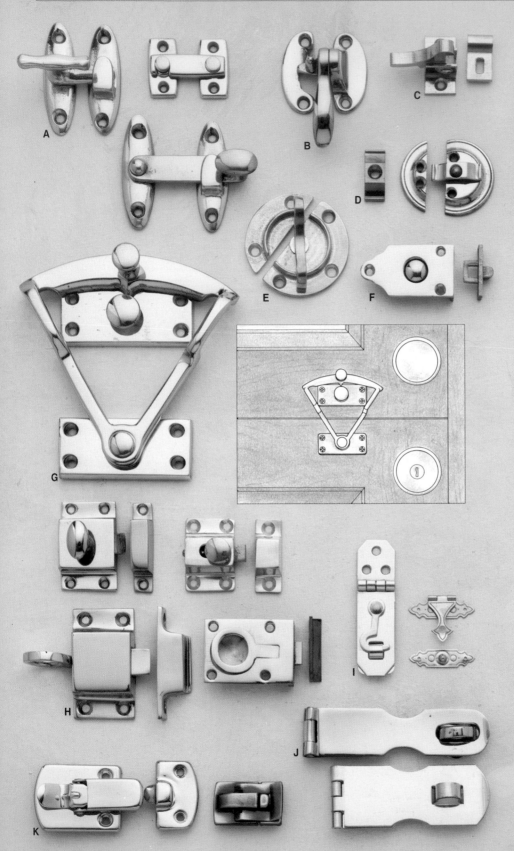

To keep a door or lid closed, latches and catches are mounted on furniture, cabinets and boxes. They come in various sizes and functions for different needs. Small locks add some degree of privacy, but not security.

Turn catch (A) holds shutters and cupboard, cabinet and other small doors closed. Space the plates carefully so the arm fits the matching plate. When using the catch on two neighbouring doors, secure one door with an interior latch, such as (C), mounted at the top or bottom of the door.

Spring-loaded catch (B) holds small doors closed. To open the door, pull up the catch's handle. A spring pulls the handle down when it is released.

Elbow latch (C) is for small doors. Open it by pushing down the handle with either your hand or your elbow.

Button catch (D) holds a light-duty door in place with the turn of its catch. Screw it on near the door's edge. It also comes attached to a plate.

Table catch (E) is screwed to the underside of a table that accepts extensions. The catch pulls the sections tightly together and holds them level.

Secretary catch (F) is recessed into the work. The button is attached to a spring clip, which releases the catch.

Stable door quadrant (G) holds two sections of a stable door closed. The plate with the quadrant is screwed to the lower section, the other plate to the top section. For added security, mount a deadbolt to the door's top section.

Cupboard latch (H) has a spring latch that slides into a strike plate. Draw the latch back by turning the knob (top) or pulling out the lever (bottom, left) or the flush ring handle (bottom, right).

Hasp (I) is ideal for holding lids closed on small boxes. The arm is held in place with a snap clip or hook.

Hasp and staple (J) has an arm that swings over the screw plate, preventing an intruder from removing screws. A padlock slips onto the staple.

Suitcase lock (K), for boxes, holds the lid in place with an arm that snaps over the opposite plate.

Ball catch (A), with a spring-loaded ball in a cylindrical case, fits into the edge of a flush cabinet door. When the door is closed, the ball fits into a recess in the cupboard wall. The strike plate provides a finished look.

Double-ball catch (B) can be used on flush, overlay and inset cabinet doors. Two balls snap over the strike plate from the front or side.

Double-roller catch (C) operates on the same principle as the double-ball catch. The roller arms are spring-loaded.

Spring-pressure catch (D), has a roller that fits into the strike plate's hook. Attach the catch shown at top to the door's bottom edge, the strike plate to the frame's base. Mount the other catch on the cabinet's vertical frame, the strike plate on the door. To open the door, push against it.

Magnetic catch (E) holds a cabinet door closed by magnetically pulling in a metal strike plate. Screw the catch to the inside of the cabinet and the strike plate to the inside of the door. Use a handle to open the door.

Magnetic pressure catch (F) combines magnetic and spring-pressure catches. No handles are necessary; simply push the door to open it. Attach a metal strike plate to a wooden door.

Glass-door catch (G) works just like the magnetic pressure catch, but the strike plate is designed to slide onto the glass door, eliminating drilling through the glass.

Cupboard lock (H) has a bolt that operates left and right. Surface-mount the lock; cut a recess to hold the bolt.

Drawer lock (I) has a double keyhole, letting you set the lock in a vertical or horizontal position. Mount it in a recess in a desk, cabinet or other furniture.

Mortise lock (J) is ideal for sliding doors, rolltop desks and other furniture. The model at far right has a spring-loaded dust cover.

Cylinder lock (K) comes in different designs for drawers and cabinet doors. Surface-mount the lock by drilling a hole through the surface, or fit it into a mortise. The lower lock at far right is designed to fit glass cabinet doors; to install it, you must drill a hole through the glass.

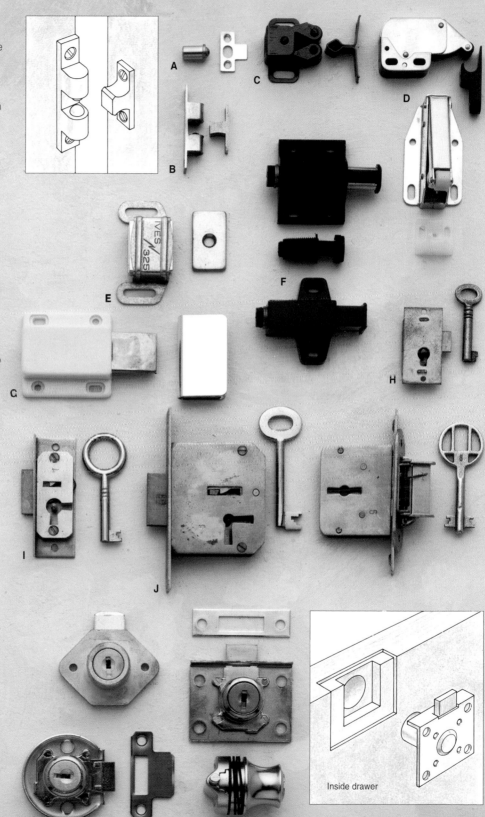

Inside drawer

DOORKNOBS AND LOCKS

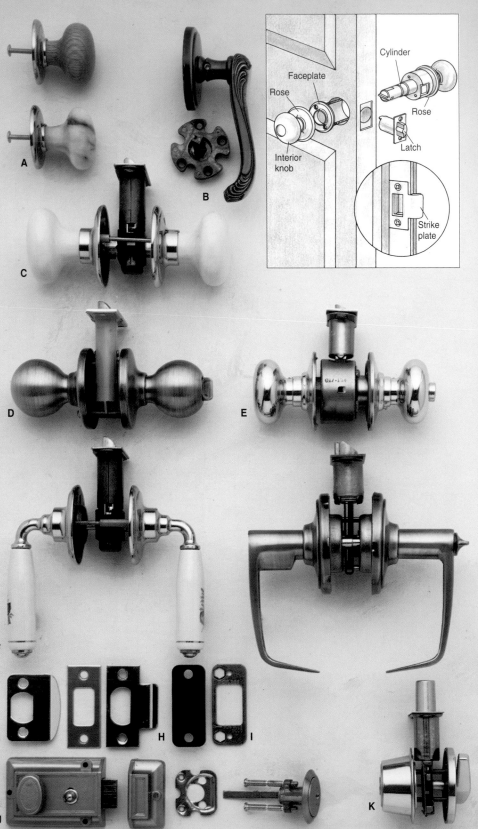

The installation of doorknobs and locks involves drilling one or two holes into the door and making a mortise in the door-jamb. Designs vary, so follow the manufacturer's instructions.

Dummy doorknob (A) attaches to a closet door to pull it open. Drill a pilot hole through the door; insert the screw from the closet side of the door; from the other side, slip on the rose and thread the knob onto the screw. To keep the door closed, install a catch.

Dummy lever handle (B) comes with mounting plate that fits into a 25 mm diameter hole. Drill a hole deep enough to flush fit the rose and, in the centre, another hole through the door for the backplate stem. Fit handle over stem, then tighten backplate screws.

Passage lockset (C) has a cylindrical lock with a spring latch to hold the door closed. Use the supplied template to drill a hole through the door face for the spindle and into its edge for the latch. Make a mortise in the doorjamb to accommodate the latch.

Privacy lockset (D) for bedroom and bathroom doors adds a turncatch or button on the inside knob to lock the door from within. It can be unlocked from outside by pushing a narrow rod into the hole in the outside knob.

Key-in-knob lockset (E) is a privacy lockset with an outside knob that locks with a key. Installation is the same as the passage lockset. To remove a knob, look for a tab or pin.

Lever handle (F) is available in passage, privacy and key-in-lever locksets. The design of the handle allows disabled people, and people with full hands, to open the door easily.

Strike plate (G) for latches and bolts fits into mortise made in doorjamb. Fix it with the longest screws that will fit. Use it alone or, preferably, with a strike box **(H)** and reinforcing plate **(I)**.

Night latch (J) is mounted at the door's edge 15 cm above the knob for additional security. The bolt slides into the strike plate installed on the jamb.

Deadbolt (K), also for extra security, has a single cylinder that moves only with a key or thumb turn. Install it in the same way as the above locksets.

Exterior lockset (A), used on a front door, comes in a variety of designs. This one has a deadlocking latch; it's similar to a spring latch, but it has a piece projecting in front of the latch that stops it from being pushed back by an intruder. To install, drill holes through the door face and into the edge; make a mortise in the jamb for the latch. From the outside, the latch is opened by depressing the thumb-piece after unlocking with a key. From the inside, just turn the knob.

Combination exterior lockset (B) has a spring latch in the lockset but also includes a deadbolt for additional security. The design and finish on the lockset and the deadbolt match. Two separate installations are required.To install the deadbolt (top), you'll have to drill an additional hole through the door face and edge and make a second mortise in the doorjamb, about 150 mm above the lockset mortise.

Interconnected exterior lockset (C) also utilizes a spring latch and dead-bolt, but they are joined together by the decorative escutcheon. Installation is slightly more difficult because the two sets of holes and mortises must be precisely spaced. A template is supplied to mark out the right locations. As with many other locksets, the handles, latch and bolt can usually be reversed to fit either a right- or a left-hand door.

Interconnected exterior lockset (D), another variety of lockset, uses a deadlocking latch in combination with a deadbolt. In some models, two separate keys operate the lockset. Installation calls for precise marking-out in the same way as fitting other interconnected locksets.

Coded combination lockset (E) with a deadlocking latch is installed like other locksets that require two holes and a mortise. To unlock the unit, you must push the buttons in a programmed order. The combination can be given out to as many (or as few) people as you wish, and it can also be changed as often as you like. (Make sure that you keep the instructions in a secure place.)

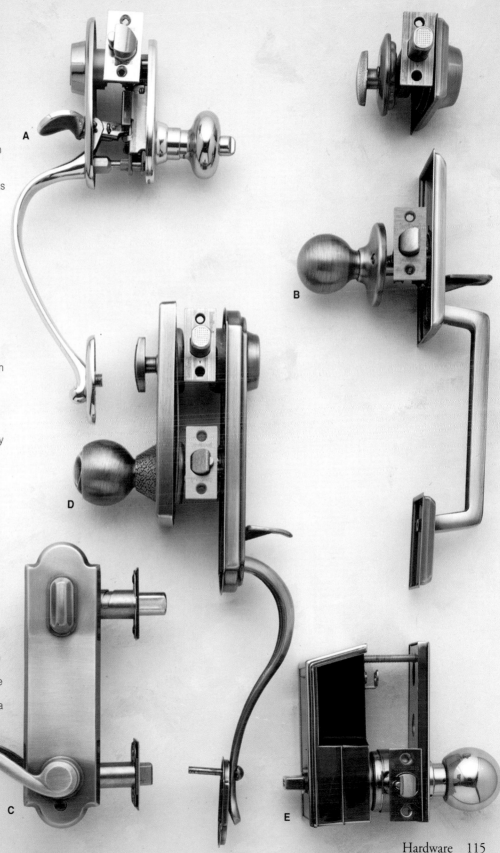

OTHER DOOR HARDWARE

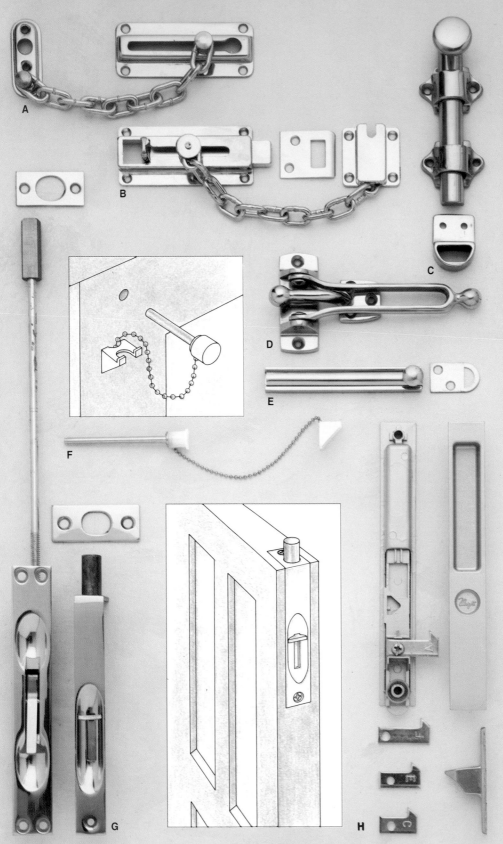

For doors that require minimal security, use the locks on this page. The additional accessories on the facing page add convenience to standard door use.

Door chain guard (A) lets you open a door partway to view visitors or for ventilation. Attach the slide piece to the door; screw the chain piece to the doorjamb or frame. Make sure you use the longest screws you can.

Deadbolt and chain guard (B) gives added security with a deadbolt. Attach the long slide plate in a horizontal position on the surface of the door, flush with the edge. Screw the chain plate to the door frame, opposite the slide plate. Position the strike on the doorjamb so the bolt can slide into it; the strike may have to be mortised.

Stable-door bolt (C) is mounted vertically on a stable-type split door. Attach the bolt to the top half of the door; secure the strike plate on the surface of the lower half of the door, near the top edge. Or attach the bolt at the top of a conventional door, using a flat strike plate (not shown) on the head jamb.

Swing bar guard (D) is stronger than a door chain guard. Attach the long arm piece to the door frame, and the smaller piece to the front surface at the edge of the door, about 18 mm away from the long arm piece. Both parts should be level, their edges parallel.

Surface bolt (E) can be used in a vertical or horizontal position on doors and cupboards. Position it with the slide bolt on the door and the strike on the jamb, making sure the bolt will easily pass through the strike.

Patio door pin (F) slips through a hole drilled through the sliding door and into the stationary door. Secure the plastic pin-holder with a screw.

Extension flush bolt (G) holds the inactive door of a pair of doors in place. It's installed in a recess cut into the door's edge. The door must be at least 35 mm thick. The smaller latch (left) is for wood doors; the other one (far left) has a longer bolt for metal doors.

Patio door latch (H) is sold to replace existing latch; select one of the proper length. Place the inside assembly in the door frame; fasten the outside plate to it. Attach the strike plate to the jamb so that the latch engages it.

Skirting buffer (A) stops an opening door before its handle hits the wall. Allowing clearance for a vacuum cleaner extension, install the rigid buffer (top) by drilling a pilot hole, then screwing the buffer in place. The flexible buffer (below) bends to make it easier for you to vacuum under it. To install one, screw in its detachable base; push the buffer onto the base.

Floor doorstop (B) screws into the floor to stop a door from opening any wider. Position the stop with the rubber pad flat against the door. (Make sure door handle does not touch wall.)

Hinge-pin buffer (C) fits onto a loose-pin door hinge. To attach one, remove the pin, slip the stop onto the pin and place it back in the hinge.

Kickdown doorstop (D), attached near the bottom of a door, holds the door open in any position. To use it, kick down the tip so that it rests flat on the floor. When the stop is not in use, the tip should point up.

Wall-mounted buffer (E) stops a doorknob from damaging a wall. Screw the buffer onto the wall, make sure it aligns with the knob.

Door knocker (F) comes in a variety of styles. When installing one on an external door, centre it horizontally 1 500 mm from the bottom of the door.

Door viewer (G) allows a normal or wide-angle view through a door. Drill a hole through the door; insert the tube and screw it into the threaded ring.

Postal slot (H) is installed with a template. Use a reciprocating saw to cut a hole in the door. Attach the outside plate cover, then the inside plate.

Pneumatic closer (I) pulls shut a screen door without slamming it. Attach it to the door rail and jamb with brackets and connecting pins provided.

Door spring (J) comes in several styles. The upper one pulls shut a light door, while the lower one, with the heavier spring, will close a heavy door or garden gate.

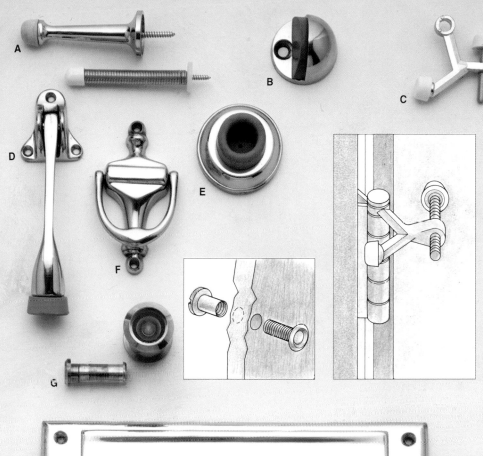

WINDOW HARDWARE

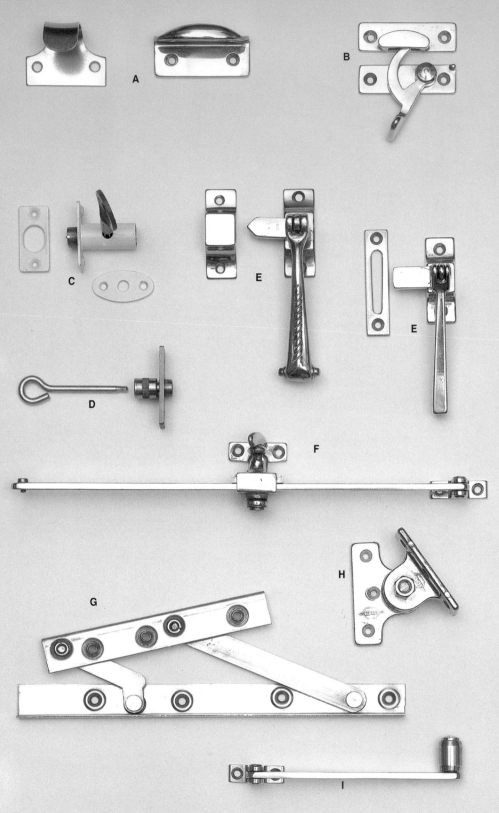

Opening, closing and securing a window is easy when it is fitted with the proper hardware. Some items here are accessories, others are replacement parts.

Sash lift (A) is screwed into the face of the lower sash's bottom rail. Grasp the lift to pull the sash up or down.

Sash latch (B) draws the upper and lower sash windows together to reduce draughts and rattling. The strike plate is attached to the top edge of the upper sash's bottom rail. Make sure the plate is centred. Align the other piece, then attach it to the top edge of the lower sash's top rail.

Rack bolt (C) is a security device operated by a splined key and may be recessed in the frame of either a casement or sash window. The bolt plate is screwed over a hole drilled in one of the outer stiles of the window. There is a smaller plate for the keyhole.

Sash lock (D) prevents sash windows being opened beyond a pre-set gap determined by the placement of the receiving plate on the upper sash. The locking barrel can be removed only with a special key.

Drop-handle casement lever (E) has a projecting tongue that engages with a grooved plate that may be flush-mounted (left) and recessed (right). For extra security, some versions are fitted with a built-in lock that blocks movement of the lever.

Sliding rod (F) operates a casement window. The rod, attached to the frame, slides through a holder installed on the rail. Tighten the knob to secure the rod in place.

Friction stays (G), fitted to the top and bottom of casements, hold them open up to 90°. The frame is not hinged at its edge, so both sides of the pane can be cleaned from inside the room when the window is fully open.

Friction pivot (H) serves as hinge and stay on fanlights. Like friction stays (G), it is not much affected by wind.

Roller stays (I) allow bottom-hinged, inward-opening fanlight to stay open in fixed position for ventilation. A stay is fitted to each vertical member of the frame, the amount of opening being determined by the length of the stays and their distance from the hinge.

BATHROOM HARDWARE

The easiest way to give your bathroom a face-lift is to replace the existing accessories. Keep in mind that surface-mounted fixtures cannot be installed where recessed ones were removed. Many brass items have a protective finish. To clean, wipe them with a soft dry or damp cloth, then buff with a dry cloth.

Towel rail (A) has a rod that's held in place with two endpieces, or bases, which are secured with toggle bolts or wall anchors. To install it, measure and mark the position of the bases on the wall. Attach one base; slide the rod into the indentation in its side. Slip the second base over the other end of the rod; secure it to the wall. The porcelain and brass rail has bases that are screwed into the wall. The bases of the white rail slide onto brackets – first screw the brackets into the wall.

Double towel rail (B) has two rods spaced apart, allowing clearance for towels to dry. Brackets hold the rail in place. Make sure they are level, correctly spaced and installed with toggle bolts. Slip the bases onto the brackets and secure them with setscrews on the bottom edge of the bases.

Towel ring (C) needs less space than a towel rail; it's installed with only one bracket. Screw the bracket to the wall; slip the base onto the bracket; tighten the setscrew in the bottom of the base.

Grab handle (D) provides support above bath tub or in the shower. Screw it to the wall vertically into plugs or diagonally with toggle bolts.

Toothbrush and mug holder (E) can be screwed in place on the wall above a sink, or it may slide onto a bracket attached to the wall. Secure the glass holder to the bracket with a setscrew. The brass holder has a dome-shaped knob that screws into the bracket.

Soap dish (F) is placed above a sink, using a bracket. The blue porcelain dish is permanently attached with plaster of Paris. Clean the back of the dish and the wall where it will sit. Wet both surfaces, apply the plaster; hold the dish in place until the plaster sets.

Toilet-roll holder (G) can be screwed in place, attached like the double towel rail (above), or recessed into a ceramic tile wall as it's installed.

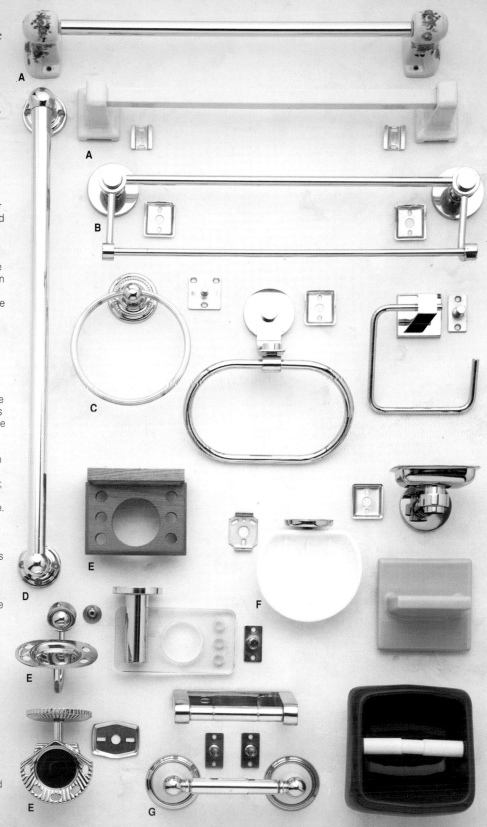

FURNITURE HANDLES

The handles and knobs needed to open drawers and cabinet doors come in a wide variety of styles, shapes and materials. Nylon, chrome, marble, plastic and glass are ideal for fitting to kitchen and bathroom furniture, and can give other rooms a modern, functional look. Wood, brass and enamel lend elegance to living room and bedroom furniture, and are available in many modern designs (this page) as well as in antique styles (facing page).

Simple handle (A) can be installed vertically on a door or horizontally on a drawer. Position the handle, mark the door or drawer where the ends of the handle touch it, and drill screw-holes at these marks. Then hold the handle in position and drive the screws into it from inside the drawer or door.

Semicircular handle (B) can be used singly or paired to make a single circular handle. You can also mount one semicircular handle on each door of a cabinet to form a full circle when the doors are closed.

Furniture knob (C) is installed like a handle but with only one screw. If the knob has a plate, slide it onto the screw between furniture and knob.

Drop handle (D) is only a bit more complicated to install. Drill a screw-hole for each post, slide on the back-plate and screw one of the small posts into place with the hole in its surface facing in the direction of the other screw hole. Slide one of the pins in the handle into the hole in the installed post, slide the other pin into the hole in the second post and screw the second post to the drawer. If the handle is already attached to the posts, install it as you would a standard handle.

Recessed handle (E) is used mainly on sliding doors. To install a recessed handle, chisel out a mortise, or hollow, just large enough to accept it. If the handle is circular, use an electric drill with a hole saw to start the mortise, then finish it with a chisel. Sand the edges of the opening smooth, and firmly wedge the handle in place. On some recessed handles you must glue the handle into place or fasten it with screws, which are usually supplied.

William and Mary period drop handles **(right)** use *snipes* (doubled-over pins) instead of screws. Position the handle and drill a hole for the snipe. Force the bail (drop) over one leg of the snipe and push it down into the bend in the snipe. Slide the backing plate over the snipe behind the bail, thread the snipe through the hole in the door or drawer, and bend its legs against the furniture, using pliers with the jaws taped to prevent scratching. Gently hammer the ends of the snipe against the inside of the furniture.

Other antique styles (right and below) include Queen Anne, Sheraton, Chippendale and Hepplewhite. If a handle uses decorative bolts and nuts in place of snipes or screws, countersink the nut on the inside of the drawer or door and saw off the protruding end of the bolt to give a smooth, snag-free surface. If you are replacing a handle and the original bolt holes are up to 3 mm too far apart or close together, stretch or push together the arms of the new bail to make it fit. If this doesn't work, install a new pull with a plate that will cover the old holes.

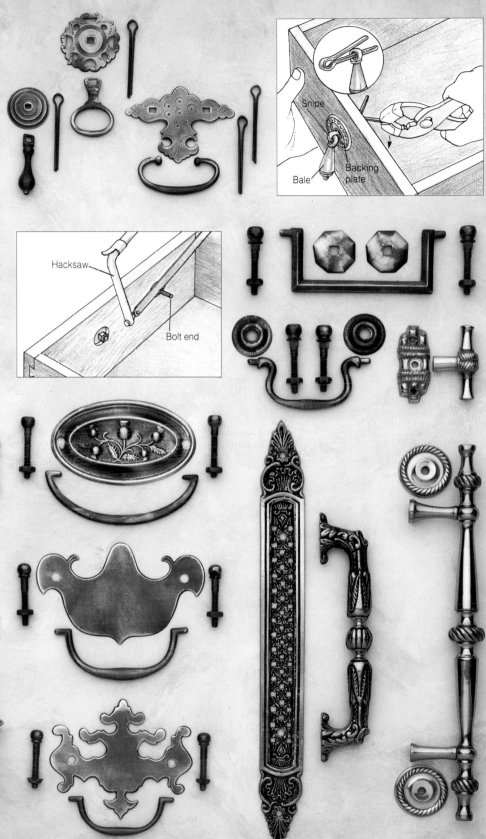

When building or repairing a piece of furniture, you may find that some of the items on this and the facing page will add to its function or decor.

Furniture glide (A) has a nail or screw end to fit into a furniture leg. Apply a glide to each leg to make it easier to move the furniture and to help protect the floor from scrapes.

Furniture leveller (B) fits into universal socket in furniture leg or into a drilled 8 or 9 mm-diameter hole. Turn threaded leveller until furniture is level.

Stem castor (C) has a rod that slides into the bottom of a hollow leg or a threaded end that screws into the leg. The castor wheel or ball bearing (near left) allows you to roll the furniture across the floor with ease.

Ferrule castor (D) slides onto the furniture leg. The socket must match the shape and size of the leg. Screw the castor to the leg to secure it in place.

Plate castor (E) has a mounting plate that is screwed to the bottom of furniture. Because of the short height of the ball bearing castor, it's ideal where headroom is limited. Some castors have brakes that lock them into place.

Flap stay (F) works in left- and right-hand pairs to hold desktop and other flaps in a 90° open position. Screw the plate with the knob inside the desk, the pivotable plate to the flap.

Lid stay (G) holds a jewellery box or chest lid open. Screw one plate to a vertical surface inside the box, the other plate to the lid. Some stays have a locking mechanism to hold the lid open. The stay at far left has a pivot mechanism that lets you use it as either a right- or a left-hand stay.

Drawer runner (H) guides a drawer open and closed. One section slides along the other one. Screw one runner to each side of the drawer and the furniture carcass. Other types attach to the bottom of the drawer.

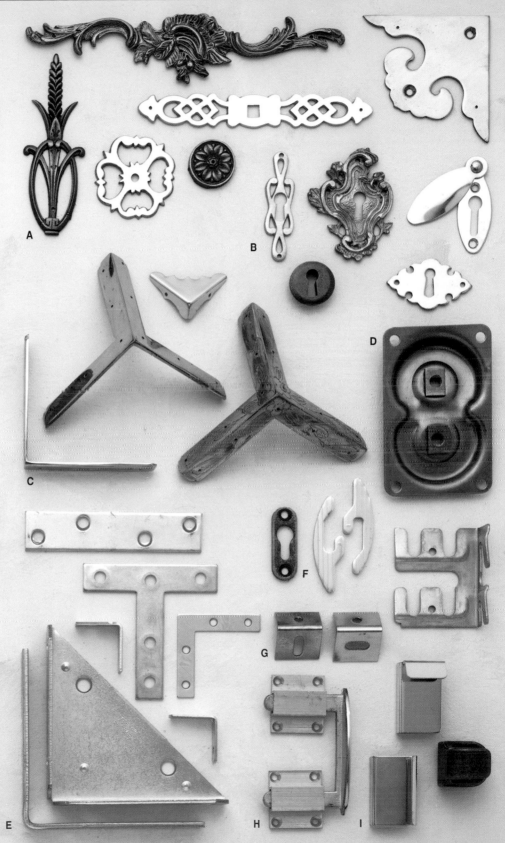

Decorative plates (A) come in an unlimited number of shapes, sizes and styles. They can embellish store-bought furniture or pieces that you make yourself. They work especially well on antique reproductions. To install a plate, screw or nail it in place through the small holes in the plate. Some plates have larger holes to accept drawer or door handles.

Keyhole escutcheon (B), a type of decorative plate, fits over a small keyhole. If you install the lock yourself, place the escutcheon over the hole as the last step. The escutcheon can also serve as a dummy, giving the appearance of a lock where none is installed.

Decorative angle plates (C) are available in a variety of shapes and sizes. Wrap the L-shaped plate and the Y-shaped plate (near right) around a piece where two sides meet. Fit the corner plate and the Y-shaped plate (farther right) over corners where three sides meet. Nail the plates in place.

Leg plate (D) firmly holds a chair or table leg in place. Attach the plate to the top of the leg with a bolt; screw the plate to the underside of a chair seat or table surface. Two settings allow you to set the leg straight or angled.

Brace and plate (E) provide support on wooden joints during initial assembly or subsequent repair. The straight plate joins two abutting pieces, the T-plate a horizontal and a perpendicular piece. The L-shaped and flat corner braces support right-angle pieces. The three-sided corner brace is for heavy-duty use.

Knockdown fitting (F) joins pieces temporarily, allowing you to take apart and re-assemble them when necessary – for instance, to move heavy furniture. They come in many styles.

Shrinkage brace (G) has one plate with a vertical or horizontal slot, allowing wood to move as it shrinks or expands with humidity changes.

Table fork (H), for expandable table, has two plates and a U-shaped fork. Mount one plate under stationary section, the other plate on the leaf; slide the fork into the plates to hold the two sections together. Use two table fork latches for each leaf.

Glass door handle (I) slides over the edge of a glass cabinet door. An inside pad prevents damage to glass.

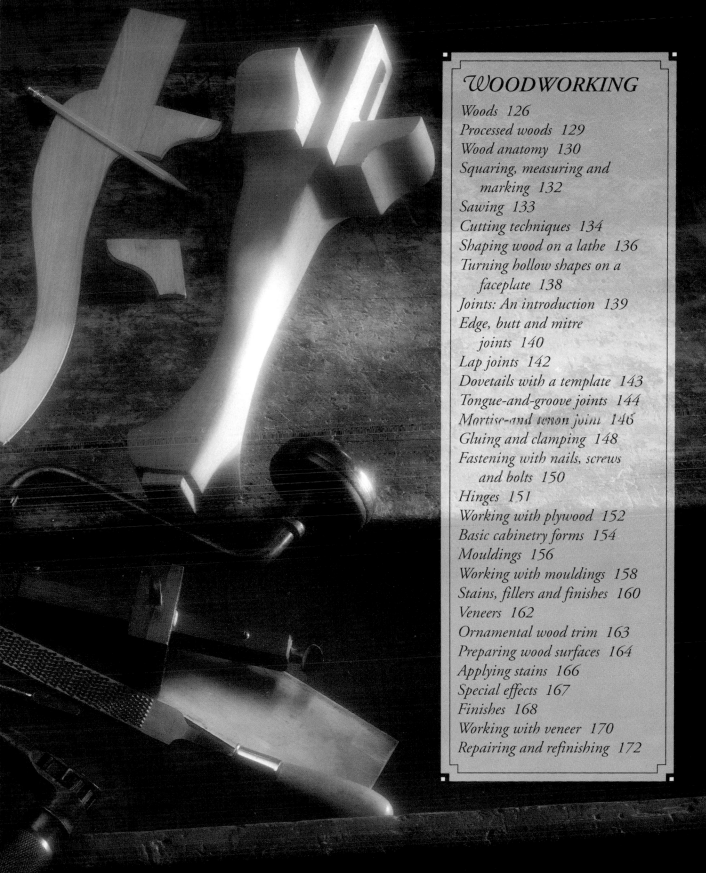

WOODWORKING

WOODS

A primary building and crafts material, wood offers strength and beauty or a combination of both. Sizes range from thick beams for houses to paper-thin strips of veneer for furniture.

Of the hundreds of wood species, only a few, mostly indigenous softwoods, are used in the building trade. Wood from trees grown in managed forests is sold in hardware stores and timberyards as construction timber, boards and manufactured products such as mouldings and doors. The hobbyist or furniture-maker uses both indigenous and imported woods. Available in forms such as boards and carving blocks, these woods must usually be ordered well in advance or bought from specialist timber dealers.

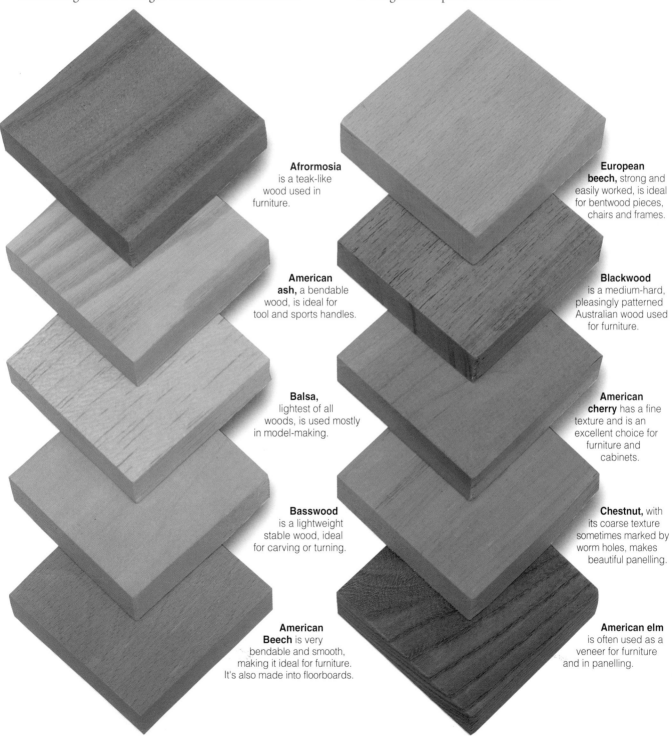

Afrormosia is a teak-like wood used in furniture.

American ash, a bendable wood, is ideal for tool and sports handles.

Balsa, lightest of all woods, is used mostly in model-making.

Basswood is a lightweight stable wood, ideal for carving or turning.

American Beech is very bendable and smooth, making it ideal for furniture. It's also made into floorboards.

European beech, strong and easily worked, is ideal for bentwood pieces, chairs and frames.

Blackwood is a medium-hard, pleasingly patterned Australian wood used for furniture.

American cherry has a fine texture and is an excellent choice for furniture and cabinets.

Chestnut, with its coarse texture sometimes marked by worm holes, makes beautiful panelling.

American elm is often used as a veneer for furniture and in panelling.

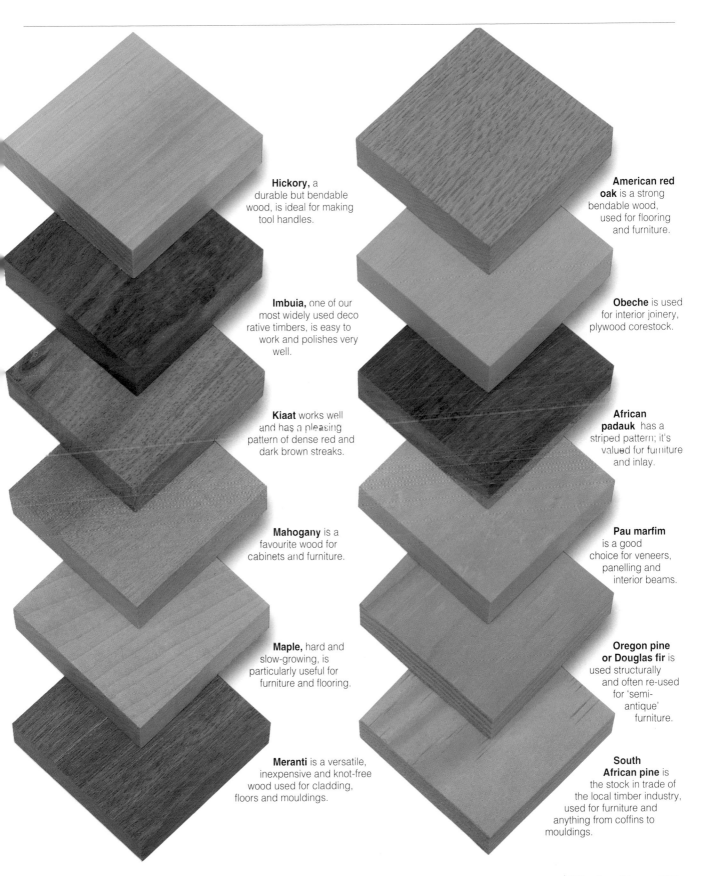

Hickory, a durable but bendable wood, is ideal for making tool handles.

American red oak is a strong bendable wood, used for flooring and furniture.

Imbuia, one of our most widely used decorative timbers, is easy to work and polishes very well.

Obeche is used for interior joinery, plywood corestock.

Kiaat works well and has a pleasing pattern of dense red and dark brown streaks.

African padauk has a striped pattern; it's valued for furniture and inlay.

Mahogany is a favourite wood for cabinets and furniture.

Pau marfim is a good choice for veneers, panelling and interior beams.

Maple, hard and slow-growing, is particularly useful for furniture and flooring.

Oregon pine or Douglas fir is used structurally and often re-used for 'semi-antique' furniture.

Meranti is a versatile, inexpensive and knot-free wood used for cladding, floors and mouldings.

South African pine is the stock in trade of the local timber industry, used for furniture and anything from coffins to mouldings.

Poplar is found in stained and painted furniture, as a plywood veneer and in mouldings.

American red wood weathers well and is ideal for decks and outdoor furniture.

African rose wood has deep, rich colours and is much sought after for cabinet-making.

Saligna is a heavy, gummy wood used for flooring, ladders, mouldings and furniture.

Sapele is a mahogany-like wood used as a veneer and in general furniture and panelling.

Stinkwood, in-digenous hardwood, has a lovely grain for enduring furniture.

Sucupira, strong and durable, is ideal for flooring, veneers and inlay work.

American sycamore is commonly used in furniture and flooring.

Tatajuba is used in carpentry, civil and marine construction.

Teak is excellent for outdoor furniture, boats, and as veneer.

American walnut is frequently used in fine cabinetwork.

Yellowwood gives a mellow golden glow to furniture, flooring and panelling.

PROCESSED WOODS

An alternative to solid wood, processed wood extends our natural resources by laminating or compressing layers of wood or wood fibres to form panels. The best known of these is plywood, which is made up of an odd number of thin timber veneers bonded so that the grain of each veneer is at right angles to that of the veneers on either side of it. Softwood plywood, made up of laminated layers, is graded according to whether it is for interior, exterior or marine use. Many exotic hardwood veneers are available. Similar materials made from wood or wood products include particleboard or chipboard, hardboard and pegboard, blockboard and fibreboard. Some types of processed board can be routed, moulded and edge-profiled while others are made for specific installations, such as skirting board, quadrant and cornice. Most processed boards are available in a range of thicknesses, while laminated structural beams are made in lengths up to 24 m.

Core thickness varies from 3 to 32 mm and thicker. From left to right are a hardwood-veneer panel; two plywood samples (the number of layers are referred to, for example, as 3-ply or 5-ply); two types of particleboard or chipboard – the one on the right, with larger particles, is also known as oriented strand board.

Hardwood-veneer plywood (below, top) is pre-sanded and ready for finishing. The superior-quality outer veneers may be sealed or stained. Use the panel where appearance is important. Birch (shown) and oak veneer are the most readily available; others can be ordered.

Industrial pine plywood (below, bottom) has softwood outer veneers that are graded from A down to D. They may be knotty. Interior (UF) and exterior (PF) grades are determined by the glue used in their manufacture.

Tongue-and-groove panels are suitable as a moisture- and termite-resistant flooring and roofing underlay. They are made from plywood and wood particles. Ends have tongues and grooves for tighter installation.

Particleboard, (below, top) also known as chipboard, is made from bonded and compressed wood particles in a variety of wood-veneer and synthetic finishes.

Blockboard (below, centre) has a timber core of laminated pine and is veneered on both surfaces.

Fibreboard (below, bottom) is stable and machines well. Use it for painted cabinet doors and also as a veneer substrate.

All trees belong in one of two broad divisions, *hardwoods* or *softwoods,* depending on whether they are broad-leaved or coniferous. But when it comes to actual characteristics, distinctions between the two types tend to blur, and certain softwoods may actually be harder than some soft hardwoods. Because hardness and strength go hand in hand, the strongest woods (facing page) are also the most difficult to work and require the sharpest tools. These dense woods are also less forgiving of careless joinery.

All woods have *grain,* a term that describes the direction of longitudinal cells in a board. Relative cell size, which can determine whether a wood needs a filler before finishing, is called *texture.* The attractive patterns of various boards, or *figure,* are caused by deviations from a tree's normal growth.

Freshly sawn timber has a high moisture content and should be seasoned, or dried, before working. Timberyards usually sell kiln-dried wood with a moisture content between 6 and 18 per cent. Wood that has less than 10 per cent moisture content is recommended for furniture-making; the range above 10 per cent is suitable for structural uses.

After seasoning, wood continues to shrink during dry spells and to swell with humidity. This tendency is critical to the woodworker because it can cause warped boards, loose joints or swollen-shut drawers. To combat this movement, you can choose a stable type of wood. Buy kiln-dried boards in advance and store them indoors for about a month to acclimatize them to the moisture content of your home. After working, apply a sealing finish on all surfaces to retard further moisture exchange.

Wood comes in various grades. In hardwood, *prime* boards are about 85 per cent defect-free; *select* and *comsells,* about 65 per cent. Timber is usually sold in standard lengths, starting at 1,8 m and going up by increments of 300 mm to 4,8 m. Timber may be sold according to its *nominal size,* which refers to the dimensions before surfacing or planing, or in its *planed all round (PAR)* size – sometimes known as *dressed all round (DAR), dressed four sides (D4S)* and *surfaced four sides (S4S).* Construction timber is usually sold in its rough-sawn state, and wood for cabinetry as PAR. Specify the finish when ordering. Some rare woods, especially indigenous hardwoods such as stinkwood, may be sold by volume.

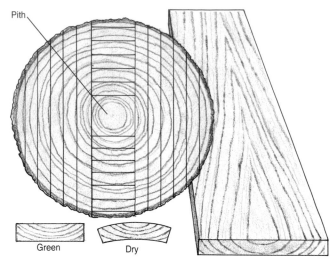

Pith

Green   Dry

Plain-sawing, or flat-sawing, yields boards whose growth rings intersect the surface at less than 45°. Boards containing the pith (the soft wood at the trunk's centre) will cup severely or split, and so are usually ripped into two narrower boards. Plain-sawn boards warp as they dry.

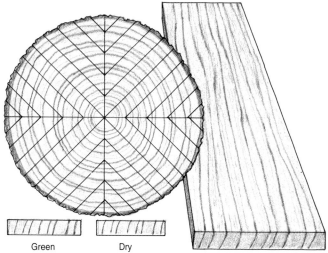

Green   Dry

Quartersawing produces wood with a close, even grain pattern because the growth rings form an angle of 45° to 90° to the board surface. Quartersawing results in more waste than plain-sawing, so boards milled this way are more expensive. While quartersawn wood may check (facing page), it is less prone to warp.

Types of grain

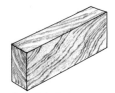

Straight grain is strong and runs parallel to board edges.

Irregular grain occurs when normal growth pattern is altered by defects in the wood.

Wavy grain, weaker than straight, has attractive figure but is difficult to work.

Spiral grain is a natural growth pattern ascending a trunk. Wood may twist.

Interlocked grain results from successive layers of wood spiralling in opposite directions. These boards, sliced from one block, show how the wood fibres changed course.

Defects in wood

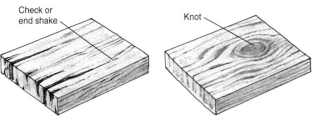

Check or end shake

Knot

Wood dries more quickly along the grain than across it. The resulting uneven moisture loss causes cracks, called checks, on board ends. Knots occur when a tree branch dies and the tree trunk grows around it. They can vary from 6 to 40 mm or more in diameter.

Storage: Stacking timber

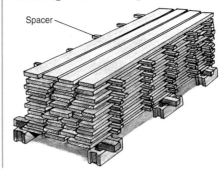

Spacer

To ensure good air circulation and to minimize warp, separate layers of boards with dry 25 x 25 mm strips of wood as spacers. Place spacers at each end of the stack and about every 500 mm along the length of the boards.

Types of warp

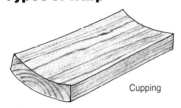

Cupping

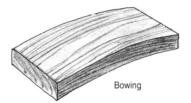

Bowing

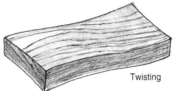

Twisting

Wood distorts when it shrinks or swells unevenly. The stress thus produced in the fibres causes a deviation from the board's flatness.

Wood types

Wood	Characteristics	Texture	Ease of working	Ease of finishing
Ash	Very strong, very stable	Coarse	Fairly difficult	Sands and stains unevenly
Basswood	Fairly strong, very stable	Fine	Very easy, but dents easily	Easy; usually painted or stained and varnished
Beech	Very strong, stable	Fine	Fairly difficult	Easy to oil or varnish
Birch, yellow	Strong, fairly stable	Medium	Fairly difficult, hard to plane	Easy to oil or varnish, but colour may be bland
Cherry, black	Strong, stable	Fine	Easy	Very easy to oil or varnish
Douglas fir	Fairly strong, very stable	Medium	Easy	Fairly difficult because of knots
Hickory	Very strong, stable	Coarse	Difficult, dulls cutting edges	Easy to oil or varnish
Imbuia	Very strong, stable	Medium	Easy	Easy to oil or varnish
Kiaat	Strong, stable	Fine	Easy	Easy to oil or varnish
Mahogany	Strong, very stable	Medium	Easy	Easy to varnish; harder to obtain lustrous oil finish; may need filler
Maple, sugar	Very strong, fairly stable	Fine	Fairly difficult	Very easy to oil or varnish
Oak, red	Very strong, stable	Coarse	Easy, but can splinter	Easy to oil or varnish; can be filled
Pine, white (softwood)	Fairly strong, very stable	Medium	Very easy	Very easy to paint or varnish; harder to obtain lustrous oil finish
Poplar	Fairly strong, stable	Fine	Very easy, but dents easily	Easy to paint or varnish; may require many coats of oil for lustrous finish; colour may be bland
Rosewood	Very strong, very stable	Fine	Difficult, hard to glue	Easy; usually oiled
Sapele	Strong, very stable	Medium	Easy	Easy to varnish, but difficult if lustrous oiled finish required. May need filling.
Teak	Very strong, very stable	Coarse to medium	Easy, but hard to glue	Easy; usually oiled
Walnut	Strong, very stable	Medium	Easy, but can dent	Very easy to oil or varnish

SQUARING, MEASURING AND MARKING

Squaring: getting it straight

The first step in any woodworking project is to choose the best board face of each member and make it exactly flat. Additionally, each piece must have one level edge that is squared to the first face. These two surfaces will become the reference for all measuring, marking and cutting operations on the opposite surface and edge, and at each end.

If you have access to a jointer and a thickness planer, you can buy timber rough-sawn in nominal dimensions (the least expensive kind) and then mill one face and each edge on the jointer and the other face on the planer. If you have only hand planes, you may want to buy more expensive boards that are surfaced, or dressed, to thickness and width. Even more expensive are those cut to exact length, thickness and width, but even these must be levelled and squared. Use a jack plane, followed by a smoothing plane; then square the edge with a jointer or jack plane (p 134).

Check flatness on best face with straightedge along dotted lines (right). Light will show at low spots. Mark high spots with pencil; plane smooth.

Check for twisting by placing a straight piece of wood at each end of the board and sighting down their top edges. Mark and plane the high spots.

On best edge, check for high spots and squareness of corner, using planed face as reference. Mark spots to be planed both across edge and along it.

Measuring and marking

To reduce the length of rough-sawn timber to manageable dimensions, mark the boards about 25 mm oversize before cutting. For dressed timber with accurate reference surfaces, you can cut pieces to their finished lengths. But mark and cut it 1 to 1,5 mm oversize in width, to allow for smoothing with a jointer plane. Once you've squared the face and edge of a board, mark the reference face with a loop and the reference edge with a V. These marks will help you orient the pieces in the right direction. Then measure and mark the cuts for your project.

A sharp scribing tool is the most accurate for marking, but if you prefer a pencil, choose one with a hard lead, sharpened to a chisel point. Use the same tools for the entire project, and avoid changing marking-gauge settings until you've marked all parts having the same measurements. Locate hole centres with crossed pencil lines and pencil a circle around the cross for clarity. Heavily marked stock can be confusing to interpret, so make pencil notes beside the marks on the waste side to avoid cutting errors.

Finally, re-measure everything before sawing; finding a mistake after you've made the cut may mean having to start over with a new piece of stock.

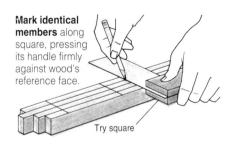

Mark identical members along square, pressing its handle firmly against wood's reference face. Try square

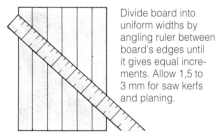

Divide board into uniform widths by angling ruler between board's edges until it gives equal increments. Allow 1,5 to 3 mm for saw kerfs and planing.

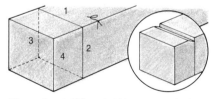

To mark cutoff line, hold try square stock on reference surface; mark lines in sequence. Chisel recess in waste to guide saw.

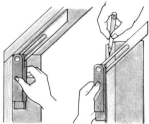

Setting an angle. Align protractor's index line to starting point on board edge; mark. Connect the two points with straightedge. Degree scale

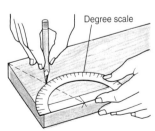

Copying an angle. Adjust the bevel-gauge blade to the angle you want to copy; transfer this angle to new piece.

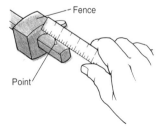

Setting marking gauge. Loosen thumbscrew; push fence away from point with ruler. Tighten screw; check setting. Fence Point

Drawing a gauged line. Grasp the handle tightly, tilt gauge, and pull toward you (shown here) or push away, trailing pin on line.

SAWING

Most sawing involves cutting a straight line along the grain (ripping), across the grain (crosscutting), or at an angle to it (mitre or bevel cut). Here are the commonest woodworking saws: For ripping – ripsaw, bowsaw, table, radial arm, band, circular; for crosscutting – crosscut, bowsaw, table, band, radial arm, circular; for angles – tenon saw, coping, circular, table, radial arm, mitre, band; for sizing plywood – crosscut, table, circular; for curves – compass, coping, band, jigsaw; for joinery – tenon saw, dovetail, bowsaw, table, radial arm.

Wood should not move or vibrate while being cut. When handsawing, support the wood on a bench or sawhorses. Hold the saw at about a 60° angle to the wood surface for ripping and at about 45° for crosscutting. Because wood can splinter where the saw teeth exit, place the good side up when cutting with a hand- or table saw, or when crosscutting with a radial arm saw. Put the good side down when using a circular saw or when ripping with a radial arm saw. Saw on the waste side of the lines, or the board will be short by the width of the saw kerf (3 mm on a table saw).

When you are ripping, the saw may bind (the kerf closes, pinching the blade). A circular saw tends to bind if it twists off a straight line or exposes too much blade. When a circular saw blade binds, the saw will kick back, or jump dangerously toward you. To keep hand- and circular saws from binding, drive wedges into the kerf. On a table saw, a splitter is part of the guard or is mounted as an accessory. Boards that are not held securely on a table saw may shoot back at you. To prevent kickback when ripping on a table saw, press the board against the fence with a clamped guide or feather board. You can buy one from a supplier or cut kerfs at 6 mm intervals in an angled board to make 'fingers'. Another safety tool is the push stick, a notched stick that guides narrow pieces.

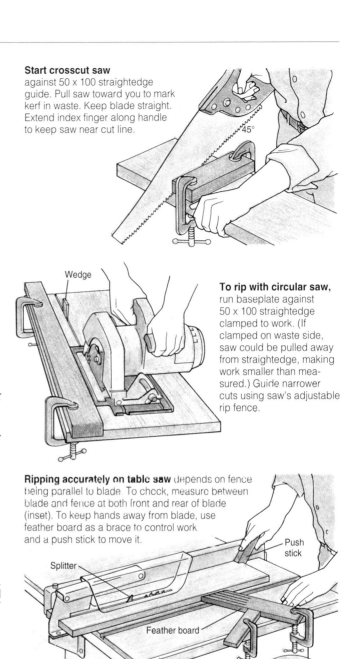

Start crosscut saw against 50 x 100 straightedge guide. Pull saw toward you to mark kerf in waste. Keep blade straight. Extend index finger along handle to keep saw near cut line.

Wedge

To rip with circular saw, run baseplate against 50 x 100 straightedge clamped to work. (If clamped on waste side, saw could be pulled away from straightedge, making work smaller than measured.) Guide narrower cuts using saw's adjustable rip fence.

Ripping accurately on table saw depends on fence being parallel to blade. To check, measure between blade and fence at both front and rear of blade (inset). To keep hands away from blade, use feather board as a brace to control work and a push stick to move it.

Push stick

Splitter

Feather board

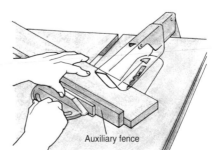

Auxiliary fence

Mitre cuts on table saw. For safety and accuracy, screw auxiliary fence, made from straight piece of hardwood or plywood, to mitre gauge. Sandpaper glued to fence will prevent wood from shifting as you slide it into blade.

► SAFE PRACTICES ◄

General rules
▷ Let saw reach full speed before cutting. Keep work clear of blade until you are ready to cut.
▷ Keep locks and clamps tight. Support work firmly.

Table saw
▷ Make sure guard and splitter, which holds cut stock open after cut, are in place and properly adjusted. Set blade to protrude 3 mm above work.
▷ Use a push stick when ripping stock less than 75 mm wide. Clamp a feather board behind saw blade and brace it from the side.
▷ Keep widest part of board between blade and fence. Hold on to work until completely clear of blade. If work is narrow, use a push stick.
▷ Hold stock against fence or mitre

gauge. Never cut freehand.
▷ To guard against kickback, never stand in area directly behind saw blade and fence.
▷ Make deep cuts in two or more passes; adjust blade each time.

Circular saw
▷ Clamp work firmly so it won't shift. Make sure the blade is sharp and clean.
▷ Never remove or wedge up the retractable blade guard.
▷ Support waste for a long cut.
▷ Stand to one side of the saw, out of the way of kickback.
▷ Stand with weight firmly on both feet; don't reach too far with the saw. Don't let saw drop at end.
▷ Always adjust the blade to the height needed for a particular job. Before adjusting, unplug the saw. (More safety tips, pp 12–13.)

Two types of hand tools shape wood: cutting and scraping. Cutting tools (chisels, drawknives, planes and spokeshaves) carve the wood, leaving a smooth surface. And because they tear out end grain, they are most efficiently used to work along the grain of straight-grained woods. Scraping tools (files, rasps and Surform-type tools) pull the fibres off wood rather than cut them, leaving a fuzzy surface. Use them in any direction, regardless of grain.

Precise planing depends on a keen blade, a flat sole and correct adjustment. Set the plane throat according to the work: with the opening widest on a jack plane, medium on a jointer plane and narrow on a smoothing plane. In addition, you may have to file smooth the chip breaker, which keeps the blade from tearing the wood, to make it fit snugly to the plane blade. Move the chip breaker about 1 mm away from the blade edge – set it closer for fine work, further away for rough.

Because taking too thick an initial cut can jam the blade in the wood, adjust the plane for a fine shaving and test the cut; then gradually increase the shaving thickness. For the smoothest surface, finish planing with progressively finer cuts. To prevent end grain from chipping, support it by clamping or gluing a piece of scrap wood to the work before you begin planing, or plane end grain from the ends of the wood toward the middle.

Although it's sometimes necessary to work directly across the grain, chisels are best used *along* the grain, so that the blade doesn't catch or split off hunks of wood. When chiselling a groove, use a chisel that is slightly narrower, or it will chip the groove sides. Control the depth of the cut by working with the chisel's bevel down; raise the handle to go deeper, lower it to cut parallel to the surface. Make a stop cut across the grain to prevent splitting of the grain. For safety, secure the work so it can't move, and always keep your hands behind the cutting edge. Never cut towards yourself.

Drawknives and spokeshaves are useful for curved work. A drawknife resembles a chisel in that it can remove both large and small amounts of wood depending on how you manipulate it. A spokeshave is closer to a plane, with its blade enclosed by a sole. Choose cylindrical handles for an easy grip and ball-shaped handles for carving wood.

Handles level with the blade allow control of heavy cuts, bent handles offer a natural hand position, and dropped handles are good for precise work. When drawknifing, keep both hands on the handles. For safety and accuracy, keep your body balanced as you pull the blade toward you, so you can stop cutting at any moment if the grain splits. Store all cutting tools on a rack – leaving them lying on a work surface is asking for an accident.

Files, rasps and Surform tools are primarily used to rapidly shape curved work. All cut on the push stroke and leave surfaces that must be smoothed with a plane, cabinet scraper or sandpaper. For greatest versatility, choose a half-round tool. Work a rasp or file diagonally, with one hand pushing the handle while the heel of the other hand guides the tool toe. A Surform, which is useful for rounding off square corners, is worked the same way, but because it's shaped like a plane, it's easier to hold. The teeth of files and rasps clog; clean them often with a special brush called a *file card,* pulling it in the direction of the file's lines or teeth. To clean a Surform, you must pull the shavings out.

Using a plane

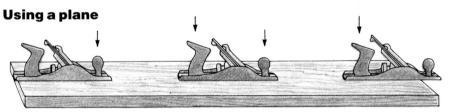

Begin a pass with pressure on the plane's toe, equalize pressure in mid-pass and end with pressure on the heel. Keep the plane sole flat on the wood. Supplement the force of your arms with back and shoulder power, and shift your weight from rear foot to front foot as you finish each stroke.

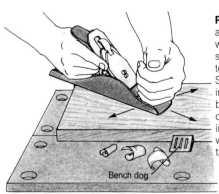

Plane diagonally across wide board with overlapping strokes; this avoids tearing the grain. Stretch your rear index finger along blade edge for extra control. Finish planing along the grain, with blade set to take a fine shaving.

Bench dog

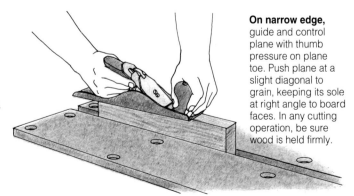

On narrow edge, guide and control plane with thumb pressure on plane toe. Push plane at a slight diagonal to grain, keeping its sole at right angle to board faces. In any cutting operation, be sure wood is held firmly.

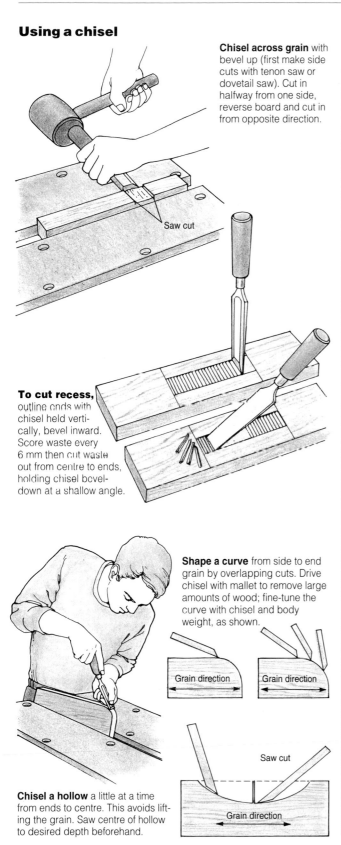

Using a chisel

Chisel across grain with bevel up (first make side cuts with tenon saw or dovetail saw). Cut in halfway from one side, reverse board and cut in from opposite direction.

To cut recess, outline ends with chisel held vertically, bevel inward. Score waste every 6 mm then cut waste out from centre to ends, holding chisel bevel-down at a shallow angle.

Shape a curve from side to end grain by overlapping cuts. Drive chisel with mallet to remove large amounts of wood; fine-tune the curve with chisel and body weight, as shown.

Grain direction

Grain direction

Saw cut

Grain direction

Chisel a hollow a little at a time from ends to centre. This avoids lifting the grain. Saw centre of hollow to desired depth beforehand.

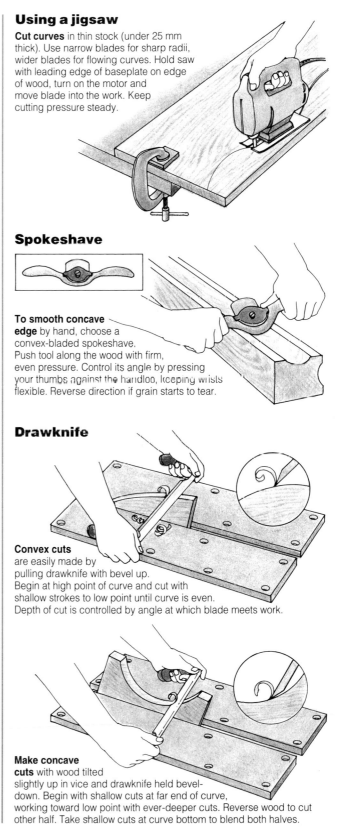

Using a jigsaw

Cut curves in thin stock (under 25 mm thick). Use narrow blades for sharp radii, wider blades for flowing curves. Hold saw with leading edge of baseplate on edge of wood, turn on the motor and move blade into the work. Keep cutting pressure steady.

Spokeshave

To smooth concave edge by hand, choose a convex-bladed spokeshave. Push tool along the wood with firm, even pressure. Control its angle by pressing your thumbs against the handloo, keeping wrists flexible. Reverse direction if grain starts to tear.

Drawknife

Convex cuts are easily made by pulling drawknife with bevel up. Begin at high point of curve and cut with shallow strokes to low point until curve is even. Depth of cut is controlled by angle at which blade meets work.

Make concave cuts with wood tilted slightly up in vice and drawknife held bevel-down. Begin with shallow cuts at far end of curve, working toward low point with ever-deeper cuts. Reverse wood to cut other half. Take shallow cuts at curve bottom to blend both halves.

SHAPING WOOD ON A LATHE

In spindle turning (centre work), the wood, held between the headstock and tailstock of a lathe, is shaped into chair or table legs, stair balusters, and other cylindrical objects. Knot-free straight-grained hardwood with fine to medium texture is easiest to turn; coarse-textured wood may splinter. Softwood is usable, but it's hard to turn crisp details. Wood may be seasoned or wet (green), but green wood may split or shrink unevenly as it dries. Large or very thin pieces take more skill to turn. Start with a blank 50 to 75 mm square.

To set up, check that the cup centre of the tailstock is tight to the wood, but not so tight that the wood doesn't turn freely. Adjust the tool-rest position so the scraping tool will be at the top edge of the wood's centreline (raise it a bit higher for a cutting tool) and close to the wood (without hitting it). Move the tool rest inward as you reduce the wood's diameter.

Caution: Wear a face shield and turn off the lathe before you adjust the tool rest or measure your progress.

Scraping tools – round-nose scrapers and diamond-points – are easier for beginners to handle. These tools can carve many shapes, but they leave a rough surface that must be sanded. Experienced turners cut or slice work with cutting tools: gouges, skew chisels and parting tools. Cutting tools shave the work, leaving a clean finish that needs little or no sanding. All tools must be sharp (pp 198-199).

First, with the lathe running at slow speed, rough out or remove corners of the blank in small sections. As the wood becomes round, increase the speed. Begin the first section 25 mm from one end, and make a series of passes from alternating directions. To avoid splits when starting the next section, move your tool toward the turned section. Rough

Mounting the wood

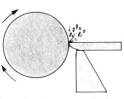

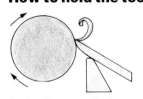

Preparing the blank. Draw two diagonal lines on each end of stock to find exact centre. With handsaw on headstock end, score lines; drive spur centre into saw cuts. Mark centre of X with awl on tailstock end (inset). If stock is more than 50 mm square, plane or saw off each corner so blank is more octagonal.

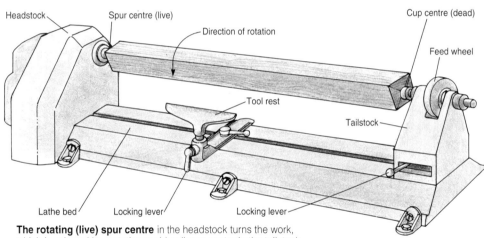

The rotating (live) spur centre in the headstock turns the work, which is gripped by a stationary (dead) cup centre in the tailstock. Use lubricant on the wood at the dead cup centre end. Begin roughing with the lathe running slowly; smooth the rounded work at higher speed, and refine shapes at highest speed.

How to hold the tool

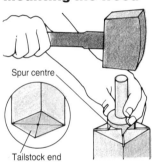

Cutting (cross section)

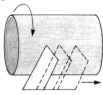

Cutting (side view)

To cut a shape, rub bevel of skew chisel on wood, then lift handle to angle bottom half of cutting edge into wood; move in direction of work.

Scraping (cross section)

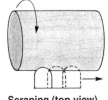

Scraping (top view)

To scrape, hold round-nose tool level to floor (or slightly down) and flat on rest, ease edge into work, and scrape lightly along the blank.

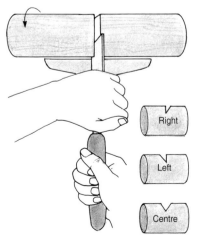

V-cutting. Score centreline of V-cut with point of skew chisel. Holding tool 90° to the work, cut V-bottom with heel of skew cutting edge. To make a right or left V-shape (keeping one side of V at 90°), cut right or left side of centreline at 45° or desired angle with bevel edge of skew. For centred V-cut, cut each side to bottom, widening the shape as necessary.

out the end sections with repeated passes, moving from the ends toward the middle. To scrape, move a round-nose scraper parallel to the ground along the tool rest. To cut, place the centre edge of a square-end gouge against the revolving wood; then roll it slightly in the direction of travel with your lower hand and move it along the rest with your upper hand. To avoid catches, grasp the tool firmly and aim for gentle, steady pressure – never force it into the wood.

To sand your work as it rotates on the lathe, remove the tool rest and press a small pad of sandpaper (backed with a scrap of leather to protect you from heat buildup) against the work, or hold both ends of a sandpaper strip under (not over) it. Start with 180- to 220-grit abrasive on smooth work, 80-grit on rough. Remove work from the lathe with a dovetail saw or parting tool held 90° to the rotating work.

From rough to final shape

Grip gouge overhand to begin rounding. Cup fingers to steady tool; brace handle against body.

Finish truing diameter with round-nose scraper held underhand and parallel to floor.

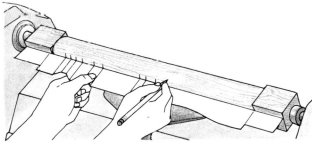

To lay out a design, hold uncut edge of hardboard template against cylinder; mark lines where cuts will be made (shown). Next, hold pencil on rest, its point on marks; hand-rotate wood to sketch lines on cylinder.

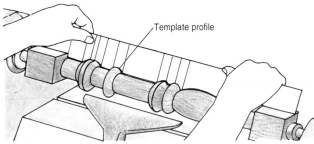

Template profile

Check work against template profile. Stop lathe often to compare your work with a cut profile of your design. For small jobs, measure diameters with outside callipers.

Turned shapes

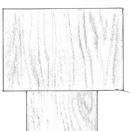

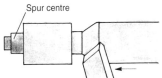
Spur centre

Square shoulder. Score shoulder line with point of skew chisel. With lower half of edge (but not heel), cut away wood leading to shoulder. Then smooth vertical wall of shoulder. Repeat until shoulder cut is correct depth.

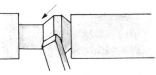

Bead. Make V-cut (facing page) on both sides of bead. Round one side of bead by rolling skew downhill from bead centre towards V-cut in one smooth, flowing motion. End with blade edge vertical. Repeat rounding motion on other side.

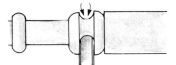

Cove. Start cut with gouge rolled on side. Raise handle to engage wood, and roll tool, rubbing bevel on wood, through cut from a shoulder to cove centre. At end of cut, gouge top faces up. Cut in from other shoulder.

Urn shape. Beginning at key wide and narrow diameters, rough out shape with skew to within 2 mm of final size. Roll skew from high to low points. Cut small concave shapes with gouge, similar to motion for coves.

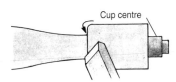
Cup centre

Round shoulder. Start cut at highest point of shoulder, engage edge of skew near heel, and roll skew downhill so heel drops into valley. Finish with blade vertical.

Woodworking **137**

TURNING HOLLOW SHAPES ON A FACEPLATE

In faceplate work, a block of wood, mounted first on a faceplate and then screwed onto the headstock, can be sculpted, as for a bowl. You remove wood across and along its grain. It's best to use finely textured hardwoods because they produce smoother turnings than softwoods and coarse-grained hardwoods, which tear out. Irregular grain patterns show well, but you should avoid wood with knots or splits. If you are just learning, work on blocks that are 150 to 200 mm in diameter and 50 mm thick. Use scraping tools; round-nose and diamond-point scrapers are easier to handle than gouges and chisels and are less likely to mar or catch in the wood.

Before mounting a blank on the lathe, true the base and round off the edges – square corners are dangerous. If a backer is needed, make it from hardwood. Softwood and plywood won't hold the screws. Wood up to 300 mm in diameter and 50 mm thick can be mounted to the backer with hot glue from a glue gun. Trace the outline of the backer (to which a faceplate has been screwed) onto the blank. Then, working quickly, run a bead of glue around the edge of the backer and inside the matching line on the blank. Hold the pieces together for a minute, then mount the work.

To turn a bowl in one mounting, shape the exterior first. True the outer edge with the lathe running slowly. Then change to medium speed and begin shaping. During the final shaping, switch to higher speed. Keep the tool flat on the rest, and work with a light touch. Before hollowing the interior, measure the stock's thickness and determine the desired bowl depth. (Never cut below 7 mm thickness.) To sand, remove the tool rest and use 60-, 80-, 120- and finally 180- or 220-grit paper. To sand large-diameter work, run the lathe at slow speed; for small-diameter work, run it at faster speed. Separate the work and sand the glue off the foot. If desired, shape a base or foot with a chisel.

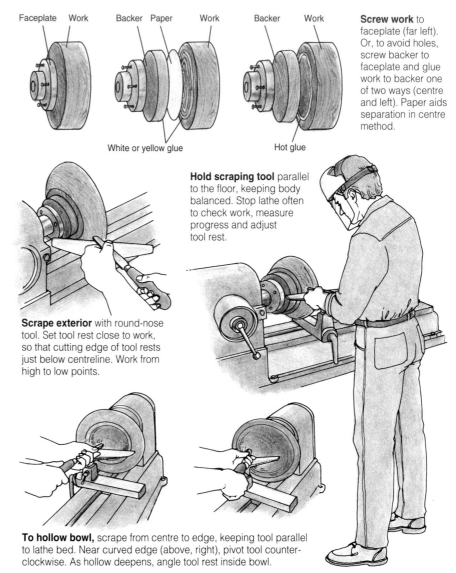

Faceplate Work   Backer Paper   Work   Backer   Work

White or yellow glue   Hot glue

Screw work to faceplate (far left). Or, to avoid holes, screw backer to faceplate and glue work to backer one of two ways (centre and left). Paper aids separation in centre method.

Scrape exterior with round-nose tool. Set tool rest close to work, so that cutting edge of tool rests just below centreline. Work from high to low points.

Hold scraping tool parallel to the floor, keeping body balanced. Stop lathe often to check work, measure progress and adjust tool rest.

To hollow bowl, scrape from centre to edge, keeping tool parallel to lathe bed. Near curved edge (above, right), pivot tool counterclockwise. As hollow deepens, angle tool rest inside bowl.

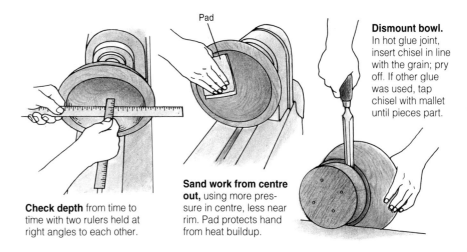

Pad

Check depth from time to time with two rulers held at right angles to each other.

Sand work from centre out, using more pressure in centre, less near rim. Pad protects hand from heat buildup.

Dismount bowl. In hot glue joint, insert chisel in line with the grain; pry off. If other glue was used, tap chisel with mallet until pieces part.

JOINTS: AN INTRODUCTION

A woodworking project is only as strong as the joints used to build it. Hundreds of joints have been developed, most derived from six groups (see chart). The dovetail, for example, can be made with visible pins and tails (through dovetail) or varied so the pins and tails are half visible (half blind) or fully hidden (blind). Tenons are often mitred when they meet in a mortise, as in a table leg, or are wedged for strength.

How do you pick the best joint for the job? Strength is a major consideration, but appearance, your expertise and the tools you own are important factors as well. Cutting a joint without the right tools and skills is risky – loose-fitting joints will have a poor glue bond; overtight joints will have to be forced together, which can damage the wood fibres and split one of the pieces of the joint. As a general rule, select the least complex joint that will work for the project.

The strength of a joint depends on the amount of gluing surface the joint provides and on whether that surface is long grain (parallel to the wood fibres) or end grain (across the fibres). Long grain holds the glue on the surface for a strong bond; end grain absorbs it, resulting in poor adhesion. The strongest joints interlock, such as dovetail pins and tails, or have maximum long-grain to long-grain gluing surfaces and minimum end-grain surfaces, such as edge joints. Joints that mate end-grain surfaces, such as butt joints, usually are reinforced with nails, screws, splines or wooden biscuits. These devices can be used to reinforce other joints as well.

Common joints

Type		Tools to use	Uses	Strength	Ease of making
Butt and edge		Tenon or cross-cut saw; table, circular or radial arm saw. Finish edge joints with plane or jointer	Butt: rough carpentry	Butt: weak; reinforce with fasteners	Butt: very easy
			Edge: large surfaces	Edge: strong	Edge: cuts must be accurate, edges straight and smooth
Face and edge mitres		Mitre box, tenon saw and plane; power mitre saw; table saw	Frames and mouldings	Weak, strengthen with dowels, keys, or splines	Difficult to cut accurately with hand tools; easier with power saw
Lap		Tenon saw and chisel; router; radial arm saw; table saw with dado head	Frames, frame-and-panel doors and interlocking grid construction	Fairly strong	Easy
Interlocking joints: dovetail, finger		Bowsaw or dovetail saw and chisel; router with template; table saw	Drawers, cabinets and boxes	Extremely strong when cut by hand; strong when cut by machine	Difficult with hand tools; easier with power tools
Grooved joints: rebate, groove, rebate-and-groove, tongue-and-groove		Tenon saw and chisel; router; radial arm saw; table saw with dado head	Drawers, cabinets, boxes and shelves	Rebate: fairly strong	Rebate: fairly easy
				Groove: weak	Groove: easy
				Tongue-and-groove: strong	Tongue-and-groove: fairly easy
Mortise-and-tenon		Hand drill and chisel; router; drill press; table saw	Frames and legs for tables and chairs, frame-and-panel cabinets	Strong	Fairly difficult with hand tools; easier with power tools

Although wide surfaces in cabinetry are often veneer-covered plywood, some fine table- or desktop projects may call for solid boards joined edge to edge. Because edge joints have plenty of gluing surface and no porous end grain, they may be assembled with glue alone. To help align the boards, you may use dowels, biscuits or splines. For a precise joint – critical to strength – the mating edges must be smooth, straight and squared to the faces. Before gluing, dry-clamp the assembly to locate any gaps. Sight along the joints with a lamp shining behind the work; mark high spots (where no light shows through), plane them and recheck.

When gluing, tighten the clamps enough so that the glue oozes beads, but don't overtighten – this will squeeze out too much glue. To keep excess glue from adhering to the straightedges or reacting with the metal clamps, put a layer of wax paper or plastic wrap wherever they touch.

Butt and mitre joints, even when precisely cut, are inherently weak because of the smaller gluing surface and the presence of end grain, which doesn't accept glue well. These joints need reinforcement with mechanical fasteners (nails or screws), dowels, wooden biscuits, keys, splines or glue blocks (blocks glued and nailed or screwed to the inside corners of joints). Although visible nails and screws are fine on rough cabinets and shelves, more refined work calls for countersunk or counterbored screws and filled nail holes (p 150).

Dowels can be either blind (hidden) or through (ends exposed). A doweling jig aids in drilling perfectly aligned holes to the proper depth, or you can use a home-made guide.

Oval-shaped biscuits are an easy alternative. To install them, you need a machine known as a biscuit or plate joiner. Biscuits, made from textured compressed wood, absorb the glue and expand, creating a very strong joint. They come in three sizes – choose the largest that will work with your stock. Biscuits are not recommended for joining warped or bowed plywood panels; use dowels or splines instead.

Caution: Never use a biscuit joiner freehand. Clamp the work, and butt the machine against the work or a stop block. Watch for kickback and keep your fingers away. (For more on mitre joints, see pp 133, 149 and 158–159.)

Blind-dowel butt joint

Pre-cut flutes (or a hand-sawn kerf) along dowel length allow excess glue to escape. Drill holes 1 to 2 mm deeper than dowel to contain excess glue. Chamfer ends for easy driving.

Pre-assemble frame. Mark dowel positions on faces. Square marks to mating surfaces.

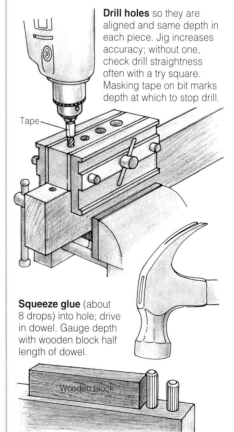

Drill holes so they are aligned and same depth in each piece. Jig increases accuracy; without one, check drill straightness often with a try square. Masking tape on bit marks depth at which to stop drill.

Tape

Squeeze glue (about 8 drops) into hole; drive in dowel. Gauge depth with wooden block half length of dowel.

Wooden block

Making an edge joint

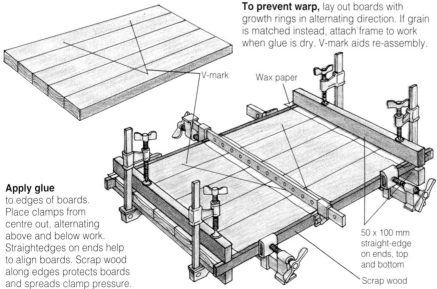

V-mark

To prevent warp, lay out boards with growth rings in alternating direction. If grain is matched instead, attach frame to work when glue is dry. V-mark aids re-assembly.

Wax paper

Apply glue to edges of boards. Place clamps from centre out, alternating above and below work. Straightedges on ends help to align boards. Scrap wood along edges protects boards and spreads clamp pressure.

50 x 100 mm straight-edge on ends, top and bottom

Scrap wood

Making biscuit joints

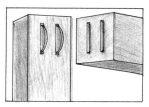

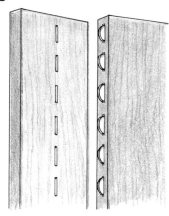

Wooden biscuits can substitute for nails, screws or dowels in butt joints and can be used instead of mortise-and-tenon joints (though they're not as strong) or splines. Wood must be wider than the length of the smallest biscuit slot. Some angle grinders will take a biscuit-joiner attachment.

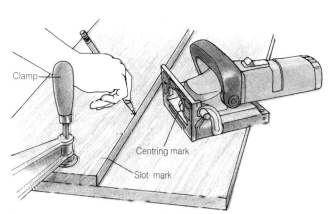

To measure and mark, clamp mating boards together. Mark slots for biscuits in both pieces, using centring mark on biscuit joiner. In butt joints, the closer the slots, the stronger the joint (strengthen frame construction by using two biscuits equally spaced on centre).

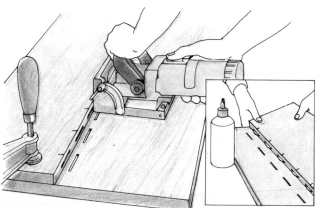

To cut, align centring mark on joiner base with pencil mark, and plunge in the blade; when it springs back, go to next mark. For slots in bottom piece, position joiner vertically with its base against edge of mating board.

Put glue in slots with applicator or thin wood scrap; insert biscuits. Clamp joint until biscuits swell from glue moisture, at least 10 minutes.

Strengthening mitre joints

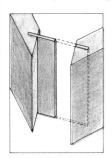

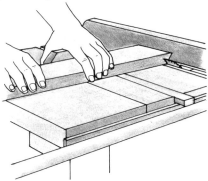

Edge mitre joint (p 159) is stronger with spline placed closer to inner corner. Spline is cut from plywood or hardwood scrap.

To cut spline slots, tilt the table saw blade 45°. Hold the work securely against the mitre gauge with one hand; press it against rip fence with the other.

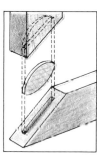

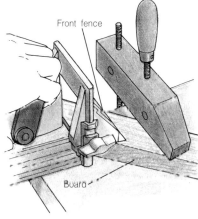

Face mitre has biscuit located at 90° angle to mitre cut.

To cut slot in end grain, place biscuit joiner against mitre cut on board, and lock front fence into place. Clamp the work securely so that it won't shift.

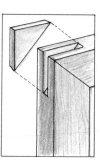

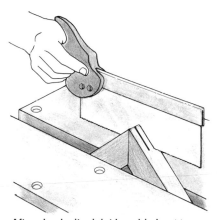

Mitre key (triangle of wood) is one-third thickness of joint but may be as thin as 2,5 mm.

After glued mitre joint has dried, cut two parallel slots into corner with dovetail saw. Chisel out waste and test-fit key. Apply glue to key and tap in with hammer. Let dry, saw key flush, and plane smooth.

LAP JOINTS

Easy to cut but somewhat weak, lap joints connect two boards at an angle, usually at 90°. *End lap joints,* at the ends of boards, are made with wide, flat cuts. *Cross lap joints,* formed by two notches, join boards at any point between the ends. A third type, called a *middle lap,* has an end lap and an intersecting cross lap and forms a T-shape. Middle laps that have to endure tensile (pulling) stress are best dovetailed.

You can make a lap joint with boards of equal or of unequal thickness. With equally thick boards, cut half their thickness; otherwise, cut no more than half the thickness of the thinner piece. Because the grains of the pieces cross, keep the lap width under 100 mm, or the wood may split when it shrinks and swells as its moisture content changes. Mark the cutting lines on the board edges with a square or

a marking gauge. Mark the shoulders of the dovetail lap with a square; use a marking gauge on the cheek. With a T-bevel, mark the dovetail angle between 8° and 12° (a 1:5 to 1:8 ratio of flare to length).

Although end laps are most easily cut with a table saw equipped with a dado head, you can make repeated cuts with a standard blade or use hand tools. After marking the joint on the wood, saw the shoulder (cross-grain cut) with a dovetail saw; then remove the waste by turning the piece on end and sawing along the grain with the same saw. To cut accurate cross laps, first score the shoulder lines on the waste side with a wide chisel held vertically. Then, with the chisel held bevel-up at an angle, remove a sliver on the waste side of the line to form a groove in which to start the saw cut.

End lap joint

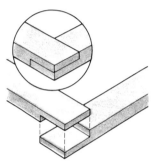
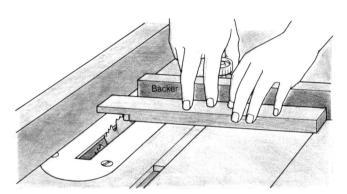

Set height of standard blade using mark on board edge as reference. Screw backer to mitre gauge to prevent tearout as blade exits. Fine-tune depth of cut on scrap. Start at end and work toward shoulder, overlapping passes. Pare rough cut with chisel. You can also use a dado head (p 144), or make an initial shoulder cut with a standard blade, then clamp work in tenoning jig (p 147) and remove waste.

Cross lap joint

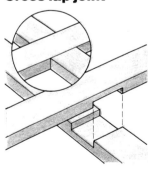
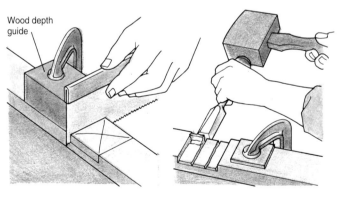

Wood depth guide

For straight cut when cutting sides of notch, press saw against wood depth guide, which should be just thick enough so that the rib atop the saw hits the guide when cut is right depth. Make a cut at each side, then score the waste at 20 mm intervals with dovetail saw. Remove waste with a mallet and chisel, held bevel-up and working from edges toward centre. Trim corners with chisel held bevel-down.

Dovetail lap joint

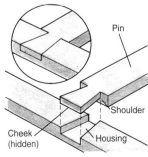

Pin

Shoulder

Cheek (hidden)

Housing

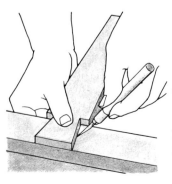
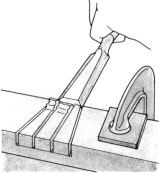

Mark pin's shoulders, cheek and dovetail angle. Saw dovetail shoulders, cheek and angle, in that order, with dovetail saw. For an accurate fit, use the finished dovetail as the template to mark the housing on mating piece. Saw and chisel the housing as you did for the cross lap joint.

DOVETAILS WITH A TEMPLATE

These decorative joints are fairly easy to cut with a router and a dovetail fixture. The fixture holds a template and has bar clamps and stop screws to hold both sides of the joint in proper alignment. The router, fitted with a dovetail bit and a guide bushing, follows the template, cutting the tails and the sockets simultaneously. For bits up to 12 mm in diameter, the bushing should have a diameter 1,6 mm greater.

Make a few test cuts in scrap wood of the same width and thickness as the workpieces. Place each board in the fixture so it butts against its stop screw and is flush with the mating piece (see illustration below). Make the initial shoulder cut in the tail board, guiding the bit along the tips of the template fingers. Advance the router from left to right with slow, steady pressure. Next, guide the bit in and out of the template's fingers, cutting deep into the recesses of the template. Make a second pass from right to left. Test-fit the joint. If the fit is loose, increase the bit's depth of cut. If it's too tight, decrease the depth of cut. If the tails don't fit all the way into the sockets, move the template back slightly. If the tails are too deep in the sockets, slide the template forward.

Once the test joint fits perfectly, you're ready to cut the actual workpieces. If you are making a drawer or box, mark a

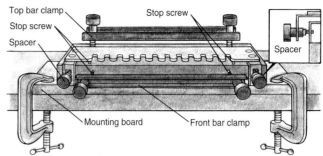

Dovetail fixture. Bar clamps hold two workpieces at right angle to each other. Stop screws establish the proper offset. Spacers hold template; adjust them up and down, forward and back, to correct depth of cut.

letter on the inside surface of all four pieces; mark each bottom edge. Cut the grooves for the bottom panel before routing the dovetails. When clamping the pieces in the fixture, always place the boards with the same edge (either bottom or top) butted against the stop screws, lettered surface facing out. Note that two joints must be cut on the right side of the fixture and two on the left side (see chart). The socket pieces (front part A and back part C) are always clamped to the top of the fixture, the tail pieces (side pieces B and D) to the front.

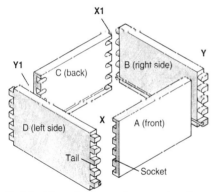

Mark inside surfaces near bottom edge. Cut grooves for bottom piece before routing X- and Y-joints. Front and back pieces have blind dovetail sockets; sides have through tails.

Setting up the workpieces

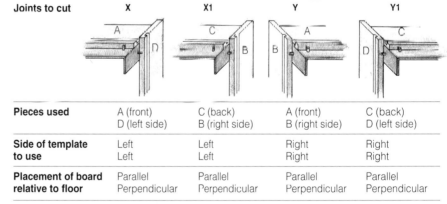

Joints to cut	X	X1	Y	Y1
Pieces used	A (front) D (left side)	C (back) B (right side)	A (front) B (right side)	C (back) D (left side)
Side of template to use	Left Left	Left Left	Right Right	Right Right
Placement of board relative to floor	Parallel Perpendicular	Parallel Perpendicular	Parallel Perpendicular	Parallel Perpendicular

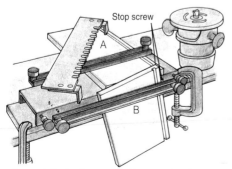

Set up joint Y. Clamp side B as a guide for front piece A. Butt A against side B and top right stop screw. Re-position B flush with top edge of A and bottom right stop screw.

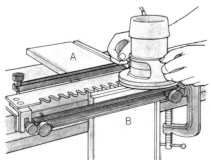

Make the first pass from left to right across tips of template's fingers. This shallow groove helps prevent splintering when the pins and sockets are cut.

Rout tails and sockets, advancing the router from left to right. Keep bushing that guides bit in contact with template at all times. Make another final pass from right to left.

HOUSING JOINTS

Housing joints join a board end-on to an upright, giving an accurate assembly with great load-bearing strength. The cut-out groove or housing may continue right across the upright, while the stopped-housing joint, which is concealed on the front, is the better joint for display and cabinet work. The depth of a housing is typically one-third the thickness of the upright. In the case of a stopped-housing, the cut-out usually ends about 18 mm from the front edge of the upright. Both types can be dovetailed by cutting inward-sloping angles on the sides of the housing and on the end edges of the cross-member. Assemble housing joints with glue and nails or screws. Strengthen the joint, if needed, by fastening a hard-wood cleat beneath each end of the cross-member. Glue and

screw the cleats to the cross-members and to the sides or the back of the support pieces or uprights.

Grooves can be made by hand with a router plane or with a tenon saw and chisel. Or you can use a router with a straight bit or a table saw equipped with a standard blade or a dado head. A dado head consists of two outer blades and four inner cutters, known as *chippers*. It cuts a groove in one pass, whereas a standard blade takes several passes.

To set up a dado head, stack as many chippers as needed between the two blades to obtain the desired width of cut. Replace the saw's narrow throat plate – the slotted plate that frames the blade – with a dado-head throat plate, available from the saw manufacturer, or make one as follows from

Through-housing

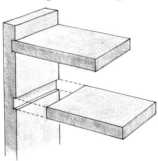

Stopped-housing

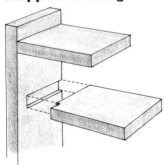

Through-dovetail

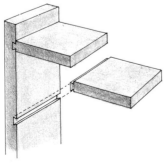

Cutting housings on a table saw

Through-housing. Mark groove width on work (inset). Add extension to mitre gauge. Adjust rip fence so work is desired distance from assembled dado head. Turn on saw; push mitre gauge forward.

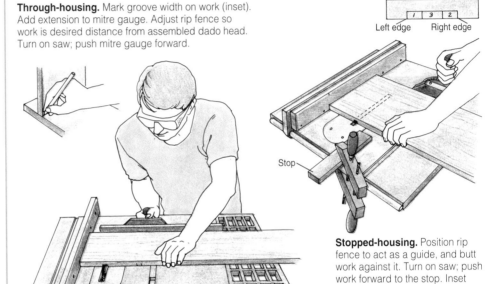

Stop

Throat plate

Stopped-housing. Position rip fence to act as a guide, and butt work against it. Turn on saw; push work forward to the stop. Inset (above) shows sawing order for a standard blade or for wide grooves (as a lap joint) with a dado head.

Through-dovetails with a router

Cutting groove. Guide router against T-square. Remove most of waste with straight bit equal in size to narrowest part of correct dovetail bit. Install dovetail bit; finish groove in one pass.

T-square

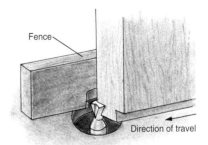

Fence

Direction of travel

Mating dovetail. Mount router in table. Make a wood fence with slot for dovetail bit. Clamp fence to router table. Practise on scrap. Start router, push stock against fence, and move it from right to left. Reverse stock and repeat.

12 mm plywood. Remove the standard plate and install the dado head. Cut a plywood blank to match the outline of the standard plate. Hold the plywood blank on the saw table by placing a board over the blank and clamping it to the front and back edges of the saw table. Be sure that the clamped board is positioned on one side of the blank, not where the dado head will come through. Start the motor, and slowly raise the dado head to cut an opening.

Caution: Never use the chippers by themselves without the outer blades.

Test-cut all grooves in scrap wood. To prevent the saw blade, dado head, or router bit from splintering the workpiece as it exits the cut, back the edge with scrap wood. Cut routed grooves in two or three passes by increasing the depth of cut with each pass. This reduces vibration and chatter of the router bit and produces a cleaner cut. A blind or stopped groove stops short of the board's edge and is hidden from view when assembled. To cut a stopped groove with a router, clamp a stop block to the work and guide the router along the straightedge. If you are using a table saw to cut a stopped groove, guide the work to a stop block that is clamped to the table or to the fence. Square the stopped corners with a chisel. Notch the front corners of the cross-member to fit the stopped end of the groove.

Dovetail or sliding grooves are strong, decorative interlocking joints. This groove, with its angled sides, can be cut with a backsaw or a router fitted with a dovetail bit. When routing a dovetail groove, make the initial cuts with a straight bit. On the last pass, cut the angled shape with a dovetail bit. To rout the mating dovetail ends of the shelves, mount the router in a router table or use a router jig. Practise on scrap wood, test fit the board and re-adjust the bit height or fence.

Rebate joints can be cut with a router or with a table saw and a dado head. (If you prefer hand tools, use a rebate plane or a backsaw and chisel.) Rout rebates with either a straight bit or a piloted bit. With a straight bit, you must use either an edge guide or a straightedge to control the cut.

Rebate joints

Single   Double

Piloted rebating bit has ball bearing that rolls against workpiece edge to control the width of rebate. No straight-edge guide is needed. For greater control, pull router toward you and always travel left to right.

Edge guide attachment allows you to rout rebates with straight bit. Guide fastens to router's base and rides against edge of workpiece.

Groove-and-rebate joints

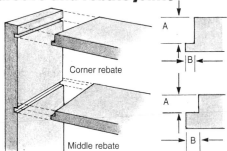

A
B

Corner rebate

A
B

Middle rebate

Corner rebate's depth (A), is ¾ thickness of rebated board; width (B) is ¼ thickness of grooved board. In a middle rebate, A can equal ½ to ⅔ thickness of the rebated board, and B is ⅓ thickness of grooved board.

T-square

Rout multiple joints side by side. Clamp squared boards and T-square securely to work surface. Test cut on scrap first. Shoulder plane (below) trims rebate if fit is too tight.

Through mortise-and-tenon

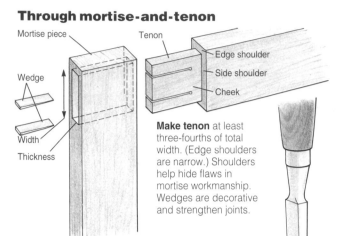

Mortise piece

Wedge

Width

Thickness

Tenon

Edge shoulder

Side shoulder

Cheek

Make tenon at least three-fourths of total width. (Edge shoulders are narrow.) Shoulders help hide flaws in mortise workmanship. Wedges are decorative and strengthen joints.

1. Set mortise gauge pins to mortise thickness. Adjust gauge fence to scribe lines centred on stock. Select mortise chisel, needed for squaring ends, 2 mm narrower than mortise thickness.

Fence

In these strong framework joints, the projecting piece, or tenon, should fit snugly into the opening, or mortise. A tight fit allows the large amount of long-grain glue surface on both pieces to adhere well. On wide stock, maximize the long-grain glue surface by spacing multiple mortises and tenons evenly across the board (facing page).

Mortise-and-tenon joints may be through or hidden (blind or stub), and each kind can have from one to four shoulders. Rounding the tenon profile with a file, a rasp or a router makes a more decorative but slightly weaker through joint. On wide boards you can make multiple rounded joints by using a jig and a router.

The size of the stock determines the dimensions of the joint. On pieces of equal thickness, the mortise and each side shoulder of the tenon usually equals one-third the thickness of the stock. A larger mortise piece (as in a table leg) can take a thicker tenon. The edge shoulders of a three- or four-shouldered tenon vary from a few millimetres to one-quarter the width of the tenon piece. When marking several mortise-and-tenon joints, always orient the mortise gauge fence against the equivalent stock face. If a piece is to have a tenon on both ends, calculate the distance between the two joints by measuring between the length lines (step 5).

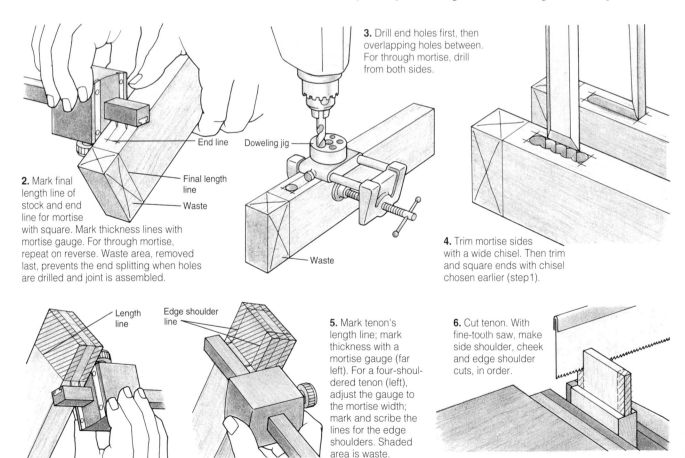

End line

2. Mark final length line of stock and end line for mortise with square. Mark thickness lines with mortise gauge. For through mortise, repeat on reverse. Waste area, removed last, prevents the end splitting when holes are drilled and joint is assembled.

Final length line

Waste

Doweling jig

Waste

3. Drill end holes first, then overlapping holes between. For through mortise, drill from both sides.

4. Trim mortise sides with a wide chisel. Then trim and square ends with chisel chosen earlier (step 1).

Length line

Edge shoulder line

5. Mark tenon's length line; mark thickness with a mortise gauge (far left). For a four-shouldered tenon (left), adjust the gauge to the mortise width; mark and scribe the lines for the edge shoulders. Shaded area is waste.

6. Cut tenon. With fine-tooth saw, make side shoulder, cheek and edge shoulder cuts, in order.

First, cut the mortise. Set the mortise gauge pins and mark the thickness of the mortise. (Cut a blind mortise 2 mm deeper than the tenon length to allow for the glue.) Drill the mortise holes on a drill press, or use a doweling jig and a hand drill fitted with a twist bit (its diameter the same as the mortise thickness). Drill a through mortise from both sides to prevent tearout. Mortises can also be made with a plunge router (see illustration) or with a standard router and jig. For a standard router, clamp the mortise piece and jig to a workbench. Tilt the router; begin cutting slightly short of the end of the mortise; remove 3 to 6 mm of stock on each pass. Cut the tenon to fit with a handsaw or power saw.

Wedges inserted into a through tenon (facing page) strengthen the joint. Before gluing, mark two cuts in the tenon's end, drill a 3 mm hole at the base of each cut to prevent splitting, and saw the cuts. Assemble the joint, and tap the wedges into the cuts with a mallet.

The number, width and thickness of multiple mortises and tenons are determined by the size of the tenon piece. To find equal spacing between tenons, as well as the width of the two edge shoulders, measure the width of the tenon piece and decide the number and width of the tenons you want. Add the total tenon width and subtract it from the tenon piece width. Divide remaining space by the number of tenons plus one. For example: four 20 mm-wide tenons will be needed on a 140 mm-wide board. Thus, 4×20 mm = 80 mm; 140 mm – 80 mm = 60 mm; 60 mm ÷ 5 = 12 mm between tenons and 12 mm ÷ 2 = 6 mm per edge shoulder.

Tools that speed the work

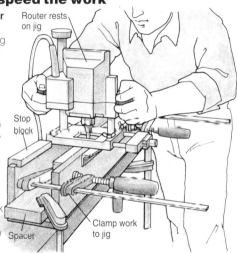

Use plunge router with a straight bit and home-made jig to cut mortise. Jig, a trough made of 20 mm plywood, glue and screws, supports router base. Front and back stops on one side of jig set mortise width. Spacer blocks bring stock to top of jig. Make repeated passes, removing no more than 3 mm of stock per pass. Square rounded ends with a chisel.

Router rests on jig
Stop block
Clamp work to jig
Spacer

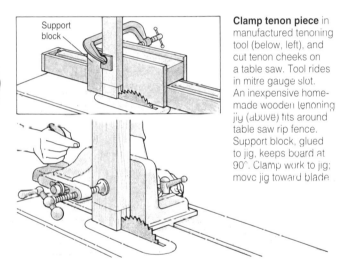

Support block

Clamp tenon piece in manufactured tenoning tool (below, left), and cut tenon cheeks on a table saw. Tool rides in mitre gauge slot. An inexpensive home-made wooden tenoning jig (above) fits around table saw rip fence. Support block, glued to jig, keeps board at 90°. Clamp work to jig; move jig toward blade.

Multiple mortises-and-tenons

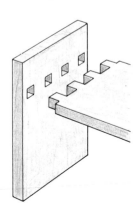

Tenon 'fingers' fit into matching mortises in wide stock. Joint may be hidden (stub or blind) or through.

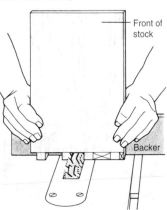

Front of stock
Backer

Cut waste between tenons with a dado head. Support work with backer and mitre gauge. Align cuts visually. To prevent tearout, first scribe depth line on back of stock with knife.

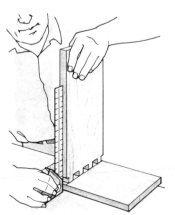

Position and mark mortises using a square and the tenon piece as a template. Scribe and mark waste areas with an X.

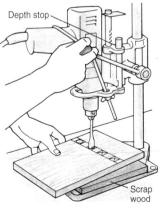

Depth stop
Scrap wood

Drill waste with a drill press and spur bit or brad point bit. Lock depth stop. Clean and square mortises with a chisel slightly narrower than mortise.

GLUING AND CLAMPING

When selecting a glue for a job, ask yourself these questions: What type of materials am I gluing; will the piece be indoors or outdoors; does the glue need to be water-resistant or water-proof; are the joints loose; how much stress will be placed on the glue and the joint? For a repair job, what glue was used before? Use the chart (below) and the container label to help you choose.

Whatever your choice, follow these basic rules: Apply the glue evenly and smoothly on both surfaces. If the end grain of wood is part of the joint, apply two coats. Allow the first to dry before applying the second. Put the project together within the glue's assembly time (how long the glue can be worked and the pieces adjusted). Drying time may be longer if a wood's moisture content is above 10 per cent or the air temperature is below 20°C. Always allow a way for excess glue to escape (for example, by ensuring that the bottom of a blind mortise is deeper than its tenon).

Caution: When using a toxic glue, follow safety precautions on the label carefully. Work in a well-ventilated area and avoid getting glue in your eyes or on your skin. Keep glue well away from any open flame. When using epoxy or contact cement, extinguish pilot lights.

Before applying glue, dry-fit (test-assemble) all joints to make sure they

Gluing

Apply glue to both pieces. Spread evenly with brush. You can spread white or yellow glue with your fingers.

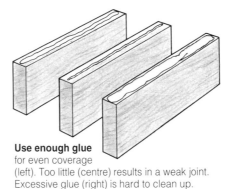

Use enough glue for even coverage (left). Too little (centre) results in a weak joint. Excessive glue (right) is hard to clean up.

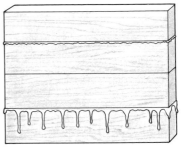

Glue line squeeze-out (top) shows a strong joint. No excess (middle) means a weak joint; too much is messy (bottom).

A glossary of glues

Type of adhesive	Assembly time	Clamping time	Uses	Characteristics	Solvent
White glue (PVA, polyvinyl acetate)	7–10 min	8 hr	Indoor non-stress wood joints; paper, ceramics	Ready-to-use liquid; non-staining, odourless, water-soluble; tends to 'creep' with age; dries clear	Soap and warm water
Yellow glue (carpenter's, aliphatic resin)	7–10 min	1 hr	Indoor furniture and cabinets	Ready-to-use liquid; less brittle than white glue; sands easily; water-soluble; dries clear	Warm water
Polyurethane	15 min	45 min at 20°C	Boat repair, outdoor furniture, shutters and window frames	The slight amount of moisture normally present in wood acts as catalyst. High heat resistance	Cool water before hardening
Epoxy	Follow label instructions	5 min – 12 hr (depending on type of epoxy)	Dissimilar materials (metal to glass); non-porous materials (china); wood	Liquids mixed in equal parts; water- and oilproof; fills holes; doesn't shrink; sands easily; dries clear or brown; toxic (follow cautions on label)	Acetone (in some nail polish removers)
Urea formaldehyde	20–30 min	16–20 hr at 20°C 9–13 hr at 24°C	Indoor and outdoor furniture, cabinets, laminating, veneering	Powder mixed with water; water-resistant; fills poorly; dries light brown; won't cure below 20°C	Soap and warm water before hardening
Polychloroprene (contact glue)	10–20 min	No clamping required	Indoor veneers and decorative work	Instantaneous bonding between many different materials and woods when both surfaces coated and dried	Lacquer thinners
Pearl glue	1 min (when cool)	1 hr	Occasionally used for antique furniture repairs	Granules soaked in water and heated to 55°C in double boiler; water-soluble; fills poorly; incompatible with white or yellow glues	Warm water

fit properly. This allows you to make adjustments for a better fit, to decide on the number and type of clamps needed and to establish the assembly sequence – gluing a piece in place too early can cause others to fit badly or not at all. For example, to assemble a bookcase with grooved sides, place one side with the grooves facing up. Next, insert the shelves in the grooves, check for fit and adjust as needed. Then align the grooves of the other side piece, and

re-adjust if needed. Disassemble, noting the order. In the actual glue-up, follow exactly the same sequence.

When clamping, work on a level surface such as a workbench or, for a large project, the floor. Unless your clamps have covers, their jaws should never touch the work. (Unprotected metal clamps may react with the glue and stain the piece.) Insert plastic wrap or wax paper between the jaws and the work. This prevents the pieces from

adhering to the clamp or to the scrap wood used to spread the pressure.

When workpieces are clamped with the right amount of glue, a small bead of glue will be forced from the joint. Immediately wipe off this excess glue with the correct solvent. This is especially critical because wood-stains and finishes will not penetrate dried glue. Clamping pressure should never be so tight that it forces out most of the glue or deforms the project.

Clamping

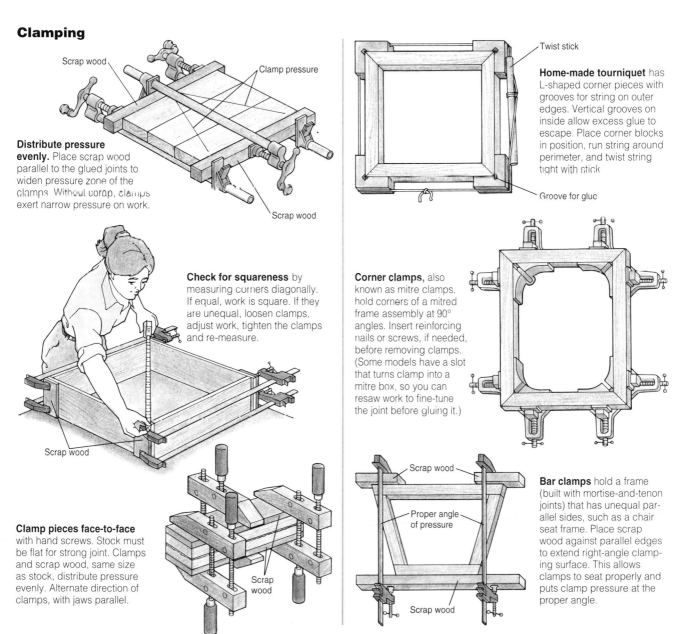

Distribute pressure evenly. Place scrap wood parallel to the glued joints to widen pressure zone of the clamps. Without scrap, clamps exert narrow pressure on work.

Check for squareness by measuring corners diagonally. If equal, work is square. If they are unequal, loosen clamps, adjust work, tighten the clamps and re-measure.

Clamp pieces face-to-face with hand screws. Stock must be flat for strong joint. Clamps and scrap wood, same size as stock, distribute pressure evenly. Alternate direction of clamps, with jaws parallel.

Home-made tourniquet has L-shaped corner pieces with grooves for string on outer edges. Vertical grooves on inside allow excess glue to escape. Place corner blocks in position, run string around perimeter, and twist string tight with stick.

Corner clamps, also known as mitre clamps, hold corners of a mitred frame assembly at 90° angles. Insert reinforcing nails or screws, if needed, before removing clamps. (Some models have a slot that turns clamp into a mitre box, so you can resaw work to fine-tune the joint before gluing it.)

Bar clamps hold a frame (built with mortise-and-tenon joints) that has unequal parallel sides, such as a chair seat frame. Place scrap wood against parallel edges to extend right-angle clamping surface. This allows clamps to seat properly and puts clamp pressure at the proper angle.

FASTENING WITH NAILS, SCREWS AND BOLTS

Holes for screws are usually perpendicular to the stock. A drill press does the job for you, provided its table is level. With a hand or electric drill, use a drill guide or a pre-drilled hardwood block clamped to the stock to keep the bit straight. When drilling at an angle, mark the starting point with a centre punch and start the hole with a smaller bit to keep the final bit from drifting.

Pilot holes, drilled slightly narrower than the diameter of the threads, allow screws and bolts to enter straight and easily. Control the hole depth with a drill stop, a depth gauge or a piece of tape wrapped around the bit. To prevent tearout on through holes, drill from both sides or drill into a scrap block clamped to the back of the stock.

Screws and bolt heads may be flush with a surface or they may be recessed. If desired, fill the recess with a plug or with wood filler.

Drive screws with a screwdriver tip the same width as the screw's slot; one too wide gouges the stock, too narrow damages the screwhead. To drive a nail into hardwood, first drill a pilot hole slightly narrower and shorter than the nail. Strike the nail squarely; at the end of the blow, slide the hammer forward or backward to emphasize the level position of the hammer. This lessens the chance of bending the nail.

To remove a bent nail, use a claw hammer or a nail puller. Avoid marring the surface by placing a small piece of scrap wood or metal between the tool and the stock. Grasp headless and finishing nails with end-cutting pliers and pull them straight out, wiggling them a little if necessary.

Installing screws and bolts

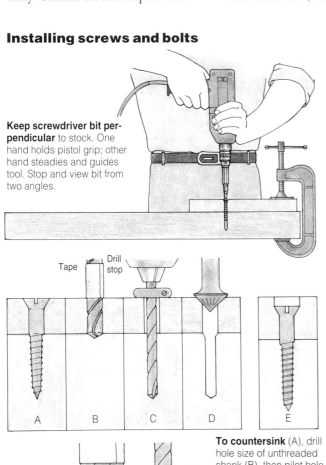

Keep screwdriver bit perpendicular to stock. One hand holds pistol grip; other hand steadies and guides tool. Stop and view bit from two angles.

Tape

Drill stop

A B C D E

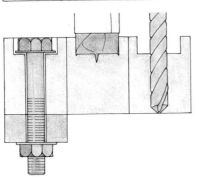

To countersink (A), drill hole size of unthreaded shank (B), then pilot hole the diameter of shank minus threads (C). Finish with countersink bit (D). To drill a counterbored hole (E), first drill recess, then follow countersink steps. To save time, use a combination bit.
For bolts (left), first drill recess the diameter of the washer.

Nailing techniques

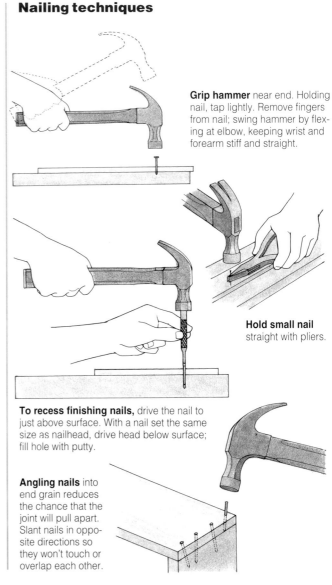

Grip hammer near end. Holding nail, tap lightly. Remove fingers from nail; swing hammer by flexing at elbow, keeping wrist and forearm stiff and straight.

Hold small nail straight with pliers.

To recess finishing nails, drive the nail to just above surface. With a nail set the same size as nailhead, drive head below surface; fill hole with putty.

Angling nails into end grain reduces the chance that the joint will pull apart. Slant nails in opposite directions so they won't touch or overlap each other.

HINGES

The style and position of the hinge knuckle determine the swing action of a hinge. For a simple hinge with two equal leaves, place the knuckle at the intersection of the two pieces. To mark for a mortise, measure the width of the leaf to the centre of the hinge knuckle with a marking gauge. If you are making many mortises of the same size, consider buying or making a jig that you can use with a router.

A drop-leaf table, hinged with one long and one short hinge leaf, has a recess chiselled into the mortise under the tabletop to hold the hinge knuckle. Before mounting a drop-leaf hinge, make a rule joint by routing the mating tabletop and leaf edges with matching cove and rounding-over bits.

On typical house doors, hinges spaced unevenly look even at eye level. Put the lower hinge farther from the bottom of the door than the upper hinge is from the top; place the middle hinge, if any, slightly above the halfway point between the others.

Mortising with a router

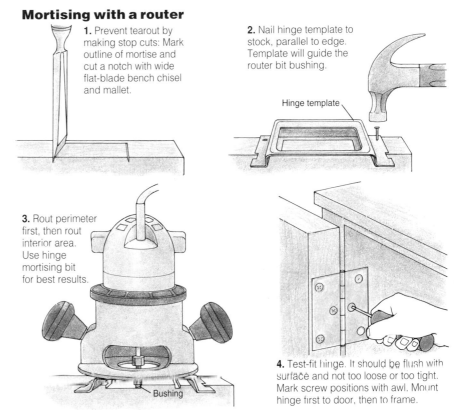

1. Prevent tearout by making stop cuts: Mark outline of mortise and cut a notch with wide flat-blade bench chisel and mallet.

2. Nail hinge template to stock, parallel to edge. Template will guide the router bit bushing.

Hinge template

3. Rout perimeter first, then rout interior area. Use hinge mortising bit for best results.

Bushing

4. Test-fit hinge. It should be flush with surface and not too loose or too tight. Mark screw positions with awl. Mount hinge first to door, then to frame.

Setting a drop-leaf hinge

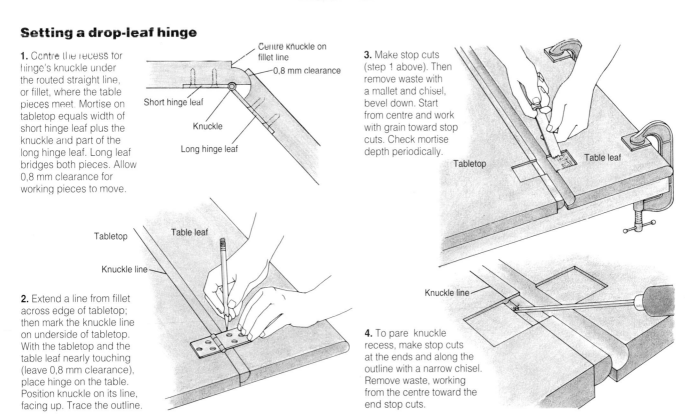

1. Centre the recess for hinge's knuckle under the routed straight line, or fillet, where the table pieces meet. Mortise on tabletop equals width of short hinge leaf plus the knuckle and part of the long hinge leaf. Long leaf bridges both pieces. Allow 0,8 mm clearance for working pieces to move.

Centre knuckle on fillet line
0,8 mm clearance
Short hinge leaf
Knuckle
Long hinge leaf

Tabletop
Table leaf
Knuckle line

2. Extend a line from fillet across edge of tabletop; then mark the knuckle line on underside of tabletop. With the tabletop and the table leaf nearly touching (leave 0,8 mm clearance), place hinge on the table. Position knuckle on its line, facing up. Trace the outline.

3. Make stop cuts (step 1 above). Then remove waste with a mallet and chisel, bevel down. Start from centre and work with grain toward stop cuts. Check mortise depth periodically.

Tabletop
Table leaf

Knuckle line

4. To pare knuckle recess, make stop cuts at the ends and along the outline with a narrow chisel. Remove waste, working from the centre toward the end stop cuts.

Thin layers or laminations of real wood, called *plies,* are glued together to make the sheet material known as plywood. The three grades of plywood available in South Africa are interior, exterior and marine. Although interior plywood is almost as strong as exterior, the plies will separate if it is soaked. Marine plywood is strong enough and flexible enough to be used for boatbuilding. All types of plywood should be finish-sealed with paint or varnish.

Plywood's large (2,44 × 1,22 m) sheets have advantages over solid wood. The sheets are strong and relatively stable. You can get wide expanses, as for a door or a tabletop, without edge joints. However, its size makes it awkward to transport, handle and store. When storing, avoid damp areas that will damage plywood fibres and cause warping.

The secret of plywood's strength and stability lies in the

Face / Veneer core / Back

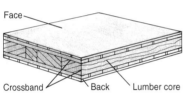

Face / Crossband / Back / Lumber core

crisscross layering of the plies. The centre ply, or *core,* varies in thickness according to the type of plywood and may be sandwiched between *crossband* layers. The outer plies are the *faces* or, if not of equal quality, the *face* and the *back*. If the outer layers are thin and you must hand-sand them, use very fine grit paper.

When sawed, plywood splinters where the saw exits. To avoid splintering the good face, place it up when cutting with a table saw, down when using a circular saw. With handsaws, use a plywood or tenon saw and work with the good face up.

When joining plywood, choose joints that cover the edge. Tongue-and-groove (facing page), multiple mortise-and-tenon (p 147), router dovetail (p 143), biscuit and dowel joints (pp 140–141) work well. Nails and screws fasten plywood to solid wood or to another piece of plywood. In some cases a combination of nails or screws and glue is necessary. Plywood resists splitting, so nails and screws can be placed close together and close (3 mm) to the edges of sheets on the face and back. Screws driven into plywood edges will split the layers apart. However, knock-down fittings, such as cross dowels (facing page), create a strong interlocking joint and allow for easy disassembly (and reassembly) of a project. For hinges, choose a wrap-around style that allows screws in the edge and the face of the plywood piece.

Cover exposed plywood edges with moulding or with veneer tape that matches the plywood's face. Depending on the type of tape you buy, apply it with glue, iron it on or peel and stick it on. For edges that will get hard use, such as a tabletop, choose solid wood moulding.

2nd cut

1st cut

Lay out project pieces on plywood sheet, being careful to avoid odd grain patterns and awkward, unnecessary cuts. Allow for power saw blade kerf (3 mm). Make all lengthwise cuts first for easier handling of large sheet. Measure again after each cut.

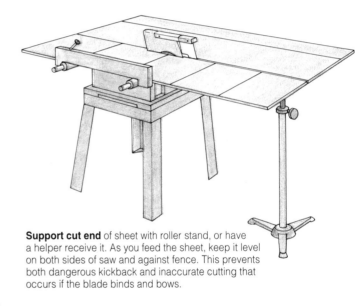

Support cut end of sheet with roller stand, or have a helper receive it. As you feed the sheet, keep it level on both sides of saw and against fence. This prevents both dangerous kickback and inaccurate cutting that occurs if the blade binds and bows.

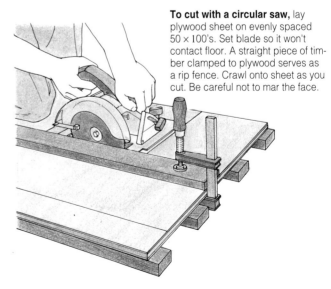

To cut with a circular saw, lay plywood sheet on evenly spaced 50 × 100's. Set blade so it won't contact floor. A straight piece of timber clamped to plywood serves as a rip fence. Crawl onto sheet as you cut. Be careful not to mar the face.

Plywood joints

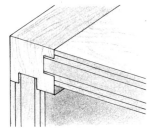

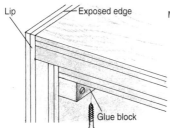

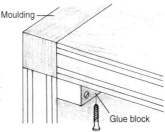

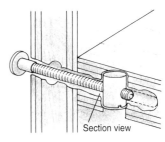

Tongue-and-groove joint is strong. Tongue is one-third stock thickness and should fit snugly into the groove. Corner piece hides plywood ends.

Double rebate joint. A lip of face veneer and crossband in side piece covers mating piece's edge. Add glue blocks; cover exposed edge with veneer tape.

Hide plywood edges with moulding. Align moulding and plywood with wood biscuits or dowels (pp 140–141), then glue. Glue blocks add more strength.

Cross dowel. Drill bolt's countersink and shank holes, then intersecting dowel hole. Insert dowel; align its opening with screwdriver. Slide bolt into hole through dowel.

Edge treatments

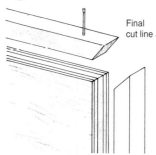

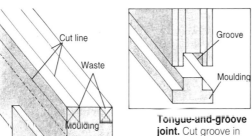

Cover edges with plain or decorative moulding. Measure and mitre corners carefully. Attach with glue and finishing nails. To prevent hardwood moulding from splitting, drill pilot holes for nails.

Tongue-and-groove joint. Cut groove in plywood edge, using router and straight bit or slotting cutter. On table saw use a standard blade or dado head. Next rout, saw or plane tongue on moulding.

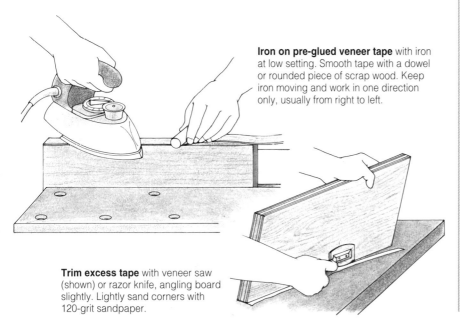

Iron on pre-glued veneer tape with iron at low setting. Smooth tape with a dowel or rounded piece of scrap wood. Keep iron moving and work in one direction only, usually from right to left.

Trim excess tape with veneer saw (shown) or razor knife, angling board slightly. Lightly sand corners with 120-grit sandpaper.

Frame and panel

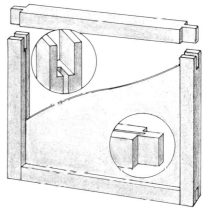

Bridle, or slip, joint is U-shaped mortise and two-shouldered tenon. Cut panel groove in each frame piece first (same thickness as plywood, usually 6 to 9,5 mm). Extend groove into tenon to accept panel corners. Cut mortise (below); then cut tenon to fit (pp 146–147).

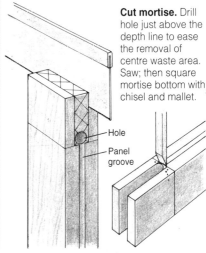

Cut mortise. Drill hole just above the depth line to ease the removal of centre waste area. Saw; then square mortise bottom with chisel and mallet.

Hole

Panel groove

Plain or fancy, a cabinet is basically a box. Large cabinets often consist of a solid wooden frame supporting either processed or solid wooden panels. Smaller boxes don't require the support of a frame.

The easiest drawer to fit in a cabinet is an overlay drawer, which has a front face that covers part of the cabinet frame. More challenging to build is the flush drawer, which fits within its opening. (Options for cabinet door styles are similar to those for drawers. If the piece has both doors and drawers, make them in the same style.)

To make a drawer, rout grooves along the bottom edges of the drawer front and sides to accept a thin plywood or hardboard bottom panel. (The back is narrow and rests on top of the bottom panel, so it needs no groove.) Cut grooves for the back in the side pieces and construct two dovetail, finger, or tongue-and-groove joints for the front corners. Next assemble the front, sides and back. Slide the bottom panel into its grooves from the back (this helps square the box) and nail or screw the bottom to the back.

Shelves, if they are adjustable, rest on clips inserted into the holes of a metal track (above, right) or on wooden dowels or metal pins inserted into holes drilled in the cabinet sides. Fixed shelves can slot into grooves.

Doors may be of solid plywood or *frame-and-panel* construction – a solid wooden frame around a panel of plywood or solid wood. The frame is joined with mortise-and-tenon, mitred spline or stile joints (facing page).

Tables, chairs, beds and the bases of some cabinets use *leg-and-rail* construction, made usually with dowel or mortise-and-tenon joints. Tenons can be either stub (at least 25 mm long) or mitred to avoid meeting within the leg. To reinforce leg-and-rail joints, fasten blocks with screws (right).

For more on joints, see pp 139–147; on hinges, p 151; on frames and panels, p 153; on plywood, pp 152–153; on building boxes, pp 143 and 149.

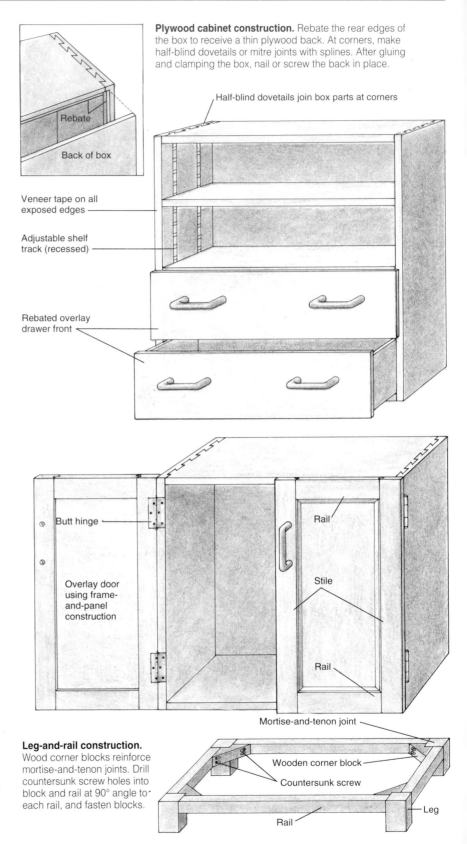

Plywood cabinet construction. Rebate the rear edges of the box to receive a thin plywood back. At corners, make half-blind dovetails or mitre joints with splines. After gluing and clamping the box, nail or screw the back in place.

Rebate

Back of box

Half-blind dovetails join box parts at corners

Veneer tape on all exposed edges

Adjustable shelf track (recessed)

Rebated overlay drawer front

Butt hinge

Overlay door using frame-and-panel construction

Rail

Stile

Rail

Mortise-and-tenon joint

Leg-and-rail construction. Wood corner blocks reinforce mortise-and-tenon joints. Drill countersunk screw holes into block and rail at 90° angle to each rail, and fasten blocks.

Wooden corner block

Countersunk screw

Leg

Rail

Drawers and supports

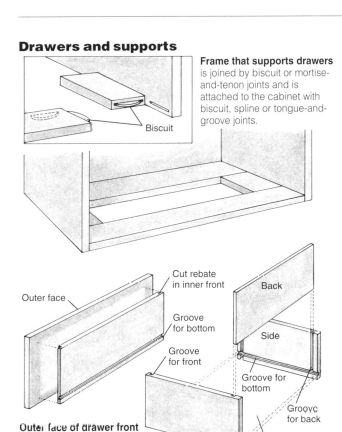

Biscuit

Outer face

Cut rebate
in inner front

Back

Groove
for bottom

Side

Groove
for front

Groove for
bottom

Groove
for back

Bottom

Frame that supports drawers is joined by biscuit or mortise-and-tenon joints and is attached to the cabinet with biscuit, spline or tongue-and-groove joints.

Outer face of drawer front overlays frame. Lay out and cut rebates on inner front. Join the inner front, sides and back. Check that outer face covers cabinet frame equally on all sides. Glue outer front.

Side-hung drawers ride on matching wooden glides screwed inside the case. Before assembling drawer, rout side grooves. (If grooves end shy of front, they function as a drawer stop.)

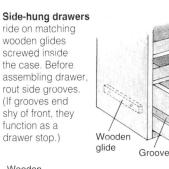

Wooden
glide

Groove

Centre-guide drawers have a grooved wooden slide mounted on the drawer bottom. The slide runs on a wooden guide that is attached to the drawer frame inside the cabinet.

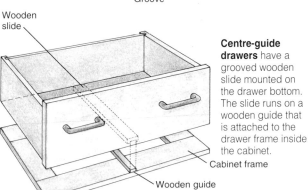

Wooden
slide

Cabinet frame

Wooden guide

Frame-and-panel construction

Rout stile joints with a matched pair of bits called stile and rail cutters. Mount the router upside down in a router table. On the four inner frame edges, cut grooves for the panel with a beading (moulding) stile bit (A); change to a beading rail bit; then cut rail ends (B) to fit stile moulding.

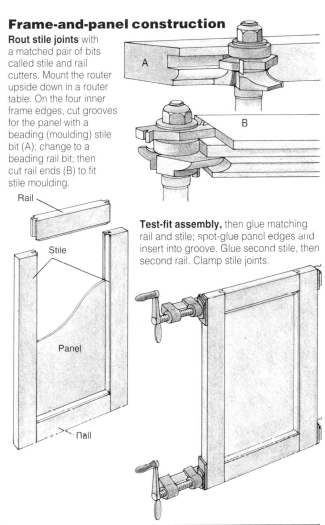

A

B

Rail

Stile

Panel

Nail

Test-fit assembly, then glue matching rail and stile; spot-glue panel edges and insert into groove. Glue second stile, then second rail. Clamp stile joints.

Building a table

Support solid wooden top with slotted metal brackets which let screws move with wood. For maximum length and strength, mitre tenon ends (inset); allow 1,5 mm gap for glue pocket.

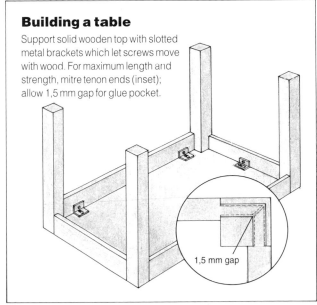

1,5 mm gap

MOULDINGS

Install moulding to create an attractive, finished look and to hide flawed joints where walls meet floors, ceilings, and door and window frames. Moulding protects vulnerable edges, holds window sashes in place, stops the swing of a door in its frame, and sheds water away from the top of a window.

Carefully select mouldings that are to be joined. Every mill makes different profiles, and slight variations occur even in the same profile from the same mill. Make sure that every piece you buy is consistent from end to end and that the profiles of pieces to be used in the same project are matched. Most mouldings come in standard lengths of 1,8 m, 2,4 m and 3 m. You can buy mouldings with 'standard' profiles in knot-free grades of South African pine, Oregon pine, meranti and oak ; you can order them in other woods.

Pre-finished mouldings are available in wood to match panelling and in foam, rigid plastic or veneered wood. Order custom mouldings through your timber supplier, or make them to your own designs with a router.

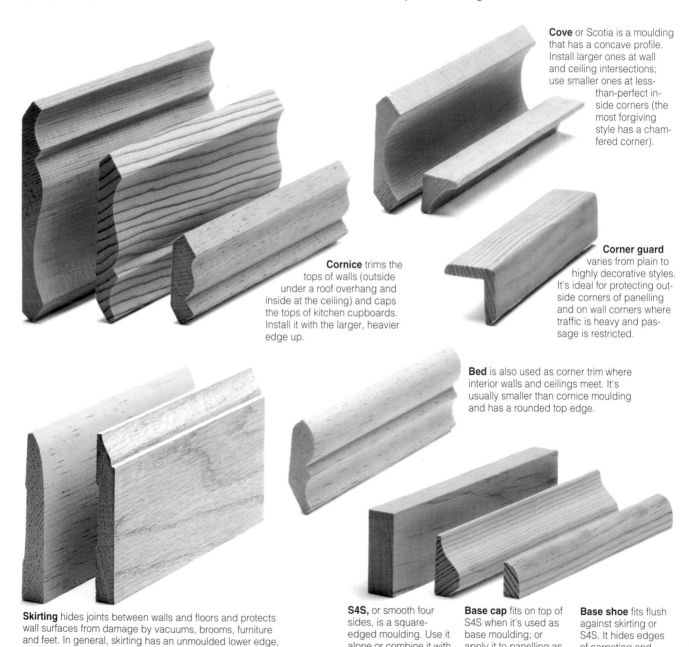

Cove or Scotia is a moulding that has a concave profile. Install larger ones at wall and ceiling intersections; use smaller ones at less-than-perfect inside corners (the most forgiving style has a chamfered corner).

Cornice trims the tops of walls (outside under a roof overhang and inside at the ceiling) and caps the tops of kitchen cupboards. Install it with the larger, heavier edge up.

Corner guard varies from plain to highly decorative styles. It's ideal for protecting outside corners of panelling and on wall corners where traffic is heavy and passage is restricted.

Bed is also used as corner trim where interior walls and ceilings meet. It's usually smaller than cornice moulding and has a rounded top edge.

Skirting hides joints between walls and floors and protects wall surfaces from damage by vacuums, brooms, furniture and feet. In general, skirting has an unmoulded lower edge, allowing you to add a base shoe. The top is often decorative, making an extra base cap unnecessary.

S4S, or smooth four sides, is a square-edged moulding. Use it alone or combine it with other mouldings to create a decorative look.

Base cap fits on top of S4S when it's used as base moulding; or apply it to panelling as a finishing touch.

Base shoe fits flush against skirting or S4S. It hides edges of carpeting and other flooring.

Quadrant, an easy-to-find moulding, fits into corners. You can also combine it with other mouldings to build a profile.

Half round is ideal for finishing shelf edges. It also adds a decorative element to furniture and as part of a built-up moulding profile such as one that surrounds a fireplace.

Chair rail protects walls against chair backs. It visually lowers wall height and serves as a horizontal dividing line between two surfaces, such as wallcovering and paint.

Picture rail supports paintings and picture frames, which are suspended from it with hooks. The moulding should continue around the room's complete circumference, close to the ceiling.

Wainscot cap or dado rail sits on top of wainscot (wood panelling on the lower portion of a wall). It protects the wood end grains and enhances the overall appearance.

Small moulding adds a finished look to shelves, screens, furniture and frames. Also use it to create built-up moulding profiles.

Plinth block covers exterior window and door frames. The moulding's thickness allows bricks and other types of siding to butt against it.

Architrave for windows and doors covers the gaps between the frames and the wall. It stiffens the frame and anchors it in the opening. It comes in plain and moulded profiles, such as colonial (far left) and clamshell (centre), and in several widths. Apron molding (left) can also be applied under windowsills.

Handrail is a thick moulding made from sturdy wood to support people as they go up and down stairs. It's often supported by brackets, which must be securely anchored to plugs in the wall.

Casing stop is added to door or window frames to stop the swing of a door or window and to hold a sliding or hung unit in place. It also serves to hide the joint and, to a degree, seals against air infiltration and sound transmission.

Decorative moulding finishes the edges of furniture, built-in cupboards and rooms. Skirting board lies flat against the wall, with the inside corners joined with coped butt joints, outside corners with edge mitres. Angled ceiling moulding, or *cornice,* is similarly mitred and coped, except that the outside corners are compound mitred – the end of each board has both a face and an edge mitre cut (p 141). To saw a compound mitre by hand, place the cornice in a mitre box with the ceiling edge down. Slit the paper binding with a knife before sawing.

Plasterboard cornice can be held by galvanized clout nails about 1 m apart, and special glue. Support the cornice with a row of nails part-hammered into the wall on the lower cornice line. Fibre wall plugs 1 m apart are convenient for driving screws or nails into when attaching moulding.

To tightly fit a moulding with butt ends, taper each end (cut the face 2 mm long and slightly undercut the back edge); snap the moulding into place. To span a long wall, join the pieces with scarf or lap joints (parallel mitres). Nail across the joint and into a

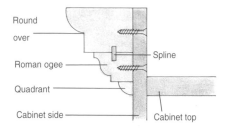

fibre wall plug. To avoid splits in hardwood moulding, pre-drill all nail holes. Nail the moulding 12 mm from the edges and 25 mm from each end.

With a router, you can create your own special mouldings (above).

Cornice installation

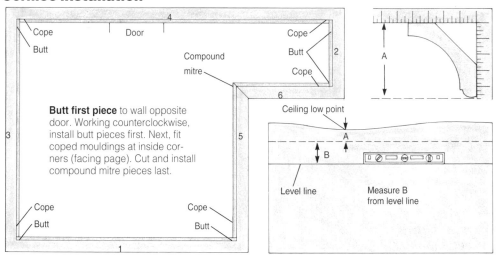

Butt first piece to wall opposite door. Working counterclockwise, install butt pieces first. Next, fit coped mouldings at inside corners (facing page). Cut and install compound mitre pieces last.

To find A, the distance from top edge (ceiling) to bottom edge (wall) of a cornice, hold it against a square (near left).

Draw a level line around room at a convenient height. Measure up from line at intervals to find ceiling's low point. From this low point, measure down distance A and mark. Then find B by measuring from level line up to A mark. On each wall, transfer same distance (B) from level line for bottom edge of cornice.

Install cornice with finishing nails anchored in plugs or studs and ceiling joists or furring strips (one-third of nail should penetrate framing); recess nails. Fill holes and gaps; sand smooth when dry.

Making a cornice compound mitre

Exploded view of cornice moulding shows how it angles away from the corner of a wall. To cut correct angle automatically, place moulding in a mitre box with the ceiling edge down.

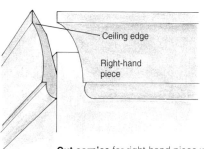

Cut cornice for right-hand piece with ceiling edge down and wall edge against fence; waste is to right of saw. For left-hand moulding, saw on opposite diagonal, with waste to left of saw.

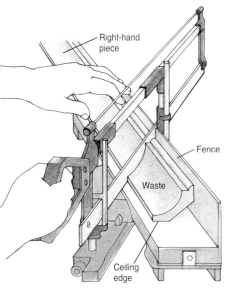

Test fit; if necessary, trim back edge of mitre on right-hand piece with block plane. Keep blade away from front moulded edge.

Skirting board installation

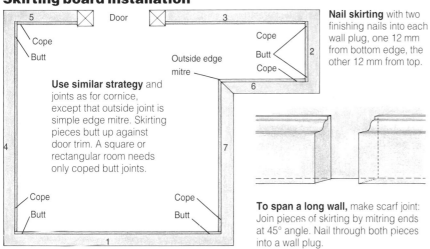

Use similar strategy and joints as for cornice, except that outside joint is simple edge mitre. Skirting pieces butt up against door trim. A square or rectangular room needs only coped butt joints.

Nail skirting with two finishing nails into each wall plug, one 12 mm from bottom edge, the other 12 mm from top.

To span a long wall, make scarf joint: Join pieces of skirting by mitring ends at 45° angle. Nail through both pieces into a wall plug.

Making an outside edge mitre

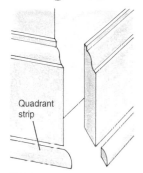

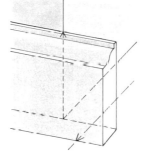

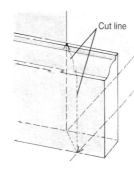

Skirting board edge mitres must match exactly for good joint. Strip moulding, such as quadrant, nailed to skirting board, covers gaps between floor and skirting.

1. Place uncut skirting boards in turn against wall. Draw the lines on the floor where they intersect and V-marks on each piece at wall corner and floor intersection.

2. Draw perpendicular lines from V-marks on front and back of each piece. Connect these lines across top and bottom edges to mark exact cut line (about 45°).

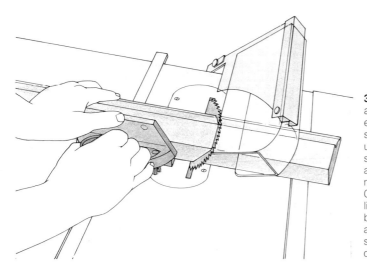

3. On table saw, angle blade for edge mitre; place skirting board face up. Test-cut on scrap side of lines about 12 mm from marked mitre. Compare cut to lines; adjust the blade. When the angle matches, saw mitre cut in one pass.

Coped butt joints

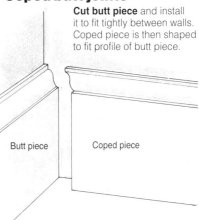

Cut butt piece and install it to fit tightly between walls. Coped piece is then shaped to fit profile of butt piece.

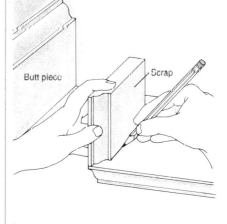

1. Trace profile from scrap piece of skirting onto back of piece to be coped. Hold sharp pencil at 45° angle to scrap.

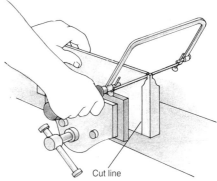

2. With coping saw at 90° to skirting back and blade angled, saw curved part of profile. Turn piece upside down; cut straight part with dovetail saw or backsaw. Test fit. Use file to adjust profile, then to undercut (bevel) back.

STAINS, FILLERS AND FINISHES

Stains, fillers and finishes can enhance wood's natural grain, cause it to reflect or absorb light, enrich or change its colour or texture, or obscure an unsightly surface. To choose the right one, first determine exactly what you want it to do. Most offer some degree of protection from sunlight, abrasion, water and chemicals. Almost all readily available stains and finishes come mixed and ready to use. Others must be prepared by mixing powder with solvents, and most can be altered to create your own unique products, but try them first on scrap wood or on a part of the workpiece that won't show on assembly. The skills and tools needed to create and apply a finish vary with the product, surface and technique.

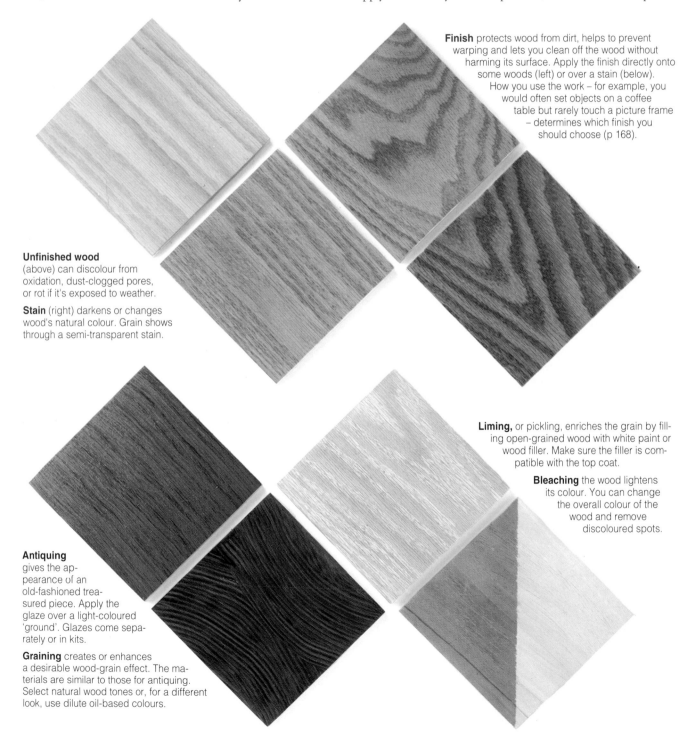

Finish protects wood from dirt, helps to prevent warping and lets you clean off the wood without harming its surface. Apply the finish directly onto some woods (left) or over a stain (below). How you use the work – for example, you would often set objects on a coffee table but rarely touch a picture frame – determines which finish you should choose (p 168).

Unfinished wood (above) can discolour from oxidation, dust-clogged pores, or rot if it's exposed to weather.

Stain (right) darkens or changes wood's natural colour. Grain shows through a semi-transparent stain.

Liming, or pickling, enriches the grain by filling open-grained wood with white paint or wood filler. Make sure the filler is compatible with the top coat.

Bleaching the wood lightens its colour. You can change the overall colour of the wood and remove discoloured spots.

Antiquing gives the appearance of an old-fashioned treasured piece. Apply the glaze over a light-coloured 'ground'. Glazes come separately or in kits.

Graining creates or enhances a desirable wood-grain effect. The materials are similar to those for antiquing. Select natural wood tones or, for a different look, use dilute oil-based colours.

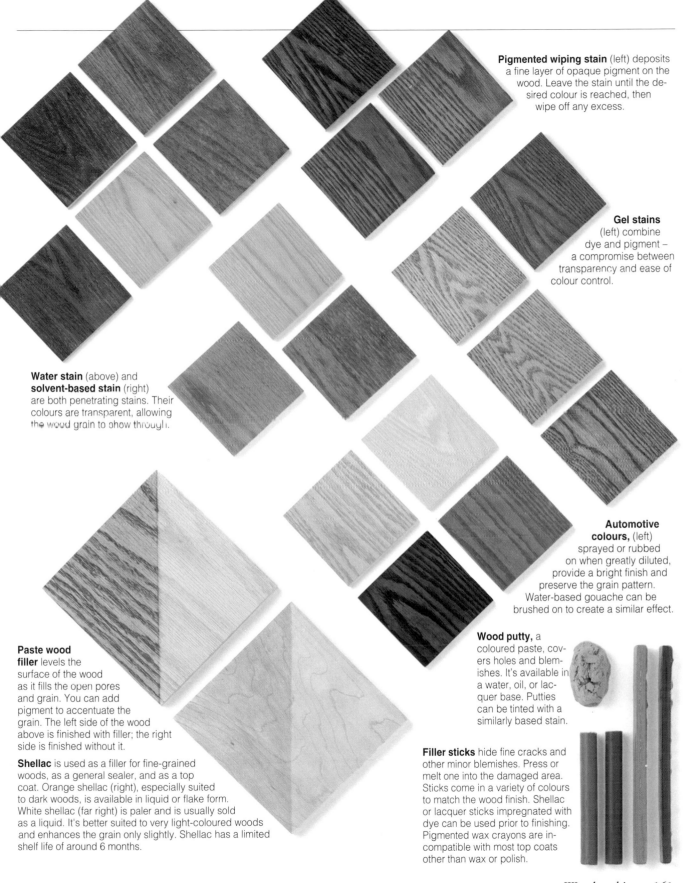

Pigmented wiping stain (left) deposits a fine layer of opaque pigment on the wood. Leave the stain until the desired colour is reached, then wipe off any excess.

Gel stains (left) combine dye and pigment – a compromise between transparency and ease of colour control.

Water stain (above) and **solvent-based stain** (right) are both penetrating stains. Their colours are transparent, allowing the wood grain to show through.

Automotive colours, (left) sprayed or rubbed on when greatly diluted, provide a bright finish and preserve the grain pattern. Water-based gouache can be brushed on to create a similar effect.

Paste wood filler levels the surface of the wood as it fills the open pores and grain. You can add pigment to accentuate the grain. The left side of the wood above is finished with filler; the right side is finished without it.

Shellac is used as a filler for fine-grained woods, as a general sealer, and as a top coat. Orange shellac (right), especially suited to dark woods, is available in liquid or flake form. White shellac (far right) is paler and is usually sold as a liquid. It's better suited to very light-coloured woods and enhances the grain only slightly. Shellac has a limited shelf life of around 6 months.

Wood putty, a coloured paste, covers holes and blemishes. It's available in a water, oil, or lacquer base. Putties can be tinted with a similarly based stain.

Filler sticks hide fine cracks and other minor blemishes. Press or melt one into the damaged area. Sticks come in a variety of colours to match the wood finish. Shellac or lacquer sticks impregnated with dye can be used prior to finishing. Pigmented wax crayons are incompatible with most top coats other than wax or polish.

VENEERS

Whether you're hiding imperfections in solid wood or covering a processed wood such as particleboard, veneer adds an attractive look to any project. You can apply it to furniture, to an inexpensive door, to shelves or almost any object where a decorative finish is desired. Veneers offer access to a variety of woods that would otherwise be unavailable because of expense or unsuitability as a solid wood.

Veneer sheets are stored and sold by suppliers in consecutive order, primarily to facilitate matching procedures (p 170) but also to ensure uniform figure, colour and texture in a finished piece. Veneer is shipped flat or rolled, according to the size of the sheet. Be sure to order on the generous side, allowing about 20 to 30 per cent waste for cutting and matching. And handle veneer with great care – it is very fragile.

Veneer sheets (right) are identified according to the wood species, the cutting method used to produce the veneer, the part of the tree from which it was cut (it may have a burl or crotch) and its figure. These variables give an endless selection for your project.

Edge trim (right) comes in strips up to 100 m long. It may have an adhesive backing or you may have to apply it with glue. Cover the exposed edges of plywood with it.

Inlay strips (right) create a decorative band around or near the edge of a workpiece. Thin strips of natural wood are pre-assembled in geometric designs, greatly simplifying the amount of work that goes into a project. They are easily laid into shallow grooves that are routed into the workpiece. The strips are available in lengths of 2,8 m and are 15 to 20 mm wide. They may be bought from some picture-framers and hardware stores.

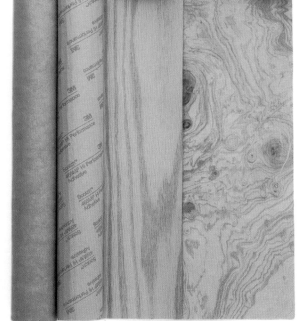

Decorative inlays may be available on special orders only. Naturally or artificially coloured woods are combined to create patterns. Recess the veneer into the workpiece or glue it as an overlay onto the surface.

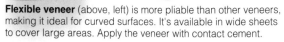

Flexible veneer (above, left) is more pliable than other veneers, making it ideal for curved surfaces. It's available in wide sheets to cover large areas. Apply the veneer with contact cement.

Pressure-sensitive veneer (above, right) has a backing that is coated with an adhesive. To apply the veneer, peel off the protective paper, position the veneer, and press it in place.

ORNAMENTAL WOOD TRIM

As the last touch before staining and finishing a surface, create an impressive look by adding one or more ornamental trims. Or add specially ordered reproduction trim to replace pieces when restoring an old piece of wooden furniture. Most of these trims are made in walnut, oak, cherry and other hardwoods, as well as in synthetic materials for painting. Ornamental trims are easy to apply and will accept almost any type of finish. Availability may be a problem in South Africa but you may find some among suppliers' old stocks. Second-hand dealers may have pieces from scrapped items.

Pre-shaped pieces come in a variety of configurations and sizes to use on a piece of furniture such as a chair or baby crib, and for creating architectural details. Some items, such as the galley railing (left), are pre-assembled.

Decorative carvings have embossed (not carved) patterns in beech, birch and other hardwoods. Some are moulded in wood-tinted plastics.

Decorative half-round mouldings are suitable for cabinetry, picture framing, and trim or borders for walls, ceilings, doors or windows.

Wood filigree, often seen on antique furniture (especially around glass cabinet doors), comes in a variety of intricate designs. You can apply it to fancy boxes, storage chests and picture frames. Remember that it can present dusting problems on horizontal surfaces.

The finish that you put on a piece will magnify any imperfections in the wood, so prepare all surfaces carefully. (On new construction, prepare the pieces before assembly.) Although some hand-sanding is always necessary, the amount can be sharply reduced by using a scraper. Proper scraping leaves lacy shavings. When you create dust instead of shavings, sharpen the blade (pp 198–199).

Power tools speed the sanding process. For rough work use a belt sander, follow with a finishing sander (orbital or oscillating) and end with light hand-sanding. Always work through a sequence of grits. For rough work, use 80-grit. On smooth surfaces, start with 120-grit (fine), then 180 (very fine) and finally 220 or 240. Sand parallel to the grain, or scratches will show. Clean the wood between grits with a tack rag. Make your own rag by dampening a piece of cheesecloth with turpentine, then kneading a little varnish into it. If your finish is water-based, dampen the cloth with water.

Caution: Wear a dust mask. When power-sanding, connect your sander to a dust bag or vacuum cleaner.

For a high shine on open-grain woods such as oak or walnut, fill the pores with paste wood filler. This comes in wood tones or neutral – you can tint the latter with universal tinting colours. (See p 167 for special effects.) Filling is unnecessary for a natural look or for wood with small pores, such as pine and meranti.

Before staining, prime surfaces and porous end grain with a sealer so they will absorb the stain uniformly (especially important with softwoods). Brush two medium coats on the wood; let each coat dry, then sand the surface with 240-grit paper. For sealer, use about one-twentieth dilution of your intended final finishing product.

Scraping

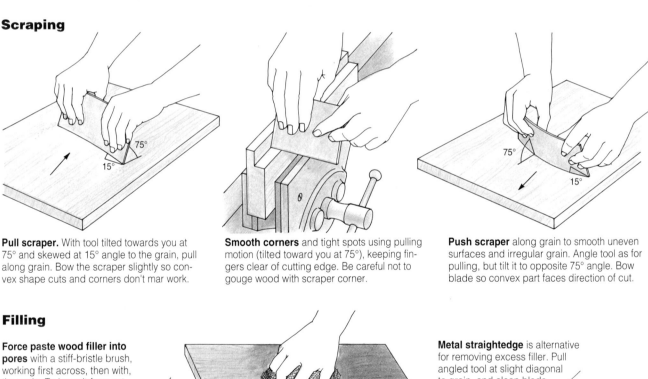

Pull scraper. With tool tilted towards you at 75° and skewed at 15° angle to the grain, pull along grain. Bow the scraper slightly so convex shape cuts and corners don't mar work.

Smooth corners and tight spots using pulling motion (tilted toward you at 75°), keeping fingers clear of cutting edge. Be careful not to gouge wood with scraper corner.

Push scraper along grain to smooth uneven surfaces and irregular grain. Angle tool as for pulling, but tilt it to opposite 75° angle. Bow blade so convex part faces direction of cut.

Filling

Force paste wood filler into pores with a stiff-bristle brush, working first across, then with, the grain. To keep it from settling, stir filler occasionally as you work.

Wad of hessian removes excess filler when glossy appearance dulls, usually after 15 to 20 min. Use vigorous circular rubbing motion. Dry overnight; then sand with 220- or 240-grit paper.

Metal straightedge is alternative for removing excess filler. Pull angled tool at slight diagonal to grain, and clean blade after each pass.

Sanding

Move finishing sander with grain in slightly overlapping parallel strokes. Keep a light touch; guide sander without exerting downward pressure.

To sand long turnings (below, left), cup sandpaper (a quarter sheet folded in thirds) over wood and move it up and down. Use gentle 'shoe-shine' motion on short sections (below, right), moving sandpaper strip over area.

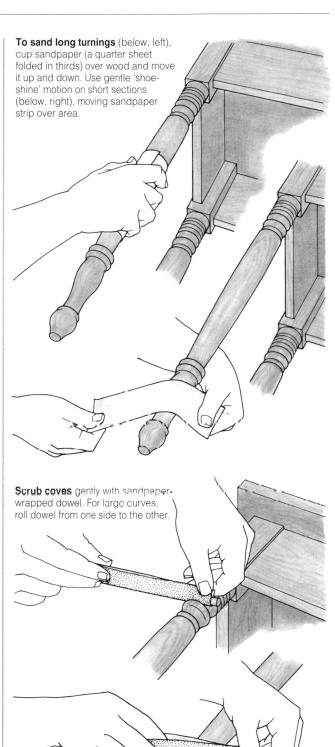

Sand small areas with palm sander, as described above. Start a power sander before it touches the wood surface.

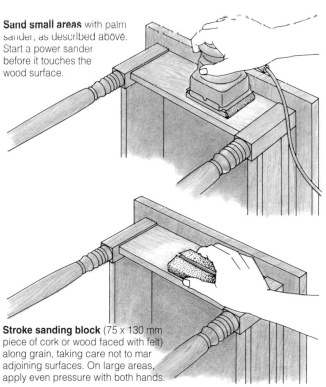

Stroke sanding block (75 x 130 mm piece of cork or wood faced with felt) along grain, taking care not to mar adjoining surfaces. On large areas, apply even pressure with both hands.

Scrub coves gently with sandpaper-wrapped dowel. For large curves, roll dowel from one side to the other.

For tight grooves, work folded sandpaper with back-and-forth motion. Alternate pressure on each side of V-cut.

Stains can enhance the natural colour of wood or change it dramatically, either highlighting or disguising the grain patterns. If you choose a penetrating stain, such as an aniline dye, expect clear, transparent colour and emphasized grain, because this type of stain actually soaks into the wood fibres. But because wood absorbs penetrating stain so readily, it may be difficult to avoid streaks and lap marks.

By contrast, pigmented stains are easy to apply, but because they leave a thin film of colorant on the surface of the wood, muddy grain often accompanies the rich colour. A third category, the varnish-stain, combines stain and finish in one step. While these products may result in a fast finish, it is often inferior to the conventional two-step finish.

When choosing a stain and finish, consider their solvents; the stain and finish must be compatible. (It's always safest to use one manufacturer's products on a project.) Both penetrating and pigmented stains are available in water- and oil-soluble forms. Combination products usually have an oil base.

Water-soluble stains are easy to clean up but can be more difficult to apply than oil-soluble ones. Perhaps the biggest disadvantage is that almost all water-soluble stains will swell the wood fibres, requiring you to raise the grain before staining. Alternatively, you can use a non-grain-raising (or solvent-based) stain (NGR), a pre-dissolved aniline dye that contains no water. To achieve the best results, NGR stains should be sprayed on.

Gel stains are expected to become available soon. Because they don't run, they are particularly easy to apply.

When selecting a stain, pick a shade slightly lighter than the desired colour – it's easier to darken a light stain than to lighten a stain that's over-dark. The colour produced will vary according to the wood, so first test the stain on a hidden area. Apply stain with a lint-free cloth or a synthetic-bristle brush, according to the manufacturer's directions. In small areas, use a foam brush.

Some woods, such as pine and fir, do not take stain well. (When properly finished, any wood may be beautiful without staining.) If you stain these woods, seal the wood first (p 164) and choose a water-base in a colour that's a little darker than the natural tone.

You can lighten a wood's overall colour by applying a commercial two-step bleach. Follow the label's directions. It is difficult, however, to remove disfiguring stains in wood, unless you know exactly what the stain is. For example, the blue-green to grey-black streaks found on an old mahogany, maple or oak piece are usually caused by a reaction between iron hardware and the tannin in the wood. Oxalic acid, a liquid commonly sold as a deck brightener, will remove the stain without changing the colour of the wood. Apply the acid and allow to dry. Thoroughly wash the dried crystals off the piece.

Caution: Oxalic acid and substances that contain highly volatile organic compounds (VOC), such as bleaches and alkyd resin- and oil-based stains and finishes, are toxic. (Some products are being re-formulated.) Ventilate your work area well, follow the manufacturer's guidelines closely and wear rubber gloves and goggles.

Basic techniques

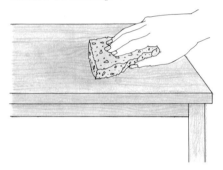

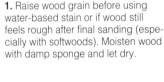

1. Raise wood grain before using water-based stain or if wood still feels rough after final sanding (especially with softwoods). Moisten wood with damp sponge and let dry.

2. Smooth off raised fibres with 180-grit sandpaper (pp 164–165), then vacuum all sanding dust from surface. Don't use a tack rag because it may leave a residue on the wood that will interfere with staining.

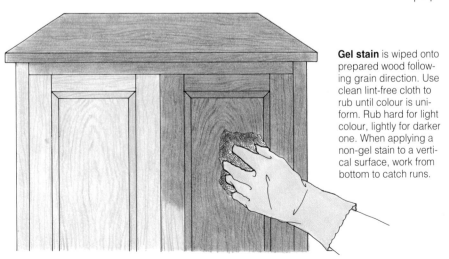

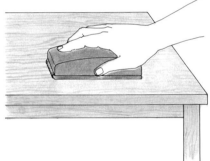

Gel stain is wiped onto prepared wood following grain direction. Use clean lint-free cloth to rub until colour is uniform. Rub hard for light colour, lightly for darker one. When applying a non-gel stain to a vertical surface, work from bottom to catch runs.

SPECIAL EFFECTS

Liming (pickling) and antiquing are two ways to artificially age a furniture piece. Liming involves filling the wood pores with white paint or with paste wood filler before finishing, creating a two-tone effect. Antiquing consists of top-coating enamelled or painted wood with a contrasting glaze, then wiping it off to create the illusion of wear. Graining, the art of producing imitation wood grain on bland surfaces, uses the same two-step procedure as antiquing. Because none of these decorative finishes protects wood surfaces (pp 168–169), finish the piece with the surface finish recommended on the label of the products you buy.

Liming

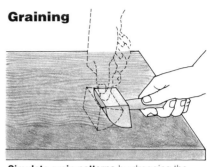

Brush on paste wood filler; then scrub off excess across grain with a wad of burlap, leaving filler in pores. Let dry for 24 hr before sealing.

Graining

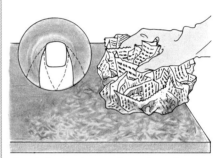

Simulate grain patterns by dragging the coarse side of the graining comb through the glaze with a twisting and rocking motion. Or use a stiff brush or whisk broom.

Create texture by pressing a piece of crumpled newsprint into glaze (experiment on scrap first). To make knots, twist thumb, leaving some 'grain' in the knot.

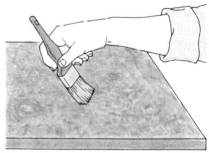

For added realism, brush over completed grain with dry brush. Angle brush as shown, and feather out grain lines with a light stroke.

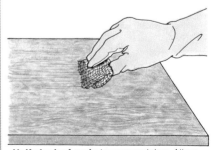

Unify look of grain by overgraining. Allow first coat of glaze to dry, then with a pad of coarse cloth, apply a second grain pattern in straight parallel lines.

Antiquing

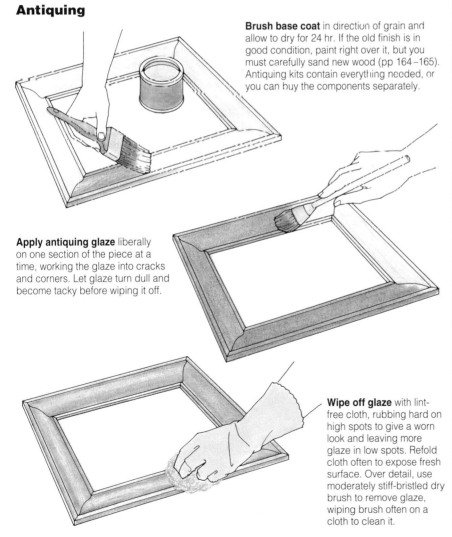

Brush base coat in direction of grain and allow to dry for 24 hr. If the old finish is in good condition, paint right over it, but you must carefully sand new wood (pp 164–165). Antiquing kits contain everything needed, or you can buy the components separately.

Apply antiquing glaze liberally on one section of the piece at a time, working the glaze into cracks and corners. Let glaze turn dull and become tacky before wiping it off.

Wipe off glaze with lint-free cloth, rubbing hard on high spots to give a worn look and leaving more glaze in low spots. Refold cloth often to expose fresh surface. Over detail, use moderately stiff-bristled dry brush to remove glaze, wiping brush often on a cloth to clean it.

The type of finish you choose depends on the use the object will receive and the appearance you desire. Surface finishes (varnish, polyurethane, lacquer) build up a protective film on the surface of the wood. Penetrating finishes (oils) sink into the wood, hardening within its fibres.

Surface finishes resist stains and abrasion better than penetrating finishes, but they are more difficult to spot-repair. Surface finishes may look too shiny unless they are hand-rubbed, while penetrating finishes produce a soft sheen that emphasizes the wood's colour and grain.

Consider the composition of the finishing material. While all penetrating finishes have a solvent base, varnish, lacquer and polyurethane are also available with a water base. Water-based

types are non-flammable and non-toxic, but they can be difficult to apply correctly and may raise the wood grain. In addition, these finishes may not be compatible with oil-based stains and fillers. If there's doubt about compatibility, contact the manufacturer.

All finishes magnify imperfections in the wood, so you must sand to a very fine grit – at least to 220 – before finishing. Treat all parts of the object the same – back, front, underside and top – so that they will react evenly to moisture changes and won't warp. If working with softwood, seal the wood first (p 164). For best results, the air temperature should be moderate, the humidity low. Consult the label for specific instructions. Allow the finish to dry between coats as recommended on the product label.

Minimize draughts while a surface finish is still wet, or specks of dust could settle in. Air bubbles are another problem, so stir a surface finish slowly, gently and thoroughly. Never drag the brush against the can rim to remove the excess. Instead, tap the brush lightly against the inside edge of the can. Dip a third of the brush into the finish and flow it on.

For a lustrous sheen, polish a dried surface finish as follows. Apply a liberal amount of rubbing oil to a cloth or felt pad and sprinkle some fine pumice onto the cloth. Rub the oil on the surface, stroking along the wood grain. When the surface is satiny smooth, wipe off the oil with a clean soft cloth, and apply two coats of paste wax. For a glossier look, repeat the process using rottenstone and oil before waxing.

Type	Surface effect	Application	Solvent	Considerations
Oil-based varnish	Durable built-up finish, matt or gloss. Darkens wood slightly	Brush on liquid type; wipe on gel type. Apply 2–3 coats	Mineral spirits or turpentine	General-purpose protection. Spar (marine) varnish good for exterior work. Gel types need more coats to achieve thickness of brushing types
Water-based varnish	Same as above, but may darken wood less	Brush on. Apply 2–3 coats	Water	Environmentally safe. May raise the wood grain. Dries faster than solvent varnishes
Polyurethane	Extremely durable finish, matt or gloss; can look plastic. Darkens wood slightly	Brush on liquid type, wipe on gel type. Apply 2–3 coats	Mineral spirits or turpentine	Extremely durable; good for objects subject to heavy wear
Synthetic-borne lacquer	Matt or glossy, accents grain of wood. Darkens wood less than other finishes, but may appear yellow	Brush or spray on; apply at least 3 coats. Brushing types may leave lap marks	Lacquer thinners	More protection than oils but less than varnishes. Highly flammable. Apply in explosion-proof spray booth
Water-based lacquer	Same as synthetic-borne lacquer, but less tendency to yellow	Brush, spray or wipe on. Apply 2 coats if brushing or spraying, 3 if wiping	Water	Non-flammable and non-toxic; raises wood grain
Tung oil	Natural-looking matt sheen. Enhances colour and grain of wood	Brush or wipe on. Apply 2–3 coats; rub in vigorously	Mineral spirits or turpentine	Suitable for all interior objects, especially carvings. Little protection against abrasion; somewhat resistant to staining
Danish oil	Natural-looking matt finish that enhances wood grain. Clear or colours available; all darken wood	Wipe on. Apply 3 coats, 4 for objects receiving heavy use	Mineral spirits or turpentine	Good for interior objects, but offers less protection than tung oil. Special types available for oily woods
Tung-oil varnish	Durable finish; looks more natural than other varnishes. Darkens wood slightly	Brush or wipe on. Apply 3 coats	Mineral spirits or turpentine	Affords more surface protection than oils but less than other varnishes

Brushing techniques

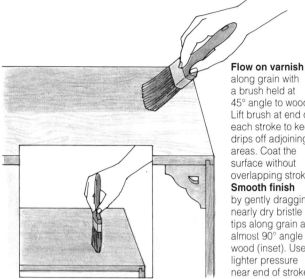

Flow on varnish along grain with a brush held at 45° angle to wood. Lift brush at end of each stroke to keep drips off adjoining areas. Coat the surface without overlapping strokes.
Smooth finish by gently dragging nearly dry bristle tips along grain at almost 90° angle to wood (inset). Use lighter pressure near end of stroke.

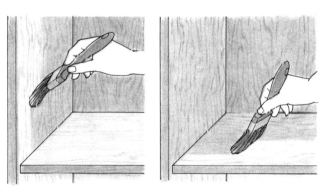

On inside corners, apply varnish first to the vertical surface, from bottom up. Then coat the horizontal surface. Work from the back corner towards front edge, brushing out any drips from the vertical face.

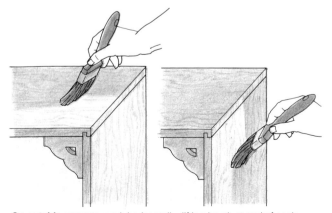

On outside corners, work horizontally, lifting brush at end of each stroke. To keep varnish from sagging, begin vertical stroke from bottom, catching any drips from horizontal face as you work.

Stripping

Paint strippers dissolve the old finish so it can be lifted off the surface. Strippers containing methylene chloride (a suspected carcinogen) work quickly (usually within 15 minutes) and effectively, but must be used with great caution. Non-toxic water-based strippers work more slowly and because they may raise the grain, necessitating light sanding after stripping, they may not be the right choice for valuable or veneered pieces. Apply all strippers the same way – pat on a thick coat with a cheap paint brush, wait the recommended time and then scrape off the old finish. Re-apply stripper to any stubborn patches.

Caution: Apply methylene chloride stripper outdoors or in an amply ventilated workspace. Wear a respirator fitted with an organic filter that will protect you from harmful vapours (other filters screen out only solid particles). Always wear safety goggles and heavy rubber gloves, not the thin latex type. Protect the floor with newspaper, not plastic drop-cloths. Keep fresh water and clean rags nearby, in case the stripper splashes on your skin or in your eyes.

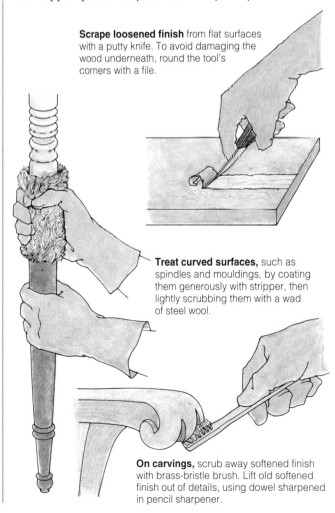

Scrape loosened finish from flat surfaces with a putty knife. To avoid damaging the wood underneath, round the tool's corners with a file.

Treat curved surfaces, such as spindles and mouldings, by coating them generously with stripper, then lightly scrubbing them with a wad of steel wool.

On carvings, scrub away softened finish with brass-bristle brush. Lift old softened finish out of details, using dowel sharpened in pencil sharpener.

Veneering is the process of gluing a thin layer of decorative wood over a thicker plain base. Most veneers are between 0,5 and 1 mm thick for cabinet-making. Thinner, flexible veneers are available for curved surfaces. Veneer is sold by the square metre in various lengths, in sheets or rolls. Flatten pieces of veneer before use by spraying them lightly with water, stack them in a pile and separate the layers with brown paper. Lay a plywood panel on top of the stack and weight it with bricks. When the veneer is flat, let it dry for 5 days in the weighted stack, changing the paper daily.

Veneer is usually either rotary cut or sliced. In rotary cutting, the veneer is peeled off a log held in a giant lathe, much like unwinding a roll of paper towels. The grain of rotary-cut veneer looks stretched out – the growth rings are more widely spaced than in the uncut log. Sliced veneer, which is

Slip matching

Book matching

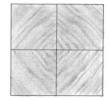

Diamond pattern

cut across the log, has the lively grain of sawn wood. Veneer is packed in the order it is cut. To keep the slices in sequence, number each one with chalk as you unpack it. The veneers may be arranged different ways. In slip matching, you slip consecutive veneers off the pile, lay them next to each other and join them edge-to-edge, creating a repetitive pattern. In book matching, you remove sheets from the pile as you

Edge-joining veneer

1. Overlap two veneer sheets by about 10 mm; clamp straightedge along centre of overlap. Cut with veneer saw, using multiple light strokes. Remove waste veneer.

2. On good face, tape across joint every 150 mm with veneer tape, then tape along joint. Carefully lift panel to light to check for fit. Light shows through if joint is not tight.

3. Place veneer, tape side down, at edge of work surface; open joint so that one piece hangs down. Apply thin coat of white glue to edges. Close, wipe off excess glue and cover with wax paper and weights.

Gluing to substrate

Roll or brush yellow glue evenly onto the substrate. Apply veneer to both sides. Protect first veneered side with plain paper. Then weight or clamp as at right.

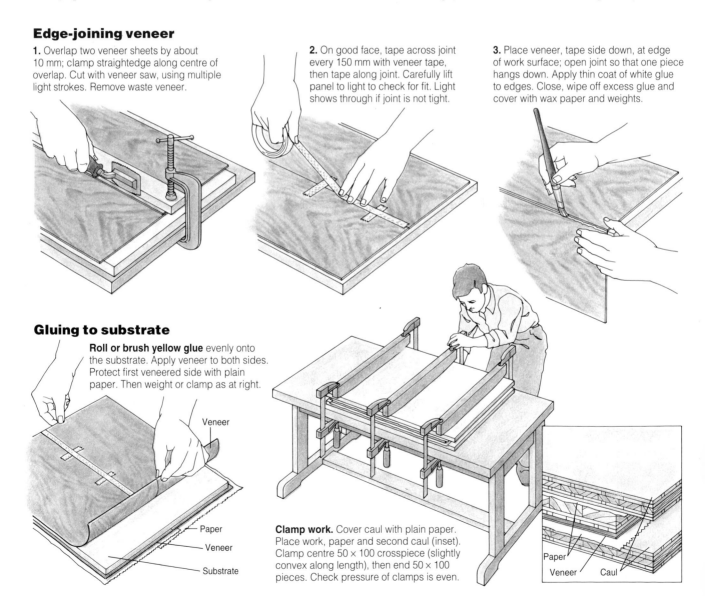

Veneer

Paper

Veneer

Substrate

Clamp work. Cover caul with plain paper. Place work, paper and second caul (inset). Clamp centre 50 × 100 crosspiece (slightly convex along length), then end 50 × 100 pieces. Check pressure of clamps is even.

Paper

Veneer   Caul

would turn the pages of a book, producing a mirror-image effect. To create a diamond pattern, cut four identical squares or rectangles of veneer so that the grain is diagonal. Then position the squares to form a pattern of either concentric diamonds or radiating lines.

Most materials can be veneered, if they are clean and smooth (bumps transmit through the veneer). Apply veneer with its grain perpendicular to the grain of processed wood. To prevent warping, veneer both sides of each piece.

Cut veneer with a craft knife, single-edge razor blade or veneer saw held at 90°. Whenever possible, cut with the back face up. Veneer should overhang the surface being covered (the substrate) by about 20 mm on all sides. Trim the waste with a veneer saw after the veneer has been glued but before scraping off the veneer tape. When both sides have been veneered, cut the work to size and cover the edges with veneer edging tape (pp 152–153).

To form a strong glue bond between veneer and its substrate, place even pressure on the work, adding slightly more force on the centre. Weight small areas of veneer with bricks or concrete blocks. If clamping, set one clamp every 2,5 cm. When using a veneer press, the plywood *cauls* (protective panels) should be larger than the work on all sides and the crosspieces should have convex bottoms. Weight hard-to-clamp areas with a sand-filled plastic bag.

Veneered surfaces break fairly easily, especially on their edges. Before patching, smooth the broken edges of the old veneer and square them with a craft knife so that they are at a right angle to the substrate. Before repairing veneer, make sure that the substrate is smooth and free of old adhesive.

Edge border

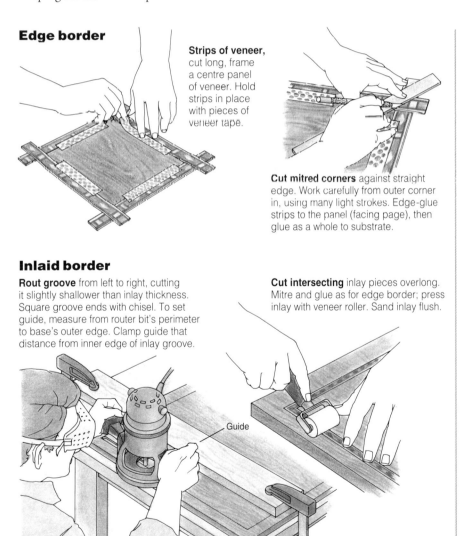

Strips of veneer, cut long, frame a centre panel of veneer. Hold strips in place with pieces of veneer tape.

Cut mitred corners against straight edge. Work carefully from outer corner in, using many light strokes. Edge-glue strips to the panel (facing page), then glue as a whole to substrate.

Inlaid border

Rout groove from left to right, cutting it slightly shallower than inlay thickness. Square groove ends with chisel. To set guide, measure from router bit's perimeter to base's outer edge. Clamp guide that distance from inner edge of inlay groove.

Cut intersecting inlay pieces overlong. Mitre and glue as for edge border; press inlay with veneer roller. Sand inlay flush.

Guide

Repairs

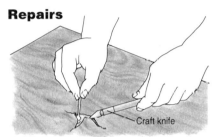

Craft knife

Blister. Slice in line with grain and gently lift veneer. Push in white glue with toothpick or glue injector. Press with flat roller; cover with wax paper and weight with a heavy object.

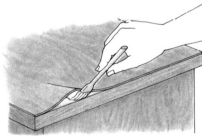

Raised veneer. Remove dried glue with craft knife or pin. Apply fresh glue with small brush or toothpick, and weight as above.

Hole. With white paper over hole, rub patch pattern with pencil; then rubber-cement drawn template to face side of patch. Cut patch with many light strokes on waste side of cut line. Test-fit patch; trim to fit, then glue and clamp.

Gluing and clamping repairs

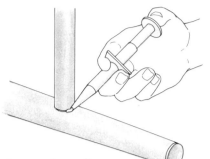

Re-glue without disassembly.
Insert glue injector into loose joint; push plunger to force in glue. Small hole may be drilled to accept tip.

Force angled joint together by wrapping rope in figure-8 pattern. Tighten rope with a twist stick.

Twist stick

Try the gentlest approach first when reviving a patch of worn finish. If the finish is sound but lifeless, a thorough cleaning with a mild detergent or a de-waxer may be enough. Specialist suppliers may stock compounds known as restorers or amalgamators, both of which act by dissolving a thin layer of the old finish. It is then either replaced by or blended with the new finish. These products, however, are more satisfactory where entire surfaces – rather than just small sections – are treated.

Disguise small scratches with dye-impregnated wood markers, stick shellac or even crayons. Deeply scratched pieces may require sanding and a complete refinishing.

To remove water rings, dampen a soft cotton cloth (old towelling is fine) with mineral oil, dip the cloth into fine pumice stone or rottenstone, and gently rub the ring until it disappears.

To raise a dent, prick it several times with a pin, cover it with a damp cloth and press it with an iron on the steam setting for a few seconds. Allow the area to dry, and repeat if needed.

Disassemble a piece cautiously when many joints need repair, when a part needs replacing, or when repairing one part will damage another part. Begin by reviewing the overall assembly. Invert tables to see how the apron and top are attached to the legs. Peer inside frame-and-panel cabinets to

locate glue blocks and screws. To aid re-assembly, note the order of disassembly and mark mating pieces.

Loose joints can be tapped apart with a rubber mallet, but forcing tight joints can break the pieces. Try softening the glue: drill or prick several small holes into the joint, then with a glue injector, inject a 1:1 mixture of white vinegar and water; wait 1 to 2 hours and tap the joint apart.

Breaks along the wood grain usually re-glue well, but cross-grain breaks do not. Strengthen the latter with dowels or splines. Tighten a loose dowel joint by gluing string or a layer of cheesecloth around the dowel to increase its diameter. You can also widen the end of a dowel on a disassembled piece by kerfing the end and inserting a hardwood wedge. Tighten a loose tenon by gluing wood shims to it; then trim them to fit. Build up a loose finger or dovetail joint with veneer pieces. For a good bond, always clean old glue out of all joints before re-gluing.

Troublesome doors often respond to one of several repairs. Check for high spots by rubbing chalk on the door's edge and then closing the door. Plane the spots where the chalk was removed. Plug a stripped screw hole tightly with glue and toothpicks and re-drill. Check hinge mortises. Chisel shallow ones deeper, and shim those that are too deep with pieces of veneer.

Repairing a split

Gently pry apart the pieces of a lengthwise break with a putty knife or an old screwdriver.

Wedge pieces far enough apart to allow insertion of a small glue brush. Coat both surfaces of split with glue. Remove wedge.

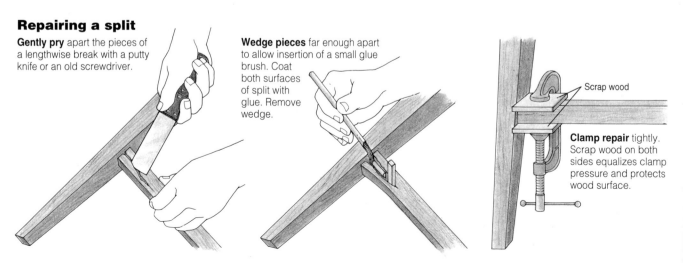

Scrap wood

Clamp repair tightly. Scrap wood on both sides equalizes clamp pressure and protects wood surface.

Fixing a doweled rung

Saw off broken wood on rung. Drill dowel hole, making hole half the width of rung and 3 mm deeper than necessary (for excess glue). Test-fit new grooved dowel in rung.

In mating leg, fill all gaps by gluing a dowel in old hole; let dry. Saw off excess dowel filler and drill a hole in leg to accept new dowel. Test-fit pieces. Coat dowel with glue; insert into rung. Lightly tap rung into leg with mallet.

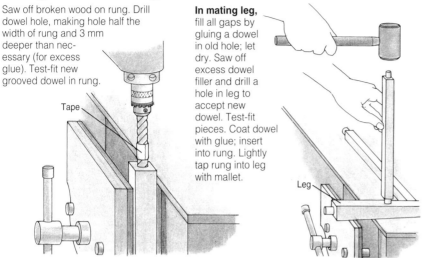

Tape

Leg

Broken mortise-and-tenon

Saw off remains of broken tenon. Within outline of tenon, drill holes for mortise at least 25 mm deep plus 3 mm for excess glue. Trim mortise with chisel (p 146). Drill or chisel out remains of tenon in old mortise.

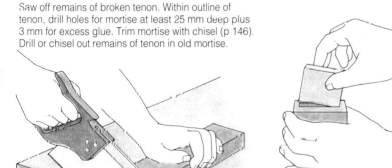

Cut wood spline to fit new and old mortises. Test-fit to ensure that the mating pieces meet tightly. Pare an oversize spline to fit. (If too loose, make a new spline.)

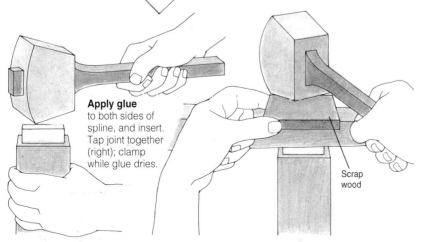

Apply glue to both sides of spline, and insert. Tap joint together (right); clamp while glue dries.

Scrap wood

Drawer repairs

Remove bottom. Pull nails with nippers and slide out panel. Replace, if needed, with 3 to 6 mm-thick hardboard or plywood (9,5 mm for large drawers).

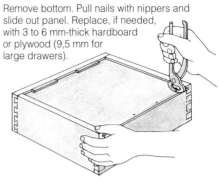

Replace piece. First, knock apart corner joints. Analyse joints to determine direction of mallet blows. Soften glue (facing page). Wood block protects wood during blows. Insert new part, glue and clamp.

Wooden block

Replace uneven or worn runners. Plane down high spots. Shave front corner area with chisel. Cut hardwood strips to fit.

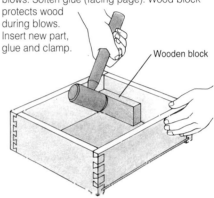

Runner

Scrap wood

Glue and align hardwood strips along drawer edges. Place clamps every 150 mm, protecting wood with scrap. When dry, test-fit drawer. Plane or sand high spots on new strips.

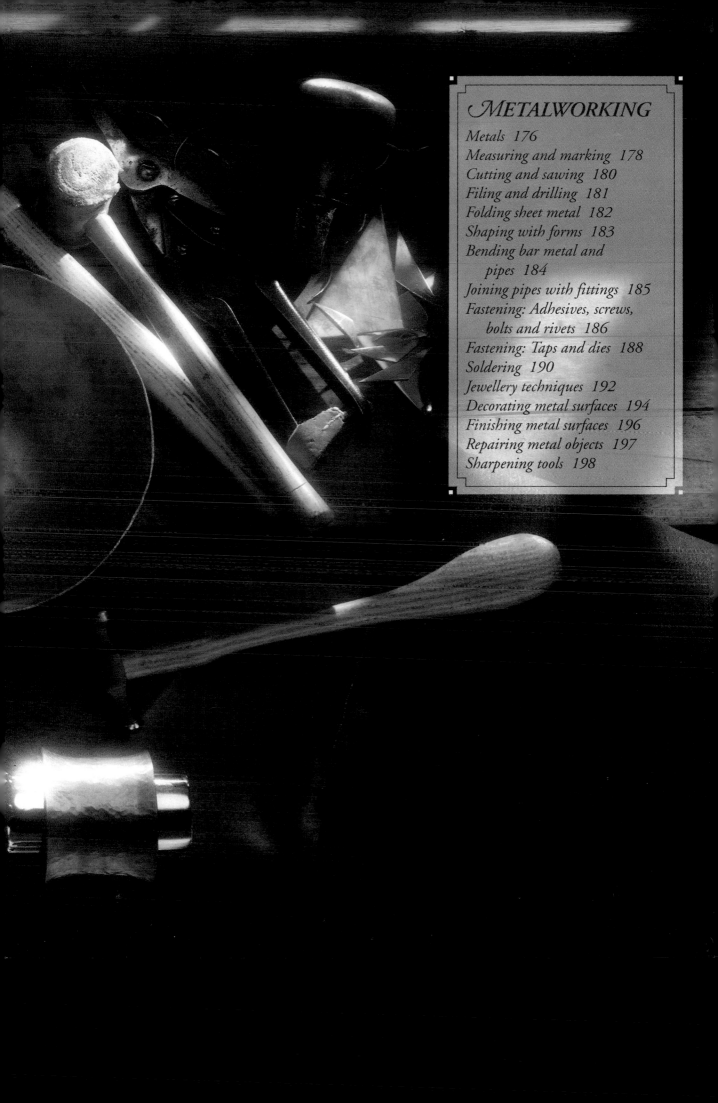

METALWORKING

Although replaced to a degree by plastics, metals are still put to a wide variety of uses around the home, as in flashing, siding or cladding, window frames, cabinets, pipes and ducts. Metals may be soft or hard, beautiful or nondescript, malleable or rigid, thick or paper-thin. They are divided into two broad categories: ferrous (containing iron) and non-ferrous, which includes all the other base metals (such as copper, aluminium, nickel and zinc) and the precious metals (gold, silver and platinum). Often two or more elemental metals are combined (alloyed) to alter their visual properties or working and performance characteristics such as hardness, strength, corrosion resistance and melting points. The metals you are most likely to work with are sterling silver, copper, brass, steel and aluminium alloys. Metals are sold in sheets (less than 5 mm thick), in plates (5 mm thick or more), and in bars, which include strips and flats (narrow sheets and plates), round, square and hexagonal rods and tubing, angles and channels, and various other shapes.

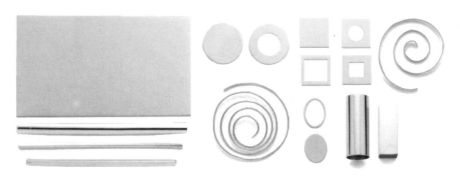

Silver and the other precious metals (gold and platinum) are highly stable chemically and resist oxidation and corrosion from acids. Silver and gold are also plastic and easy to work. They are available in standard or pre-formed sheets, plates, standard wire, flat bezel wire, tubing and rods. Also available are foil, leaf, shot (granules) for casting and alloying, and prefabricated chains, clasps, earring posts and jump rings, called findings, that simplify jewellery-making.

Copper is often used in rigid water-supply piping and fittings. It is also available in sheets of different thicknesses, including thin foil, rolls of tapelike foil for stained-glass work, wire, tubes, flats and bars. Circular sheets are ideal for shaping bowls, and small pre-shaped pieces of sheet copper can be used in jewellery-making or decorative items. Copper is also the chief component of brass and bronze alloys.

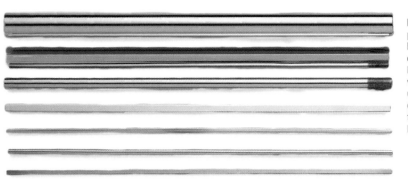

Brass, an alloy of copper and zinc, is sold as sheets, plates, tubes, rods, angles and wire. It's stronger and harder than copper and resists corrosion, although decorative items are usually coated to prevent tarnish. Thin brass-plated steel pipe is also available. Solid brass is widely used for pipe fittings, including nipples and unions and flare, compression and threaded fittings (below). Banding (bottom) is used for decorating furniture, boxes, lamps and bowls. Bronze, a copper-tin alloy, has properties superior to those of ordinary brass.

Plain carbon steels, alloys of iron and carbon only, are the steels used in home workshops. They come in three varieties: low-, medium- and high-carbon. The most widely used is low-carbon, or mild, steel, which is easily drilled, cut and bent. It is available in a vast array of shapes including rods, tubing, angles and flats, as shown at right, and is ideally suited for threaded pipes and fittings (below). Medium-carbon steel, a harder alloy, is found in castings and in many workshop tools. High-carbon steel is extremely hard, making it ideal for cutting tools.

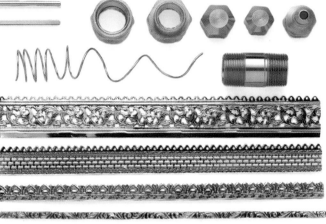

Aluminium, too soft to use alone, is always used as an alloy. It is lightweight and easily drilled and cut, but it cannot be soldered and is difficult to weld. Although aluminium resists atmospheric corrosion, *anodizing,* an electro-chemical coating process, dramatically improves its performance. It comes in sheets, pre-shaped flashing and rods, as well as in many other forms, including angles, pre-formed thresholds, TV antennas and framework for windows and patio doors.

Metalworking   177

Working with metal, whether forming original work or making repairs, requires careful preparation and good materials. Sources for metal and supplies are diverse. For non-ferrous metals (copper, brass or aluminium) try hardware, building or plumbing supply stores. For ferrous metals (iron or steel) visit a sheet-metal or welding shop, or a scrapyard. Craft shops and jewellery suppliers carry metals, other materials and special tools for jewellery-making.

Metal thickness is sometimes expressed in gauge numbers – the lower the gauge number, the thicker the metal. In South Africa, however, metal sheet or plate is referred to by its thickness in millimetres, there being one system for mild steel and galvanized iron, and another for aluminium, brass, copper and stainless steel.

A gauge plate can roughly measure metal thickness, but a micrometer or a vernier calliper is precise, measuring any piece to hundredths of a millimetre. Mark the measurement on any leftover metal for future use.

Before bending, cutting or drilling, mark the metal accurately. Check angles or find centre points with a combination tool. Mark straight lines with an indelible pen or a scriber and a steel rule, curves and circles with dividers, and points with a centre punch.

Some standard thicknesses in mm	
Mild steel and galvanized iron	Aluminium, brass, copper, stainless steel
0,203	0,102
0,230	0,152
0,460	0,203
0,500	0,230
0,600	0,460
0,800	0,500
1,000	0,700
1,200	0,900
1,600	1,200
2,000	1,600
2,500	2,000
3,000	2,500
5,000	3,000
6,000	4,000
8,000	4,500

Measuring metal thickness

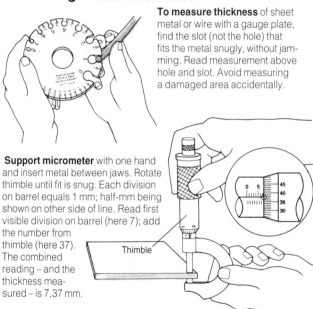

To measure thickness of sheet metal or wire with a gauge plate, find the slot (not the hole) that fits the metal snugly, without jamming. Read measurement above hole and slot. Avoid measuring a damaged area accidentally.

Support micrometer with one hand and insert metal between jaws. Rotate thimble until fit is snug. Each division on barrel equals 1 mm; half-mm being shown on other side of line. Read first visible division on barrel (here 7); add the number from thimble (here 37). The combined reading – and the thickness measured – is 7,37 mm.

Thimble

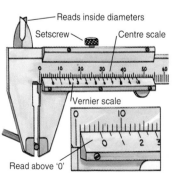

Reads inside diameters
Setscrew
Centre scale
Vernier scale
Read above '0'

Vernier calliper has a centre scale marked in millimetres, with a sliding vernier scale beneath it marked in twentieths (0,05mm) of a millimetre. Read the centre scale above '0' on the sliding scale (here 20 mm). If a line meets exactly, that's the measurement. If not, look right for first vernier line that meets a line on the centre scale (here at 0,1 mm). Add the two readings to find the dimension measured – in this case 20,1 mm or 2,01 cm.

Marking metal

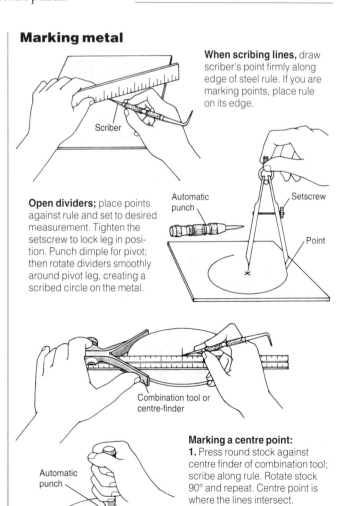

Scriber

When scribing lines, draw scriber's point firmly along edge of steel rule. If you are marking points, place rule on its edge.

Open dividers; place points against rule and set to desired measurement. Tighten the setscrew to lock leg in position. Punch dimple for pivot; then rotate dividers smoothly around pivot leg, creating a scribed circle on the metal.

Automatic punch
Setscrew
Point

Combination tool or centre-finder

Automatic punch

Marking a centre point:
1. Press round stock against centre finder of combination tool; scribe along rule. Rotate stock 90° and repeat. Centre point is where the lines intersect.

2. Place tip of automatic punch on centre point. With one hand, press down on sleeve until punch recoils, forming a slight dimple.

Making a pattern

When creating any metal object, start by making a full-size pattern, or template, on heavyweight paper or thin cardboard. Original designs for two-dimensional items, such as plaques or pieces of jewellery, can be drawn on graph paper first, then transferred to pattern paper by tracing over carbon paper. Cut out the pattern and fasten it to the metal with rubber cement. Then cut the metal directly around the pattern. For larger objects – or for three-dimensional objects such as ducts, decorative pieces or the box shown on this page – make a pattern called a stretch-out, which shows all parts of the object unfolded and flattened.

Draw a stretch-out with a sharp pencil and an accurate straightedge. Check all measurements twice. Use one line as a base line from which to measure, to avoid compounding any errors. Distinguish cut lines from fold lines, and calculate allowances for seams and edges. When you have finished, cut along the cut lines with scissors or a utility knife (use a steel rule to guide the blade); then assemble the pattern to test the design and to establish a logical sequence of work steps to follow when creating the actual object. (For folds, refer to the work sequence on p 182.) For a complicated project, make a written list of these steps so you can refer to them.

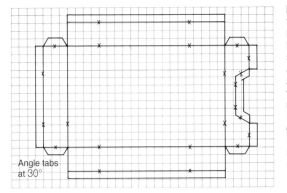

Making a stretch-out: 1. For a three-dimensional object, begin by drawing the bottom or base. Extend all dimensions to form the sides, adding the appropriate amounts for seam and edge tabs. Angle the ends of the tabs towards each other at about 30° to make them easier to fold. Mark lines indicating folds with X's. Cut out the pattern and test it by folding it to its final shape, holding the seams temporarily closed with masking tape.

Angle tabs at 30°

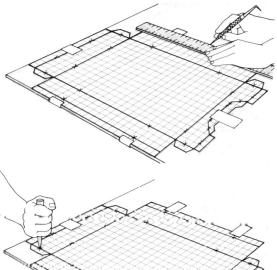

2. To scribe the pattern onto sheet metal, fasten it securely to the metal with masking tape. Using a steel rule as a straight-edge, lightly trace the pattern's outline onto the metal with a scriber. Align rule carefully with the pattern's edges, and always keep scriber's point against the rule's bottom edge.

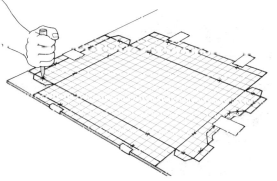

3. With a scratch awl or a punch, mark fold lines and any internal cut lines by punching gently through the pattern in at least two places along each line. Remove the pattern. Using the scriber and rule, scribe along fold lines lightly to avoid weakening the metal, then scribe over the outline and any other cut lines more firmly, making these lines deeper.

Holding work securely

Accidents happen quickly in metal-working. Avoid them by securing the work with clamps or in machinist's or engineer's vice so that it cannot move during an operation. In a home work-shop, fasten the vice at one corner of the workbench, near or over a leg. The vice's fixed jaw should project about 12 mm beyond the bench's edge. Read the safety precautions on pp 10–13. In particular, wear eye protection to prevent injury from metal splinters, and heavy gloves and long sleeves to protect against sharp edges.

Swivel lock

For safety and control, tighten swivel and vice jaws firmly. Working close to jaws lessens chattering and movement of metal and reduces strain on vice.

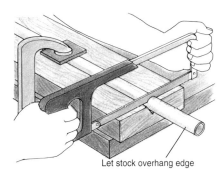

Let stock overhang edge

Wooden V-block holds round stock securely for drilling, sawing or shaping. Clamp stock in single V-block or use two V-blocks in machinist's or engineer's vice.

There are many ways to cut metal, depending on the type, size and amount of stock to be cut. Thin metal, such as aluminium cladding, can be cut by scoring with a utility knife several times along the cut line, using a steel rule as a straightedge. Most wire can be cut with side-cutting pliers. For sheet metal thinner than 1,2 mm, use snips. Aviation snips, with their compact size and compound leverage, handle well. Ordinary tin snips leave a smoother edge. If you must make long or multiple cuts, investigate power shears or a nibbler. Both make curved and straight cuts quickly, but a nibbler cuts a channel through the metal, leaving a smoother edge. Before cutting with these power tools, lubricate along the cut line with light machine oil.

A circle cutter, available through jewellery suppliers, forms small discs and other shapes (such as half-moons or semi-circles) for decorative or jewellery work. For thick metal plate and round stock, cut with a hacksaw or – for soft or thinner metals – an electric jigsaw fitted with a metal-cutting blade. A cold chisel struck with a hammer will cut rough openings in metal too thick for snips and can shear through solid stock such as bolt shafts.

Caution: Read the safety precautions on pp 12–13. In particular, protect your hands and eyes against flying metal chips and sharp edges. Always clamp or grip workpieces securely, and file rough edges smooth immediately after they have been cut.

Cutting techniques

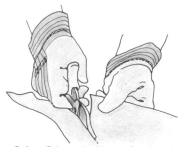

Snips. Grip work with your free hand and slightly angle straight-cutting snips above surface. Work on waste side of cut line; don't close blades completely. Curl waste aside.

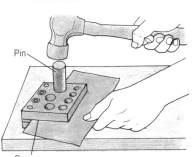

Circle cutter. To make shapes from sheet metal, first remove all pins. Slide metal into groove under hole (for varied shapes, position metal partially under hole). Insert pin in hole; strike with hammer to punch out piece.

Power shears. Let waste overhang work surface. Cut slowly for thick metal or tight cuts, faster for thin sheets or long cuts. Curl waste aside. Wear safety goggles.

For inside curves, first drill or punch a starter hole. Using right- or left-cutting aviation snips, make first cut close to line, then trim remaining metal.

Cold chisel. For inside shapes, grip chisel loosely and tilt. Strike chisel with ball-peen hammer, slicing metal with chisel blade.

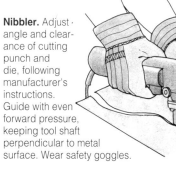

Nibbler. Adjust angle and clearance of cutting punch and die, following manufacturer's instructions. Guide with even forward pressure, keeping tool shaft perpendicular to metal surface. Wear safety goggles.

Sawing metal

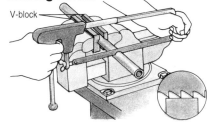

Hacksaw. Blade should have at least three teeth touching edge of metal for efficient cutting. Hold saw at both ends. Cut on forward stroke. Rotate round stock to complete cut.

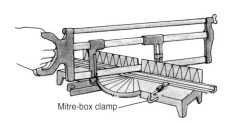

Angled cuts. Cut soft metal to specific angles in a mitre box. Clamp or hold metal in box. Use metal-cutting blade with mitre box saw, or use hacksaw, as at left.

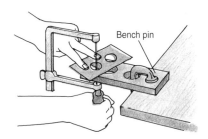

Jeweller's saw. Install blade through drilled hole in metal. Hold work against bench pin with fingers and keep centred in bench pin slot. Keep blade vertical and cut on downstroke only.

For shaping and smoothing metal edges, mill files are usually the best choice, but for soft metal, particularly aluminium, choose a curved-tooth file with deeply cut teeth. Single-cut files, having a single series of parallel teeth, cut more slowly than double-cut files; the latter have a second row of teeth overlapping the first at an angle. Most files come in three grades – smooth cut, second cut, and bastard (coarsest) – but longer files, regardless of grade, leave a coarser surface than shorter files. Choose a file shape that matches the work, whether round, square, triangular or flat.

Always put a handle on a file before working – it is safer and gives better leverage. Place the handle on the file's tang, and strike the handle against a hard surface until it is tight.

Hold the file at both ends and push it with long, slow strokes. (Draw-filing, shown on this page, is an exception.) Using your arms and shoulders as well as hands, apply even pressure. Maintain a steady rhythm, but lift the file on the return stroke to avoid dulling its teeth.

Prevent clogged teeth by rubbing chalk over a file before use, and regularly clean files by brushing with a file card.

Cross-file to remove burrs from a cut edge. Lay file diagonally across workpiece edge, square to sides. Push file forward and sideways.

Draw-file to produce smooth, finished edge. Hold file flat against surface, square to work's sides. Pull tool towards you, using fresh teeth for each stroke.

Round file smooths tight curves. Push file forward and sideways along curve (as in cross-filing) while rotating blade.

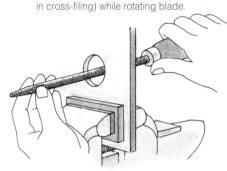

Drilling holes in metal

Drill holes in metal for fasteners, decoration, or instead of sawing when making large holes. A drill press provides stability, accuracy and control, but a portable electric drill mounted in a stand can also drill through sheet metal and small stock. Make holes in thinner metal and stationary pieces with a variable-speed portable drill.

Choose sharp high-speed twist bits. Mark the location of the hole by denting the centre with a punch (p 178) and back the metal with scrap wood. Apply several drops of light household or motor oil to the bit and the hole as you work. When drilling thick metal or steel, make a well with modelling clay to contain the oil. Drill slowly and exert firm but not undue pressure, slowing the drill speed if the bit squeaks, and pausing if it turns bluish or if smoke appears. Raise the bit frequently to clear waste and to add oil.

Caution: Wear safety goggles to protect your eyes from metal chips, and clamp all workpieces firmly unless they are stationary.

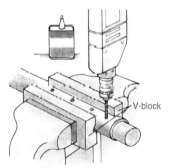

To drill holes in tubing, clamp tubing in V-blocks or vice. Insert dowel to reinforce thin walls and to guide bit straight through other side. Be sure bit can exit freely.

For holes over 3 mm wide, back metal with wood. Insert step bit into drill, mark desired diameter on bit with tape. Drive the bit through the metal until bit reaches tape mark and the hole is desired size.

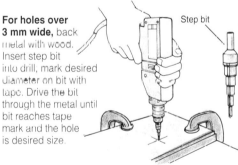

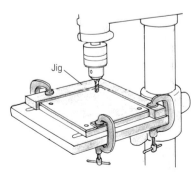

Drill press. For uniformly placed holes, make a two-sided jig. Back metal with wood. Clamp the jig firmly on drill press table; rotate metal for each hole.

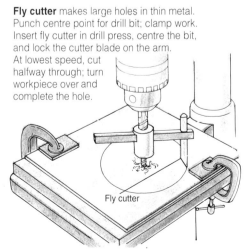

Fly cutter makes large holes in thin metal. Punch centre point for drill bit; clamp work. Insert fly cutter in drill press, centre the bit, and lock the cutter blade on the arm. At lowest speed, cut halfway through; turn workpiece over and complete the hole.

When working with sheet metal, first bend it with gloved hands before moving on to bending and striking tools. Fold gradually by working along the entire fold line in stages, starting in the middle and working towards the ends. A bending brake, available at metalworking suppliers, provides greatest accuracy. A homemade brake can consist of two pieces of hardwood clamped together – align the metal's fold line between them and bend along it.

Complete bends and folds with a flat-faced mallet, and finish edges with a wedge-faced hammer. Never use a damaged wooden, plastic or rawhide mallet. Polish steel hammer faces (p 196) to remove nicks and scratches.

Plan the work sequence beforehand by assembling the stretch-out pattern (p 179). File rough edges smooth and complete any decorative surface work (pp 194–195), then form the edges and seams. Complete the object by making inside folds.

Folding sequence for a box begins with top edges, then each side and the seam tabs. For final inside folds, or when box will no longer fit in bending brake, use a hatchet stake.

Hand seamer makes edges and narrow folds. Align edge of tool with fold line and tighten jaws with screws. Bend in stages along fold line by lifting tool upward. Close seam with mallet.

Hatchet stake can be made of hardwood with a bevelled top edge. Align fold line over edge of stake. First make fold with hands; then make a crisp crease with wooden mallet.

Hatchet stake

Bending brake folds sheet metal that is thinner than 1,6 mm. Adjust brake jaw for metal thickness. Clamp metal so fold line aligns with edge of plate and push plate up to fold sheet to desired angle.

Edges

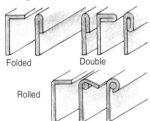

Folded   Double

Rolled

Edge treatment strengthens and smooths edges, and provides neat appearance. Rolled, or wired, edge (right) is strongest.

Rolled edge: 1. Width of fold should be 2,5 times diameter of wire. Bend edge upward along fold line with hand seamer or brake. Hold wire in place; close fold with mallet.

2. Support seam with block of wood. Curl edge around wire with wedge-faced hammer. Snip off excess wire with diagonal-cutting pliers.

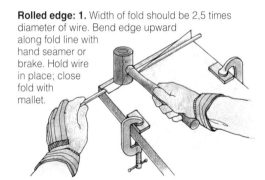

Seams

Butt joint

Flat lap

Locked seam

Seams are metal joints that can be soldered or fastened with rivets or screws. Locked seam (right) needs no fasteners or solder.

Locked seam: 1. Bend folds of equal width on both edges, one opposite the other. Lay scrap wood inside each fold; hammer down until almost closed; then remove wood and interlock edges (inset). Place seam over clamped pipe and flatten with mallet.

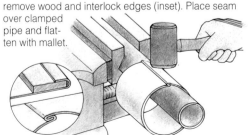

2. Fit channel of appropriate-size hand groover over seam. Strike handle of groover with ball-peen hammer as you move channel along the seam.

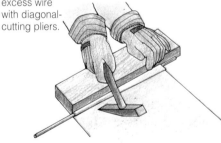

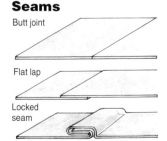

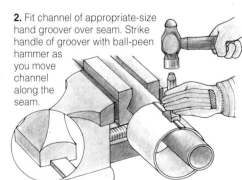

SHAPING WITH FORMS

Because metal is ductile – it flows, rather like modelling clay – it can be shaped by striking it against a form with a hammer or a mallet. You can create such objects as vases, bowls and trays using two basic forming techniques – *raising* and *sinking*.

Deep objects are raised by striking their outer surface against solid forms called *stakes*. Various stakes are available at metalworking suppliers, but you can improvise with pieces of metal or hardwood. Jewellers use tapered stakes called *mandrels* for shaping rings and bracelets (p 193).

When sinking a shallow object, strike its inner surface against a hollow form such as a sandbag or a mould made by gouging a bowl-shaped depression in the end grain of a hardwood block. Strike the metal squarely with the tool's face, not its edge, and use gentle, even blows. Keep steel hammer faces free of nicks (p 196).

Prolonged beating hardens most metal and it ceases to flow, becoming brittle and likely to crack. *Annealing,* or heating, the metal will restore its malleability. (Do not anneal aluminium, lead or pewter.) After annealing, remove oxide residue by cleaning the object in pickle (pp 190–191).

To finish a formed piece, decorate or planish it if desired (pp 194–195), then polish and buff it (p 196).

Annealing. Set piece on firebrick; heat all over with bushy torch flame until metal glows dull red. Allow to cool; then quench in water. Wear gloves and handle metal with tongs.

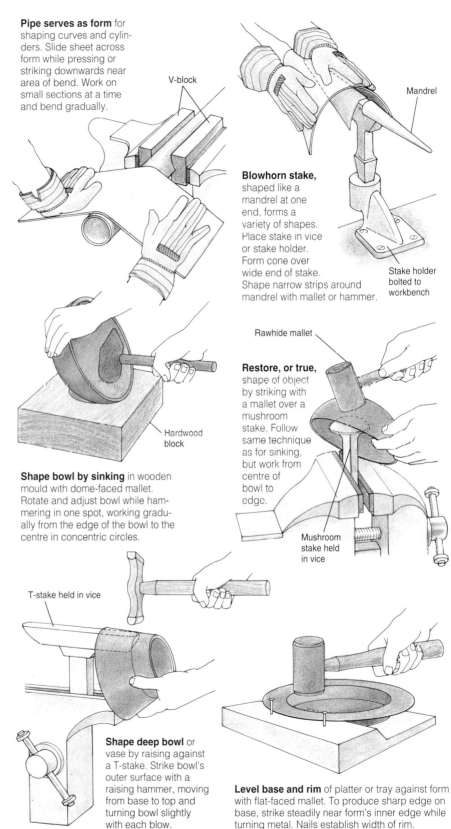

Pipe serves as form for shaping curves and cylinders. Slide sheet across form while pressing or striking downwards near area of bend. Work on small sections at a time and bend gradually.

V-block

Mandrel

Blowhorn stake, shaped like a mandrel at one end, forms a variety of shapes. Place stake in vice or stake holder. Form cone over wide end of stake. Shape narrow strips around mandrel with mallet or hammer.

Stake holder bolted to workbench

Rawhide mallet

Restore, or true, shape of object by striking with a mallet over a mushroom stake. Follow same technique as for sinking, but work from centre of bowl to edge.

Mushroom stake held in vice

Hardwood block

Shape bowl by sinking in wooden mould with dome-faced mallet. Rotate and adjust bowl while hammering in one spot, working gradually from the edge of the bowl to the centre in concentric circles.

T-stake held in vice

Shape deep bowl or vase by raising against a T-stake. Strike bowl's outer surface with a raising hammer, moving from base to top and turning bowl slightly with each blow.

Level base and rim of platter or tray against form with flat-faced mallet. To produce sharp edge on base, strike steadily near form's inner edge while turning metal. Nails establish width of rim.

BENDING BAR METAL AND PIPES

Bar metal is classified as strips and flats as well as shaped rods (pp 176–177). Bending and twisting techniques apply to all varieties of bar metal. In general, ferrous metals are harder to bend than non-ferrous. For tubing, use special bending tools.

Most bar metal up to 6,35 mm thick and 12,5 mm wide can be bent cold, but tight curves can overstretch metal, so make allowances when laying out. A bend of 90° will lengthen the outside of the curve by half the metal's thickness and shorten the inside of the curve by the same amount.

Align the workpiece exactly perpendicular or parallel to the vice jaws, protecting soft metal with V-blocks or scrap wood. Bend gradually and smoothly, by small amounts, checking the angle of the bend several times with a template or T-bevel. Use hand pressure first, then strike the metal with a hammer or mallet. For an exact shape, bend around a stationary form, such as a pipe clamped parallel to the vice jaws.

Heating metal makes it easier to bend and increases the amount it will stretch. Heat the area of the bend with a gas (LPG) torch until you can bend the metal smoothly.

Caution: Remove all nearby flammable objects and direct the torch flame only towards the area of bend. Wear gloves and protective clothing. Do not heat aluminium.

Cold-bending. Mark point of bend on metal strip. Clamp metal in vice and bend by hand for looser curve. For extra leverage, slip a length of pipe over strip's free end. For tight curve, strike metal just beyond edge of vice.

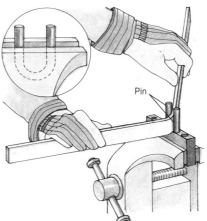

Bending jig makes scrolls and other bends. Set distance between pins slightly larger than the metal's thickness and feed metal between pins while bending. Homemade jig (inset) is a U-shaped rod clamped in vice.

Pin

Twisting strips. Clamp one end of strip in vice. Grip other end with adjustable wrench or locking pliers. Twist with steady pressure to produce spiral.

A bending spring shapes copper tubing without kinking. Slide tubing into spring until coils cover area of curve. Bend with thumbs as fulcrum or against knee to desired curve.

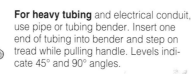
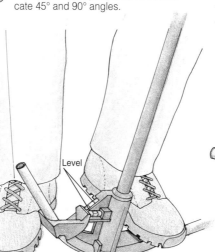

For heavy tubing and electrical conduit, use pipe or tubing bender. Insert one end of tubing into bender and step on tread while pulling handle. Levels indicate 45° and 90° angles.

Level

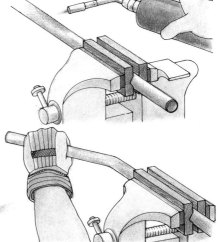

Bend flats, strips and rods secured in vice by heating area of bend with torch until metal glows red. Extinguish torch, grasp free end of metal with gloved hand and bend sideways.

JOINING PIPES WITH FITTINGS

Rigid bronze and steel pipe are joined with threaded fittings. Flexible copper tubing is joined with compression or flare fittings, and both flexible and rigid copper tubing can be soldered (pp 190–191). Certain fittings require threaded pipe. For these, pipe can be purchased pre-threaded or threaded to order at hardware, building or plumbing suppliers. Special fittings join incompatible materials. When buying fittings, specify the pipe's inside diameter, the material and whether it forms part of a water supply system or a drainage system.

Make careful calculations before cutting pipe to length – with rigid pipe, adjustments are seldom possible. Calculate both the width of the fitting and the amount it will overlap the pipe. Cut the ends of pipes exactly square, using a tubing cutter or, for bronze or steel pipe, a hacksaw (p 180). To prevent disturbed waterflow inside pipes, remove burrs – the rough edges produced by cutting – by reaming the ends.

Tighten and loosen threaded fittings with two pipe wrenches. Holding the pipe stationary with one wrench prevents damage to other joints on the line. Hold a pipe wrench so its jaws face the direction in which force is applied.

Caution: Before modifying a plumbing system, check with your local authority. Building and plumbing regulations may require that some repairs and installations should be done only by a licensed professional. Shut off the water supply and drain a plumbing pipe before working on it.

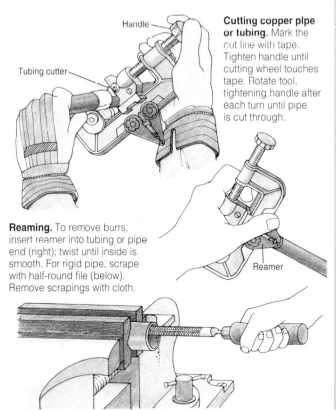

Cutting copper pipe or tubing. Mark the cut line with tape. Tighten handle until cutting wheel touches tape. Rotate tool, tightening handle after each turn until pipe is cut through.

Reaming. To remove burrs, insert reamer into tubing or pipe end (right); twist until inside is smooth. For rigid pipe, scrape with half-round file (below). Remove scrapings with cloth.

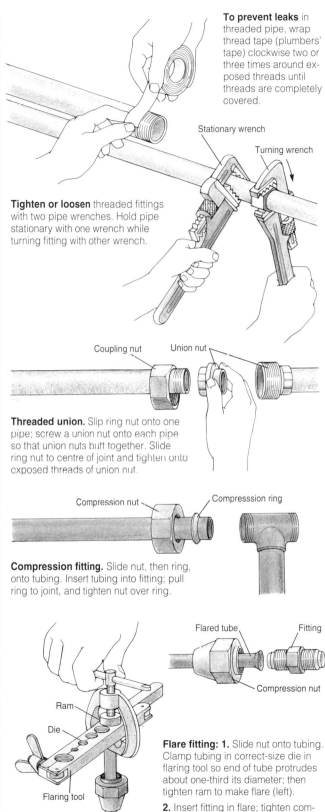

To prevent leaks in threaded pipe, wrap thread tape (plumbers' tape) clockwise two or three times around exposed threads until threads are completely covered.

Tighten or loosen threaded fittings with two pipe wrenches. Hold pipe stationary with one wrench while turning fitting with other wrench.

Threaded union. Slip ring nut onto one pipe; screw a union nut onto each pipe so that union nuts butt together. Slide ring nut to centre of joint and tighten onto exposed threads of union nut.

Compression fitting. Slide nut, then ring, onto tubing. Insert tubing into fitting; pull ring to joint, and tighten nut over ring.

Flare fitting: 1. Slide nut onto tubing. Clamp tubing in correct-size die in flaring tool so end of tube protrudes about one-third its diameter; then tighten ram to make flare (left).

2. Insert fitting in flare; tighten compression nut onto fitting (above).

Adhesives

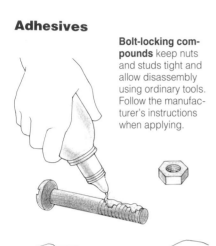

Bolt-locking compounds keep nuts and studs tight and allow disassembly using ordinary tools. Follow the manufacturer's instructions when applying.

Cyanoacrylate adhesive forms quick bond between non-porous materials. Apply a drop to one surface; press parts together and hold for 30 sec.

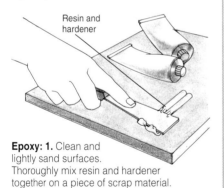

Epoxy: 1. Clean and lightly sand surfaces. Thoroughly mix resin and hardener together on a piece of scrap material.

Resin and hardener

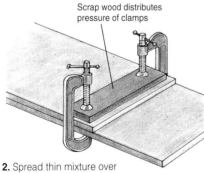

Scrap wood distributes pressure of clamps

2. Spread thin mixture over both pieces; clamp together until adhesive sets. Wipe away excess adhesive immediately.

Adhesives can create a strong bond for metal, but it is important to use the correct high-quality adhesive and to clean the surfaces thoroughly (degrease metal by wiping with denatured alcohol or a commercial degreasing agent). Follow the manufacturer's instructions for application and drying time.

To prevent threaded fasteners from loosening during ordinary running (particularly fasteners in engines and other vibrating machinery), coat them with bolt-locking compound, available at hardware and automotive stores. Small metal objects that receive little stress, such as costume jewellery and appliance trim, can be bonded with cyanoacrylate adhesive, also known as superglue. Select the right viscosity: liquid cyanoacrylate for tight-fitting flat surfaces; a thicker gel formula for pieces that fit together more loosely. Use epoxy where moderate stress is likely, when bonding metal to a non-porous material or where metals are rough-textured and fit loosely. Resin and hardener must be in correct proportions – too much hardener causes a weak joint; too little retards drying.

Caution: Work in a well-ventilated area when using adhesives and don't smoke, eat or drink. If cyanoacrylate or epoxy adhesive contacts your skin, remove it promptly with acetone (found in most nail polish removers).

Stronger than most adhesives are threaded fasteners and rivets. Fasteners are available in a variety of metals. If possible, match the fastener to the metal being joined, but where rust may occur use non-ferrous fasteners, such as aluminium or brass.

Screws

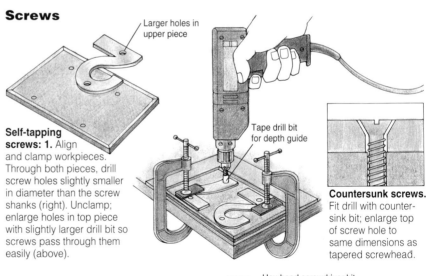

Larger holes in upper piece

Tape drill bit for depth guide

Self-tapping screws: 1. Align and clamp workpieces. Through both pieces, drill screw holes slightly smaller in diameter than the screw shanks (right). Unclamp; enlarge holes in top piece with slightly larger drill bit so screws pass through them easily (above).

Countersunk screws. Fit drill with countersink bit; enlarge top of screw hole to same dimensions as tapered screwhead.

2. Align pieces. Install screws; threads should bite into sides of holes in bottom piece. First drive all screws moderately tight; then fasten each screw securely.

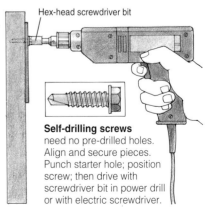

Hex-head screwdriver bit

Self-drilling screws need no pre-drilled holes. Align and secure pieces. Punch starter hole; position screw; then drive with screwdriver bit in power drill or with electric screwdriver.

Screws for joining sheet metal are usually self-tapping. Driven with a screwdriver or a spanner, they cut threads inside a pre-drilled hole. Self-drilling screws create both a pilot hole and the threads inside. Check with the manufacturer for the maximum thickness of pieces to be joined. (To remove stuck threaded fasteners, try the methods shown on p 189.)

For thicker pieces accessible from both sides, use bolts. Machine bolts with fine threads have greater holding power than stove bolts. Lag or carriage bolts can be used to attach metal to wood. A tightened bolt should extend beyond the nut by two or three threads. Allow for the additional thickness of washers, which serve to distribute pressure under the bolt head and the nut. A variety of specialized nuts is available; use cap nuts when fastening children's equipment (or wherever safety is a concern) and wing nuts for bolts that will need to be unfastened. If necessary, you can thread bolt holes yourself (p 188).

Blind rivets are strong enough only for light sheet-metal work like gutters and aluminium cladding or for automobile body repairs, but they are easy to install with a blind-rivet tool and are more versatile than tinner's rivets. The work can be accessible from only one side, but there must be room for the rivet to form on the other side.

Bolts

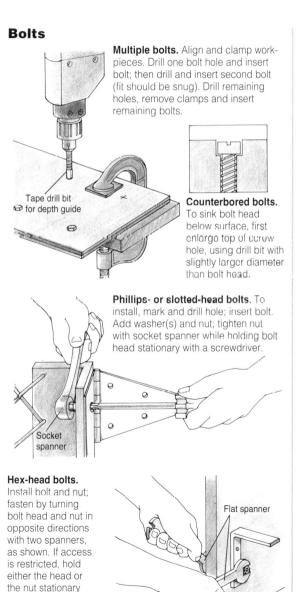

Multiple bolts. Align and clamp workpieces. Drill one bolt hole and insert bolt; then drill and insert second bolt (fit should be snug). Drill remaining holes, remove clamps and insert remaining bolts.

Tape drill bit for depth guide

Counterbored bolts. To sink bolt head below surface, first enlarge top of screw hole, using drill bit with slightly larger diameter than bolt head.

Phillips- or slotted-head bolts. To install, mark and drill hole; insert bolt. Add washer(s) and nut; tighten nut with socket spanner while holding bolt head stationary with a screwdriver.

Socket spanner

Hex-head bolts. Install bolt and nut; fasten by turning bolt head and nut in opposite directions with two spanners, as shown. If access is restricted, hold either the head or the nut stationary with a spanner and tighten other part with a socket spanner.

Flat spanner

Rivets

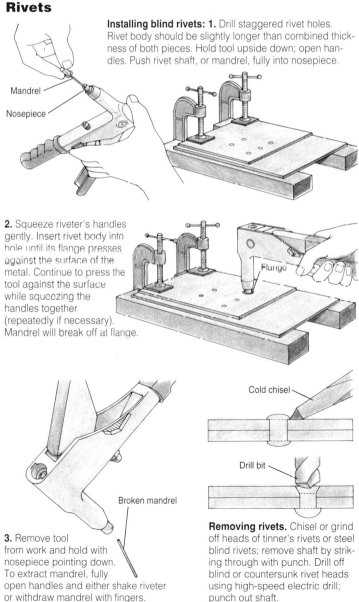

Installing blind rivets: 1. Drill staggered rivet holes. Rivet body should be slightly longer than combined thickness of both pieces. Hold tool upside down; open handles. Push rivet shaft, or mandrel, fully into nosepiece.

Mandrel

Nosepiece

2. Squeeze riveter's handles gently. Insert rivet body into hole until its flange presses against the surface of the metal. Continue to press the tool against the surface while squeezing the handles together (repeatedly if necessary). Mandrel will break off at flange.

Flange

3. Remove tool from work and hold with nosepiece pointing down. To extract mandrel, fully open handles and either shake riveter or withdraw mandrel with fingers.

Broken mandrel

Cold chisel

Drill bit

Removing rivets. Chisel or grind off heads of tinner's rivets or steel blind rivets; remove shaft by striking through with punch. Drill off blind or countersunk rivet heads using high-speed electric drill; punch out shaft.

Taps are used for cutting threads in holes; dies for threading rods. Both tools are often used for renewing damaged threads when repairing automobile parts, small-engine machinery (such as lawn mowers and chain saws,) and household appliances.

Although the metric system is commonly used in South Africa, there are many different types of thread. Check the thread required by using a thread pitch gauge (below) or ask your hardware supplier to identify the type and size of taps that you need.

Taps are usually supplied in sets of three, consisting of a *taper tap*, used for starting the thread or when thin material is being tapped; the *intermediate tap*, to extend the thread, and the *bottoming tap*.

Fully tapped hole goes through workpiece.

Blind hole ends inside workpiece.

Drill the hole to be tapped using the drill bit size indicated by a chart (often provided with tap and die sets) or by reading the markings directly on the taps. A blind hole must be drilled deeper than the required thread to prevent the tap from binding on contact with the bottom of the hole. Complete blind holes with the bottoming tap, which cuts threads to the base of the hole, withdrawing the tap occasionally to clear metal chips from the hole.

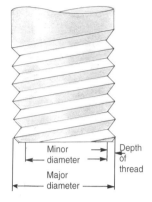
Thread anatomy. Major diameter of threads determines size of tap or die to use for cutting. Drill bit for pilot hole is slightly larger than minor diameter.

Drilling tap holes

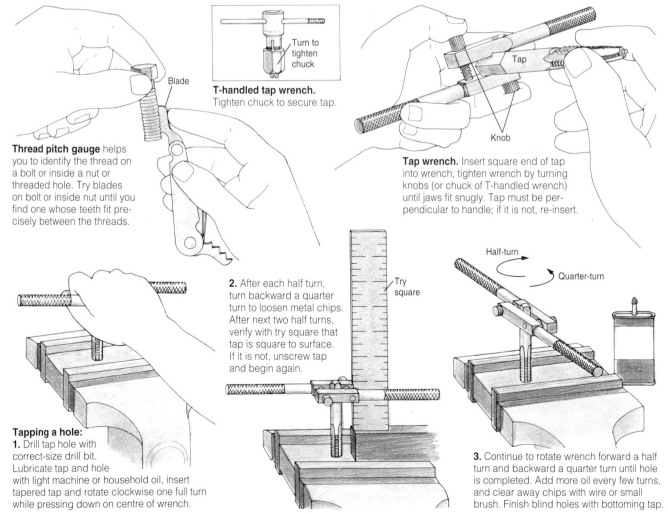

Thread pitch gauge helps you to identify the thread on a bolt or inside a nut or threaded hole. Try blades on bolt or inside nut until you find one whose teeth fit precisely between the threads.

T-handled tap wrench. Tighten chuck to secure tap.

Tap wrench. Insert square end of tap into wrench; tighten wrench by turning knobs (or chuck of T-handled wrench) until jaws fit snugly. Tap must be perpendicular to handle; if it is not, re-insert.

Tapping a hole:
1. Drill tap hole with correct-size drill bit. Lubricate tap and hole with light machine or household oil, insert tapered tap and rotate clockwise one full turn while pressing down on centre of wrench.

2. After each half turn, turn backward a quarter turn to loosen metal chips. After next two half turns, verify with try square that tap is square to surface. If it is not, unscrew tap and begin again.

3. Continue to rotate wrench forward a half turn and backward a quarter turn until hole is completed. Add more oil every few turns, and clear away chips with wire or small brush. Finish blind holes with bottoming tap.

Extracting broken fasteners

A broken or rusted bolt or screw can often be removed by soaking it with penetrating oil for 15 min. Then, if the head is accessible, twist out the fastener with locking pliers.

Another method is to strike a prick punch with a ball-peen hammer against one edge of the fastener head, turning the fastener counterclockwise.

For fasteners broken off below the surface, use a screw extractor. Most have left-hand threads; some have straight flutes along the shank. Both are turned counterclockwise with a wrench to extract the broken fastener.

Tape drill bit as a guide

Removing a broken fastener:
1. Punch starting point in centre of broken fastener. With a drill bit smaller than the fastener, drill at least 9,5 mm into broken shaft.

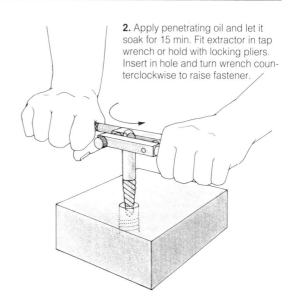

2. Apply penetrating oil and let it soak for 15 min. Fit extractor in tap wrench or hold with locking pliers. Insert in hole and turn wrench counterclockwise to raise fastener.

Threading rods with dies

Dies are held in a special wrench called a *diestock*. Some diestocks have an adjustable collar called a *diestock guide* that fits snugly around the rod to keep the die perpendicular to the handle.

Most tap and die sets include several dies. Choose a die whose diameter corresponds to the size of the rod to be threaded. *Adjustable dies* can be made larger or smaller with a setscrew on one side. To test the fit of an adjustable die, cut the threads first with the die fully open. Screw a nut onto the rod. If the fit is too tight, adjust the die so it is smaller and re-cut the threads.

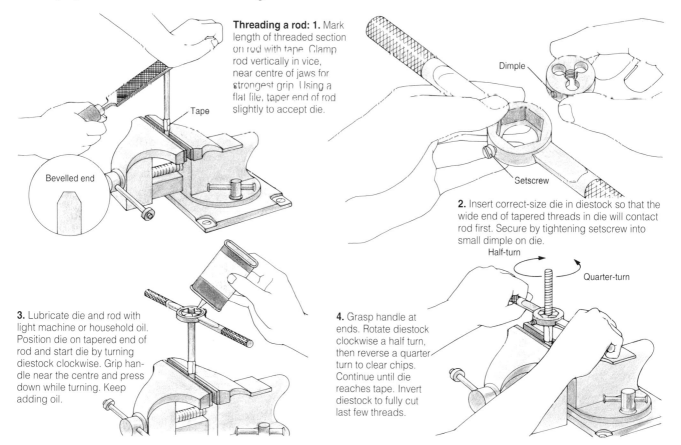

Threading a rod: 1. Mark length of threaded section on rod with tape. Clamp rod vertically in vice, near centre of jaws for strongest grip. Using a flat file, taper end of rod slightly to accept die.

Tape

Bevelled end

Dimple

Setscrew

2. Insert correct-size die in diestock so that the wide end of tapered threads in die will contact rod first. Secure by tightening setscrew into small dimple on die.

Half-turn

Quarter-turn

3. Lubricate die and rod with light machine or household oil. Position die on tapered end of rod and start die by turning diestock clockwise. Grip handle near the centre and press down while turning. Keep adding oil.

4. Grasp handle at ends. Rotate diestock clockwise a half turn, then reverse a quarter turn to clear chips. Continue until die reaches tape. Invert diestock to fully cut last few threads.

SOLDERING

Soldering joins metals by melting between them an alloy, called solder, that acts as a glue. For *soft-soldering*, the usual method for joining sheet metals and electronic parts, the solder is made chiefly of tin and lead. Copper pipes should be joined with lead-free solder. These solders melt at 370°C or under – too low a temperature to cause changes in the metals being joined. *Hard-soldering* creates stronger joints and is needed to join silver or for fine craftsmanship. Hard solder contains precious metals, such as silver, with melting points between 590°C and 900°C. Heating a metal to accept hard solder creates microscopic spaces into which the solder can flow; thus hard-soldered joints have more strength than soft-soldered joints and can be filed flush without weakening. *Brazing* is a type of hard-soldering generally used to join steel or dissimilar metals; it requires a brass solder with a melting

point between 1000°C and 1650°C. Brazing requires considerable skill and the high heat created by an air/fuel torch.

An electric soldering pencil or gun provides sufficient heat for soft-soldering stained-glass joints or small electronic components. To soft-solder metal objects, use an electric soldering iron. A propane torch produces a flame suitable both for soldering copper pipes and for hard-soldering.

Before soldering, clean well and cover surfaces with the appropriate flux to avoid the formation of oxides, a dark scaly film that prevents solder from adhering. For soft-soldering all except electronic items, use a zinc chloride flux, wiping away any excess with a wet cloth after soldering. Delicate electronic work requires a rosin flux, which is non-corrosive. For hard-soldering, use fluxes containing borax or fluoride. After hard-soldering, remove oxides with *pickle,* a cleaning solution that may contain sulphuric acid. Use a non-sulphuric-acid pickle, available from craft shops and jewellery suppliers.

Soft-soldering with an iron

1. File tip of iron if it is pitted or has a dark coating. Clamp iron in vice; protect it with blocks of wood. File sides of tip with coarse or bastard file until metal shines.

2. Tin tip to allow uniform heat transfer from iron to pieces being soldered. Heat iron until it smokes, then immediately brush tip with flux. Touch the tip with solder, coating it thinly and evenly.

3. Prepare surfaces to be joined by cleaning them with a wire brush and then polishing them with steel wool. Do not touch polished areas with fingers. Test the fit of the pieces. Solder will not bond across visible gaps.

4. Apply flux to both pieces. To make cleaning finished seam easier, try to brush flux only onto areas that are to receive solder.

5. Bind pieces with utility wire. Apply solder by first holding hot iron against seam. Then touch seam with solder just ahead of tip. When solder flows, gradually draw both iron and solder along seam until full.

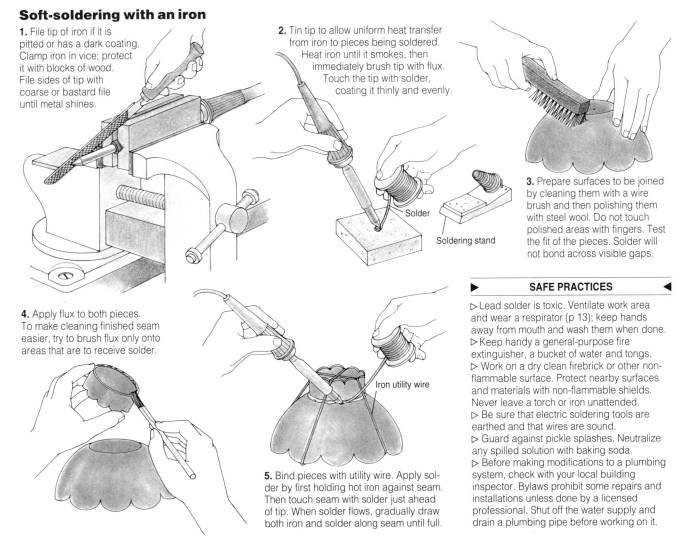

Soldering copper tubing

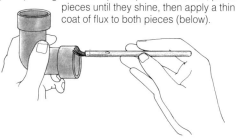

1. Clean all parts. Ream inside tubing to remove burrs (p 185). Using steel wool (above) or a wire brush, polish pieces until they shine, then apply a thin coat of flux to both pieces (below).

2. Heat joint area. Tack a piece of non-flammable material to nearby surfaces. Brush entire joint with torch flame to heat it evenly throughout, concentrating more heat on heavier part of fitting.

3. Apply solder to joint. When flux bubbles, touch solder to side of fitting opposite flame. At correct temperature, solder will melt instantly and flow around seam. Hold flame away from seam as solder flows. Wipe off excess solder with damp cloth.

Hard-soldering with a torch

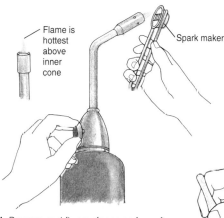

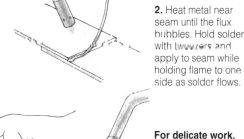

Flame is hottest above inner cone

Spark maker

1. Prepare and flux surfaces as for soft-soldering, using appropriate flux. Light torch by holding tank upright, opening valve about half a turn, then igniting gas with spark maker held alongside nozzle. Adjust flame to produce pointed inner cone.

2. Heat metal near seam until the flux bubbles. Hold solder with tweezers and apply to seam while holding flame to one side as solder flows.

For delicate work, cut solder sheet into small squares; place them where pieces will join. Apply flame evenly to both pieces; as metal heats, solder will melt into joint.

3. Clean oxidized pieces by dipping into pickle. Follow manufacturer's instructions for heating solution – do not boil. Hold piece with copper tongs only – steel or iron may affect metal. Rinse pieces under running water.

Welding and blacksmithing

Welding joins metals – usually steel – by melting them so that they fuse together. The high heat required can come from a torch that mixes fuel with pure oxygen or from a powerful electric transformer called an *arc welder*. Strong welded joints are required for repairs to machinery, metal furniture and outdoor equipment, as well as to tools and to metal used for structural purposes. Though fairly simple in theory, welding requires expert instruction and much practice. Technical colleges and art schools may offer courses in welding, and rental centres carry welding equipment.

Blacksmithing has seen a revival of interest in recent years. Ample space and equipment are needed, including a forge for heating metal and a selection of hammers and stakes for beating it into shape. Craft items like fireplace tools, decorative hardware and cooking utensils are the stock-in-trade of most modern-day smiths. Technical colleges may be able to advise on courses in blacksmithing. Equipment can be homemade or bought at flea markets and auctions. A smith who shoes horses is a *farrier* – for instruction, consult farming, equestrian or veterinarians' groups.

Wire – round, half-round, square and rectangular – serves as stock for many jewellery and metalworking projects. Wire can be pulled through a metal drawplate (a process called *drawing*) to change its shape and thickness and it can be decoratively twisted by itself or with other wires. It can be fashioned into jump rings, then used to form chain or create *findings,* the basic elements of many jewellery pieces.

Finger rings are made with wire or with strips cut from sheet metal. Use a graduated ring mandrel, which has standard ring sizes marked at intervals along its length, to form new rings or to re-shape damaged ones. Calculate the length of metal needed to form a given ring size by using the linear scale provided on some mandrels or by forming a template from a strip of paper. First wrap the paper around the desired ring size on the mandrel, then add twice the thickness of the metal stock for the template's total length.

The metal found in commercial chain is sometimes filled with solder, which lowers its melting point, making it difficult to repair by soldering. Homemade solid wire jump rings, however, make durable links and chains. Making circular jump rings is shown; you can also create oval and square jump rings by winding the wire around a form with the desired shape.

Buy commercial findings – such as settings for stones, clasps for necklaces and bracelets, and posts for earrings and cufflinks – at craft shops or jewellery suppliers, and use them to replace broken findings or to form new pieces. Unless you're experienced, don't try to repair or set valuable stones – it is easy to lose or damage them.

Hard-soldering with the technique for delicate work shown on p 191 is the best way to join metal jewellery pieces. For a project with many joints, use solder designated high-, medium- and lower-temperature in succession to avoid melting completed joints while heating others. Glue together any pieces that can't be heated (p 186).

Working with wire

Drawing wire. File wire tip to 25 mm taper; then lubricate it with beeswax or light household oil. Clamp drawplate in vice; insert wire from plate's unnumbered side into smallest possible hole of desired shape. Hold tip; pull wire through hole. Pull through successively smaller holes until wire reaches desired gauge. Anneal frequently (below).

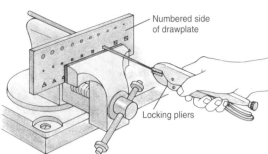

Numbered side of drawplate

Locking pliers

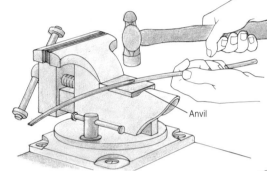

Anvil

Flattening wire. Anneal wire; then place on a smooth flat metal surface. Hold wire and strike squarely and evenly with ball-peen hammer along wire's entire length. For square wire, turn on edge and strike that side until both sides are equal.

Annealing wire. Coil wire closely, with no loose strands. Bind coil with soft iron utility wire. Place on firebrick and heat with constantly moving torch until metal glows dull red. Quench in water, remove binding utility wire, and pickle (p 191).

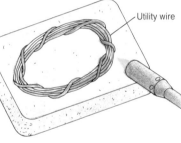

Utility wire

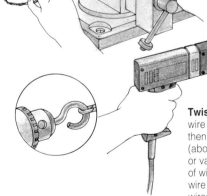

Twisting wire. For a double twist, select a piece of wire twice the length needed plus 25 mm. Anneal wire, then fold in half and fasten loose ends securely in vice (above, left). Secure a cup hook in chuck of hand drill or variable-speed electric drill (inset); slip doubled end of wire over hook. With wire taut, operate drill slowly; wire will twist (above). To twist single wire or several wires together, fasten wire ends directly in drill chuck.

Twisted wire designs

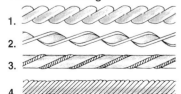

1.
2.
3.
4.

Twisted wire can form rings and patterns on flat brooches, earrings or bracelets. To make a bracelet, loop wire to desired diameter and solder ends together.
1. Double-twist round wire, then flatten.
2. Twist single strand of flat wire.
3. First twist single square wire, then double-twist round wire and wind together by hand.
4. Twist together several strands of round wire.

Forming a ring

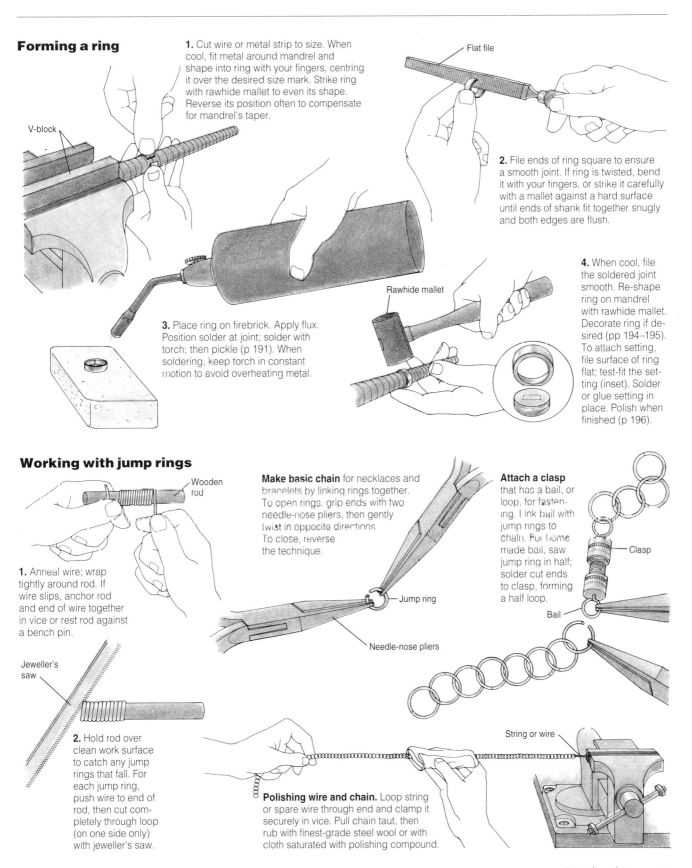

1. Cut wire or metal strip to size. When cool, fit metal around mandrel and shape into ring with your fingers, centring it over the desired size mark. Strike ring with rawhide mallet to even its shape. Reverse its position often to compensate for mandrel's taper.

V-block

Flat file

2. File ends of ring square to ensure a smooth joint. If ring is twisted, bend it with your fingers, or strike it carefully with a mallet against a hard surface until ends of shank fit together snugly and both edges are flush.

4. When cool, file the soldered joint smooth. Re-shape ring on mandrel with rawhide mallet. Decorate ring if desired (pp 194–195). To attach setting, file surface of ring flat; test-fit the setting (inset). Solder or glue setting in place. Polish when finished (p 196).

Rawhide mallet

3. Place ring on firebrick. Apply flux. Position solder at joint; solder with torch; then pickle (p 191). When soldering, keep torch in constant motion to avoid overheating metal.

Working with jump rings

Wooden rod

1. Anneal wire; wrap tightly around rod. If wire slips, anchor rod and end of wire together in vice or rest rod against a bench pin.

Jeweller's saw

2. Hold rod over clean work surface to catch any jump rings that fall. For each jump ring, push wire to end of rod, then cut completely through loop (on one side only) with jeweller's saw.

Make basic chain for necklaces and bracelets by linking rings together. To open rings, grip ends with two needle-nose pliers, then gently twist in opposite directions. To close, reverse the technique.

Jump ring

Needle-nose pliers

Attach a clasp that has a bail, or loop, for fastening. Link bail with jump rings to chain. For home made bail, saw jump ring in half; solder cut ends to clasp, forming a half loop.

Clasp

Bail

Polishing wire and chain. Loop string or spare wire through end and clamp it securely in vice. Pull chain taut, then rub with finest-grade steel wool or with cloth saturated with polishing compound.

String or wire

Metal objects can be decorated by a variety of techniques, including hammering, etching and colouring with chemicals. Decoration must be applied at the appropriate point during construction. For example, items like bowls or vases that are shaped by raising or sinking cannot be decorated until after they are formed. But a box or other item with flat sides can be decorated before it is folded or attached to other pieces. Practice decorative techniques on pieces of scrap metal before attempting them on the actual workpiece.

Planishing is the technique of hardening and smoothing metal by hammering. A skilfully planished surface has many small indentations that add texture and sparkle to the piece. Polished hammers are reserved for planishing. Keep their faces smooth (p 196). A ball-peen hammer can also be used to create patterned surfaces – reflecting the various contours of either the face of the hammer or the surface it strikes. Always wear safety goggles when striking metal with hammers.

Pointed tools and punches are struck with hammers to create intricate designs on metal surfaces. Punching holes to form a pattern in the metal is called *piercing*. In *chasing*, blunt punches are used to create a pattern in shallow relief on the surface. When the pattern is also raised in relief by hammering it from behind, the technique is

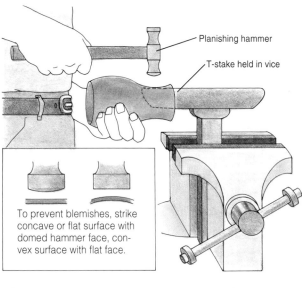

To prevent blemishes, strike concave or flat surface with domed hammer face, convex surface with flat face.

Planishing hammer
T-stake held in vice

Planishing. Hold piece on stake or against other hard surface. Work with light in front of you. Strike squarely and evenly with planishing hammer, working in a spiral from base to rim, (for a bowl, work from centre outward). Deliver blows from wrist; overlap points of impact.

Chasing and repoussé

Chasing hammer
Chasing tool

1. Heat pitch and mount work face-up in pitch bowl so that metal is supported at all points. Trace outline and details with chasing tool by striking tool end lightly with hammer. Hold tools firmly to avoid slips; deliver blows from wrist.

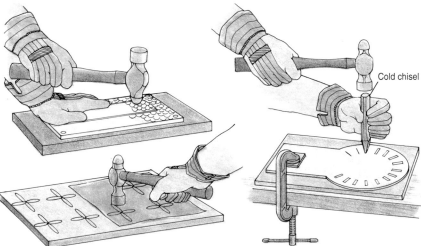

Cold chisel

Impact and hammer textures. For dimpled pattern, hold work against a hard surface and strike work with round hammer face (top). To reproduce a surface texture, hold workpiece against surface; strike workpiece all over with flat face until design is imprinted (bottom).

Piercing. Scribe pattern of holes; clamp work on scrap wood. Use nails, a prick punch or a cold chisel with a sharp edge (shown) to pierce holes in the metal, striking the tool with flat face of a ball-peen hammer. Aim for uniform results over the entire piece.

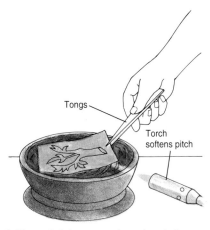

Tongs
Torch softens pitch

2. Warm pitch to remove chased work. For repoussé work, anneal (p 183); then mount work face-down in pitch and emboss with repoussé tools, using the same hammer technique as for chasing. Proceed alternately on front and back until design is defined.

called *repoussé.* You strike chasing and repoussé tools with a lightweight chasing hammer, and do both techniques on a surface that yields slightly. Pitch set in a special bowl is ideal (it is available at metalworking suppliers), but softwood or a sandbag can also serve as a work surface. Heat pitch with a torch to soften it before positioning or removing an object, but do not ignite it. To remove excess pitch, soak the metal in lacquer thinners.

In *etching,* a design is created on metal by dissolving part of the surface with a corrosive *mordant.* The mordant for most metals is usually nitric acid; its use is best left to professionals. However, copper and brass can be etched with ferric chloride, a safer, less caustic salt solution available at crafts and electronics suppliers. Parts of the design to be protected from the mordant are coated beforehand with a *resist,* usually wax or a substance called asphaltum.

Exposing metals to certain chemicals creates a thin layer of corrosion that changes their patina, or texture and colour. After treatment, polish the metal if desired (pp 196–197), then protect it from further coloration by giving it a coat of lacquer or wax.

Caution: Wear safety goggles and rubber gloves when working with chemicals and follow any other precautions for handling, storage and disposal listed by the manufacturer.

Etching

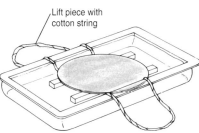

Metal scriber

1. Cover areas to be protected from mordant by brushing on resist (wax or asphaltum). Either coat surface and scribe design into resist for etching (above), or cover metal with stencil of design and paint resist over uncovered areas (below), then remove stencil. Let the resist dry.

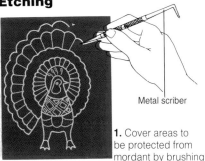

Stencil

Lift piece with cotton string

2. Submerge piece upside down in mordant in glass or plastic container, with patterned face on plastic supports. Stir often with a feather or a string to dislodge bubbles.

3. After 30 min, rinse piece with water and check progress. Repeat every 15 min until metal has dissolved to desired depth. Remove resist with soft cloth soaked in turpentine.

Protecting finished surfaces

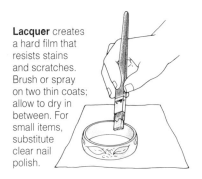

Lacquer creates a hard film that resists stains and scratches. Brush or spray on two thin coats; allow to dry in between. For small items, substitute clear nail polish.

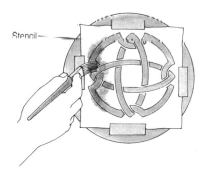

Wax seals out air and moisture where hard finish is not desired. Select a fine-quality furniture wax that contains no silicone. Apply, allow to harden, then buff with clean soft cloth. Repeat until desired sheen is achieved.

Creating a patina

When treating metal objects to create a surface patina, adjust the recipes below proportionately if greater or smaller amounts are needed for the size of the object. The effect of the treatment will vary depending on the type of metal and the surrounding conditions. Try recipes on scrap metal first. Before treatment, wash metal thoroughly in a bucket of water mixed with household detergent and 1 tbsp of ammonia. (When the metal is clean, water will no longer form beads on the surface.) Dry the metal with a clean soft cloth, and from then on handle it only by the edges. Mix chemicals in a glass or porcelain container and use only distilled water. Check the object frequently to gauge its progress. Follow the manufacturer's instructions for storage and handling of chemicals.

To darken silver or copper, mix 1 tbsp liver of sulphur (potassium sulphide, available from jewellery and crafts suppliers) in 1 cup warm water. Hold the piece with tongs and dip it into the solution. Rinse under running water.

To darken steel, aluminium or bronze, apply gun blue, available at gun shops. Rub the blue over the metal with fine-grade steel wool until you achieve the desired effect.

To give copper a variegated blue pattern, wet the piece, then sprinkle it with table salt. Place the piece beside an open bowl of ammonia, and cover both with a plastic bucket or small plastic tent. Leave until the desired effect is achieved (sometimes several days).

To colour copper, brass or bronze green, mix 1 tbsp ammonium chloride (sal ammoniac, available from jewellery and crafts suppliers), 1 tbsp table salt and 2 tbsp ammonia in 1 litre warm water. Pour solution into a plastic spray bottle and spray the piece all over. Allow to dry; repeat until the desired effect is achieved.

To turn copper dark brown, coat your fingers with a thin film of linseed oil, then rub the piece all over, applying just enough oil to cover the surface. Warm the piece evenly with a propane torch until the oil just starts to smoke. Wipe off excess oil with a clean cloth.

FINISHING METAL SURFACES

The final stages of many metalworking projects are sanding, which smooths the surface, and buffing, which creates lustre. (Filing removes rough edges and burrs; see p 181.) Complete polishing consists of rubbing with successively finer grades of abrasive, beginning by hand with abrasive paper (or by using an attachment on a portable power drill), and then buffing with an electric polishing machine, such as a bench grinder.

Start with a medium (100-grit) or very fine (200-grit) abrasive and, when the surface is uniform, switch to an extra-fine (300-grit) abrasive. For a fine polish, work up to at least a 400-grit abrasive, then buff.

Buff on a bench grinder fitted with a cloth disc called a *buffing wheel*. To buff rings and other small objects, fit a *cone buff* over a *tapered spindle,* both of which are available at hardware stores or jewellers' suppliers. Follow the tool manufacturer's instructions for changing wheels and installing a tapered spindle on the motor shaft – you will first have to remove the side housing panel. It's safe also to remove the eye guard and tool rest from the tool, but wear safety goggles, and allow no one to stand where they might be hit by an item pulled from your grasp by the wheel. Hold large items in your hands and brace smaller or flat items against a board. The wheel should always rotate downward toward you.

Apply buffing compounds directly to the wheel. Select compounds to suit the metal of your workpiece – one type is best for zinc, aluminium and steel, while another is suited to copper, brass and other non-ferrous metals. Install a separate wheel for each compound. After using each, clean the metal by washing it with a mixture of household detergent, water and a few drops of ammonia.

A portable power drill fitted with a buffing pad attachment and clamped into a horizontal drill stand can substitute for buffing with a bench grinder. Apply polishing compound and buff as you would with a grinder.

Preliminary polishing. Secure piece; rub metal with abrasive cloth or paper wrapped around stick, file or dowel. Use two or more grades of abrasive; change direction of strokes with each successive grade.

Sanding block

Polishing hammer face. Clamp hammer in vice; polish as described above but with abrasive material wrapped around wood block or secured in sanding block. To buff, coat leather-covered block with buffing compound and rub hammer face with circular motion.

Portable drill speeds up polishing. Fit abrasive disc (shown) or buffing pad on a drill arbor according to manufacturer's instructions. If object is not stationary, clamp it securely. Running tool at high speed, move disc across surface at even rate, using light pressure. Wear goggles and gloves.

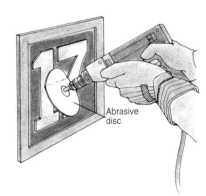

Abrasive disc

Buffing with a bench grinder

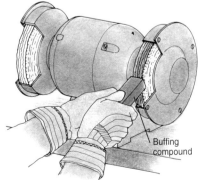

Buffing compound

Preparing wheel. Wear goggles and gloves. Touch end of compound stick to moving wheel below centre-line. Coat wheel evenly with compound every 5 min during use. When surface becomes shiny, hold buff rake (or an old fork) against surface of pad until the cloth is no longer compacted, then re-apply compound.

Buffing. Grip work tightly with fingers and hold it below wheel's centreline. Turn piece constantly to expose whole surface. Clean work before changing to a wheel that has been coated with another compound.

Buffing small items. Install tapered spindle on motor shaft and screw cone buff onto spindle. Coat the buff with compound. Press small items gently and firmly onto spinning buff. Change cones and clean workpiece between compounds. Rubber gloves make handling easier.

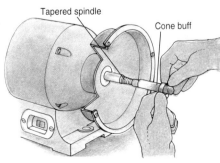

Tapered spindle

Cone buff

REPAIRING METAL OBJECTS

Metal objects with minor rust and damage can usually be repaired, but rust destroys metal quickly. Prevent it by painting outdoor tools, toys and other items with rust-resistant paint and storing them in a dry place, and by using galvanized metal for outdoor fasteners, railings and fencing.

Clean metal with mild detergent and water, and brighten tarnished metal by rubbing it with commercial polish. Careful tapping on a sandbag or stake, or with the aid of a dolly block (a polished steel block available through auto supply stores), flattens dents. Solder small cracks (p 190); or patch cracks and holes with a two-part fibreglass repair kit, available at hardware and auto supply stores. Read the kit manufacturer's instructions before use – these compounds are not suitable for making structural repairs or repairs to containers of liquid or gas.

An alternative to sanding away rust is *liquid rust-converter*. Scrape off all loose rust, then apply the converter. It hardens and seals the remaining rust, creating an irregular but rustproof surface that can be primed and painted.

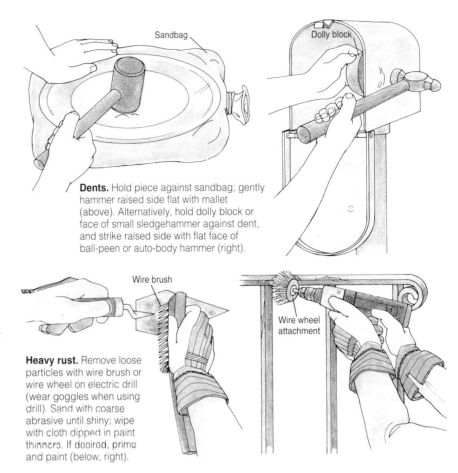

Dents. Hold piece against sandbag; gently hammer raised side flat with mallet (above). Alternatively, hold dolly block or face of small sledgehammer against dent, and strike raised side with flat face of ball-peen or auto-body hammer (right).

Heavy rust. Remove loose particles with wire brush or wire wheel on electric drill (wear goggles when using drill). Sand with coarse abrasive until shiny; wipe with cloth dipped in paint thinners. If desired, prime and paint (below, right).

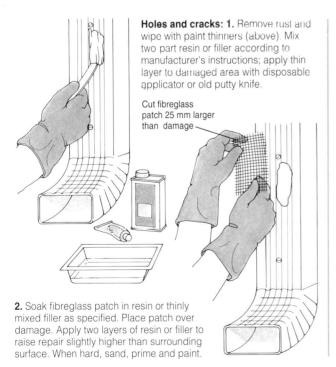

Holes and cracks: 1. Remove rust and wipe with paint thinners (above). Mix two part resin or filler according to manufacturer's instructions; apply thin layer to damaged area with disposable applicator or old putty knife.

Cut fibreglass patch 25 mm larger than damage

2. Soak fibreglass patch in resin or thinly mixed filler as specified. Place patch over damage. Apply two layers of resin or filler to raise repair slightly higher than surrounding surface. When hard, sand, prime and paint.

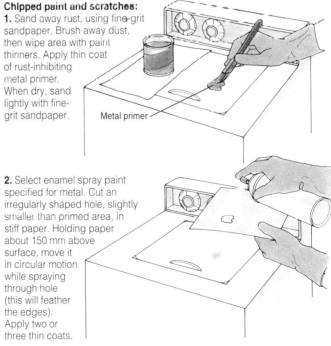

**Chipped paint and scratches:
1.** Sand away rust, using fine-grit sandpaper. Brush away dust, then wipe area with paint thinners. Apply thin coat of rust-inhibiting metal primer. When dry, sand lightly with fine-grit sandpaper.

Metal primer

2. Select enamel spray paint specified for metal. Cut an irregularly shaped hole, slightly smaller than primed area, in stiff paper. Holding paper about 150 mm above surface, move it in circular motion while spraying through hole (this will feather the edges). Apply two or three thin coats.

Inspect tools before each use. A blunt tool is neither efficient nor safe. With practice and good equipment, you can sharpen most straight-edged tools. But saw blades, carbide-tipped tools and other hardened or contoured edges are best sharpened professionally.

Sharpening causes the sides of a blade to meet at an angle, called a bevel, the steepness of which is crucial to the blade's performance. In general, re-sharpen a blade to its original bevel. Chisel and plane blades come with bevels ranging from 15° to 30°. You can add a narrow secondary bevel five degrees greater. This speeds honing by reducing the cutting area. *Hollow-grinding* (grinding the primary bevel against the edge of the bench grinder wheel until the blade is slightly concave) produces a similar result.

Primary bevel

Secondary bevel

Hollow-ground

A bench grinder speeds sharpening and is helpful for re-shaping damaged edges. Buy new grinding wheels as needed and install a medium- and a fine-grit wheel to use as a pair.

When grinding, follow the safety precautions listed below and on pp 12-13. Improper use of a bench grinder not only is extremely dangerous; it can destroy the tool's *temper* – its hardness and resilience.

Hand-sharpen and hone blades with flat sharpening stones and curved slipstones. A good selection might include a combination medium/fine oilstone and a few waterstones. Keep stones well lubricated when in use, and store each in its own box, away from workshop dust. For a keen edge, finish up with a leather strop.

Sharpening with a bench grinder

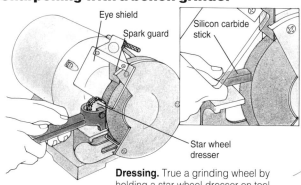

Eye shield

Spark guard

Silicon carbide stick

Star wheel dresser

Dressing. True a grinding wheel by holding a star wheel dresser on tool rest and, while running the grinder, slide dresser lightly from side to side against wheel's edge (above). To restore clogged wheel, use same technique, but with silicon carbide stick (inset).

Hollow grinding. Set tool rest to desired bevel angle. Hold tool with both hands; place on rest and slide from side to side against edge of wheel. Keep forefinger against bottom edge of rest to steady tool.

Tool rest

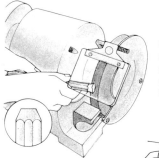

Cold chisel. Grind away mushroomed or split head of cold chisel to reduce chances of splintering, which can cause injury. Taper ground end (inset) to reduce chance of future damage.

Drawknife. Before grinding, ensure that blade can move freely across grinder wheel. Bevel blade by sliding it across the wheel, supported on the tool rest. To hone, clamp one handle of tool in vice. Start at opposite end and slide sharpening stone along blade's bevelled side. To remove burr, reverse tool and repeat on other side.

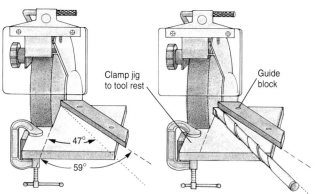

Clamp jig to tool rest

Guide block

47°

59°

Drill bit. Make jig for sharpening twist drill bit against side-grinding wheel. Clamp jig to level tool rest; place bit on jig against guide block. Press one side of tip against wheel; roll bit clockwise while slowly pivoting it to guideline at 47°. Repeat for other side.

Honing a sharp edge

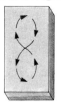

To prevent uneven wear on stone, move blade in figure-8 pattern. Simpler technique is back-and-forth motion.

Hone primary bevel on chisels, plane blades and spokeshaves by rubbing blade over medium stone (above, right) until you can feel a burr on blade's flat side. To create secondary bevel, raise blade 5 degrees (inset) and rub over fine stone until burr forms. Remove burr both times (right) by gently rubbing blade's flat side on stone until blade is smooth.

Honing guide helps keep angles uniform. Model below rolls along flat work surface, allowing blade to travel over entire stone. Fit tool and set bevel angle according to manufacturer's instructions. Stroke tool firmly along stone; reset angle for secondary bevel.

Angle gauge

Roller guide

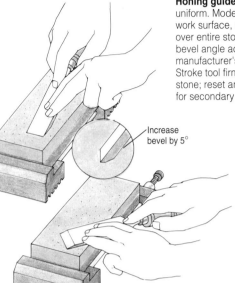

Increase bevel by 5°

Stone holder

Strop on leather that has been lightly coated with fine polishing compound. Hold blade against strop; draw back several times on each side of blade. Alternatively, hone on a very fine stone (6000 grit).

Leather strop

Special techniques

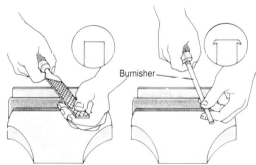

Burnisher

Scraper. Clamp in vice; protect with scrap wood. Make edge perfectly square with file or stone (left). (For bevelled cabinet scrapers, file bevel to original angle.) Create burr (hooked edge) by pushing burnisher along edge while pressing down firmly (right). On final strokes, tilt tool downward slightly to make burr curl over.

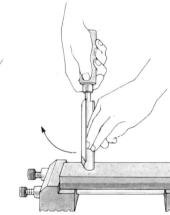

Gouges. On gouge with outside bevel (shown), follow the existing bevel angle as you slide the edge with a rotating motion along a flat stone. Remove burr on inside edge by stroking with a slipstone. On gouge with inside bevel, sharpen by stroking with slipstone at existing bevel angle. Remove burr with flat stone.

Slipstone

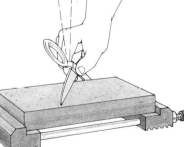

←10°→

Knife. With cutting edge leading, draw blade across stone from handle to tip. Maintain bevel angle. Turn blade over and repeat. Use same number of strokes for each side. Strop for razor edge.

Slipstone

Serrated knife. Clamp knife in vice with bevelled side of serrations facing you. Sharpen each serration by stroking lightly with curved edge of slipstone held at bevel angle. Remove burrs by rubbing unbevelled side of blade on flat stone.

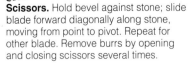

Scissors. Hold bevel against stone; slide blade forward diagonally along stone, moving from point to pivot. Repeat for other blade. Remove burrs by opening and closing scissors several times.

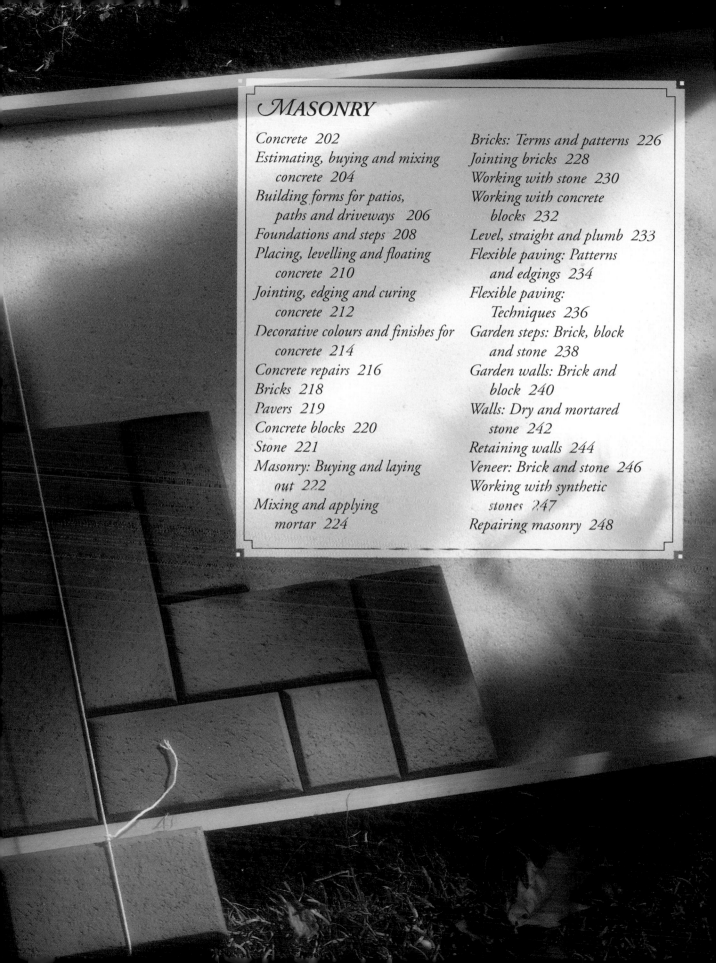

MASONRY

Concrete is a mixture of sand and coarse aggregate – either gravel or crushed stone – held together by Portland cement. When mixed with water, the cement hardens as the result of a chemical reaction. Depending on the size of your project, you may decide to buy separate ingredients and mix your own concrete or to buy bags of dry ready-mixed concrete to which only water needs to be added. A third choice, if you need a cubic metre or more of concrete, may be to hire a motor-driven concrete mixer or to order the concrete delivered mixed and ready for casting or throwing.

The standard colour of Portland cement is grey, but you can create other colours by adding powdered pigments, generally known as 'oxides'. Sprinkle the pigment on the wet surface before the final levelling and screeding, and work over the surface with a plasterer's trowel. Colouring oxides that are usually readily available are black, red, green and yellow. You can also liven up a concrete surface before it sets by roughening it, carving designs into it, adding exposed aggregate or by stamping it with a pattern (see p 215).

Concrete cures best in moderately cool weather. Very hot weather may cause the concrete to dry so fast that it becomes impossible to work satisfactorily. Before embarking on a project that involves casting concrete, check with your local authority that you will not be contravening their regulations.

False flagstone effect can easily be hand-tooled into concrete before it sets. If you wish, add a colour pigment before the concrete sets. Smooth the poured concrete with a float, cut the outlines of flagstones into the surface with a brick pointing tool and smooth the surface again. Apply a sealing solution when the concrete is hard.

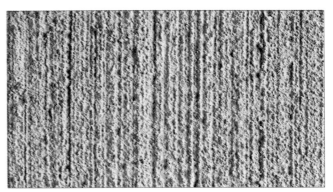

Brooming, produced by dragging the bristles of a stiff broom over wet concrete, gives a rough-textured non-slip surface. The 'grain' generally runs straight, either along the length of the surface or across it, but there are many decorative variations, including wavy grain, diagonals and alternating diagonals. Colour can be added to the concrete.

Pebbled surface, or exposed aggregate finish, offers a more variable type of rough-textured surface than brooming. Sprinkle decorative aggregate at random or in a pattern over the surface of poured concrete (coloured or not) before it sets. When the concrete is firm, wash and brush the surface to expose the tops of the aggregate.

Decorative aggregates used in textured concrete vary widely in colour and shape according to the type of rock. In fact, even pieces of the same type of aggregate may vary. You can use any kind, but rounds and cubes cover best; rough textures bond better and flat stones tend to dislodge.

Basket weave

Herringbone

Square

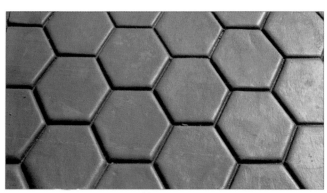

Hexagon

Charcoal cobblestone

Yellow-ochre cobblestone

Stamping offers a quick method of creating a false finish with a re-peated pattern. By pushing a stamping tool into wet concrete (usually coloured), you can fashion any number of designs to make a driveway, walk or patio floor look as though it is paved with bricks, cobblestones, slate, granite, concrete pavers or tiles.

A few of the patterns available in commercially made stamping tools are shown here. You can use a single pattern for an entire area, or com-bine two or more to create a more fanciful design or to add a border or separate a section. Seal the stamped concrete after it has hardened.

Compared with hand-laid pavers, stamped concrete is less likely to tilt out of level because of local ground subsidence, and there are no spaces between units for grass and weeds to grow through. On the other hand, if the surface is damaged, you may have to replace a large section of the slab, rather than just one or two individual pavers.

Running bond brick

ESTIMATING, BUYING AND MIXING CONCRETE

A successful concrete project requires careful planning and preparation. First, determine the composition of your concrete. Choose aggregate that is no larger in diameter than one-third the slab's thickness. Aggregate larger than 19 mm is hard to spread and to compact with hand tools. Mixed cement is the 'glue' that holds the aggregate and sand together, so determine how much cement and water you'll need (the thicker the paste, the stronger the concrete) as well as the proportions and quantities of sand and aggregate. The recipes below should be checked against your local building regulations.

To estimate how much concrete you need, use mathematical formulas (p 344) or graph paper (below). Add 5 to 10 per cent for contingencies. For strength, a concrete slab for footpaths and patios should be at least 90 mm thick, and driveways for light traffic – ordinary sedans and light delivery vehicles – should be at least 100 mm thick. Again, check the local authority requirements.

Use only enough water to make the mixture workable. Excess water may 'bleed' to the surface when the concrete is compacted and screeded, carrying cement with it and resulting in a poorly bonded layer. When the concrete has been placed, allow about 24 hrs for setting and keep it covered with wet sacking for several days.

Measuring based on weight is more accurate than that based on volume because sand increases in volume when wet. The recipes in the chart below assume wet sand – for damp or overly wet sand, increase or decrease the water. Then make a trial batch and test the consistency (facing page).

For projects requiring 1 cu m or more, consider having the concrete professionally mixed and delivered. Place your order well in advance and specify the quantity, the strength (generally equal to 20 megapascals) and the *slump*, a measure of consistency or workability (usually 80 mm). Have the site prepared and helpers on hand when the truck arrives. In practice, you may find suppliers reluctant to deliver the relatively small amounts needed for most home projects.

For small jobs, you can buy pre-mixed concrete with all the dry ingredients correctly proportioned. Just add clean water and mix with a hoe, shovel or trowel. Or you can buy the dry ingredients in separate bags from most hardware stores.

Caution: Contact with wet concrete can cause serious burns or skin irritation. Wash concrete splashes off your skin with water as soon as you can. Wear long sleeves and trousers, rubber boots and gloves (wet concrete has a corrosive-like effect on leather) and goggles.

Estimating concrete quantities

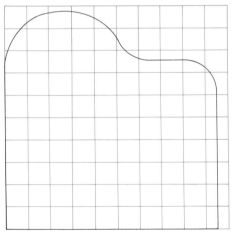

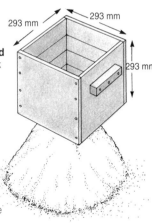

Find volume of irregular shape. Lay out the design on the ground, staking it at its widest points. Measure; then draw the shape to scale on graph paper with one square equivalent to 1 sq m. Count all the filled squares and those that are one-third or more filled. Then multiply the area (number of counted squares) by the required thickness of the slab to find cu m of concrete mixture required.

Determine moisture content of sand by squeezing. Damp sand won't stick together. Properly wet sand (above) forms ball but leaves no noticeable moisture on palm. Overly wet sand forms ball and leaves palm moist.

To measure by volume, build a bottomless box with inner dimensions of 293 × 293 × 293 mm to contain 25 ℓ. Mark sides for quarter amounts. Use one of formulas below. Place box on flat surface at mixing site. Fill, then lift box away. It takes 40 of these boxes to make 1 cu m.

293 mm · 293 mm · 293 mm

Formulas based on half-pocket mixes suitable for hand-placing:

	High strength				Medium strength			
	Aggregate size 6-13 mm		Aggregate size 19-26 mm		Aggregate size 6-13 mm		Aggregate size 19-26 mm	
	kg	25 ℓ box	kg	25 ℓ box	kg	25 ℓ box	kg	25 ℓ box
Cement	25	0,75	25	0,75	25	0,75	25	0,75
Wet sand		1,5		1,5		2,25		2,25
Coarse aggregate		1		1,5		1,5		2,25
Water	Add 15 ℓ initially and then just enough for workability. Remember that water is easy to add but almost impossible to remove.							

Working with concrete

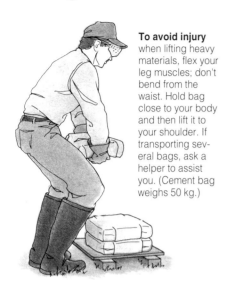

To avoid injury when lifting heavy materials, flex your leg muscles; don't bend from the waist. Hold bag close to your body and then lift it to your shoulder. If transporting several bags, ask a helper to assist you. (Cement bag weighs 50 kg.)

Power mixing

Anchor mixer with sandbags and mix a trial batch. Before starting the mixer, load the coarse aggregate and half the water. Start mixer. Add the sand, cement and remaining water, in that order. Mix for at least 3 min or until all ingredients are blended and uniform in colour. Shovel a portion onto a flat surface and test the consistency (below). **Caution:** To avoid injury, keep your head, hands and shovel away from the blades when the mixer is on. Don't wear loose clothing that might get caught in outer moving parts.

Mixing concrete by hand: 1. Spread measured amount of sand on mixing surface. Add measured amount of cement; mix until streaks disappear. Add measured amount of aggregate; mix again by turning ingredients at least three times.

2. Heap up ingredients and form depression in centre. Slowly add two-thirds of the water. Mix by pulling dry ingredients little by little into the centre and pushing over-wet mixture to the sides. Gradually add remaining water.

3. Test mixture for proper proportions by smoothing surface with hoe, then making a row of narrow troughs. Correctly mixed concrete will hold peaks. Aggregate should be barely discernible throughout the mix. If necessary, adjust proportions on paper. If the mixture is lumpy, reduce the aggregate or add more sand, cement and water. If soupy, reduce the water. Mix a new batch (don't try to adjust a poor one).

BUILDING FORMS FOR PATIOS, PATHS AND DRIVEWAYS

Site preparation

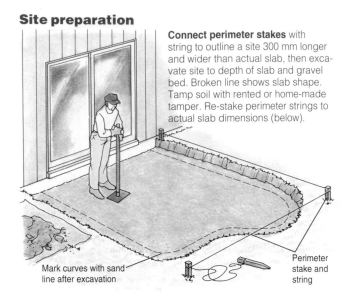

Connect perimeter stakes with string to outline a site 300 mm longer and wider than actual slab, then excavate site to depth of slab and gravel bed. Broken line shows slab shape. Tamp soil with rented or home-made tamper. Re-stake perimeter strings to actual slab dimensions (below).

Mark curves with sand line after excavation

Perimeter stake and string

Setting the levels

String guideline

1. Mark high point of slab surface: Drive stakes on both sides 40 mm outside final slab location to allow space for forms to be nailed to stakes. Stretch and level chalked string; then snap it against the house. Drive the tops of stakes level with snapped line. Stretch new perimeter string guidelines to mark placement of graded stakes for the fall of the slab.

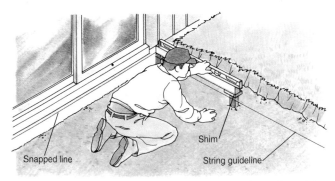

Snapped line

Shim

String guideline

2. Drive stake 1 m away from house with inner face against string guideline. Nail 10 mm-thick shim beneath one end of 1 m-long straight 50 × 100. Place spirit level and 50 × 100 across stakes, with shim down and away from house; drive stake until 50 × 100 is level. Continue to end and repeat on other side. Nail the forms flush with tops of stakes.

Forms mould and support concrete when it is poured. Because of the extreme pressure wet concrete exerts, forms must be sturdy and well braced, and are usually nailed to 50 × 50 mm stakes driven into the ground. The tops of the forms serve as guides when pouring and as bearing surfaces when smoothing the concrete (pp 210–211).

Although most forms are temporary and designed to be removed after the concrete has cured, they must be securely assembled to withstand the pressure of the concrete. Coating the form timbers with used engine-oil will make them easy to remove once the concrete has set. When constructing forms for a slab that is to be poured in stages, place and stake temporary partition forms called stopboards. A bevelled strip or 'key' may be nailed to one side of the stopboard to create a joint to interlock with the next section (pp 212–213). Straight forms may be made of composite board, exterior-grade plywood, or 50 × 100 or wider planks. (Measure the actual width of your planks and, if necessary, fill the gap below the forms with gravel.) Make gradual curves by kerfing 20 × 100's of softwood, sharper curves with plywood or hardboard. Green wood is easier to bend than kiln-dried timber, and it draws less moisture away from the concrete (which can be weakened) during curing.

Sometimes forms are left in place permanently for decoration, in which case they also serve as control joints, reducing cracking in large slabs (pp 212–213). To retard decay, use pressure-treated wood or, before use, coat untreated timber with an appropriate sealer. Cover the top edges of all permanent forms with masking tape to prevent staining.

To drain properly, slabs should have a fall or slope of at least 10 mm per metre of length or width. Good drainage makes walks and driveways less slippery when wet and keeps water on an uncovered patio away from the house. To create a slope, drive stakes to progressively graded heights and fasten forms flush with their tops. To create a slope from the middle towards both sides of a wider slab, as for a driveway, set the central divider boards the required distance higher than the forms along the sides. When screeding the concrete, place the screed across the central form and a side form to grade the slab to the correct slope.

Prepare the site by excavating an area deep enough for the slab and a gravel layer, and 300 mm wider on all sides to provide room for nailing. A slab thickness of 100 mm will suffice for light motor vehicles, 125 mm for heavy. (Replace the turf and topsoil when landscaping around the slab.) Gravel supports the slab and drains water that collects under it. Drainage is important in all climates, especially in areas subject to heavy showers. In low-lying areas or where the soil is heavy clay, compact a 100 mm-thick layer of 20 mm gravel beneath a slab. Local building codes may regulate concrete construction, so check with the building inspector or town engineer's department before starting a project. You may have to build perimeter footing or add reinforcing bars (p 208).

Building a temporary form

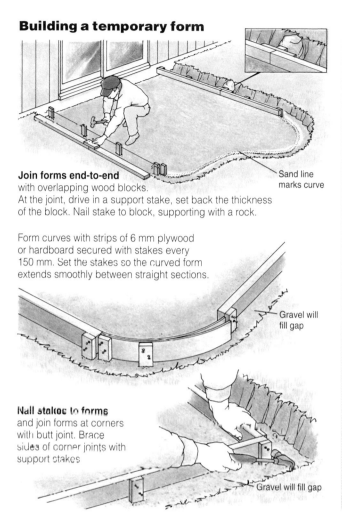

Join forms end-to-end
with overlapping wood blocks.
At the joint, drive in a support stake, set back the thickness
of the block. Nail stake to block, supporting with a rock.

Form curves with strips of 6 mm plywood
or hardboard secured with stakes every
150 mm. Set the stakes so the curved form
extends smoothly between straight sections.

Gravel will
fill gap

Nail stakes to forms
and join forms at corners
with butt joint. Brace
sides of corner joints with
support stakes

Gravel will fill gap

Making a permanent form

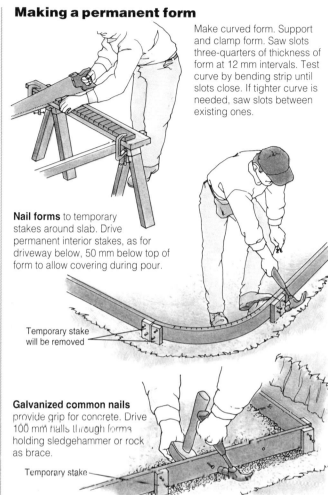

Make curved form. Support
and clamp form. Saw slots
three-quarters of thickness
of form at 12 mm intervals. Test
curve by bending strip until
slots close. If tighter curve is
needed, saw slots between
existing ones.

Nail forms to temporary
stakes around slab. Drive
permanent interior stakes, as for
driveway below, 50 mm below top of
form to allow covering during pour.

Temporary stake
will be removed

Galvanized common nails
provide grip for concrete. Drive
100 mm nails through forms
holding sledgehammer or rock
as brace.

Temporary stake

Sand line
marks curve

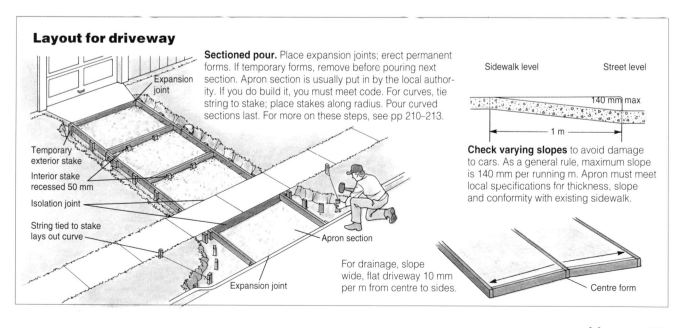

Layout for driveway

Sectioned pour. Place expansion joints; erect permanent
forms. If temporary forms, remove before pouring next
section. Apron section is usually put in by the local authority. If you do build it, you must meet code. For curves, tie
string to stake; place stakes along radius. Pour curved
sections last. For more on these steps, see pp 210–213.

Expansion
joint

Temporary
exterior stake

Interior stake
recessed 50 mm

Isolation joint

String tied to stake
lays out curve

Apron section

Expansion joint

For drainage, slope
wide, flat driveway 10 mm
per m from centre to sides.

Sidewalk level   Street level

140 mm max

1 m

Check varying slopes to avoid damage
to cars. As a general rule, maximum slope
is 140 mm per running m. Apron must meet
local specifications for thickness, slope
and conformity with existing sidewalk.

Centre form

Laying out a foundation

1. Place levelled batterboards. Lay out the foundation corners and outer perimeter with strings (p 233). Dig a trench deep enough for sand and foundation, and wide enough for a 150 mm work area on each side of foundation. Place, tamp and level sand. To mark the outer perimeter, pour contrasting colour sand over strings.

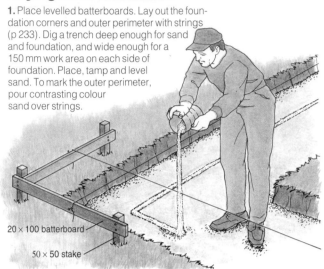

20 × 100 batterboard

50 × 50 stake

2. Drive long stakes (equal to foundation depth, sand fill, and 100 mm below trench) along outside of sand line. Check with level. Nail forms (pp 206–207). Locate stakes for inner form boards with spacer cut to exact width of foundation plus thickness of two form boards.

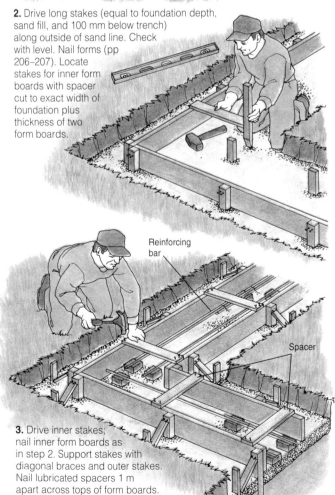

Reinforcing bar

Spacer

3. Drive inner stakes; nail inner form boards as in step 2. Support stakes with diagonal braces and outer stakes. Nail lubricated spacers 1 m apart across tops of form boards. If regulations call for reinforcing rods or bars, prop them on bricks or rock chips so bars will rest in centre of foundation.

Concrete foundations or footings support the weight of vertical structures and hold them in place. In planning any project, check your local building regulations. Before excavating, obtain necessary permits. Follow inspection schedules. For example, some regulations require that forms for foundations be inspected before the concrete is poured.

It is critical that the foundation surface is smooth to ensure a level base and that the sides are straight and plumb (p 233). Pier footings, consisting of concrete columns sunk into the ground, are used as spot supports for fence posts, decks and storage sheds. For a concrete landing and steps up to 750 mm high (facing page) and pier-and-panel walls (pp 240–241), pier footings may give enough support and require less excavation than a continuous foundation. (Steps higher than 750 mm are usually supported by a continuous foundation, which is also required by most garden walls.) Depending on bond and building material used, a 1,2 m-high wall may need a concrete footing 230 mm thick.

When excavating for foundations, dig a trench that is deep enough to hold a layer of compacted coarse sand 100 mm thick. The sand provides a stable support for the foundation. In areas that experience extreme cold, the base of the foundation should rest below the frost line.

In hard, compacted soil, wooden forms may not be needed for continuous foundations. A straight-sided trench with a layer of sand in the bottom may suffice. Pier footings can often be made by pouring concrete into a hole partly filled with gravel; but if the soil is loose or the piers project above ground level, it may be possible to use a form of sectioned cement-pipe securely bound or bolted together.

Concrete steps. When planning, keep safety and ease in mind. The risers and treads must be uniform – 150 mm risers are the easiest to climb, while 175 mm is the maximum height. Treads should be deep enough to stand on easily – at least 280 mm and preferably 300 to 350 mm. To increase the depth of the treads, angle the risers inward 15° from top to bottom. For drainage, concrete treads must slope 20 mm per m from back to front. Extend landing at least 150 mm beyond the door on either side, or as specified by regulations.

Side forms for steps up to 750 mm high can be made of 20 mm plywood. Riser forms can be plywood or nominal 25 mm-thick timber. To allow for smoothing the treads prior to removing the forms, bevel the bottom edges of the riser forms. Brace all forms well and lubricate the insides (p 210). To use less concrete, you may fill some space within the forms with compacted gravel; leave at least 100 mm of depth on all sides for the poured concrete.

The grain of the wood forms will show on the concrete. When you remove the forms (about 3 days after the pour), smooth the step sides by brushing on grout made of 1 part cement to 1,5 to 2 parts sand and diluted with enough water to resemble thick paint. Let it dry for 1 to 2 hours; then rub off any excess with dry sacking.

Building steps

Mark perimeter and height of steps with levelled strings stretched between stakes; then excavate to depth of 150 mm. Dig 200 mm-diameter holes 100 mm below frost line for pier footings at front corners. Compact 100 mm of gravel in holes and fill with concrete. To tie steps to house, insert reinforcing bars into solid concrete foundation (p 213).

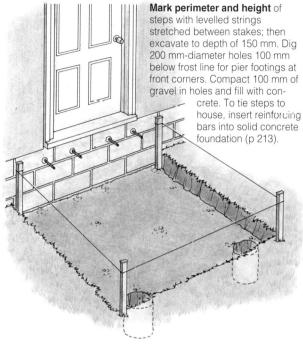

Layout for landing, treads and risers. Allow enough area for landing so door can open. To find number of steps, divide the height of the steps by the riser height. Build riser form with 15° forward tilt, tread with slope of 20 mm per m for drainage.

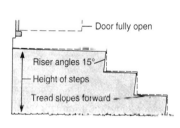

- Door fully open
- Riser angles 15°
- Height of steps
- Tread slopes forward

Cut two step profiles, including 150 mm below ground level and riser forms. Stake and brace profiles, then riser forms. Add gravel and compact it. Pour concrete into lowest tread first. Allow it to stiffen about 30 min (time varies with temperature and stiffness of mixture when placed), so it will resist pressure when successive treads are poured.

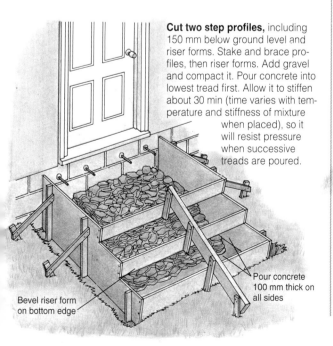

Bevel riser form on bottom edge

Pour concrete 100 mm thick on all sides

Setting a post

1. Dig post hole. With handles parallel, raise post-hole digger and thrust it into ground. Open handles and rock or rotate tool as you remove it to excavate soil. Repeat until depth is a minimum of half of total post length or 100 mm below frost line (whichever is greater). For multiple holes or rocky soil, consider hiring a professional with a power auger.

2. Add 100 to 150 mm of gravel. Drive nails into a pressure-treated wood post. (Nails provide gripping surface for the concrete.) Place the post; adjust with a level until two adjacent sides are vertical. Brace in this position with stakes on two sides.

3. Put second post in its hole; align posts. Hang taut line level between posts; adjust height of second post, if needed, so heights are uniform; adjust second post's vertical position (step 2).

4. Fill post holes with concrete until holes are at least three-quarters full. There should be four times as much concrete as gravel. Fill the remaining space with compacted soil, sloped at the surface to shed water. Remove the braces.

Soil

Concrete

Gravel

Masonry 209

Preparation

1. Prepare forms and gravel bed (pp 206–209). Then wet down all interior surfaces to minimize settling and to keep moisture from being drawn away from the concrete during curing.

2. To prevent concrete from sticking, coat the inside of wet wooden forms with a thin film of form-release agent.

Whether you mix concrete by hand, in a portable mixer or have pre-mixed concrete (ready-mix) delivered by truck, you must plan ahead. To prepare for on-site mixing, erect platforms large enough to hold the ingredients and to function as the mixing site. Then lay planks for transporting concrete to the pouring location via wheelbarrow.

Avoid delays when working with concrete, but don't reduce mixing times – always mix until colour and consistency of the mixture are uniform. Wheelbarrows should be watertight and only about one-third filled. If there's a hold-up in getting the wheelbarrow to the pouring site, re-mix the concrete by giving it a few turns with a shovel before pouring.

Any surface against which concrete is to be placed – such as earth foundation trenches – must be thoroughly wetted beforehand. This will prevent water being drawn from the fresh mix. To prevent excessive dilution, see that there is no free water standing where the concrete is to be placed. When using reinforcing bars, ensure that they do not come into contact with form-release agent.

Dump or pour concrete as near as possible to its final position and avoid overworking it. Overworking weakens concrete, producing a sheen of surface water during smoothing – suspend further smoothing until the sheen has evaporated.

Concrete poured in hot weather stiffens rapidly, shortening the time available for finishing. Surface drying is a problem on days when the humidity is low or when there is a wind. Do not pour concrete onto frozen ground or into forms containing snow or ice.

Poured concrete must be fully compacted – either by hand or by machine – to expel air and to force the mixture up against the forms.

Caution: Concrete is caustic and can cause chemical burns on skin. It will corrode leather, cloth and other material unless promptly washed off.

Pouring

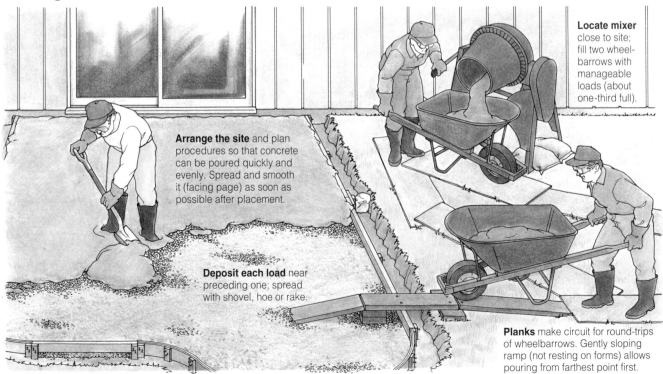

Arrange the site and plan procedures so that concrete can be poured quickly and evenly. Spread and smooth it (facing page) as soon as possible after placement.

Deposit each load near preceding one; spread with shovel, hoe or rake.

Locate mixer close to site; fill two wheelbarrows with manageable loads (about one-third full).

Planks make circuit for round-trips of wheelbarrows. Gently sloping ramp (not resting on forms) allows pouring from farthest point first.

Spreading

Tamp concrete with straight 50 × 100 on edge. Start at far end of pour; deliver vertical blows. Move board half its thickness with each blow.

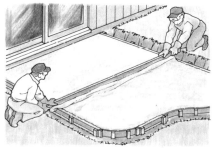

Strike off, or screed top by sawing back and forth with board used for tamping. Raise the board's leading edge slightly on forward stroke. Excess concrete ahead of board fills hollows.

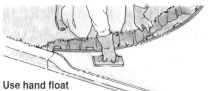

Use hand float to screed transition areas such as apron where driveway meets curb. Tamp, then smooth surface with tool. Fill hollows with spare concrete.

Handling ready-mix

Be ready when truck arrives; or you may be charged for overtime. Move chute to farthest point of pour. Dampen chute and forms with hose; then signal driver to release concrete. Re position chute as form fills. If your crew can't keep up, direct the driver to release concrete more slowly. Signal driver to stop when concrete in chute will complete job.

Plunge spade into the mix to thoroughly fill corners, eliminate gaps and to settle the mix.

Tamp to push aggregate below surface, then level by screeding (see left).

Floating

Smooth screeded surface with bull float (skip) after surface water has evaporated. Push tool at right angle to screed marks, with front edge slightly raised. Pull tool back with blade flat.

Use darby for smaller areas. Sweep tool in wide arcs, pressing lightly on blade's trailing edge. Work from centre to edges. On wide slabs, support yourself on kneeboards.

Move hand float in circles to smooth bull float or darby marks. Lean on second float for support. Keep floating to a minimum. For a skid-resistant surface, finish with broom texture (p 215).

Expansion and control joints

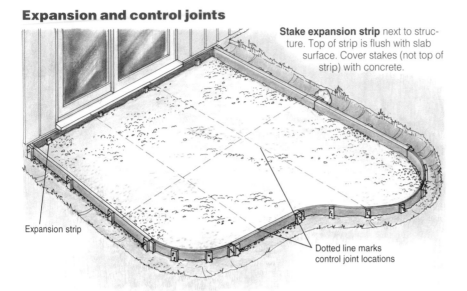

Stake expansion strip next to structure. Top of strip is flush with slab surface. Cover stakes (not top of strip) with concrete.

Expansion strip

Dotted line marks control joint locations

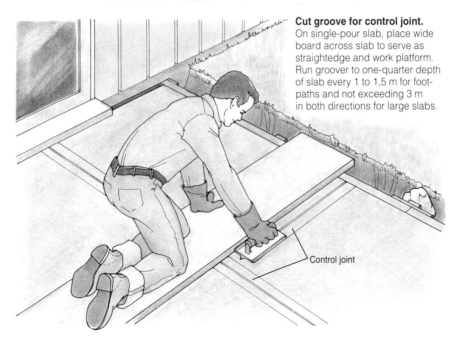

Cut groove for control joint. On single-pour slab, place wide board across slab to serve as straightedge and work platform. Run groover to one-quarter depth of slab every 1 to 1,5 m for footpaths and not exceeding 3 m in both directions for large slabs.

Control joint

Construction joints

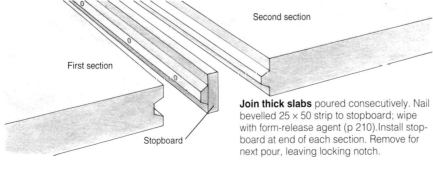

Second section

First section

Join thick slabs poured consecutively. Nail bevelled 25 × 50 strip to stopboard; wipe with form-release agent (p 210). Install stopboard at end of each section. Remove for next pour, leaving locking notch.

Stopboard

Concrete shrinks as it dries and hardens. It continues to shrink and expand with seasonal temperature changes. Under these conditions, cracks can develop. Three types of joints – expansion, control and construction – minimize cracking in different situations.

Expansion joints, or isolation joints, separate new concrete from adjoining building materials or older cured concrete. This allows the new concrete to move at its own rate, unaffected by the different rate of the adjoining material. (If the two were bonded, they would probably crack apart.) Create an expansion joint by placing a 12 mm-thick strip of expansion joint material, available from building suppliers, against an existing material when the new concrete is poured.

Control joints are grooves tooled into fresh concrete or sawn into cured concrete (use a circular saw equipped with a masonry-cutting blade). These grooves create weak areas that induce cracks to occur beneath them, where they are less visible and not harmful.

Use construction joints where concrete is poured in sections (with a 30-minute interval or longer). For slabs 100 mm thick, insert a straight-sided temporary form, or stopboard, between pours. Join thicker sections with a locking, or keyed, joint: fasten a bevelled strip to a stopboard that is the same width as the thickness of the slab.

To prevent chipping, round over all edges and joints in fresh concrete with an edger. (Cover wet concrete after the initial smoothing. Uncover small areas for finishing, then re-cover immediately to slow drying.) After jointing and edging, concrete needs time to cure, or harden. Curing continues for 5 days after pouring, and for 7 days or more in cold weather (below 10°C). Keep the concrete moist by sprinkling it with water or covering it with water-retaining material, such as straw or hessian, that is kept continuously damp. Protect newly poured concrete from frost by insulating it with a cover of straw or sacking.

Edging and curing

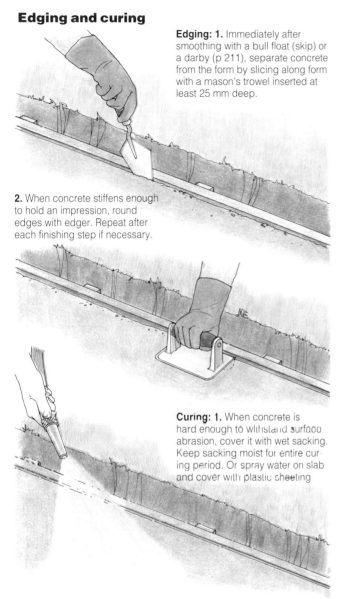

Edging: 1. Immediately after smoothing with a bull float (skip) or a darby (p 211), separate concrete from the form by slicing along form with a mason's trowel inserted at least 25 mm deep.

2. When concrete stiffens enough to hold an impression, round edges with edger. Repeat after each finishing step if necessary.

Curing: 1. When concrete is hard enough to withstand surface abrasion, cover it with wet sacking. Keep sacking moist for entire curing period. Or spray water on slab and cover with plastic sheeting

Tying steps to a foundation

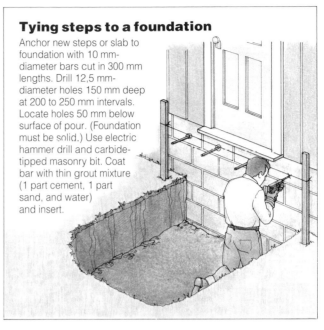

Anchor new steps or slab to foundation with 10 mm-diameter bars cut in 300 mm lengths. Drill 12,5 mm-diameter holes 150 mm deep at 200 to 250 mm intervals. Locate holes 50 mm below surface of pour. (Foundation must be solid.) Use electric hammer drill and carbide-tipped masonry bit. Coat bar with thin grout mixture (1 part cement, 1 part sand, and water) and insert.

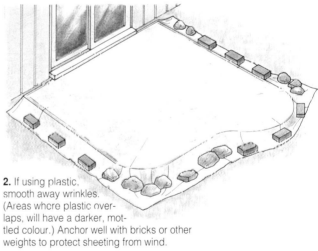

2. If using plastic, smooth away wrinkles. (Areas where plastic over-laps, will have a darker, mot-tled colour.) Anchor well with bricks or other weights to protect sheeting from wind.

Anchoring wooden posts to concrete

Metal bases embedded in concrete piers (right) or foundation walls secure wooden sills and posts used in house framing. Embed base according to manufacturer's instructions. Bases should be held in position temporarily until concrete has hardened. To position base A, place a wood brace in U of base, and nail. Position tubular mould in hole; then pour concrete. Place base and brace in wet concrete across top of the form (inset). To position elevated post base B in wet concrete, place it atop 50 × 50 spacer boards. Allow concrete to cure 7 days before attaching the post.

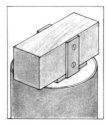

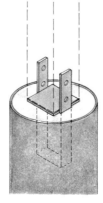

A

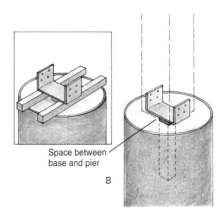

Space between base and pier

B

DECORATIVE COLOURS AND FINISHES FOR CONCRETE

Colouring the top layer

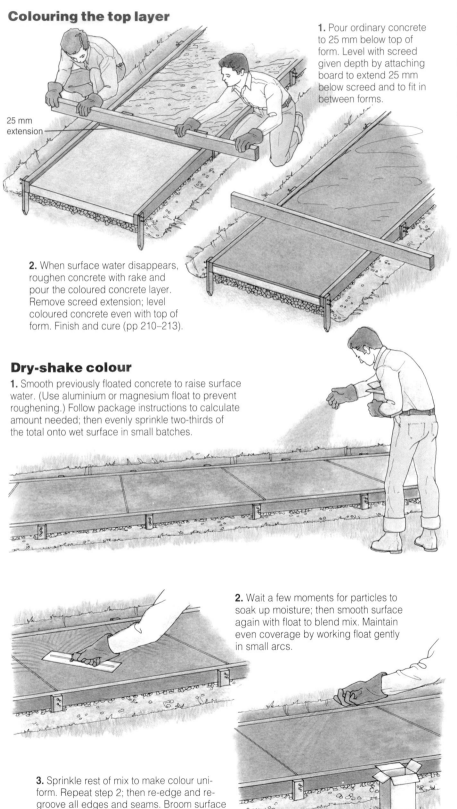

1. Pour ordinary concrete to 25 mm below top of form. Level with screed given depth by attaching board to extend 25 mm below screed and to fit in between forms.

25 mm extension

2. When surface water disappears, roughen concrete with rake and pour the coloured concrete layer. Remove screed extension; level coloured concrete even with top of form. Finish and cure (pp 210–213).

Dry-shake colour

1. Smooth previously floated concrete to raise surface water. (Use aluminium or magnesium float to prevent roughening.) Follow package instructions to calculate amount needed; then evenly sprinkle two-thirds of the total onto wet surface in small batches.

2. Wait a few moments for particles to soak up moisture; then smooth surface again with float to blend mix. Maintain even coverage by working float gently in small arcs.

3. Sprinkle rest of mix to make colour uniform. Repeat step 2; then re-edge and re-groove all edges and seams. Broom surface for skid resistance, if desired (facing page).

Cement or concrete surfaces need not be drab – it's fairly easy to add colour or texture, and textured surfaces also make slabs and paths less slippery.

There are two main ways to colour concrete: by blending powdered mineral pigment (available from concrete suppliers) with the mix and by dusting poured concrete with pigment after the concrete has been smoothed with a float (p 211). The latter material, called dry-shake, may contain hardeners that increase the surface's resistance to wear. Concrete can also be painted or stained with products made for the purpose. However, the results vary and are not as long-lasting as the other two methods.

Pigments for concrete consist of mineral oxides and should be used according to the manufacturuer's recommendations. Read the instructions on the container and consult the supplier for specific advice.

To save money, use concrete made with standard ingredients (without pigment) for the bulk of the pour. Screed the bottom layer, then immediately mix the ingredients for the coloured layer, being careful not to add too much water. Pour, screed and finish the coloured layer.

Experiment before using pigments on the site. Colour test-blocks, then damp-cure and let them dry before judging the results.

Ordinary (grey) Portland cement can successfully be coloured buff, yellow, brown, red, pink, grey, blue or green. For light pastel shades, use white Portland cement (WPC), which is much more expensive than ordinary cement, and white sand and stone. Many blues and greens, however, tend to fade on exposure to sunlight, so check with the manufacturer of the pigments that they are suitable for outdoors.

Proprietary pigmented white-cement and concrete mixes are sometimes available, and require only the addition of water and thorough mixing before use. Use of these pre-mixes, especially on small or critical jobs, should save time and ensure uniformity of results.

Brooming

Hold broom at low angle and drag bristles across concrete to produce ridged non-slip surface. Don't let brush strokes overlap or cross each other at angles. Use soft bristles to create fine lines, stiff bristles to make a deeper design.

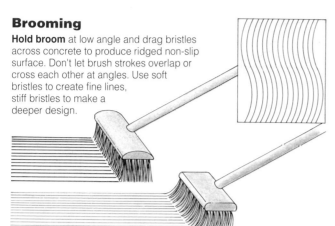

Stamping brick design

Place two stamp tools across width of floated concrete; third begins new row. Step on each one. Move first two to finish new row and begin next. Pour and stamp small areas so design imprints well. Easiest slabs to fill have 90° angles and are designed so tools fit evenly. Home-made hand tools can fill in other shapes and gaps between forms.

Pebbled texture

1. Wet clean round pebbles or other smooth stones 20 to 30 mm in diameter. Pour and screed small section of concrete. Sprinkle pebbles evenly (shown), or create a mosaic pattern on surface.

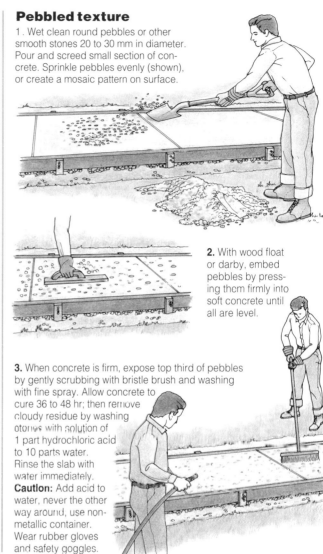

2. With wood float or darby, embed pebbles by pressing them firmly into soft concrete until all are level.

3. When concrete is firm, expose top third of pebbles by gently scrubbing with bristle brush and washing with fine spray. Allow concrete to cure 36 to 48 hr; then remove cloudy residue by washing stones with solution of 1 part hydrochloric acid to 10 parts water. Rinse the slab with water immediately. **Caution:** Add acid to water, never the other way around, use non-metallic container. Wear rubber gloves and safety goggles.

False flagstone

1. After smoothing concrete with float, carve outlines of flagstone design with a brick pointing tool.

2. Smooth and re-tool the concrete to finish the flat surfaces and to deepen the outlines.

3. Brush outlines carefully with a dry paintbrush to smooth their edges and to remove particles.

Despite its sturdiness, concrete can deteriorate with age and with exposure to severe weather, and it can suffer damage from settling or blows. (Overworking concrete also weakens a slab.) To repair concrete successfully, you must clean the area well and create a good bond between the damaged surface and the patching compound.

You can fill cracks and holes with a home-made compound of 1 part Portland cement, 2,5 parts sand and enough water to make a stiff paste for vertical surfaces, or a thin one for horizontal surfaces. However, this mixture doesn't adhere well if applied in a thin layer. The repair surface must be at least 25 mm deep, and the edges must be undercut with a cold chisel.

An easier method is to buy a patching compound containing latex, epoxy or other polymers. These don't require the shaping work and they usually bond well, even when filling small cracks and mending scaling surfaces. These products are expensive and, on drying, may tend to be much darker than the surrounding concrete. An economical strategy for repairing larger holes is to use home-made and commercial products together.

To reduce a dusty or powdery condition, sweep and vacuum the slab, then wash it with soapy water and a wire brush (use powdered detergent). Scrub the surface again with more soapy water and a softer brush, then rinse it with clean water. If the concrete continues to dust, apply a commercial hardener containing magnesium and zinc fluorosilicates or sodium silicate (available from concrete suppliers). Follow the manufacturer's directions.

To prevent crazing on a new slab, begin slow-curing procedures early – within a few minutes of the final trowelling in hot, dry weather. Avoid overworking the concrete, which is one of the chief causes of localized surface-breakdowns known as blistering. **Caution:** Wear safety goggles and long sleeves, and also don thick rubber gloves when applying repair compounds to concrete.

Filling cracks with commercial compound

1. Remove loose or cracked material with small sledgehammer and cold chisel. Hold chisel at slight angle.

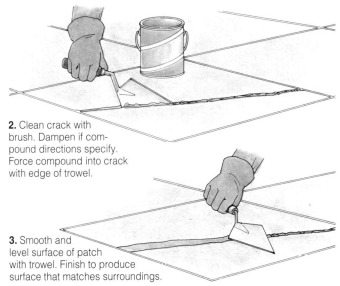

2. Clean crack with brush. Dampen if compound directions specify. Force compound into crack with edge of trowel.

3. Smooth and level surface of patch with trowel. Finish to produce surface that matches surroundings.

Patching large holes in layers

1. Chisel sides of hole so they are vertical; prepare hole as for cracks. Brush with grout (mix 1 part cement and 1 part sand; add water to consistency of housepaint).

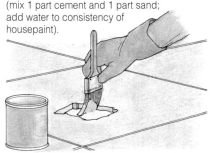

2. Fill hole to within 7 mm of surface with home-made compound (see text above). Avoid over-wetting mix; this weakens it.

3. Apply finish layer of commercial patching compound, following package directions. Feather edges of patch. Finish to match surrounding concrete.

Rebuilding edges and corners

1. Chisel away loose particles and brush damaged area thoroughly to remove dust. Mix patching material according to maker's directions. Dampen concrete before applying if directions specify.

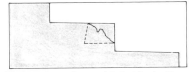

Undercut repair area (dotted line) with chisel if using home-made patching mix.

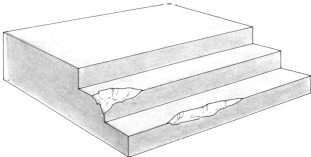

2. Erect, lubricate and brace form to contain and shape patch. Apply compound. Smooth surface with trowel and edger (pp 206–213).

Replacing a broken slab

Break up damaged slab with sledgehammer. Slab will crack along control joint. Remove broken pieces and cover with layer of gravel as for new slab (pp 206–207). **Caution:** Bend knees as you lift and lower hammer. Straighten knees a little at top of swing. Let the hammer fall of its own weight. Check the hammerhead often for looseness. Wear goggles and heavy work gloves.

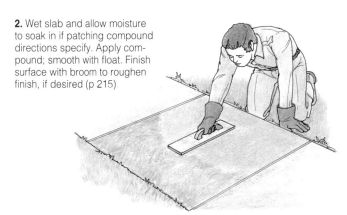

Control joint

Expansion joint

Erect forms level with existing pavement. Install isolation joint material to separate new pour from older concrete. Pour concrete and finish as for new slab. (See pp 206–213.)

Resurfacing

1. Remove damaged surface by chiselling at an angle or by striking with a 1,5 kg sledgehammer. Avoid heavy blows that might crack slab. Clean slab thoroughly with wire brush and broom.

2. Wet slab and allow moisture to soak in if patching compound directions specify. Apply compound; smooth with float. Finish surface with broom to roughen finish, if desired (p 215).

Brick is a kiln-fired solid masonry unit made with clay or shale. Although some bricks are manufactured essentially the same way they have been for millennia (with soft 'mud' in moulds), most modern bricks are made by compressing and extruding a stiffer mix through a die to make long bars, which are then wire-cut into shorter units. These 'green' bricks are dried, sometimes glazed and then fired in a kiln to harden them. To a large degree, a brick's colour and some of its other properties are determined by the raw materials that make up the mud. However, the final result can be adjusted by adding chemicals or surface colouring to the mud and by controlling the firing.

Today, bricks are available in hundreds of sizes and shapes and in a variety of colours for many applications, making brick one of the most versatile of all building materials. Only a few of the available styles are shown below.

Bricks are classified as common, for hidden work, or face, for exposed work. They may be solid, cored or have indentations, or frogs, and they may be glazed. Most bricks are modular – they relate in size to each other or to other units, such as concrete blocks, to allow mixing of different units.

Rounded edges or ends on bricks, originally designed to reduce water penetration, are now used by architects and designers to add dimension to flat walls and to form decorative details. These bricks can also be used to frame doors or windows or to form cornices.

Maxi brick is larger than the standard brick and is popular with builders because fewer are needed to cover the same area as standard bricks, yet the maxi weighs about the same and has the same ease of working as the standard brick.

Curves and corners may require special bricks. Internal and external radial bricks (top) form sweeping curves. The internal angle and single cant bricks (bottom) offer alternatives to simple squared-off corners.

Other bricks include the half-round coping (above, left) and the double cant (above, right), the plinth stretcher (lower, left) and the plinth external return (lower, right). All of these are designed to cap walls and to shed water quickly, preventing saturation of the masonry. Purely decorative bricks are available in hundreds of designs, colours and shapes. They can be inserted singly or combined to form almost unlimited design details. Custom bricks can be made to fit special designs, but are expensive, and you may need your local authority's approval to use them in a structure.

PAVERS

Traditionally bricks and flat-cut stones (p 221) have been used as pavers. Bricks are probably the more versatile of the two, as they can be laid in a number of attractive patterns or be set on end at an angle to form a picket-like edging. Equally versatile are pavers made of concrete that is pressed in a mould under extreme pressure and compacted with high-frequency vibrators. Both brick and concrete pavers are highly resistant to wide fluctuations of temperature and, laid on adequate foundations, they are also able to withstand the weight of the heaviest vehicles.

Brick pavers are suitable for industrial and residential pavements, and can also withstand light vehicular traffic. Coping pavers with rounded edges (right) are ideal for slight overhangs, as on stairs or pool borders.

Cobblestone concrete paver lets you add a dash of Old World charm to a patio or other outdoor area. These popular pavers are generally available in single units (left), with special edging pieces (far left) to square off the paved area. Double cobble stone pavers (below) are also available. Cobblestones come in a variety of colours, as do the other concrete pavers.

Split-faced paver is made in one piece and then split in half, offering a roughened surface that simulates stone.

Concrete pavers come in shapes and colours to suit just about any purpose. Copy traditional patterns or freely mix shapes, sizes and colours to create your own design. When developing your own pattern, work out the details on graph paper first.

CONCRETE BLOCKS

Made of Portland cement, graded aggregates and water, concrete blocks, or concrete masonry units, are pre-cast in a wide range of sizes, shapes, colours, textures and profiles. They may also be solid or hollow, and are designed to meet various requirements of strength, fire resistance and thermal and sound insulation. Comprehensive specifications have been drawn up by the South African Bureau of Standards (SABS), and blocks produced by a manufacturer who holds a valid SABS permit, are of a very high standard. Because blocks come in a variety of modular sizes (sizes that fit with one another), structures are easily planned and built without the need to cut the masonry units into smaller sizes, as must be done with stonework. An advantage of hollow-core blocks is that they can be filled with insulation or reinforcing.

Stretcher block (right), the basic wall unit, has flanged ends and generally two or three hollow cores (cells) separated by partitions (webs) that may taper from top to bottom.

Stretcher end (far right) has one or both ends flush. This one is called semi-solid, with one end of its cells closed for extra bearing or for the tops of walls (closed side up).

Sash block (left) has narrow slots for anchoring a metal sash. This split-faced unit has a rough stonelike appearance.

Half sash (below, left) has traditional texture.

Half sash, half stretcher (below, right) is a fluted split-ribbed unit.

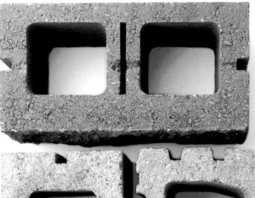

Narrow hollow block with both ends flush is one of a vast number of variations on the basic form. The block shown measures 390 × 140 × 190 mm.

Rock-face block adds a false but impressively realistic stone surface to the interior or exterior of a house. The block shown is a split faced concrete block that has been manufactured with a simulated rough stone appearance.

Partition blocks are narrow units designed for partition walls inside a house, garage or other building. The ground-down surfaces of the blocks shown make them aesthetically pleasing for indoor use. The red block has a single score in its face. The white one is a semi-solid block.

Screen block creates decorative designs in walls and fences. A wall of screen blocks allows for privacy without cutting out all light. Screen blocks are ideal for closing in patios or swimming pools. An almost unlimited number of patterns is available, ranging from simple to intricate and lacy.

STONE

For a combination of strength, diversity, durability and natural beauty, few building materials are equal to stone. Stone can be roughly shaped, cut to precise dimensions or used as it is found in nature. Its surface can be rough and irregular, smooth and flat, or polished to a high gloss that is impervious to stain. Because of its versatility, it is used for interior and exterior walls and floors, fireplaces and chimneys, countertops, roofing, walkways and driveways and countless other landscaping and architectural applications.

Stones for walls or veneer are generally sold by the tonne; flagstones, slate, tiles and other flat units, by the square metre. In rubble masonry, rough uncut stones of various shapes and sizes are fitted together. In ashlar masonry, cut stones with squared-off surfaces are tightly fitted. In either case, the stones may be coursed (layered in rows) or random. Stone walls may be set dry (without mortar) or with or without the mortar showing. Ashlar mortar joints are no more than 12 mm wide; usually they are 3 to 6 mm wide.

Shale (right) is sometimes used in mortarless construction. The section of wall shown here is made up entirely of strips, as flat stones are called. Indurated, or hard, shale lasts longest.

Slate (far right) is available in several colours ranging from greys and greens to reds. It is shown here in a section of floor that has been laid in a geometric pattern.

Prairie granite (right), with its flat surface and irregular shapes, can be laid in a mosaic pattern with 12 mm mortar joints, as demonstrated in the section of wall shown here.

Salt-and-pepper granite (far right), cut into large squared blocks and strips, is ideal for walls. The section of wall shown here has 12 mm pointed mortar joints.

Sandstone (right), a richly coloured stone, can be arranged in random strips to form a mortarless wall. The variety of sizes keeps spaces between the stones to a minimum.

Rough-textured marble (far right), like all other types of marble, is very difficult to cut; always buy it pre-cut. Pink marble is shown here in a section of an ashlar wall with tight 3 to 6 mm joints.

When planning a masonry project, choose the material that best suits your ability and the finished look that you have in mind.

Bricks and concrete blocks are uniform in size and lend themselves to geometric designs. Although both are available in many sizes, the dimensions of individual units usually are proportionally related. This makes them easy to fit together in patterns, reduces the amount of skill and time required to build with them, and simplifies estimating materials. These projects are relatively easy to design because their dimensions can be based on the size of the individual units. Also, their uniform shape, texture and colour allow you to predict the appearance of a finished project.

Stones that are uniformly shaped, or dressed, can be treated like brick or block. Roughly dressed stones (with protrusions cut off but not squared) and undressed stones vary in size, shape and surface features. This variety tends to create less structured designs that emphasize texture and colour more than precise or repeating geometric patterns.

Working with undressed and roughly dressed stones requires much more creativity, skill and time than working with bricks, blocks or dressed stones. Every piece must be chosen or cut to fit with its neighbours like pieces of a jigsaw puzzle, so you need to have many stones on hand to choose from. (As a rule, the more irregular the stones, the more stones you will need.) Furthermore, it is difficult to predict precisely the appearance of

Grades of undressed stones

Suitable   Irregular, needs shaping   Poor (unsuitable)

the finished project, but these types of stones have considerable aesthetic appeal, and the labour associated with this work is well rewarded.

Bricks are classified according to use. Face bricks are graded as FBS (face brick, standard), FBX (face brick, extra) and FBA (face brick, aesthetic). The first two are selected for their durability, and uniformity of shape, size and colour while FBA, although equally durable, are noted for the artistic effect derived from their differences of size, shape and colour.

Non-facing plastered (NFP) bricks are used for general work that is to be plastered. Non-facing extra (NFX) bricks are suitable for both plastered and unplastered structures and also for use on permanently damp sites. Non-facing bricks are also known as common, stock or non-plaster units.

The actual size of a standard brick is approximately $222 \times 106 \times 73$ mm, but bricks are usually sold according to their nominal size, which includes an allowance of 12 mm for mortar joints. The nominal size of a standard brick is $234 \times 118 \times 85$ mm. To determine the number of bricks needed for a project, calculate the size of the area in square metres (p 344) and subtract the areas of openings or unpaved sections. When

estimating quantities of bricks for projects involving mortar, use the nominal size.

The rule of thumb is that between 48 and 54 standard bricks are needed per square metre of wall, assuming nominal vertical and horizontal joints of 12 mm. For a wall more than one brick thick, multiply the result by the number of bricks making up the structure's thickness. Add 5 per cent to allow for wastage as a result of cutting and breakages.

Where bricks are to be laid close together without mortar (as on a patio or path with sand in the joints), use the actual dimensions; allow about 42 standard bricks per square metre.

New standard bricks are usually sold on wooden pallets and are bound in stretch tape in units – known as 'packs' – of 500 bricks. Each pack measures 1,2 m on each side and weighs about 1 500 kg. When bricks are delivered, make sure they are not unloaded in such a way as to obstruct any property, public or private, other than your own. For long-term storage, cover bricks with a plastic tarpaulin.

Blocks are made of concrete and contain a variety of aggregates for different uses. Quantities are estimated as for bricks, calculating the number of blocks of a particular size per square metre of wall. The most widely used modular concrete block has an actual size of $390 \times 190 \times 190$ mm and is laid with a standard joint thickness of 10 mm of mortar, giving a nominal size of $400 \times 200 \times 200$ mm.

Depending on the type of aggregate used in its manufacture, one concrete block of this size may weigh up to 17,5 kg. Concrete masonry units are

Estimating bricks for 10 sq m single-skin wall

	Nominal dimensions	Units	Mortar*cu m
Standard brick	$234 \times 118 \times 85$	510	0,191
Maxi brick	$234 \times 127 \times 102$	336	0,144
Concrete block	$400 \times 200 \times 200$	125	0,107
Maxi concrete brick	$232 \times 125 \times 100$	340	0,142

*Add 25% to 50% more for waste. Amount varies according to size of job and skill of mason.

also made in the same size as the standard clay brick. The range of masonry units varies from one manufacturer to another.

Before ordering concrete blocks, find out whether the supplier has a valid certificate from the South African Bureau of Standards. Concrete blocks are available from reputable manufacturers in several approved strength categories for particular applications, and the use of substandard or substrength units will lead to serious structural problems. Blocks that are suitable for a single-storey house, for instance, may not be adequate for a double storey.

Concrete blocks have acquired an undeserved reputation for cracking, chiefly because of faults in manufacture, wrong application and inadequate curing. Blocks should be cured by being allowed to dry, slowly and naturally, for at least four weeks before being used.

Smaller concrete units, called pavers or paving stones, are laid without mortar on beds of sand and make durable and decorative paths, patios, steps and driveways (pp 234–239).

Caution: because they respond differently to moisture, temperature and stress, clay bricks and concrete blocks should not, as a general rule, be mortared together in the same wall. They may, however, be used in separate skins of the same wall, as in a cavity wall, and linked with wall-ties.

Stones that are suitable for building purposes range from granite, which is very hard, to softer limestones and sandstones, and slates are split along their layers to form paving stones.

Successfully cutting or dressing stone is a skill acquired only after long practice, so select stones that require the minimum of dressing and will lie straight in a wall, supporting stones above themselves.

Local stone, which may be suitable for basic projects, can usually be obtained from a nearby quarry. Be careful not to injure yourself or overload your vehicle if you transport it yourself.

Bricks

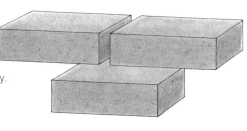

Place modular bricks with mortar joints of recommended thickness (12 mm) to form horizontal increments of 85 or 118 mm. Joints are staggered for strength and durability.

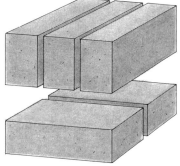

Thickness of three standard modular bricks plus mortar joints equals the length of a similar brick.

Turn a simple corner by alternating position of whole bricks. This offsets the mortar joints at intersecting walls.

Concrete blocks

Webs and face shells taper slightly so blocks can be unmoulded at the factory. Others flare, providing a little more mortar surface. Place blocks with thicker side up.

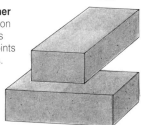

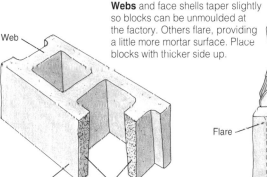

Web

Face shell

Taper

Flare

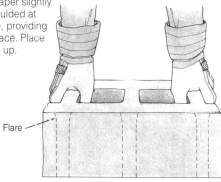

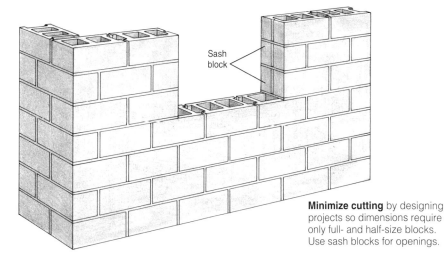

Sash block

Minimize cutting by designing projects so dimensions require only full- and half-size blocks. Use sash blocks for openings.

Mixing mortar

Mix dry ingredients thoroughly; then add water in small amounts. Blend with hoe until mortar is smooth and sides of a test furrow hold their shape without crumbling or sagging.

Mortar is the cement mixture used to bond bricks, concrete blocks and stones together. Unlike concrete, which weakens if overworked by excessive mixing or smoothing, mortar can be spread and trowelled repeatedly until it begins to harden. Masons *throw* mortar beds and *butter* bricks. It is crucial to mix and spread mortar correctly; practice throwing mortar on a 50 × 100.

Select the mortar recipe appropriate to your needs from the chart below. The types shown are suitable for most do-it-yourself projects except stone-work. (Stones should fit together well and rely on the force of gravity rather than the strength of the mortar.) Before restoring brickwork more than 100 years old, consult an experienced mason about the proper mortar mix. Mortar that is too strong may cause bricks in such masonry to crack.

There are three ways to mix mortar: from scratch using Portland cement, hydrated builder's lime, and sand; from masonry cement (Portland cement pre-mixed with lime) and sand; and from bags containing all the ingredients (ready-mix). Buy materials for mortar from a builders' supplier to be sure of getting the right kinds. Sand must always be clean, finely graded and salt-free. Use only clean tap water.

Mix mortar in a wheelbarrow or mortar pan in batches of up to about 30 ℓ. This is about as much as one person can use within an hour and a half, the time it usually takes for hardening to begin. Mortar not used within two hours of mixing should be discarded. The standard builder's wheelbarrow has a capacity of between 60 and 65 ℓ.

Follow the instructions for mixing concrete by hand (pp 204–205). Add enough water to achieve the right consistency. Mortar that is too wet will run out between the joints; if it is too dry, the bond will be weak. With a power mixer, add three-fourths of the water, half the sand and all the masonry cement (or all the Portland cement and lime) required. Mix briefly, add the remaining water and sand and mix again for at least three minutes.

Caution: Wear waterproof gloves when working with mortar.

Mortar recipes

Type	Use	Strength	Portland cement	Lime*	Sand	Masonry cement	Sand
I	Highly stressed, high-strength masonry units as in multi-storey buildings	Strongest	50 kg	0-10ℓ	130ℓ	50 kg	100ℓ
II	Normal load-bearing – parapets, free-standing walls and those exposed to severe damp	About 75% of Type I	50 kg	0-40ℓ	200ℓ	50 kg	170ℓ
III	Lightly stressed walls, such as single-storey and not exposed to severe damp	About 33% of Type I	50 kg	0-80ℓ	300ℓ	50 kg	200ℓ

*The use of lime is optional and cement and sand volumes stay the same if it is omitted. Lime improves the plasticity and cohesiveness of fresh mortar and gives the hardened mortar additional resistance to cracking.

Loading the trowel

1. Chop a slice of mortar from the mound on mortar board (600 mm-square piece of 20 mm plywood) – enough to cover three or four bricks. When chopping, hold trowel perpendicular to board with thumb extended along top of handle; relax forearm and let blade drop.

2. Without changing grip, use flat surfaces of trowel to shape slice into rounded loaf or wedge, whose length equals that of the trowel's blade.

3. Rotate wrist to scoop up loaf by sliding trowel underneath it. Forearm and palm of gripping hand should face up. Lift loaded trowel and flick it down and up rapidly to settle mortar firmly on blade.

Throwing a mortar line

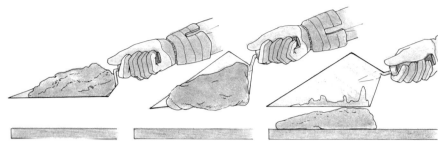

1. Hold tip of loaded trowel at starting point, parallel to ground, with palm of gripping hand facing up.

2. Throw the mortar by rotating your wrist and flicking trowel downward while pulling tool toward you in a straight line.

3. End with trowel perpendicular to surface and mortar along centreline of bricks or practice 50 × 100. If mortar is off-line, return it to board. Try again using fresh bricks.

4. Draw back of trowel along centre of mortar to smooth it into a uniform 12 mm-thick bed that covers entire surface of three or four bricks.

Buttering a brick

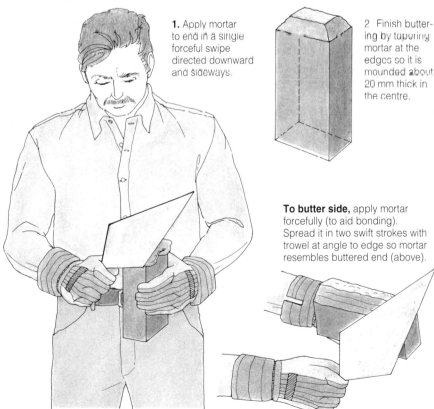

1. Apply mortar to end in a single forceful swipe directed downward and sideways.

2 Finish buttering by tapering mortar at the edges so it is mounded about 20 mm thick in the centre.

To butter side, apply mortar forcefully (to aid bonding). Spread it in two swift strokes with trowel at angle to edge so mortar resembles buttered end (above).

Brick positions

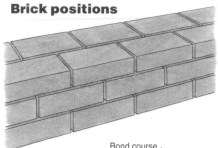

Stretcher is placed horizontally with its long narrow side exposed. This is the most common position for bricks and forms the basis of running, stack and open bonds.

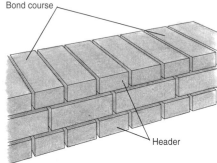

Bond course

Header

Header shows end of brick with wider surface on horizontal. Headers are a common structural bond in double-skin walls and combine with stretchers to make the decorative feature of many pattern bonds.

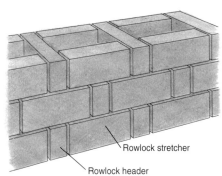

Rowlock stretcher

Rowlock header

Rowlock is laid with long narrow side down. Rowlock stretchers, also called shiners, reveal a brick's long wide surface; rowlock headers reveal ends. The former are used for pattern bonds; the latter for capping walls and windowsills.

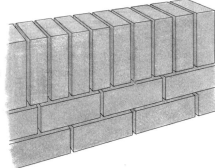

Soldier stands on end with long narrow side exposed. Soldiers are commonly used within pattern bonds to simulate arches over doorways and windows.

Sailor stands on end with wide side exposed. Narrow support surfaces at top and bottom limit use to non-structural pattern bonds and edging for paths and patios.

Bricklaying is an intricate skill that has many aspects of an art. Over the centuries, bricklayers have developed colourful yet precise terms to describe every feature of bricks and the ways they are used.

In a wall or other structure, bricks are identified by their position when installed (see left). The exposed surface of an installed brick is called its *face*. The horizontal layer of mortar on which bricks are laid is called a *bed*. A layer of bricks in a structure is called a *course*. A vertical section, or wall, of masonry that is one brick thick is sometimes called a *withe,* though it is more commonly known in South Africa as a single-skin or single-brick wall. A wall two bricks thick is a double-skin or, if there is a space between skins, a *cavity wall*. A row of bricks overlapping more than one skin is called a *bond course;* if the face of a course consists of the ends of bricks, it is called a *header course*.

Any piece that is less than a whole brick is called a *bat*. A *half bat* is a brick split to divide its length in half ; a *three-quarter bat* and a *quarter bat* are three-quarters and one-quarter of the length, respectively. Short bats that are used at corners to maintain joint spacings are called *closures*.

The term *bond* describes three different ways that bricks are tied together in a structure: A *pattern bond* implies the arrangement of the bricks; a *mortar bond* refers to the adhesion of that material with the masonry units; and a *structural bond* refers to metal ties or anchors used in masonry construction, and to the overlapping of masonry units to stagger and thereby strengthen their vertical joints.

Pattern bonds are named to reflect their appearance; they also may or may not have important structural qualities. Some are suitable only for veneer work (p 246). Before selecting a bond, check with your local authority to make sure it is permissible for your project.

Decorative design

Garden wall pattern places a header after every two stretchers in each course. Use a brick of contrasting colour to outline diamond shape. To create a larger diamond pattern, place the header after every three stretchers. Before building, draw your project and its pattern on graph paper.

Forming patterns with stretchers

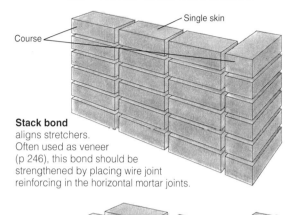

Stack bond
aligns stretchers.
Often used as veneer
(p 246), this bond should be
strengthened by placing wire joint
reinforcing in the horizontal mortar joints.

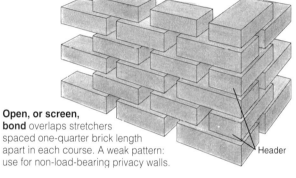

**Open, or screen,
bond** overlaps stretchers
spaced one-quarter brick length
apart in each course. A weak pattern:
use for non-load-bearing privacy walls.

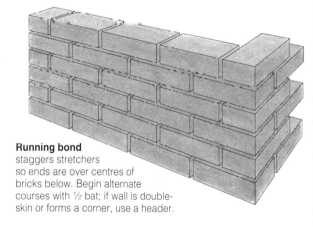

Running bond
staggers stretchers
so ends are over centres of
bricks below. Begin alternate
courses with ½ bat; if wall is double-
skin or forms a corner, use a header.

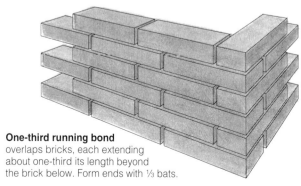

One-third running bond
overlaps bricks, each extending
about one-third its length beyond
the brick below. Form ends with ⅓ bats.

Combining headers and stretchers

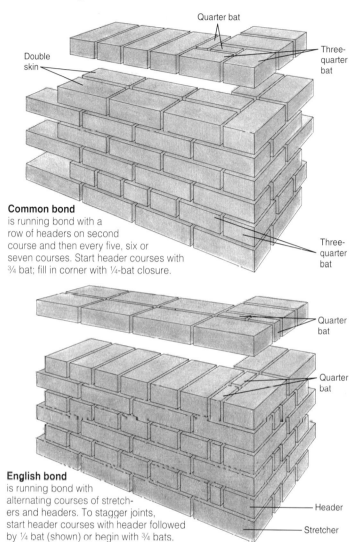

Common bond
is running bond with a
row of headers on second
course and then every five, six or
seven courses. Start header courses with
¾ bat; fill in corner with ¼-bat closure.

English bond
is running bond with
alternating courses of stretchers and headers. To stagger joints,
start header courses with header followed
by ¼ bat (shown) or begin with ¾ bats.

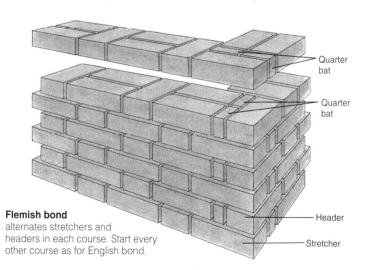

Flemish bond
alternates stretchers and
headers in each course. Start every
other course as for English bond.

JOINTING BRICKS

Joints are the layers of mortar between bricks. They are named for their position in the structure: horizontal joints are called *bed* joints; vertical joints between bricks in a course are *head* joints. If a wall is more than one brick thick, the vertical joint between the skins is called a *collar* joint.

When laying bricks, apply the mortar forcefully to aid its adhesion (p 225). Then push the bricks into place with one motion; don't move them further except to tap them gently immediately afterward, using the handle of a mason's trowel, to settle and level them. Re-positioning them breaks the seal between the mortar and the bricks, interfering with the bond and causing cracks in the mortar. If a brick is too low or is misaligned, remove it together with the mortar in the joint; then clean and replace the brick, using fresh mortar. Check your work often with a level and stretched string to make sure bricks and courses are placed properly (p 233).

The mortar is ready to be finished when it is hard enough to retain a thumbprint without leaving any residue on your thumb. Finishing shapes and compresses the joints, strengthening them and sealing them against moisture. Using a trowel to finish joints is called *striking;* using a special tool is called *pointing*. As a rule, it is best to work from bottom to top.

Many styles of mortar joints have been developed. Some are purely decorative and only for indoor use; others are designed to shed water and are best for outdoor work. After the initial shaping and trimming, clean all joints by brushing them with a medium-soft bristle brush, sacking or carpet scrap. After brushing, rework the joints if necessary to sharpen their details and remove any imperfections.

While mortar joints form the main structural bond for masonry, expansion joint material inserted at certain points (facing page) allows the bricks and the mortar to expand and contract with changes in temperature and humidity. These expansion joints are placed every 6 m in brick walls and at strategic points in rigid (mortared) brick patios and walks. However, you do not need to use expansion joints in a project, vertical or flat, that is less than 6 m long or in any type of sand-set (flexible) brickwork.

Laying bricks

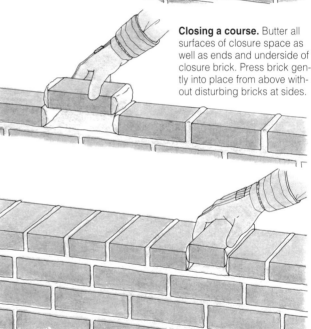

To place stretcher or header in course, butter one end or side of brick; push brick down and against previous brick to produce uniform head and bed joints. Level by tapping brick with trowel handle.

Closing a course. Butter all surfaces of closure space as well as ends and underside of closure brick. Press brick gently into place from above without disturbing bricks at sides.

Pointing head and bed joints

Trim away tags of excess mortar by slicing upwards with edge of trowel. Repeat step after pointing head and bed joints.

Shape head joints first. Press and slide the tool over vertical seams to smooth and compact the mortar before it hardens.

Smooth bed joints next, using the same tool, to create continuous horizontal lines. Avoid gouging joints with tool or knuckles.

Mortar joints and shapes

Weathered. Sheds water well. Form by running trowel tip against underside of upper course while pressing tip inward at 30° angle. Shape of head joints is the vertical equivalent, all slanting in the same direction.

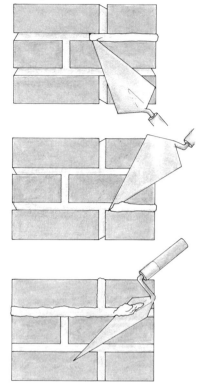

Struck. Opposite of weathered. Sheds water poorly. Work from above to form; recess lower edge of mortar by pressing trowel tip inward against top of lower brick course. Head joints are same as for weathered.

Flush. Moderately water-resistant but not strong because mortar is not compressed. Form by slicing away excess mortar with trowel to leave flat surface. Best for use beneath plaster, giving an even surface.

Concave. Most common joint. Sheds water well. To form, see facing page. You can use pipe, dowel or back of kitchen spoon instead of convex forming tool. All tools should be 6 mm wider than joints.

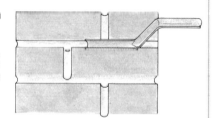

V. Dramatic appearance. Sheds water well. Form with V-pointing tool or tip of mason's trowel. Practise first to avoid unevenness. Centreline of joint must be spaced evenly between brick courses.

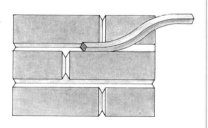

Raked. Not water-resistant; use indoors to create strong shadow lines. Form by removing 6 to 12 mm of mortar from joints with raking tool. Clean exposed surfaces thoroughly afterwards.

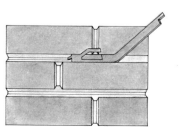

Expansion joints in mortared paving

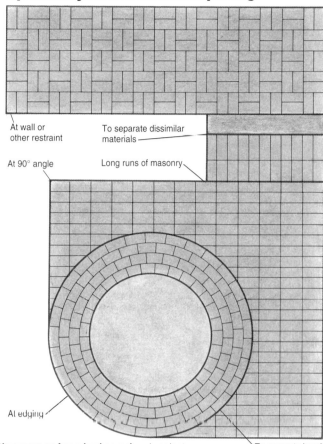

At wall or other restraint

To separate dissimilar materials

At 90° angle

Long runs of masonry

At edging

To separate bond patterns

Neoprene or foam backer rod and sealant expansion joints allow for differing expansion and contraction of bricks and mortar. Pour concrete slab (pp 204–213) prior to laying rigid flatwork.

How to cut a brick

Cut line

Mark cutting line around brick with pencil and straightedge. Place brick on ground or board. Score brick. Place brick bolster on cutting line, with bevelled edge facing waste. Strike tool gently with hammer. To cut brick, insert bolster in scored line, and strike sharply with hammer. Grip bolster around shaft, not blade, to avoid injuring fingers.
Caution: Wear heavy gloves and goggles.

Lifting stones

To lift a stone safely, bring it close to your body. When rising, 'hug' the stone, using your thigh muscles to stand. Keep your back straight. Avoid carrying stones more than a few metres. A stone 300 mm square and 150 mm thick can weigh 35 kg or more.

Pry stone from ground with levers. Start with long steel digging bar; then insert 50 × 100 planks and lever alternately with these until one plank can serve as a ramp on which to slide the stone. Place wood blocks beneath planks to keep them from sinking into sides of hole. Do not reach beneath the stone when rolling it free.

Because stone is heavy and working with it requires physical conditioning, a novice should start a project gradually. Have a medical examination, warm up before working by doing stretching exercises that include touching your toes, and spend no more than 4 to 6 hours daily lifting and moving stones until your muscles are developed. Always wear protective clothing, including heavy leather work gloves, sturdy boots with steel toes, and safety goggles (when cutting).

Rely on mechanical aids to save physical effort and to avoid injury. To lift stones, use digging bars, ramps and hand or power winches. When using a winch, wrap a chain – not the winch cable – around the stone and attach the winch cable to the chain. A winch cable can break if it is looped around an object and then hooked to itself.

For hauling stones over short distances, get a sturdy wheelbarrow with solid arms and a pneumatic tyre. (For maximum manoeuvrability, load stones so most of the weight is in the rear.) Or place stones on a wooden plank and roll the plank along on logs or pipes. For hauling stones long distances, use a pickup truck (bakkie) with heavy-duty suspension, or a flatbed trailer pulled by a similar powerful vehicle. To avoid losing control, drive cautiously when hauling stones. Inspect the brakes beforehand, and upgrade them if necessary so they are in excellent condition. When hauling flat or thin stones, place them on edge and wedge them to keep them from falling; if laid flat, they can break when bounced.

Dry stone (mortarless) masonry is the best type for novices because it requires fitting stones together and relies on gravity to hold them in place, the key to all stonework. Shaping the stones is an important part of dry stonework; for best results use a 1,5 kg sledgehammer or a stonemason's hammer and at least two chisels: a broad-bladed *stone chisel* or a *pitching tool* for scoring and for splitting grained stones; and a *point,* tapered on all sides like a sharpened pencil, for focusing blows over small areas. When shaping stones, support them on a firm but resilient surface (p 236). Professional stonemasons use a sturdy home-made wooden table, padded with sawdust or several layers of carpet. The height of such a table should be about 150 mm below the user's waist.

The properties of stone

Type	Physical characteristics	Workability	Durability*	Use
Granite	Hard, dense; coarse-grained or speckled; grey, blue, pinkish	Difficult; hard to cut	Excellent	Walls, foundations, chimneys (not cut to fit)
Limestone	Medium-soft; light to dark grey	Easy; cuts well	Medium to poor	Walls, foundations, chimneys
Sandstone	Soft to medium-hard; golden brown to reddish	Easy to medium (there are soft and hard sandstones)	Medium	Hard types: walls, foundations, chimneys. Soft types: interior veneer
Slate	Soft; dark grey or black	Medium; splits between layers; cut across grain with masonry saw	Medium to poor	Patios, paths, shingles

*Includes resistance to weather

Moving stones

Roll stone onto a plank resting on logs or pipes. Push plank forward, or lever it from behind with a 50 × 100, while removing rollers from rear and setting them in pathway ahead. On soft ground, place boards beneath rollers for support.

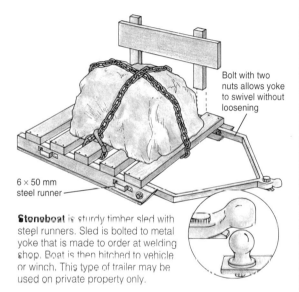

Bolt with two nuts allows yoke to swivel without loosening

6 × 50 mm steel runner

Stoneboat is sturdy timber sled with steel runners. Sled is bolted to metal yoke that is made to order at welding shop. Boat is then hitched to vehicle or winch. This type of trailer may be used on private property only.

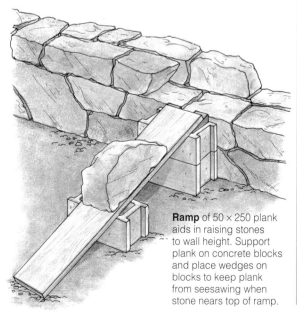

Ramp of 50 × 250 plank aids in raising stones to wall height. Support plank on concrete blocks and place wedges on blocks to keep plank from seesawing when stone nears top of ramp.

Splitting stones

To split stone along the grain, mark line around the stone with soft pencil; then drive metal wedges or series of chisels along grain. Strike in succession, one blow each with 1,5 kg hammer until crack widens and stone splits apart.

Cutting and fitting stones

Choose stones by analysing space that needs filling. Select the stone with closest shape. Stones in a wall should tilt towards the centre and exert chiefly vertical pressure. Successive courses should cover vertical joints between stones below.

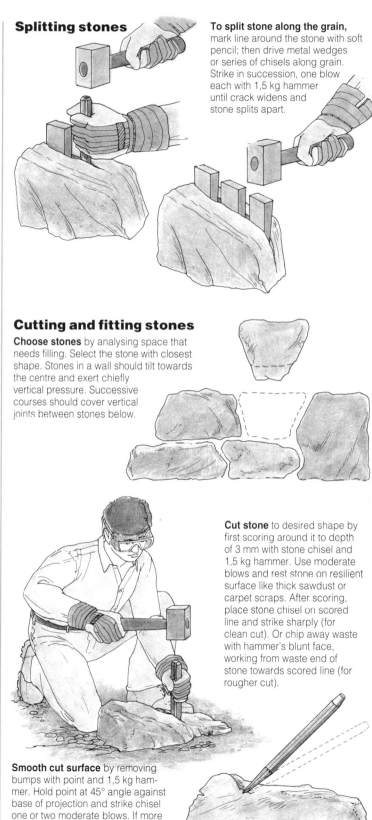

Cut stone to desired shape by first scoring around it to depth of 3 mm with stone chisel and 1,5 kg hammer. Use moderate blows and rest stone on resilient surface like thick sawdust or carpet scraps. After scoring, place stone chisel on scored line and strike sharply (for clean cut). Or chip away waste with hammer's blunt face, working from waste end of stone towards scored line (for rougher cut).

Smooth cut surface by removing bumps with point and 1,5 kg hammer. Hold point at 45° angle against base of projection and strike chisel one or two moderate blows. If more blows are needed, lower point to 30°.

Laying blocks in courses

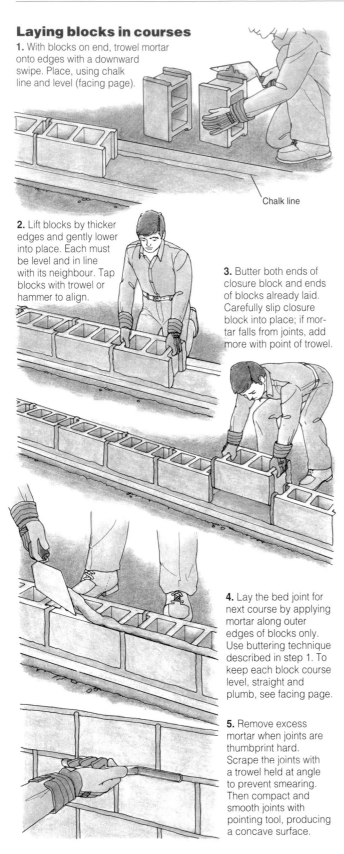

1. With blocks on end, trowel mortar onto edges with a downward swipe. Place, using chalk line and level (facing page).

Chalk line

2. Lift blocks by thicker edges and gently lower into place. Each must be level and in line with its neighbour. Tap blocks with trowel or hammer to align.

3. Butter both ends of closure block and ends of blocks already laid. Carefully slip closure block into place; if mortar falls from joints, add more with point of trowel.

4. Lay the bed joint for next course by applying mortar along outer edges of blocks only. Use buttering technique described in step 1. To keep each block course level, straight and plumb, see facing page.

5. Remove excess mortar when joints are thumbprint hard. Scrape the joints with a trowel held at angle to prevent smearing. Then compact and smooth joints with pointing tool, producing a concave surface.

Many find that laying concrete blocks is faster and easier than laying bricks. You can butter several blocks at one time; in addition, because of their weight, you set the blocks in place without pushing them. Their larger size means that levelling and aligning require less time.

Concrete blocks take the same type of mortar as bricks, and the joints are a standard 10 mm. The mortar bed beneath the first concrete block course must cover the entire area; you apply mortar for subsequent block courses only to the block's outer edges. Lay blocks with their thicker edges uppermost; the wider surfaces hold more mortar (p 223). Cover stored concrete blocks with a sturdy plastic tarpaulin to keep out moisture and dirt.

In certain walls control joints – deliberately weakened vertical seams – are necessary to reduce cracking by accommodating the movement of the masonry. These walls have large openings, intersect other block walls, are restrained at each end or have varying heights or thicknesses. In addition, concrete blocks that are joined to other structural materials also require control joints. Place control joints where the greatest stresses occur and at intervals along the wall's length equal to its height or up to 1,25 times its height. For example, a wall 4 m high will have control joints every 4 to 5 m along its length.

Because control joints act as a focus for cracking and, therefore, occasionally crack themselves, gasket material keeps the wall in alignment as it shifts. You can buy blocks designed to house the various types of gaskets.

Control joints

Cruciform gasket strip of nylon or plastic fits groove in sash blocks. Firmer support is provided by galvanized steel channel fixed to cast columns and fitting the grooves of sash blocks or open-ended hollow units. Metal bars and ties are also used.

Mortar in control joint acts as backer for sealing compound. Rake out mortar to a depth of 18 mm, then fill the joint with sealing compound. (First brush primer into the joint if caulking instructions specify.)

LEVEL, STRAIGHT AND PLUMB

In all types of masonry, aligning the building units accurately is crucial to success. To build straight walls that do not lean or bulge, each brick or concrete block must be checked three ways – lengthwise, across its width and vertically – as it is set in place, and if necessary, adjusted before proceeding.

To ensure straightness, mark the length of a wall by snapping a chalk line on the foundation. So that the chalk line won't be covered with mortar, snap it at a uniform distance – say, 50 mm – from foundation's edge. Every time you place a brick or block, measure between it and the line at both ends to make sure the unit and the line are exactly parallel.

Masons build the ends of a wall first; then they fill in the centre of the wall. The built-up ends of walls are called *leads*. If the walls form corners, the ends are called *corner leads*. Stretch a mason's line between the ends as a guide.

A home-made *course rod* allows you to check that your mortar joint is the proper thickness as you build each course. To make a course rod, mark squared lines on a 25 × 50 mm board at intervals equal to the thickness of your masonry unit plus a mortar joint. Make as many marks as there are courses in the wall. Hold the pole next to the construction to check the mortar joint for each course.

Building a wall lead

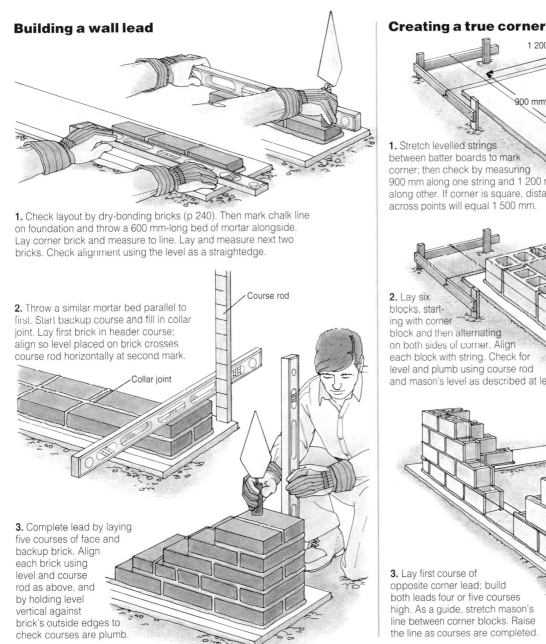

1. Check layout by dry-bonding bricks (p 240). Then mark chalk line on foundation and throw a 600 mm-long bed of mortar alongside. Lay corner brick and measure to line. Lay and measure next two bricks. Check alignment using the level as a straightedge.

2. Throw a similar mortar bed parallel to first. Start backup course and fill in collar joint. Lay first brick in header course; align so level placed on brick crosses course rod horizontally at second mark.

Course rod

Collar joint

3. Complete lead by laying five courses of face and backup brick. Align each brick using level and course rod as above, and by holding level vertical against brick's outside edges to check courses are plumb.

Creating a true corner

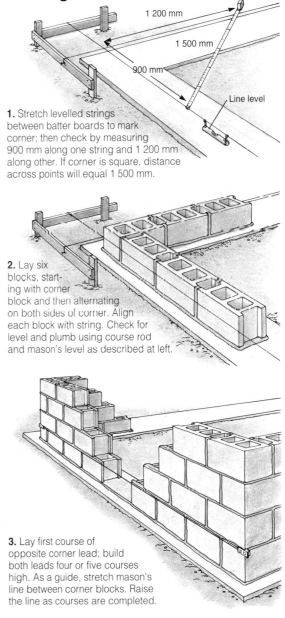

1 200 mm

1 500 mm

900 mm

Line level

1. Stretch levelled strings between batter boards to mark corner; then check by measuring 900 mm along one string and 1 200 mm along other. If corner is square, distance across points will equal 1 500 mm.

2. Lay six blocks, starting with corner block and then alternating on both sides of corner. Align each block with string. Check for level and plumb using course rod and mason's level as described at left.

3. Lay first course of opposite corner lead; build both leads four or five courses high. As a guide, stretch mason's line between corner blocks. Raise the line as courses are completed.

When used in flatwork, bricks and concrete pavers are often laid in sand (without mortar) on a flat, firm base and anchored with an edging. This method, called *flexible paving,* is easy to install and repair.

Brick paving is usually laid in classic patterns: running bond, stack bond, basket weave and herringbone. Of these, herringbone is the most durable and stable because the bricks interlock at right angles. Concrete pavers are available in many shapes and the more intricate ones come with installation instructions.

Flagstone (slasto) is also popular for flexible paving. Because no edging is required, it is easier to lay out an area for flagstone than for bricks or concrete pavers. In addition, you can space the sand joints irregularly. But make sure the flagstones are well supported underneath, otherwise they may break when stepped on. (For more on flagstone paving, see pp 236–237.)

With sandy, well-drained soil in areas where freezing seldom occurs, excavate the site to the depth of the paving plus 60 mm for a bed of compacted sand. (The sand will keep the paving from shifting.) With other soils and in cold climates, excavate 100 mm deeper to add a layer of compacted gravel under the sand. Gravel permits drainage and helps prevent masonry from being pushed upward when the ground alternately freezes and thaws.

When laying out a project, base its shape on the dimensions of the paving units in order to minimize cutting. You can cut bricks fairly easily by hand (p 229), but you will need to rent a splitter to cut pavers. (Pavers that create special patterns usually come with half blocks for filling in outside edges.)

Edging can be anchored with stakes or spikes. Use pressure-treated timber strips or landscaping ties (old railway sleepers are ideal, being rot-resistant and relatively cheap.) Alternatively, you can anchor strips of polyvinyl chloride (PVC) with 10×250 mm metal spikes. Or you can dig a narrow ditch and add a brick edging (facing page). To minimize the effects of frost heave, where this is noticeable, dig the ditch 50 mm deeper and pour in a layer of gravel before placing the bricks.

To reduce the chance of tripping over wood or PVC edging, place the top surface 6 mm below the paving. The paving will settle more and the two will eventually be level.

Patterns

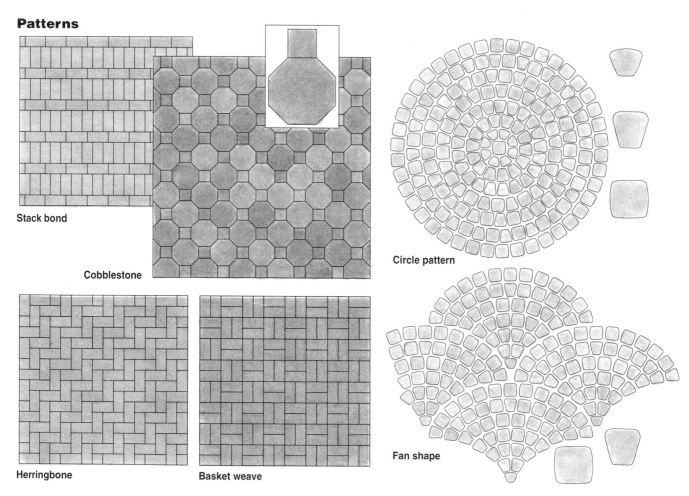

Stack bond

Cobblestone

Circle pattern

Herringbone

Basket weave

Fan shape

Brick edging

Lay out project. Position corner stakes so that connecting strings outline edges of project. Mark edges with a sand line (p 208). Dig a ditch equal to length of bricks (plus 50 mm for gravel, if used). Keep outer sides vertical.

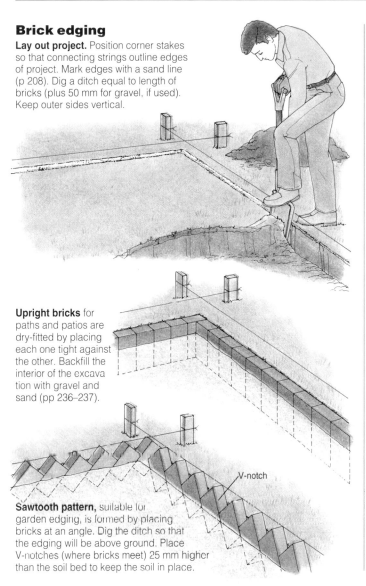

Upright bricks for paths and patios are dry-fitted by placing each one tight against the other. Backfill the interior of the excavation with gravel and sand (pp 236–237).

Sawtooth pattern, suitable for garden edging, is formed by placing bricks at an angle. Dig the ditch so that the edging will be above ground. Place V-notches (where bricks meet) 25 mm higher than the soil bed to keep the soil in place.

V-notch

Wood strip edging

Dig level ditch that is wide enough to allow work area outside perimeter. Place edging. Drive stakes at 1 m intervals and where boards join. Recess stakes 25 mm below top of edging. Fasten with nails or screws.

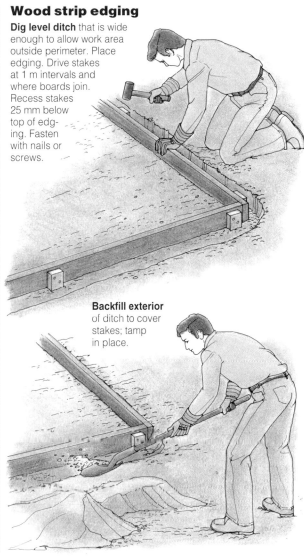

Backfill exterior of ditch to cover stakes; tamp in place.

Two ways to set landscaping ties

Set ties (old railway sleepers) flat on excavation. Butt-join them with 250 mm nails driven at an angle and staggered. To hide nails, drive them into sides of ties. Add gravel, sand and paving. Backfill exterior.

At each end and in centre, drill 16 mm holes with spade bit. Insert 12 × 450 mm mild-steel rods. With short-handled sledge-hammer, drive rods into holes until flush with edging. Lay paving; backfill exterior.

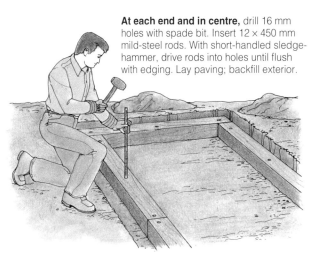

Paving with bricks

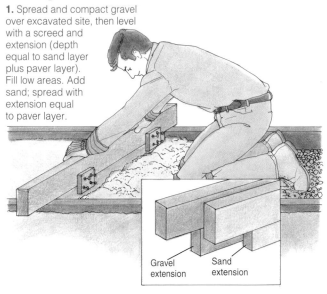

1. Spread and compact gravel over excavated site, then level with a screed and extension (depth equal to sand layer plus paver layer). Fill low areas. Add sand; spread with extension equal to paver layer.

Gravel extension   Sand extension

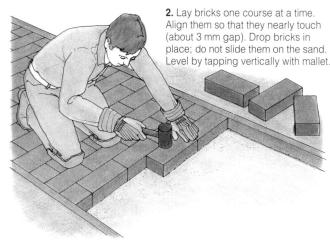

2. Lay bricks one course at a time. Align them so that they nearly touch (about 3 mm gap). Drop bricks in place; do not slide them on the sand. Level by tapping vertically with mallet.

3. Spread coarse sand over bricks after all are laid, then sweep sand into cracks. Spray site with garden hose to moisten and settle sand. (Do not tamp bricks.) Repeat two or three times until joints are filled.

To lay out areas for sand-laid paving, tie strings to stakes or batterboards as for poured concrete and mortared masonry projects (pp 206–208, 233). The strings determine the perimeter and establish a height from which to measure downwards when excavating the site. To outline curved areas, lay a garden hose or rope on the ground. Drive stakes along the hose or rope outline, and stretch strings between them. (The strings need not follow the curve exactly.)

If the paved surface is to be flat, use a line level to adjust each string. If the surface must slope to promote drainage away from a building, the strings that are stretched in the direction of the slope should slant downward 22 mm for every metre of their length.

The most crucial step in building with flexible paving is site preparation; a firm and flat site minimizes the settling of the paving. As a rule, it is easier to excavate the entire site to the depth required and then install the edging and paving. If you install anchored wood edging (pp 234–235) before laying the pavers, you can use it as a guide when levelling the sand and gravel beds on which the paving will rest.

To use the edging as a levelling guide, rest the ends of the screed (pp 211, 214) on it and drag the extension over the gravel, then the sand. If the area is wider than the screed, or if you prefer to install the edging last (as you might for vertical or angled brick edging), place temporary strips of wood equal to the height of the edging on the ground before adding the first layer of fill. Use these to support the ends of the screed. After levelling the beds, remove the strips and fill the areas by adding material with a trowel.

Take extra time to make sure that the gravel bed (or the excavation if gravel is not used) is compacted and level. You can compact small areas with a hand compactor or tamper (p 206), but for best results, compact large areas with a plate compactor, a motor-powered tool that can usually be hired.

Caution: Plate compactors are noisy; wear ear protectors.

Don't compact a sand bed. Until the paving is laid, protect the bed from rain either by covering the sand with plastic sheeting when you have finished for the day or by spreading the sand in areas of one square metre just before installing the paving. Stay off sand bed by working from outside the perimeter or by kneeling on previously laid sections.

When paving with flagstones (slasto), first fit as many uncut stones together as possible to minimize the amount of shaping you have to do. To cut flagstones, support them on sand-covered ground. If you will be cutting a number of stones, raise the work to a more comfortable height and reduce back strain by building a sturdy sand table to rest them on. Make the table surface out of 20 mm plywood, use 50 × 100 mm legs to support the table, and add a rim of 25 × 50 mm strip to contain the layer of sand.

Place flagstones with their more level and attractive side up. Avoid using small stones; they tend to sink into the ground or to tip when stepped on.

A patio of concrete pavers

1. Prepare 100 mm-thick gravel base with screed (facing page). To compact large area, move plate compactor across base several times. Spread and smooth 50 mm of coarse sand. Do not compact.

2. Lay pavers starting at 90° corner. Align edge units precisely; set all pavers in place without disturbing sand. Follow manufacturer's suggested sequence when using irregularly shaped units.

3. Keep pavers aligned by following string stretched parallel with courses. Complete patio, then compact pavers with plate compactor. Sweep sand into joints and compact pavers again with compactor. Do not wet. Repeat until joints are full.

Shaping flagstones

Place flagstone so edge to be cut overlaps edging or previously laid stone. Determine cut line by eye, and mark both sides with grease pencil.

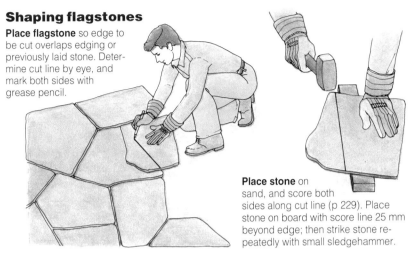

Place stone on sand, and score both sides along cut line (p 229). Place stone on board with score line 25 mm beyond edge; then strike stone repeatedly with small sledgehammer.

Laying flagstones

1. Lay flagstones about 12 mm apart. Arrange largest stones around perimeter of site to help keep the rest from shifting. Place stone on ground and test fit; then lift stone and re-grade area underneath by removing or adding sand to accommodate stone's uneven surface.

2. Tap stones lightly with a mallet to settle them. Lay several stones, then place a mason's level across them in several directions to check that all are the same height and that there are no high edges or irregularities that can cause tripping.

3. Finish project by filling joints with sand and wetting it as for flexible brick path (facing page). Use scrap wood to tamp sand between stones after each application.

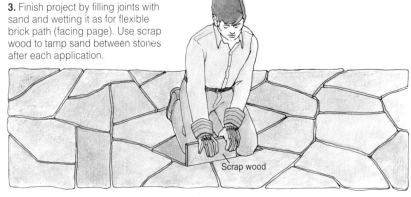

Scrap wood

GARDEN STEPS: BRICK, BLOCK AND STONE

Above-ground steps generally require a foundation to prevent settling and cracking, and often a railing for safety. Steps leading into a building should be wider than the doorway and, if the door opens out, should have a landing that is deeper than the door. Steps that are built into a steep slope may also need retaining walls at the sides (pp 244–245). Before you begin construction, consult your local building inspector to find out what codes apply.

As a general rule, steps (or risers) should have a maximum height of 180 mm and a minimum tread depth of 280 mm. Along gently sloping paths, long landings (1,85 to 2,45 m) divided by low risers, or a series of landings interrupted by pairs of identi-

cal steps, are often more comfortable and appealing than a single compact flight. These designs are safer too, especially if the steps tend to be slippery.

Lay out steps by measuring the slope's *rise,* or height, and its *run,* or horizontal distance. Often the rise is fixed by the physical constraints of the site. For example, the position of a house entry door and its height above ground level determine the rise of above-ground steps. When this is the case, the run can usually be adjusted as necessary to fit the steps. With in-ground steps, both rise and run measurements may be more flexible.

To calculate the number of steps, divide the rise (in mm) by a divisor, less than or equal to 175, that goes

into the rise equally. Determine the number of treads by dividing the run measurement by a tread depth (at least 280 and no more than 450 mm) that goes into the run equally. If the rise or the run of the steps happens to divide awkwardly, spread the remainder evenly among the treads or risers, or adjust the overall measurement.

For example, take a 950 mm rise with a 2 100 mm run. The run divides into seven 300 mm treads, requiring six risers. The rise divides into six risers that are 158 mm high.

You can also design steps by transferring the run and rise measurements to graph paper and sketching uniform riser/tread combinations (to scale) to comfortably and safely fill the space.

Above-ground steps

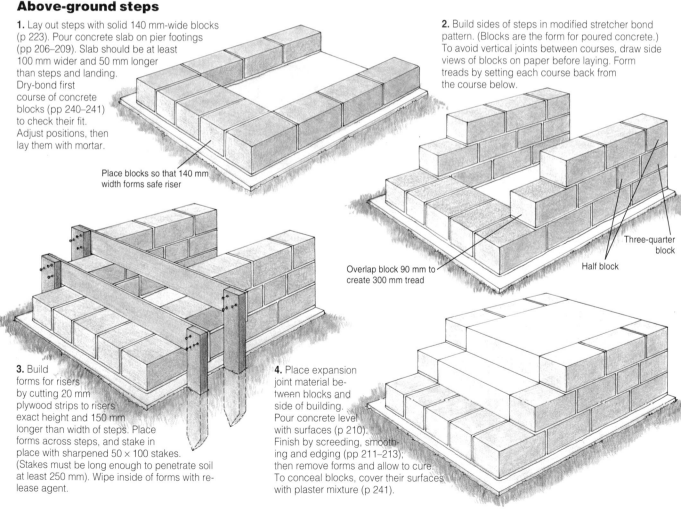

1. Lay out steps with solid 140 mm-wide blocks (p 223). Pour concrete slab on pier footings (pp 206–209). Slab should be at least 100 mm wider and 50 mm longer than steps and landing. Dry-bond first course of concrete blocks (pp 240–241) to check their fit. Adjust positions, then lay them with mortar.

Place blocks so that 140 mm width forms safe riser

2. Build sides of steps in modified stretcher bond pattern. (Blocks are the form for poured concrete.) To avoid vertical joints between courses, draw side views of blocks on paper before laying. Form treads by setting each course back from the course below.

Three-quarter block

Half block

Overlap block 90 mm to create 300 mm tread

3. Build forms for risers by cutting 20 mm plywood strips to risers exact height and 150 mm longer than width of steps. Place forms across steps, and stake in place with sharpened 50 × 100 stakes. (Stakes must be long enough to penetrate soil at least 250 mm). Wipe inside of forms with release agent.

4. Place expansion joint material between blocks and side of building. Pour concrete level with surfaces (p 210). Finish by screeding, smoothing and edging (pp 211–213); then remove forms and allow to cure. To conceal blocks, cover their surfaces with plaster mixture (p 241).

In-ground steps

1. Drive stakes at top and bottom of slope. Using string and a line level, measure between stakes to find the run. Measure the height of the taller stake from the ground to the string to find the rise. Calculate uniform step dimensions (facing page).

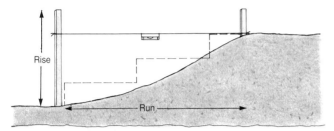

2. Side view of plan for steps shows the position of railway sleepers used as landscaping ties. They are about 2,1 m long and embed the steps well into the slope. Steel rods anchor each tie to the one below it.

Flagstone (slasto) steps

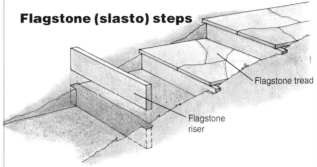

Flagstone tread

Flagstone riser

Lay out as for other in-ground steps. Excavate, allowing for stone tread and 50 mm layer of sand above 100 mm bed of compacted gravel. Then dig narrow, straight trenches for flagstone risers. Install risers, then add fill. Lay flagstone treads so they overlap risers, trimming edges if necessary. Check treads often with a level, and reposition them as needed to ensure flat surfaces (pp 236–237).

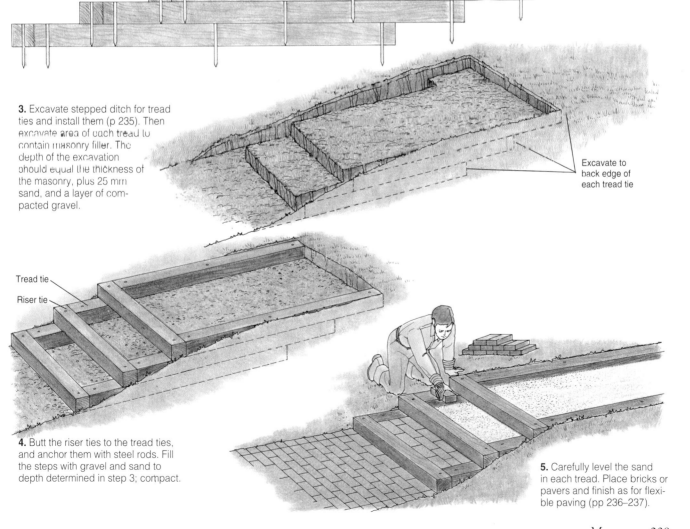

3. Excavate stepped ditch for tread ties and install them (p 235). Then excavate area of each tread to contain masonry filler. The depth of the excavation should equal the thickness of the masonry, plus 25 mm sand, and a layer of compacted gravel.

Excavate to back edge of each tread tie

Tread tie

Riser tie

4. Butt the riser ties to the tread ties, and anchor them with steel rods. Fill the steps with gravel and sand to depth determined in step 3; compact.

5. Carefully level the sand in each tread. Place bricks or pavers and finish as for flexible paving (pp 236–237).

Masonry   239

Local regulations govern virtually all types of masonry walls and boundary fences, so you should consult your local authority's building department before beginning a wall project. In almost all cases, you'll have to supply plans and have them approved.

Support your wall with a foundation that conforms in thickness and depth to the local requirements and, in very cold areas, rests below the frost line (pp 208–209).

Depending on local conditions such as wind and drainage, you may be required to build double-skin walls, although exceptions may be made in the case of reinforced pier-and-panel walls. These are easier to construct than double-skin masonry and require fewer bricks and less excavation. Pier-and-

panel walls derive their strength from steel reinforcing bars embedded vertically in the piers. The size of the piers and the panels must be designed to suit the individual site and conditions, as well as local regulations.

Reinforcing bars should be spaced properly within grout-filled centres. When placing the first courses, you may need to support the bars in position with braces staked to the ground on either side of the wall.

Many non-load-bearing walls of concrete block do not require reinforcing. But walls built with screen blocks, a decorative variety used for privacy walls, should be reinforced with pilasters, whose function is similar to that of piers. Pilasters are constructed with special pilaster blocks and, like

piers, they contain reinforcing bars. In addition, wire joint reinforcing should be embedded between every other course to compensate for the inherent weakness of the stack bond pattern (pp 226–227) in which screen blocks are usually laid.

Cap all walls to protect them from moisture and to provide a finished look. On brick walls, lay a rowlock course or place a course of decorative capping bricks. On concrete block walls, lay a course of solid units or apply a rounded layer of mortar.

Plaster can be applied to masonry for both appearance and protection. A typical formula for plaster is 1 part masonry cement and 3 to 5 parts very fine sand, mixed with clean water to the consistency of creamy cake icing.

Double-skin brick wall

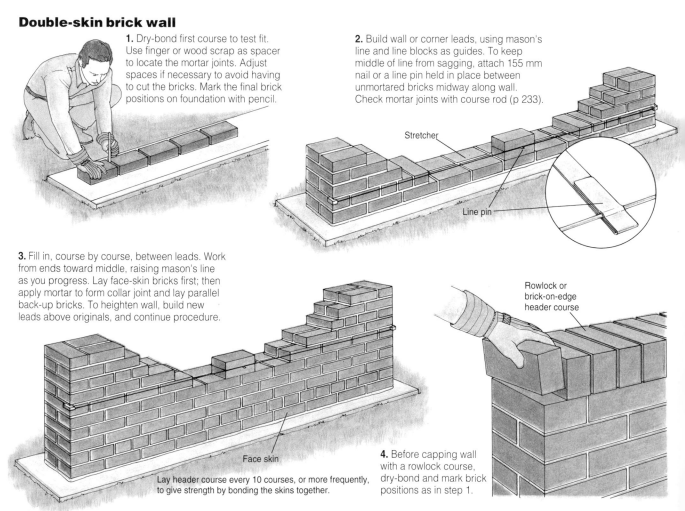

1. Dry-bond first course to test fit. Use finger or wood scrap as spacer to locate the mortar joints. Adjust spaces if necessary to avoid having to cut the bricks. Mark the final brick positions on foundation with pencil.

2. Build wall or corner leads, using mason's line and line blocks as guides. To keep middle of line from sagging, attach 155 mm nail or a line pin held in place between unmortared bricks midway along wall. Check mortar joints with course rod (p 233).

Stretcher

Line pin

3. Fill in, course by course, between leads. Work from ends toward middle, raising mason's line as you progress. Lay face-skin bricks first; then apply mortar to form collar joint and lay parallel back-up bricks. To heighten wall, build new leads above originals, and continue procedure.

Face skin

Lay header course every 10 courses, or more frequently, to give strength by bonding the skins together.

Rowlock or brick-on-edge header course

4. Before capping wall with a rowlock course, dry-bond and mark brick positions as in step 1.

Pier-and-panel wall

1. Excavate and pour pier footings. When concrete stiffens, insert reinforcing bars cut to wall height. Brace bars with spacers and wire ties. Lay each brick course; fill pier cores with grout. Embed wire reinforcing horizontally in every other course as for privacy wall (below).

Pier   Panel

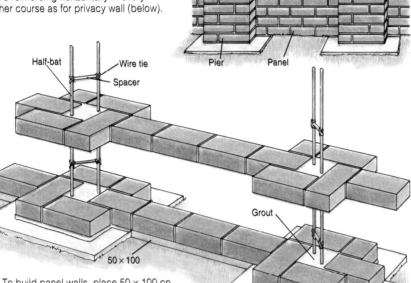

Half-bat   Wire tie
Spacer
Grout
50 × 100

2. To build panel walls, place 50 × 100 on ground as bearer to provide level base for first panel course. Lay first course of bricks (with no mortar bed on bearer). Tie odd and even courses into piers in alternating design. Remove bearer after wall has cured.

Privacy wall

Wire reinforcing

Decorative cap
Reinforcing bar

Screen blocks come in many sizes and patterns

Pilaster block

Embed reinforcing bar in stiff concrete foundation. Place end and intermediate (not shown) pilaster blocks around bar in mortar bed; fill centres with concrete. Throw mortar bed 12 mm thick and 100 mm wide on foundation; lay screen blocks. Embed wire joint reinforcing in horizontal joints of every second course. Top wall with decorative cap.

Plastered wall

1. Dampen wall; brush on liquid bonding agent. Apply first coat of plaster 10 mm thick by spreading it forcefully with steel trowel or float.

2. Score first coat with scarifier or other raking tool. Keep surface damp for 48 hr by spraying or by covering with plastic sheeting.

3. Apply final coat of plaster 6 mm thick with plasterer's trowel. Mix pigment into plaster to add colour. To add texture, pattern your strokes.

Masonry   241

The courses of a stone wall can be *random,* or irregular, using uncut, roughly dressed or dressed stones in no particular pattern, or they can be regular, with the stones fitted tightly in level courses.

Walls can be laid with or without mortar. Novices should begin with a *dry stone* wall (one built without mortar) that is a maximum of 1 m high. Because dry stone walls move with extreme temperature cycles, they are more flexible than mortared ones. Dry stone walls need no concrete foundations and require an excavation of only about 150 mm.

Gravity is the force that holds well-built walls together and pulls apart poorly laid ones. The following guidelines will help you work effectively with gravity and maximize the friction between the stones. Tilt the stones slightly towards the centre of the wall. You can also taper, or *batter,* the faces of a wall a minimum of 25 mm for every 600 mm. (In dry retaining walls you must taper the outer face or slant the inner face, pp 244–245.) Fit each stone so that it contacts the adjacent stones in as many places as possible. Place the stones 'one over two', staggering vertical joints by laying one stone over the joint between the two below. For stability, make the wall at least two stones thick. (A wall 1 m high should be about 600 mm thick.) Use a bonding, or *tie,* stone every square metre. These stones, ideally as long as the wall is thick, are laid crossways to hold the stones together.

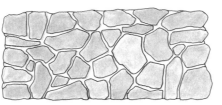

Coursed dry stone wall with shaped stones

Random mortared wall with undressed stones

A mortared, or *wet,* wall can be built with the mortar visible or recessed so that it is hidden from view. Either way, mortar improves the bonding between stones, permitting higher walls and vertical faces. But the same principles for working with gravity apply: Mortar is not as durable as stone, and when it fails, gravity and friction take over.

A mortared wall is relatively inflexible. Instead of moving slightly to adjust to the forces of freezing and thawing or of growing tree roots, a mortared wall cracks. To minimize movement, build a wall on a foundation just below the frost line. On sloping land install a pipe on the uphill side to drain the water behind the wall (pp 244–245). Never lay more than three courses (or 600 mm of wall height) in a day, so that the mortar can set enough to withstand the weight of the next courses. A standard mortar mixture for stone is 1 part lime, 3 parts Portland cement and 9 parts sand. Add water slowly until the mixture stands in peaks like whipped cream. Keep the mortar off the stones' faces because the lime will stain the stones.

Caution: Wear waterproof gloves when working with mortar and protect your eyes with goggles.

Keep a just-built wall cool and damp for about a week to extend the curing time and strengthen the mortar. Mist the wall with a hose and cover it with plastic sheeting. If necessary, build a temporary shading device.

Putting gravity to work

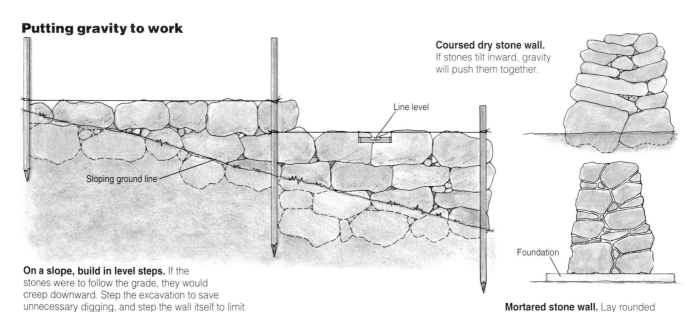

Coursed dry stone wall.
If stones tilt inward, gravity will push them together.

Line level

Sloping ground line

Foundation

On a slope, build in level steps. If the stones were to follow the grade, they would creep downward. Step the excavation to save unnecessary digging, and step the wall itself to limit its height. Make sure each step is level by running a line level between two stakes. Dig out to accommodate large or irregular stones.

Mortared stone wall. Lay rounded stones so they have maximum contact. Place small wedge-shaped stones to hold the rounded stones in place.

Laying a dry wall

Place the first course on firm, level ground, using stakes and level lines to guide the construction. Place the larger, more irregular stones on the bottom, digging as needed so they slope slightly down towards the centre of the wall. Fill the centre with smaller stones. As you add courses, stagger the vertical joints.

Turn corners by overlapping long and short stones from each leg in alternating courses. These stones tie the two legs together.

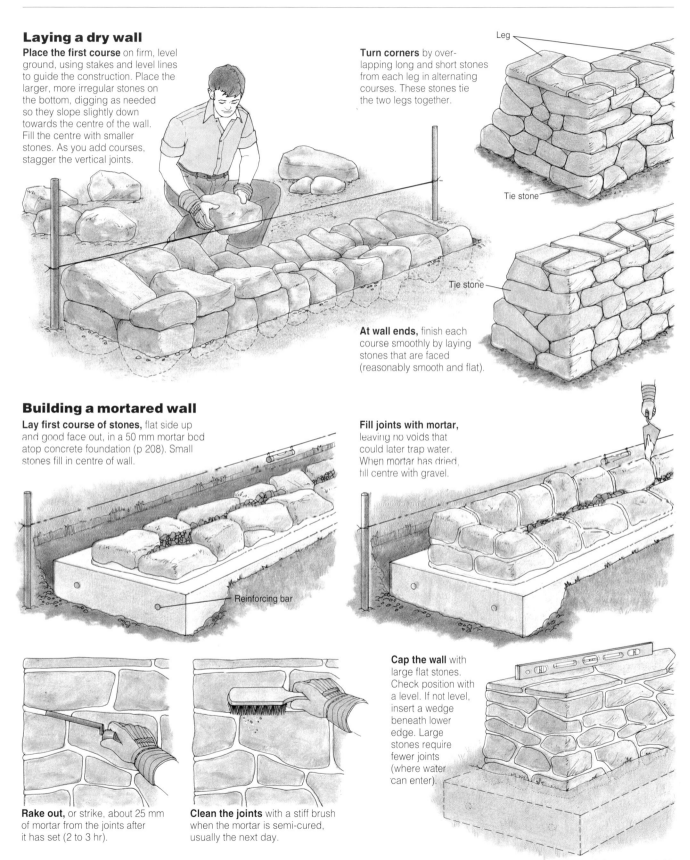

Leg

Tie stone

Tie stone

At wall ends, finish each course smoothly by laying stones that are faced (reasonably smooth and flat).

Building a mortared wall

Lay first course of stones, flat side up and good face out, in a 50 mm mortar bed atop concrete foundation (p 208). Small stones fill in centre of wall.

Fill joints with mortar, leaving no voids that could later trap water. When mortar has dried, fill centre with gravel.

Reinforcing bar

Cap the wall with large flat stones. Check position with a level. If not level, insert a wedge beneath lower edge. Large stones require fewer joints (where water can enter).

Rake out, or strike, about 25 mm of mortar from the joints after it has set (2 to 3 hr).

Clean the joints with a stiff brush when the mortar is semi-cured, usually the next day.

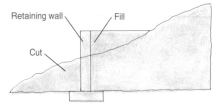

On sloping land, retaining walls hold back the soil, preventing erosion and creating a more usable landscape. These walls are commonly made of stone or concrete block – either the standard kind or a variety of interlocking blocks that require no mortar. The design of the wall depends on the building material you choose and such technical factors as the soil type, the wall height and the site conditions.

A straight vertical wall of concrete block is tied with bars to a reinforced foundation (p 208) that is set deeply into the sloped bank. A stone wall, if laid dry, requires no foundation and should slope, or batter, in toward the bank. Whether it is made of stone or concrete block, a gravity wall, thick at the bottom and tapering gradually, relies on its mass to hold back the soil.

Soils vary in their ability to absorb or drain water as well as the ways they react when wet or frozen. Generally, soils that drain well and remain stable when wet (such as gravel and sandy gravel) will not put as much pressure on a retaining wall as those that absorb water or lack cohesiveness (such as soft clay and silt). In addition, soils differ in their ability to bear weight – a factor for high walls only. Consult your local authority's building department for advice about local soil conditions. If the soil conditions are a concern, or if you are unsure, backfill the area behind the retaining wall with gravel rather than with the soil found on site.

Site conditions. A rainy climate, a high water table (the level of a site's groundwater), or the presence of a nearby lake, stream or spring may affect the design of a wall. When soil becomes wet, its load-bearing capacity is reduced, its weight increases and it tends to move laterally. In cold climates, wet soil freezes and expands, putting tremendous pressure on the wall. To reduce increased soil pressure, install special drainage for all types of retaining walls over 600 mm high, even dry stone walls. Drainage can be provided by weep holes, gravel backfill, drainage pipe or a combination of these elements. A damp-proofing coat will help to prevent water from seeping through the wall itself and should prevent efflorescence (p 248).

Wall height. Retaining walls may be governed by local building regulations. In general, the higher the wall and the steeper the slope of the supported bank, the stronger the wall – and the foundation below it – must be. To hold back a steeply sloping bank, a series of low walls (terraced effect) is an attractive and less demanding alternative to a single high wall. Consider having a contractor build walls over 1,2 m high and have an engineer or architect design retaining walls over 2,4 m high or those that involve complicating factors – for example, if the wall is below a driveway, it will have to be designed to accommodate truck and car traffic.

Caution: In areas subject to earth tremors, special reinforced designs may be required.

Concrete block retaining walls

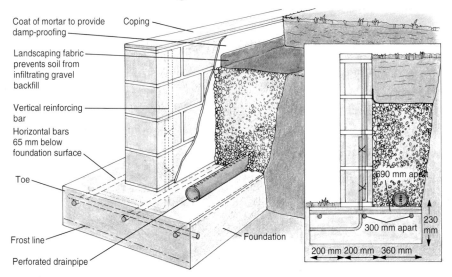

Coat of mortar to provide damp-proofing

Coping

Landscaping fabric prevents soil from infiltrating gravel backfill

Vertical reinforcing bar

Horizontal bars 65 mm below foundation surface

Toe

Frost line

Perforated drainpipe

Foundation

690 mm apart

230 mm

300 mm apart

200 mm 200 mm 360 mm

Foundation for typical 1 to 1,2 m-high retaining wall of 190 × 190 × 390 mm block (above) extends 360 mm into bank. To tie wall to foundation, vertical reinforcing bars run through the courses every 860 mm and are bent to extend into toe of foundation. Horizontal bars are placed 300 mm apart along length and 690 mm apart across width of foundation.

Gravity wall (right) has a vertical face and a stepped-back profile, with a base equal to at least half the height. This depends on its weight and on friction between the wall and the ground for its ability to resist horizontal pressure. Use blocks of 190 mm and 290 mm widths to build stepped wall with staggered mortar joints.

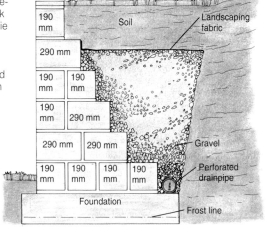

190 mm

Soil

Landscaping fabric

290 mm

190 mm 190 mm

190 mm 290 mm

290 mm 290 mm

Gravel

190 mm 190 mm 190 mm 190 mm

Perforated drainpipe

Foundation

Frost line

Dry stone retaining wall

Excavate to firm subsoil and lay stone courses. Backfill with gravel as you build, extending large stones into the hill. Excess water drains through dry wall joints. For clay soil, add a drainpipe behind wall.

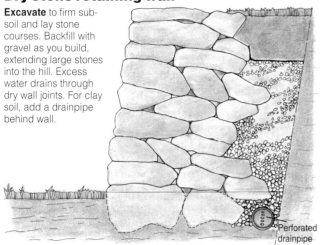

Perforated drainpipe

Vertical-face dry wall

Slant back of wall into slope. Lay narrow base course; backfill with gravel or soil, and pack it with digging bar (p 230). Repeat, laying gradually thicker courses. The top course of a 1 m wall should be about 600 mm thick.

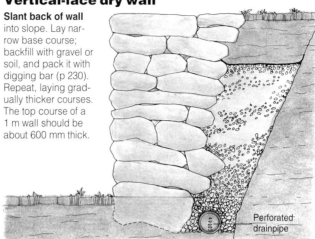

Perforated drainpipe

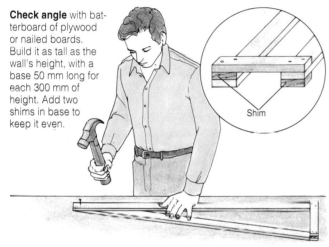

Check angle with batterboard of plywood or nailed boards. Build it as tall as the wall's height, with a base 50 mm long for each 300 mm of height. Add two shims in base to keep it even.

Shim

Mortared retaining wall

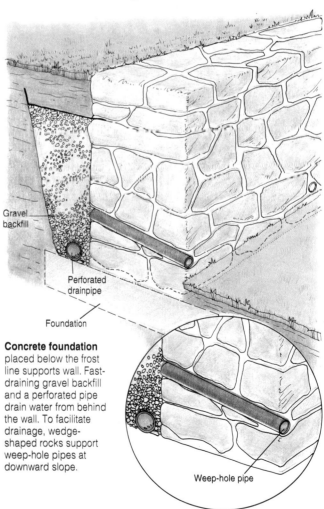

Gravel backfill

Perforated drainpipe

Foundation

Concrete foundation placed below the frost line supports wall. Fast-draining gravel backfill and a perforated pipe drain water from behind the wall. To facilitate drainage, wedge-shaped rocks support weep-hole pipes at downward slope.

Weep-hole pipe

Place batterboard against the wall as you lay each course. For a long wall you can stake several batterboards 1 or 1,2 m apart and add a levelled line.

Veneer masonry is a decorative sheathing that enhances the face of a structure. It can be made of brick, natural stone or a synthetic stone that is lighter in weight and easier to install than natural stone. Applying full-size bricks or stones as veneer (bottom of page) requires using traditional masonry techniques. These include building a foundation to bear the weight of the materials (the foundation must be below the frost line if the veneer is outdoors) and arranging and mortaring the bricks or stones so that those on the bottom support those on top. In addition, metal ties or wire reinforcing is needed to fasten the veneer to the wall or other structure being sheathed.

Veneer bricks, also called thin bricks, measure only 25 mm thick and are lightweight. Individual pieces can be arranged in any pattern. You can also buy them in panels and in kits that contain face and corner units, spacers, thin-bed adhesive and pre-mixed mortar. Cut thin bricks with tile cutter or circular saw fitted with masonry blade.

Synthetic veneer masonry. These products come as panels or individual pieces resembling various kinds of bricks or building stones. Many are suited for both outdoor and indoor use and some are designed especially for hearths. Synthetic masonry is easy to install almost anywhere. If it will be visible from the side, install it with corner pieces. These units have a 90° angle that allows the 'stones' to turn corners.

When preparing surfaces and installing synthetic veneer, follow the manufacturer's instructions. Set thin bricks in a layer of adhesive and fill the joints with mortar. For synthetic stones, apply a scratch coat of mortar, then let it dry. (Spread mortar directly on bare masonry; cover other surfaces with reinforcing mesh first.) Apply mortar to the back of each piece and press into place. Fill joints with mortar.

Thin bricks for interiors

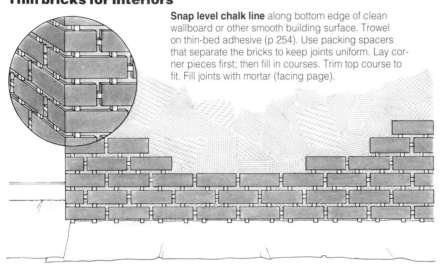

Snap level chalk line along bottom edge of clean wallboard or other smooth building surface. Trowel on thin-bed adhesive (p 254). Use packing spacers that separate the bricks to keep joints uniform. Lay corner pieces first; then fill in courses. Trim top course to fit. Fill joints with mortar (facing page).

Brick skin on block retaining wall

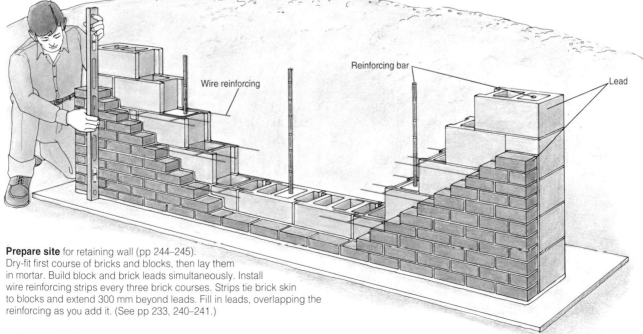

Prepare site for retaining wall (pp 244–245). Dry-fit first course of bricks and blocks, then lay them in mortar. Build block and brick leads simultaneously. Install wire reinforcing strips every three brick courses. Strips tie brick skin to blocks and extend 300 mm beyond leads. Fill in leads, overlapping the reinforcing as you add it. (See pp 233, 240–241.)

WORKING WITH SYNTHETIC STONES

Setting the stones

Lay hearth pieces, if any, first (bottom of page). Protect them with plastic sheeting. If necessary, staple or nail reinforcing mesh to studs in wall at 150 mm intervals. Apply mortar scratch coat. Attach units, working from top down.

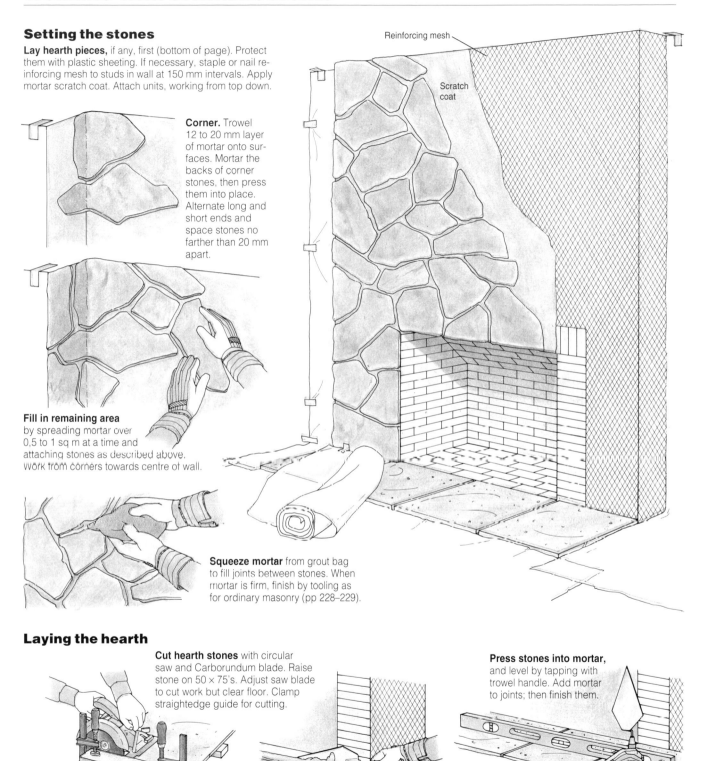

Corner. Trowel 12 to 20 mm layer of mortar onto surfaces. Mortar the backs of corner stones, then press them into place. Alternate long and short ends and space stones no farther than 20 mm apart.

Reinforcing mesh

Scratch coat

Fill in remaining area by spreading mortar over 0,5 to 1 sq m at a time and attaching stones as described above. Work from corners towards centre of wall.

Squeeze mortar from grout bag to fill joints between stones. When mortar is firm, finish by tooling as for ordinary masonry (pp 228–229).

Laying the hearth

Cut hearth stones with circular saw and Carborundum blade. Raise stone on 50 × 75's. Adjust saw blade to cut work but clear floor. Clamp straightedge guide for cutting.

Press stones into mortar, and level by tapping with trowel handle. Add mortar to joints; then finish them.

Install hearth stones. Throw lines of mortar, each 75 mm wide and 20 mm thick, on base. Space lines 25 mm apart.

Masonry should be repaired as soon as the damage is discovered. If neglected, small problems that are relatively easy to fix can become major ones. Most masonry damage is caused by moisture, settling, or impact – in that order.

Efflorescence, a white powder commonly found on new masonry surfaces, is usually caused by moisture introduced during construction. The moisture should dry in a few months and rain usually washes away the powder.

If efflorescence continues or if it appears on older masonry, look for an entry point for moisture, such as cracks, crumbling mortar, deterioration around windows, doors and chimneys, and dampness caused by moisture-saturated soil against masonry below ground. Repairing all but the last usually involves replacing damaged

building materials, applying a patch, or caulking. Once you have solved the moisture problem, remove the efflorescence by scrubbing it with a stiff brush and water or a detergent solution.

Before repairing cracks in mortar joints, seal off any entry points of moisture. If cracks re-develop, consult an engineer. For tuck-pointing, use mortar that is 1 part masonry cement, 3 parts sand and enough water to make the mix the consistency of soft ice cream. Consult your local authority or museum before repairing masonry more than 100 years old. Special mortar may be required.

Dampness in embedded masonry is more difficult to cure, as the soil around it must be drained. If the masonry is a foundation wall, first check that gutters are not clogged and that

channels are placed beneath downpipes to carry away runoff. You may have to re-grade the ground surface so that it slopes away from the masonry.

Clear blocked downpipes with a drain auger if you can reach their openings (they may empty directly into a stormwater drain). In basements, a high water-table causes dampness. Installing a sump pump beneath the floor, and perhaps perimeter drainpipes leading to it, may solve the problem. For severe or persistent moisture problems, consult an engineer. The solution is often to dig along the outside of the wall (or the high side of a retaining wall), install a drainpipe surrounded by a layer of gravel, and place damp-proof material and porous drainage fabric against the wall before backfilling (pp 244–245).

Tuck-pointing cracked mortar joints

1. With cold chisel and ball-peen or small sledgehammer, drive out old mortar to depth of 12 to 20 mm. Wear goggles and thick gloves. Chisel a square-sided groove, exposing bare stone on at least one side of each joint. Blow or brush away chips and dust.

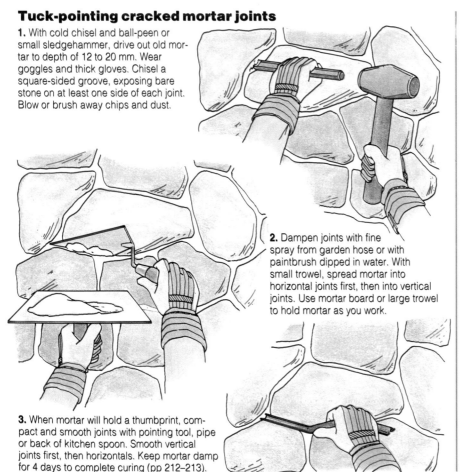

2. Dampen joints with fine spray from garden hose or with paintbrush dipped in water. With small trowel, spread mortar into horizontal joints first, then into vertical joints. Use mortar board or large trowel to hold mortar as you work.

3. When mortar will hold a thumbprint, compact and smooth joints with pointing tool, pipe or back of kitchen spoon. Smooth vertical joints first, then horizontals. Keep mortar damp for 4 days to complete curing (pp 212–213).

Replacing a broken brick

1. Chisel away damaged brick and surrounding mortar. Clean wall cavity and dampen it. Spread mortar on bottom surface.

2. Dampen new brick; mortar top and sides, then slide into place from board or trowel. Add extra mortar to joints if necessary.

Filling large cracks

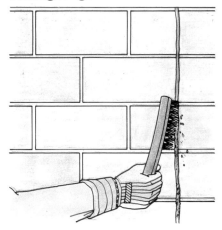

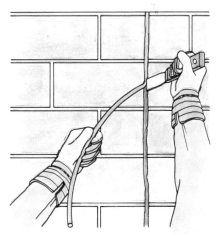

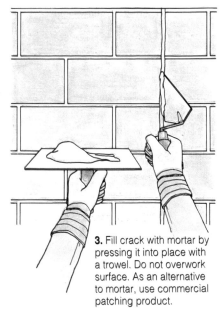

1. Brush or blow out all debris carefully. In concrete block masonry it is better not to chisel out a crack, as you would for concrete. Mortar will adhere to a clean crack in a block, and chiselling may damage the relatively thin face shell of the block.

2. Pack cracks with flexible backer rod (available at building supply stores). Next, dampen the crack and brush all surfaces with a commercial bonding agent or home-made grout (equal parts cement and sand, mixed with water to consistency of thick paint).

3. Fill crack with mortar by pressing it into place with a trowel. Do not overwork surface. As an alternative to mortar, use commercial patching product.

Rebuilding a broken block

1. Carefully chisel off loose or weak sections of damaged face shell. Dampen area and apply mortar to webs.

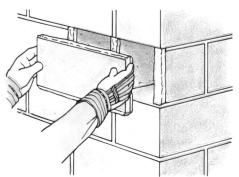

2. Cut face shell from new block. Apply mortar and press block into place. (Mortar fills gaps between cut shell and repair area.) Finish joints as for whole blocks (p 232).

Repairing plaster

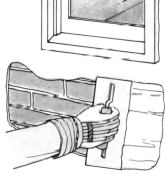

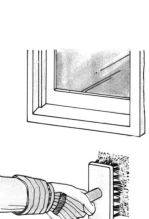

1. Correct any structural or moisture problems. Chisel away loose plaster; brush repair clean. Dampen area, then trowel on plaster until it is level with surrounding surface.

2. Compact and smooth new plaster with straightedge (p 211). Add more plaster if necessary. Disguise repair by feathering plaster beyond borders of patch with trowel.

3. Keep plaster damp for 5 days until cured. Then mix and apply finish-coat plaster with float. If desired, add texture by using freehand strokes or by spattering with a brush.

CERAMICS, GLASS AND PLASTICS

In addition to being beautiful, ceramic tiles are durable and easy to clean. They come in various colours and may be plain or hand-painted. Grout, the material placed between tiles, comes in colours to match or contrast with the tiles.

When choosing tiles, consider where they will be used. This will determine what the composition should be (p 254). Then think about appearance – large patterns will look out of place in a small room. And remember that although tiling a whole section with hand-painted tiles may be too expensive for most budgets, you can select a few as accent pieces to fit in with more affordable tiles. Because manufacturers make tiles in different thicknesses, whenever you mix tiles be sure that their thicknesses match. When you visit a designer or tile supplier, take colour swatches, photos and dimensions.

Floor tiles are made to withstand traffic. All of the tiles shown here can be used in heavy-traffic areas with the exception of the small hexagonal tile, which is made for use in light-traffic areas such as bathrooms.

Mosaic tiles are easy to install. They come in mesh- or paper-backed sheets or are joined with rubber or plastic. Some are pre-grouted. To customize a design, replace individual tiles.

Wall tiles are designed specifically for walls. If you install them on a floor they will probably crack under the weight of people and furniture. They also scratch easily. You can create your own geometric patterns by selecting plain tiles of different colours and arranging them as you want. Tiles may come designed for complementary arrangements, including tiles with matching patterns (far right, top) or repeating patterns (far right, centre). Some manufacturers also make matching border tiles.

Speciality tiles come in a variety of shapes and sizes to create a smooth transition between adjacent surfaces or to give a finished appearance by forming rounded edges or corners. They are usually designed to match standard tiles.

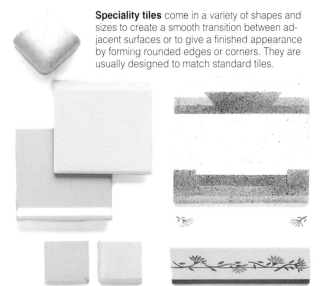

Dual-use tile (above) is suitable for walls and floors. If installed on a floor, make sure dual-use tiles are rated for use in light-traffic areas. These tiles are not suitable for floors exposed to heavy traffic.

Insert tiles (above) accent or border wall tiles. Some are strong enough for floors.

Border tiles come with different patterns and profiles. You can use them in single rows or stack them to create a distinctive look. Use the tiles to accent the tops of tiles that end part of the way up a wall or to break up a solid block of plain tiles.

Ceramics, Glass and Plastics 253

Ceramic tiles provide a durable, attractive covering for surfaces as diverse as walls, countertops, floors and hearths. Tiling a surface is not difficult, but careful planning and installation will pay off – careless work can result in cracked, uneven or loose tiles.

Before choosing a type of tile, consider the degree of water resistance, strength, slipperiness and stain resistance necessary for the location. Most tiles are classified for use on either walls or floors. Most wall tiles are not strong enough to be set on floors or high-use areas. Many floor tiles are too large for countertops and too heavy for walls. Glazed tiles are easier to keep clean while unglazed tiles are less slippery underfoot but are more easily stained. Sealing unglazed tiles with a commercial tile sealant will make them stain-resistant but more slippery; renew the sealer on these tiles annually. Tiles with a textured surface also wear well and are less slippery than regular tiles.

Glazed tiles generally absorb less water than unglazed tiles, but water resistance is gauged by the amount of water the *bisque,* or body, of a tile absorbs. In descending order of absorption, tiles are classified as non-vitreous (readily absorbs water), semivitreous, vitreous, and impervious (absorbs less than ,05 per cent of its weight). Tiles may also be designated as standard grade, second grade or decorative thin wall tile. Most tiles sold are standard grade; second-grade tiles may have imperfections in the shape or glaze.

Tiles can be either set on a thick mortar bed (best left to professionals) or laid over a substrate thinly coated with adhesive (known as thin-bed installation). The type of substrate may vary, but it must be clean, flat and very stable – movement causes tiles to loosen and crack. (If in doubt about the strength of a countertop, add extra cross braces underneath.) An ideal substrate is 12 mm chipboard, available from hardware stores. It can be installed over most flat surfaces, including wallboard and plywood (p 257). Flexible hardboard can be used for curved surfaces or if a thinner substrate is required.

Tile adhesive is usually bought ready to use. The two main types are based on resin or on powdered cement. Both types may be used as thin-bed adhesive (3 to 6 mm thick), and the cement-based type may be used as a thick-bed adhesive (up to 12 mm). Cement-based adhesives are generally stronger than resin-based types which are more easily affected by heat and water.

Refer to the chart below when choosing tiles and matching them with the correct substrate and adhesive. Plan the layout, and install the tiles following the steps on pp 256–257.

Special techniques for preparing the substrate and installing floor tile are shown on pp 334–336. Mosaic tile sheets, commonly set on a mesh backing, are described on p 258. Pre-grouted sheets of larger tile are laid out and set in much the same way as individual tiles. However, it's easier to snip or tear individual tiles off the backing sheet before cutting them.

If you have many tiles to cut, a hired wet saw is the best tool. A portable cordless tile saw fitted with a diamond blade can make straight cuts in tile, but make sure the tile is securely held on a stable surface before cutting.

Ceramic tile is extremely hard – use carbide-tipped drill bits and fit power saws with blades specified for cutting ceramic tile. To avoid chipping the glaze, drill and cut through the face of the tile, not the back.

Caution: In addition to following the safety precautions on pp 12–13, inspect all rental tools for sound cutting edges and proper guards before leaving the store. When cutting or drilling tile or mixing powdered adhesive, wear goggles and a dust mask. Also wear ear protection when using power tools. When using adhesives, work in a well-ventilated area and extinguish all open flames (including pilot lights). Water keeps bits and blades cool, but never submerge part of the body of a power tool in water.

Choosing tile

Location	Tiles	Substrate	Adhesive
Indoor floors	Glazed floor tiles, pavers (must be sealed), quarry tile, terracotta, monocoturra, mosaic	Wooden floor, concrete slab, plywood	Thin-bed for dry concrete slab; thick-bed for rough slab; latex additive for non-rigid floor
Outdoor floors	Some glazed floor tiles, mosaic, pavers, quarry tile	Wooden floor, concrete slab	As for indoor floors but check adhesive is waterproof
Wet walls (such as shower surrounds)	Glazed wall tiles, mosaic	Plastered walls	Thin-bed with latex additive
Countertops	Glazed wall tiles (for low-use areas), small glazed floor tiles, mosaic, monocoturra	Chipboard, plywood, plastic laminate	Thin-bed with latex additive
Indoor walls and backsplashes	Glazed wall tiles, mosaic, small glazed floor tiles	Plasterboard, wallboard, plaster, plywood	Thin-bed with latex additive

Cutting tiles to fit

Tile nippers trim irregular cuts. Nibble away waste from ends to centre of cut. To avoid ragged edges, keep jaws parallel to pencilled cut line, and place only two-thirds of jaw surface on tile for each bite.

Snap cutter for straight cuts can be hired. Place tile in cutter, and score by drawing marking wheel lightly once across cut line (inset). To snap tile, set wings on tile close to the rule, then strike handle with heel of your hand. If wings might mar tile, wrap them with masking tape.

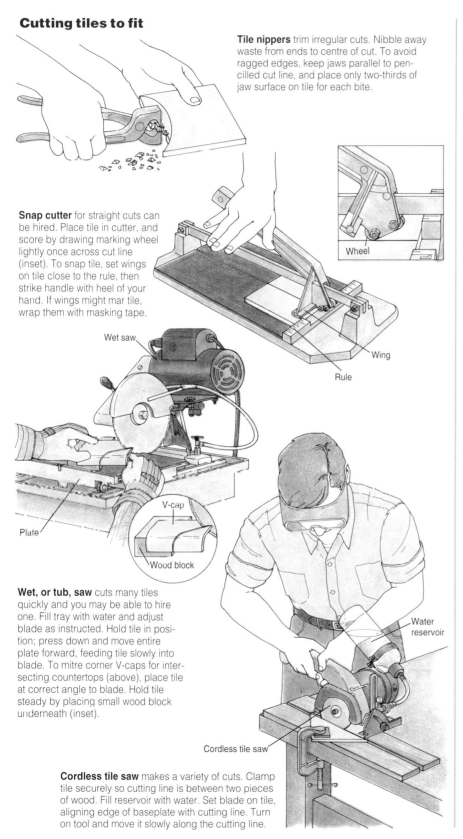

Wet, or tub, saw cuts many tiles quickly and you may be able to hire one. Fill tray with water and adjust blade as instructed. Hold tile in position; press down and move entire plate forward, feeding tile slowly into blade. To mitre corner V-caps for intersecting countertops (above), place tile at correct angle to blade. Hold tile steady by placing small wood block underneath (inset).

Cordless tile saw makes a variety of cuts. Clamp tile securely so cutting line is between two pieces of wood. Fill reservoir with water. Set blade on tile, aligning edge of baseplate with cutting line. Turn on tool and move it slowly along the cutting line.

Drilling holes

To cool bit, fill a well of putty with water. Place tile on cardboard. Fit drill with carbide-tipped masonry bit; start drill at low speed, then run at faster speed.

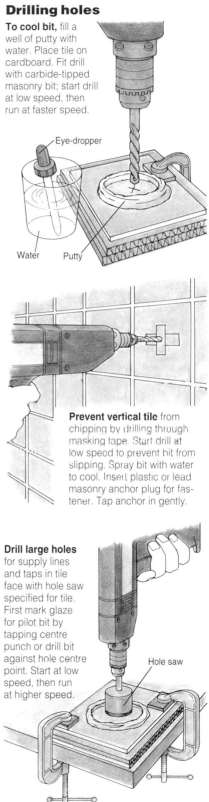

Prevent vertical tile from chipping by drilling through masking tape. Start drill at low speed to prevent bit from slipping. Spray bit with water to cool. Insert plastic or lead masonry anchor plug for fastener. Tap anchor in gently.

Drill large holes for supply lines and taps in tile face with hole saw specified for tile. First mark glaze for pilot bit by tapping centre punch or drill bit against hole centre point. Start at low speed, then run at higher speed.

Choose a tile to match the size of your room – large pavers suitable for an expansive hallway would overwhelm a small bathroom. See p 347 to calculate the amount of tile you need. Buy 15 per cent extra to allow for breakage.

The key to a successful tile job is an accurate layout. The tiles must be equidistant and evenly arranged on the substrate before you set them in adhesive. On a vertical surface, use a layout rod to mark the position of the tiles. For a horizontal surface, you can use the tiles themselves. If it's necessary to cut tiles at the ends of rows, they should be the same size at each end and more than half a tile wide. Working around irregular shapes can be tricky. A round sink, for example, will require curved cuts in all the surrounding tiles.

Grout joints should be 3 to 6 mm wide. Some tiles have built-in lugs to ensure consistent joint size; otherwise, place tile spacers between tiles or use pre-set sheets of tile (check grout joints between sheets with a straightedge). Spacers are most useful when the tiles are uniform, but for all types, check that the tiles are parallel to the layout lines.

If the surface is not square, you can make corrections in the layout, such as cutting end tiles at a gradual taper. To protect countertop tiles from cracking with any substrate movement, leave a 3 to 6 mm caulk-filled gap between the tiles and the backsplash or wall, or if the tiles continue on the vertical surface, install cove tiles (p 259). Leave a small caulk-filled gap between the substrate and the backsplash, if possible.

Set most tiles with a square-notched trowel – with 3 mm notches for tiles with lugs or ribs on the back or with 6 mm notches for other tiles. Lift a tile from the setting bed to see if its entire back is covered with adhesive. If not, switch to a trowel with larger notches.

Grout can sometimes be coloured to match your tiles. (Lighter shades are more prone to staining.) A light grout used with dark tiles, and vice versa, can look dramatic but will exaggerate any mistakes in the installation.

Layout patterns

Straight or continuous is easier to install than running bond. Turn straight 45° for diagonal design.

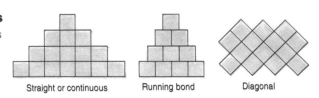

Straight or continuous   Running bond   Diagonal

Marking the layout

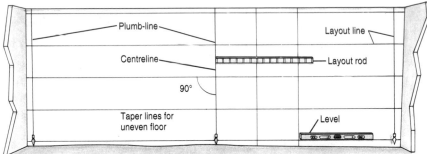

Plumb-line · Layout line · Centreline · Layout rod · 90° · Taper lines for uneven floor · Level

To mark wall layout, first snap a plumb-line from ceiling to floor at the wall's centreline or at a focal point (door or window). Then use the layout rod to mark layout lines approximately every 600 mm in all directions, carefully checking horizontal lines for level. Mark corner plumb-lines from the last possible joint on the layout rod; then adjust width of cut tiles on ends as needed. Taper end tiles to accommodate irregularities at wall edges.

To make layout rod, mark tile and joint widths along a 2 m-long 20 x 50 timber strip.

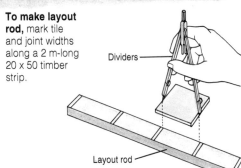

Dividers · Layout rod

Straight counter

Centreline · End tile · Trim tile

L-shaped counter

Cove tile · Backsplash · Mitred corner

Mark countertop centreline at counter's centre or at a focal point such as the sink above. First determine position of trim or end tiles, then main tiles, avoiding narrow cuts along edges. On an L-shaped counter (above, right), start layout at inside corner and work out in both directions. (Mitre trim tiles at corner, if desired.) When layout looks right, snap chalk lines to guide installation in 600 mm sections. Mark tiles to fit sink and tap cutouts (right); transfer the cut line to the tile's top for cutting. If possible, install sink and tap on top of the tile; otherwise, fill space between sink or tap and tile with caulk.

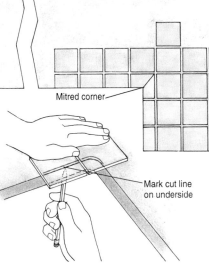

Mark cut line on underside

Tiling on waterproof board

1. Fibre-cement board or waterproof chipboard must be rigidly braced with non-corrosive screws spaced at 300 mm. Seal joints between pieces of board with silicon sealer. Prepare the board with a slurry consisting of a keying agent mixed with cement or cement-based adhesive.

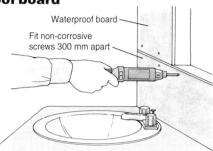

Waterproof board

Fit non-corrosive screws 300 mm apart

2. Spread 1 mm layer of slurry with plastic applicator and let dry 24 h. Use flexible tile adhesive mixed with bonding additive and mix grout with bonding agent, not with water.

Use grout mixed with bonding agent

Setting tile

1. Spread adhesive with the trowel's smooth edges; comb with the notched edges to form ridges, keeping the trowel angle consistently at 30° to the surface. Work in 600 mm-square areas.

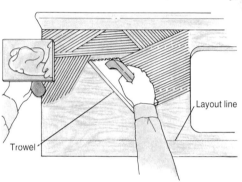

Layout line

Trowel

Spacer

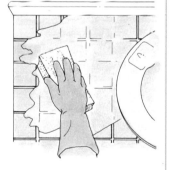

2. Insert spacers, if used, and position tile with firm twisting motion – don't slide. Clean excess adhesive off the face of the tiles and at least halfway into the joints.

3. Seat tiles in adhesive with mallet and wood block. After laying several rows, check that installation is level and square. When finished, remove spacers with utility knife.

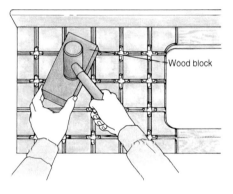

Wood block

Applying grout and caulk

Grout trowel

Pack grout into joints (left) with a grout trowel held consistently at 45° to the tile surface.

Clean off excess grout immediately with damp sponge (right); then remove hazy residue after an hour. When dry, polish with a clean cloth.

Caulk around edges of sink and bathtub with flexible caulk. Shape bead with wet finger. Also caulk under rim of sink before installation. To open bathtub seam before caulking, fill tub with water.

Sealing grout and tiles

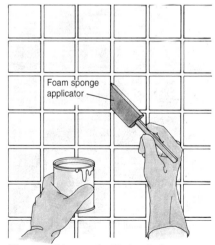

Foam sponge applicator

Allow grout to cure for 30 days before sealing grout and tiles with penetrating sealer. (Highly porous tiles, such as terracotta, may require specialized sealer.) Brush on several light coats of sealer with foam sponge applicator. Wipe sealer off the face of glazed tiles and tiles that will be exposed to food. Keep joints clean with commercial grout cleaner; re-seal grout joints once a year.

Trimming edges

Set trim tiles last. For a V-cap, butter the horizontal edge of substrate with adhesive; then butter back of tile's vertical edge (below).

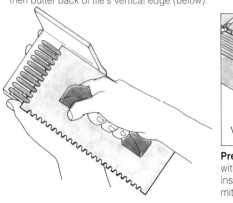

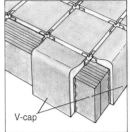

Press tile firmly into place without sliding. At corner, install special trim tile or mitre-cut V-caps (p 255).

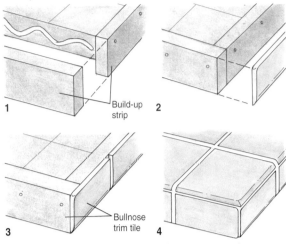

Support trim tile on build-up strips where countertop is too thin. Apply 25 × 50 mm solid wood or plywood strips to the edges of counter before laying tile. Secure strips with cold glue and nails or screws.

Install cove tile to minimize cracking at joints between horizontal and vertical surfaces. Set horizontal tiles first. Next, set a row of cove tiles, then the vertical tiles. Fill the joint on the horizontal surface with flexible caulk.

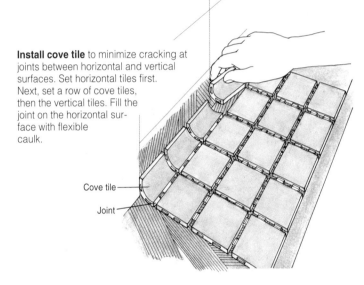

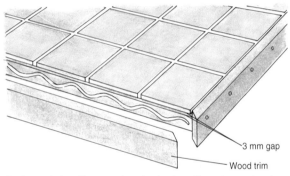

Seal wood trim with several coats of polyurethane to repel moisture. Secure with cold glue and wood screws; countersink screwheads. Allow 3 mm gap between wood and tiles, and fill it with flexible caulk.

Installing fixtures

To stick fixtures directly to wall, set them in contact adhesive or in plaster of paris mixed with acrylic latex grout additive. Coat fixture and wall with adhesive, position fixture, and hold in place overnight with strips of masking tape. Clean off excess adhesive. Do not use fixture for at least 24 hr.

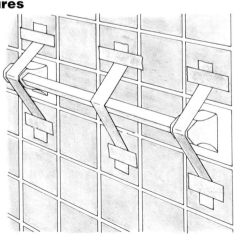

To fit fixtures on existing tile surface, first drill hole for clip-on fixture in centre of tile (p 255). Install clip; slide fixture over clip; then caulk narrow joint between fixture and wall.

Installing mosaic tile

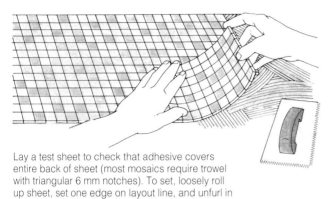

Lay a test sheet to check that adhesive covers entire back of sheet (most mosaics require trowel with triangular 6 mm notches). To set, loosely roll up sheet, set one edge on layout line, and unfurl in place. Check for square every 600 mm; grout as shown on page 257. Soak off any mounting paper.

Tiling a curved surface

To lay tiles around a gradual curve, first cut tile into lengthwise pieces. Work in 600 mm-square rows across surface. Align pieces carefully, and fully cover back of tiles with adhesive. (Do not use spacers on curved surface.) For 90° corners, buy corner tiles.

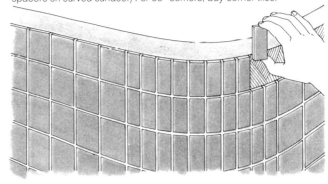

Repairing grout

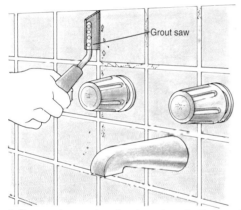

Grout saw

1. Remove damaged or discoloured grout with a grout saw or cordless tile saw, working from top of joint (wear goggles with tile saw). Clean away all debris with a damp sponge. If crumbling or cracking of grout is extensive, consult a professional.

2. Dampen joint and apply new grout with a gloved finger. Make sure to compact grout in joint. For repairs over 0,1 sq m, use a grout float. Seal grout (p 257).

Replacing tile

1. Remove grout around tile as shown at left. Break up tile with chisel and small sledgehammer, or make small plunge cuts with cordless tile saw. Wear gloves and safety goggles.

2. Scrape off old adhesive with a putty knife, without gouging substrate. Clean away all debris; vacuum area around repair thoroughly.

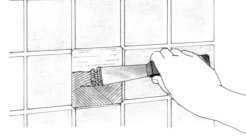

3. Apply new adhesive to substrate and to back of tile. Fit tile in place, twisting it slightly as you position it. Wipe off excess adhesive. Let dry, and re-grout.

Margin trowel

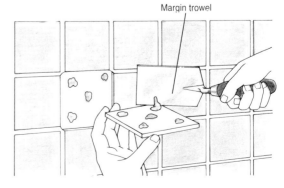
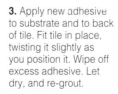

Modern glass has the same humble beginnings as ancient glass – molten silica sand. To create a polished surface, glass is floated on a bath of molten tin. It is then annealed (heated and slowly cooled). When plastic is laminated between two layers of glass, the 'sandwich' can be safely used as a car windscreen. If it is broken, the pieces remain attached to the plastic. Some glass has wire mesh embedded in it. This glass is ideal where security is an issue, such as in a window next to a front door. Transparent metal coatings on low-emissivity (low-E) glass make it reflect heat while admitting light. Subtle texturing makes glass non-reflective for glazing picture frames; dense patterns produce an obscure finish ideal for privacy. You can even change a speciality glass from an obscure to a clear finish (and vice versa) simply by flicking a switch.

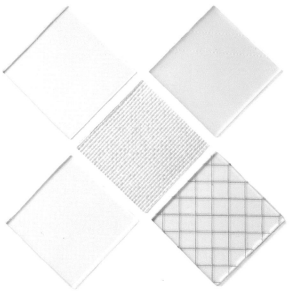

General-purpose glass suits many home uses, including clear glass for windows, light-diffusing ground glass for light fixtures and patterned glass for bathroom windows. Special glass is laminated with plastic (bottom, left) or has wire set in the glass (bottom right). This prevents flying shards by holding them in place.

Glass block, the original insulating glass, is available in many textures, sizes and shapes (including some for curved walls). Use it to make an exterior wall, a translucent room divider or a floor.

Stained glass is found in the world's most beautiful windows and lampshades. Specialist glass suppliers stock many types of stained glass in a variety of textures and colours, both translucent and opaque. The glass is coloured by adding metal alloys such as copper, iron and cobalt. Antique-style glass is hand-made; other glass is machine-made. The names of the glass are as exciting as their appearance: (top to bottom, far left) fracture streamer, ring mottle, stipple; (top to bottom, centre) iridized, single glue chip, crackle; (top to bottom, left) hand-blown 'antique', opal and flashed.

WORKING WITH GLASS

Thicknesses and types of glass vary, so ask a retailer which glass is best for your application. Always carry and store glass upright, otherwise it may break under its own weight.

Caution: When you handle glass, protect yourself by wearing goggles and heavy gloves. Dispose of shards in a closed container, or wrap them with several layers of paper; then discard.

Although a supplier will make long cuts, you can make short ones using the techniques shown below and on p 262. First wipe the glass clean with commercial cleaner, then back it with scrap softwood. The cutting – really controlled breaking of the glass – is done in two steps: scoring with a glass cutter, and then breaking the glass along the score (known as *breaking out* the score). Score patterned glass on its smooth side, mirrored glass on its uncoated side. Score curved shapes around a stiff paper template; slight curves can be broken out in the same way as straight cuts; sharper curves and circles require radial lines.

Lubricate the cutter's wheel with light oil, and grip it comfortably. Score briskly and steadily – a sizzling sound indicates the correct pressure; white flakes mean you've pressed too hard. Never go over an imperfect score; this can damage the cutter. Break out the glass immediately after you have scored it, starting at the score's finished end.

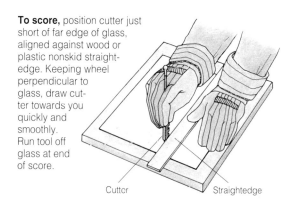

To score, position cutter just short of far edge of glass, aligned against wood or plastic nonskid straight-edge. Keeping wheel perpendicular to glass, draw cutter towards you quickly and smoothly. Run tool off glass at end of score.

Cutter   Straightedge

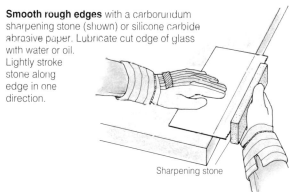

Break out glass 3 mm thick or thicker over a pencil in line with and at end of the score. Gently press down on both sides of the score.

Pencil

For thinner glass, or small pieces, place thumbs on either side of score and snap.

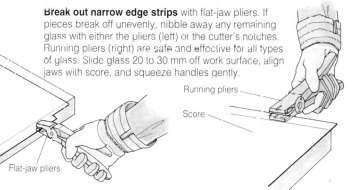

Break out narrow edge strips with flat-jaw pliers. If pieces break off unevenly, nibble away any remaining glass with either the pliers (left) or the cutter's notches. Running pliers (right) are safe and effective for all types of glass. Slide glass 20 to 30 mm off work surface, align jaws with score, and squeeze handles gently.

Running pliers
Score
Flat-jaw pliers

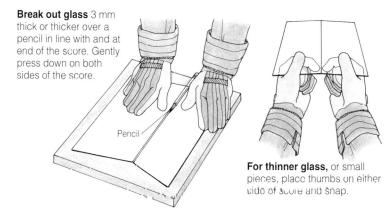

Smooth rough edges with a carborundum sharpening stone (shown) or silicone carbide abrasive paper. Lubricate cut edge of glass with water or oil. Lightly stroke stone along edge in one direction.

Sharpening stone

Cutting circles and sharp curves

1. For circles, place glass on corrugated cardboard. Position circle cutter on glass with suction cup in centre. Score circle by rotating cutter arm around cup with even pressure. (Score sharp curves against a stiff paper template.) Turn piece over and press down gently along score with thumbs, not quite breaking it out.

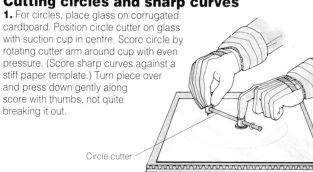

Circle cutter

2. Turn piece back over; remove cardboard; then score freehand radial lines from glass edges to just short of (not touching) the original score. Break out radial lines with running pliers; circle or curved shape will now break out completely.

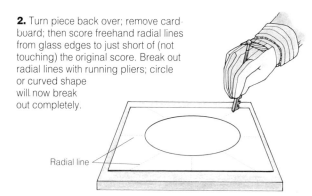

Radial line

Safety glass is available in three types: laminated, wire (security) and tempered. Although tempered glass cannot be cut, both laminated and wire glass can be scored and broken out (p 261), with an additional step of separating the non-glass material. In the case of laminated glass, this material is a sheet of plastic sandwiched between two layers of glass. Wire glass has a layer of wire mesh embedded in it. Laminated glass must be scored on both sides; after breaking out each score, sever the plastic sheet as shown below.

Small 'bull's-eye' breaks in car windshields need not lead to replacement of the windscreen, but can be repaired – usually within 30 min – by some auto and glass suppliers, using an epoxy solution.

When removing broken panes of glass, wear heavy gloves and goggles, and work from the top down to prevent injury from falling shards. If the pane does not have broken pieces that make removal easy, tape the glass with masking tape in a crisscross pattern, then break it with a hammer. Describe the application of the glass to your dealer to help determine the correct type and thickness for its replacement. Make a cardboard template for odd shapes, such as diamonds or ovals. To determine the type or thickness of glass you need for particular frames, especially those enclosing large areas, ask your local authority's building department.

Glazing putty, used to bed and seal the glass in the frame, is available in sealed packs for application with a putty knife for small jobs. You can also bed the glass with a self-adhesive foam strip. Install the foam around the inside of the frame's rebate, hold the glass in place by hand or with small metal points called glazing sprigs, and seal the glass with putty.

Caution: Do not try to replace or repair sealed units; they should be worked on only by a professional.

Cutting safety glass

Laminated glass: 1. Score and break out glass on top, then score and break out on bottom (p 261). Heat exposed plastic along score with heat gun until it's pliable.

2. Pull glass apart just far enough to insert a utility knife, and cut the plastic along the length of the score.

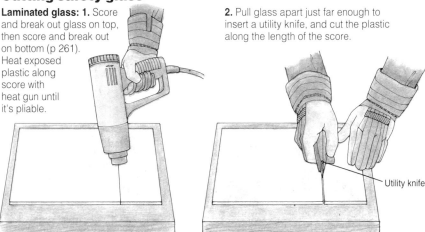

Utility knife

Wire glass. Score glass on smooth side, and break out. Slowly turn one side up (like the page of a book) until wires snap.

Installing fasteners

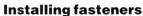
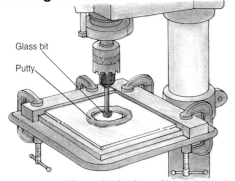

Glass bit

Putty

1. Drill holes up to 25 mm wide in glass with special spade-shaped bit in drill press or hand drill. (Have supplier drill larger holes; or use a circle cutter, p 261.) Drill into a well of putty filled with water. Run bit at low speed, feeding it evenly into glass. Drill no closer than 25 mm to glass edge.

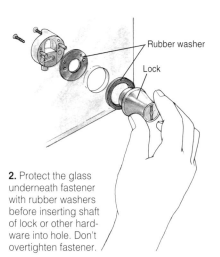

Rubber washer

Lock

2. Protect the glass underneath fastener with rubber washers before inserting shaft of lock or other hardware into hole. Don't overtighten fastener.

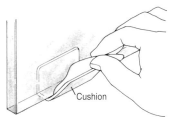

Cushion

Magnetic catch. Install self-adhesive cushion of two-part hardware first; then slide catch into place.

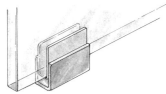

Replacing glass in a metal frame

Solid frame: 1. With pliers, pry out rubber gasket from frame. If damaged, buy new gasket. Remove any glass and clean out frame with wire brush. Measure frame from inner edges; cut or order glass 1,5 mm smaller in length and width.

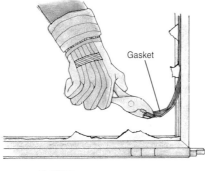

Gasket

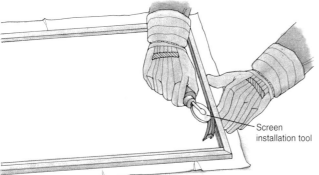

Screen installation tool

2. Coat inside of frame with the adhesive recommended by glass supplier. Position glass in frame. Using screen installation tool or fingers, press gasket under frame lip all around. If gasket is too short, lengthen it by stretching as you insert it.

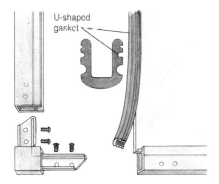

U-shaped gasket

Three-sided frame:
To disassemble frame, unscrew two corners (or remove rivets, p 187), releasing one side. Gently slide out U-shaped gasket and glass. Cut or buy new pane; then fit new gasket around it. Slide glass and gasket into sash, position the side piece, and screw or rivet corners together.

Replacing glass in a wood frame

1. Working from outside, remove broken glass; use putty knife to remove old putty and glazing sprigs. (Soften hard compound with heat gun.) Newer windows may have foam strip instead of putty.

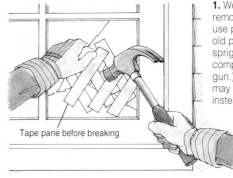

Tape pane before breaking

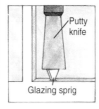

Putty knife

Glazing sprig

2. Clean out rebate with a wire brush and coat with a wood sealer. Measure to inside of rebate. Order or cut glass

Glazing sealant applied with caulking gun

1,5 mm smaller in length and width. Spread a thin layer of putty (or foam strip) inside rebate, then press in glass. Hold pane in place and press in glazing sprigs every 100 mm.

3. Cover sprigs and seal glass with putty or other sealant. Smooth with wet finger or flexible putty knife, forming 45° bevel so that putty is invisible from inside. Paint when compound dries, in several days.

Minor repairs

Fixing a windshield 'bull's eye'. Align adhesive seal and pedestal over the cleaned damage. Empty the chemicals into injector and shake. Press injector into pedestal; then follow manufacturer's directions to shoot resin into repair. Leave whole assembly in place for 4 hr; then use a razor blade to scrape away excess resin and free the pedestal.

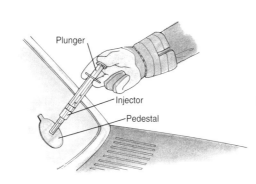

Plunger

Injector

Pedestal

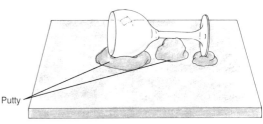

Putty

Gluing glassware. Clean object; then support it with putty (or improvise another way to hold it steady). Glue with epoxy adhesive specified for glass, following safety precautions given with adhesive.

Traditionally pieces of stained glass are arranged in a rigid framework of lead *came* that is soldered only at the joints. Although lead came is suitable for windows and large decorative pieces, it can overpower small or intricate designs. For these, the copper-foil technique shown here is more appropriate. Soldered copper-foil seams look delicate, yet they are strong enough to support sturdy boxes and lamps.

Begin by pencilling a full-size drawing, or *cartoon,* on plain paper. Keep your design simple – straight lines are easiest for novices to cut. Then make two copies. Cut one copy into templates for use when cutting the glass. The other copy is a guide onto which you will place the pieces of glass after edging them with foil. Cut the glass and smooth its edges (p 261), then clean it with commercial glass cleaner.

Adhesive-backed copper foil comes in different sizes; for most work, use foil that is 6 mm wide and 0,025 mm thick (for the perimeter, you can use slightly wider foil). Wrap outside corners as you would a parcel, folding down one side of the foil, then pressing the second side over the first. To avoid splitting the foil on curved edges, ease it gently around the curve. Immediately after wrapping each piece,

Joining glass with copper

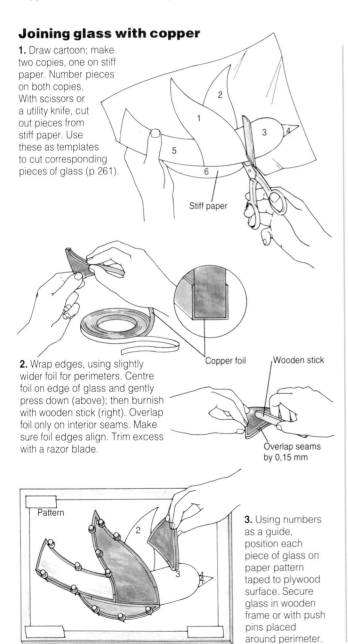

1. Draw cartoon; make two copies, one on stiff paper. Number pieces on both copies. With scissors or a utility knife, cut out pieces from stiff paper. Use these as templates to cut corresponding pieces of glass (p 261).

Stiff paper

2. Wrap edges, using slightly wider foil for perimeters. Centre foil on edge of glass and gently press down (above); then burnish with wooden stick (right). Overlap foil only on interior seams. Make sure foil edges align. Trim excess with a razor blade.

Copper foil

Wooden stick

Overlap seams by 0,15 mm

Pattern

3. Using numbers as a guide, position each piece of glass on paper pattern taped to plywood surface. Secure glass in wooden frame or with push pins placed around perimeter.

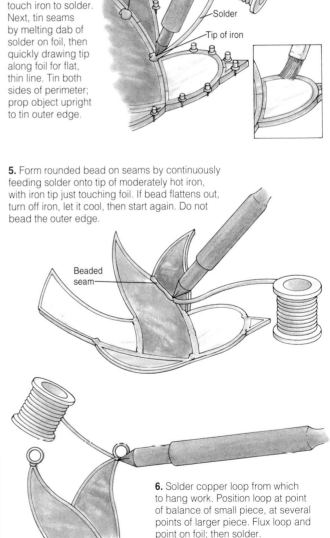

4. Brush oleic acid flux along seams (inset). To tack, hold solder over each seam; lightly touch iron to solder. Next, tin seams by melting dab of solder on foil, then quickly drawing tip along foil for flat, thin line. Tin both sides of perimeter; prop object upright to tin outer edge.

Tacked seam

Solder

Tip of iron

5. Form rounded bead on seams by continuously feeding solder onto tip of moderately hot iron, with iron tip just touching foil. If bead flattens out, turn off iron, let it cool, then start again. Do not bead the outer edge.

Beaded seam

6. Solder copper loop from which to hang work. Position loop at point of balance of small piece, at several points of larger piece. Flux loop and point on foil; then solder.

position it on its corresponding number on the paper pattern.

Follow the soldering instructions on p 190. Tin the tip of the soldering iron with the same 60/40 lead/tin solder you'll use for the seams, and flux the seams so the solder adheres. Most copper-foil seams are first *tinned*, which creates a thin flat surface, and then *beaded* for a gently rounded seam. The perimeter need only be tinned.

Manipulating the iron and spool of solder requires practice – if you are having difficulty, switch them to the opposite hands, work more slowly, or change to a more comfortable grip.

Immediately after soldering, dust the work with talc and rub it with a soft cloth. If desired, apply a liquid patina, available at crafts suppliers, to colour the seams either copper or black. Wearing rubber gloves, dip a

sponge into the patina and wipe it along a seam. Wait a few seconds, and then rub the seam with a dry cloth. To brighten the patina, rub it with brass polish. Prevent dark corrosion from building up on copper foil by rubbing it periodically with fine steel wool.

Caution: Lead is toxic. Ventilate the work area well. Wash hands after handling lead, solder or patina; dispose of these materials carefully (p 11).

Three-dimensional objects

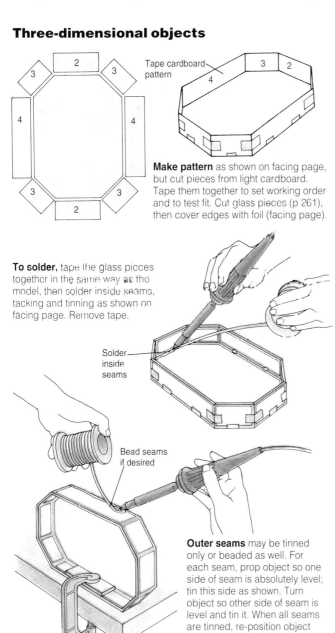

Make pattern as shown on facing page, but cut pieces from light cardboard. Tape them together to set working order and to test fit. Cut glass pieces (p 261); then cover edges with foil (facing page).

To solder, tape the glass pieces together in the same way as the model, then solder inside seams, tacking and tinning as shown on facing page. Remove tape.

Solder inside seams

Bead seams if desired

Outer seams may be tinned only or beaded as well. For each seam, prop object so one side of seam is absolutely level; tin this side as shown. Turn object so other side of seam is level and tin it. When all seams are tinned, re-position object and bead seams, if desired.

Repairing lead-came glass

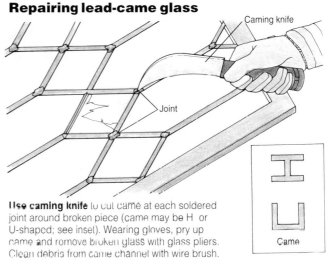

Caming knife

Joint

Use caming knife to cut came at each soldered joint around broken piece (came may be H or U-shaped; see inset). Wearing gloves, pry up came and remove broken glass with glass pliers. Clean debris from came channel with wire brush.

Came

Trace outline of broken piece on light cardboard. Cut glass to outline, insert glass into came, then lightly push came down on glass. Push glazing putty into opening between glass and came, then fully push came down.

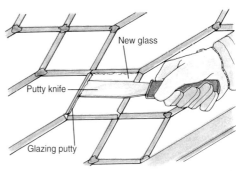

New glass

Putty knife

Glazing putty

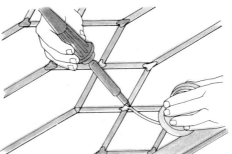

To re-solder came at joints, first brush on oleic acid flux. Holding solder to seam, touch iron to both came and solder until solder flows, then quickly move iron away. When soldering is done, colour seams with patina to match rest of piece.

INSTALLING GLASS BLOCKS

Glass block makes strong, attractive walls and windows that are easy to maintain and keep clean. The blocks are laid in mortar and require some masonry skills to install, but few special tools are needed. Most supplies, including plastic spacers, expansion strips, reinforcing wire and panel anchors, can be purchased from your glass block dealer. Before incorporating corner and end blocks in your design, find out if they're offered in the pattern and size you want to use.

Because glass blocks are non-load-bearing (they cannot support building weight from above), you'll need to frame a block wall with a header (such as a 50 × 100 or 50 × 150 secured to wall plugs), a wood or concrete sill and at least one side jamb – consult the block manufacturer for details on installing block in a particular framework. Show your design to a building inspector or other qualified professional to determine whether extra floor joists and support blocking will be necessary to bear the wall's weight. Panel anchors help secure the wall to its frame, and expansion strips prevent the wall from cracking with any structural movement.

The upper courses of block can squeeze wet mortar out from between the lower courses before it hardens. Avoid this by inserting plastic spacers, which keep the blocks evenly spaced. After the mortar has set, remove the visible part of the spacer, leaving a section between the blocks. Cut the spacers into T- or L-shapes to insert at the edges of each course. Buy at least 50 per cent more spacers than blocks.

Use pre-mixed white glass block mortar, or make your own from 1 part white Portland cement, 0,5 part hydrated lime, and 4 parts clean white sand. (For wet areas, use waterproof cement or a waterproofing additive.) Mix the dry

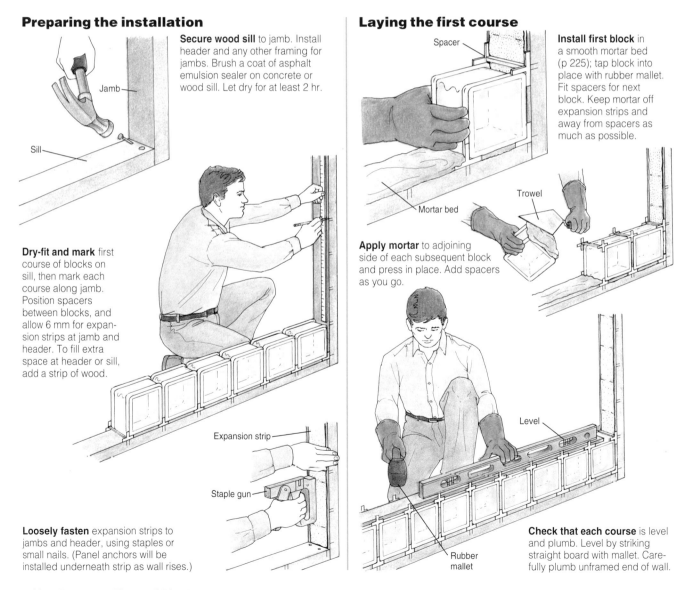

Preparing the installation

Secure wood sill to jamb. Install header and any other framing for jambs. Brush a coat of asphalt emulsion sealer on concrete or wood sill. Let dry for at least 2 hr.

Jamb

Sill

Dry-fit and mark first course of blocks on sill, then mark each course along jamb. Position spacers between blocks, and allow 6 mm for expansion strips at jamb and header. To fill extra space at header or sill, add a strip of wood.

Expansion strip

Staple gun

Loosely fasten expansion strips to jambs and header, using staples or small nails. (Panel anchors will be installed underneath strip as wall rises.)

Laying the first course

Spacer

Install first block in a smooth mortar bed (p 225); tap block into place with rubber mallet. Fit spacers for next block. Keep mortar off expansion strips and away from spacers as much as possible.

Mortar bed

Trowel

Apply mortar to adjoining side of each subsequent block and press in place. Add spacers as you go.

Level

Rubber mallet

Check that each course is level and plumb. Level by striking straight board with mallet. Carefully plumb unframed end of wall.

ingredients, then add water – the mortar is thick enough when it no longer slides off a vertical surface (p 224). Mix only what you will use in an hour. Build up a wall in sections of 1 to 1,5 m per day, leaving time to strike the joints and ensure that the wall is not out of alignment. As each course rises, check that the wall is level and plumb. If one end of a block wall will be unframed, suspend a plumb bob from the free end of the header and check that the wall is straight.

Glass block can sometimes be purchased pre-assembled, but you'll need help to position these heavy panels. Panels that are designed to replace windows may come with built-in adjustable louvre vents. A mortarless system for installing glass block is also available. You insert thin plastic strips between the blocks and then seal them with silicone caulk; full instructions are provided by the manufacturer of the system.

Building up the wall

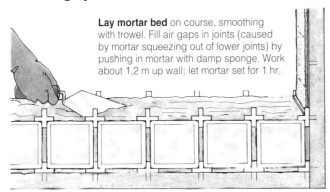

Lay mortar bed on course, smoothing with trowel. Fill air gaps in joints (caused by mortar squeezing out of lower joints) by pushing in mortar with damp sponge. Work about 1,2 m up wall; let mortar set for 1 hr.

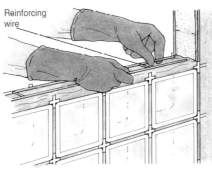

Reinforcing wire

For larger walls (over 2 sq m), embed strip of reinforcing wire in mortar of horizontal joints every third course of 150 mm block, every second course of 200 and 300 mm block.

After second course, install panel anchor. Cut 600 mm. anchor in half and bend a 100 mm leg. Slit and lift expansion strip; screw leg to jamb. Re-secure strip over anchor. Repeat every other course. At second to top course, attach anchors to header in same fashion, running anchors down every other vertical joint.

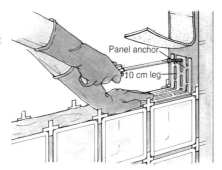

Panel anchor

10 cm leg

Finishing the wall

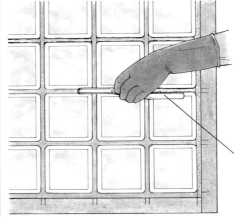

Remove visible part of spacers. Smooth and compact joints by sliding striking tool along them, working from bottom up. Wipe off cement haze with cloth; scrub any mortar flecks on glass with dry non-metallic abrasive pad.

Striking tool

For spaces between expansion strip and blocks at jambs and header, fill with a bead of flexible caulk. (With any structural movement, mortar would crack at these locations.) Smooth caulk with a wet gloved finger.

Curves and corners

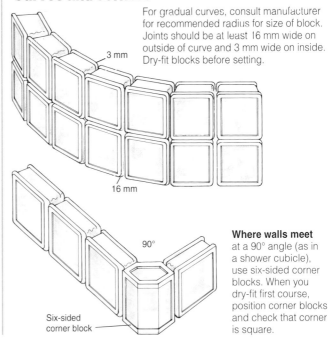

For gradual curves, consult manufacturer for recommended radius for size of block. Joints should be at least 16 mm wide on outside of curve and 3 mm wide on inside. Dry-fit blocks before setting.

3 mm

16 mm

90°

Where walls meet at a 90° angle (as in a shower cubicle), use six-sided corner blocks. When you dry-fit first course, position corner blocks and check that corner is square.

Six-sided corner block

Ceramics, Glass and Plastics   267

The variety of plastics on the market makes them among the most versatile of all do-it-yourself materials. For example, chlorinated polyvinyl chloride (CPVC) never corrodes, sweats, or allows scale build-up. As clear as glass, sheet acrylic is easy to shape, resists sunlight and doesn't break readily. Polycarbonate, a virtually unbreakable but lightweight plastic, is simple to install. Fibreglass patching materials, when

layered and saturated with liquid resin, make extremely strong repairs in fibreglass, metal and wood products. Sheet laminate creates an inexpensive countertop that is easy to maintain. Acrylic and polyester resin solid-surface materials are also ideal for countertops. They cost more than sheet laminate, but they can be custom-edged with your choice of router bit, and scratches can be sanded away.

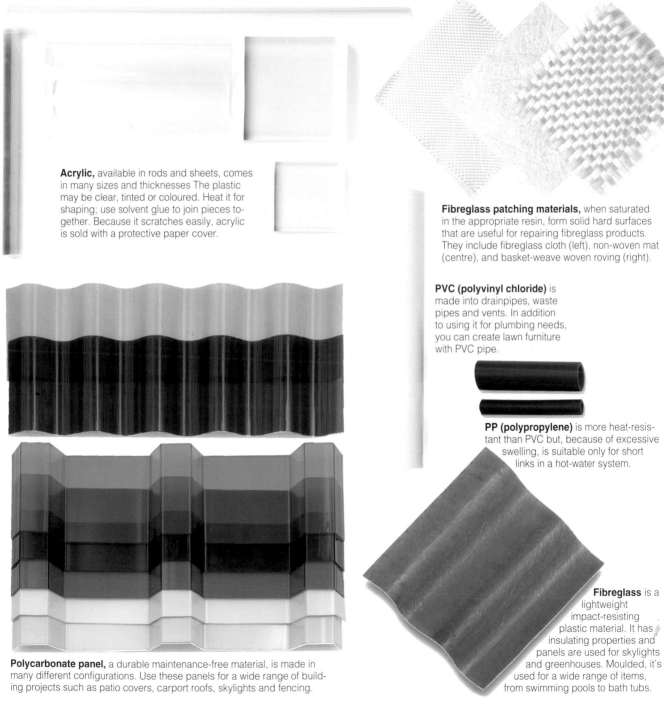

Acrylic, available in rods and sheets, comes in many sizes and thicknesses The plastic may be clear, tinted or coloured. Heat it for shaping; use solvent glue to join pieces together. Because it scratches easily, acrylic is sold with a protective paper cover.

Fibreglass patching materials, when saturated in the appropriate resin, form solid hard surfaces that are useful for repairing fibreglass products. They include fibreglass cloth (left), non-woven mat (centre), and basket-weave woven roving (right).

PVC (polyvinyl chloride) is made into drainpipes, waste pipes and vents. In addition to using it for plumbing needs, you can create lawn furniture with PVC pipe.

PP (polypropylene) is more heat-resistant than PVC but, because of excessive swelling, is suitable only for short links in a hot-water system.

Fibreglass is a lightweight impact-resisting plastic material. It has insulating properties and panels are used for skylights and greenhouses. Moulded, it's used for a wide range of items, from swimming pools to bath tubs.

Polycarbonate panel, a durable maintenance-free material, is made in many different configurations. Use these panels for a wide range of building projects such as patio covers, carport roofs, skylights and fencing.

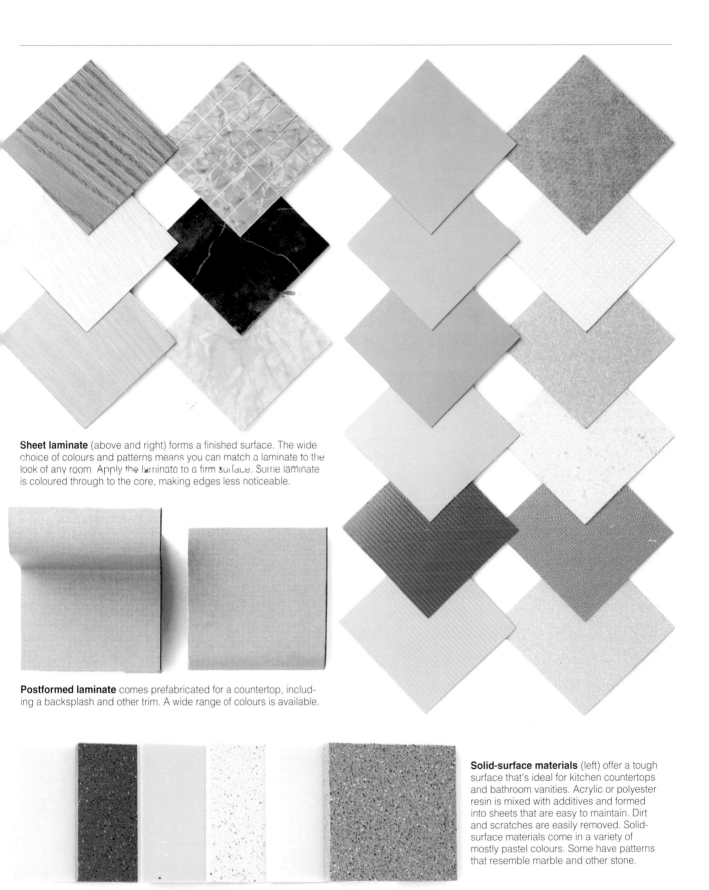

Sheet laminate (above and right) forms a finished surface. The wide choice of colours and patterns means you can match a laminate to the look of any room. Apply the laminate to a firm surface. Some laminate is coloured through to the core, making edges less noticeable.

Postformed laminate comes prefabricated for a countertop, including a backsplash and other trim. A wide range of colours is available.

Solid-surface materials (left) offer a tough surface that's ideal for kitchen countertops and bathroom vanities. Acrylic or polyester resin is mixed with additives and formed into sheets that are easy to maintain. Dirt and scratches are easily removed. Solid-surface materials come in a variety of mostly pastel colours. Some have patterns that resemble marble and other stone.

Ceramics, Glass and Plastics 269

Clear acrylic sheets and other shapes are used in crafts objects, for making furniture, and as a substitute for glass. PP (polypropylene) and PVC (polyvinyl chloride) are two types of rigid plastic tubing: PP tubing forms cold-water supply lines and short runs in the hot-water system. The wider PVC tubing is used for waste plumbing, drainpipes, electrical conduit, and lightweight or outdoor furniture. To work with any of these plastics, you will need a combination of basic woodworking, metalworking and glazing skills.

Special tools and supplies are available for working with plastics – follow the manufacturer's specific instructions for plastics. For example, when cutting acrylic with a jigsaw, running the tool at high speed can melt the plastic behind the blade. The plastic may then fuse together, ruining the cut.

Despite its toughness, acrylic is easily scratched and so comes coated with protective paper. Leave as much of the paper on the plastic as possible until the project is completed. To remove the paper, lift it at one corner and pull it off the sheet. Scratches on plastic are best removed with a commercial scratch remover. To prevent sagging, store acrylic sheets either upright or flat and fully supported.

Acrylic sheets can be joined with threaded fasteners, rivets, or posts and screws, but pieces are usually cemented with a special solvent. The most common technique is cementing along the seams by capillary action (facing page). If solvent spills on an unprotected piece of acrylic, quickly wipe it with a clean soft cloth. PP and PVC can also be joined with a solvent cement, but use only the cleaner, primer and cement specifically recommended for joining each plastic.

Most plastics can be bent if they have been heated first, but for PP and PVC the temperature must be controlled so precisely that doing it

Cutting and drilling

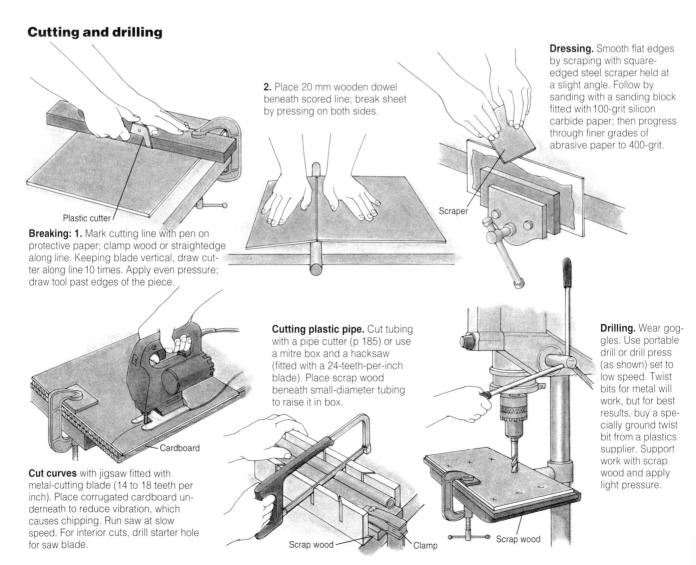

Breaking: 1. Mark cutting line with pen on protective paper; clamp wood or straightedge along line. Keeping blade vertical, draw cutter along line 10 times. Apply even pressure; draw tool past edges of the piece.

Plastic cutter

2. Place 20 mm wooden dowel beneath scored line; break sheet by pressing on both sides.

Dressing. Smooth flat edges by scraping with square-edged steel scraper held at a slight angle. Follow by sanding with a sanding block fitted with 100-grit silicon carbide paper; then progress through finer grades of abrasive paper to 400-grit.

Scraper

Cut curves with jigsaw fitted with metal-cutting blade (14 to 18 teeth per inch). Place corrugated cardboard underneath to reduce vibration, which causes chipping. Run saw at slow speed. For interior cuts, drill starter hole for saw blade.

Cardboard

Cutting plastic pipe. Cut tubing with a pipe cutter (p 185) or use a mitre box and a hacksaw (fitted with a 24-teeth-per-inch blade). Place scrap wood beneath small-diameter tubing to raise it in box.

Scrap wood   Clamp

Drilling. Wear goggles. Use portable drill or drill press (as shown) set to low speed. Twist bits for metal will work, but for best results, buy a specially ground twist bit from a plastics supplier. Support work with scrap wood and apply light pressure.

Scrap wood

yourself is not recommended. It is easy to bend acrylic using a strip heater, available (often as a kit) from a plastics supplier or hardware store.

Caution: When using power tools to cut, sand or drill plastic, wear safety goggles and a dust mask. Wear heat-proof gloves while heating and bending plastic. When cementing, follow the precautions listed by the manufacturer. Work in a well-ventilated area and do not get solvent on your skin. Before modifying a plumbing system, check with your local building inspector that the modification is legal. Shut off the water supply and drain a pipe before working on it.

Smoothing edges

Buff edges with 10 mm drill fitted with buffing pad. First coat the pad with either tripoli or rouge polishing compound (available at crafts suppliers). Finish with a non-stitched disc of clean muslin or flannel. Do not buff seam edges.

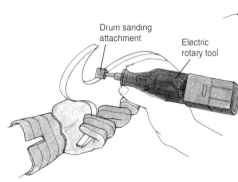

Buffing pad

Drum sanding attachment

Electric rotary tool

Sand and polish curves and tight spots with an electric drill or with a small rotary tool specified for working with acrylic. Sand edges with drum sanding attachment; buff with hard felt and muslin or flannel discs. To avoid overheating plastic, use a light touch and low speed.

Joining plastic tubing

Preparing joints. With a sharp knife or reamer, remove burrs on cut ends; bevel walls slightly. Smooth ends of fitting and tubing with 120-grit sandpaper. Assemble tubing and fitting to test fit. Mark a line across both pieces with a pencil. Detach the pieces and clean them by swabbing with the appropriate cleaning fluid, using the applicator supplied. After cleaner dries, apply primer (to remove gloss); then apply the cement.

Joining. Apply a second coat of cement to tubing and immediately insert in fitting with marks mis-aligned by a quarter turn. Quickly twist until marks align. Hold together for at least 30 sec then wait 24 hr before applying full pressure. A thin line of cement should be visible entirely around the new joint.

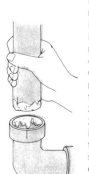

Bending with heat

Heating. Mark area of bend; remove 100 mm-wide strips of paper from both sides of sheet. Centre uncovered area just above heating element; turn sheet several times for even heating. Hold for 1 to 5 min until the plastic softens.

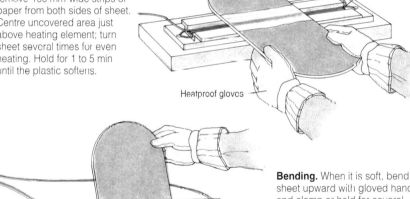

Strip heater

Heatproof gloves

Bending. When it is soft, bend sheet upward with gloved hands, and clamp or hold for several minutes until it cools. To make adjustments, flatten sheet by reheating, then bend again.

Joining acrylic sheets

Remove paper near edges; place pieces to be joined so seams are horizontal. Tape, clamp or brace pieces together. Edges must be even so pieces fit with no gaps. Then carefully draw needle-nose applicator along seam, squeezing gently to dispense solvent evenly. Don't blot excess solvent; allow capillary action to draw it into joint.

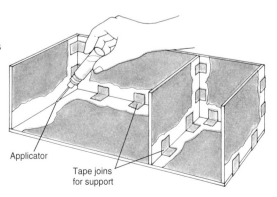

Applicator

Tape joins for support

Ceramics, Glass and Plastics   271

Fibreglass, a material made from threads or fragments of spun glass, comes in different forms. As a building material, it is moulded into hard panels. For shaped objects, it is matted or woven into a fabric, which is then bonded with resin.

Pre-formed fibreglass panels are easy to work with and can be cut with a jigsaw fitted with a fine-tooth blade. For an outdoor project such as a patio roof, heavyweight corrugated or ridged panels are best. For indoor use or where rigidity is not necessary, use lighter flat panels. Supplies for building with the panels, such as flashing and corrugated closure strips, are also available. To clean the panels, hose them with water; if they discolour, apply a refinisher recommended by the manufacturer. Fibreglass panels will not bear a person's weight; never attempt to walk on them.

Fibreglass laminate is used to make shaped objects such as car bodies, boats, swimming pools and bath tubs. Layers of fabric are bonded together with a liquid resin that cures with the addition of a catalyst, forming a tough, durable shell. Holes up to 12 mm in diameter in fibreglass laminate can simply be filled with putty – a mixture of resin and filler. Larger areas of damage are repaired by patching with layers of fabric and resin. However, if you suspect that the damage may have affected the structural integrity of an object, consult a professional before attempting the repair.

A repair patch (p 274) usually consists of alternating layers of mat and cloth. In large projects, woven roving is sometimes used. A successful repair depends upon choosing the correct fabric and resin; the chart on the facing page will help you determine the best combination for a particular repair.

Polyester resin – used for most laminate repairs – is easier to work with and less expensive than epoxy. There are two types: *air-dry,* or *tack-free,* contains wax, which floats to the surface of the repair, sealing off the air and allowing the resin to cure with a hard surface. The other type, *air-inhibited,* cures to a tacky surface unless covered with wax paper or polyvinyl alcohol spray (PVA), which can be found at marine supply stores. The PVA is washed off with warm water after the resin cures. Fabric will bond better if you use air-inhibited resin for the inner layers of a repair. If you use air-dry resin for the outer layers, it will harden so that the surface can be sanded more easily.

Epoxy resin cures hard, but slowly. It will bond well with many materials but is more difficult to work with than polyester. If in doubt whether to use epoxy or polyester resin for a repair, contact the manufacturer of the object or try a small test patch on an inconspicuous spot.

The outer finish coat of fibreglass laminate is the *gel coat,* a specially formulated polyester resin. Wash the gel coat frequently with detergent and water (or wipe it with a solvent such as acetone), and buff with wax to protect it. Scratches that do not penetrate too far beneath the gel coat can easily be repaired with a mixture of gel coat and filler, often available in a kit at marine supply stores.

Working with fibreglass panels

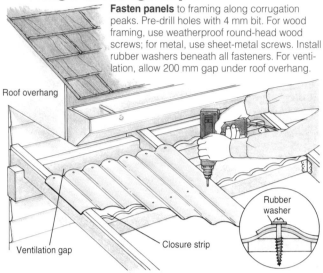

Fasten panels to framing along corrugation peaks. Pre-drill holes with 4 mm bit. For wood framing, use weatherproof round-head wood screws; for metal, use sheet-metal screws. Install rubber washers beneath all fasteners. For ventilation, allow 200 mm gap under roof overhang.

Roof overhang

Rubber washer

Ventilation gap

Closure strip

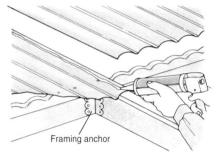

Seal panels by applying permanently flexible (non-drying) mastic or clear silicone caulk to seam area on corrugation's peaks. Also, before installing flashing (below), caulk along length of peaks that will be covered by flashing.

Framing anchor

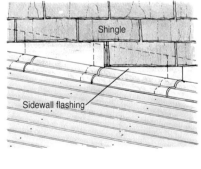

Shingle

Sidewall flashing

Install flashing where panels meet sidewalls; match aluminium flashing corrugations to those in panels. Slide flashing under cladding or shingles. If cladding is fastened at lower edge, install flashing over cladding with galvanized screws and rubber washers.

For masonry walls, secure sidewall flashing every 200 mm with masonry anchors. Cover with step flashing: First saw or chisel a small groove in mortar joint. Fold back top edge of flashing, and insert in groove as shown (inset). Fill joint with urethane caulk.

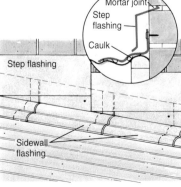

Mortar joint

Step flashing

Caulk

Step flashing

Sidewall flashing

PATCHING FIBREGLASS LAMINATE

Material	Characteristics	Use	Hints
Fibreglass mat	Fairly thick and stiff; easily moulded to curves; adds adhesion	Alternated with cloth or roving for general repairs	Use as first and final layers; for thin repairs, use 250 g mat; for thick repairs, use 450 g mat
Fibreglass cloth	Thin and strong; leaves a smooth finish	Alternated with mat for small repairs	Make small cuts in cloth when moulding to curved surfaces so fabric lies flat; in general, use 450 g cloth
Woven roving	Thick, heavily textured; provides stiffness, strength and bulk	Alternated with mat for large repairs	Handle carefully as it tends to unravel; do not place directly under gel coat; for large repairs use 600 g roving
Polyester resin	Tough, water-resistant, compatible with many laminated objects; easy to work with	General laminating, especially fibreglass boats; do not use on objects that may contain polystyrene foam	Shelf-life may be limited; use within 90 days; use air-inhibited for inner layers of repair, air-dry for outer layer; clean equipment with acetone
Epoxy resin	Creates a stronger bond and is more water-resistant than polyester; can be difficult to work with – cures more slowly than polyester	Bonds fibreglass to dissimilar materials, such as wood, metal and many household plastics	Requires precise mixing and temperature control; clean equipment with acetone
Gel coat	Hard, glossy, waterproof; can be tinted by mixing with pigment; can be mixed with filler to add bulk	Forms waterproof, protective colour coat on finished surface of repair	Air-dry type is best. When mixing, add pigment and test colour after adding catalyst; thin with acetone before spraying
Putty	Depending on filler, adds hardness or bulk	Fills flaws that have penetrated beneath gel coat	Use fumed silica filler for small flaws; microsphere filler for large areas or where light weight is important; sand after patch dries

Mixing chemicals

Measure ingredients, following manufacturer's instructions carefully. For polyester resins, vary proportions according to temperature. In cool conditions use more catalyst; in warm conditions use less. Do not work in extreme temperatures or direct sunlight. Make several test batches to evaluate curing time and quality of mixture. Prepare only as much resin as you can apply in 20 min (once cured, it cannot be used).

Repairing minor damage

1. Clean damaged area by wiping with acetone. Protect surface around repair with tape. Fit 10 or 6 mm drill or a rotary electric tool with drum sanding attachment and make V-shaped groove along damage.

Drum sanding attachment

2. Sand edges of groove, then blow away dust (do not touch). Mix gel coat with catalyst and filler according to manufacturer's instructions. Pack groove with mixture, building up 1,5 mm above surface.

Plastic applicator

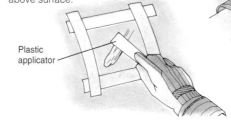

3. Spray with PVA, or cover with wax paper and push squeegee across surface to force out air. After 2 hr, wash off PVA with warm water or remove paper. Sand and buff area (p 274).
(Continued p 274)

Preparing the damaged area

Grind damaged area with electric drill fitted with sanding attachment. Use coarse abrasive paper; taper edges back 50 mm from opening (on front and rear if possible). If damage is inaccessible from rear, grind hole to a roughly oval shape. Wipe with acetone.

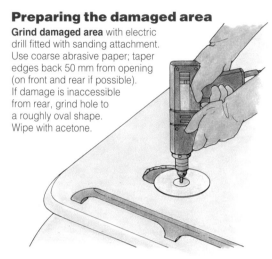

If rear is accessible, tape a piece of cardboard over front of damage. From rear, build up three layers of fabric and resin (p 273), as shown below. Remove cardboard and continue repair from front.

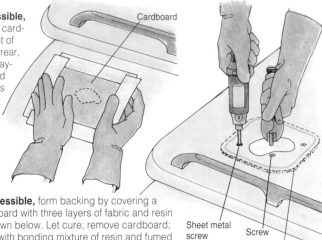

Cardboard

Sheet metal screw

Screw

Bonding mixture

If rear is inaccessible, form backing by covering a piece of cardboard with three layers of fabric and resin (p 273), as shown below. Let cure; remove cardboard; edge backing with bonding mixture of resin and fumed silica. Insert through hole; hold against rear with screw and pliers. Secure with sheet-metal screws; let cure.

Building up the patch

Protect area around front of damage with tape. Remove screws. Cut a piece of mat slightly larger than the sanded area; then cut progressively larger pieces of alternating fabric. Saturate first piece of mat with resin, and brush resin around sanded edges. Press piece into place over hole.

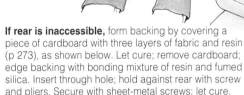

Mat

Add successive layers of fabric and resin, pressing with laminate roller to remove all air bubbles. Complete repairs more than 3 mm thick in two stages, allowing first layers to cure before continuing.

Laminate roller

Finishing the patch

When patch has cured, sand area with palm sander fitted with medium, then fine, abrasive paper. Wipe area with acetone.

Palm sander

Gel coat spray

Fill uneven spots with gel coat mixed with filler (p 273). Sand once more; then spray entire area with gel coat mixed with catalyst and thinned with acetone to near-watery consistency. Cover repair with wax paper or spray with PVA. Let cure overnight.

Remove paper, or wash off PVA with warm water. Wet-sand with fine abrasive paper, followed by extra-fine. Remove tape. Coat an electric drill buffing attachment with rubbing compound formulated for fibreglass. Buff the patch (below); then apply car polish or liquid wax with a soft cloth.

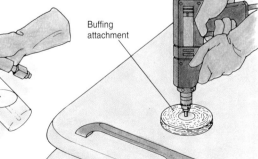

Buffing attachment

Postformed countertops are made of plastic laminate bonded to a core material (generally plywood or particleboard). The front edge of countertops is rounded and often the rear edge curves up to form a backsplash. They come in standard widths and are usually cut to length by the retail supplier. L-shaped countertops come in two sections with a mitred corner. You join the sections with hardware supplied with the countertop. Also supplied are pre-glued strips of laminate called *end caps*. Apply these after you have built up the edges as shown on page 276.

Before removing an old countertop, shut off the water, gas and electricity supply to any fixtures or appliances. Then remove the sink and appliances, noting how they are installed so that you can put them back correctly. (Have an electrician disconnect and remove built-in items such as a garbage disposal unit or a cooking hob.) Working from inside the base cabinets, remove any fasteners retaining the countertop; then free the countertop by levering up against it, again from the inside, with a flat pry bar.

Take measurements for a new countertop as shown below and make a detailed sketch of the cabinet layout to take with you when ordering.

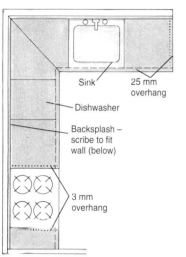

Measuring a countertop. For L-shaped top (left), measure along rear of each run of base cabinets, from corner to far end. Also measure from the wall to the front of the cabinets. Add 25 mm where edges overhang cabinets; add 3 mm where cabinets abut an appliance or a wall. For a new sink or appliance, measure inside base cabinets.

Sink
25 mm overhang
Dishwasher
Backsplash – scribe to fit wall (below)
3 mm overhang

Levelling. With the countertop removed (right), check if top edges of cabinets and wall anchors are level. If not, insert shims under or behind cabinets – first loosening the cabinets from the wall if necessary – or tack strips of wood to top edges. If needed, install corner and cross braces to support the new countertop and provide fastening surfaces. Ensure that corners are square; otherwise the countertop will not fit.

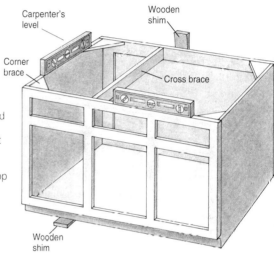

Carpenter's level
Wooden shim
Corner brace
Cross brace
Wooden shim

Belt sander

Installing a countertop: 1. Place countertop in position. If end section abuts an uneven wall, scribe the contours of the wall onto the edge. Wearing goggles and a dust mask, sand the edge to match the scribed line. Re-fit the countertop, and repeat for rear edge of backsplash (above).

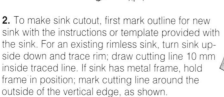

Frame

2. To make sink cutout, first mark outline for new sink with the instructions or template provided with the sink. For an existing rimless sink, turn sink upside down and trace rim; draw cutting line 10 mm inside traced line. If sink has metal frame, hold frame in position; mark cutting line around the outside of the vertical edge, as shown.

3. To cut sink opening, first drill starter holes in corners of outline, turn piece over, and redraw guidelines. Wearing a dust mask and goggles, remove waste with jigsaw fitted with fine-tooth blade. File or sand edges smooth.

Tighten bolt with spanner

4. Spread glue or adhesive caulk along top's mitred edges. Fit sections together so surfaces are flush; secure with fasteners provided (above). Let adhesive dry overnight. Then, with a helper, position top on cabinets. Install wood screws in top's underside through corner braces. Apply clear flexible caulk to any gaps along the backsplash and ends.

Sheets of laminated plastic for use on countertops, and on other flat or curved surfaces, are available in many patterns and colours. Most have a dark core that is visible at the edges, but a variety called colour-through laminate has a single colour throughout. When choosing laminate, avoid glossy or patterned styles in kitchens – heavy use can dull them. Light-coloured laminates show wear less readily and are easier to match. Buy vertical-grade laminate for use on walls and cabinets.

Sheet laminate can be applied over nearly any smooth, level surface. Particleboard is used most often as a substrate for countertops, although plywood (more expensive) is stronger and less likely to absorb moisture, which can cause laminate to lift and buckle. For cabinets, use plywood – it is lighter than particleboard and holds fasteners more securely. Make cutouts for a sink (p 275) or other appliance in the substrate before covering it with laminate. Sand irregularities in the substrate and fill depressions with spackling compound; then wipe clean.

Attach laminate to both sides of the substrate unless (as with a countertop)

Cutting laminate

Scoring and breaking.
Pencil a cutting line on face of laminate. With metal straightedge as a guide, score along line several times with a plastic cutter; then break by lifting edge of sheet. For small strips, clamp straightedge along cutting line, score and lift sheet.

Plastic cutter

Cutting narrow strips.
For strips 100 mm wide or less, fit laminate trimmer with slitter attachment and solid carbide straight-cutting bit. Clamp laminate to bench; fit piece between slitter's baseplates with guide on edge. Push tool along cutting line.

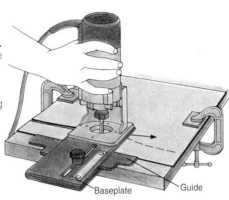

Baseplate   Guide

Laminating a vertical surface

1. Apply contact cement with narrow roller or paintbrush: two thin coats to the substrate, one to the laminate. Allow both coats to dry until adhesive appears hazy and is not sticky.

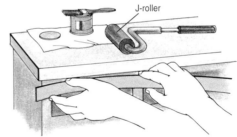

J-roller

2. Carefully align individual strip against edge; press into place, and roll with J-roller or tap with wooden block and hammer. (Attach strips to opposite ends of substrate first; trim; then attach any remaining strips.)

Installing pre-glued laminate.
For bendable strips (and for end caps, p 275), first ensure that surface is clean and dry. Set heat gun to medium; hold several cm from strip. As laminate softens, press strip down.

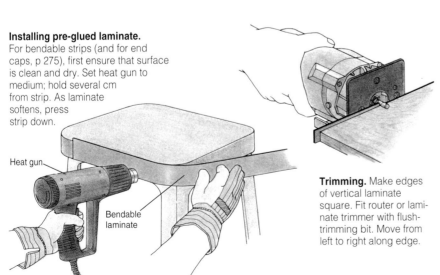

Heat gun

Bendable laminate

Trimming. Make edges of vertical laminate square. Fit router or laminate trimmer with flush-trimming bit. Move from left to right along edge.

Edge treatments

Build up an edge
and cover with laminate or pre-glued end cap. Attach build-up strip of wood with white glue and finishing nails.

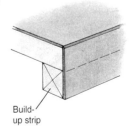

Build-up strip

Solid wood edging
is stronger and more durable than laminate. Flanged edging fits groove routed in the substrate panel. Secure with white glue.

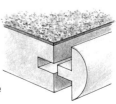

it is securely fastened to a frame; otherwise it will warp. Laminate vertical surfaces before horizontal ones, and fit pieces to the back and sides of an object first, then to the front.

Glue laminate to the substrate with contact cement; other adhesives will work but require extensive clamping. Non-flammable contact cement is safer than the flammable variety.

Laminate can be cut with a laminate trimmer, or with a circular saw, jigsaw or table saw fitted with a laminate blade. Keep leftover pieces to use for repairs. Bevel exposed edges with a router or laminate trimmer, then file to prevent chipping, applying pressure on the downward stroke. When trimming with a router or trimmer, use only self-guiding solid carbide bits.

Despite its toughness, sheet laminate is subject to burns, scratches and stains. Try to remove stubborn stains by dabbing with bleach for 1 min and then rinsing with water.

Caution: When sanding, cutting or trimming laminate, wear goggles and a dust mask. If applying contact cement, work in a well-ventilated area and wear a respirator (p 13).

Laminating a horizontal surface

Applying adhesive. Apply contact cement to substrate and laminate. Lay dowels or cardboard strips on substrate (these will not stick) and set laminate on top. Do not let laminate touch substrate until it is in position. Then remove dowels individually, starting at end of surface, as you press laminate into place.

Smoothing. Roll entire surface with J-roller or rolling pin, working from centre of panel towards edges. Exert strong pressure to remove all air bubbles.

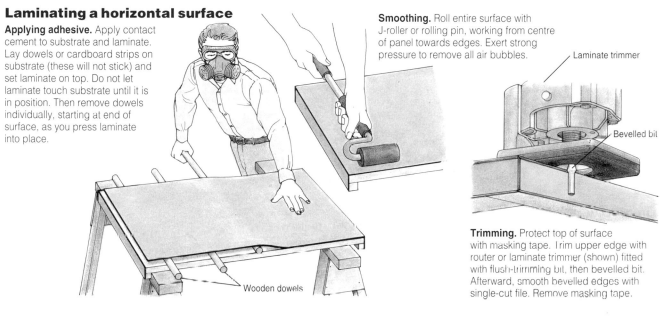

Wooden dowels

Laminate trimmer

Bevelled bit

Trimming. Protect top of surface with masking tape. Trim upper edge with router or laminate trimmer (shown) fitted with flush-trimming bit, then bevelled bit. Afterward, smooth bevelled edges with single-cut file. Remove masking tape.

Cutouts and backsplashes

Cutting sink opening. If there is no sink cutout in substrate, cut opening as shown on p 275. If cutout exists, first apply laminate to substrate, then drill starter hole in laminate. Insert router fitted with flush-trimming bit; guide router to edge of cutout, then clockwise around cutout.

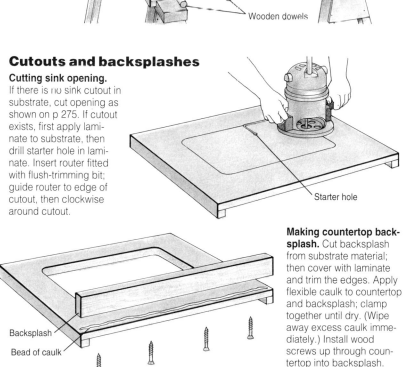

Starter hole

Backsplash

Bead of caulk

Making countertop backsplash. Cut backsplash from substrate material; then cover with laminate and trim the edges. Apply flexible caulk to countertop and backsplash; clamp together until dry. (Wipe away excess caulk immediately.) Install wood screws up through countertop into backsplash.

Making repairs

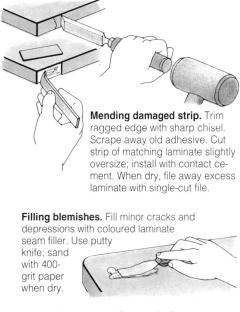

Mending damaged strip. Trim ragged edge with sharp chisel. Scrape away old adhesive. Cut strip of matching laminate slightly oversize; install with contact cement. When dry, file away excess laminate with single-cut file.

Filling blemishes. Fill minor cracks and depressions with coloured laminate seam filler. Use putty knife; sand with 400-grit paper when dry.

Solid plastic sheets known as solid-surface material, or solid surfacing, have the best features of marble and alabaster, which they resemble, yet they can be worked with power tools and joined with nearly invisible seams. Usually formed from a blend of acrylic or polyester resin combined with a mined mineral, these synthetics are heavy, durable and stain-resistant. You must round off all inside and outside corners; custom-profiling (shaping the edges with a router) is optional.

More expensive than many other materials, solid surfacing is available at kitchen and bathroom showrooms. Before selecting a brand, check that its warranty extends to do-it-yourself installation. Study the manufacturer's instructions carefully. If you don't have the basic carpentry skills necessary to work with the material, consult an installer trained by the manufacturer.

Before beginning to work, check that all sheets have the same batch number, and peel off the protective coating. For countertops, measure the

Cutting sheets

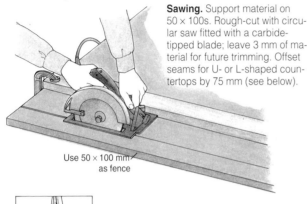

Sawing. Support material on 50 × 100s. Rough-cut with circular saw fitted with a carbide-tipped blade; leave 3 mm of material for future trimming. Offset seams for U- or L-shaped countertops by 75 mm (see below).

Use 50 × 100 mm as fence

Sink cutout. To make a template, calculate sink outline (p 275). Enlarge outline by the distance between router bit and the edge of its base, and saw a plywood template to this measurement. Clamp template to piece, drill a starter hole, and rout away the cutout, using a 12 mm single-flute straight-cutting carbide bit. Sand edges smooth with 100-grit paper.

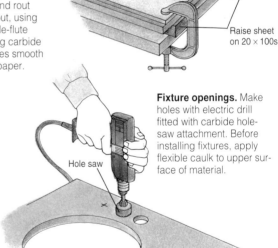

Edge of template

Sink outline

Raise sheet on 20 × 100s

38 mm

Mark cut line using template

Outside corners. First make a template to radius of 38 mm. Mark a 38 mm square at the corner of a small piece of plywood. Place a compass on the inside point of the square and scribe an arc across the corner (inset). Cut template along this arc, mark cut line on material, then rough-cut material to cut line with jigsaw (left). Clamp template to underside of corner, smooth with router fitted with a self-guiding straight-cutting bit.

Fixture openings. Make holes with electric drill fitted with carbide hole-saw attachment. Before installing fixtures, apply flexible caulk to upper surface of material.

Hole saw

Joining sheets

1. Clamp sheets 6 mm apart, and rout along edges with double-flute straight-cutting carbide bit. Guide router with straightedges clamped parallel to gap (inset). Clean edges with denatured alcohol, and position sheets 3 mm apart. Mix seaming compound and fill seam according to manufacturer's instructions; clamp sheets together until compound hardens.

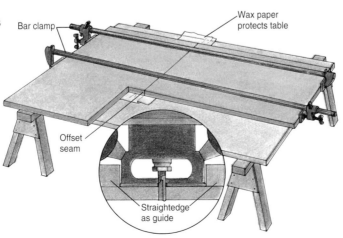

Bar clamp

Wax paper protects table

Offset seam

Straightedge as guide

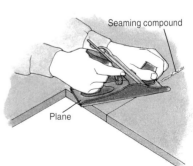

Seaming compound

Plane

2. Remove excess dried compound with sharp plane (to avoid gouging material, round corners of plane iron with file); then sand with 100-grit paper. Finish surface (facing page).

base cabinets as described on p 275. Remove the old countertop, and attach supporting strips (using drywall screws) of 100 mm-wide 20 mm plywood over the top edges of the cabinets. Add cross braces spaced 600 mm apart if you are using 20 mm-thick surfacing, or at 450 mm intervals for 12 mm-thick surfacing. Also add cross braces from front to back where sinks and other openings will be located and where countertop seams will lie.

Caution: Wear a dust mask when cutting, routing and sanding solid surfacing. Seaming compound is very flammable. Use it only in a well-ventilated area, and follow all safety precautions listed by the manufacturer.

Finishing

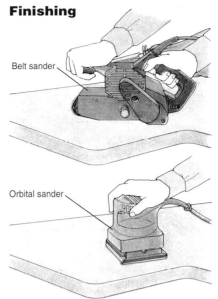

Belt sander

Orbital sander

For mat finish, power- or hand-sand entire surface (top) with 100-grit paper followed by 180-grit; then polish with fine plastic abrasive pad secured to orbital sander (above).

Adding dropped edges

1. To give the appearance of thicker edges, first turn over piece. Cut 38 mm-wide strips of surfacing to fit exposed sides. Roughen mating surfaces with 60-grit sandpaper. Test-fit strips; then apply seaming compound to strips. Secure with spring clamps at 100 mm intervals until compound hardens.

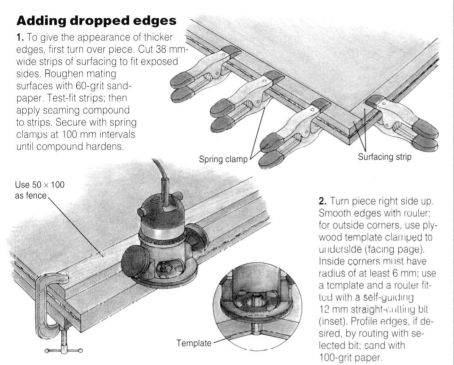

Spring clamp

Surfacing strip

Use 50 × 100 as fence

Template

2. Turn piece right side up. Smooth edges with router; for outside corners, use plywood template clamped to underside (facing page). Inside corners must have radius of at least 6 mm; use a template and a router fitted with a self-guiding 12 mm straight-cutting bit (inset). Profile edges, if desired, by routing with selected bit; sand with 100-grit paper.

Buffing pad

For glossy finish (for low-use surfaces), sand with 220-, then 320-grit paper. Fit a drill with a buffing pad and polish until glossy with liquid car polish.

Adding a backsplash

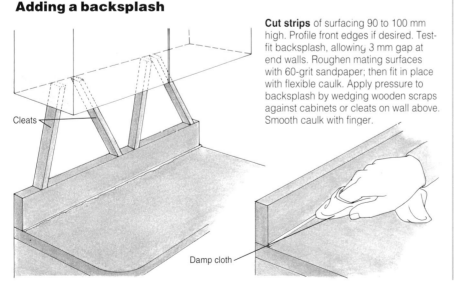

Cleats

Damp cloth

Cut strips of surfacing 90 to 100 mm high. Profile front edges if desired. Test-fit backsplash, allowing 3 mm gap at end walls. Roughen mating surfaces with 60-grit sandpaper; then fit in place with flexible caulk. Apply pressure to backsplash by wedging wooden scraps against cabinets or cleats on wall above. Smooth caulk with finger.

To remove blemishes, scrub with abrasive cleanser or sand with 100-grit paper. For deep flaws, grind away damage with an electric rotary tool, then fill depression with seaming compound. Finish surface.

Ceramics, Glass and Plastics 279

PAINT AND WALLCOVERINGS

Paint is basically pigment, which provides a particular colour, and a binder in an oil- or water-based solvent. As the paint dries, the solvent evaporates, leaving an opaque film.

Some oil-based paints have highly volatile solvents that speed drying. When using them, wear a respirator or ensure that the room is well ventilated. Newer oil-based paints leave more brush strokes than their old counterparts, but they also dry faster and sag less than the old linseed-oil-based paints.

Most water-based paints have a latex binder, which may be vinyl, rubber, polyvinyl acetate (PVA) or acrylic resins. PVA paint offers excellent colour retention, easy cleaning and low toxicity, making it an ideal choice for house paint.

Thick textured paint, with granular additives, hides defects as it adds character to a surface. It comes pre-mixed and as a dry powder. You can create special effects with textured paint (below) or with glaze applied over a paint (facing page).

Textured paints

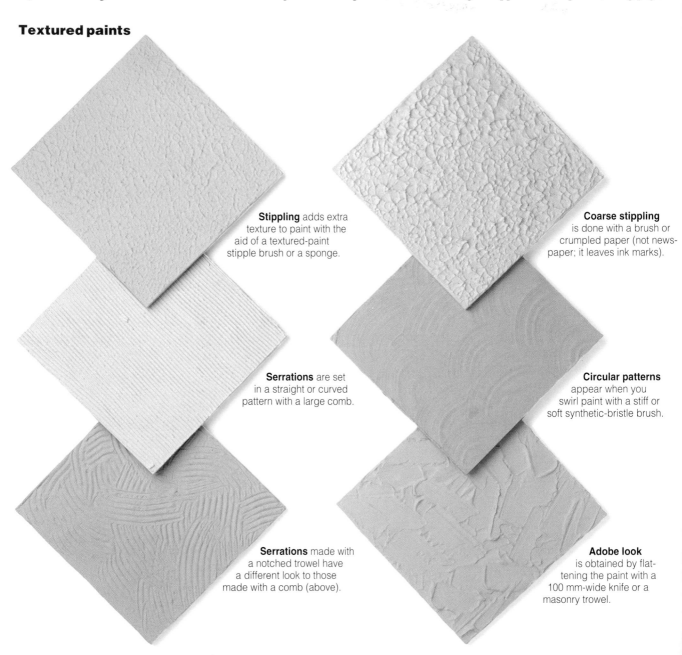

Stippling adds extra texture to paint with the aid of a textured-paint stipple brush or a sponge.

Coarse stippling is done with a brush or crumpled paper (not newspaper; it leaves ink marks).

Serrations are set in a straight or curved pattern with a large comb.

Circular patterns appear when you swirl paint with a stiff or soft synthetic-bristle brush.

Serrations made with a notched trowel have a different look to those made with a comb (above).

Adobe look is obtained by flattening the paint with a 100 mm-wide knife or a masonry trowel.

Glazed paints

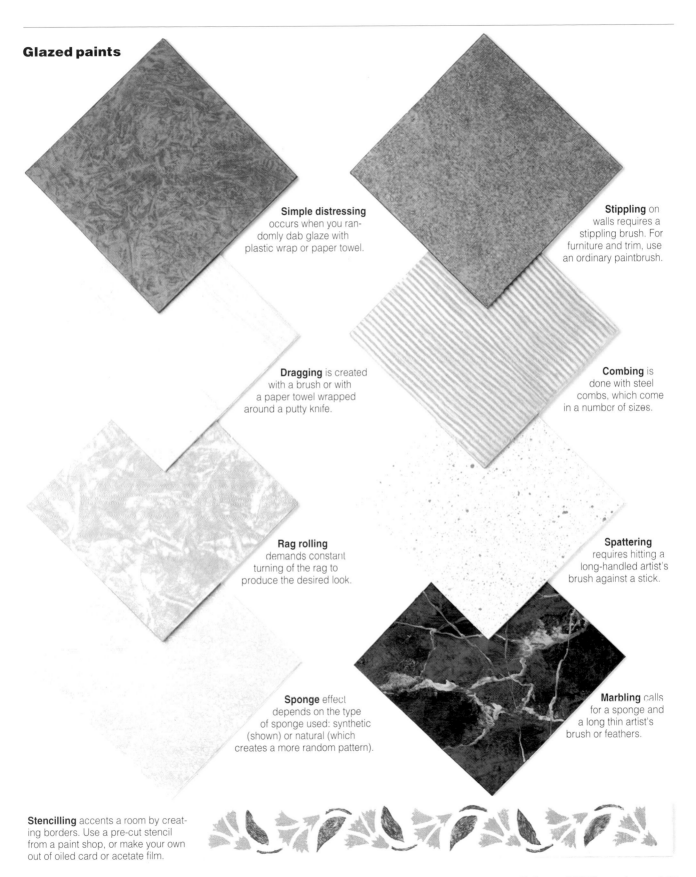

Simple distressing occurs when you randomly dab glaze with plastic wrap or paper towel.

Stippling on walls requires a stippling brush. For furniture and trim, use an ordinary paintbrush.

Dragging is created with a brush or with a paper towel wrapped around a putty knife.

Combing is done with steel combs, which come in a number of sizes.

Rag rolling demands constant turning of the rag to produce the desired look.

Spattering requires hitting a long-handled artist's brush against a stick.

Sponge effect depends on the type of sponge used: synthetic (shown) or natural (which creates a more random pattern).

Marbling calls for a sponge and a long thin artist's brush or feathers.

Stencilling accents a room by creating borders. Use a pre-cut stencil from a paint shop, or make your own out of oiled card or acetate film.

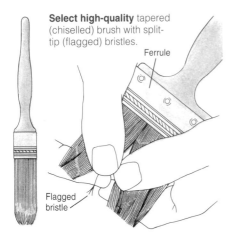

Select high-quality tapered (chiselled) brush with split-tip (flagged) bristles.

Ferrule

Flagged bristle

For an attractive, durable paint job, buy the best quality tools and materials you can afford. A well-made brush has flagged and chiselled bristles (left) and a sturdy metal ferrule. Because natural bristles absorb water, losing their shape, select synthetic-bristle brushes for latex (water-based) paint. Choose either synthetic- or natural-bristle brushes for enamel (oil-based) paint. Roller covers (p 294) come in synthetics or lamb's wool. For latex paint, choose a synthetic roller cover; lamb's-wool covers hold and spread enamel

paints better. Less expensive rollers hold paint poorly and tend to shed fluff. Take care of your tools by cleaning them thoroughly after each use and storing them as shown on pp 292 and 294.

Premium paints may seem expensive when compared with their cheaper counterparts, but any saving is usually illusory. Although the less expensive paints may advertise good hiding qualities (the ability to cover the previous colour), they generally cover less area, may be more difficult to apply and

Paint	Location	Characteristics	Comments
Latex (water-based)	Most surfaces, except some metals; many premium brands can be used on aluminium and vinyl cladding	Little odour; dries quickly; easy clean-up; withstands sunlight, moisture, mildew, and wood shrinkage or expansion; good colour retention; may adhere poorly to problem surfaces; brush marks tend to show	Do not apply over enamel paint unless it has been sanded and primed; use water as solvent
Enamel (oil-based)	Most surfaces except aluminium cladding; preferred for interior wood trim	Strong odour and fumes; dries slowly; clean-up messier than latex; colour may fade; when dry, is easy to wash; brush marks less evident	Do not apply over latex unless it has been sanded and primed; use paint thinners as solvent
Primer	Most surfaces except some metal, such as aluminium; use enamel for exteriors, wall-coverings and bare wood; otherwise, use same type as finish coat	Flat; white, unless tinted to match finish coat; most rust-inhibiting metal primer is bright yellow; many wood-primers are pink	Use appropriate solvent; always check label for information on compatibility of primer with undercoat and finish coat
Masonry paint	Interior and exterior concrete, aggregate, brick, stone and other masonry	Bonds to concrete and masonry walls; usually flat sheen	Specially formulated latex paint
Epoxy	Non-porous surfaces, such as porcelain, plastic, fibreglass and tile; many bathroom surfaces; concrete floors	Exceptionally durable and moisture-resistant; glossy; colour may yellow over time	May be latex or enamel – use appropriate solvent; may have two parts that require mixing
Heat-resistant paint	Metal objects subject to high temperature, including grills, fireplace screens, radiators and pipes	Resists heat up to very high temperature; limited sheen and colour choices available	Specially formulated silicone enamel paint
Metal paint	Any ferrous metal	Rust- and corrosion-resistant	Specially formulated latex or enamel paint
Whitewash	Interior and exterior walls, especially where a rough-plastered, rustic appearance is desired	Completely matt, with soft and powdery texture; can be tinted to warm, earthy colours; poor waterproofing qualities	Also known as distemper or limewash; oil-bound distemper and limewash give better waterproofing
Stoep and floor paint	Interior or exterior wood floors, concrete porches, or steps	Resists wear from foot traffic	Specially formulated enamel paint
Textured paint	Walls and ceilings where surface pattern is desired	Covers damaged, stained or uneven surfaces; reduces reflective glare; various patterns can be created (p 299)	Specially formulated or can be made from plaster-filler and PVA paint

About sheen

All paints are designated with a certain sheen or lustre.

Flat and eggshell sheens are the least shiny and reflective. They are often used on walls and ceilings in living areas and hallways, where they tend not to show surface flaws and brush or roller marks.

Medium sheens (satin and semi-gloss) are often used on kitchen and bathroom surfaces and in rooms where a soft but somewhat shiny look is desired.

Glossy sheens are easiest to wash and are best for high-wear areas such as kitchen and bathroom surfaces, children's rooms and woodwork or trim. Higher-gloss enamels are glossier than similar latex paints, and are also more durable and washable; any paint containing enamel will also have these characteristics, but may become brittle and yellow with age. (In South Africa, the terms 'oil-based', 'alkyd' and 'enamel' are generally used interchangeably.)

care for, and don't wear as well as better brands. When applied with a roller, good quality paint will go on smoothly, without spattering or forming blemishes. Because the quality of a paint isn't always obvious from the information on the tin, follow the advice of a reputable retailer or be guided by the experience of friends.

Many surfaces can be covered with more than one type of paint. Review the chart at left when choosing paint for a specific location and surface. Because latex paint is easily cleaned up, it is usually preferred for interior walls and ceilings.

Enamel paint has a stronger odour and requires mineral spirits, turpentine or another solvent for cleaning up. Enamel paint is less likely to retain brush marks when dry, so it is often used for interior woodwork. When working with it in confined spaces or in the absence of a through draught, wear a respirator.

Both latex and enamel paints come in all sheens, from flat to high gloss, but latex is never quite as glossy as its enamel counterpart. If you like the natural look of wood for trim or furniture, apply a stain or a clear finish such as varnish (pp 164–167).

An undercoat of primer will help the finish paint coat adhere and keep its colour uniform. If you are repainting with the same colour and paint type, just spot-prime any stains or patches of spackling compound. But if you are painting fresh wallboard, changing the colour of the room, or have done many repairs, prime all surfaces with a primer that you have tinted to match the final coat. If you are unsure whether a previous coat is latex or enamel, apply primer; latex paint applied over enamel is likely to peel off in time. When selecting a primer, check labels to make sure that primer and finish coat are compatible.

Caution: Follow the preparation and safety recommendations given on p 291. When you have finished, dispose of paint properly (p 307).

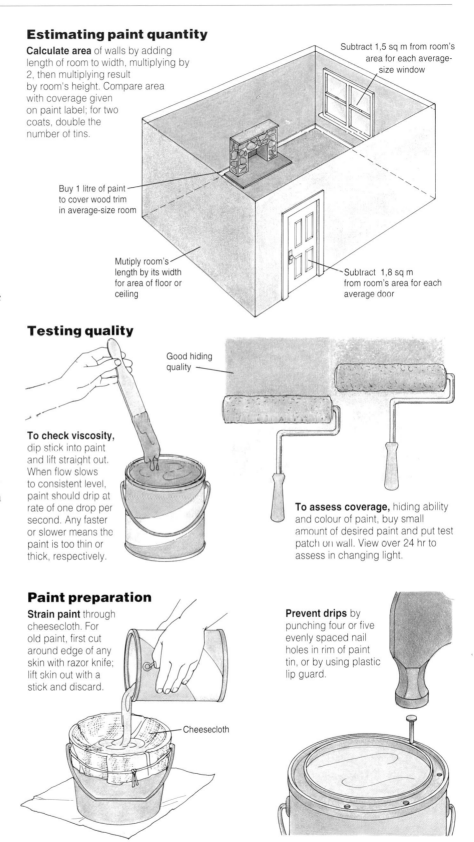

Estimating paint quantity

Calculate area of walls by adding length of room to width, multiplying by 2, then multiplying result by room's height. Compare area with coverage given on paint label; for two coats, double the number of tins.

Subtract 1,5 sq m from room's area for each average-size window

Buy 1 litre of paint to cover wood trim in average-size room

Mutiply room's length by its width for area of floor or ceiling

Subtract 1,8 sq m from room's area for each average door

Testing quality

To check viscosity, dip stick into paint and lift straight out. When flow slows to consistent level, paint should drip at rate of one drop per second. Any faster or slower means the paint is too thin or thick, respectively.

Good hiding quality

To assess coverage, hiding ability and colour of paint, buy small amount of desired paint and put test patch on wall. View over 24 hr to assess in changing light.

Paint preparation

Strain paint through cheesecloth. For old paint, first cut around edge of any skin with razor knife; lift skin out with a stick and discard.

Cheesecloth

Prevent drips by punching four or five evenly spaced nail holes in rim of paint tin, or by using plastic lip guard.

When developing a colour scheme, work with the colour wheel as your basic tool. Combine your own colour preferences with the information it provides to achieve the effects you want. Colours opposite one another on the wheel are known as *complementary* colours. They work well together, as do adjacent or related colours (next to each other on the wheel). An accent in a complementary colour can enliven a monochromatic scheme (one that has different shades of the same color).

Colour influences people's moods; avoid having too little or too much of it in one place. Combine wall colours with the existing elements in the room – artwork, curtains, furniture and carpeting. Exterior colours should be influenced by your home's surroundings. When decorating from scratch, you can begin with the colour of one element and then build your scheme around it.

Warm vs cool. Red and yellow and the combinations made from these primary colours are called warm colours – they energize and heat up a room. In cool climates and in sunny rooms, warm colours create a feeling of cosiness. The cool colours are blue, green and purple. In hot climates, these colours make a room feel cooler.

By adding white, you lighten the shade of a colour. Lighter shades can brighten rooms that have little natural light. By adding black, you darken a colour's shade. Darker shades create a feeling of intimacy. Light shades appear lighter when placed against a dark background. Against a light background, dark shades seem darker.

Colour can help to improve a room's proportions. Lighter shades reflect light, making walls appear to recede and giving the impression of a larger room. Darker shades make a room seem smaller and cosier. For a long, narrow room, paint the end walls a darker shade or a warmer colour than the side walls. This appears to bring in the end walls and widen the room. To make a room seem larger, paint all the walls and the trim the same colour. This will also unify an irregular space. Paint the ceiling a darker shade to

Outer colour wheel has 12 colours. Red, yellow and blue are primaries. Each secondary colour (orange, green and purple) is a combination of two primaries. When you blend colours you change their basic character, creating a wide variety of choices.

Inner colour wheel shows how neutrals may be warm (those on right side) or cool (those on left side). Combine neutrals with brighter colours to create satisfying schemes.

visually lower it and a lighter shade to give the effect of height.

Colour intensity. An intense colour is known as *highly saturated* and, warm or cool, it attracts the eye. Use intense colours as accents and for dramatic effect – on a single wall, for instance. In some spaces, such as hallways, an intense colour can be chosen as a main colour because the room is only for passing through. A glossy finish makes a colour stand out; the same colour in a semi-gloss is less obtrusive.

To draw attention to a particular wall or to an interesting feature such as a carved moulding, introduce a new colour or a glossier finish. On the other hand, you can minimize an awkward feature, like a badly placed door or serving hatch, by painting it the same colour as the background and in a less glossy finish.

For variety, introduce new colours in different rooms. But maintain unity by featuring a main colour from one room as an accent elsewhere. A multi-coloured wallcovering, mixing some or all of your colours on some walls (for example, in a hallway), can also unify a colour scheme throughout the house.

Choose indoor colours one shade lighter than you think you want. Once they have dried on the wall, they will be darker than they appear on the colour card. Before making a final decision, try the colour card test described below, or buy a small tin of the desired paint and paint a sample board. Hang the board up for a day, assessing the colour as the paint dries and the light changes.

Shades

Adding white or black changes a colour's shade, permitting many gradations within a single colour. Different colours can also be blended together – brown, for instance, is a mixture of red, yellow and black.

Paint colour cards

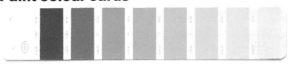

Use colour cards to help you choose shades. Cut the same shade from four cards and tape them together. Compare with furnishings and accessories, and tape to wall to observe in different lighting.

Interior colours

Semi-gloss coral-red walls make for a stimulating room. Usually red is an accent, but red walls can also wake up a quiet room and lend a cosy, intimate feeling. Try red for dining areas, south facing rooms and rooms used mainly at night.

Cool colours are serene and relaxing. Here, the soft grey-green of the walls is picked up in accessories such as the scatter cushion, picture and drapery fabric. Use cool colours in hot climates, in rooms that receive morning or afternoon sun and for modern decor.

Shades of the same colour – in this case white – are used to create a simple look that won't go out of style. You can brighten up neutral colours with contrasts (such as the green here). Such a scheme would suit children's rooms, kitchens and sun rooms.

Exterior colours

When choosing paint colours, keep in mind these factors: a small house will seem larger if you paint the entire structure, including trim, the same light colour (right). Light colours also make a house appear closer to the street, while dark colours make it appear to recede. Any paint with a glossy finish will exaggerate surface flaws.

A three-colour exterior scheme (below) with neutral or mid-tone walls, darker trim and a complementary-colour door emphasizes architectural features. Change colours only where a surface changes, and harmonize colours with brick or any other features whose colour cannot be easily altered. (If cleaning your masonry will alter its colour, clean it before selecting paint colours.)

Sunlight makes any colour seem lighter; select a slightly darker shade than the one you actually desire. Strong colours fade more rapidly outdoors than light colours. A house's surroundings change with the seasons; choose colours that will be pleasing year-round.

It is essential that you clean and repair all surfaces before painting. First remove wallcoverings (p 312), curtains and all hardware except switch plates and outlet covers (remove them only after you have washed the walls). Scrape old paint from screw slots, then turn out the screws with a screwdriver. Working up from the bottom, sponge-wash walls and trim with a solution of sugar soap or domestic detergent, then rinse. Before washing the ceiling, cover the floor with paper or drop cloths. Observe ladder safety precautions (pp 290–291).

If paint is thickly layered on the trim, remove it with a heat gun, as shown here, or with a chemical stripper. After applying the stripper, let the paint soften and then scrape and sand as you would when using a heat gun.

Caution: Unless you are certain that the paint does not contain lead (p 307), wear an appropriate respirator (p 13). Dispose of all debris properly.

Patch minor wallboard damage (facing page). For larger holes, saw back to the framing on each side of the damage and screw nailing strips to the framing. Cut a wallboard patch to match the hole, and screw the patch to the strips. Cover the seams with wallboard tape and layers of joint compound. In plaster, large or widening cracks, or cracks radiating from window or door corners, may indicate structural problems; have these professionally evaluated. Also do this wherever you see water damage.

Removing paint

Stripping paint:
1. Soften paint by holding heat gun 75 to 150 mm away. Move it back and forth until paint blisters.
Caution: To avoid scorching wood, keep tool moving. Wear gloves, goggles and a respirator.

2. Immediately scrape softened paint from flat surfaces with a narrow putty knife. (Round corners of knife to avoid gouging wood.) Either heat paint or scrape it – doing both at the same time could damage wood.

Shavehook

3. Scrape contoured wood with shavehook or four-edged blade scraper. For intricate carving, use pointed object such as an awl. Do entire surface until bare wood is visible.

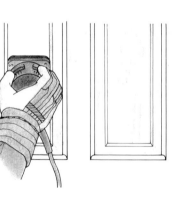

4. When most of the paint is gone, let dry; then remove remaining paint with palm sander or sanding block fitted with successively finer grits of abrasive paper.

Repairing wood trim

Scrape away loose paint with a stiff putty knife. Dig away any rotten wood. Brush wood sealer on bare wood and rotten areas.

Patching compound

Fill depressions with wood-patching compound and let dry. Smooth and feather edges with coarse then fine abrasive paper.

Popped nail

Nail set

Popped nails: 1. For doors, windows and other trim, re-seat nails with nail set or punch. Fill holes and joints with compound or paintable caulk.

Spray primer

2. Spray wood with a fast-drying primer or brush on regular primer. Let dry, then sand lightly.

Repairing damaged wallboard

For popped nails, drive new wallboard screw 50 mm below or above nail, then sink nailhead below surface by striking with nail set. Fill any dent (below).

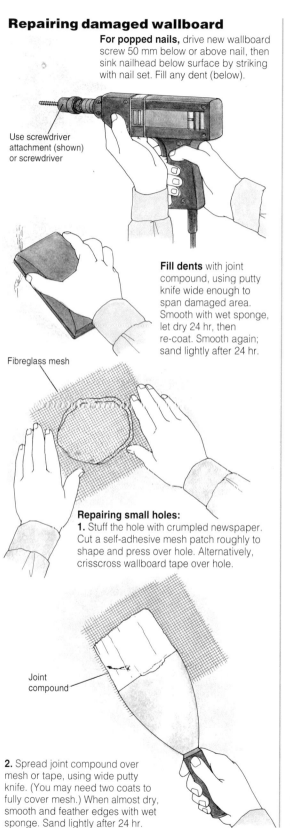

Use screwdriver attachment (shown) or screwdriver

Fill dents with joint compound, using putty knife wide enough to span damaged area. Smooth with wet sponge, let dry 24 hr, then re-coat. Smooth again; sand lightly after 24 hr.

Fibreglass mesh

Repairing small holes:
1. Stuff the hole with crumpled newspaper. Cut a self-adhesive mesh patch roughly to shape and press over hole. Alternatively, crisscross wallboard tape over hole.

Joint compound

2. Spread joint compound over mesh or tape, using wide putty knife. (You may need two coats to fully cover mesh.) When almost dry, smooth and feather edges with wet sponge. Sand lightly after 24 hr.

Filling holes in plaster

Scrape away loose paint from area around hole, using large putty knife. (Wear goggles and a dust mask.) Then scrape loose plaster from hole, taking care not to remove sound plaster. Undercut hole's inside edge with utility knife or tin-opener.

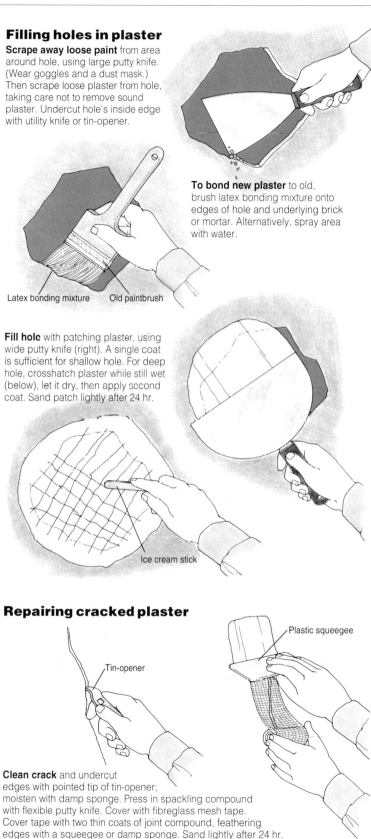

To bond new plaster to old, brush latex bonding mixture onto edges of hole and underlying brick or mortar. Alternatively, spray area with water.

Latex bonding mixture   Old paintbrush

Fill hole with patching plaster, using wide putty knife (right). A single coat is sufficient for shallow hole. For deep hole, crosshatch plaster while still wet (below), let it dry, then apply second coat. Sand patch lightly after 24 hr.

Ice cream stick

Repairing cracked plaster

Plastic squeegee

Tin-opener

Clean crack and undercut edges with pointed tip of tin-opener; moisten with damp sponge. Press in spackling compound with flexible putty knife. Cover with fibreglass mesh tape. Cover tape with two thin coats of joint compound, feathering edges with a squeegee or damp sponge. Sand lightly after 24 hr.

Reducing clutter and carefully masking the work area will help your project go smoothly and make cleaning up easier. Remove curtains, floorcovering, and any light furniture. Move the heavier pieces to the centre of the room. Wash and repair the walls, ceiling and trim (pp 288–289), then vacuum and dust the area thoroughly.

Remove all hardware such as window locks, curtain rods and picture hooks; tape the fasteners to the hardware so they don't get lost. Use drop cloths or masking material to cover everything that won't be painted. Inexpensive plastic cloth is fine for furniture, walls and cabinets, but old

sheeting is best for floors because it absorbs paint splatters. If you do use plastic cloth, cover it with newspaper or old sheets to absorb the paint. Cover wood trim with good quality masking tape or self-adhesive masking paper, available in many widths at paint supply stores. To prevent paint from leaking behind the tape or paper, press its edge down with a flexible putty knife. Remove the masking material when the paint dries – it may damage the trim if left too long.

Before removing the cover plate of a switch or outlet, or wrapping a ceiling or wall fixture in plastic, turn off the electricity to the room. Unscrew

a fixture's cover plate and slide it away from the surface. Don't let a fixture's wires bear its weight. Instead, support the fixture with a piece of rope tied through the mounting strap.

Masking window glass saves time, but if you have only one window and a steady hand, it's easier to scrape dried paint off the glass with a single-edge razor blade. An alternative is to coat the glass with liquid glass coating (a wax-based masking product), but keep it off the frame and glazing bars.

Caution: Keep children and pets out of the work area. Before leaving for any length of time, clean up or store your paint and materials (p 307).

Preparing to paint

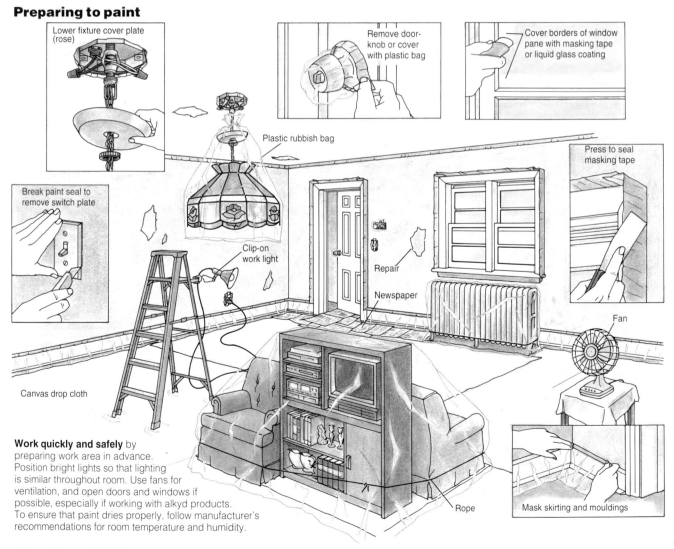

Lower fixture cover plate (rose)

Remove doorknob or cover with plastic bag

Cover borders of window pane with masking tape or liquid glass coating

Plastic rubbish bag

Press to seal masking tape

Break paint seal to remove switch plate

Clip-on work light

Repair

Newspaper

Fan

Canvas drop cloth

Work quickly and safely by preparing work area in advance. Position bright lights so that lighting is similar throughout room. Use fans for ventilation, and open doors and windows if possible, especially if working with alkyd products. To ensure that paint dries properly, follow manufacturer's recommendations for room temperature and humidity.

Rope

Mask skirting and mouldings

WORKING WITH LADDERS AND SCAFFOLDING

Usually one ladder is required when painting a room; for exteriors, you will often need at least two ladders. Stairs call for special set ups (p 297). Indoors use stepladders – if you need an extension ladder to reach a high ceiling, wrap the tops of its side rails with cloth to protect the wall. Scaffolding can be constructed with ladders and planks. For large set ups, you can hire more elaborate scaffolding from a supplier. Whenever you climb, even a short fall can result in serious injury, so read and follow the basic safety rules given here.

Stepladder

Position ladder so feet are level and steady on floor. For balance, lean your body into ladder. When you can no longer comfortably reach work surface, get down and move ladder. Don't overreach, or ladder may topple.

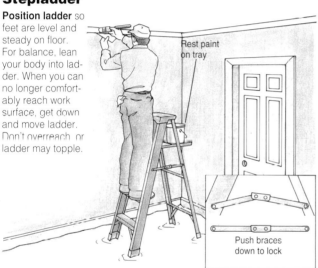

Rest paint on tray

Push braces down to lock

Scaffolding

Construct scaffold from strong, straight 50 x 100 or 50 x 300 plank set between two stepladders. Extend plank at least 300 mm beyond steps. For spans over 1,5 m, double planks for extra strength.

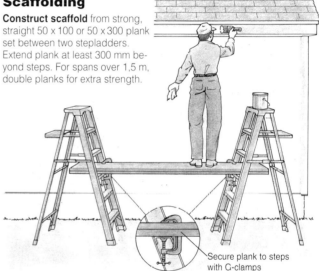

Secure plank to steps with C-clamps

Extension ladder

To raise, set unextended ladder on ground with its feet near foundation and walk up, hand over hand, against wall. When ladder is in position, extend to desired height and pull base out to correct angle.

Angle ladder so distance between its feet and wall equals one-fourth the ladder's height. Both feet should be an equal distance from the wall, so that ladder does not rock. On a hard or slippery surface, have a helper hold the ladder steady.

One-fourth ladder's height

Haul up supplies with container on rope, or have someone hand them to you. Hang paint tins and supplies from notched rod that fits through top rung of ladder.

You can paint the woodwork in a room first, then mask it off (p 290) and paint the ceiling and walls. Or if you are wary of splattering newly painted trim, begin by painting the ceiling and walls and paint the woodwork last. When painting large surfaces, first use a 50 or 75 mm brush to outline or 'cut in' around windows, doors and other trim and at the intersections of ceilings and walls where a roller can't reach. Then cover the remaining surface using a wide brush or a roller (pp 294–295). Paint windows and exterior doors early so you can close them at night without the paint sticking.

Start painting in a corner near a window. For an even coat, use the entire tip of the brush to apply the paint. Hold the brush in a comfortable grip, your thumb supporting its underside, but shift your grip now and then to avoid fatigue. When you need to reload the brush with paint, smooth out or 'feather' your strokes by gradually lifting the bristles off the work surface during the stroke. To avoid lap marks, work towards the most recently painted section, slightly overlapping the wet edges. Don't take time off in the middle of an unbroken section – you may end up with colour variations.

Using a paintbrush

Load brush, covering one-third of bristle length. To remove excess paint, lift brush straight up and slap it lightly against inside of tin. Don't drag brush over rim.

Cut in at ceiling with narrow edge of brush if wall and ceiling colours are different. Keep paint off adjacent surface. Remove smudges with a putty knife wrapped in paper towel.

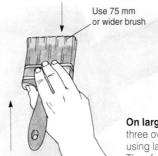

Use 75 mm or wider brush

On large areas, apply paint with two or three overlapping diagonal brush strokes, using largest brush that is comfortable. Then feather paint with vertical strokes until coverage is smooth.

At corners, around woodwork and wherever roller won't reach, cut in using width of brush. Work slowly to prevent splatters.

Caring for a paintbrush

Remove excess paint with a brush comb before washing brush. Alternatively, work brush back and forth across newspaper.

Brush comb

Wash latex (PVA) paint out of brush with warm water, separating bristles with your fingers. For enamel paint, clean with turpentine.

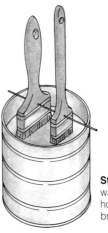

Store brushes overnight in water or paint thinners by drilling hole in handle and suspending brushes on piece of stiff wire.

For long-term storage, wrap brushes in their original plastic wrappers or wrap bristles in paper or foil.

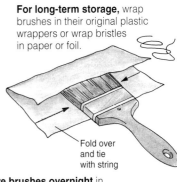

Fold over and tie with string

Painting a window

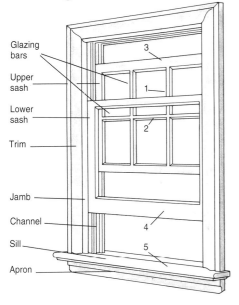

Glazing bars
Upper sash
Lower sash
Trim
Jamb
Channel
Sill
Apron

Work order: First remove locks and handles. Paint vertical glazing bars, then horizontal, then the rest of the sash. For double-hung windows, paint as much of upper sash as possible, reverse sash positions, and paint lower parts of upper sash. Then paint lower sash. Finally, paint jamb, apron, sill and trim. If you paint sash channels, sand them first. To prevent sashes sticking, move them while paint is still wet.

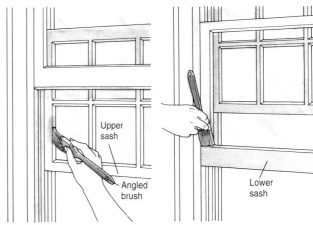

Upper sash

Angled brush

Lower sash

Begin in middle of unpainted area, using 38 mm sash brush. Brush out in both directions, then stroke toward wet areas. For convenience, put paint in small container.

Check sash corners occasionally for paint buildup and drips – remove by gently dabbing with dry brush. Remove drips at bar intersections in same way.

Painting a door

Frame
Jamb
Rail
Stile
Wedge

Work order: Before painting, remove or cover doorknob and firmly prop door open with pair of wedges. If door is new, paint bottom edge before hanging, to prevent wood from absorbing moisture and warping. Paint side and top edges of door first. Then paint panel edges. Follow with panel surfaces. Finish with rails, then stiles.

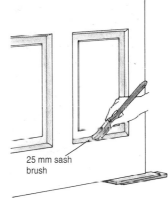

25 mm sash brush

For panels, paint edge with 25 mm sash brush, working from top to bottom. To prevent drips, dab paint into corners.

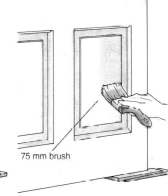

75 mm brush

Paint panel surfaces with 50 or 75 mm brush, working from centre of panel to edge. Feather strokes to smooth paint.

Painting trim

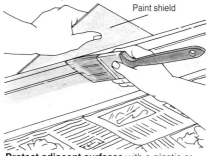

Paint shield

Protect adjacent surfaces with a plastic or metal shield, wiping it frequently with a clean cloth. Paint with the wood grain. Use two coats.

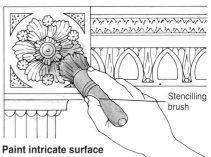

Stencilling brush

Paint intricate surface with stiff-bristle brush, such as a stencilling brush. Force paint into all crevices; remove paint buildups and drips.

Paint and Wallcoverings 293

PAINTING WITH ROLLERS AND PADS

Match the thickness of a roller's nap to your job. A 12 mm nap is fine for most flat and semi-gloss paints on smooth surfaces. For high-gloss paint, choose a 6 mm nap or a foam roller sleeve. For textured paint (p 299) or concrete, use a 20 mm nap. Before painting, dampen a roller with water (for latex) or turpentine (for enamel), then blot excess on paper towels.

A power roller requires the same techniques as a manual roller. Even though its speed makes it a tempting investment, the time needed to clean it may cancel out any savings in application time. Painting pads are less messy than rollers, but they can be slower to use. Certain pads are handy for painting over irregular surfaces or over textured paint and for reaching tight

spots (p 298); edger pads make it easy to get clean coverage next to trim.

Apply each coat of paint without interruption so that wet paint won't overlap dry. If you must stop, do so at a natural break in the surface, such as a window or door. When painting new wallboard, wait for the first coat of paint to dry, then fill visible seams and repairs before applying the next coat.

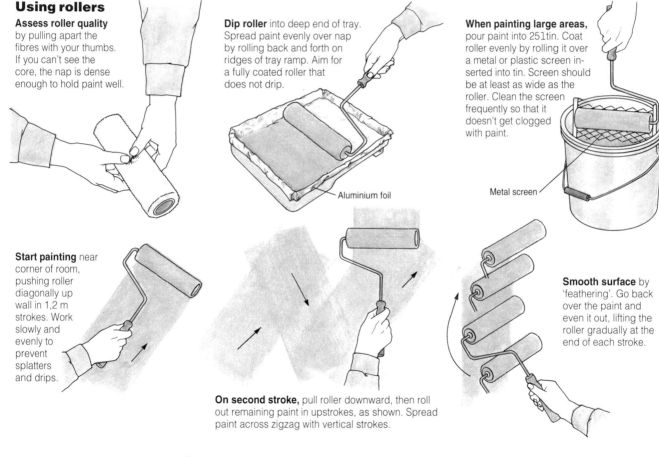

Using rollers

Assess roller quality by pulling apart the fibres with your thumbs. If you can't see the core, the nap is dense enough to hold paint well.

Dip roller into deep end of tray. Spread paint evenly over nap by rolling back and forth on ridges of tray ramp. Aim for a fully coated roller that does not drip.

Aluminium foil

When painting large areas, pour paint into 25 l tin. Coat roller evenly by rolling it over a metal or plastic screen inserted into tin. Screen should be at least as wide as the roller. Clean the screen frequently so that it doesn't get clogged with paint.

Metal screen

Start painting near corner of room, pushing roller diagonally up wall in 1,2 m strokes. Work slowly and evenly to prevent splatters and drips.

On second stroke, pull roller downward, then roll out remaining paint in upstrokes, as shown. Spread paint across zigzag with vertical strokes.

Smooth surface by 'feathering'. Go back over the paint and even it out, lifting the roller gradually at the end of each stroke.

Cleaning and storing

Remove excess paint with curved side of brush comb, then wash roller cover with soap and hot running water for latex (PVA) paint or with turpentine for enamel paint. Wear rubber gloves while rubbing turpentine into nap.

Brush comb

Store cover when dry, wrapped in paper or aluminium foil. If you use plastic, punch a few air holes in it to prevent damage caused by damp or mildew.

Painting ceilings and walls

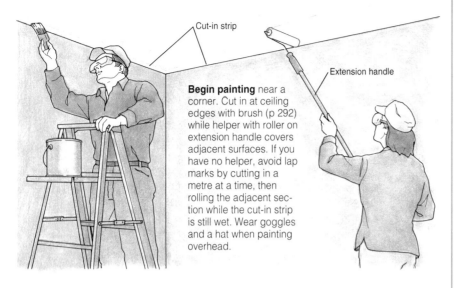

Cut-in strip

Extension handle

Begin painting near a corner. Cut in at ceiling edges with brush (p 292) while helper with roller on extension handle covers adjacent surfaces. If you have no helper, avoid lap marks by cutting in a metre at a time, then rolling the adjacent section while the cut-in strip is still wet. Wear goggles and a hat when painting overhead.

Roll on paint in diagonal strokes, as shown on facing page. Cover only a 1 m section at a time, then feather the surface to even out coverage. Move from a dry section into a wet one, overlapping edges to prevent streaks. Roll slowly to minimize splattering.

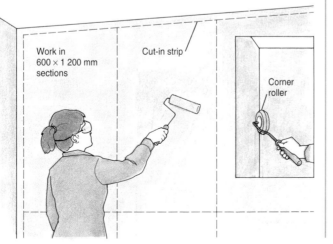

Cut in and paint walls after ceiling. A corner roller works well for 90° or acute angles (inset). Starting in upper corner, work in 600 × 1 200 mm sections, working towards lower corner. Apply and distribute the paint as shown on facing page.

Work in 600 × 1 200 mm sections

Cut-in strip

Corner roller

Painting with pads

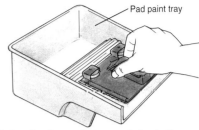

Pad paint tray

Before loading pad, dampen it first (with water for latex paint, turpentine for enamel paint). Then press it into paint until fibres are saturated. Blot off excess on tray's ridges.

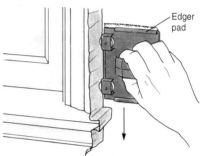

Edger pad

Position guide wheels of edger pad against trim and paint with long straight strokes. Move pad in one direction only, not with the back-and-forth motion you'd use with a brush.

Clean pad by blotting it on paper to remove paint. Then rinse in water (for latex paint) or turpentine (for enamel paint).

Blot pad on newspaper to remove excess moisture; then air-dry thoroughly. Wrap in paper or aluminium foil for storage.

Paint and Wallcoverings 295

PAINTING WITH SPRAYERS

Spray-painting saves time, especially when you need to paint irregular surfaces such as fences and furniture, but it takes some practice before you can produce an even, drip-free coating. A typical sprayer requires more paint than a brush or roller for the same surface. And all sprayers require thorough cleaning after use. Before buying or hiring a sprayer, balance these factors against the reduced painting time. If you do decide to spray, match the tool to the job. For instance, the 1 litre airless paint sprayer shown here may not

be suitable for painting an exterior (pp 306–307). Although most paints can be sprayed, some sprayers can't spray thick paints. Have the sprayer's operation explained by your dealer or agent, and request an instruction manual in case problems arise.

Before filling the sprayer, strain the paint (p 285) to avoid clogging the nozzle; then thin the paint by about 10 per cent with water or paint thinners, depending on the type of paint. Select the correct nozzle and clear it of any debris. Because spraying produces

a lot of overspray, mask all surfaces you want to protect. Practise your technique on scrap material. If the paint is thin enough, it will evenly cover the surface in an elliptical pattern.

Caution: A paint sprayer forces paint out at high pressure – you can cause serious injury by actually injecting paint into your flesh. Never point a sprayer at anyone or anything other than the surface you wish to paint. Unplug the sprayer before filling, cleaning or servicing it. Always wear the appropriate respirator (p 13).

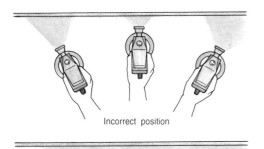

Incorrect position

Correct position

Move spray gun parallel to surface, at a distance of about 300 mm. To maintain even coverage, keep sprayer upright and bend your wrist; don't swing sprayer in an arc.

Overlap each pass by about a third of its width (right), stepping from side to side (rather than overreaching) to keep sprayer aimed directly at surface; don't tilt sprayer. If your arm tires, support the sprayer with both hands.

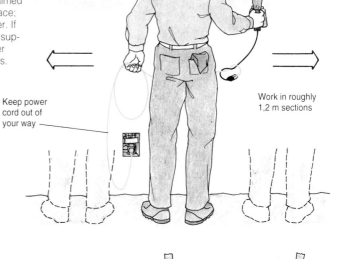

Keep power cord out of your way

Work in roughly 1,2 m sections

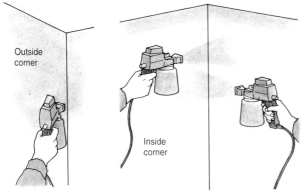

Outside corner

Inside corner

At corners, keep spray gun moving to feather edges of sprayed area. For outside corners, aim directly at intersection of walls; for inside corners, aim at each wall in turn. If ceiling and wall colours differ, cut in at top of wall (p 292).

Extension   Cut in where colours differ

Spray ceiling or floor with a flexible extension. (Paint should be of thinner consistency than for regular spray nozzle.) Support base of sprayer with one hand.

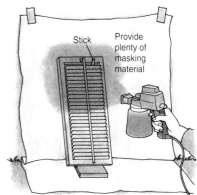

Stick   Provide plenty of masking material

Cover intricate shapes with horizontal strokes. To avoid drips, spray past the edges of object on each pass. For a shutter, hold slats open with a stick.

Reaching the ceiling and upper walls of a stairwell usually requires scaffolding. You can hire scaffolding or make your own with 50 × 100 or 50 × 300 planks supported on a combination of sawhorses, extension ladders, and stepladders. Make sure the planks are straight and knot-free.

For extra strength on spans longer than 1,5 m, double the planks. Don't try to span a gap longer than 3 m without extra support from beneath. When erected, the scaffold planks should be level and should extend beyond the end supports by at least 300 mm. Clamp or nail the planks to their supports. To reduce the risk of falling, position the scaffold no further than your body's width from the wall and, as you work, keep the scaffold free of extra paint, tools and materials.

Mask and cover the area under and beyond the edge of the work platform. Paint banisters and railings with paint mittens, steps with brushes and small rollers. Cut in around ceilings and walls as you would normally (p 292).

Caution: When working at heights, follow the safety information given on p 291, in particular making sure that your platform is secure. To prevent a ladder from slipping, nail a wooden cleat to the floor to brace its feet (if possible, lift up any carpet to do this). Block access to the stairs, and either leave doors wide open or block them closed to prevent them from being opened into the scaffold.

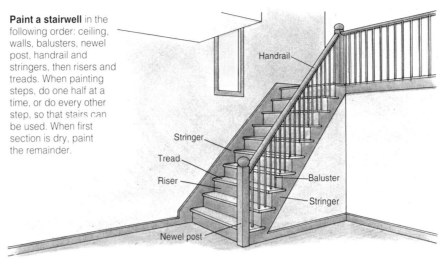

Paint a stairwell in the following order: ceiling, walls, balusters, newel post, handrail and stringers, then risers and treads. When painting steps, do one half at a time, or do every other step, so that stairs can be used. When first section is dry, paint the remainder.

Handrail
Stringer
Tread
Riser
Baluster
Stringer
Newel post

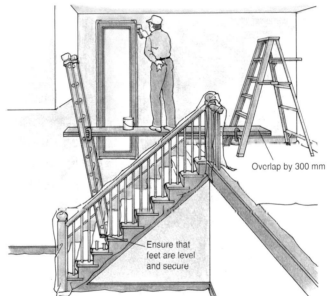

Overlap by 300 mm

Ensure that feet are level and secure

Rig a tall scaffold to reach upper wall area by arranging step- and extension ladders as shown. Lodge the extension ladder firmly against a step riser; wrap rails with cloth to protect walls. Run two planks of 50 × 100 or 50 × 300 between the ladders, securing them to the rungs with clamps or nails. If space is limited at upper part of stairway, use a stepladder or sawhorse leaned against the upper wall.

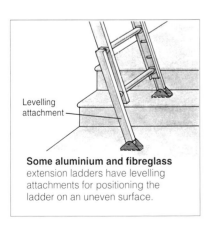

Levelling attachment

Some aluminium and fibreglass extension ladders have levelling attachments for positioning the ladder on an uneven surface.

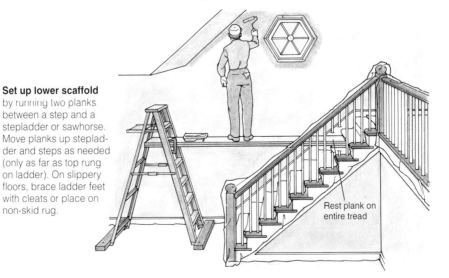

Set up lower scaffold by running two planks between a step and a stepladder or sawhorse. Move planks up stepladder and steps as needed (only as far as top rung on ladder). On slippery floors, brace ladder feet with cleats or place on non-skid rug.

Rest plank on entire tread

SPECIAL PAINTING TECHNIQUES

Most paint jobs include at least one hard-to-reach area or an irregular surface. While it's possible to paint almost anything with a combination of brushes and rollers, some items require the special techniques or tools shown below.

Reaching all the surfaces of kitchen and bathroom cupboards can be difficult. To manoeuvre more easily in tight spaces, try a brush with a short handle. Before painting cupboards, remove the doors, drawers and fittings, and wash all surfaces. Lightly sand new or previously painted wood. To prevent warping from uneven moisture absorption, use an equal number of coats of paint on all the cupboard's surfaces.

An airless sprayer (p 296) will quickly paint decorative metalwork and louvred shutters, but you can get similar, if slower, results with a paint mitten or a flexible paint pad.

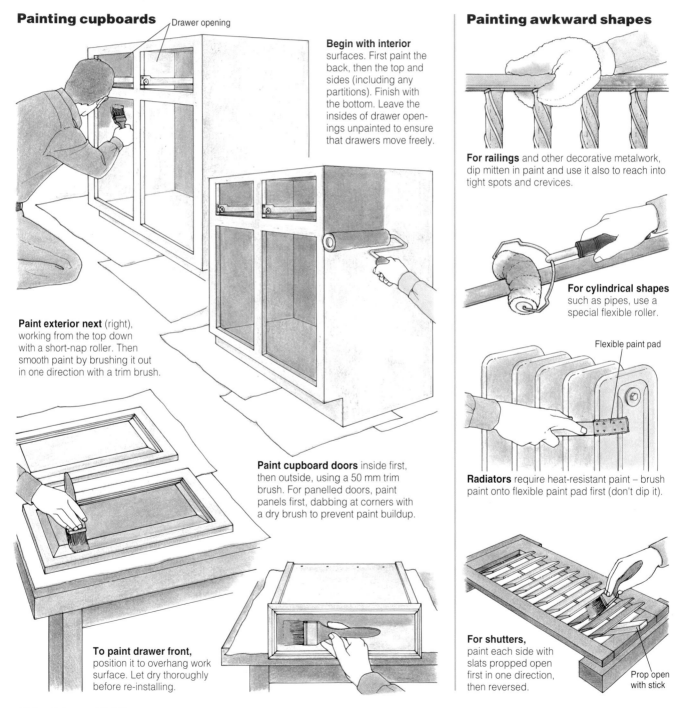

Painting cupboards

Drawer opening

Begin with interior surfaces. First paint the back, then the top and sides (including any partitions). Finish with the bottom. Leave the insides of drawer openings unpainted to ensure that drawers move freely.

Paint exterior next (right), working from the top down with a short-nap roller. Then smooth paint by brushing it out in one direction with a trim brush.

Paint cupboard doors inside first, then outside, using a 50 mm trim brush. For panelled doors, paint panels first, dabbing at corners with a dry brush to prevent paint buildup.

To paint drawer front, position it to overhang work surface. Let dry thoroughly before re-installing.

Painting awkward shapes

For railings and other decorative metalwork, dip mitten in paint and use it also to reach into tight spots and crevices.

For cylindrical shapes such as pipes, use a special flexible roller.

Flexible paint pad

Radiators require heat-resistant paint – brush paint onto flexible paint pad first (don't dip it).

For shutters, paint each side with slats propped open first in one direction, then reversed.

Prop open with stick

PAINTING WITH TEXTURED PAINT

In addition to providing a decorative surface, textured paint hides cracks and other flaws in walls and ceilings. Once applied, it's difficult to remove, but it can be freshened or have its colour changed with a coat of paint. After you apply textured paint, pattern it with the simple techniques shown. Pre-mixed latex paints have a thinner texture; powder that you mix with water or latex paint provides a heavier coat.

Before applying the textured paint, practise your pattern on heavy cardboard. Fill any large holes or dents in the surface of the wall (pp 288–289); the paint itself will fill minor flaws. Prime the wall with an appropriate primer and apply the textured paint. Let it dry for the time specified on the label, then create the final pattern. Before painting textured paint another colour, let finished pattern dry for 24 hours.

Applying textured paint

Mix textured paint to desired consistency. With specified roller, cover 1 m-square sections until paint is 1,5 mm thick. Create pattern (below); then cover next 1 m section.

To colour the texture, paint over it with flat latex. First cut in around trim and wall edges with a brush. Dab paint into all crevices, then smooth it out.

For remaining surfaces, use a roller fitted with 20 mm-nap roller cover. Roll on latex paint in W or M shape; then fill in spaces. Alternative is to use a paint sprayer (p 296).

A selection of patterns

Circular pattern. Position a slightly damp natural sponge against paint, then rotate.

Ridges. Rake notched trowel across paint in curved or straight motion.

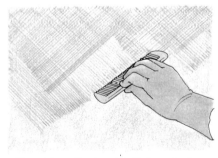

Fine ridges. Comb paint with large-tooth plastic or metal hair comb.

Rustic look. Dab and twist paint slightly with concrete finishing trowel or putty knife.

Swirls. Twist stiff-bristled brush against paint; softer bristles create more subtle look.

Stipple. Repeatedly press crumpled piece of wax paper or plastic against paint.

With a few improvised tools, glaze that you make yourself, and the techniques shown here, you can decorate surfaces in a variety of ways. More subtle than patterned wallpapers and more elaborate than plain painted surfaces, decorative paint finishes can dramatically alter the appearance of a room. You can treat a whole room or use one effect to accent a single wall, an architectural detail, a piece of furniture, or a craft item.

Glaze – the basic material of much decorative painting – is a translucent paint that you apply over a base coat. The glaze is *distressed* in such a way that the base coat shows through the glaze unevenly, creating a pattern. The most common technique is to brush or roll the glaze over the base coat, then distress it (facing page), resulting in a smooth, subtle finish. You can also apply the glaze over the base coat with the distressing tool, producing a more clearly defined pattern. Or you can combine these techniques, using several paints or glazes of different colours for a multi-layered effect.

Formulas for concocting the glaze abound; a simple, effective recipe that combines enamel paint, solvent and glazing liquid is given below. (Commercial glaze has become available in South Africa only recently.)

Because it's difficult to match consecutive batches exactly, mix a bit extra.

The base coat over which you put the glaze can be either latex or enamel, but it should be a satin or semi-gloss finish. Let a new base coat dry for 24 hrs before you apply the glaze. Enamel glazes dry slowly, giving you time to distress the glaze. Latex glazes dry fast, and so are recommended only for small areas or items.

Once the glaze is dry, you can apply a clear varnish, which provides a protective coating and gives the surface its final sheen. Varnish is almost always used when marbling (p 302), and on furniture or craft objects.

Before choosing a finish, consider the condition of the surface. Combing, stippling and dragging produce a linear effect that can highlight any imperfections in the surface. Before tackling a project, practise your technique on mat board. Mask and prepare the room as you would for any painting job (p 290). For an entire room, work on one wall, then its opposite, to avoid overlaps in the corners.

Caution: Some enamel-based paint products may be toxic, so wear a respirator (p 13) and rubber gloves. Work in a well-ventilated area, keep pets and children away, and dispose of materials properly (p 307).

Making your own glaze

Stir together 1 part each of enamel paint and paint thinners; then add 1 part glazing liquid. Mix glaze thoroughly, stirring up from bottom of container. Test on painted mat boar – glaze should be thin but not runny. To thicken, add more paint. To thin, add paint thinners. To increase transparency, add more glazing liquid.

Applying glaze

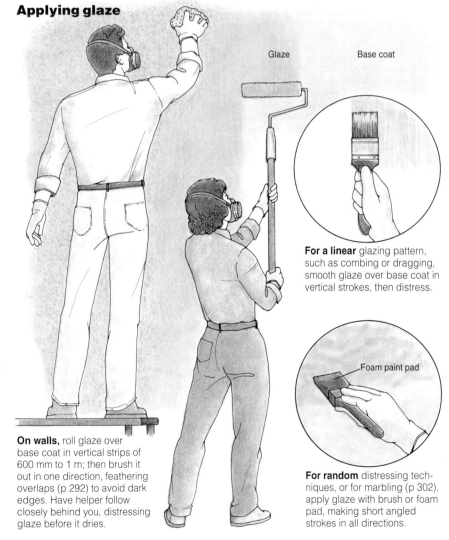

On walls, roll glaze over base coat in vertical strips of 600 mm to 1 m; then brush it out in one direction, feathering overlaps (p 292) to avoid dark edges. Have helper follow closely behind you, distressing glaze before it dries.

For a linear glazing pattern, such as combing or dragging, smooth glaze over base coat in vertical strokes, then distress.

For random distressing techniques, or for marbling (p 302), apply glaze with brush or foam pad, making short angled strokes in all directions.

Ways of distressing glaze

Simple distressing. Dab firmly at glaze with a paper towel, a clean lint-free cloth or a piece of lightweight plastic. To keep the pattern random, rotate material in your hand often. Periodically expose clean surface of material or change to a fresh piece.

Sponging. Pat solvent-dampened sea sponge against surface, frequently changing its position in your hand. Hold the sponge delicately, without squeezing it. Synthetic sponge gives a more defined, regular look.

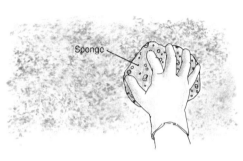

Sponge

Stippling. Firmly press stippling brush (or less expensive stainer's brush) into wet glaze; for crisp pattern, avoid sliding. Frequently wipe glaze off brush with clean cloth. Keep bristles at right angle to surface.

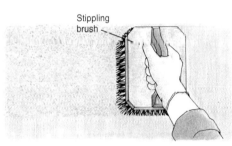

Stippling brush

Rag-rolling. For pattern resembling crushed velvet, shape a clean lint-free cloth about 300 mm square into a loose sausage shape, and roll it down the surface in vertical strips. Overlap the strips slightly.

Combing. Place steel or rubber comb at 45° angle to surface; drag down to etch pattern into glaze, forming straight, wavy or zig-zag lines, as you prefer. Don't overlap rows; clean comb at end of each row. Use comb with narrow teeth for tight spots.

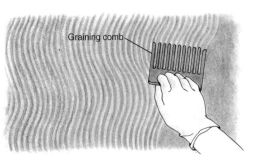

Graining comb

Spattering

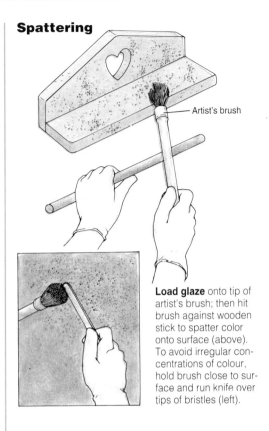

Artist's brush

Load glaze onto tip of artist's brush; then hit brush against wooden stick to spatter color onto surface (above). To avoid irregular concentrations of colour, hold brush close to surface and run knife over tips of bristles (left).

Dragging

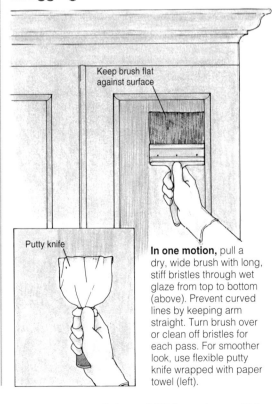

Keep brush flat against surface

Putty knife

In one motion, pull a dry, wide brush with long, stiff bristles through wet glaze from top to bottom (above). Prevent curved lines by keeping arm straight. Turn brush over or clean off bristles for each pass. For smoother look, use flexible putty knife wrapped with paper towel (left).

The easiest way to create the look of marble is to gradually build up a clouded effect over a base coat with one or two colours of glaze, blending them with distressing tools to create a subtle effect. After this clouding has dried, use a feather or an artist's brush to paint on the glaze veins.

Two often-reproduced marbles are *verde* (which is shown here and has a black base with green clouding and grey veins) and *Carrara* (composed of a white base with light grey clouding and medium grey veins).

Before beginning to work, assemble the tools and glazes (p 300–301) you will need. Then practise your technique (especially the veins) on a sample board. Refer to a real piece of marble or to a photograph for help in making your 'marble' realistic.

Good marbling projects for beginners are objects that could actually be made of marble, such as tabletops or fireplace mantels. If you choose to tackle a larger area, such as a wall or a floor, divide it into 300 mm-square sections and work on one at a time. However, for a realistic effect, flow the clouding and veins across the sections.

Just about any paintable surface can be marbled, as long as it is clean and smooth. Remove old paint only if it is thick or flaking. Sand the surface smooth with fine abrasive paper, and then apply the base coat, which can be either latex or enamel paint (but make sure that it is compatible with the existing surface).

Most marbled projects are finished with several coats of clear oil- or water-based varnish (p 168), to enhance the deception. All varnishes yellow with age, oil-based ones more than water-based. This can eventually dull a marbling job, so a water-based varnish is preferable. A too-glossy finish will highlight surface irregularities. Ask your paint dealer about the best type of varnish for your marbling project.

Caution: When you are working with enamel-based glazes, follow the safety measures described on p 300.

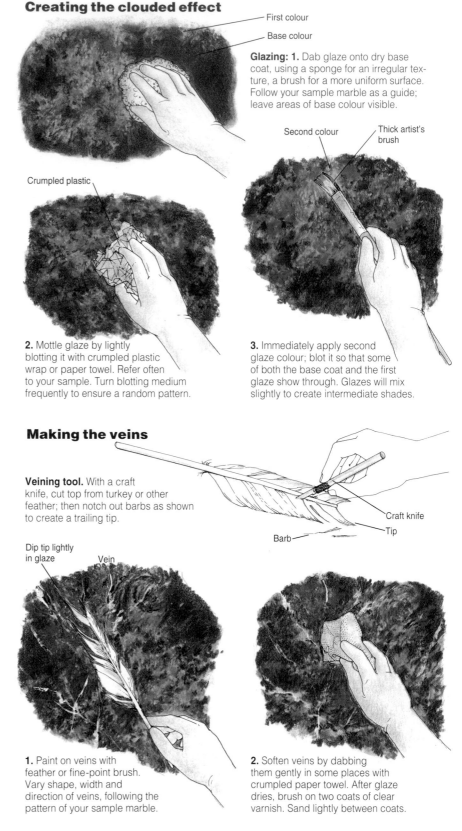

Creating the clouded effect

First colour

Base colour

Glazing: 1. Dab glaze onto dry base coat, using a sponge for an irregular texture, a brush for a more uniform surface. Follow your sample marble as a guide; leave areas of base colour visible.

Second colour

Thick artist's brush

Crumpled plastic

2. Mottle glaze by lightly blotting it with crumpled plastic wrap or paper towel. Refer often to your sample. Turn blotting medium frequently to ensure a random pattern.

3. Immediately apply second glaze colour; blot it so that some of both the base coat and the first glaze show through. Glazes will mix slightly to create intermediate shades.

Making the veins

Veining tool. With a craft knife, cut top from turkey or other feather; then notch out barbs as shown to create a trailing tip.

Barb

Craft knife

Tip

Dip tip lightly in glaze

Vein

1. Paint on veins with feather or fine-point brush. Vary shape, width and direction of veins, following the pattern of your sample marble.

2. Soften veins by dabbing them gently in some places with crumpled paper towel. After glaze dries, brush on two coats of clear varnish. Sand lightly between coats.

STENCILLING

Creating the stencil

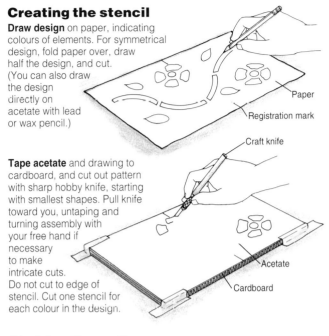

Draw design on paper, indicating colours of elements. For symmetrical design, fold paper over, draw half the design, and cut. (You can also draw the design directly on acetate with lead or wax pencil.)

Paper

Registration mark

Craft knife

Tape acetate and drawing to cardboard, and cut out pattern with sharp hobby knife, starting with smallest shapes. Pull knife toward you, untaping and turning assembly with your free hand if necessary to make intricate cuts. Do not cut to edge of stencil. Cut one stencil for each colour in the design.

Acetate

Cardboard

Marking the wall

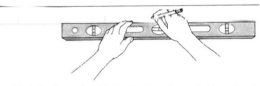

Mark horizontal guideline for top of stencil. Use a level and mark very lightly with a sharp, hard lead pencil.

Walls, ceilings, floors, furniture and decorative objects can be made brighter or given a more traditional look with the application of a stencilled pattern. This pattern can be a continuous border, a design that completely covers a surface, or simply an accent for a focal point. You can purchase stencils ready-made, copy a design from a pattern book (available at paint and art supply stores) or create your own design. Enlarge or reduce the pattern as necessary (p 338).

Stencilling requires few materials. If you're making your own stencil, you'll need acetate or stencil paper. Acetate is easier to cut, and because it's transparent, it's easier to align with registration marks. Protect the work surface with heavy cardboard, and cut out the stencil with a sharp craft knife.

When painting, tape stencils to the surface with draughting tape. Paint the stencil with either special stencil paint or artist's acrylics. Thin paint can bleed behind the stencil and smudge, so thin the paint just to a creamy consistency with paint thinners (for oil-based paint) or water (for latex paint). Apply the paint with a stippling brush or, for a more mottled look, a sponge. You can stencil on most surfaces, but for best results, stencil over flat latex or enamel paint.

Follow the steps at left to measure and mark out registration marks along a horizontal wall border, fine-tuning the spacing as necessary to compensate for uneven walls or obstacles. Complete one colour at a time, and let the paint dry before positioning the stencil sheet for the second colour – wet paint can easily be smudged. If you have a complicated design (even if using only one colour), you can also avoid smudging by 'leap-frogging' around the room, doing every other stencil repeat. When you have finished, go around the room again to fill in the missing spaces.

Registration mark

Length of stencil

Divide each wall by length of stencil to determine number of pattern repeats. Adjust spaces between repeats to avoid awkward pattern breaks at corners and obstacles. Lightly pencil registration marks along horizontal guideline, working out from centre of each wall to both corners.

Painting the stencil

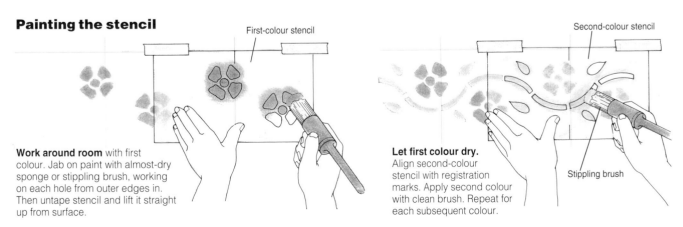

First-colour stencil

Second-colour stencil

Stippling brush

Work around room with first colour. Jab on paint with almost-dry sponge or stippling brush, working on each hole from outer edges in. Then untape stencil and lift it straight up from surface.

Let first colour dry. Align second-colour stencil with registration marks. Apply second colour with clean brush. Repeat for each subsequent colour.

If you spend time properly preparing your house for painting, you'll be rewarded with professional-looking, durable results. Start by diagnosing any problems. For example, peeling paint on the wall outside a kitchen may indicate a need for improved ventilation. Mildew may be caused by heavy shade or overgrown shrubbery – trim the trees and shrubs and choose a paint containing a fungicide.

Work your way around the house, making repairs as needed. Then remove hardware such as lamps, downpipes, shutters and awnings. Cover the perimeter with canvas or plastic drop cloths (taking care not to damage delicate plants). Enclose everything else you don't want painted, such as electricity meters, window sills and face brick, with taped plastic sheet.

All surfaces must be thoroughly cleaned. A hired power washer is fast and also removes most peeling paint. Then stabilize and prime bare wood, repairs and flaking surfaces. (Flaking produces a fine light powder. Power-washing will remove it, but you must stabilize and prime to prevent it from recurring.) Stabilizing primers seal and waterproof porous walls and prevent too much paint from being absorbed. For a strong bond between paint and primer, paint the house within two weeks of priming it.

To calculate the number of litres of paint needed per coat, multiply the house's wall height by its perimeter, then divide the result by the coverage claimed on the paint tin. Generally, 1ℓ of masonry paint covers 6 to 10 sq m of a smooth surface, about 5 sq m of a medium-textured surface and up to 4 sq m of a deep texture. Pick a dry, clear day to paint. Start with the fascia, then paint the walls and windows. Finish with doors, porches or decks, thresholds, steps and shutters.

Caution: Wear goggles when sanding and scraping paint and, unless you are certain that the paint does not contain lead (p 307), wear a respirator (p 13). Dispose of all debris properly. When power-washing, wear goggles and protective clothing, and aim only at wood or masonry – the spray might break glass or injure someone.

Preparing to paint

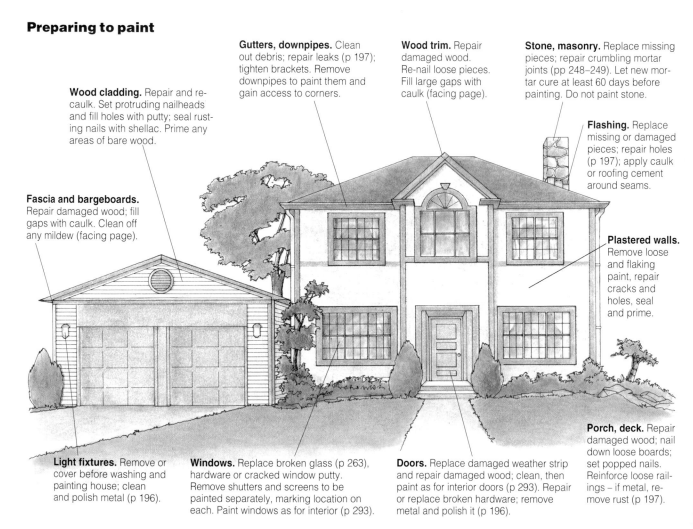

Wood cladding. Repair and re-caulk. Set protruding nailheads and fill holes with putty; seal rusting nails with shellac. Prime any areas of bare wood.

Gutters, downpipes. Clean out debris; repair leaks (p 197); tighten brackets. Remove downpipes to paint them and gain access to corners.

Wood trim. Repair damaged wood. Re-nail loose pieces. Fill large gaps with caulk (facing page).

Stone, masonry. Replace missing pieces; repair crumbling mortar joints (pp 248–249). Let new mortar cure at least 60 days before painting. Do not paint stone.

Flashing. Replace missing or damaged pieces; repair holes (p 197); apply caulk or roofing cement around seams.

Fascia and bargeboards. Repair damaged wood; fill gaps with caulk. Clean off any mildew (facing page).

Plastered walls. Remove loose and flaking paint, repair cracks and holes, seal and prime.

Light fixtures. Remove or cover before washing and painting house; clean and polish metal (p 196).

Windows. Replace broken glass (p 263), hardware or cracked window putty. Remove shutters and screens to be painted separately, marking location on each. Paint windows as for interior (p 293).

Doors. Replace damaged weather strip and repair damaged wood; clean, then paint as for interior doors (p 293). Repair or replace broken hardware; remove metal and polish it (p 196).

Porch, deck. Repair damaged wood; nail down loose boards; set popped nails. Reinforce loose railings – if metal, remove rust (p 197).

Cleaning exterior surfaces

Remove dirt from small areas with garden hose. For tougher stains, use car-washer attachment. Scrub mildew with solution of 1 ℓ bleach, ⅓ cup household detergent (no ammonia), and 3 ℓ warm water.

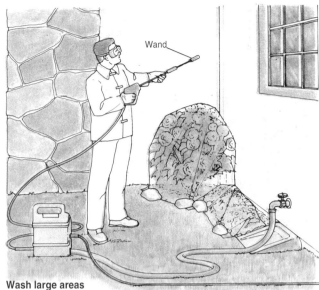

Wash large areas with a hired power washer, varying the strength of the spray and the distance of the wand from the surface to avoid damaging woodwork. Hold the wand at an angle of 45° to the wall and at least 300 mm away. Move jet in gentle loops and add a fungicide to the spray if necessary. Use power washers cautiously on tile or shingle roofs.

Preparing exterior surfaces

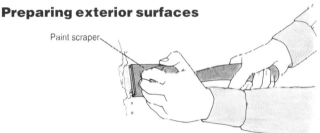

Scrape loose paint not removed by power washing with long-handled scraper. Blend edges of scraped area into surrounding paint by feathering with sander (right).

Smooth new plaster with palm sander, keeping it moving to avoid oversanding. In tight spots, you'll have more control if you hand-sand.

Scrape joints between plaster and window or door trim to remove old, crumbling caulk. Refill joints with paintable caulk. Add caulk under windowsills and thresholds.

Cut tip at 45° angle

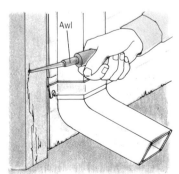

Probe rotten wood with awl to determine depth of damage. If minor, sand or scrape down to sound wood. Powdered wood and tiny holes indicate insect damage; consult a professional.

Fill deep rot pockets with epoxy wood filler, after mixing according to product instructions. Sand dried filler before painting it.

When all the surfaces of your house are clean and smooth, you are ready to begin priming and then painting. To avoid unattractive lap marks in the finish coat (caused by the edge of a paint stroke drying out before you overlap it with the next stroke), work on the shady side of the house so that the sun won't dry the paint too quickly. Begin with the fascia and work down the walls, moving from left to right and working from one natural break to the next, such as from a window to a door. Where there are no natural breaks, paint across the width of the house, coating only an area big enough to be comfortably completed before the previous area starts to dry.

After completing the walls, tackle the other parts of your house, following the order of work described on p 304. Paint doors and windows the same way as their interior counterparts (p 293). When painting the edges of an exterior door, match the colour of the hinge edge to the colour of the exterior, the colour of the latch edge to the interior trim. When painting steps, patios, or decks, block off their entrance with sawhorses or rope to prevent traffic over wet paint.

Fences and other outdoor structures are probably best painted with a paint sprayer. A portable sprayer (p 296) will cover small areas, but a larger airless or compressor-type sprayer will speed major jobs. Select one with a capacity of at least 25 litres and a long hose. If you hire the sprayer, ask the agent to show you how to use and clean it. Read the information given on p 296 before beginning to use the sprayer.

Cladding

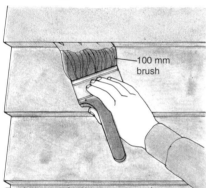

Begin by coating bottom edge of each course of boards with a brush. Clear up drips immediately with your brush. Do several courses at a time.

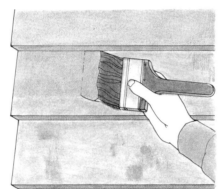

Next, paint along length of each course with short strokes of wide brush. Force paint into any cracks. To avoid lap marks, do entire course before starting next one.

Shingles

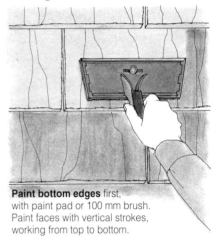

Paint bottom edges first, with paint pad or 100 mm brush. Paint faces with vertical strokes, working from top to bottom.

Exterior trim

Hold paint shield over areas adjacent to trim to protect them from paint. Alternatively, cover these areas with masking material.

Patio or deck

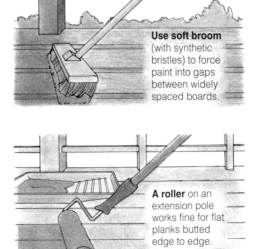

Use soft broom (with synthetic bristles) to force paint into gaps between widely spaced boards.

A roller on an extension pole works fine for flat planks butted edge to edge.

Concrete

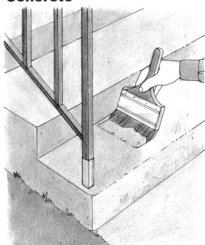

Apply stoep paint by stroking 100 to 150 mm coarse-bristle brush first in one direction, then the other. Force paint into angles and surface irregularities. Mask base of railings with tape.

Using a sprayer

Spray wooden cladding in two steps. Paint bottom edges first (inset). To paint the faces, hold spray gun 200 to 250 mm from surface and at right angle to it (p 296). For even application, overlap strokes by about one-third on each pass.

For fences, furniture, and other items that don't have solid surfaces, choose a windless day and block overspray with a shield such as a large piece of cardboard braced against a ladder.

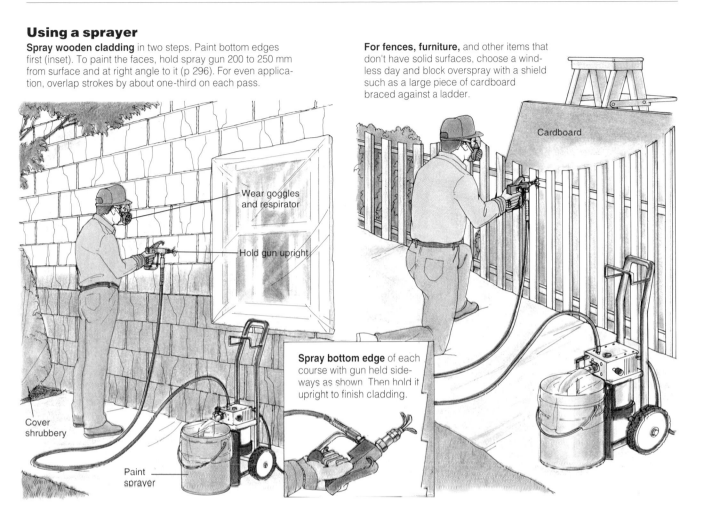

Wear goggles and respirator

Hold gun upright

Cover shrubbery

Paint sprayer

Cardboard

Spray bottom edge of each course with gun held sideways as shown. Then hold it upright to finish cladding.

Paint and plasterwork

The rate at which paint deteriorates depends on how well the surface was prepared and on exposure to wind, rain and, especially, direct heat. In general, the outside of a house needs painting about every five years. Try to schedule painting during a dry spell, and avoid painting on windy days – dust and dirt will adhere to the new surface. If it starts to rain, stop painting at once and wait until the surface has completely dried out before you start painting again – never paint a damp surface. In addition to the information given here, see also pp 290-296.

If scraping and high-pressure spraying (p 305) fail to produce a surface suitable for re-painting, try brushing the affected areas. Use a stiff wire brush and work from the top down.

Most of the stains on plasterwork are caused by rust originating with gutters, downpipes and their fasteners. The metal causing the rust stains will almost always need to be replaced so, where possible, use galvanized or other non-rusting materials. If you can't replace the rusted parts, scrape or sand them until you reach shiny metal, then prime them carefully before repainting. (Many chemical rust-removers are available, but not all are satisfactory.)

Make sure that all exposed cement or concrete, including new repairs and patches, is properly primed before you begin painting. Alkali-resistant or stabilizing primer should be used.

For painting a very deeply textured finish, try using a thickly bristled dust-pan brush loaded with paint from a roller tray. It's less tiring than using a conventional brush over rough surfaces and the sweeping motion spreads the paint well.

If downpipes and walls are to be coated with different paints, wrap a collar of paper as protection around each pipe before you start painting the wall behind it.

Never throw away tins containing wet enamel paint or solvent – the liquid could ignite spontaneously. To recyle solvents, pour the used liquid into a container, seal it, and allow the paint particles to settle out. Then pour off the clean solvent for re-use.

Because of the wide variety of patterns and styles available, choosing a wallcovering can be difficult. Before selecting a covering, consider the room's dominant architectural style and its furniture and furnishings. The covering should be compatible with its surroundings.

The covering's colour, pattern, texture and overall design will influence a room's look. 'Advancing' warm and dark colours make surfaces appear closer or larger, whereas 'receding' cool colours make surfaces seem farther away or smaller.

Vertical stripes or patterns with an upward movement add height. Borders and friezes can be used effectively near ceilings, as chair rails and as frames around architectural elements to enhance or alter a room's appearance.

Generally, choose patterns in proportion to the room size, and if you're mixing coverings, keep the colours alike but vary the pattern sizes. Look at the whole picture, especially if rooms flow into one another, and remember that many wallcoverings have companion fabrics and borders.

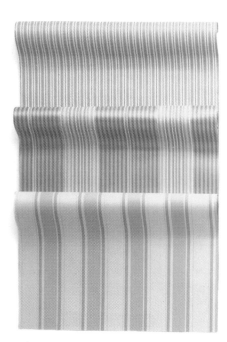

Stripes (left) are easy to match. But if the walls are bumpy or aren't plumb, the straight lines will show up these defects.

Random patterns (right) don't need matching unless one side of the sheet is 'shaded' (darker than the other). Wall defects will not be as noticeable as with striped coverings.

Small patterns (below, left) are best used in small areas, such as a kitchen where cupboards leave little uncovered wall space, but they can also be used in large rooms with matching upholstery. When hanging sheets, some patterns will match straight across; others are drop patterns – the sheets must be staggered to align the patterns.

Large patterns (below, centre and right) are best suited to big rooms. Light colours are less likely to overwhelm the room. You may want to use a large pattern on one wall and a smaller related pattern on the other walls.

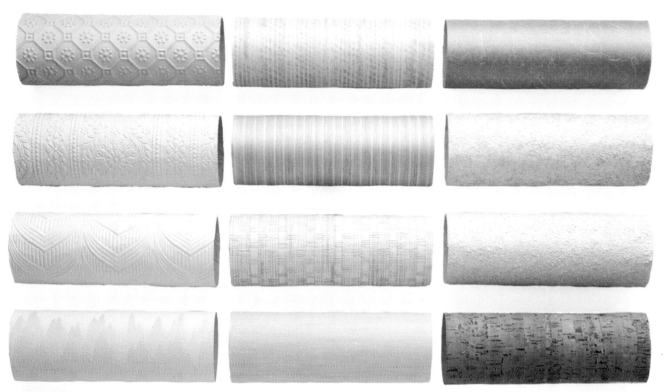

High-relief and expanded vinyls are embossed. High-relief vinyls (top three) have patterns that stand out noticeably; apply paint after hanging the covering. Expanded vinyl (bottom) is raised slightly to add texture.

Natural-look coverings include string, hessian and grass-cloth materials. Although the textures don't require matching, the colour will vary from roll to roll. The individual rolls may also 'shade'. Before hanging these coverings, arrange the sheets to match the colour.

Exotic coverings include, from top to bottom, rice paper backed with paper (unbacked versions have a translucent look); ceramic chips and false stone (their bumpy surfaces make it more difficult to cut clean seams); and cork, which should be hung over a lining

Lining (right) is necessary under silk, unbacked fabrics, cork and foils. It gives a smooth, uniformly porous surface that has a neutral pH. It may also eliminate shrinkage and absorb excess moisture.

Plaster-saturated coverings are ideal for covering wallboard, concrete block, cracked plaster and other problem walls.

Borders are made to complement wallcoverings and to be used by themselves as trim on painted walls. They may have, for instance, floral designs or patterns that appeal to young children, or the borders may be embossed to imitate architectural details.

Three kinds of patterns

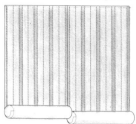

Random match. Easy to hang; design either may not align or may align anywhere.

Straight-across match. Easy to hang; design flows across strips when top edges align.

Drop match. Harder to hang; design runs diagonally; every other strip aligns at ceiling.

Creating illusions with wallcovering

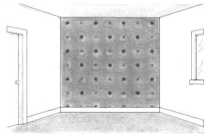

Create a cosy feeling in a high-ceilinged room by adding a wide border at the top and bottom of the walls.

Foreshorten a long, narrow room by covering one short wall. Choose a pattern that suits the room's proportions.

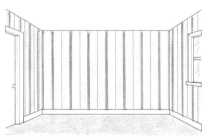

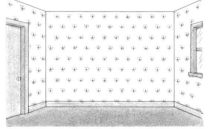

Add height to a room by choosing a vertical pattern, but avoid straight-line designs if walls are badly damaged.

Expand a confined space, or hide wall irregularities, by covering the walls with a medium-size overall pattern.

Estimating quantity

Find area of room by multiplying length by width, multiplying the result by 2, and then multiplying that result by the room's height. To determine number of rolls needed, divide square metres of room by that of roll; then add 1 roll. Straight-across patterns with large repeats may require extra rolls.

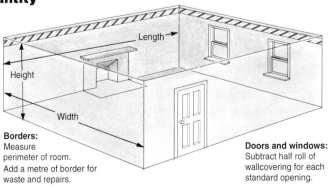

Borders: Measure perimeter of room. Add a metre of border for waste and repairs.

Doors and windows: Subtract half roll of wallcovering for each standard opening.

Wallcoverings are classified by the base material, or ground, onto which the design is printed – it may be paper, vinyl or fabric. Often this ground provides the background colour for the design. In thicker products, the ground is laminated to a backing, or substrate. In thinner ones the ground and the substrate may be one and the same. Other terms refer to ease of care and removal. *Washable* coverings can be sponged with mild detergent; *scrubbable* ones can withstand more vigorous scrubbing (p 319). Both the ground and the substrate of a *strippable* material can be removed, but the substrate of a *peelable* covering must be removed separately (p 312).

When you set out to choose a wallcovering, take along some fabric samples and paint chips or colour cards from the area you are decorating. If you plan to mix two patterns, remember that the colours must match but the scale needn't. In fact, the greater the difference in scale, the better. Even a flowered border can complement a striped covering if the colours are a good match. However, you must also consider durability (see table) and ease of installation. Many coverings come pre-pasted; you can either cover the back with water or soak the strips in a water tray. For unpasted wallcoverings, you cover the back with the appropriate adhesive.

The sample book or the roll's packaging should indicate the amount of wall space a roll will cover. A single standard roll is 10 m long and 530 mm wide, although not all come in metric sizes. (To convert square feet to square metres, multiply square feet by 0,093. To obtain sq ft, multiply sq m by 10,8). Avoid colour variations by making sure all rolls have the same lot number. (To minimize variations on some random-match patterns, install them with alternate strips reversed top to bottom.) Take samples of your choices home and tape them to the wall for 24 hrs to see how you like them under changing light conditions.

Sorting out wallcoverings

Type	Description	Typical location	Ease of hanging	Cleaning	Durability	Cost*
Paper	Traditional wallcovering; consists of single layer of patterned or coloured paper	Dry medium- to light-wear areas, such as living rooms, bedrooms	Medium (tends to tear easily)	Non-washable	Poor	R
Vinyl-coated paper	A paper substrate with a thin layer of vinyl sprayed on during manufacture. Usually pre-pasted. Strippable	Any room	Easy	Medium	Medium	R
Fabric-backed vinyl	Fabric substrate covered with solid vinyl ground	Any room	Easy	Easy	Very durable	RR
Solid vinyl	These have a paper or fabric substrate onto which has been laminated a solid vinyl film	Heavy-wear areas, such as children's and recreation rooms, or rooms prone to moisture, such as bathrooms, laundry rooms, and kitchens	Medium	Easy	Very durable	RRR
Expanded vinyl	During manufacture the surface of a solid vinyl sheet is 'expanded', raising relief patterns for an embossed look. Sometimes called 'foamed vinyl'	Medium-wear areas, such as bedrooms, living rooms, dining rooms. Good for uneven surfaces	Easy	Medium	Medium	RR
High-reliefs (Lincrusta, Anaglypta)	Moulded wallcoverings with highly defined relief patterns. Some are permanently attached to the surface; others are used for borders	Good for cracked or uneven surfaces	Medium to difficult (requires painting after mounting). Some require professional installation	Medium	Very durable	RRR
Mylar	Metallic-looking wallcoverings with paper or fabric substrate. May have a thin vinyl coating	Smooth surfaces only Used for decorative effect in hallways, small rooms. Bright sun or lighting creates undesirable reflective glare	Difficult **	Medium	Medium	RR
Hand prints, screen prints	Hand-made patterns applied over wall-covering with paper or fabric substrate. Most have thin vinyl coating over pattern. Paint texture creates relief in some; others can be custom-coloured	Dry light wear surfaces	Difficult **	Medium	Least durable	RRR
Naturals	Made of grass cloth, string or other material over paper substrate	Clean, dry light-wear surfaces	Difficult **	Non-washable	Poor	RRR
Cork	Layers of cork over paper substrate. Available in varying thicknesses and textures	Light-wear surfaces where additional sound insulation is desired.	Difficult **	Medium	Medium	RRR
Fabrics	Wallcoverings made of a textile or fabric, usually with no substrate	Clean, dry light-wear surfaces	Difficult **	Non-washable	Poor	RRR
Rice paper	Translucent type has no substrate; opaque type has paper substrate. Usually has a thin vinyl coating	Light-wear surfaces	Difficult **	Non-washable	Poor	RRR
Ceramic chip, false stone	A layer of tiny rough chips or flakes on a paper substrate	Medium- to light-wear areas, such as living rooms, bedrooms	Difficult	Non-washable	Poor	RRR
Plaster-saturated	Gypsum-saturated material. Can be covered with other wallcovering	Damaged, unsightly surfaces	Difficult	Easy	Very durable	RR
Lining paper	Unpatterned paper or fabric. Often applied under delicate special coverings or used to cover damaged surfaces	Damaged or uneven surfaces, or wherever specified for installation under specialty coverings	Easy (pp 312–313)	Not necessary	Very durable	R

*Cost: R – Inexpensive, RR – Medium price range, RRR – More expensive
** Requires professional installation

Although you can apply new wallcovering over old, it's generally better to strip off the old covering and adhesive (and if you are hanging vinyl wallcovering, it's essential). Buy a commercial remover product from your wallcovering supplier or hardware shop and follow the manufacturer's instructions for mixing it into a solution.

To remove built-up layers of wallcovering, or covering that has been painted over, you may be able to hire a steamer. Learn how to operate the steamer before leaving the supplier or hire centre, and check occasionally during use to make sure that the water tank doesn't run dry. Follow all safety instructions included with the tool, and wear goggles and gloves.

Whatever stripping method you choose, protect the room (p 290) before starting. Lay a disposable drop cloth on the floor, tape it to the skirting board and cover it with newspapers to absorb the solution. When you have finished, gather up the papers in the drop cloth and dispose of them.

If your walls are rough-textured or damaged, disguise the flaws by choosing a high-relief or fabric-backed vinyl covering. Even after repairing holes and dents (pp 288–289), you may need to cover irregular surfaces with

Removing wallcovering

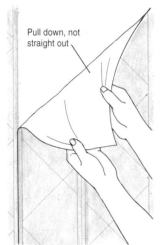

Pull down, not straight out

For strippable and peelable coverings: Loosen covering at corner and gently peel each strip from wall. For peelable covering, soak remaining substrate and adhesive with wallcovering remover for 10 min, then scrape with wide putty knife.

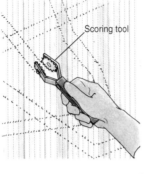

Scoring tool

Stripping with solution: 1. First score covering in crisscross pattern with scoring tool or utility knife so that solution can penetrate to the adhesive layer. Be careful not to damage wallboard or plaster.

2. Roll or sponge solution onto walls (or spray onto surface with a tank-type garden sprayer). Let soak into covering for amount of time specified on remover's label. When paper bubbles up, it's ready to be stripped.

3. Soak tight spots (such as corners or narrow strips beside cupboards) by applying solution with a plastic spray bottle.

4. Scrape off wallcovering with scraper or wide putty knife. Then saturate adhesive with remover solution and scrape off. Rinse surface with clean hot water. Allow it to dry, then apply sealer or size.

Using a steamer

Steamer

1. Fill unit with clean water before plugging it in. Steamer is ready to use when vapour emerges from holes in baseplate.

Baseplate

2. Hold steamer against (but not touching) surface for 15 sec or until area around plate is moist. Scrape with scraper or wide flexible putty knife with one hand while steaming adjacent area with the other.

Stiff nylon brush

3. After scraping, clean surface by scrubbing with nylon brush and solution of either phosphate-free trisodium or 1 part bleach to 4 parts water. Allow surface to dry; then apply sealer or size.

lining paper. This improves both the appearance and the adhesion of a wallcovering, and it is essential for certain delicate coverings. Leave a 3 mm gap at the edges and seams of lining paper, and plan the wallcovering seams to fall elsewhere than on the paper seams.

Some surfaces should also be prepared with a primer/sealer. A sealed wall is uniform and will prevent moisture and residue from affecting the covering's adhesive. A 'universal' acrylic latex primer is easy to clean up and can be tinted to match the background of the wallcovering. Use it in high-moisture areas such as bathrooms and over new wallboard, existing wallcoverings that cannot be removed and surfaces that have been repaired.

You can also improve the adhesion of a wallcovering by first applying liquid *size* to a prepared wall. In addition, size makes it easier to slide the wallcovering into place. Size is not required if you use a pre-mixed vinyl adhesive.

Lightly sand painted surfaces and wash with detergent. (Sanding gives 'tooth' to glossy surfaces and improves the adhesion of the wallcovering.) Rinse with clean water and let dry. After preparing the surfaces, paint the ceiling and trim to avoid splattering paint on the new wallcovering.

Applying sealer and size

Spread sealer or size evenly over surface with short-nap roller or 150 mm paste brush. Allow 1 hr to dry before hanging wallcovering.

After repairing painted walls, cover repairs with sealer, then wash walls.

Hanging lining paper

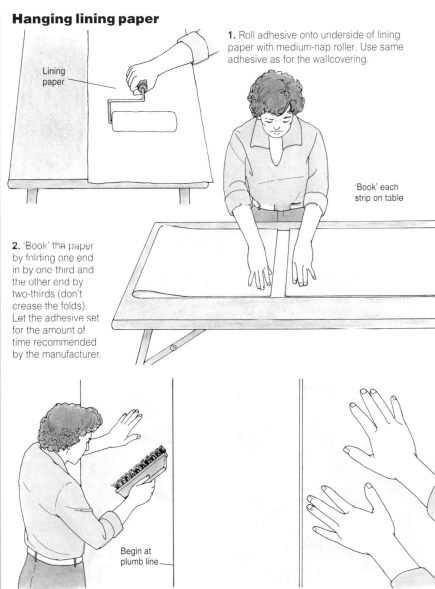

1. Roll adhesive onto underside of lining paper with medium-nap roller. Use same adhesive as for the wallcovering.

Lining paper

'Book' each strip on table

2. 'Book' the paper by folding one end in by one-third and the other end by two-thirds (don't crease the folds). Let the adhesive set for the amount of time recommended by the manufacturer.

Begin at plumb line

3. Carry liner to wall and unfurl on wall as you smooth it with a 300 mm smoothing brush. Leave a slight space at wall edges and trim.

4. Do not butt strips at seams. Let paper dry for 36 hr, or until it does not indent when pressed with a finger.

Planning the layout

Plan a mismatch in an inconspicuous corner. You may start hanging at this point, or use it as an end point, beginning directly across the room and working back towards it, first from one direction, then the other.

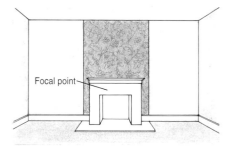

If pattern is large or room has strong focal point or wall, centre a strip (or seam) at focal point. Work out from both sides until you reach the end point.

Mark location of each strip around room with level (mark width of strip on level with tape). Re-arrange guidelines as needed to avoid awkward pattern breaks and so that strips at corners will be no less than 75 mm wide.

To guide installation, snap chalked plumb line at starting point for each wall.

Before you begin, establish both where you will start and where you will finish hanging the strips, and decide how you will handle potentially awkward areas such as corners and around windows and doors (pp 316–317). To help prevent errors, pencil in guidelines to indicate the position of each strip. Because paper and pre-pasted strippable wallcoverings may expand up to 12 mm when wet, you must determine a strip's true width before marking guidelines. To do so, cut a 50 mm strip from the roll, briefly submerge it in water, let it expand for 10 minutes and then measure its new width.

Some wallcoverings have arrows printed on the back to indicate which way the pattern should run. Decide how you want to break the pattern at the intersection of the wall and the ceiling. It's usually best not to cut through a design element, particularly if the design is strong. Remember that you'll be adding 50 mm to both the top and the bottom of each strip for trimming at the ceiling and skirting board, so allow for this in your measurements. For a drop-match pattern, align the second strip to the first by eye before cutting it (facing page). Cutting a drop-match pattern from alternating rolls reduces waste. With a straight-match pattern you can cut as many strips as possible from each roll.

Check for flaws in every roll by re-rolling it in the opposite direction – this also helps to uncurl and loosen the wallcovering. Plan to cut and paste two strips of covering first – then if there are no problems, continue to cut several strips at a time (most manufacturers will not accept returned rolls from which more than two strips have been cut). Sometimes unpatterned or textured wallcoverings will be over-inked, and thus slightly darker, along one edge. To even out the colour across the wall, turn every other strip upside down so that similarly shaded edges meet.

To hang unpasted covering, you'll need a good-size work table and a paint roller or paste brush for applying the paste. Choose the type of paste recommended by the wallcovering manufacturer, and follow the directions for mixing it. A kitchen whisk is useful for stirring out lumps.

You can purchase a special water tray in which to wet a pre-pasted covering. Follow the instructions on the wallcovering about soaking time – oversoaking may wash off some of the adhesive. An alternative to soaking a pre-pasted covering in a tray is to place the covering on the table and use a damp paint roller to wet the back of the strip thoroughly. Don't add any paste to a pre-pasted wallcovering. It may be incompatible with the existing adhesive.

After hanging each strip, smooth out any air bubbles with a 300 mm smoothing brush (choose short bristles for vinyl, longer for paper) or a plastic smoother. You'll also need a seam roller to smooth seams and edges. As you finish hanging each strip, sponge off excess adhesive with clean water, then dry the covering with a clean cloth. It's best to keep all surfaces clean while you're working – if you try to remove dried adhesive later, you may damage the covering.

Cutting a drop-match covering

Cut strip from first roll (A) to length plus 50 mm at top and bottom (for trimming), using utility knife and straightedge. Mark top with T. Weight strip to prevent it slipping off table.

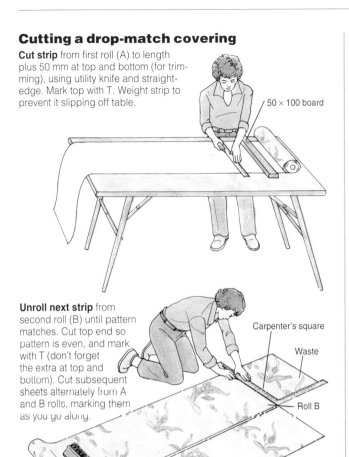

50 × 100 board

Unroll next strip from second roll (B) until pattern matches. Cut top end so pattern is even, and mark with T (don't forget the extra at top and bottom). Cut subsequent sheets alternately from A and B rolls, marking them as you go along.

Carpenter's square

Waste

Roll B

Roll A

Pasting the strips

Re-roll pre-pasted covering from bottom to top (with pattern facing in), and submerge in water tray (right) for about 10 sec. Or unfurl strip on table and wet back with saturated paint roller (see box below).

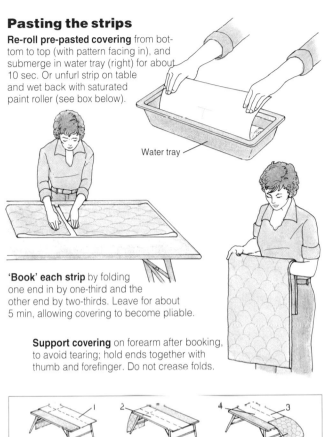

Water tray

'Book' each strip by folding one end in by one-third and the other end by two-thirds. Leave for about 5 min, allowing covering to become pliable.

Support covering on forearm after booking, to avoid tearing; hold ends together with thumb and forefinger. Do not crease folds.

Book end

For unpasted covering, keep extra adhesive off work surface (where it could damage the covering) by working out from centre of strip toward surface edge, re-positioning covering as shown. Make sure to paste all edges completely.

Hanging the covering

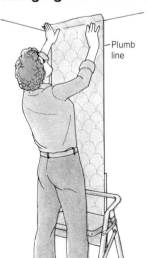

Plumb line

Align first strip against plumb line, smoothing upper section first and overlapping ceiling by 50 mm (left). Then unbook and position lower section. Work out air bubbles from centre to edges with smoothing tool. Trim top and bottom by holding straightedge tool against end and cutting with utility knife (below).

Seam roller

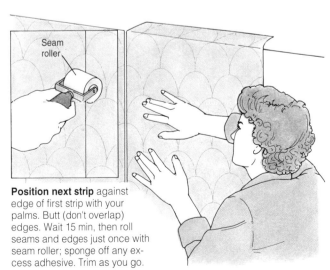

Position next strip against edge of first strip with your palms. Butt (don't overlap) edges. Wait 15 min, then roll seams and edges just once with seam roller; sponge off any excess adhesive. Trim as you go.

Paint and Wallcoverings 315

Fitting around doors and windows

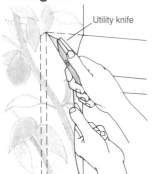

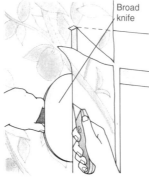

Let strip hang over door or window. Cut to rough shape, leaving 50 mm all around for trimming. Then make a diagonal cut from the outer corner of the frame.

Smooth the covering into place against side of frame; then trim away excess with razor or utility knife, guiding the blade against a tool with a straight edge.

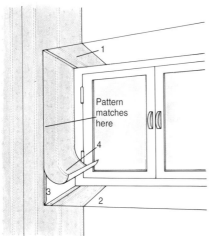

Recessed window. Let strip hang over recess. Cut horizontal line to 25 mm from edge of recess, then cut and paste to upper (1) and lower (2) parts of recess. Trim at edges. Paste 25 mm vertical flap around side edge (3). Cut an additional strip of covering to fit side of recess (4), making sure to match the pattern with strip on wall. Overlap this strip at upper and lower edges.

The walls of most rooms are likely to present some challenges. At the very least, you'll have to fit wallcovering around one door and, usually, one window. Use the techniques shown here to make clean edges at windows, doors, fireplaces, built-in bookcases and cupboards. Never try to measure and pre-cut wallcovering around obstacles. It's much easier to fit when it's up, and if you make a mistake there's usually time to re-position the wallcovering before it dries.

The broad, unobstructed surface of a typical ceiling makes it relatively easy to hang wallcovering there, but because you have to work overhead, the job can be tiring. If possible, enlist the aid of a helper to unfold the wet strips and hand them to you for positioning and smoothing. A sturdy scaffold (p 291) is a necessity for most ceiling work. If you plan to cover both the ceiling and the walls, do the ceiling first or you may damage the finished walls.

When you are using a patterned wallcovering on both ceiling and walls, remember that you will probably be able to achieve a perfect match at only one wall/ceiling intersection, so make this match at the most conspicuous place. Mismatches are less obvious in small random patterns.

If you are working on stairwell walls, you may need to stand on a scaffold (p 297). While you are on the scaffold, fitting the covering to the upper part of the wall, have a helper stand on the stairs below to fit and smooth each strip to the lower part of the wall. Be especially careful not to splash water from a wallcovering tray onto a scaffold or ladder, where it could easily cause you to slip.

Covering a room's switchplates to match the walls is a common way to finish off a wallcovering job. If you don't want to cover the plates yourself, you may be able to buy kits that allow you to simply insert a piece of the covering behind a clear plate.

Turning a corner

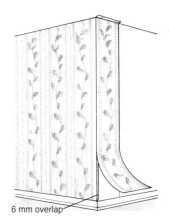

Inside corner: 1. Measure from edge of last strip to corner at top, middle, and bottom; cut the next strip 3 mm wider than the widest dimension.

2. Hang cut strip, wrapping 3 mm around corner. Measure narrowest part of remainder of cut strip; mark plumb line on new wall this distance from corner.

3. Position remainder of strip with factory (uncut) edge against plumb line. Smooth covering into corner on top of 3 mm overlap. Trim at top and bottom.

Outside corner. Measure first strip as for inside corner, but add 6 mm allowance for corner overlap. Plumb second wall and hang strip as for inside corner.

Covering ceilings

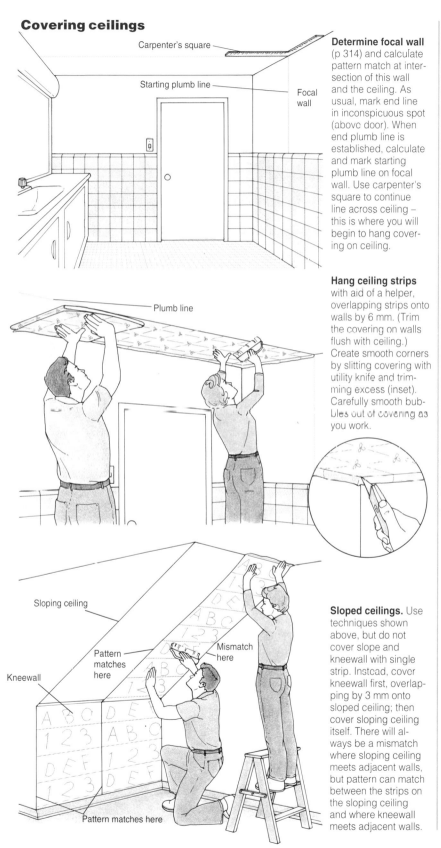

Carpenter's square

Starting plumb line

Focal wall

Plumb line

Sloping ceiling

Pattern matches here

Kneewall

Mismatch here

Pattern matches here

Determine focal wall (p 314) and calculate pattern match at intersection of this wall and the ceiling. As usual, mark end line in inconspicuous spot (above door). When end plumb line is established, calculate and mark starting plumb line on focal wall. Use carpenter's square to continue line across ceiling – this is where you will begin to hang covering on ceiling.

Hang ceiling strips with aid of a helper, overlapping strips onto walls by 6 mm. (Trim the covering on walls flush with ceiling.) Create smooth corners by slitting covering with utility knife and trimming excess (inset). Carefully smooth bubbles out of covering as you work.

Sloped ceilings. Use techniques shown above, but do not cover slope and kneewall with single strip. Instead, cover kneewall first, overlapping by 3 mm onto sloped ceiling; then cover sloping ceiling itself. There will always be a mismatch where sloping ceiling meets adjacent walls, but pattern can match between the strips on the sloping ceiling and where kneewall meets adjacent walls.

Covering curved archways

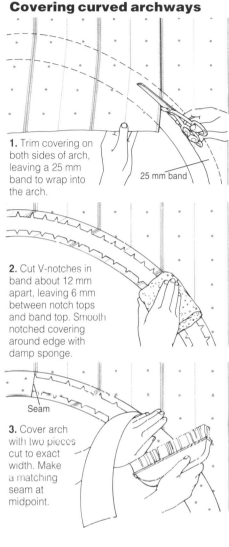

1. Trim covering on both sides of arch, leaving a 25 mm band to wrap into the arch.

25 mm band

2. Cut V-notches in band about 12 mm apart, leaving 6 mm between notch tops and band top. Smooth notched covering around edge with damp sponge.

Seam

3. Cover arch with two pieces cut to exact width. Make a matching seam at midpoint.

Working around obstacles

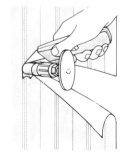

Fixtures. Cut from closest seam to fixture; fold covering back and trim around fixture, using notch-shaped cuts. Press covering down; roll seam.

Outlets and switchplates. Turn off power. Remove cover plate; make diagonal cuts in covering at corners; then trim off at edges with knife and straightedge.

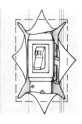

A border near the ceiling can make a room feel cosier; at chair-rail height it makes a room feel loftier. Borders can also add interest to a plain room (particularly a child's room), fill a narrow space between cupboard tops and the ceiling, or frame windows and doors. As with any wallcovering, first take home samples so that you can check them with your decor and lighting.

Prepare painted walls by sanding them with fine sandpaper. Then wash away the dust and apply a coat of wallcovering primer. On covered walls, coat the area that will accept the border with wallcovering primer (with tack). Apply a border over new wallcovering only after the latter has dried for at least 48 hours. However, if you allow for the border while planning the wallcovering layout, you can then cut each wallcovering strip to allow the border to be inset above or within it. This method yields smoother seams, but it also requires more time and skill.

Borders are usually sold in 5 m rolls. Cut pieces the length of each wall, plus 6 mm to wrap into the corners. To avoid awkward design positions at corners or obstacles, calculate the border's positioning before you hang it. If the border will frame a window or a door, avoid the problem of having a directional pattern going sideways or upside down by selecting a random pattern. When framing with a border, mitre the corner seams as shown. Use only an adhesive recommended by the border manufacturer.

Hanging a border

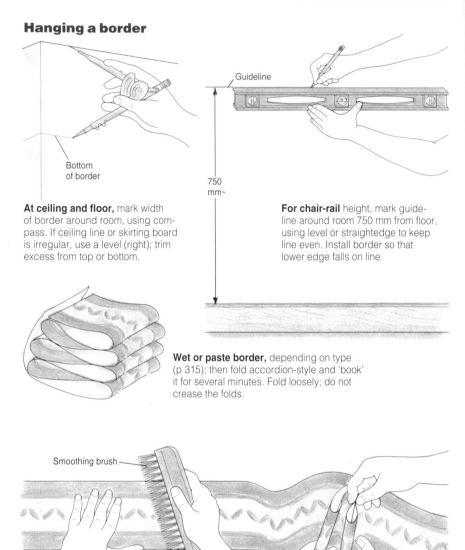

At ceiling and floor, mark width of border around room, using compass. If ceiling line or skirting board is irregular, use a level (right); trim excess from top or bottom.

For chair-rail height, mark guideline around room 750 mm from floor, using level or straightedge to keep line even. Install border so that lower edge falls on line.

Wet or paste border, depending on type (p 315); then fold accordion-style and 'book' it for several minutes. Fold loosely; do not crease the folds.

Hang border in manageable sections, with helper assisting you. Push border into place with your fingers; then smooth out air bubbles with brush or smoother.

Making tight seams

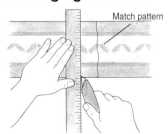

Butting seams: 1. Overlap ends and cut through both layers with a utility knife along a straightedge.

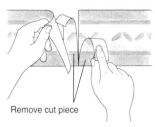

2. Remove cut pieces of both layers. Smooth ends in place with sponge; wait 15 min; then roll seam smooth.

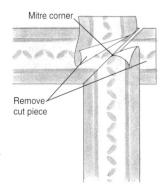

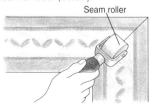

Mitre-cut corners by overlapping pieces, then cutting through both layers at 45° angle (left). Remove cut pieces of both layers, and roll seam smooth (below).

CARING FOR WALLCOVERINGS

Clean wallcoverings twice a year, following the manufacturer's directions. Wash scrubbable coverings with brush and mild detergent. Washable coverings can be lightly rubbed with a solution of water and mild detergent applied with a damp cloth or a nearly dry sponge. You can vacuum some cloth and flocked wallcoverings with a brush attachment, but delicate wallcoverings such as silk or hessian (p 311) must be professionally cleaned. Commercial cleaning solutions are also available for various types of wallcovering. Whichever product or technique you choose, first test-clean a small

patch in an inconspicuous area to ensure the cleaner won't stain or damage the wallcovering.

Many stains on non-washable coverings can be removed with either an artist's gum eraser or wallcovering cleaning dough (available at wallcovering stores). Stroke the eraser or dough downwards against the wallcovering, overlapping strokes until the stain lifts off. As the material picks up dirt, turn it to expose a fresh surface.

To remove grease or wax, cover the stain with blotting paper or paper towels, and iron over it on low heat for several seconds. Repeat, using clean

paper each time, until the spot is gone. If this doesn't work, wipe the stain with cheesecloth dampened with turpentine. If ironing causes the wax from crayons to be absorbed, gently rub off the coloured residue with moist baking soda on a damp cloth.

Stains that can't be removed any other way may be patched (below). Whenever you re-decorate, save extra wallcovering for this purpose, but remember that because of aging, a patch is bound to be a slightly different shade to the installed wallcovering. Use ordinary pre-mixed wallpaper paste or seam adhesive for patching.

Loose or torn seams and edges

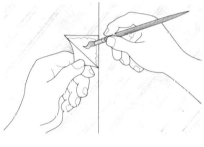

1. Brush adhesive onto wall surface and underside of covering. Press covering into place and hold for several minutes.

2. Smooth flat, and remove excess adhesive with a slightly dampened sponge. Roll seam after 15 min.

Fixing bubbles

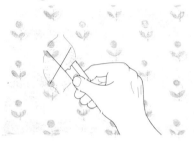

Slit bubble in X-pattern with razor blade, fold back edges and use tweezers or brush to remove grit. Insert adhesive as shown at left; smooth with sponge.

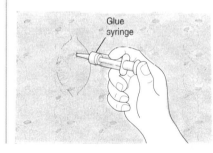

Glue syringe

For glue syringe, (often available in a kit), first make small slit with razor blade. Press out air; inject adhesive. Smooth area with seam roller or sponge.

Patching a hole or stain

Damage

Patch

Cut patch 75 mm larger than damaged area, making sure pattern matches. Tape patch over damage with draughting tape.

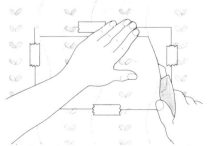

Cut through both layers beyond edge of damaged area. If possible, cut along design elements to disguise cut lines.

Remove both layers of wallcovering, scraping old covering if necessary (p 312). Paste patch in position; after 15 min, roll edges.

FLOORING

WOOD FLOORING

More resilient than stone or tile, wood flooring has a natural warm appearance that enhances almost any home. It's available in blocks, strips and planks (either solid or laminated). The flooring is sold unfinished, requiring sanding and finishing, and it's also available pre-finished. Be sure to describe the intended use of the flooring as well as what you want visually.

The final appeareance of the floor will depend on what you choose: the type of flooring (planks or blocks), the species and grade of the wood, and the finish. Have a good look at what's available, and don't make your decision on the basis of samples only. Try to examine an installed floor of the type and wood that you want, before you place your order.

Solid and laminated blocks, with small wood pieces laid in a pattern, are sold ready to install. They are also available in separate pieces, which you assemble yourself. Because the blocks are laid down side by side, complex geometric designs can be formed. Tongue-and-groove edges help align the pieces.

Parquet, a type of wood block, has small wood pieces attached to a paper backing or wire splines. They must be individually glued down. Parquet comes in the same designs as solid and laminated blocks. Although the ones shown are not finished, they are available pre-finished.

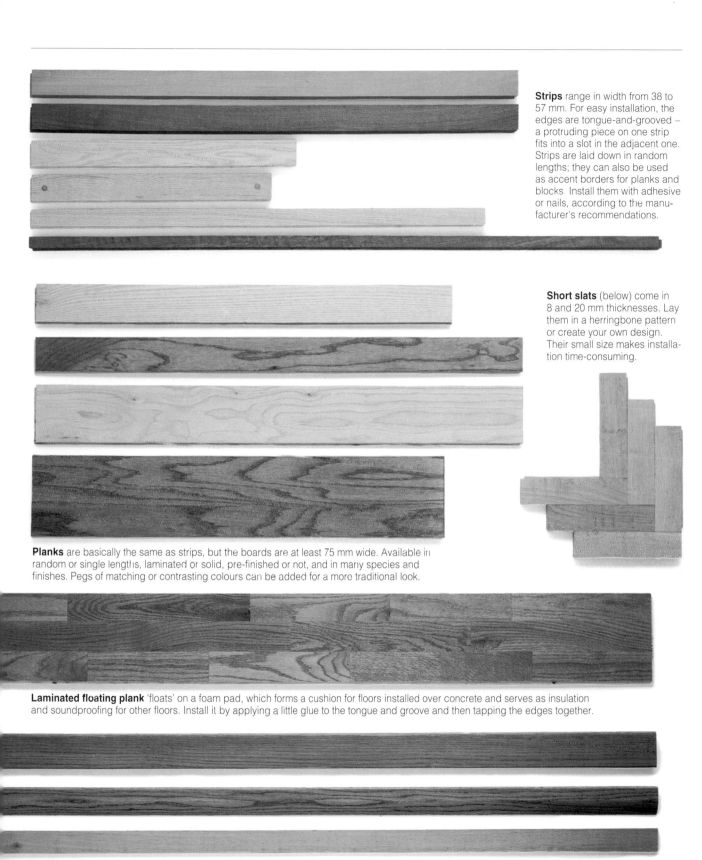

Strips range in width from 38 to 57 mm. For easy installation, the edges are tongue-and-grooved – a protruding piece on one strip fits into a slot in the adjacent one. Strips are laid down in random lengths; they can also be used as accent borders for planks and blocks. Install them with adhesive or nails, according to the manufacturer's recommendations.

Short slats (below) come in 8 and 20 mm thicknesses. Lay them in a herringbone pattern or create your own design. Their small size makes installation time-consuming.

Planks are basically the same as strips, but the boards are at least 75 mm wide. Available in random or single lengths, laminated or solid, pre-finished or not, and in many species and finishes. Pegs of matching or contrasting colours can be added for a more traditional look.

Laminated floating plank 'floats' on a foam pad, which forms a cushion for floors installed over concrete and serves as insulation and soundproofing for other floors. Install it by applying a little glue to the tongue and groove and then tapping the edges together.

Reducer strips create a transition between two types of flooring at different elevations: one of wood; the other of ceramic tile, carpeting, vinyl or another wood. These strips are useful where two rooms, such as a dining room and living room, flow into each other.

RESILIENT FLOORING

Because it is affordable and easy to install and maintain, re-silient flooring is a good choice for bathrooms and kitchens. Today's resilient flooring is usually made of vinyl (the actual vinyl content varies from product to product). It's available in 230 and 300 mm square tiles and in 2 m-wide rolled sheets. Tiles are either solid vinyl or a vinyl composition; the latter resists stains better. Sheet flooring has a base layer topped with a vinyl resin or, for added scuff resistance, a vinyl resin-urethane or vinyl resin-melamine finish. It may be cushioned with a high-density foam. Designs with texture and colour variations are better at concealing seams, scratches, substrate irregularities and dirt.

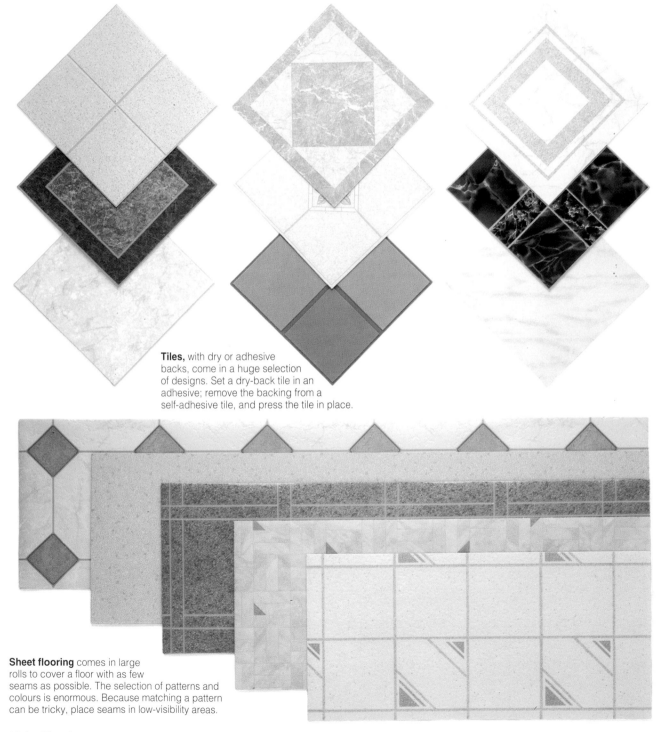

Tiles, with dry or adhesive backs, come in a huge selection of designs. Set a dry-back tile in an adhesive; remove the backing from a self-adhesive tile, and press the tile in place.

Sheet flooring comes in large rolls to cover a floor with as few seams as possible. The selection of patterns and colours is enormous. Because matching a pattern can be tricky, place seams in low-visibility areas.

PREPARING A FLOOR

Before installing wood or resilient flooring or ceramic tile, make sure the surface beneath is flat, smooth, stable and structurally sound. If it is not, the new flooring may soon crack or buckle.

The existing floor need not be made absolutely horizontal to prepare it for a new covering. Many floors in older houses sag or tilt because of settling, and if the condition is not severe, new flooring usually can be installed over the old with satisfactory results. But be alert to sagging caused by structural damage. Have an experienced builder or engineer examine subflooring, joists and other framing that appears to be weak or decayed.

To prepare an existing subfloor or a finished wood floor, vacuum and clean it thoroughly and re-seat any protruding fasteners. Then walk over the entire floor, bouncing on it as you go. Squeaks signal loose flooring; springiness indicates weak support underneath.

Also check the floor for bumps and hollows. Uneven wood flooring can be sanded (pp 332–333), but often the best way to obtain a flat, smooth surface is to cover it with liquid floor-levelling compound or a suitable filler available at hardware stores. Choose a compound that is compatible with the subfloor and the new flooring adhesive. Mix the compound according to the manufacturer's instructions, and follow all safety precautions.

Both resilient flooring and ceramic tile can be covered directly with flooring, but apply floor-levelling compound first if the surface is uneven. Before applying compound or any new flooring to a concrete slab, perform a test (right) to check for excess moisture seeping through the concrete.

Caution: Never sand or remove existing resilient flooring unless you are absolutely certain that it does not contain asbestos. (If it does, the dust created would be hazardous.) Before removing resilient flooring of uncertain age or type, call your local health department for advice on safe handling techniques and local regulations.

Checking for flatness

Use straightedge board or long level to find bumps and hollows over 3 mm high; sand or fill. If possible, level raised flooring by re-securing or removing it.

Stiffening a springy floor

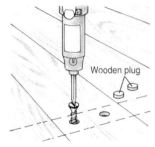

Eliminate squeaks by driving glue-coated shims between joists and flooring (far left). Do not use wedges; they will lift flooring. If repairs cannot be made from underneath, fasten loose flooring to joists with screws from above (left); fill holes with wood plugs.

Close a long gap between flooring and warped joist by attaching 50 × 100 or wider timber along upper edge of joist (right). Brace springy joists by installing rows of wood or metal cross-bridging strips at 2 to 2,5 m intervals (far right).

Applying floor-levelling compound

Spread levelling compound with trowel or wooden float. For concrete slab, first perform a moisture test (inset): Clean and sand a small area and cover it with multipurpose vinyl adhesive. Tape down a patch of resilient sheet flooring. Remove after 72 hr; if adhesive is still wet, moisture is seeping through slab.

An underlay provides a smooth, flat surface for all types of new flooring. It gives extra support for heavy materials such as ceramic tile, provides a good nailing surface for a solid wood floor, and can provide moisture resistance. Choose an underlay that is appropriate for the type of flooring you wish to install and be sure that it is thick enough to cover any unevenness and imperfections in the subfloor.

Removing moulding

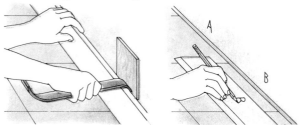

Pry moulding gently from wall with flat pry bar or stiff-bladed putty knife (left); work gently to minimize chipping or splintering. Protect wall with scrap wood. Label pieces and wall areas with matching letters to simplify re-installation (right). If moulding is old and damaged, or if splintering and chipping are unavoidable, consider replacing the moulding.

Installing plywood underlay

Place panels so surface grain is 90° to joists. Stagger end joints. Leave 3 mm gap between panels and 12 mm gap between panels and walls. Nail panels through joists. Fasten every 15 mm at the joists at panel edges and every 250 mm at inner joists.

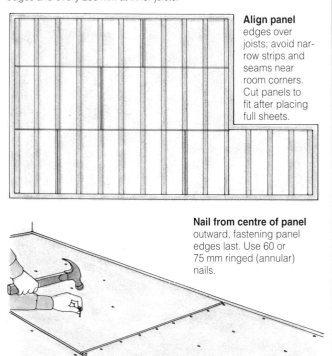

Align panel edges over joists; avoid narrow strips and seams near room corners. Cut panels to fit after placing full sheets.

Nail from centre of panel outward, fastening panel edges last. Use 60 or 75 mm ringed (annular) nails.

Before installing new flooring, you can take measures to reduce moisture and increase comfort. For example, if the floor is over an earth bed, lay damp-course sheet on the earth to act as a moisture retarder. If the floor is above a living space, add a layer of insulation to muffle sounds.

Existing floors. Some types of flooring can be installed directly over existing flooring. However, you should always remove carpeting and make sure that the floor is clean, dry and grease-free. Find positions of underfloor joists and make a mark opposite their ends low on the wall. Underlay panels can be installed over flooring that is dry, flat and securely attached to the subfloor. Adding an underlay and the new flooring will raise the floor's height. If the difference is pronounced, install threshold reducer strips and cut doors and frames as necessary (p 329).

Caution: Resilient flooring can create hazardous dust and waste when it is removed.

To prepare a floor for ceramic tile or wood parquet, use 25 mm exterior-grade plywood; for other wood flooring and for resilient flooring, use 19 mm exterior grade plywood or 12 mm hardboard. Flooring-grade chipboard may also be used. (Never use fibreboard or particleboard as underlay.)

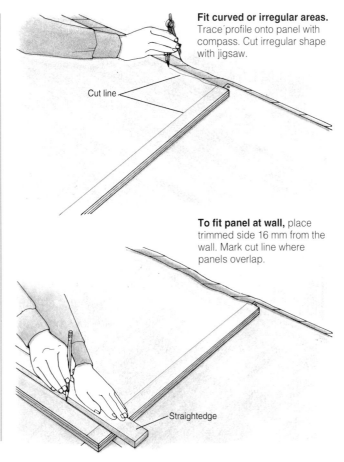

Fit curved or irregular areas. Trace profile onto panel with compass. Cut irregular shape with jigsaw.

Cut line

To fit panel at wall, place trimmed side 16 mm from the wall. Mark cut line where panels overlap.

Straightedge

Lay flooring-grade chipboard where extra moisture resistance is needed under ceramic tile. Whether you install flooring-grade chipboard or plywood, always leave a small gap between the panels, and between the walls and the underlay, to allow the panels to expand or move. Fill the gaps between the chipboard and the wall with a flexible caulk; leave the gaps in a plywood underlay unfilled.

Concrete slab. Parquet, laminated strip and plank flooring, ceramic tile, and all types of resilient flooring can be glued with adhesive or mastic directly to dry, sealed concrete (p 325). (Never glue down planks or strips of solid wood.) If the concrete slab is below ground level, you will need to provide a moisture barrier. For solid wood flooring, embed short lengths of 50 × 100 timber, called *screeds* or *sleepers,* in mastic as shown at right. Strip or plank flooring up to 100 mm wide can be attached to the screeds; to support wider planks, attach a plywood underlay. For ceramic tile, spread thinbed adhesive and lay in it a moisture barrier of polythene specifically designated for this purpose.

Exterior concrete slab. Ceramic tile can be laid over an exterior concrete slab if it drains well and has been laid with the correct expansion joints (pp 206–207, 212–213).

Installing chipboard

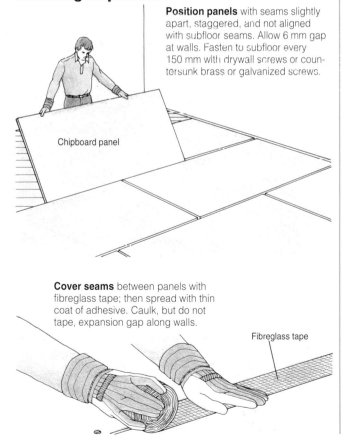

Position panels with seams slightly apart, staggered, and not aligned with subfloor seams. Allow 6 mm gap at walls. Fasten to subfloor every 150 mm with drywall screws or countersunk brass or galvanized screws.

Chipboard panel

Cover seams between panels with fibreglass tape; then spread with thin coat of adhesive. Caulk, but do not tape, expansion gap along walls.

Fibreglass tape

Preparing a concrete slab

1. Clean a slab when it is completely dry, and if necessary even it out with levelling compound (p 325). Then spread waterproofing mastic with a notched trowel. Start at far corner and work towards doorway.

2. Allow to dry following maker's directions. Then cover mastic with polythene film. Begin at doorway and roll film towards corners. Overlap sheets by 100 mm. Press film against mastic over entire area.

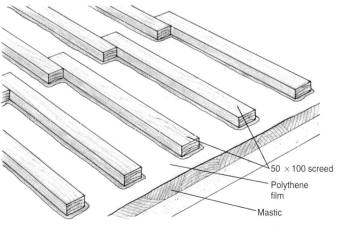

50 × 100 screed

Polythene film

Mastic

3. To attach screeds, spread runs of mastic onto polythene at 300 mm intervals on centre and perpendicular to direction of finish flooring. Embed 50 x 100 timber strips (screeds) in mastic, overlapping strips by 100 mm. (In areas of high humidity, cover screeds with an additional layer of polyethylene.) Add 20 mm underlay for planks wider than 100 mm.

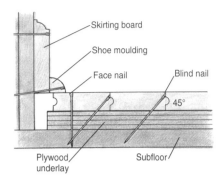

Skirting board
Shoe moulding
Face nail
Blind nail
45°
Plywood underlay
Subfloor

Strip and plank boards require a strong support system that will hold the fasteners securely. The flooring can run either perpendicular to or diagonally across the floor joists or screeds. Leave a 20 mm expansion gap between the flooring and the two walls that run parallel to the flooring (none is needed at the end walls).

First of all, find out how square the room is and how parallel the walls are. (Variation is likely so cut and taper pieces to fit as described.) To determine how close to square the corners are, measure between diagonal corners (p 149). To locate unparallel areas, measure between walls that will be parallel to the flooring strips. Variation between end walls matters less because you can easily cut ends to fit.

To accurately align the flooring, string a baseline on the floor parallel to the intended direction of the floorboards. In a small or average-size room, locate the baseline close to the longest or most noticeable wall. In a room over 6 m wide, locate the baseline near the centre so that the flooring can be installed by working outward from it in each direction.

Measure between the baseline and the wall every foot or so. If the wall is bowed or snakes, use a jigsaw to shape the first course, or row, of boards. If the room is less than 25 mm out of parallel, taper the last course; if more than 25 mm, divide the variation between the first and last courses. Mark the pieces that need tapering (p 326); then rip the boards to the correct taper. To make the adjustment less obvious, plane the grooved edge and the tongue (or deepen the groove) of pieces in several courses. Install the shaped pieces where least noticeable.

Select the straightest pieces for the first two or three and the final three or four courses. Slightly warped boards can be pried into place; check severely warped boards for straight sections that can be cut off and used.

Face-nail the first course of flooring, grooved edge towards the wall, with a row of 60 or 75 mm nails driven vertically 25 mm from the groove. Don't nail through the groove. Sink the nails with a nail set and fill the holes. Continue fastening the first course by *blind-nailing* it at an angle through the tongued edge and into the bottom of the floorboard and the subfloor (the face and blind nails are staggered); drive these heads flush. Blind nails are hidden when the next board is put in place. Blind-nail all but the final courses. Face-nail the last two courses.

Getting started

Locate baseline. Near each corner of the wall where you will begin installing boards, measure and mark the width of your flooring plus 20 mm for expansion joint.

Roll out building felt over plywood underlay, overlapping pieces by 100 mm. Felt minimizes squeaks in the flooring.

Stretch string between nails driven into baseline marks in each corner. Test-fit first strip parallel to baseline. Mark irregular areas.

Lay out several courses before nailing. Arrange strips so that joints are staggered at least 150 mm apart from course to course. Avoid clustering short boards and creating distracting patterns. Strips at ends of courses should be at least 200 mm long.

Fitting pieces

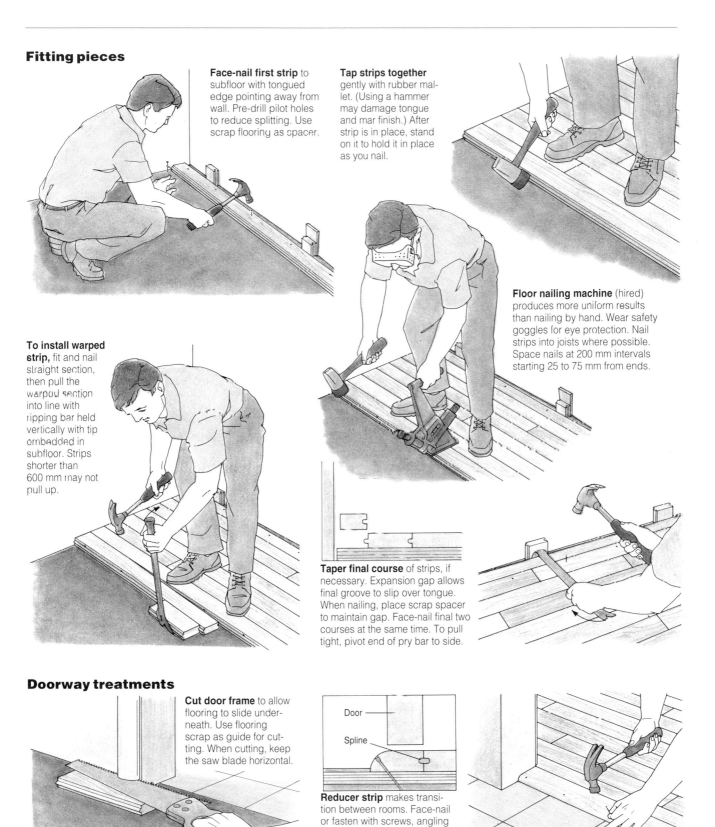

Face-nail first strip to subfloor with tongued edge pointing away from wall. Pre-drill pilot holes to reduce splitting. Use scrap flooring as spacer.

Tap strips together gently with rubber mallet. (Using a hammer may damage tongue and mar finish.) After strip is in place, stand on it to hold it in place as you nail.

Floor nailing machine (hired) produces more uniform results than nailing by hand. Wear safety goggles for eye protection. Nail strips into joists where possible. Space nails at 200 mm intervals starting 25 to 75 mm from ends.

To install warped strip, fit and nail straight section, then pull the warped section into line with ripping bar held vertically with tip embedded in subfloor. Strips shorter than 600 mm may not pull up.

Taper final course of strips, if necessary. Expansion gap allows final groove to slip over tongue. When nailing, place scrap spacer to maintain gap. Face-nail final two courses at the same time. To pull tight, pivot end of pry bar to side.

Doorway treatments

Cut door frame to allow flooring to slide underneath. Use flooring scrap as guide for cutting. When cutting, keep the saw blade horizontal.

Door

Spline

Reducer strip makes transition between rooms. Face-nail or fasten with screws, angling them toward new flooring. If no tongue and groove, glue spline into routed grooves.

WOOD LAMINATE AND PARQUET FLOORING

Laying a floating floor

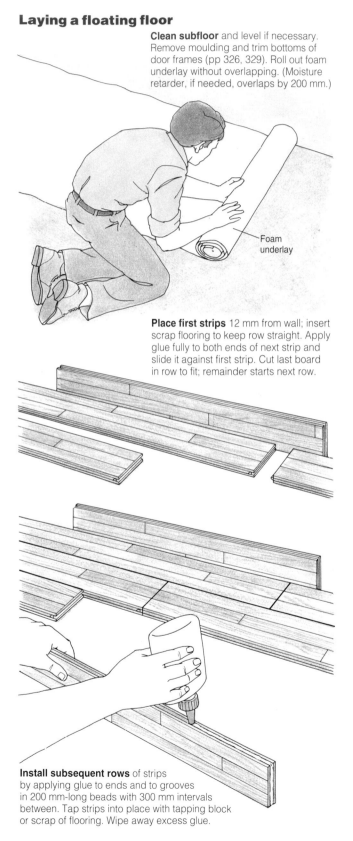

Clean subfloor and level if necessary. Remove moulding and trim bottoms of door frames (pp 326, 329). Roll out foam underlay without overlapping. (Moisture retarder, if needed, overlaps by 200 mm.)

Foam underlay

Place first strips 12 mm from wall; insert scrap flooring to keep row straight. Apply glue fully to both ends of next strip and slide it against first strip. Cut last board in row to fit; remainder starts next row.

Install subsequent rows of strips by applying glue to ends and to grooves in 200 mm-long beads with 300 mm intervals between. Tap strips into place with tapping block or scrap of flooring. Wipe away excess glue.

The easiest type of flooring to install is laminated strip flooring. It requires no nailing; you either glue the pieces to each other, creating a *floating* floor, or embed them in mastic applied to the sub-floor, creating a *glue-down* floor.

To prepare for a floating floor, flatten the sub-floor with floor-levelling compound (p 325), then cover it with a layer of foam sheeting supplied by the flooring manufacturer. On a concrete slab, place a layer of polythene sheeting beneath the foam as a moisture retarder.

A glue-down floor also requires a flat sub-floor and, if the floor is below ground, a layer of polythene sheeting set in mastic. If the floor is concrete, dry and above ground, you can stick most types of laminated flooring directly to it. But if the slab is at or below ground level, first glue down a sheet of polythene and install a subfloor of sleepers and plywood underlay. Then lay the flooring in mastic on the plywood. (For more on preparation, see pp 325–327.)

Parquet patterns may look best only when running in a certain direction – arrange a dozen or more squares on the floor as a test. Parquet, like ceramic and vinyl tiles, requires two perpendicular baselines that act as guides for the alignment of the tiles. Follow these lines precisely when laying parquet – the tiles may not always be exactly square.

For best results, use the special installation tools, materials and adhesives recommended or supplied by the maker. Tools include tapping blocks and pry bars designed for fitting strips into place without damaging their tongued edges or disturbing the mastic, and a trowel with precisely notched edges for applying the mastic. Cork material (available in strips, sheets and tile-size squares) fills an expansion gap that is needed between the flooring and the walls.

Mastics vary in their content, but all require a waiting period after they are applied (the length of time depends on the type). Mastic is ready to accept the tiles when it has become tacky. It stays that way for a specified time, so set the tiles during this *open* period. Trowel mastic over only as much area as you can tile in that time.

Caution: The solvents for many mastics are toxic and may be flammable. Follow the maker's safety precautions.

As you work, select squares randomly from several cartons to maximize colour uniformity over the entire floor. Before kneeling on just-laid squares, cover them with a plywood sheet. This helps embed the squares and prevents them from sliding apart. Before the mastic hardens, walk on each square or roll the floor with a hired 75 kg roller to make certain the squares adhere completely. Finish the floor except for the perimeter. Trowel mastic onto this area only after all the tiles have been cut to fit.

Caution: Trim parquet by hand or with a bandsaw or jigsaw – a table saw or a radial arm saw will cause kickback.

Allow new flooring to harden for 24 hours or as long as the maker suggests. Then cover the gaps with moulding and install a reducer strip where different floorings meet (p 329).

Layout for parquet

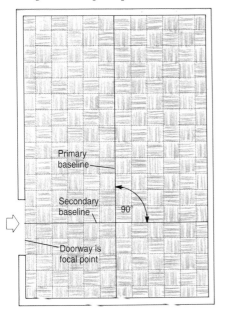

Primary baseline

Secondary baseline

90°

Doorway is focal point

Snap primary baseline parallel to longest wall. Then mark secondary baseline at 90° angle to primary line. They should cross at focal point or room's centre. To check corner for squareness: Measure 900 mm on one line, 1 200 mm on other; distance between must be exactly 1 500 mm.

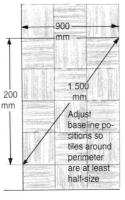

900 mm

1 200 mm

1 500 mm

Adjust baseline positions so tiles around perimeter are at least half-size.

Complete half of room. Repeat for second half

Work in one quadrant at a time

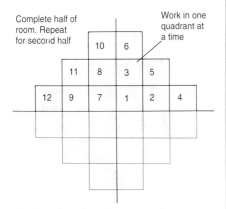

	10	6	
11	8	3	5
12	9	7	1	2	4

Starting where baselines cross, lay squares in a pyramid pattern, placing squares next to baseline and tile or in a corner formed by two tiles. This technique ensures straight rows.

Installing parquet

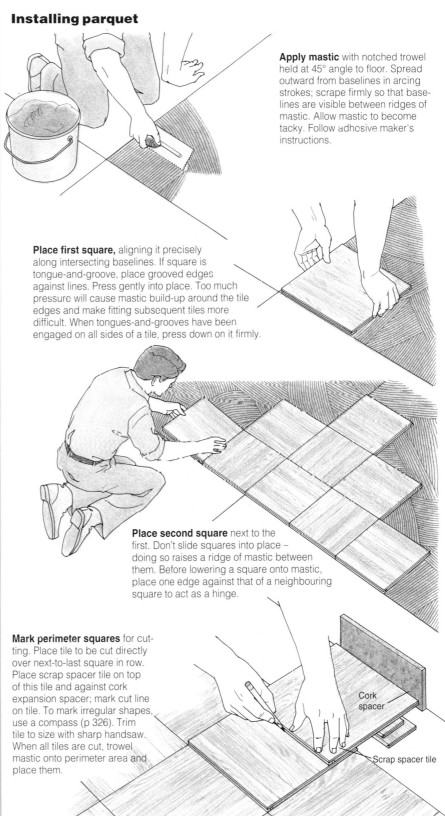

Apply mastic with notched trowel held at 45° angle to floor. Spread outward from baselines in arcing strokes; scrape firmly so that baselines are visible between ridges of mastic. Allow mastic to become tacky. Follow adhesive maker's instructions.

Place first square, aligning it precisely along intersecting baselines. If square is tongue-and-groove, place grooved edges against lines. Press gently into place. Too much pressure will cause mastic build-up around the tile edges and make fitting subsequent tiles more difficult. When tongues-and-grooves have been engaged on all sides of a tile, press down on it firmly.

Place second square next to the first. Don't slide squares into place – doing so raises a ridge of mastic between them. Before lowering a square onto mastic, place one edge against that of a neighbouring square to act as a hinge.

Mark perimeter squares for cutting. Place tile to be cut directly over next-to-last square in row. Place scrap spacer tile on top of this tile and against cork expansion spacer; mark cut line on tile. To mark irregular shapes, use a compass (p 326). Trim tile to size with sharp handsaw. When all tiles are cut, trowel mastic onto perimeter area and place them.

Cork spacer

Scrap spacer tile

Solid wood floors that are at least 19 mm thick can be restored several times during their life by sanding off the old finish and applying a new one. Thinner floors and some parquet flooring can be restored this way once or twice. Laminated flooring has a thin surface layer. Sanding will probably expose the backing underneath, so it is usually sold pre-finished.

Sanding a floor is a big job that must be done carefully. Rather than use an ordinary belt sander or a disc sander attached to an electric drill, which can easily gouge the wood, hire three large power tools – a drum sander, a special disc sander called an edger, and a buffer. The drum sander does the bulk of the work; the edger sands the perimeter of the room and wherever the drum sander cannot reach; the buffer prepares the sanded floor for each finishing coat. These machines must be handled carefully to avoid gouging the wood. Have an expert show you how to load and operate them. Obtain plenty of sandpaper, steel wool or screen for each tool. You can usually return unused portions.

Before you begin sanding, empty the room and seal all interior openings to contain the dust. Then inspect the floor for protruding nails, staples or tacks. Glue down any large splinters.

Sand the entire floor with coarse (60-grit) sandpaper, then vacuum the floor and sand it again with medium (80-grit) paper. Vacuum again and sand the floor with fine (120-grit) sandpaper. Then fill any cracks and flaws in the floor with filler. When it has dried, sand the floor with the buffer fitted with a 100-grade screen disc or 00-grade steel wool. Using a screen, called *screening,* gives a smoother surface than the steel wool.

Next apply either a stain or the first coat of finish. When it is dry, screen the surface with the buffer, and then thoroughly vacuum the floor and wipe it with a tack cloth (p 164). Repeat the process until as many coats of finish as necessary have been applied.

Caution: Follow the manufacturer's instructions exactly. Non-water-base products and their vapours are toxic, and even water-base versions can be harmful. Ventilate the area well and wear safety goggles, an SABS-approved respirator, and rubber gloves. Extinguish all pilot lights and stoves and switch off electric motors to avoid the risk of sparks setting off an explosion. To prevent exposure to fumes, the premises should be vacated for at least 24 hours after the finish has been applied.

For more on sanding, staining and finishing wood, see pp 164–169.

Sanding direction

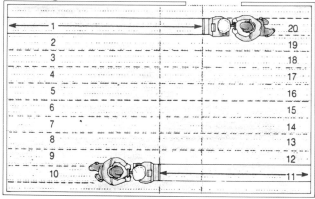

Move parallel to grain of strip or plank floor. Cover two-thirds of room by moving sander back and forth. When reversing, retrace your steps without turning machine. On forward cuts, overlap previous pass by 50 to 100 mm. When ready to sand final third of floor, switch off machine and turn sander 180°. Overlap the sanded area by 600 mm.

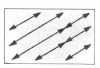

Sand parquet floor with medium-grit paper at a 45° angle, using similar sequence as for strip and plank flooring.

Make second pass with fine grit at 90° angle to first pass. Start at diagonally opposite corner.

Final pass with extra-fine grit should be parallel to room's long walls. Finish sanding with buffer and a screen.

Wood floor finishes

Finish type	Durability	Application	Upkeep and repair
Polyurethanes	Oil-base type is extremely durable; water-base type has fair durability. Both have excellent water resistance	Brush on with lamb's-wool applicator. Oil-base type dries in 12–24 hr, is easier to apply. Water-base type dries in 2–4 hr; spread carefully to avoid surface bubbles	Damp-mop to keep floor free of grit. Never apply wax or cleaner containing oil. Sand dull floor; re-coat with new finish
Varnishes	Moderate durability and water resistance. Avoid spar (marine) varnish, which is too soft for flooring	Spread with brush; usually needs 3 coats. Water-base type dries faster than solvent- or oil-base types but may raise wood grain. Keep room dust-free until dry	Dust often to remove grit. Apply wax to protect against moisture. Most repairs require stripping and re-finishing
Penetrating sealers	Fair durability; strengthens and seals wood but does not protect surface	Easiest finish to apply. Spread with lint-free cloth or lamb's-wool applicator; let stand for a time (see directions); then wipe off excess	Dust often to remove grit. Apply wax to protect against moisture. To repair, sand and apply new finish or refurbisher

Sanding and filling

Gradually lower moving drum of sander while pushing tool at start of forward motion. Walk evenly to avoid rocking sander from side to side. Near end of pass, raise drum gradually, pushing sander as far forward as possible. To continue, begin walking backward while gradually lowering drum. Place cord over your shoulder.

Start edger while it's off the floor. Gradually lower tool and move left to right in small overlapping circular strokes. Overlap edger into area covered by drum sander. In areas too narrow for drum sander, such as a closet, move edger in zigzag pattern but parallel to wood grain.

Hand scraper removes old finish beneath fixtures like radiators and below cupboard toe kicks. Follow with hand-sanding to blend with other sanded areas.

Push filler across floor with wide putty knife, forcing it into cracks. Work from corners towards centre of room. Remove excess filler from floor as you go, to avoid interfering with subsequent sanding. Most filler dries hard in 1 hr.

Finishing

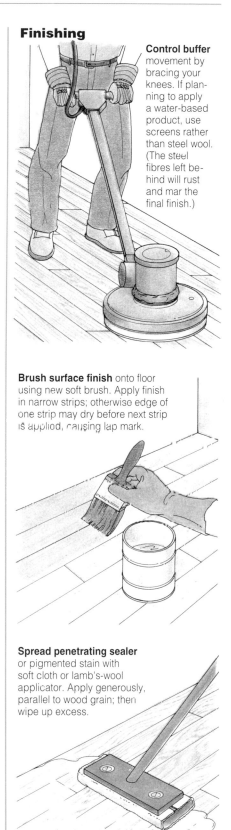

Control buffer movement by bracing your knees. If planning to apply a water-based product, use screens rather than steel wool. (The steel fibres left behind will rust and mar the final finish.)

Brush surface finish onto floor using new soft brush. Apply finish in narrow strips; otherwise edge of one strip may dry before next strip is applied, causing lap mark.

Spread penetrating sealer or pigmented stain with soft cloth or lamb's-wool applicator. Apply generously, parallel to wood grain; then wipe up excess.

RESILIENT AND CERAMIC TILE FLOORS

Installing resilient and ceramic tile is similar to installing parquet flooring and ceramic tile countertops. The floor must be flat, and an underlay is needed for support (pp 325–327).

Modern no-wax resilient tiles are usually made of vinyl, come in a wide range of colours and patterns, and are typically 300 mm squares. Accent tiles – larger or smaller or in different shapes – are also available; with these you can create borders or design your own patterns. Newer resilient tiles can usually be removed by heating them with a heat gun. This allows you to change accent tiles to update the floor's appearance, rather than change the entire floor. However, do not remove existing tiles if there is any chance that they contain asbestos (p 325).

Most resilient tile is fastened by gluing it to the floor with special adhesive. (The tile manufacturer or dealer will specify which kind to use.) Some tiles are self-adhesive – their backs are coated with contact cement covered by paper or plastic film. Remove the covering just before installation. Both types of tiles must then be pressed down with a floor roller to secure them completely. You can hire a floor roller; this may weigh 75 kg but can be disassembled for easier carrying.

Ceramic floor tiles are similar to those used for countertops and walls but are generally larger and stronger. Powdered thinbed adhesive is the best choice for do-it-yourself installation. Wear a dust mask when mixing it with

Planning a diagonal layout

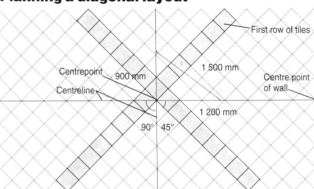

Centrepoint · Centreline · 900 mm · 1 500 mm · Centre point of wall · 1 200 mm · 90° 45° · First row of tiles

Draw a plan on graph paper, letting each square represent a tile (add grout spaces for ceramic tiles). Find room's centre point by snapping chalk lines between centre points of opposite walls. To verify 90° angle, mark out from centre point 900 mm along one line, 1 200 mm along the other. Distance between two marks should be 1 500 mm. If not, adjust by redrawing one centreline without changing centre point. Bisect 90° with carpenter's square for 45° angle; verify with combination square.

Border of tiles placed parallel to walls simplifies trimming to compensate for room that is out of square.

Lay down first row (without adhesive) along 45° line. If necessary, adjust the row without changing its angle so that the end tiles are equal in size and at least half a tile wide. Mark additional guidelines every 600 mm. Mark border with separate colour to avoid confusion.

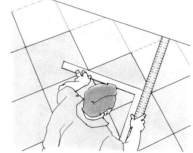

Border

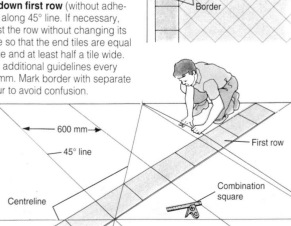

600 mm · 45° line · Centreline · First row · Combination square

Installing resilient tiles

Remove backing from self-adhesive tile, or spread tile adhesive with notched trowel (facing page). Lay tile in place without twisting, using edge of adjoining tile as a 'hinge'.

'Hinge'

To mark perimeter tiles that are not full-size, run a straightedge ruler from the wall to the corner of the tile in preceding row (ensure that straightedge is at 90° to wall by holding a carpenter's square across centrelines of adjoining tiles). Transfer measurement to new tile and cut tile with utility knife held against straightedge.

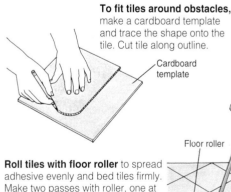

To fit tiles around obstacles, make a cardboard template and trace the shape onto the tile. Cut tile along outline.

Cardboard template

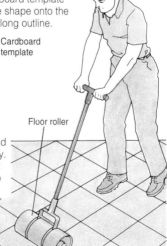

Floor roller

Roll tiles with floor roller to spread adhesive evenly and bed tiles firmly. Make two passes with roller, one at right angles to the other. Be sure to cover entire floor.

water. For more information on choosing, cutting and repairing ceramic tiles, see pp 254–259.

Typically, tiles are laid either parallel to the walls or at a 45° angle to them. When designing a parallel layout, follow the same procedures as for parquet floors (pp 330–331), but allow for the width of grout joints with ceramic tile. Where a room is significantly out of square or has many obstacles, adapt the layout method on pp 328–329. Select one wall as a focal point, mark a baseline two or three tile widths from it, and then proceed with a parallel or diagonal layout.

Tiles can hide a room's defects. Vertical lines appear to lengthen a room; a border will make it appear smaller. Hexagonal tiles should be laid with their sides, not their corners, parallel to two opposite walls. For your first tile floor, keep the design simple.

Whatever the layout, work first on graph paper. Estimate the amount of tile you need based on the size of the room and that of your chosen tile (plus any grout joints), adding 10 per cent extra for breakage and for future repairs. Test the design first by doing a dry run on the floor, making adjustments as needed to compensate for obstacles and the room's dimensions.

Be careful not to apply adhesive over areas that are too large to cover with tiles before the adhesive hardens. Similarly, never apply more grout than you can easily spread and clean before it begins to set.

Laying ceramic tiles

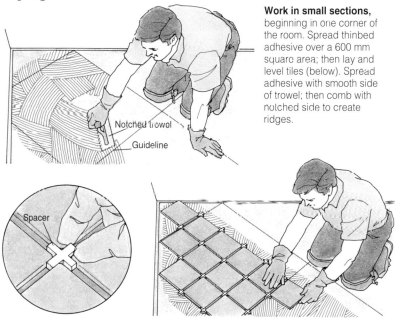

Work in small sections, beginning in one corner of the room. Spread thinbed adhesive over a 600 mm square area; then lay and level tiles (below). Spread adhesive with smooth side of trowel; then comb with notched side to create ridges.

Notched trowel

Guideline

Spacer

Lay tiles in adhesive, fitting them in place with a slight twist to spread the adhesive. Remove excess from joints with knife or grout saw. Place spacers at corners to maintain uniform gap between tiles (inset). Never walk on newly laid tiles.

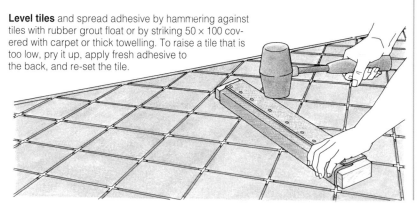

Level tiles and spread adhesive by hammering against tiles with rubber grout float or by striking 50 × 100 covered with carpet or thick towelling. To raise a tile that is too low, pry it up, apply fresh adhesive to the back, and re-set the tile.

Grouting and cleaning the tiles

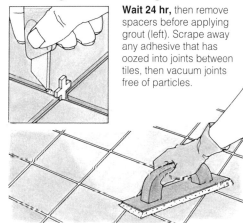

Wait 24 hr, then remove spacers before applying grout (left). Scrape away any adhesive that has oozed into joints between tiles, then vacuum joints free of particles.

Spread grout over tiles with rubber grout float held firmly at 30° angle. Wipe away excess immediately by scraping with float held nearly perpendicular to floor.

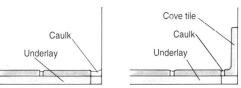

Cove tile

Caulk

Caulk

Underlay

Underlay

Apply caulk, not grout, in expansion joints such as joint around perimeter of floor (left) or where cove and floor tile meet (right). Use caulking gun to push flexible waterpoof caulk firmly into joint.

Clean tiles before grout dries. Wipe several times with sponge squeezed nearly dry (rinse sponge often); then remove hazy residue with clean towel.

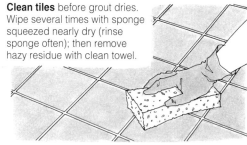

Laying the flooring

1. Ventilate the area well. Unroll flooring, starting at longest un-interrupted wall. Allow excess to curl up at edges; adjust sheet so pattern is square to walls.

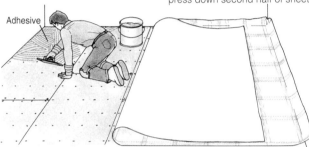

Adhesive

2. Fold back half of sheet, without creasing, to expose underlay. Apply adhesive to floor with notched trowel and immediately press down sheet. Fold back other half of sheet, cover remainder of floor with adhesive and press down second half of sheet.

3. Flatten sheet with floor roller or rolling pin to spread adhesive and remove bubbles. Work from centre of floor outward.

Floor roller

Usually made of vinyl, resilient sheet flooring comes in many different colours, patterns and textures. Quality and prices vary; premium grades have a durable top, or wear layer, that disguises underlay flaws. So-called no-wax types have a wear layer made of thermoplastic or other resins.

Most sheet flooring is available in rolls up to 2 m wide. If possible, select a width that allows you to cover the floor with a single piece. Sheets can be joined, but it is difficult to match patterns and textures at a seam. If a seam can't be avoided, plan so that it will occur in an inconspicuous area.

You can apply sheet flooring over almost any smooth hard surface, even over existing resilient flooring. (To flatten or strengthen the underlay, see pp 325–327.)

The flooring manufacturer will specify whether the flooring should be laid using the full-adhesion method shown here or whether it should be laid loose. To loose-lay flooring, follow the steps shown here to position and trim it, but leave a 6 mm gap along the walls and do not apply adhesive. Then secure the edges as directed by the manufacturer.

Resilient flooring can be difficult to manipulate. Avoid bending it sharply as you lay it, or it may crease or rip. Even after it has been rolled, fully adhered flooring usually develops bubbles, caused by gas escaping from the adhesive. If these have not disappeared within a week, prick them with a pin in an inconspicuous spot and then press the flooring flat.

When moving heavy items over resilient flooring, lay down a sheet of thin plywood or heavy cardboard to protect it. Clean flooring often with a slightly damp mop (the flooring is not waterproof). Special cleaners recommended by the flooring manufacturer will preserve or restore a glossy finish.

Trimming

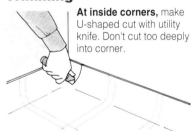

At inside corners, make U-shaped cut with utility knife. Don't cut too deeply into corner.

Trim excess along walls by pressing flooring close to wall and using straightedge as a guide. Leave a 3 mm gap between flooring and wall.

At outside corners, trim with utility knife, making vertical slits through excess flooring.

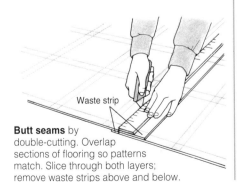

Waste strip

Butt seams by double-cutting. Overlap sections of flooring so patterns match. Slice through both layers; remove waste strips above and below.

Finishing touches

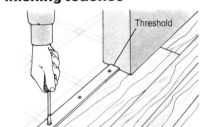

Threshold

Cover flooring at doorways and where flooring meets different material. Cut strips of metal or other threshold material to precise length and secure with matching fasteners.

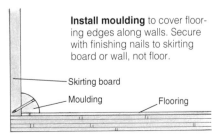

Install moulding to cover flooring edges along walls. Secure with finishing nails to skirting board or wall, not floor.

Skirting board

Moulding

Flooring

REPAIRING FLOORING

Strip and plank flooring

Drill holes with a spade bit at each end of damaged area. Chisel out board.

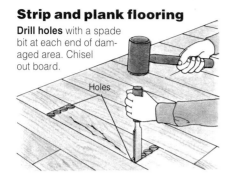

Holes

Cut to length a new strip of tongue-and-groove flooring; reverse board and remove lower lip of groove with chisel, saw or plane.

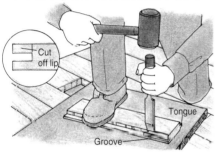

Cut off lip

Tongue

Groove

Fit tongue of new board into groove of adjacent floorboard. Tap into place with mallet and scrap block. Fasten with nails and finish to match floor.

To stretch the time between major refinishings, dust floors often to remove grit and wipe up spills promptly to avoid stains. For general cleaning, and to maintain a bright finish, use commercial cleaners recommended by the flooring manufacturer or installer.

On wood floors, avoid water-base products. On floors finished with polyurethane, don't use cleaners containing any kind of oil, grease or solvent. Synthetic floor finishes – such as Swedish finish and acrylic – resist penetration by most liquids. On the other hand, floors finished with shellac, lacquer, conventional varnish and wax are easily damaged by almost any liquid that is allowed to remain for more than a few minutes, especially liquids containing solvents like alcohol.

To repair minor scratches in a nonsynthetic finish, rub the spot with very fine steel wool (No 0000) and then apply a dab of paste wax. Extensively damaged or stained finish may have to be stripped and replaced. To repair a synthetic finish and the finish on resilient flooring, use only the products and techniques recommended by the flooring manufacturer.

Stained wood flooring can sometimes be sanded or bleached If not, or if floorboards are splintered or broken, the damaged area must be removed as shown (far left).

Lighten stained ceramic tile grout with special cleaners, available at tile suppliers. For instructions on sealing tiles and grout and repairing damaged ceramic tile, see pp 257 and 259.

In resilient flooring, you can sometimes fill small gouged areas with a paste made of grated flooring material and clear nail polish. (Grate resilient flooring only if you are certain that it does not contain asbestos, p 325). However, you'll usually get better-looking results by patching the area.

Parquet tile

Drill holes from corner to corner to slightly less than the depth of the tile. Chisel away all sections.

Scrape off old adhesive; then apply new layer and fit replacement tile in place.

Resilient tile and sheet flooring

Soften adhesive with a heat gun. Scrape off the damaged tile and old adhesive. Apply the new adhesive and fit the new tile in place.

Patch

Patching sheet flooring:
1. Place a patch on top of damage, aligning pattern precisely. Tape in place; then cut through both layers with a utility knife.

2. Remove patch (below) and set it aside. Heat and pry away damaged flooring and adhesive as you would for a damaged tile.

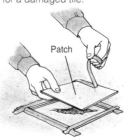

Patch

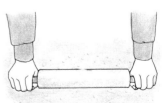

3. Spread new adhesive, using notched trowel. Fit patch into place; then press flat with rolling pin.

You will save time, money, energy and a lot of frustration if you think a project through and carefully plan each step before beginning. For almost any undertaking, large or small, you will benefit by drawing up your plans on paper. A good set of plans lets you see what tools you'll need and aids in estimating the amount and cost of the materials you'll use. It also helps you see the complexity of the entire job, so that you can determine whether or not you'll need professional help.

Drawing up plans. Begin by making a sketch or diagram of the project. It needn't be elaborate or artistic – simply clear enough to illustrate what you mean to do, showing all the parts and indicating the materials you plan to use. You can make simple outlines of the parts and use heavy dots or X's for the nails, screws or bolts.

Then, to ensure accurate results, transfer the sketch to graph paper, letting each square on the paper equal 1 m or some other clear-cut measurement. Or use measuring and layout tools to draw the plans to scale.

To make a full-size pattern from a small picture or drawing, use a pantograph (p 19), or draw a grid of intersecting vertical and horizontal lines over the original drawing and transfer the design onto graph paper square by square. Be thorough and accurate.

When designing furniture and cupboards, consider the average person's comfort and use standard dimensions. Also be sure to leave enough open space around each item (pp 340–343).

For large projects, if you don't want to draw your own plans, you can alter existing ones, purchase ready-drawn plans or copy plans from books or magazines. Or you can buy two- or even three-dimensional kits that have scaled pieces of cardboard or plastic representing furniture, cupboards and other features. These small pieces can easily be moved about inside a grid floor plan to find the best arrangement. Also available is computer software for designing a room or an entire house or for landscaping a garden. Some design companies provide personalized computer planning.

Outlining the steps. Once the plans for a project are drawn up, think the whole job through and make a list of the major steps. Put the steps in order, break them down into sub-steps, and number the steps and sub-steps.

When planning a large project, break it down into a series of small, manageable projects (see below). This allows you to make timely purchases, organize your time and spot any specialized work that goes beyond the level of your skills and requires a professional. Checking through the steps, make a list of all the tools you will want to have on hand. Then examine the steps and the plans to determine the amounts of materials you will need (pp 344–347), including fasteners and other hardware.

Other considerations. For your safety, be sure to line up one or more helpers if the project will involve transporting or working with materials that are heavy or awkward to handle. Also, plan and set up a space, either in your workshop or on site, for working on the project and storing the materials.

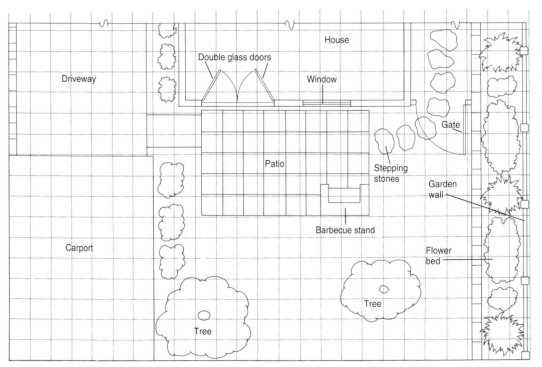

Begin a large project, such as adding a patio to your house, by drawing up a plan. Using the plan as a guide, break the project into a number of smaller, more manageable jobs, such as laying the patio floor, putting in the flower beds, building the barbecue stand, and adding the stepping stones. Then in order to see what tools and materials you'll need, break each of these smaller jobs into self-contained steps. For instance, divide the patio floor job into laying out the area, excavating the topsoil, adding the gravel and mortar, laying the stones, and adding the grout. Finally, do the work in a logical sequence, suiting your budget, your free time, and the time of year.

If a project is going to generate a lot of waste materials, decide in advance how you will recycle or dispose of them. For a major project, engage a waste-disposal company or haul the debris to an authorized dumping site.

Remember that materials such as oils, paints, lacquers and varnishes, as well as thinners, strippers and other solvents, are flammable or toxic. Some are hazardous to the environment. Use them up according to the instructions on the labels, and consult your local authority about approved methods of disposal leftovers and waste products. Until it is removed from your premises, ensure that potentially harmful material is out of the reach of children and cannot be tampered with by people who might normally investigate domestic refuse in search of useful or edible substances.

Regulations and permits. Before finalizing any building or renovation arrangements, submit plans of them to your local building department, making sure that you are familiar with any related restrictions and requirements. Generally there are separate regulations for construction, plumbing and electrical work, and these cover every aspect of the job, even down to the types of nails you must use. You may also have to have some of the work done by a licensed professional and have it inspected at various stages.

Get a permit if you need one, and arrange any neccesary inspections. Permits are usually required for major renovations, such as turning a garage into a guest room, but they may also be required for small jobs, such as walling in a patio, building a barbecue with a high chimney, breaking through a curb to install a driveway and some plumbing and electrical jobs.

When working on a project that requires digging or excavating, such as putting in a path, ask your local authority to mark the locations of underground cables and pipelines before you start digging. This will protect you from the possibity of injury, liability and disruption of services.

Hiring a Contractor

The skills portion of this book shows you what's involved in working with various materials, demonstrating all the basic techniques and some advanced ones. It can also help you assess what's involved in any projects you may plan and determine your role in them.

If, after gathering information and assessing the job's complexity, you decide to undertake a large project that involves work you don't feel comfortable doing, consider hiring a contractor to do part or all of the job. For example, for the patio project shown on the facing page, you might serve as general contractor and do some of the work yourself, but hire a labourer to excavate the soil, an electrician to install the outdoor lighting, and a plumber to put in the garden sprinkler system.

To find a contractor, compile a list of names by talking to your friends and relatives who have had similar work done, looking in the Yellow Pages of your phone book and calling local building and construction organizations. Contact several of the listed contractors who do the type of work you need, asking for references from customers who have used their services recently for a project similar to yours. Call the references and ask to look at the work.

Narrow your list to contractors with good references. In addition to customers, check suppliers for complaints against them and make sure they have the appropriate licences.

Finally, ask two or three of the contractors to tender for the work, furnishing them with drawings and specific information on the materials you want. (Most contractors provide their own materials because part of their profit is derived from the discount they receive from suppliers.)

When the tenders are in, study them carefully and choose the contractor you think is best for the job. But remember, the lowest bid is not always the best. Contractors may cut corners to bring down the price.

For your protection, get everything in writing. The contract should include start and completion dates, a detailed account of the work to be done, the types of materials to be used (including the brand names, if important), how and when waste disposal will be handled, procedures for making changes in the original plans, warranties and termination conditions.

Be sure to include the full cost of the project and a schedule of payments. Never pay everything up front; it's common to make a down payment of no more than one-third the total cost, several payments as the work progresses, and a final payment when everything is completed and you have approved the work.

Your contract should also include a lien waiver clause, requiring the contractor to show proof that suppliers and subcontractors have been paid so that you cannot be sued for non-payment of his bills. It is also a good idea to have the contractor obtain permits and be responsible for following the regulations. Ask to see certificates of damage and liability insurance from contractors and sub-contractors.

Once the work begins, keep close tabs on its progress and quickly bring any problems to the attention of the contractor – not his workers. If you want to make a change in the plans, ask how it will affect the total cost of the project and get it all in writing. Sometimes making a small change necessitates expensive changes elsewhere. For example, to add a lighting fixture an electrician may have to run an extra circuit at great expense, but he might not tell you until he presents the bill at the end.

When the job is finished, examine it carefully before making the final payment. Never pay for work that has not been done.

When designing furniture and arranging it in a room, it's best to adhere to the standard dimensions that architects have established for the average person. A table or desk must be the proper height, for example, to eat or work at comfortably. In addition, allow sufficient space for people to pass easily through a room or to walk or work around the furniture.

DINING TABLE SIZES (in cm)

	People	Minimum	Average	Ample
Square tables	2	61 × 61	71 × 71	76 × 76
	4	76 × 76	81 × 81	91 × 91
	8	112 × 112	122 × 122	132 × 132
Rectangular tables	2	56 × 71	61 × 76	71 × 81
	4	71 × 112	81 × 122	91 × 132
	6	87 × 127	91 × 168	107 × 183
	8	87 × 183	91 × 218	107 × 230
Round tables	2	56	61	71
	4	81	91	107
	6	107	127	138
	8	142	158	183

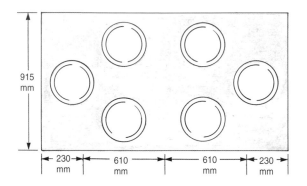

Coffee, or cocktail, table must be within easy reach of someone seated on a sofa or an armchair but far enough away to allow leg room.

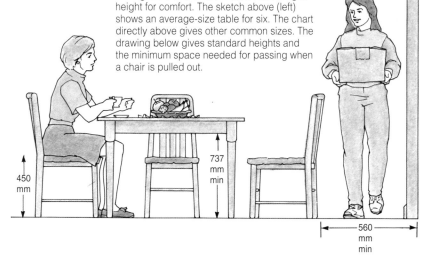

Dining table and chairs must be at the right height for comfort. The sketch above (left) shows an average-size table for six. The chart directly above gives other common sizes. The drawing below gives standard heights and the minimum space needed for passing when a chair is pulled out.

Computer centre

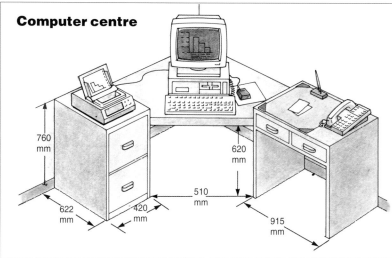

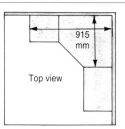

Top view

By building your computer centre into a corner, you gain more room for the monitor and keyboard and provide a partial wraparound workspace that lets you work with a minimum of moving about.

Either build or buy the elements for a computer centre. In the arrangement shown, the centre table for the keyboard (and monitor) is 140 mm lower than the rest because that is generally a more comfortable height for typing. The area at right can be reserved for writing, and the printer can be placed at left. Reverse the arrangement for a left-handed worker.

STANDARD MEASUREMENTS FOR STORAGE AREAS AND BEDROOMS

In planning storage space, always take into consideration the size of the people who need access to it. Some standard measurements are given here, but you may have to change them to suit the needs of individuals. For example, you might build low shelves in a child's bedroom but put high ones in another room for storing harmful materials out of the reach of young children. If you add extra-high shelves, use a steady ladder or step stool to reach them. Bookshelves should be shallower than wardrobe shelves, and they should not be more than 1 m long to sustain the weight of the books without sagging. When furnishing a bedroom, leave enough space for dressing and moving about.

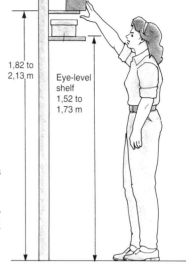

Shelves (right) should be within reach of everyone who uses them without their having to stand on tiptoes. Make high shelves shallower than lower ones.

Wardrobes (left) hold more if packed tightly; buy or build a closet organizer. Install rods for hangers at least 300 mm from wall.

Allow access space in front of cupboard doors or drawers (below).

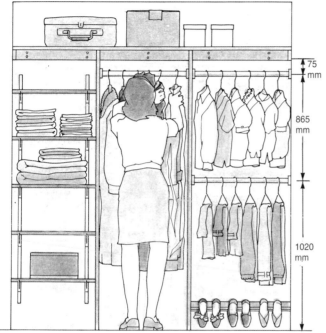

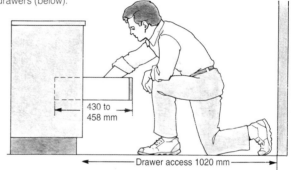

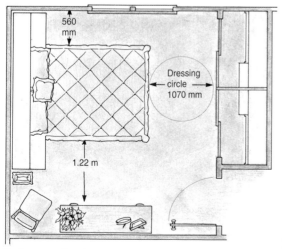

Bedroom wall unit (right) can frame any bed. Standard mattress lengths are 188 and 200. Standard widths are king-size 183 cm; queen-size 152 cm; double 137 cm; twin or three-quarter 107 cm; single 92 cm and bunk 76 cm. Allow 560 mm between twin beds. Amounts of space shown around bed (above) are minimums.

Perhaps more than any other parts of your home, the kitchen and bathroom benefit from careful planning. A well-designed kitchen can put everything at your fingertips and dramatically reduce the time you spend preparing food. A carefully laid-out bathroom ensures maximum comfort and avoids cramped spaces that cause you to bang your knee or stub your toe. You might also consider installing a hand-held shower and grab bars at convenient heights for people who might be unsteady on their feet. If someone in your household is confined to a wheelchair, you may want to make some of the adjustments shown below and on the facing page.

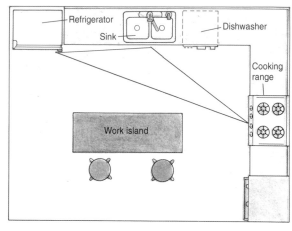

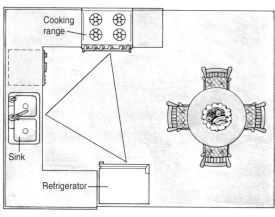

Work triangle that puts the sink, refrigerator and cooking range (stove or separate oven and hob) at its three corners is the most efficient arrangement for a kitchen. A U-shaped work triangle is shown in the layout at left, and an L-shaped kitchen with a longer, narrower work triangle is shown above. When planning a kitchen, be sure to leave enough counter space between the three points for preparing food, serving and cleaning up, but make the length of the sides of the triangle short enough to minimize walking. Never place a heat-making appliance, such as the cooking hob or dishwasher, next to the refrigerator.

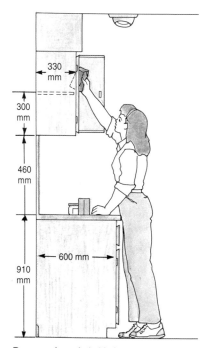

Base cupboards in kitchen are deeper than the wall cupboards, so top shelves can't be as high as shelves with no obstruction below.

Leave crouching space in front of a low oven (below) or a cupboard with swing-out doors.

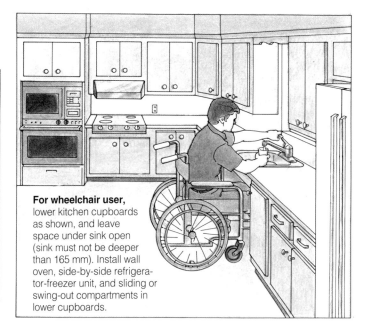

For wheelchair user, lower kitchen cupboards as shown, and leave space under sink open (sink must not be deeper than 165 mm). Install wall oven, side-by-side refrigerator-freezer unit, and sliding or swing-out compartments in lower cupboards.

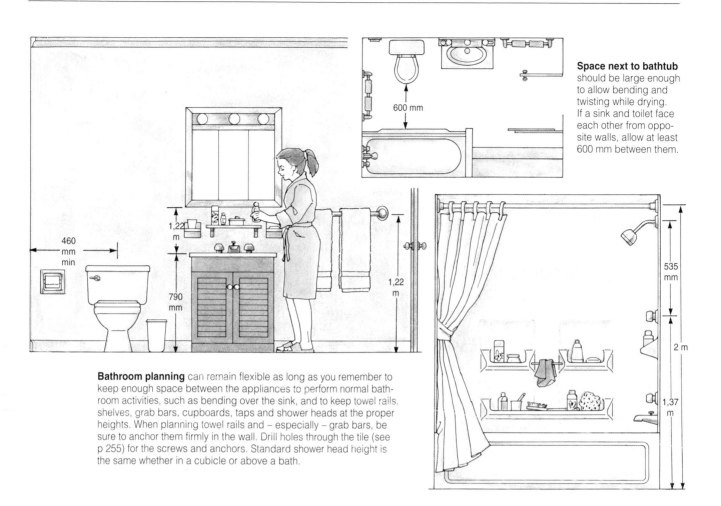

Space next to bathtub
should be large enough
to allow bending and
twisting while drying.
If a sink and toilet face
each other from oppo-
site walls, allow at least
600 mm between them.

600 mm

460 mm min

1,22 m

790 mm

1,22 m

535 mm

2 m

1,37 m

Bathroom planning can remain flexible as long as you remember to keep enough space between the appliances to perform normal bath-room activities, such as bending over the sink, and to keep towel rails, shelves, grab bars, cupboards, taps and shower heads at the proper heights. When planning towel rails and – especially – grab bars, be sure to anchor them firmly in the wall. Drill holes through the tile (see p 255) for the screws and anchors. Standard shower head height is the same whether in a cubicle or above a bath.

Bathroom for handicapped needs more grab bars and a hand-held shower. You should also lower the medicine cupboard and position it beside the sink (right). Leave enough space next to the toilet to park a wheelchair, and a circle of space at least 1,5 m across in the centre of the room to turn the chair freely (below).

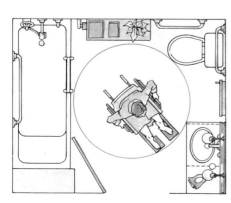

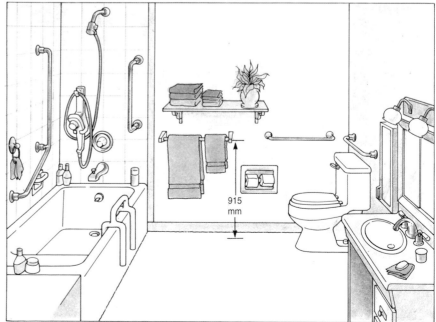

915 mm

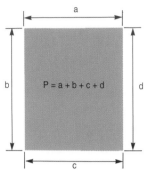

Perimeter of (distance around) a rectangle, triangle or other straight-sided shape is found by adding the lengths of all its sides.

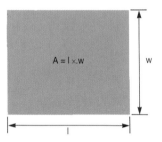

Area of a rectangle is found by multiplying its length by its width.

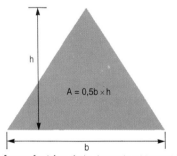

Area of a triangle is determined by multiplying half the length of its base by its height.

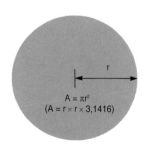

Area of a circle is found by multiplying the square of the circle's radius (half the distance across the circle) by π (3,1416).

Once you have drawn up plans for a project, start compiling lists of the materials and hardware you will need. First consider the nature of the project. How much will it be used? Is it to be permanent or temporary? Will it be visible or hidden, utilitarian or decorative? Should it match or coordinate with existing materials? Is it going to be indoors or outdoors? Will it be used by children or a handicapped person? How much are you prepared to spend? With these factors in mind, choose the type and quality of materials you want to use and, if applicable, pick the finishes (paint, stain or natural) you wish the project to have. Don't forget that you may be required to adhere to local building regulations in selecting materials and hardware.

After you have decided upon the types of materials, you'll need to work out the quantities. For materials that are installed in straight lines, such as pipes or skirting board, simply mea-

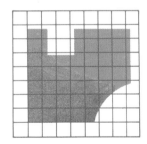

Sketch complex areas on graph paper, letting each square on the paper equal 1 sq m or 1 sq dm (100 × 100 mm). Add up whole squares and those more than one-third filled.

sure the length needed. For materials that frame or border, measure the perimeter or circumference of the piece or area to be enclosed. For many other materials, you'll need to calculate either the area to be covered or the volume to be filled. Use the formulas illustrated here to make these estimates. Then determine the amounts of materials you'll need based on these calculations. When using any formula, remember to calculate only with like things. For instance, you can't multiply millimetres by metres or feet – convert all readings to the same units (see also conversion tables on pp 348-349).

Some materials are sold and estimated in several ways. The most common are given in the pages that follow. If you want to be sure how a material is sold in your area, call and ask one or two suppliers. Wth larger projects, ask about discounts to owner-builders.

Break the job down into its individual steps (p 338), recording the type and quantity of the materials needed at each step. List every item required for building or installation, including hardware, fasteners, caulk and abrasives. Also list any tools that you may have to buy or hire.

A rule of thumb when estimating materials is to add 10 per cent to allow for under-calculations, damage, waste and future repairs. Once you have determined the quantities, multiply the amount required by the cost per unit for the total cost of the materials.

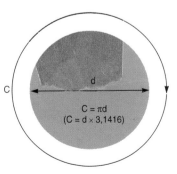

Circumference of (distance around) a full circle is found by multiplying the circle's diameter (the distance across it) by π (3,1416).

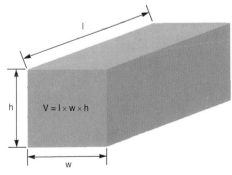

Volume, or cubic dimension, of a square or other rectangular space is determined by multiplying the length by the width by the height.

Before estimating the amount of timber you will need for a project, decide on the type and grade (pp 130–131) and find out how your supplier sells it. Both softwoods and hardwoods are generally sold in standard lengths starting at 1,8 m and increasing by 300 mm increments up to 4,8 m (or 6,6 m in the case of structural pine).

Dressed timber is sold in its nominal size – that is, according to its dimensions *before* surfacing or planing. The dressed or PAR (planed all round) size of a length of Oregon pine, for instance, may be about 85 × 20 mm but it will be described by its nominal size of 100 × 25 mm. Construction timber and most SA pine is sold rough-sawn, but you can specify finish and precise dimensions at extra cost. PAR timber for cabinet work usually needs to be squared and planed to a finer finish.

Depending on timber size and on whether it is a hardwood or a softwood, the difference between nominal and PAR sizes is usually from 2 to 15 mm, with hardwoods losing less during dressing. Standard thicknesses of sawn hardwoods are 19, 22, 25, 32, 38, 50 and 76 mm. The width depends on tree size and may range between 25 and 304 mm.

To calculate your requirements of timber sold in running or linear metres (including boards, dimensional timber, dowels and mouldings), simply measure the length needed in metres. In the case of project components, measure each component separately, and add all the measurements together to calculate the total amount of timber.

Rare hardwoods may be sold by the cubic metre, although this usually applies only when actual trees or trunks – rather than planks, for instance – are sold. (The sale of indigenous timbers from trees grown in State forests is very strictly controlled and is usually by tender.) The private individual, buying from a timber dealer, will usually be quoted a price based on dimension rather than volume.

Some dealers, however, do base their calculations of rare wood prices on volume. A common example is based on the size of a plank measured to round figures in inches and converted to metres. Thus, a plank measuring 6 feet (72 inches) by 6 inches by 1 inch – or 1,83 × 0,15 × 0,0254 m – has a volume of 0,007 cu m. To obtain the price of a plank of approximately this dimension, multiply the price per cu m by 0,007 and adjust according to the actual size. It may help you to visualize a cubic metre if you consider that it is equivalent to a 266,6 m length of timber with width and thickness of 150 × 25 mm.

Dealers in rare woods usually make an additional charge for machining the wood. This is commonly based on the time that the machine is in use, and may specify a minimum quantity of timber to be machined, or a minimum charge – usually for an hour's machine time. For special projects, such as making or repairing fine furniture, it is worth obtaining woods well in advance. Demolition contractors' yards are sometimes a surprisingly good source of second-hand rare woods.

Laminated wood. This is made in SA pine and is widely used as structural timber. It is often seen as rafters, varnished and left exposed because of its attractive appearance. Where obtainable, standard lengths range from 3 to 12 m, thicknesses from 35 to 70 mm and widths from about 150 to 300 mm. Beams of dimensions up to 24 m × 630 mm × 140 mm are available as special orders.

Sheet materials. Plywood, particleboard, panelling, hardboard and other sheet materials come in various thicknesses and standard sheet sizes. Larger sizes (both longer and wider) may be available by special order – usually at a premium price – and some suppliers sell cut panels, or cut them to order if you pay for the waste and the cutting.

To calculate the number of panels needed for a large project, such as wall sheathing, simply divide the area (in sq m) of the space to be covered by the area of a standard-size sheet. Then add a standard waste factor of from 5 to 10 per cent, allowing for more waste when dealing with odd angles, curves or irregular shapes.

If you are working on a small project or one that requires a sheet to be cut into numerous pieces, lay it out on graph paper to determine the best size sheet to buy and to devise a cutting plan that will make the most efficient use of the material, keeping in mind that plywood is stronger along its length. If it matters, show the orientation of the grain but remember that you may need additional material to match grain patterns.

Well before the timber is delivered, make sure that a responsible person will be present to receive it and to ensure that it will be stacked in a suitable storage area. If necessary, erect a temporary storage shelter of tarpaulin.

PAR timber – approximate dimensions mm	
Nominal size	Actual size
25 × 50	19 × 38
25 × 76	19 × 64
25 × 102	19 × 90
25 × 127	19 × 115
25 × 152	19 × 140
25 × 204	19 × 190
25 × 254	19 × 235
25 × 304	19 × 286
50 × 50	38 × 38
50 × 76	38 × 64
50 × 103	38 × 90
50 × 152	38 × 140
50 × 204	38 × 190
50 × 254	38 × 235
50 × 304	38 × 286
75 × 102	64 × 90
102 × 102	90 × 90
102 × 152	90 × 140
152 × 152	140 × 140
204 × 204	190 × 190

In addition to wood, you'll have occasion to estimate the amounts needed of various other building materials and hardware. Some of the most common items are discussed below.

Bricks. To estimate the number of bricks you'll need for a project, calculate the number of square metres to be covered and deduct the area of doors and windows. Divide your answer by the number of square metres in the face of the type of brick you are using. Use the nominal dimensions of the brick for a project with mortar, but use actual sizes for a mortarless project such as a patio or pathway. Allow from 5 to 10 per cent for waste.

The rule of thumb is that between 48 and 54 standard modular bricks are needed per sq m, and between 40 and 42 maxi bricks per sq m. These figures apply to single-skin walls. New bricks are usually sold singly or in units of 500 or 600 called packs, so calculate your order accordingly. (For details, see p 222.)

Concrete and concrete blocks. Concrete is sold and mixed by the cubic metre. Calculate the area in square metres and multiply that number by the thickness of the concrete (also in metres). The result is the total volume of concrete required, in cubic metres. For example, if you are pouring a 100 mm-thick concrete slab that is 5 m by 8 m, multiply 5 by 8 by 0,1 (100 mm equals 0,1 m). The total is 4 cu m. If you'd like to be safe, order an extra 10 per cent.

You can roughly estimate the number of blocks you'll need for a project by dividing the number of square metres the project will cover (less any doors, windows or other large openings) by the number of square metres in the face of the block. As a general rule, 12,5 hollow blocks measuring 390 × 190 × 190 mm or 34 maxi concrete bricks will cover 1 sq m of a single-skin straight run of wall.

Separate calculations are required to arrive at the number of special blocks you'll need. Find out the dimensions of the special blocks that are available and make the estimate based on your plans, which should be drawn to scale or marked with exact dimensions. Special blocks include sash blocks and sill blocks for windows, and solid blocks for the top courses of bearing walls.

Your supplier can probably help you estimate the amount of mortar you'll need for a project (see p 222). Remember, though, that the type of cement and the proportions of cement, sand and lime are likely to vary with the type of project.

Concrete pavers. Manufactured concrete pavers come in different sizes and shapes; some interlock. Check with the supplier for actual sizes and patterns available.

To estimate the number of pavers needed for a job, divide the area of the space to be covered by the area of each paver. For example, you've chosen pavers measuring 225 × 225 mm (each having an area of 0,05 sq m) and the area to be paved measures 3 × 3,6 m or 10,8 sq m. Thus 10,8 ÷ 0,05 = 216 pavers. Depending on the site layout, allow from 5 to 10 per cent for cutting and breakages. If you are dubious about doing your own calculation, ask your supplier to help – the manufacturer of the paver probably issues a list showing area coverage for the various patterns.

Flagstones. Flagstone, generally known in South Africa as *slasto* (from *sla*te *sto*ne) or crazy paving, is any flat stone used for a patio or pathway and usually has irregular dimensions. It is normally sold according to the area covered, but may also be sold by weight – 1 ton covers about 8 sq m.

The thickness of slasto varies, but stone between 30 and 50 mm thick is suitable for most projects and is laid on a base of coarse sand. If you can, make your own selection of colours, shapes and sizes from your supplier's stocks. Try to obtain shapes that suit the proportions of the area to be paved and select mostly large to medium pieces – small stones involve more work.

Finishes. Paint, stain, and other finishes come in containers holding from 250 ml to 25ℓ, depending on the finish and whether or not it is specially mixed. The labels on the containers sometimes indicate coverage – the area that the contents should cover.

In general, to calculate the amount of finish you'll need, divide the total area to be covered by the coverage indicated on the container; then multiply the result by the number of coats you plan to apply. For large areas such as walls, deduct for doorways, windows and other large openings (p 285).

If you apply too little paint (as most non-professionals do), you will either get away with using less paint or will need more paint for an extra coat. The type of applicator you use will also affect the amount of paint you need. Allow 10 to 15 per cent waste if you use a paint-feeding tool, such as a power roller or a spray applicator. If the surface to be painted is unusually porous, as is concrete block or new wallboard, allow 25 per cent more paint for the first coat (usually a primer). Finally, if you are applying a light colour over a dark one, you'll need to apply a heavier coat or add a coat.

Wallcoverings. Wallpaper and other wallcoverings usually come in rolls that are 10 m long by 530 mm wide, giving an area of 5,3 sq m per roll. However, not all rolls are produced in metric sizes.

To estimate the number of metric rolls you'll need, calculate the area of each wall and add all the measurements together; then subtract the total area of doors and windows and divide the result by 5,3. Remember that this will give an approximate figure only and that you will need more rolls of a drop-match pattern wallcovering. Borders are sold by the metre – measure the perimeter of the room.

For wallcoverings that are not pre-pasted, 500 g of paste will hang approximately 9 rolls of paper. Liquid sealer or sizing may be needed to prepare certain surfaces before adding the

Approximate number of wire nails per kilogram									
Length (mm)	25	32	40	50	63	75	100	125	150
Diameter (mm)	1,6	2,0	2,0	2,5	2,8	3,5	4,0	5,0	5,6
Wire nails per kg	2 400	1 200	1 000	500	300	170	100	50	30

wallcovering. If so, estimate the amount you need as you would paint.

Plastics. Plastic laminate, for countertops and cupboards, is sold in sheets measuring 1,2 × 2,4 m. Measure the length and width of the area to be covered with laminate and order a piece that is at least 12 mm wider and of equal length.

Acrylic sheets of 1,2 × 2,4 m are commonly 3,6 or 9 mm thick, but suppliers often sell smaller pieces. Calculate the area to be covered and order accordingly.

Glass. You can buy glass cut to order, or buy a large sheet and cut it yourself. If you are buying glass to replace a broken windowpane, measure the cracked pane, if possible, or measure the length and width of the inside of the window frame. Before measuring, clean the frame of all fragments of old glass and sealing putty. For ease of fit, cut or buy a piece of glass 3 mm smaller than the opening. For a large, expensive piece of glass or mirror, it's best to have the glass company assume the responsibility of taking the measurements, particularly if it must fit an opening that may not be perfectly square.

Glass blocks are available in standard thicknesses of 80 and 90 mm. The faces come in 190 and 240 mm squares. The face measurements are nominal, allowing for 6 mm mortar joints. Glass blocks are also sold in pre-assembled panels that can be slipped into place.

Pre-assembled or not, determine the number of courses you'll need by measuring the height of the space to be filled and dividing by the height of a single block (all in mm). Then measure the width of the space and divide by the width of each block to determine the number of blocks in a course. Multiply the two resulting figures for the total number of blocks needed.

Floor coverings. Sheet vinyl flooring comes on rolls in 2 m widths. Buy enough to cover the area with about 75 mm of overhang on each side. Be sure to get enough to cover the floors of any halls, closets, or odd-shaped areas that branch off the main space.

Vinyl, asphalt and carpet tiles come in 229 and 300 mm squares. Ceramic tiles come in 150, 200 and 310 mm squares, and in rectangles of 240 × 115 mm. They are all usually sold by the box, but sometimes they are sold by the piece as well.

To calculate the number of pieces you'll need to cover a large area with tiles of the same size and colour, divide the area of the space to be tiled by the area of a single tile. If you are planning to lay tiles in patterns involving mixed sizes or colours, lay out the design on graph paper (p 338) and count the number of tiles needed in each size and colour. Add 10 per cent for waste for ceramic tiles, a bit more for brittle tiles or tiles laid in a diagonal pattern, and less for the others. Then divide the number of tiles needed by the number of tiles per box to determine the total number of boxes required.

When buying ceramic tiles, be sure to check them before leaving the supplier. Ceramic tile is susceptible to breakage during storage and shipment.

Hardware and miscellaneous. When estimating the materials you'll need for a job, include hardware, adhesives and other installation materials. Buy enough nails or other fasteners for joining pieces or mounting them on walls, and don't forget anchors or toggles for use in plaster or wallboard. If you're joining pieces with nuts and bolts, remember to include any necessary washers. Be sure to buy matching nails and trim for wood panelling. When replacing a windowpane, include the caulk or putty that holds the glass. And don't forget hinges, brackets, braces, latches and knobs or pulls, if needed.

By consulting your scale-drawn plans, you can make a good estimate of all the hardware you will need. Because fasteners get lost easily and nails bend if not driven properly, it's a good idea to buy more fasteners than you will need for a job. You can always save the extras for future repairs and other jobs. Nails are sold loose or in a variety of packs (often by weight). Most other fasteners, including screws, are generally sold in small bubble packs or in larger boxes. The number of pieces is marked on the package. Depending on the type of job you're doing and especially when buying screws and hinges, don't mistake 'brassed' for the more expensive but non-rusting 'brass'. Brassed items have only a thin brassy plating that's fairly easily scratched off, leading to rusting of the iron underneath, while brass goods should be just that – solid brass.

Before placing your order, make sure that the materials you're about to request – and the items you propose to make from them – are permissible in terms of regulations such as local building bylaws. Be sure too that when goods are delivered they can be off-loaded without damaging or obstructing property, and that you have a secure and suitable place in which they can be stored safely until you need to use them.

Electricity is one of the most flexible, economical and adaptable power sources available. It provides light and heat and drives a big range of domestic and leisure equipment. But even the simplest repair to an electrical fitting or appliance can be dangerous unless you understand what you're doing.

A current of electricity flows only when it can complete a circuit that runs from the power source along a conductor (such as a wire), and back to the source. In domestic appliances and home workshops electricity flows along the brown-coated *live* wire to the appliance, and from the appliance along the blue-coated *neutral* wire. When the current bypasses the appliance and passes directly from live to neutral, a *short circuit* occurs.

Electricity flows along a conductor as the result of electrical pressure, which is measured in *volts* (V or v). The domestic supply of electricity in South Africa is standardized at 220 volts. Appliances are designed to work within a certain voltage range and may be seriously damaged or destroyed if used outside that range.

The flow of electrical current is measured in *amperes* (A), abbreviated to amp or amps. Cables, fuses, plugs and sockets are rated according to the maximum amperage that they can carry safely.

The electrical power of an appliance is measured in *watts* (W or w), and the higher the wattage, the greater the amount of electricity used. Wattage is generally calculated by multiplying amperage by voltage.

To determine the amperage of the cable, fuse and plug required for a particular appliance, divide the appliance's wattage by the voltage of your supply. The amperage and wattage of an electrical appliance is usually stamped onto a metal part of its body or onto a metal plate attached to the body.

Apart from the live (brown) and neutral (pale blue) wires, there is a third wire, coated yellow-green, known

as the *earth* (or, on some imported appliances, as *ground*). The yellow-green wire of three-core flex is connected to a piece of exposed metal on appliances and, at the plug, to the largest and longest pin.

Some modern appliances don't have any provision for an earth connection. This is because they are completely insulated from the user or operator. Such appliances are usually known as 'double insulated'.

Domestic circuits. Electricity arrives at your house via a service cable ending at a sealed fuse and an electricity meter, usually mounted in a closed box built into an external wall. Near the meter is an earth terminal to which all sub-circuits in the house are connected.

From the electricity meter, the current passes to a distribution board inside the building. On the front of the board are mounted the earth-leakage relay, a main switch and various sub-main switches connected to the building's sub-circuits, such as stove, water heater (geyser) and power plugs. Shutting off the main switch prevents incoming current from reaching the sub-circuits. Only licensed wiremen, authorized by the electricity supplier (usually the local authority), are permitted to carry out work on, or modifications to, sealed fuses, meters and distribution boards.

If an appliance is faulty, so that a metal part of it becomes live, an imbalance between live and neutral currents causes a sensitive switch known as an earth-leakage relay (ELR) to shut down the circuit. As a rule, a fault will cause a fuse to 'blow', or it will 'trip' the ELR or a circuit switch. The result of either of these is to prevent current from flowing through the circuit to which the faulty appliance is attached.

In older buildings, wire and ceramic fuses rather than circuit-breakers or trip switches may be installed. Apart from main switch fuse units, there may be additional fuse boards for the power and the lighting circuits.

When replacing 'blown' fuse wire or cartridge fuses, use replacements of the amperage for which the fuse is rated. The use of heavier wire will cause damage elsewhere in the circuit – probably to the appliance – and it will also lead to over-heating and the risk of fire.

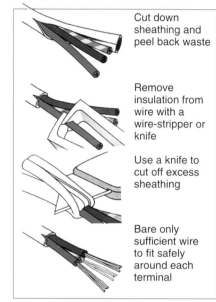

Cut down sheathing and peel back waste

Remove insulation from wire with a wire-stripper or knife

Use a knife to cut off excess sheathing

Bare only sufficient wire to fit safely around each terminal

The electricity that you use is registered on your meter as 'units'. A unit is one thousand watt-hours, also known as 1 kilowatt-hour or 1 kWh, and is equivalent to one thousand watts used continuously for one hour. Meter readings, depending on the age of the installation, may be in the form of dials or of a digital display. The number of units of electricity used is determined by subtracting the previous reading from the latest one. The unit forms the basis on which the supplier calculates charges for electricity consumption, to which are added fixed availability or distribution charges.

Finding the fault. The first thing to do when a fuse or a trip switch breaks the circuit is to correct the fault that caused the failure. Switch off and disconnect any appliance you were using or that you suspect may be faulty.

If the distribution board is fitted with fuses, switch off the main switch before removing any fuses. Use a torch for additional light, if necessary, to examine each fuse in turn until you find one with a broken or melted fuse wire. Keep a card of fuse-wire near the board, and replace the broken wire with one of the correct amperage which is stamped or cast on the body of the fuse-holder.

If fuses continue to blow after replacement, it's probably best to call an electrician or to take a suspect appliance to a repair shop. Whether or not you should open the appliance to examine it yourself depends on your own level of expertise and the equipment that you have available. Before opening or dismantling an appliance, try to find out whether you would be invalidating the terms of any warranty or other condition of sale.

Trip switches on sub-circuits automatically flick themselves off if the circuit is overloaded or if there is a fault in an appliance on the circuit. The circuit is made operational again simply by moving the switch to the 'on' position. As a rule, the trip switch lever points up when in the 'on' position, down when it has flicked off.

Circuit overload. Circuits are shut down by fuses and trip switches not only when there is a wiring fault, but also when the circuit is overloaded. This occurs when the appliances on that circuit draw more current than the circuit is designed to provide. Most domestic power circuits in South Africa – apart from those feeding electricity to stoves and water heaters, or specially installed sockets – are rated at 15 amperes (15A).

Where there's a shortage of power plugs, a socket panel is useful. Socket panels are plugged into a 15A plug socket and offer two, three or four sockets. Some are fitted with a light to indicate when they are in use, and with their own circuit-breaker switch. The use of a socket panel does not increase the rating of a power circuit but merely provides additional sockets into which to plug extra appliances. If the combined amperage being drawn by the appliances connected to the socket panel exceeeds 15A, the circuit will automatically be shut down. Switch off and unplug some of the appliances, to reduce the load, before replacing the fuse or re-setting the trip switch.

Power tools. The electric drill power unit is the average householder's most versatile power tool. The range is vast, and drill units are usually priced according to their chuck capacity (the maximum diameter of bit shank that can be secured in the chuck), or power output, which is proportional to the wattage they consume, and their sophistication. The most basic unit rotates at a fixed speed in one direction. Some have a gear selector that permits a choice of two speeds. Electronic models have a controller that permits them to be run at any speed up to maximum revolutions per minute (rpm). Variable speed control and the ability to reverse the direction of rotation are useful functions. Impact drills use a rotary motion as well as hammer-like blows – sometimes up to 50 000 blows per minute at a speed of 2 800 rpm. Cordless drill are powered by a rechargeable battery.

Accessories are available to transform the electric drill into the power unit for other tools, such as a circular saw, jigsaw, sander or even a lathe. However, the modern tendency is for tools to be custom-made for a specific purpose, rather than to be adaptable under circumstances in which safety levels or performance may drop.

Whatever the function of a power tool, the heart of it is the universal electric motor that draws its power from the electricity supply, which may be mains or battery. The electrical energy is then converted to mechanical power that is transmitted to whatever form of attachment is being used. Most power tools have a reduction gear to reduce the speed of the motor (up to 30 000 rpm) to the speed needed for a particular application, which may be from 220 rpm for drilling to 5 000 rpm or more for grinding.

Most power tools are well designed, well made, and seldom give trouble with ordinary use. If you do have trouble, however, your safest course is to take the tool to the manufacturer's agent for examination and repair.

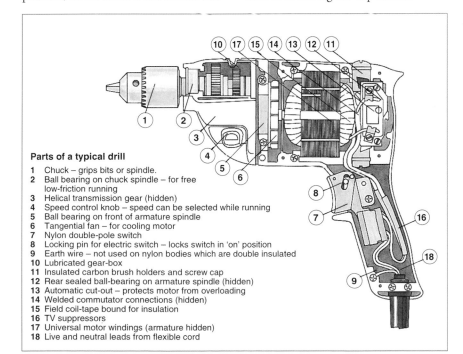

Parts of a typical drill

1. Chuck – grips bits or spindle.
2. Ball bearing on chuck spindle – for free low-friction running
3. Helical transmission gear (hidden)
4. Speed control knob – speed can be selected while running
5. Ball bearing on front of armature spindle
6. Tangential fan – for cooling motor
7. Nylon double-pole switch
8. Locking pin for electric switch – locks switch in 'on' position
9. Earth wire – not used on nylon bodies which are double insulated
10. Lubricated gear-box
11. Insulated carbon brush holders and screw cap
12. Rear sealed ball-bearing on armature spindle (hidden)
13. Automatic cut-out – protects motor from overloading
14. Welded commutator connections (hidden)
15. Field coil-tape bound for insulation
16. TV suppressors
17. Universal motor windings (armature hidden)
18. Live and neutral leads from flexible cord

Acetate A clear, acetate-based plastic film used for stencilling

Age-hardening Slow, natural process that takes place at room temperature in some alloys, especially of aluminium, after annealing. Age-hardened metal must be re-annealed before it can be worked

Aggregates Stones and sand added in pre-determined proportions to cement and water to form concrete. The usual forms of fine and coarse aggregates respectively are sand, and stone crushed to size

Alkyd paint Oil-based paint

Alloy Combination of two or more metals and other substances. The two sub-classes are *ferrous alloys* such as nickel steel and tungsten steel and *non-ferrous alloys* such as brass, bronze and pewter

Annealing Heat-treating metal to produce its softest possible working state

Architrave Moulding (usually wood) around the opening for a door or a window

Arris Sharp corner or edge

Bagged brick Type of rough finish achieved by making a wad of sacking and using it to smear the plaster onto the wall. Because of its thinness, a bagged finish is not very weatherproof

Bat Part of a brick that has been cut across its width

Batching The process of measuring out the ingredients per batch of concrete

Bedding The mortar under a brick

Bevel Any corner or angle other than a right angle

Beading Small, convex moulding with a semicircular cross-section

Bleeding (a) A fault that occurs when soluble paints or other materials on a surface dissolve and show through subsequent layers of paint

Bleeding (b) The appearance of excess water on the surface of newly placed and compacted concrete, caused by too much water having been added to the mix

Blueing Treatment to improve the corrosion resistance of metals. Metals may be heated to create a very thin skin of oxide, and then quenched in oil. Blueing, especially of weapon steel, may also be carried out by chemical processes, such as immersion in selenious acid

Bond Pattern of interlacing of bricks for strength and for decoration

Brandering Wood with dimensions of 38×38 mm, available in lengths from 1,8 m and used in ceiling construction

Brittleness Liability to break under a sharp blow. Cast iron and heat-hardened high-carbon steels are extremely brittle

Brushing out Spreading paint to form an even film over the surface

BSP British Standard Pipe thread, used for the threaded tails of some taps and metal pipe fittings

Bull float See **Skip float**

Bullnose A brick or tile with a rounded edge or end, used in frames for doors and windows and on the edge of steps. A tile or brick with two rounded ends or edges is described as being double bullnose

Butt joining Joining strips of wood or wallcovering edge to edge or side to side, so that there is no overlap

Butt joint Simple end-on joint which is inherently weak and needs to be reinforced with either screws or nails

Buttress Structure built to support a wall. Also called a **Pier**

Cam Eccentric lobe forming part of a rotating shaft and giving a reciprocating motion to part of a machine (such as a valve in a car engine)

Carcasing Timber used in the structural work of a building

Carcass The skeleton or framework of any structure, such as a building or a cupboard

Casting Producing shapes by pouring molten material into moulds

Catalyst A substance that, by its addition to other substances, enables a reaction to take place

Cement Powder, usually grey, made of a mixture of processed limestone and clay, used with water and sand to make mortar and, with the addition of coarse aggregates, to make concrete

Chamfer A narrow, flat surface at a corner or edge

Closer A part brick, cut along its length, used near a corner or end to even up the bond

Concrete A mixture of cement, water and aggregates (sand and stones, which are known as fine and coarse aggregates respectively)

Conductivity Capacity to transmit heat and electricity. Copper, silver and pure aluminium are good conductors

Course A horizontal layer of bricks, usually when mortared into a structure

Craft knife Also *hobby knife*; knife with long, extensible blade, up to about 10 mm in width and made in segments that can be easily broken off as they become dull. *Utility knife* is a larger version, with a blade width of up to about 25 mm

Crazing Fine cracks appearing in plaster that has dried too rapidly – usually because it was applied in very hot weather or in strong wind

Cross-lining Hanging lining paper horizontally so that the joints will not coincide with the vertical ones of the final layer of paper

Curing Concrete sets or becomes hard within 3 to 4 days, although reaching full strength or cure may take 28 days or longer. During the processs, concrete and mortar must be kept moist and cool to allow reaction with the water content to continue. The temperature should not fall below 10°C

Cutting in Painting up to an edge using a long steady stroke

Darby or derby float Wooden or metal board used to smooth concrete

Drawing Pulling ductile metals, especially wire, through holes in a plate to reduce their cross-section

Drawknife Knife pulled towards the user to strip wood

Drip moulding Protruding strip of plaster or wood, usually above an external door or window. It allows rainwater to drip clear

Ductility Capable of being stretched into fine wire without breaking; copper is highly ductile

Efflorescence Powdery, crystalline or furry deposit formed by evaporation and chemical action on the surface of plaster or brickwork. Particularly on a new wall, efflorescence may disappear naturally, but it can be treated with dilute acid or by brushing and sponging with water

Elasticity Ability to resume original shape after deformation. Lead is very malleable, but has little elasticity in that it does not spring back when bent and released

Emulsion Water-based paint. *See* **PVA**

Enamel paint Oil-based paint or varnish, which may be glossy (reflective) or matt

Extruding Forcing materials (such as plastics or metals) through holes to produce bars or tubes

Face side The main prepared side of a workpiece from which all marking out and assembly is done

Ferrous metals Metals composed mainly of iron, such as cast or wrought iron, carbon steel and mild steel

50 × 100 Term of convenience to describe approximate size of timber

Figure Grain characters of a particular wood

Filler Material used for filling holes and cracks

Flexible cement Rubber and cement-based adhesive used for tiling

Footing A specific section of a foundation, such as that supporting a **Pier**

Forging Shaping hot metal by hammering it

Form The mould in which concrete is cast – also known as shuttering

Form release agent Chemical compound that prevents any adhesion between cement or concrete and wood

Frog Recess in the face of a brick

Fusibility Property of a metal of liquefying – becoming liquid – when heated to its melting point

Grain The general direction, arrangement or lay of wood fibres

Groove A channel cut in the length of a piece of wood

Grout A waterproof paste used to fill the gaps between tiles. On drying, grout may be rigid or flexible

Hardening Producing maximum hardness in carbon steel by heating it until it glows bright cherry red and then cooling or quenching it in water or brine. This makes the steel brittle and is usually followed by **Tempering**

Hardness A metal's resistance to deformation, bending and cutting

Hardwood Timber from any broadleafed tree, which may not necessarily be hard

Hawk Plasterer's board for holding mortar, also known as a *tokkie*

Header Brick laid with its ends parallel to the wall face

Heartwood Central, dark-coloured core of a tree trunk, consisting of non-functioning tissue

Housing Channel, usually cut across the grain of a piece of wood, to house fittings such as shelves

Jamb Vertical side member of a door frame or window frame

Joint The layer of mortar between bricks or blocks

Knock-down fittings Fittings designed to hold pieces together only temporarily and easily removed to allow for dismantling

Knot Portion of a branch enclosed by the wood. Live knots are usually firmly held while dead knots, usually black around the edges, tend to come out easily

Knotting Solution of shellac with methylated spirit, used for sealing knots so that resin will not bleed

through the paint or finish coat

Laminated Composed of layers, usually of wood or plastic, that may be bonded or glued together

Laying off Final brush strokes that leave the surface perfectly smooth. On wood, laying off is done in the direction of the grain, and in the longest direction on metal

Length In timber, this is always the direction of the grain

Lime Hydrated builder's lime must be used – not agricultural or road lime. It improves the plasticity, cohesiveness and water retention of fresh mortar, and renders hardened mortar less susceptible to cracking

Lintel Horizontal beam, usually fitted over a door or window to support the weight of the masonry above

Load-bearing Term applied to a wall that has to support a structure

LPG Liquefied petroleum gas, usually a mixture of propane and butane , highly inflammabe and stored under pressure in metal cylinders

Malleability Ability to be rolled, beaten or hammered into a thin sheet without breaking. The most malleable metal is gold, which can be beaten into a foil only 0,001 mm thick

Mastic Putty-like filler or adhesive

Mitre A corner joint formed by cutting bevels of equal angles in each of two pieces of material

Mortar Mixture of cement, sand, water (and often lime), used for bedding and jointing masonry (bricks or blocks) and as floor toppings or screeds

Mortise Rectangular hole in a piece of wood, usually chiselled out, to take a fitting or a **tenon**

Moulding A shaped strip or edge

Mullion Fixed vertical member between the casements of a window

Nominal size The size of wood before it is planed down or dressed. A piece of wood with a nominal size of 25 × 25, may have an actual size after being planed all round of 22 × 22 mm

No-fines concrete Made in the same way as ordinary concrete, but without sand, to the usual proportions of 1 cement: 8 stone. Used for ground floors, it prevents rising damp, is warmer, cheaper and shrinks less than ordinary concrete. It is finished with a sand-cement screed.

Non-ferrous metals Metals that contain little or no iron, such as copper, tin, lead and aluminium.

PAR Planed all round

Pier Bonded-in support for a beam or support for a wall. *See* **Buttress**

Plasters Coverings – often mortar-based – applied to walls built of brick or block

Portland cement Type of widely used cement named for its resemblance, when mixed and dried, to Portland stone

Pressing Forming metal to a shape by using a press tool

Primer The first coat of paint on a new surface. It seals the surface and prevents subsequent coats of paint from soaking into it. *See* **Undercoat**

PVA Polyvinyl acetate, a synthetic resinous material used in water-based emulsion paints, adhesives and sealers

PVC Polyvinyl chloride, a synthetic material used for making chemical-resistant pipes and fittings

Quartered A log when it is sawn into quarters and then cut radially to expose the grain to the best advantage

Quoin Corner, usually of a wall

Racking back Step pattern used in building corners

Rail Horizontal frame member in a door, window or piece of panelling

Ratchet Device in which a pivoted lever, called a pawl, engages a toothed wheel to permit motion in one direction only.

Rebate Rectangular recess cut along an edge. Also called a *rabbet*

SAE Abbreviation for *Society of Automotive Engineers* and used to de-

scribe a thread-size based on fractions of an inch

Sapwood Ring of live, sap-carrying outer wood immediately below the bark. It is usually removed from sound timber and, untreated, is especially liable to attack by wood-boring insects

Scribing Marking a line on a work-piece with a knifepoint or other cutting instrument

Section The appearance of an object as it would be if cut through

Selvedge The waste strip down both sides of a roll of wallpaper that protects the pattern from damage. It must be cut off before hanging. Most papers are sold ready trimmed

Shake Any fault, split or crack in or through a piece of timber

Size Thinned adhesive or glue used as a form of primer to seal a surface before hanging wallcovering. Size prevents water in the hanging paste from being absorbed too rapidly by the wall

Skip float Rectangle of flat metal or board, usually attached to a long handle, used to smooth a large screeded surface. Also called a **Bull float**

Soffit Closure of the underside of any part of a building or structure, such as an arch, stair or eaves

Softwood Timber from coniferous (cone-bearing) trees with needle-like leaves, which may not necessarily be soft

Spackling Any compound used to fill holes, especially in wood and concrete

Spinning Process in which a fast-revolving sheet of ductile metal is forced over a wooden or metal former – a common way of producing aluminium kitchenware

Spokeshave Blade with a handle at each end. It differs from a drawknife in having an adjustable blade

Stile vertical frame member in a door, window or piece of panelling

Stopped Used to describe a groove not running the full length or width of the piece in which it is cut

Stopped end End of a wall, where courses end flush with one another

Stopping Material that can be moulded, used for filling holes and cracks in wood before finishing

Stretcher Brick laid with its long sides parallel to the wall face

Subfloor The concrete or wooden floor base on which the underlay and flooring are installed

Tempering Reducing the brittleness of steel after it has been hardened. It is done by heating the steel and then cooling it – the temperature and rate of cooling vary with the type of steel. Steel cannot be tempered without first being hardened. *See* **Hardening**

Tenacity Resistance to a pulling force – the opposite to ductility. Also known as cohesion

Tenon Projection, cut in a piece of wood, to fit into a corresponding **mortise** in another piece

Thick bed/thin bed adhesives Adhesives based on resins or powdered cement, especially when used for tiling. The same adhesive may be used as a thin bed (3 to 6 mm) or as a thick bed (6 to 12 mm)

Thread tape Also known as plumber's tape, it is bound around external threads to provide a watertight seal

Toothing The projecting of alternate courses of bricks left for bonding-in when bricklaying is temporarily suspended. See **Racking back**

Torque The force produced in a rotating shaft such as an electric drill

Undercoat Coat applied on top of a primer or other coat to provide a good key, usually for a gloss finish

Wane The natural edge of a board as cut from a trunk – it often has bark attached. Also known as *waney edge*

Warp Twist in a board or sheet of material caused by unequal internal or surface tensions

Work-hardening The hardening of metal by being hammered or bent. The metal becomes brittle and must be annealed to prevent it from cracking

In South Africa, all measurements – whether of length, area or volume – are based on the metric system. Many of the tools that you'll buy or use, however, may have been made according to the imperial system which is based on inches and feet. An inch, in turn, is divided into fractions – commonly using a denominator (or divisor) based on sixty-fourths of an inch.

Use of an electronic calculator makes it easy to metricate an imperial size or volume, but the exact equivalent is not always the standard dimension used by manufacturers. Some standard imperial and metric dimensions are given on this page. The converted figures are approximations.

Fluid measures Although both the United States and United Kingdom make use of gallons, the volumes differ. Both gallons (gall or gal) consist of four quarts (qts), or eight pints (pts) In a US pint there are 16 fluid ounces (fl oz) and in a UK pint there are 20.

United States measures	ml
1 gallon (gal, gall)	3 785
1 quart (qt)	946
1 pint (pt)	473
1 fluid ounce (fl oz)	29,6

To convert US gallons to litres, multiply by 3,785. To convert litres to US gallons, multiply by 0,2642.

United Kingdom measures	ml
1 gallon	4 546
1 quart (0,25 gall)	1 136
1 pint (0,125 gall)	568
1 fluid ounce (0,05 pint)	28,4

To convert UK gallons to litres, multiply by 4,546. To convert litres to UK gallons, multiply by 0,22.

Linear measurement The United Kingdom and (especially) the United States of America use the imperial system, in which 12 inches (in) are equal to 1 foot (ft), 3 feet (36 inches) are 1 yard (yd), 220 yards are 1 furlong and 8 furlongs are 1 mile. Most South African artisans, engineers and DIY enthusiasts refer to measurements of up to about 2 metres in millimetres (mm) rather than in centimetres (cm).

Although it would be correct, for instance, to speak of a chisel with a 2,5 cm-wide blade, or of a length of wire of 1,5 metres, custom and preference give them as 25 mm and 1 500 mm respectively.

Many items either made in America or made in other countries and intended mainly for the American market, are sold in South Africa. These usually carry their dimensions stamped in inches and fractions of an inch, although some are marked both in inches and in metric sizes. To convert inches to cm, multiply by 2,54 – or by 25,4 to obtain mm. To convert feet to metres, multiply by 0,3048. The following are typical sizes of drill bits and small tool blades, in imperial, metric and metric standard (std).

Imperial size (64ths)	(inches)	Metric (mm)	Metric std (mm)
3	3/64	1,191	1 or 1,2
4	1/16	1,588	1,5 or 1,6
5	5/64	1,984	2
6	3/32	2,381	2,4 or 2,5
7	7/64	2,778	2,8 or 3
8	1/8	3,175	3 or 3,2
9	9/64	3,572	3,5
10	5/32	3,969	4
11	11/64	4,366	4,5
12	3/16	4,7625	4,8 or 5
13	13/64	5,159	5
14	7/32	5,556	5,5
15	15/64	5,953	6
16	1/4	6,35	6,5
18	9/32	7,144	7
20	5/16	7,9375	8
22	11/32	8,731	8,5
24	3/8	9,525	9,5
26	13/32	10,319	10
28	7/16	11,1125	11
30	15/32	11,906	12
32	1/2	12,70	12,5
36	9/16	14,2875	14
40	5/8	15,875	16
44	11/16	17,4625	17,5
48	3/4	19,05	19
52	13/16	20,6375	20
56	7/8	22,225	22
60	15/16	23,8125	24
64	1 in	25,40	25

Measures of weight or mass The imperial system is based on pounds (lb) and ounces (oz) – avoirdupois, not fluid ounces – with 16 ounces to the pound. Other units that you may encounter include the stone (14 pounds or 14 lb) and the hundredweight (cwt) which, confusingly, is not 100 lb in the United Kingdom, but 112 lb. In Canada and in the United States, however, a hundredweight is 100 lb. A *metric hundredweight* is equivalent to 50 kilograms (kg). The British or long ton is 2 240 lb and the American or short ton is 2 000 lb. The metric ton (also called *tonne*) is 1 000 kg.

To convert pounds to kg, multiply by 0,4536 and to convert kg to pounds, multiply by 2,2046. To convert ounces (avoirdupois) to grams, multiply by 28,35 and to convert grams to ounces (avoirdupois), multiply by 0,0353.

Surface area In both metric and imperial systems, the basic units are squared and usually written as square feet (sq ft) or square metres (sq m or m²). To convert square inches to square centimetres (cm^2), multiply by 6,4516 and to convert cm^2 to square inches, multiply by 0,155. To convert square feet to m^2, multiply by 0,0929 and to convert m^2 to square feet multiply by 10,764.

Cubic measures Although the litre is a measure of volume, solids are usually measured by the cubic metre (cu m or m^3) with 1 m^3 being equivalent to 1 000 litres. There are approximately 35 cubic feet in 1 cubic metre. To convert cubic feet to m^3 multiply by 0,028317 and to convert m^3 to cubic feet, multiply by 35,315.

Temperature On the Centigrade or Celsius scale, water (under standard conditions) freezes at 0 degrees (0°C) and boils at 100 degrees (100°C), corresponding to 32°F and 212°F respectively on the Fahrenheit (F) scale. To convert from Celsius to Fahrenheit, multiply by 1,8 and add 32. To convert from Fahrenheit to Celsius, subtract 32 and divide by 1,8.

INDEX

Reproduction by Hirt & Carter (Pty) Ltd, Cape Town   Printed by Tien Wah Press (Pte) Ltd, Singapore